1001 DAYS
THAT SHAPED THE WORLD

1001 DAYS
THAT SHAPED THE WORLD

GENERAL EDITOR PETER FURTADO

PREFACE BY MICHAEL WOOD

◖ 8:15 A.M. August 6, 1945, Hiroshima.

 CASSELL
ILLUSTRATED

First published in Great Britain in 2008 by Cassell Illustrated
An imprint of Octopus Publishing Group Limited
Carmelite House, 50 Victoria Embankment
London EC4Y 0DZ
www.octopusbooks.co.uk

An Hachette UK Company
www.hachette.co.uk

Revised edition 2018

A CIP catalogue record for this book is available from the British Library.

ISBN-13: 978-1-78840-083-1

This book was designed and produced by
White Lion Publishing
The Old Brewery
6 Blundell Street
London N7 9BH

Senior Editor	Jodie Gaudet
Editors	Mary Cooch, Becky Gee, Ben Hubbard,
	Fiona Plowman, Frank Ritter, Andrew Smith
Assistant Editor	Philip Contos
Picture Researcher	Lorna Ainger
Update Editor	Sophie Blackman
Update Designer	Dean Martin
Production Manager	Anna Pauletti
Editorial Director	Ruth Patrick
Publisher	Philip Cooper

Printed in Malaysia

Contents

Preface

By Michael Wood, historian and broadcaster

In 2008 I had the chance to hitch a lift into Iraqi Kurdistan with a U.S. patrol out of Mosul. My goal was a historical quest. The summer heat rose with the dawn and in no time we were sweltering in our armored vests, inside a cramped armored troop carrier. We crossed the Tigris and were soon passing the ruined gates of Nineveh with its memories of Old Testament and Assyrian kings, and of Medes and Persians, "coming down like a wolf on the fold." As we headed down the old road to Babylon, the layers of Iraqi history were to be seen all around us—Assyrian Greek, Christian, Muslim—with memories of battles from the Assyrians to the Mongols and now, no less fatefully perhaps, Operation Iraqi Freedom. As I peered out from the observation hatch, I found myself reflecting that for it to be truly alive, history must always be Here and Now.

Beyond Mosul a great brown massif rears out of the plain: this is the Jabal Maqlub, or "upside down mountain," known to Iraqi Christians as Alfaf or "the hill of a thousand saints." Late in the day we walked to the top to find an epic view across to the mountains of Kurdistan. Below us in the middle of a wide plain by a dried stream bed was a steep-sided ancient mound. Now called Tel Gomel, it was once an ancient town that had taken its name from the mountain on which we stood: Gaugamela or "The Camel's Back." We were looking over the site of Alexander's greatest battle, where—so the Greeks later claimed—49,000 battle-hardened Greeks had defeated nearly one million men under the Persian emperor Darius. The battle made Alexander "Lord of Asia" and the world would never be the same again. The day was October 1, 331 B.C.E.

When I was a student at the end of the Sixties, the conventional wisdom was that great events, and the role of the individual in history, were much overrated; that "days that shaped the world" was something of a redundant idea. Left-wing historians in particular insisted that deeper forces were what really shaped history—social movements, proletariats. A little later, Fernand Braudel's great book on the Mediterranean taught us (more convincingly to my mind) that history exists on different levels: at the bottom lies the *longue durée* of landscape and climate to which the deep-rooted, long-term patterns of human life adapt themselves; then above that is the overlay of the rise and fall of civilizations; and only on the third level is *l'histoire evenementielle*—"mere events," those short-lived fireflies that briefly light up the surface of history. Braudel, I am sure, is right. But, nevertheless, it seems to me also beyond dispute that people like Alexander, and days like Gaugamela, really did change the world.

That's what makes this collection so fascinating. It's a simple idea: a reasoned list of 1001 of the most significant moments in the history of humanity. Not just events but ideas, inventions, artistic creations. For me many stories in this book evoke memories of my own travels in history over the years: hitching as a student down the heel of Italy to find Hannibal's Cannae, or around the Turkish southern shore to Issus. At Alesia one university break, I remember discovering to my amazement that faint traces of the huge entrenchments were still visible by which Julius Caesar first encircled Vercingetorix and then strangled the life out of him. Memories too of wandering around crumbling suburbs of Mexico City looking for physical traces (even oral traditions) of the fall of Mexico in 1520–1521, which Adam Smith thought the greatest event in history, and which was the beginning of the Spanish conquest of Mesoamerica.

Another intriguing aspect is the historical synchronicities that emerge from this book. Take what Karl Jaspers called the Axis Age. The idea that the Buddha, Confucius, Lao Tzu, the early Greek philosophers, and some of the Old Testament Prophets may have all been alive at the same time: what that fact means in the history of human thought is still hotly argued. Other synchronicities revealed in these pages are no less striking. During the seventh century, the course of two religions was radically altered: the Prophet Muhammad died (632 C.E.); Muslim Arab armies burst out of the Arabian peninsula to change the course of history; and Hsuan Tsang arrived in Kashmir on one of the great cultural missions of history – to bring back to China the core texts of Buddhism, which then probably had the greatest number of adherents of any religion in the world.

It is, of course, a list for our time. In a couple of generations, when India and China return to being the world's great powers and when Asia once again becomes the motor of change, future historians may revise this list and see trends in history that we haven't noticed: finding precursors to their time that we today cannot yet see. But isn't that after all the perennial fascination of history? It is never static, always changing, and, as I discovered that evening on the Camel's Back in Northern Iraq, at its most engaging it is always Here and Now. And that is the attraction of this handsome and provocative book.

Introduction
By Peter Furtado, General Editor

All day, every day, everywhere around the world, things happen. People buy and sell, build and destroy, fight and negotiate, live and die, in large ways and in small, each action a distinct event. And, imperceptibly for the most part but sometimes dramatically, the world changes a little.

Every day, everywhere around the world, people look at this chaotic mass of occurrences and try to report some of them, to make patterns out of them, to say which are important and which are less so. They look at the muddle of events, and try to find – or to give – meaning to them, to construct stories out of them, to draw them to the attention of others who might find them interesting. One result is the daily newspaper or broadcast news bulletin, which orders, prioritises and explains a minute fraction of the mass of things that happen, in order to inform, educate or entertain the rest of us.

The task of imposing order on chaos is not simple, and it is never achieved fully or entirely successfully. A reporter may discover only part of the truth, a vital detail may be hidden or missed, the links – the meaning – may be too broad or too intricate for anyone to grasp; the story may be unpalatable to preconceived ideas as to what ought to happen, and may be ignored or suppressed. So we – hopefully – have a multiplicity of reporters all working from their different perspectives, while we, the consumers, pick and choose the version of the day's events that is the most comfortable or useful to us.

A key aspect of the search for meaning is to unravel the chains of cause and effect, to look for links between the things that are happening now and those reported in the past. That search quickly takes some people deeper and deeper into the past, trying to find out not just what really did happen, but to pin down those connections, to identify carefully just how one event influenced another. The result is history.

Among historians there has always been debate about causation. It is evident that the world changes, but how exactly? There are those who emphasise underlying forces, economic, cultural or intellectual trends that form great patterns of change into which smaller events all fit; while others prefer to stress the contingent and the effects of chance, personality and human error. Was Europe's great war of the mid-twentieth century the consequence of tensions and trends stretching back decades or centuries, or was it the product of a single man's world view? Even to pose the question demonstrates how false is the choice: it is not a matter of either/or, but of both/and.

One of the pleasures of looking at the human drama of the past is realising how wide ranging it is, and just how memorable so much of it is. All human life is there. And if history offers the grandest stage of all, many of the characters who bestride it are larger than life. Whether monsters, heroes or hopeless failures in situations beyond their capabilities, the protagonists of the past – with all their ambitions and foibles – offer a vision beyond the imaginings of even our greatest playwrights. If we watch their dramas, the stories of the things they did can stay in our minds for the rest of our lives.

1001 Days that Shaped the World offers a series of tableaux from that massive drama. The series starts at the very beginning – in fact before history, before the creation of the earth – and comes right up to the twenty-first century. It ranges around the world. It covers some of the greatest things that have happened, and some rather trivial ones too, whose interest lies in the manner they have wormed their way into the popular consciousness and stayed there.

Once upon a time, schoolchildren had to be able to recite the kings and queens of England, the presidents of the United States, or the names of all the explorers of new continents. Often they could also reel off the dates of famous events, so you only had to say "1776" or "1789" and chances were that it would instantly be understood that you were referring to the American Declaration of Independence or the French Revolution. This educational practice is not so common today, and one often hears people bemoaning the loss of this knowledge of names and dates from the past. Memorable dates have several benefits. They serve as a kind of shorthand for the great events of history; and they naturally arrange themselves into chronological order. Learning dates therefore gives you a sense of what goes before, and what comes after. This is different from cause and effect, but it provides the beginning of the "big picture" of the past, into which more detailed knowledge on specific topics can slot.

This book gives you a thousand such dates, plus one for luck, and therefore offers something of the "big picture". It is not a picture that is smooth or complete – in fact, rather than being a framed oil painting, it is more like a join-the-dots drawing. But it has a clear shape, and if you try to join the dots and find the patterns within it, you will gain a sense of how the world has changed (though not an explanation as to why). And if you become intrigued enough to want to colour in some detail by following up on events that grab you, then the book will have served its function well.

Not that you have to start at the beginning of the book and read the whole thing. Each entry stands alone, and presents, within the obvious limitations of space, a glimpse of the drama of what happened that day, where it happened, and why, and what its consequences were. So you can dip in, read about things you have never heard of before, and come away with a snapshot of a key moment in time. But it must be acknowledged that, whatever the range of the entries, it is patently impossible in a book like this to cover all that could be said about the past. What we have tried to do is select memorable events, and give them a context, and a consequence. While any event might be included, we have limited ourselves to events that took place on a single day, or at least reached their climax on that day.

The evidence of history is patchy, especially so the further back you look, so it is not always possible to be sure on which exact day of which exact month a particular event occurred. Sometimes, even for the most famous events in the whole of history, there is debate even as to the years in which they occurred – the crucifixion of Jesus is one example. Lack of calendrical clarity does not mean that these events never happened at all, so we have included them. Also, confusion may result from the many different systems of calendar in use around the world at the time, or different ways of counting. Until a couple of hundred years ago, the year did not begin, in official or legal terms, on 1 January as it does now, but on 25 March (the Feast of the Annunciation, also known as Lady Day), so that an event that we think of as having occurred on, say, 30 January 1649 (the execution of King Charles I at the hands of Oliver Cromwell) was thought by people of the time as having happened on 30 January 1648. Similarly, a change in calendars means that Lenin and the Bolsheviks called their revolutionary seizure of power in Russia the "October Revolution", because in their minds the decisive seizure of the Winter Palace occurred on 25 October, even though today we say it took place on 7 November 1917.

Because it is impossible to know every detail of everything that happened in the past, sometimes it is more important to know what people thought happened. People have often, for whatever reason, accepted stories of things happening in the past that today seem inherently highly unlikely, or even totally impossible. Some historians prefer to ignore these instances, and concentrate on things that really did happen. Sometimes, though, the belief itself, however peculiar, is important because it drives those who accept it to do remarkable things that impact on the lives of many others. So, their story of the things that they thought happened is part of history too – so long as we make clear that the belief, and not just the event, is the story. Which is why you will find some events – like the "creation of the world" in October 4004 B.C.E. – that no modern historian would seriously claim ever happened: the fact that intelligent people once believed they did, and that they seriously affected the decisions those people made about their own lives, is reason enough for their inclusion. Most of these dates – like the foundation of Rome by Romulus on 21 April 753 B.C.E., after he and his twin brother Remus had been brought up by a wolf – relate to long-gone mythologies, but are, however, dates that have played an important part in the history of their associated cultures.

The stories here range from the political, dynastic and military – the raw materials of history, you might say – to the cultural, technological and scientific, and the odd piece of ephemera. While we start in prehistory, our emphasis is on the last 150 years. For this there are a number of reasons. One is that before the development of the Western empires, and the globalisation of history that has resulted, only few events resonated far beyond the borders of the lands in which they happened. While these events are included here, many other fascinating, but essentially local, developments have been passed over in silence. From the nineteenth century, events in one part of the world have affected others elsewhere with far more frequency, hence the emphasis here on the last two centuries. Another reason is that history has simply speeded up in the last two centuries: more things happen more quickly than they did in the Middle Ages, say – or at least more things happen that are reported in detail, and whose implications and roots can be tracked. As change becomes more rapid, so days that shape the world become more frequent.

No selection of 1001 days that shaped the world could ever be definitive, and I expect – or rather, hope – that you will find yourself questioning the selection. I hope, though, that you will also find things that surprise and interest you. This is all to the good. History can never be definitive: if you do not argue about it sometimes, and if it does not sometimes surprise you, then something is wrong. Either it has been badly presented, or else you think you already know everything there is to know about life. History is a dialogue between all of us – writers, readers, scholars, citizens – and all of it is open to debate. So – let us debate it.

Index by Country

The Gezer Calendar, found near Jerusalem and dating to the tenth century B.C.E., gives details of an agricultural year.

BIG BANG–1 B.C.E.

The Universe Explodes into Being

The "Big Bang" is the beginning of the universe.

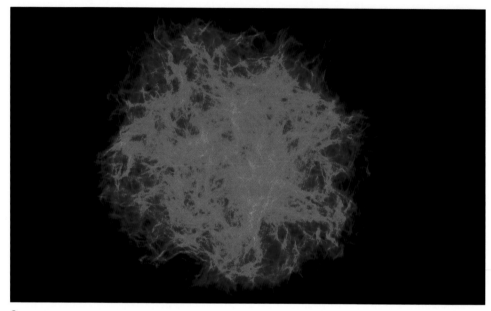

○ A conceptual, computer illustration of the explosion, showing the expansion of gas and matter that would become our universe.

There was, of course, no "bang," big or small, because there was no medium in which sound could exist. It was the beginning of time, space, matter, energy, everything—all inexplicably created out of a "singularity" in which none of these existed before. In the 1960s, scientists detected the echo of the Big Bang in the form of background radiation from across the sky. Impressively, they have produced a theoretical explanation of what must have happened in the very first second of the universe. When the universe was still tiny and incredibly hot, a sudden expansion occurred as matter moved from the minute quantum scale to that of a small but growing cosmos. Vast amounts of matter and antimatter were created, almost all of which mutually annihilated, leaving just a tiny proportion of matter. As the universe cooled from its enormous levels of energy, subatomic particles assembled. It was not for another 380,000 years that temperatures fell sufficiently for electrons and protons to come together to form atoms.

Vast clouds of hydrogen collected, cohering into ever-denser masses that compacted under the force of gravity until hydrogen atoms at the center fused into helium, releasing energy that made them burn as stars. When some of these exploded into supernovae, heavier atoms were made, which formed the raw materials for the universe as we know it.

The theory of the Big Bang was put forward in the 1950s, and it is still the unchallenged scientific explanation of the origins of the universe. **PF**

Dinosaurs Wiped Out in Asteroid Horror?

Did an asteroid striking Earth account for the demise of the prehistoric beasts?

O The K/T boundary, the black layer between Cretaceous and Tertiary rock, is made from material ejected from an asteroid impact.

Having ruled the Earth for more than 100 million years, the dinosaurs suddenly died out 65 million years ago. So too did ammonites, most marine reptiles, many species of plankton, and many marsupials. Somehow, however, the small and primitive mammals survived, plus most species of bird, insect, lizard, and amphibian. In some parts of the world more than half of all plant species also became extinct.

What happened? Scientists have long debated how quickly the extinctions occurred—whether in the space of a few catastrophic years, or several millennia. The most likely theories suggest one or several large asteroid impacts, which would have melted the Earth's crust, causing massive atmospheric disruption and creating huge tsunamis and firestorms, followed by a drastic lowering of the sea level. One site now clearly identified with this is in the sea off the coast of Yucatan, which involved the impact of an asteroid 6 miles (10 km) in diameter. Its shape suggests that it hit at an angle, scattering much debris across North America.

The end of the Cretaceous (K) and beginning of the Tertiary (T) period is known as the K/T boundary event. Yet it is not clear why some groups of animal were devastated whereas others survived. Smaller and burrowing animals were less affected than large surface dwellers, and free-swimming species suffered more than bottom-feeding marine ones. But the survival of birds suggests that the atmospheric disruptions may have been fairly short lived. **PF**

Let There Be Light!

The Bishop of Armagh examines the Bible to pinpoint the date of creation.

"In the beginning God created heaven and earth." The opening words of the Book of Genesis indicated the beginning of history for millions of Christians and Jews over the millennia—but when was that beginning? Before the eighteenth century when geological research began to suggest that the Earth was many millions of years old, the best information people had to go on were the many generations (or "begats") mentioned in the Bible itself. Using these, and the (often extraordinarily extended) life spans of some of the patriarchs, and cross-checking against astronomical cycles and what was known of Middle Eastern and Egyptian history, James Ussher, Bishop of Armagh in Ireland, estimated in 1658 that "the beginning" occurred at nightfall on Saturday, October 22, some 4,004 years before the Nativity of Jesus.

Ussher assumed that when night and day were created, they would have been equal in length, which pinpointed the date as being near the equinox. He also assumed that, in order to allow Adam and Eve food to eat, it would have been harvesttime in the Garden of Eden. Ussher's chosen date was included in the margins of many printed Bibles from the early eighteenth century until the mid-twentieth century, and became notorious.

Ussher was not the only scholar of his day to make such a calculation. A few years earlier the vice chancellor of Cambridge University, John Lightfoot, had estimated that heaven and earth came into being in September 3929 B.C.E. Previous scholars, including the Venerable Bede, Martin Luther, and Johannes Kepler, had also worked out complicated sums arriving at similar conclusions, but none of their calculations achieved the same universal acceptance as Ussher's date of creation. **PF**

Great Pyramid Finished

The Great Pyramid of Giza houses the tomb of King Khufu.

Khufu's monument is the only one of the Seven Wonders of the Ancient World to survive today. Built in 2575 B.C.E., it houses the tomb of King Khufu, who for twenty-three years had been king of Upper and Lower Egypt. Few records survive from his reign, but inscriptions suggest he campaigned both in Nubia to the south and in Canaan to the north. Despite this paucity of information, his reputation has endured for millennia. Khufu is remembered as a cruel ruler, determined to achieve two great goals: to ensure the survival of the dynasty beyond his son Khephren; and to ensure his own immortality, through the building of the Great Pyramid, the largest monument of the ancient world. The ancient Greek historian Herodotus, writing some 2,000 years later, claimed Khufu forced his daughter to work as a prostitute to raise funds for his pyramid.

The logistics of constructing such a massive object, 480 feet (146 m) high and comprising some 2.3 million blocks of stone, in a relatively short period were astounding. Yet they were obviously overcome. The building's simple design, unusual in Egypt for not being covered with inscriptions or prayers, has fascinated observers for millennia. In recent years exploration of the structure's narrow passageways using robot-mounted cameras has suggested that the pyramid was aligned with the star Orion in order to allow the king's soul to travel to the stars.

Beside the pyramid was a 141-foot-long (43 m) funeral boat in which the king was carried to his final resting place, and smaller tombs for members of his household—an unprecedented sight at the time. **PF**

◯ The famous sphinx of Giza with the Great Pyramid beyond it, which houses Khufu's tomb.

Sargon Takes Empire

Sargon defeats two kings to become the first ruler of the whole of Mesopotamia.

In 2334 B.C.E., Sargon became the first emperor in the history of the world. Sargon came from a humble background—he was brought up by a gardener—but eventually rose to the prestigious position of cup-bearer to Ur-Zababa, the king of the Mesopotamian city of Kish. Sargon later waged war on Lugalzagesi, the powerful king of Uruk, and by defeating him became Emperor of Mesopotamia.

Sargon extended his rule across the entire region, and campaigned as far west as the Mediterranean coast of Lebanon and in Anatolia. Sargon, whose

---

"Now any king who wants to call himself my equal, wherever I went, let him go."

Sargon, Emperor of Mesopotamia

---

name means "the rightful king," established his capital at Akkad, a city that has never been found, on the banks of the Euphrates. He immediately built a large bureaucracy, which took over the focal role of economic activity from the city temples of old Sumeria. Roads were built and a postal system was devised using royal seals. An attempt was also made to survey the population.

During his fifty-six-year reign, Akkadian, a Semitic tongue, became the official language of Mesopotamia. Sargon faced continuing revolts, first from Lugalzagesi and later from individual city-states. Toward the end of his reign, Akkad was besieged, but on his death in 2279 B.C.E. Sargon was able to pass his empire to his sons, and it endured for 150 years before collapsing in internal anarchy. **PF**

Hammurabi's Code

Hammurabi sets down his 282 laws, creating an enduring legal system.

King of Babylon from 1782 B.C.E., Hammurabi's main contribution to civilization lies in his laying down a code of 282 laws in 1760 B.C.E. Written in the Akkadian language on a stela, or basalt column, the code was placed prominently in the city. The laws set out detailed punishments (many involving the death penalty) for specific offenses. Their harshness aside, they embody enduring legal principles, including the importance of evidence, the presumption of innocence, and the need to avoid arbitrary justice. At the top of the stela is a depiction of the king being given the laws by the god Shamash. Although probably not the earliest law code, Hammurabi's is the most complete to have survived from this early period.

A system of professional judges was set up, and a right of appeal granted to the king—though even he was required to act within the divinely inspired, and hence immutable, code of justice. Tribal or customary vengeance was not acceptable. Property rights and a system of contracts were set out, as were the rights of owners over their slaves and landlords over their tenants. Marriage law was also established and dealt with primarily in contractual terms.

In addition to setting down a code of laws, Hammurabi strengthened his kingdom both militarily and economically. Until he inherited its throne, Babylon had been just one of several small competing Mesopotamian states. After driving off an attack by the northern Elamites, Hammurabi conquered the rival local power Larsa to create his empire in southern Mesopotamia by 1763 B.C.E.; he then expanded his own power to the north. **PF**

○ A carved stone tablet containing a fragment of Hammurabi's code, written in cuneiform characters, c.1760 B.C.E.

Volcanic Explosion Rocks Thera

The eastern Mediterranean endures one of the world's worst natural disasters.

◐ Amphorae half-buried under pumice stone and scoria from the volcanic eruption on the island of Thera.

"In a single day and night of misfortune . . . the island of Atlantis . . . disappeared."

Plato's *Timaeus*, c.360 B.C.E.

The volcanic eruption on the small Aegean island of Thera, or Santorini, is recorded in no known literature, and scientists continue to argue about when it occurred (somewhere between 1650 and 1550 B.C.E., with 1620 or a little later being the most common estimate), but its shockwaves were felt right across the eastern Mediterranean. Probably the second-largest volcanic explosion in human history—it produced four times as much atmospheric smoke and ash as Krakatoa in 1883, and carpeted the sea floor for many miles around with up to 260 feet (80 m) of pumice—it apparently caused a huge tsunami that brought catastrophic destruction to the north Cretan civilization of the Minoans, who never recovered. The explosion also created a vast caldera, or volcanic depression, on Thera itself, and buried the town of Akrotiri under 26 feet (8 m) of ash.

Egyptian records do not suggest the event had a significant impact in the Nile Valley. Although some scholars have argued that the biblical plagues of Egypt may have been related to the aftermath of the explosion, most consider that the exodus of the Jews from Egypt took place several centuries later. There are, however, suggestions that unusual weather conditions recorded in China at the time of the fall of the Xia dynasty in about 1618 B.C.E. may relate to the explosion. Some scholars have even linked Thera with the disappearance of the legendary island of Atlantis, which Plato described as the heart of a "great and wonderful empire."

From 1967, excavations of Akrotiri revealed remarkable frescoes, indicating trading and cultural links with Egyptian, Crete, and the Levant. No human remains have been found, suggesting that the inhabitants had sufficient warning to be able to leave in good time, unlike those at Pompeii. **PF**

Pharaoh Worships Sun-Disk God Aten

Amenhotep founds Amarna and briefly rewrites the rules of Egyptian kingship.

The kings of ancient Egypt, known from the Eighteenth Dynasty onward as pharaohs, were universally identified with the supreme god Amen, the Hidden One, whose cult was based at Thebes, or Ra, the sun god based at Heliopolis. All except one. In the fifth year of his reign, Amenhotep IV of the Eighteenth Dynasty overthrew the old gods in favor of his own single deity, the sun-disk Aten, and changed his own name to "One Useful to Aten."

Akhenaten founded a capital in the desert at Amarna, setting up a new priesthood and creating, with his wife, Nefertiti, an original style of naturalistic art, in which the king was depicted as a strange physical specimen, with elongated features and bulbous stomach, unlike any other Egyptian monarch. This has led scholars to suggest—on the basis of little other evidence—that he was suffering from a range of diseases. Aten's temple was open to the sun, and the king wrote a hymn to his god that has been compared to contemporary monotheistic literature, such as the Jewish psalms.

The challenge to the old order was dramatic. The new religion gave rise to great opposition in Egypt, and Akhenaten found himself unable to protect his empire in the Middle East from incursions by the Anatolian Hittites and others. After his death, his son briefly ruled as Tutankhaten before being forced to change his name and faith back to the traditional forms, becoming Tutankhamen. Though an otherwise unremarkable ruler, Tutankhamen would become the most famous pharaoh of all, thanks to his tomb being the only one (so far as is known) to survive to the modern age unmolested. Meanwhile Akhenaten's capital was abandoned and his name forcibly removed from inscriptions by those who sought to extirpate all traces of his unique religion. **PF**

○ A carved relief depicting Akhenaten and his family worshipping Aten, the disk of the sun (*c.*1350 B.C.E.).

"Birds fly from their nests, Their wings greeting your ka, All flocks frisk on their feet."

Hymn to the Aten, Inscription, Tomb of Ay

Ramses II Crowned in Egypt

One of the longest and most significant reigns in world history begins.

○ The remains of three colossal statues of Ramses II from the temple built by—and dedicated to—him at Abu Simbel.

"I charged all countries while I was alone … my chariotry having forsaken me."

Annals of Ramses II

Ramses II began his long reign in 1279 B.C.E. upon the death of the founder of the Nineteenth Dynasty, Seti I, who had restored Egypt's trading influence and power across the Levant, creating the most extensive empire of ancient Egypt. Ramses continued his work, fighting a renowned, though indecisive, battle on the borders of the empire with the Hittites at Kadesh in Syria in 1275 B.C.E., which defined the limits of power for both states, and which was described in detail on the walls of the pharaoh's funerary temple in Thebes known as the Ramesseum.

Later in his reign Ramses faced the growing power of the Assyrians. He also embarked on a series of vast and architecturally interesting building projects at Luxor, Karnak, Abydos, and Abu Simbel. At the latter, he constructed a rock-cut temple that was supposedly dedicated to the god Amum-Re, but which was fronted by four 65-foot-high (20 m) seated statues of Ramses himself. When the Aswan Dam was built across the Nile in 1959, the rising Lake Nasser engulfed the site, and the whole Abu Simbel complex, with its statues, was moved to higher ground.

Though little is directly known of the pharaoh's personal life, one of his wives—and purportedly his favorite—was Nefertari, for whom he built a fine tomb in the Valley of the Queens. It is also claimed that he fathered some one hundred children. His reputation has certainly endured as one of the great pharaohs, and following his reign Egyptian power was never again so widespread.

Ramses's mummified body was discovered at Deir el-Bayhri in the 1880s, and in the 1970s it was finally unwrapped to carry out necessary preservation work, giving modern civilizations a remarkable glimpse of the physical features of the redheaded, physically powerful, hook-nosed king. **PF**

Moses Leads His People Out of Egypt

Moses leads the Jews out of captivity across the Sea of Reeds into the eastern desert.

Although the precise date is frequently disputed, it was probably early in the reign of Seti I that the Hebrew people in Canaan, suffering from severe famine, migrated to Egypt, where they were enslaved. There is some evidence that they indeed worked in the Delta city of Pithom, as described in the Bible.

According to the book of Exodus, one Hebrew boy, Moses, was brought up as an Egyptian in the king's household. However, having discovered his true background and realizing the abuses suffered by the Hebrews, in 1250 B.C.E. Moses determined to lead his people out of captivity. With his brother Aaron, he challenged the new pharaoh Ramses to allow them to leave. When the pharaoh declined, they tried some magical demonstrations of divine favor, and then, according to the Bible, the kingdom endured a series of plagues (perhaps the result of an unusually strong Nile flood). The final plague was the death of the first-born son of every house in the kingdom, except those marked by the Hebrews with a bloody sign from a sacrificed lamb, which meant that the divine plague "passed over" the house. This event has been taken as a sign of God's first great intervention in Jewish history, and is commemorated each year at the festival of Passover (traditionally celebrated in March or April, following the spring equinox).

After this event, Moses encouraged thousands of Hebrews to move off into the eastern desert. The pharaoh sent numerous forces after them, but Moses led his people across the marshes of the Sea of Reeds (often mistakenly assumed to be the Red Sea itself), where the Egyptian chariots foundered. Safe in Sinai, Moses laid down the law for the Jews before their eventual return to the land of Canaan, traditionally after forty years of wandering. **PF**

○ A fourteenth-century depiction of the Jews leaving Egypt, led by Moses, being pursued by Pharaoh and his cavalry.

"The Lord . . . made the sea into dry land, and the waters were divided."

Exodus 14:21

Ji Fa Claims Mandate from Heaven

The Zhou become the longest-lived dynasty in any major state of China.

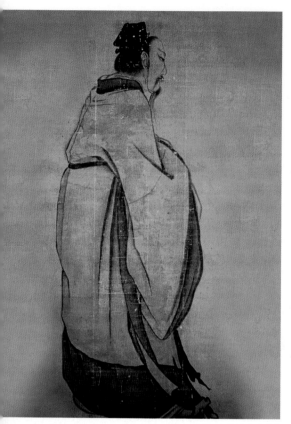

○ An undated portrait of Emperor Wu by an unknown artist, now in the National Palace Museum in Taiwan.

"Running a large country is like cooking a small fish."

Laozi, Daodejing, sixth century B.C.E.

The Zhou, a once-nomadic tribe that had settled in the region of the River Wei, came to power in 1122 B.C.E. when their leader Ji Fa defeated Dixin, the last of the Shang, in battle and set up a new capital near Xi'an. China had been unified by the Shang in the early second millennium B.C.E., but Ji Fa proclaimed the Shang rule to be corrupt, arguing that Dixin had grown cruel and despotic, more concerned with the construction of magnificent gardens than with the welfare of the people. He further asserted that the Shang were no longer justified to rule, whereas his own legitimacy as ruler derived from the Mandate of Heaven, a concept that endured in Chinese history for millennia. His period of rule, as the "Son of Heaven," under the regnal name of Wu, and the early years of the dynasty were remembered as a golden age in Chinese history.

Wu set up a powerful state that initially ruled through its cities but developed on feudal lines, with large territories of land given to nobles in return for fealty—some of these eventually developed into separate kingdoms in their own right. Agriculture, town life, and religion all continued to flourish, and the writing system developed. The new dynasty initially saw cultural continuity with the Shang: as they founded new towns, the Zhou introduced Shang populations and artisan skills, including high-quality bronze working.

The Zhou ruled from Xi'an until 771 B.C.E., when, after a defeat and sacking by northern barbarians, the capital was moved to Loyang. Thereafter, the power of the state declined into what is known as the Warring States Period, but these years paradoxically saw great growth in Chinese culture, philosophy, and art, as well as the widespread development of iron working and irrigation. **PF**

David Becomes King of Israel

Bible stories indicate that King David united the kingdoms of Israel and Judah.

After the Philistines defeated Israel, killing both Saul, the first king of Israel, and his son Jonathan, David was proclaimed king in his home region of Judah. He then conquered the Canaanite city of Jerusalem and made it his capital, bringing the Jew's holy Ark of the Covenant there. Over the ensuing years, he expanded Israel's power northward into Syria, uniting the kingdoms of Israel and Judah.

As a young shepherd boy, David had killed his enemies' champion, Goliath, with his sling. David had entered Saul's household, befriended by Jonathan, but had been driven out by the increasingly erratic king. David became a mercenary for the Philistines, although he avoided the battle in which the Philistines killed Saul.

Despite his human frailties, David is presented in the Bible as a divinely appointed monarch, whose military and political acts—as much as his spiritual activities (he is said to have composed many of the psalms)—are expressions of his response to the wishes of God. His son Solomon expanded Israel's influence across the Middle East. The Jews believed that the kings of Israel and the Messiah would come from David's descendants. He holds an important place in the Jewish, Christian, and Muslim traditions.

Beyond the Bible there is little hard, historical evidence for the existence of David. "The house of David" is mentioned on an Aramaic inscription dated to around 850 B.C.E., and in 2005 an archeologist uncovered remains in Jerusalem that she claimed were the remains of his palace, though this is disputed by other scholars. Historians still argue as to whether it is likely that Bronze Age Judah was likely to have had such a unified kingship as appears in the Bible stories, which probably were written in the late seventh century B.C.E. **PF**

○ A fifteenth-century painting of David and Goliath, attributed to the Italian Renaissance artist Andrea Mantegna.

"And thine house and thy kingdom shall be established for ever."

Yahweh's promise to David; II Samuel 7:16

Sacred Temple Built

Solomon completes the temple in Jerusalem begun by his father David.

Having made Jerusalem his capital, David planned a temple to Yahweh, and bought a site, now Temple Mount, from the Jebusites for the purpose. He assembled materials from which to build it, including vast amounts of gold and silver, but the work fell to his son, Solomon, to complete. Hiram, the Phoenician king of Tyre, made available stone, cedars, gold and bronze, and sent his best craftsmen and laborers, receiving in exchange an area around Galilee.

The temple, which was 95 feet (29 m) long and 29.5 feet (9 m) wide, took seven years to complete. It was dedicated a year later, in a seven-day ceremony at the New Year festivities, during which the Ark of the Covenant—the sacred container of the tablets on which were inscribed the Ten Commandments—was installed in the Holy of Holies, a room that could be entered only by the high priest, once a year on Yom Kippur. The entire interior was covered in gold, and the Ark of the Covenant was flanked by two huge winged figures—cherubim—carved from olive wood. Before the Holy of Holies was the Holy Place, with altars for sacrifice. Two huge bronze pillars flanked the main doorway. Water for the ritual baths was supplied in underground cisterns.

The temple was raided many times over subsequent centuries, and was finally destroyed by the Babylonian king Nebuchadnezzar in 586 B.C.E. A second temple was built in 515 B.C.E., which stood until its destruction at the hands of the Romans in 70 C.E. No undisputed remains of Solomon's temple have been found, and even its exact location on Jerusalem's Temple Mount is uncertain. **PF**

◐ A fifteenth-century illuminated manuscript depicting the building of Solomon's Temple in Jerusalem.

Dido Founds Carthage

The city of Carthage is ideally sited for control of the central Mediterranean.

According to legend—best known from the epic *The Aeneid* by the Roman poet Virgil—Carthage was founded in the aftermath of the Trojan war by Dido (also known as Elissa). She was the elder sister of Pygmalion, the King of Tyre, who killed Dido's wealthy husband, forcing her to flee west. On arriving at the Gulf of Tunis in 814 B.C.E., she asked the local Berber people for just as much land as an ox's skin could encompass, but then cut the skin into thin strips, enabling her to enclose an entire hill. She founded the city on this hill, and ruled it until the arrival of Aeneas, a Trojan prince. They fell in love, but Aeneas had to continue his journey to Italy, where his descendants Romulus and Remus were to found Rome. The distraught Dido cursed Aeneas and condemned Aeneas's people and her own to eternal enmity before committing suicide.

There is no real evidence for this story, and the oldest archaeological remains in Carthage date from one hundred years after the traditional date for its founding. The city was built on a peninsula covered with low hills with a lake behind. The site was easily defended, as just a narrow strip of land connected the peninsula to the mainland. Carthage, Rome's great rival for control of the central Mediterranean, was an outpost of the Phoenician people of the Lebanon coast, traders who from the tenth century B.C.E. roamed throughout the eastern Mediterranean. Their colony on the north African coast near modern Tunis, was eventually to outgrow the mother city, Tyre.

By the end of the sixth century B.C.E., Rome and Carthage were coming into conflict over control of Sicily and Sardinia, and wars between them continued intermittently until 146 B.C.E., when Rome utterly destroyed its rival. **PF**

Faster, Higher, Stronger

The first recorded Olympic Games are held and the tradition of holding them every four years, with an accompanying truce, lasts for more than 1,000 years.

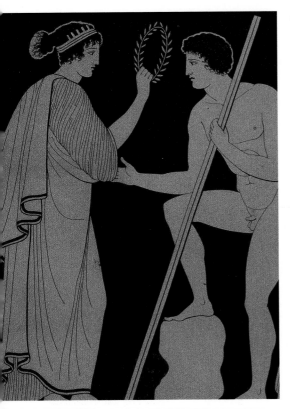

🜂 The personification of Victory giving a laurel wreath to an athlete, depicted on an ancient Greek amphora.

> **"To be a victor at the Olympic Games you must surrender yourself wholly."**
>
> **Epictetus, 2nd century c.e.**

According to one Greek myth, it was Zeus who initiated the Olympic Games to celebrate his victory over his father, Cronos. While it is certain that the Games were held regularly long before the first recorded instance in 776 B.C.E., historian Pausanias, writing in the second century C.E., states that it was the ninth-century B.C.E. king Iphitus who "arranged the games at Olympia and re-established afresh the Olympic festival and truce, after an interruption of uncertain length. At this time Greece was torn by internal strife and plague, and Iphitus asked the god at Delphi for deliverance from these evils. The Pythian priestess ordained that Iphitus himself and the Eleans must renew the Olympic Games."

From 776 B.C.E., the Games were held every four years until 394 C.E., when they were abolished by the Christian Byzantine emperor Theodosius, who saw them as an anachronistic hangover from the pagan era. So important were the Games that the Greeks used them to count the passing years. Held at Olympia in the Peloponnese in a stadium with a capacity of more than 40,000, they were primarily a religious festival in honor of Zeus, with a truce declared so that men from all Greek-speaking cities could attend.

At first there was just one event, the Stadion, which was a race over 650 feet (200 m)—one length of the stadium track. The winner in 776 B.C.E. was a local boy from Elis, a cook called Coreobus. His reward may have been no more than a branch of an apple tree, although later Greek Olympic champions in a growing list of events were crowned with olive wreaths and won great financial rewards. Although historians often refer to Greek athletes competing naked, nudity was not actually introduced until 720 B.C.E., in part as a celebration of the human body. **PF**

Wolf-Boys Found Rome

Twin brothers quarrel and Romulus becomes first king of Rome.

The history of Rome supposedly has its roots in the legend that twin brothers Romulus and Remus decided to found a city on a hill overlooking the River Tiber. While they were laying out the boundaries, the brothers started quarreling over who should be king, which came to an end only when Romulus killed Remus with a violent blow to the head. Hence Romulus became the first king of Rome, and gave the city the name by which it is still known today.

The story is of course a legend. Romulus and Remus were believed to be the sons of Mars, the god of war. Their mother was a priestess called Rhea Silvia, a descendant of Aeneas who had escaped from the city of Troy after its destruction by the Greeks. According to the legend, the baby boys were abandoned in the wild soon after their birth on the orders of their great-uncle Amulius, a local king who feared that his great-nephews might one day overthrow him. They were saved by a she-wolf who nursed them as two of her cubs.

In time the twins grew to adulthood, deposed and murdered Amulius, and placed their grandfather Numitor, the rightful king, back on the throne. They now needed a city of their own to rule and, according to tradition, chose a site close to the place where they had been abandoned on the Palatine Hill, one of Rome's seven hills.

The Romans believed that the city's founding took place on April 21, 753 B.C.E., and dated their calendar from that day. Over the centuries, they cherished and embellished the myth of Romulus and Remus. When, some 700 years later, the historian Livy wrote his great history of Rome, he drew upon these stories to show that Rome had always been destined for great things. **SK**

On the Warpath

Tiglath-pileser III succeeds to the Assyrian throne and sets up a unified state.

The Assyrians, who according to the poet Byron, "came down like a wolf on the fold," dominated the Middle East for centuries. Described as among the cruelest and most aggressive peoples in history, they massacred entire populations or deliberately destroyed tribes and their local bonds. In 745 B.C.E. Tiglath-pileser III of Assyria came to power and held sway across Anatolia, Syria, and Israel. He expanded his empire by conquering and isolating smaller states, forcing them to pay tribute to him, and he sealed off Egypt commercially and militarily in the Levant.

"All their people and all their goods I carried off to Assyria . . ."

From Tiglath-pileser's *Annals of War*

Tiglath-pileser, known in the Bible as Pul, and one of the great military leaders in world history, set up a unified state under eighty provincial governors, each of whom reported directly to him, their king. In 728 B.C.E., Ukin-zer of Babylon rebelled, so Tiglath-pileser defeated him, taking over the Babylonian throne. Even after his death two years later, Assyrian domination and aggression continued. Either Tiglath-pileser or his successor Shalmaneser was responsible for the exile of the Jews to Babylon in 722 B.C.E.

The bas-reliefs and murals from Nimrud, Tiglath-pileser's capital city, show a formidable standing army, armed with iron weapons at a time when most armies still used bronze. Tiglath-pileser also kept a formidable chariot force and the world's most sophisticated siege trains. **PF**

Jews Exiled to Babylon

Nebuchadnezzar banishes the Jews to Babylon after capturing Jerusalem.

Nebuchadnezzar II, the Chaldean king of Babylon in Mesopotamia from 605 B.C.E., attacked Judah and took Jerusalem in 597 B.C.E. He had been campaigning vigorously in the Levant, but after a heavy defeat at the hands of the Egyptians in 601 B.C.E. he had lost control of some of his vassal states and had decided to retaliate. Following the custom of the day, he exiled the king, Jehoiachin, as well as almost 10,000 Jewish subjects to Babylon.

Ten years later, the remaining Jews under King Zedekiah rebelled, and the Chaldeans launched yet

"By the waters of Babylon, we lay down and wept when we remembered Zion. . . ."

Psalm 137

another violent attack, destroying the Jews' temple. Nebuchadnezzar sent thousands more Jews into exile, where they remained—unusually for the times—as a single group, preserving their cultural identity until being permitted to return home in 539 B.C.E.

The exile period proved both traumatic and formative for the Jews. Their god, Yahweh, had promised to preserve them in Judah, so an explanation had to be found for his permitting their removal. This was developed above all by the prophets Jeremiah and Ezekiel, who had argued, even before the fall of the city, that the Jews would be punished for having fallen below the required standards.

Nebuchadnezzar is also remembered for the Hanging Gardens of Babylon, one of the Wonders of the Ancient World, built for his wife, Amytis. **PF**

Solon's Reforms

A new constitution heralds the dawn of Athens's greatest age.

It could be claimed that the great age of Athenian civilization began in 594 B.C.E. when Solon, a moderately wealthy noble (and poet), became *archon* (chief ruler) of the city and introduced unprecedented far-reaching reforms. A moderate who sought to bring justice and alleviate poverty, he repealed the harsh laws set up by Draco in 621 B.C.E., abolishing the death penalty for all offenses except murder and manslaughter. He also moved significantly away from the aristocratic bias of the old laws, which had excluded all other social classes from government

"Men keep agreements when it is to the advantage of neither to break them."

Solon

and had made many farmers, mired in debt, into virtual serfs on their own land. Solon also reformed the debt system. Although many at the time believed his reforms would soon be circumvented by the wealthy, in fact they endured for centuries, and Solon acquired the title of one of Athens's Seven Wise Men.

Politically, his new constitution gave all citizens, regardless of their social standing, the right to attend the General Assembly, and all but the poorest citizens the right to serve on the executive Council of Four Hundred. He also enhanced the rights of foreigners working in Athens. Although many people were left dissatisfied by Solon's reforms, the laws averted a very real threat of revolution and laid the solid foundations for the glories of Athenian democracy to come. **PF**

Cyrus Takes Babylon and Releases Exiled Jews

Cyrus permits the Jews to return to Judah after their enforced exile in Babylon, but the Jews find Judah full of Samaritans.

After they had been driven out of Judah by Nebuchadnezzar in 597 B.C.E., the Jews remained in exile in Babylon until the city was attacked by Cyrus, the Persian founder of the Achaemenid Empire, in 539 B.C.E. Cyrus had already secured his rule in Iran by defeating the Medes in 549 B.C.E. and Lydia in Asia Minor a few years later. In 539 B.C.E. he turned his attention to Mesopotamia, and on October 12 defeated the Babylonians at Opis, taking Babylon without bloodshed, by diverting the River Euphrates until his troops could wade across into the city. Cyrus routed Nabonidus, the Chaldean heir of Nebuchadnezzar, who had gone into hiding having lost even the support of his own priests. Cyrus then declared himself "King of the Four Sides of the World," claiming a substantial empire that extended as far as to the Mediterranean.

In one of his first acts as king in Babylon, Cyrus released the exiled Jews, who were now about 40,000 strong, most of whom chose to return to Judah. They took with them the many treasures that had been seized by Nebuchadnezzar, and rebuilt their capital and temple, but they were not permitted to reinstate their monarchy. On returning to their lost homeland, the Jews were surprised to discover other, non-exiled people living in the region, who followed a similar religion. Disputes between the two groups in time became ossified in the hostility between the Jews and the Samaritans, a problem that continued to New Testament times and beyond.

During their time in exile, the Jews had maintained their system of elders, their rituals, and essential practices, and had developed the Hebrew script. They remembered Cyrus with gratitude, even describing him as "God's anointed." **PF**

○ A medieval illustration of King Cyrus telling captured Jewish leaders they are free to leave and rebuild Jerusalem.

"I will raise up Cyrus. . . . He will rebuild my city and set my exiles free."

Isaiah 45:13

Prince Siddhartha Attains Enlightenment

After seven weeks of meditation, Prince Siddhartha attains full enlightenment and begins preaching a new religion and philosophical movement known as Buddhism.

○ A depiction of the Buddha at the Bodhi tree in Bodh Gaya, the place where he attained enlightenment.

"To depend on others for salvation is negative, to depend on oneself, positive."

Gautama Buddha

At the age of thirty-five, in circa 527 B.C.E., Siddhartha Gautama, prince of Lumbini (in the northern Ganges region of India, now Nepal), sat in meditation beside a bodhi tree at a place called Bodh Gaya. He determined not to move until he reached full enlightenment. After seven weeks of waiting, on the night of a full moon his meditation covered the full range of existence. From that time on, he was known as the Buddha, or the Enlightened One.

The fundamental understanding the Buddha achieved became known as the Four Holy Truths, which asserted the inevitability of loss and suffering as a product of humans' attachment to things and other people. He realized that attachment and the cravings it brings could be broken through adherence to a set of precepts that he laid down: the Eightfold Path.

The life of the Buddha is described only in devotional literature and is evidently embellished with miraculous details; even the century in which he lived and died is very uncertain. According to the stories, he was brought up in a palace without any experience of the pains of life. One day, however, he went out of the palace and encountered, for the first time, disease, aging, and death. Moved by these, he renounced his privileged lifestyle in favor of that of the ascetic wandering holy man. After a period of severe austerity, he concluded that this path did not hold a key to enlightenment, so he adopted a more moderate style of life, which eventually led him to the seven weeks of meditation and his enlightenment.

He spent the next forty-five years traveling and preaching to people from all walks of life, attracting many followers. By the time of his death, aged eighty, he had laid the foundations for the major religious and philosophical movement that endures to this day. **PF**

Mahavira Dies

The teacher whose ideas formed the heart of Jainism dies at Pawapuri.

At the age of seventy-two, Mahavira, or "Great Hero," died in 527 B.C.E. Often called the founder of Jainism, the third great religion of India, Mahavira is more accurately identified as the person who propagated or codified older teachings into their present form. A contemporary of Siddhartha Gautama, the Buddha, he too lived in the region of Bihar, having been born in Vaishali; his parents were King Siddhartha and Queen Trishala, of the *kshatriya* or warrior caste.

At the age of thirty he left his wife and family to become a monk. Like others of his caste at the time, he rejected some of the practices of Brahmanism, in particular the frequency of animal sacrifices, and he adopted ever more extreme practices, including refusing all possessions to the extent of going entirely naked and continually wandering. Developing the practice of *ahimsa*, or nonviolence, he refused to hurt any creature, and after twelve years he achieved *kevala*, the highest state of perception.

Over the next thirty years Mahavira collected together a variety of older teachings that he promulgated as the principles that came to form the heart of Jainism, preaching that people could save their souls through the renunciation of bodily desires and passions and of violence to any creature. He was considered the twenty-fourth and last of the *tirthankars* or saints, who had achieved enlightenment through their asceticism. By the time of his death at Pawapuri, he had thousands of followers from all walks of life, both monks and nuns; his sermons were collected and assembled into an oral tradition and were not written down until a thousand years later. Mahavira's life story, though, was recorded in a text known as the *Kalpasutra*, written about 150 years after his death. **PF**

Tarquin Flees Rome

The ruler known as the last king of Rome is overthrown in a popular uprising.

Tarquin the Proud (*Tarquinius Superbus* in Latin), the seventh and last king of Rome, was overthrown in a popular uprising. The people were angered by accusations that his son, Sextus, had raped a noblewoman, Lucretia. Tarquin, known for his cruelty, had ruled Rome for more than twenty years after murdering the previous king, Servius Tullius, and usurping his throne.

Tarquin may have been descended from Etruscans, who hailed from the area corresponding to modern Tuscany. The Etruscans, in many ways more advanced than the Romans at this time, were extending their power southward, and Etruscan inscriptions from the period have been found in Rome. If this is so, it may explain why Tarquin and his predecessors were so hated. As soon as Tarquin (and Sextus, who was found and killed) had fled from Rome, it is said that Lars Porsena, king of the Etruscan city of Clusium, attempted to seize the city but was held off by the bravery of the Romans, led by Horatius Cocles, who died while preventing the Etruscans from crossing the bridge across the River Tiber.

After more than 200 years of monarchy, the Romans decided it was time to rule themselves. Two men, known as consuls, were chosen from the senate (the council of elders that formerly advised the king), to act as joint heads of state. Their term of office lasted for one year only, and each was able to veto any action of the other, so that their power was intentionally limited. For later Romans, the overthrow of the monarchy and the foundation of the Roman republic was the most important event in their city's history, marking the beginning of Rome's independence from tyranny, and its rise to true and long-lasting greatness. **SK**

Democracy Is Born

Cleisthenes introduces an early form of democratic government to Athens.

The man who created the structure of the world's first and most influential democracy, Cleisthenes, spent a large part of his life fighting for the rights of his own prominent family against other noble factions in Athens, which included several decades in enforced exile. Eventually he achieved power by siding with the common people and seeking to implement the spirit of the reforms of the lawgiver Solon, who had attempted to balance the interests of the different communities of the city.

Cleisthenes therefore abolished the traditional forms of political organization based on family and clan, replacing it with that of ten "tribes" based on villages or *demes*, and set up a legislative council ("*boule*") in which the members were chosen by lot from among the entire citizenry, with quotas of representatives of each *deme* among its 500 members. There were strict rules about who was eligible and how long they could serve on the council, and the law courts and military command were organized in a similar manner. In doing so, Cleisthenes ensured that political participation was greatly widened and that it would be difficult for cliques to dominate the state and rule only in their own interests. The years of tyranny were over.

Although this is often seen as the beginning of direct democracy in which all citizens participated equally, Cleisthenes himself did not call this system democracy (meaning "rule by the people"), but rather *isonomia*, or equal rights for all. In many ways he left much of the traditional culture of Athens intact, but his reforms are seen as the beginning of the Golden Age of Athens, during which democracy grew and culture flourished. Little is known of his life after he introduced his reforms. **PF**

The Master's Message

Confucius leaves Lu to spread the message of good government.

In 497 B.C.E. Kong Fuzi (known in the Western world as "Confucius") left Lu, where he had been justice minister, to travel around China, searching for a state that would adopt his beliefs in the principles of good government. It was said that he disapproved of the king of Lu—where he had been justice minister—having failed to attend to proper rites during an animal sacrifice. For the next thirteen years, Confucius wandered all over China offering advice to feudal lords. His teachings, which have had a profound influence on Eastern thought up to the present day,

"Riches and honors acquired by unrighteousness are to me as a floating cloud."

Confucius, *Analects*, c.497 B.C.E.

were not immediately appreciated and he returned home unsuccessful in 484 B.C.E.

Confucius spent his last years dictating his thoughts, later collected as the *Analects*. In them, he stressed the need for ethical behavior, respect for the ancestors, and integrity. Prior to his wanderings, Confucius had been famous for his mastery of the six arts—ritual, music, archery, charioting, calligraphy, and arithmetic—and his familiarity with the traditions of poetry and history. However, it was only after his death that he attained the level of fame he now knows. His hometown is still a focus of pilgrimage, and there are temples devoted to him. **PF**

◗ A depiction of Confucius; the scrolls he is holding are indicative of his great wisdom.

Athenian Army Victorious at Marathon

Athenians defeat the Persian army on the plain of Marathon, north of Athens.

○ A seventeenth-century depiction of the Battle of Marathon, showing the Athenians defeating the Persians.

The cause of the Battle of Marathon can be traced back to 511 B.C.E., when Athens ejected Hippias, who had ruled the city as a tyrant for many years. However, when Darius of Persia sought Hippias's reinstatement, Athens became embroiled in a revolt of Greek Ionian colonies on Asia Minor against the Persian Empire. In 492 B.C.E., Darius sent an army under Mardonius to conquer Greece and her ally Eretria. The supporting fleet was wrecked in a storm, but a vast new fleet was assembled the following year that arrived at Euboea and landed on the mainland.

The Athenians sent a runner to request help from their old enemy Sparta, but the Spartans demurred, refusing to wage war during a religious festival. Athens was left without support other than the small city of Plataea. The Athenian generals were divided about whether they should attack or delay. Eventually they bravely marched northward toward the invaders.

The armies met on the plain of Marathon, north of Athens. Fewer than 10,000 Athenian hoplites (infantrymen) faced between 20,000 and 50,000 Persians, who had their backs to the sea. Realizing that the Persian cavalry was not on the field, the Athenian general Miltiades attacked at a run, surprising the Persian army. Overwhelmed, the Persians ran in confusion to their fleet. According to the Athenian historian Herodotus, some 6,400 Persians lost their lives, at a cost of only 192 Athenians. This was the first major defeat for the Persians in many years, and was a huge boost to Athenian confidence and power. **PF**

Leonidas and the Three Hundred Spartans

Victory over the Greeks comes at a huge cost for the Persian army.

○ *Leonidas at Thermopylae 480 BC (c.1814) by the French Revolutionary artist Jacques Louis David (1748–1825).*

When the massive army of the Persian king Xerxes ran into a tiny force of Spartans at Thermopylae in 480 B.C.E., it achieved both a victory and a defeat. Xerxes's army killed every one of the Spartan defenders, but the battle was to be one of the most significant defeats in the history of the world—the restraining of an Asian despotic power by the independent-minded Greeks.

To avenge the defeat of his father, Darius, ten years earlier, Xerxes raised an army perhaps 250,000 strong, accompanied by a large fleet, in an attempt to defeat Athens and conquer Greece. The Athenians decided to concentrate on fighting at sea, whereas the Spartans organized an army to defend Greece by land. The Spartan king Leonidas defended a pass through which ran the only road from the plains of Thessaly to the south. His army numbered no more than 7,000, including 300 heavily armed Spartans. For two days the well-positioned defenders held off wave after wave of attacks, but eventually a Greek farmer showed Xerxes a mountain path that would enable his troops to surround the defenders. Realizing this, Leonidas ordered all his troops other than Thebans and Spartans to withdraw. He got his remaining men to advance, but lost his life, and the Thebans, too, abandoned the fight. A final stand by the remaining Spartans was ended by Persian archers.

Despite their victory, the Persian losses were significant, whereas the Athenians' resolve to resist was strengthened. The Greek cities had begun to learn to fight together. **PF**

Xerxes Trounced

Themistocles's "wooden walls" save the city of Athens from the Persians.

After the Pyrrhic victory over the Spartan army at Thermopylae, the way was clear for Xerxes to invade Attica and attack Athens. The Athenian commander Themistocles hurriedly built a large fleet, acting on the advice of an oracle who had told him that the city would be saved by "wooden walls." Athens was evacuated, and when the Persians sacked the almost empty city and destroyed the Acropolis, Themistocles persuaded the other Greek states that it was necessary to fight the Persian fleet that accompanied—and provisioned—the invading army.

Half the Greek fleet came from Athens, but twenty other cities also contributed. Even so, it was outnumbered by more than two to one. Themistocles insisted on fighting in the narrow bay of Salamis, near Athens, but faced with disagreement by other Greek commanders he threatened to withdraw to Sicily. Hearing of this (Themistocles sent a slave with carefully filtered information), the Persians anticipated many of the defenders would withdraw at night. Even though this did not materialize, they entered the battle confidently, with Xerxes watching from a golden throne on a nearby hill.

The fight proceeded with the *triremes* ("warships") ramming one another before hand-to-hand fighting by the marines. The large Persian fleet could not easily maneuver, and after the Persian commander was killed, his fleet attempted to retreat but was driven back by the strong wind. Hundreds of Persian boats were sunk and thousands of men drowned. The whole of the Persian Royal Guard was killed. Xerxes could no longer provision his huge army and had to leave Greece. In rebuilding their city, the Athenians reached heights of cultural sophistication and political skill barely equaled since. **PF**

Sophocles Wins Prize

Aeschylus and Sophocles compete for the ivy wreath of the Great Dionysia.

In ancient Greece, theater—especially tragedy—was associated with Dionysus, god of wine. Playwrights competed over the right to have their plays put on in an annual competition known as the Great Dionysia. In 468 B.C.E. there was a contest between two of the greatest playwrights of all time.

Aeschylus, who was born in about 525 B.C.E., had fought at both Marathon and Salamis, and his earliest surviving play, which won the prize in 472 B.C.E., concerned the women of Persia suffering after the defeat of their army. Aeschylus had had his plays

> ## "I would rather miss the mark acting well than win the day acting basely."
>
> **Sophocles, *Philoctetes*, 409 B.C.E.**

performed at the Great Dionysia since 499 B.C.E., and throughout his career won the prize—a wreath made of ivy—some thirteen times.

In 468 B.C.E. Aeschylus found himself up against the novice Sophocles. Sophocles's trilogy included a play entitled *Triptolemos*, which has since been lost, and his victory began a glorious career in which he wrote 123 dramas (only seven have survived in their entirety) and won as many as twenty-four victories, the last of which was fifty-nine years after the first, in 409 B.C.E. (the winning play was *Philoctetes*).

Perhaps stung by his defeat, Aeschylus returned the following year with his famous Oedipus trilogy, of which only one play, *Seven Against Thebes*, still survives. Ironically Sophocles is best known today for his own trilogy about the ill-fated Oedipus. **PF**

Athenians Flaunt Status with Giant Statue

After the defeat of the Persians, Athens sees an extraordinary flourishing of cultural and political confidence and creativity.

Nothing symbolized Athens's preeminent status more than the marble temple astride its Acropolis, and the statue at its heart, dedicated to the goddess who protected the city and whose name it bore: Athena Parthenos ("maiden").

The building, with its subtle geometry, deep understanding of proportion, and marvelous frieze of sculptures (the remains of which are now in the British Museum in London), was the work of the architect Phidias, commissioned by the statesman Pericles in 449 B.C.E. Phidias set to work designing the statue of the goddess whose home the temple was, and in 438 B.C.E. she was finished and dedicated. Standing some 38 feet (12 m) high, the statue was made of a hollow wooden frame covered in ivory (for the flesh), silver, and more than a ton of gold. She was shown wearing a tunic, an *aegis* ("breastplate"), and a helmet, and holding a *Nike* ("goddess of victory") in her right hand and a spear in the left. A shield and a serpent rested by her side.

After finishing Athena, Phidias moved on to sculpt Zeus, father of the gods—the statue was erected at Olympia in 435 B.C.E. and became one of the Seven Wonders of the Ancient World. A few years later, however, Phidias's enemies accused him of stealing gold. He was also accused of impiety because his portrait, along with that of Pericles, appeared on Athena's shield. As a result Phidias was thrown into prison. It seems he either died there or in exile.

In 296 B.C.E., the gold was removed and replaced with bronze sheets, although the statue remained standing in the Parthenon for another 800 years. A new statue of Athena was erected in Nashville, Tennessee, in 1990, made as faithfully as possible to Phidias's original. **PF**

○ A nineteenth-century French engraving of how Phidias's statue of Athena would have looked.

"Hail Goddess . . . may you always defeat your enemies, with a spear of salvation!"

Orestes to Athena, in Aeschylus's *Eumenides*

Pericles Praises Dead from Peloponnesian War

The great political leader tries to galvanize Athens with his famous funeral oration.

○ An undated depiction of Pericles delivering his funeral oration to the Athenian people.

Late in 431 B.C.E., Pericles gave his famous oration at the public funeral held in Athens for all those who had died over the previous twelve months in the Peloponnesian War. Pericles had been preeminent in Athens for thirty years, overseeing the building of the Parthenon and the city's so-called "Golden Age," but he came to champion the use of an increasingly belligerent form of imperialism over the other Greek cities that led to the war with Sparta breaking out in 432 B.C.E. The bloody conflict was to continue for some thirty years, and ultimately result in defeat and destruction for the Athenian democracy, but in 431 B.C.E., at the outset of the war, Pericles sought to raise the spirits of the citizens of Athens with his oratory. The historian Thucydides recorded how, in the funeral procession, the bones of the dead were taken in cypress coffins, with one left empty for those whose bodies could not be recovered, to the public tomb dedicated to men who died in war. Pericles then gave the oration. Whether Pericles's words were his own or the invention of the historian cannot be known, but they included a resounding celebration of the glories of Athenian democracy, liberty, equality, and empire. Finally Pericles praised the dead, and exhorted the living to continue in the same spirit.

Despite his fine words, the Athenians grew increasingly unhappy with the way the war was going, particularly as they faced a devastating outbreak of plague. Yet Pericles retained power until, in 429 B.C.E., he too succumbed to the disease. **PF**

Socrates Forced to Drink Poison

The famous philosopher is found guilty of corrupting the youth of Athens.

○ *The Death of Socrates* (date unknown) by Charles Alphonse Dufresnoy (1611–1668).

The Athenians needed a scapegoat. Politically, the city's fortunes were at a low ebb in 399 B.C.E. after a humiliating defeat, five years before, at the hands of its traditional enemy, Sparta. There was one man in Athens who had made himself a reputation for being awkward—the philosopher Socrates. He liked to ask difficult and irritating questions; he mocked those in power and spent his time debating ideas with a band of devoted pupils. He was also known as an associate of some of Athens's discredited leaders. So Socrates was put on trial, charged with not believing in the gods and with corrupting the young men of Athens. Socrates's famous pupil Plato left an account of his trial, in which he states that Socrates could have saved himself by paying a fine, but instead refused to

answer the charges against him, claiming he had done nothing wrong. He was found guilty and was sentenced to death by drinking poison hemlock, a toxic herb that paralyzes the nervous system. Still debating questions such as the immortality of the soul with the friends who had gathered around him, Socrates took the poison calmly from the executioner and drank it in one swallow. Death followed quickly.

Socrates was one of the most significant thinkers in the course of history and, with Plato and Aristotle, was largely responsible for founding Western philosophy. He was interested in the values that make people act as they do, yet left no writings of his own. Most of what we do know of his teachings comes from the *Dialogues of Plato*. **SK**

Gauls Attack Rome and Lay Siege to the Capitol

Juno's sacred geese alert Roman soldiers and avert a catastrophe.

⬧ An engraving of the painting *The Capitol is Rescued by the Holy Geese of Juno* by Heinrich Merté (1838–1917).

"Juno's sacred geese, despite the dearth of provisions, had not been killed."

Livy, *History of Rome*, c.26 C.E.

Rome's worst defeat since its foundation came at the hands of the Gauls of northern Italy's Po Valley. In the summer of 390 B.C.E. a band of Gauls led by a warrior chief named Brennus destroyed a Roman army at the battle of Allia and went on to attack Rome itself. It was night, and the garrison had taken refuge in the Capitol, which was the highest point of the city as well as being its religious center.

The Gauls were climbing up along a rocky path approaching the Capitol when a furious cackling and flapping of wings broke out. The flock of sacred geese kept in the sanctuary of Juno—which had been spared despite the lack of food—made such a noise that the defending soldiers were warned of the Gauls' approach and the Capitol was saved. The rest of the city was plundered and destroyed, but luckily almost every one of the city's inhabitants, including the Vestal Virgins and their sacred flame, had fled already. The Gauls laid siege to the Capitol for seven months until Brennus finally agreed his troops would withdraw, in return for a large payment of gold.

The memory of their humiliation at the hand of the Gauls would haunt the Romans for generations to come. Picking itself up from defeat, the army adopted new weapons and strategy, and in 378 B.C.E. a defensive stone wall, 7 miles (11 km) long, was built around the city, large sections of which are still standing today.

The military expansion of Rome continued, but the Romans could never feel secure until, in 225 B.C.E., the Gauls of northern Italy were finally defeated and brought under the Romans' control. As for the sacred geese, each year they were allowed to sit on purple cushions, whereas the dogs that guarded the Capitol were punished for having failed to give warning of the Gauls' attack. **SK**

Into the Groves of Academe

Greek philosopher Plato sets up the world's first school for thinking.

The location for the school where Plato would go on to systematize philosophy was about a mile northwest of the Athens Acropolis. It was set in a park of olive groves, usually used for religious festivals and athletic contests, and called Academia after Hecademus, a legendary figure who was said to have given it to the city. The school—and countless schools and colleges ever since—was therefore called the "Academy."

The area had probably been used for teaching and discussion for some decades before Plato. Although it is not clear whether he set up any formal organization, Plato certainly owned a house and small garden in the area, and is said to have taught there for about forty years until his death in 348 B.C.E. For twenty years Aristotle was a regular attendee of Plato's Academy.

Plato accepted only those students he believed to be "intoxicated to learn what was in their souls." It seems, from the evidence of Plato's own writings, that he taught by walking around reading from his dialogues and lectures, and presiding over religious devotions and long meals at which the participants could "honor the gods and enjoy each other's company and refresh themselves with learned discussion." He also set up a Museion, or temple of the Muses, nearby.

The Academy survived for several hundred years, becoming renowned for the school of philosophers known as neo-Platonists. In 86 B.C.E., the olive groves were cut down by a Roman invading force, although the Academy remained. It is uncertain exactly when it closed, although some sources claim it endured until 526 C.E. At this time the emperor Justinian issued an edict to close down all "pagan" schools, and Plato's Academy may have been among them. **PF**

⊘ A mosaic of Plato's Academy, dated to the first century C.E., now in the National Archeological Museum in Naples, Italy.

> ## "The direction in which education starts a man will determine his future life."

Plato, *The Republic*, 360 B.C.E.

Alexander Educated

Aristotle is summoned to teach Alexander, the future conqueror of Asia.

The Greeks had always affected to despise Macedon, judging it a backward and barbaric place. But Philip II, who became king of Macedon in 356 B.C.E., was determined to change things. In 342 B.C.E., he invited Aristotle to travel from Athens to his capital at Pella and act as tutor his thirteen-year-old son, Alexander. Philip wanted his son's education to prepare him for his future role as a military leader. Aristotle, who had a passionate interest in nature (he identified more than 500 animal species), taught Alexander for three years. He instructed him in politics, rhetoric,

> ## "Philip sent for Aristotle, the most learned and celebrated philosopher of his time."
>
> **Plutarch (c.46–120 c.e.), *Life of Alexander***

mathematics, science, medicine, and Greek literature. In later life, Alexander drew inspiration from Homer's poem *The Iliad*, which he took on his campaigns.

Philip trained the Macedonian army using Greek fighting methods, and expanded his kingdom through military force. When Alexander was sixteen and acting as regent of Macedon, he crushed a rebellion in his father's absence. Two years later, in 338 B.C.E., he fought beside Philip at the decisive battle of Chaeronea, at which the Macedonians won an overwhelming victory over Athens, Thebes, and the other Greek city-states. Philip was now sole ruler of Greece. Aristotle meanwhile returned to Athens, where, in 335 B.C.E., he founded a school, the Lyceum, and devoted himself to study. He is recognized today as the first true scientist. **SK**

King Philip II Slain

Twenty-year-old heir Alexander wreaks vengeance upon revolting Greeks.

The Macedonian capital of Pella was crowded for the marriage of Cleopatra, daughter of King Philip II, to King Alexander of Epirus, when all was thrown into confusion—Philip had been stabbed to death as he attended the theater where the celebrations were being held. The assailant, Pausanius, of the king's noble bodyguard, was killed as he fled the scene of the crime. Some people suspected that Olympias, Philip's estranged queen and the mother of Alexander, had been involved in the murder plot.

The Macedonian army immediately proclaimed Alexander, who was barely twenty years old, as King Alexander III. At the time of his death Philip had been about to lead a Greek army in an invasion of Persia. Most of the Greek city-states now seized the opportunity to break their allegiance with Macedon, but Alexander swiftly moved to halt the revolt. He laid siege to Thebes, and when the Thebans refused to surrender, he ordered his soldiers to storm and destroy the city, and sell all the inhabitants into slavery. The other city-states immediately submitted to Alexander. Summoning their leaders to an assembly at Corinth, he gave notice of his intention to carry out his father's planned invasion of Persia. It proved to be a campaign of unparalleled conquest.

In 1977, archeologists excavating a site at Vergina in northern Greece discovered the tomb of Philip II. In the burial chamber, they found a marble sarcophagus, splendid vessels of gold and silver, and a magnificent set of royal armor. The king's cremated remains were inside a gold casket decorated with the royal star of Macedon. **SK**

○ A fourteenth-century manuscript illumination of Philip II of Macedon (382–336 B.C.E.), father of Alexander the Great.

† ἐγὼ ἐν τῷ
ἀλεξα δ ἐν ὀ
τε φ η φ ορ ω ρα
και κοσμηκε
τον τον κα
καματων και
ω ὁ ρ η μ ι κα
τᾶμ ὁ ρ ημρα ς
Ἀ ρ ου τω ο θ

Alexander Battles for Issus

Darius and his vast Persian army meet the Macedonian forces of his nemesis Alexander at the gulf of Issus, and suffer a terrible defeat.

🌢 A first-century C.E. mosaic depicting scenes from the Battle of Issus, in which Alexander defeated the armies of Darius.

"I send you mustard seed . . . that you may acknowledge the bitterness of my victory."

Letter from Alexander to Darius III

Alexander's conquest of the Middle East, which had begun with his victory at the Granicus in May 334 B.C.E. and the consequent seizure of Asia Minor, became unstoppable the following year when he met and destroyed a much larger army, led by the Persian emperor Darius III.

The Persian army was said to have numbered 600,000, which is probably a wild exaggeration, but even had it numbered a more likely estimate of 100,000 it would probably have more than doubled the Macedonian army. Alexander and his general Parmenion had joined forces, intending to attack the Persians in the south, but they discovered that Darius had already passed them and cut off their supply lines. The armies, divided by a shallow stream, met on a small plain at the head of the gulf of Issus, in the southeast of modern Turkey. Crucially, the site did not permit the Persians to take advantage of their numerical superiority.

Alexander led the charge on the right flank, and while the most important early fighting took place on the Macedonian left, by the coast, the Persian advance was held up by Parmenion long enough for Alexander's cavalry charge to destroy the Persian position. Alexander himself directly attacked Darius's position, and although the two may not actually have met (as is shown in a famous Pompeiian mosaic), desperate fighting took place around the emperor's chariot. Darius fled, and a Persian rout ensued—in which more than 50,000 men were said to have been killed. The Macedonians pursued Darius for 15 miles (24 km), capturing his treasure and family, including his mother and both of his wives. Alexander moved south through Syria to Egypt—and the imminent destruction of the Achaemenid Empire. **PF**

Alexandria Founded

Alexander becomes king of Egypt and founds his eponymous city.

After his victory over Darius at the Issus River, Alexander marched south through Jordan to Egypt, where the ancient civilization had been reduced to the state of a Persian province. The Persian governor could not resist, and Alexander was welcomed as a liberator. He sailed up the Nile to Memphis, where he sacrificed a bull to Amun and was soon after crowned King of Egypt.

In 331 B.C.E., he began searching for a site to found a new city, one that could link Egypt with the Greek world. Alexander discovered a site mentioned by

"There is an island in the much-dashing sea; Pharos is what men call it."

Homer, *The Odyssey*, recalled by Alexander

Herodotus and Homer (in *The Odyssey*) on the Mediterranean coast; protected by sea, desert, and other natural defenses, it was a central, defensible location with easy access to Greece. Alexander marked out streets, palaces, temples, defenses, and even a complex sewer system. A later story described how, having no chalk, he marked his streets in lines of barley flour, but that these were eaten by a flock of birds. Despite this drawback, a soothsayer asserted that the city would still flourish.

Shortly thereafter, Alexander left Egypt. He never saw the completed city that would in later years come to boast the Pharos of Alexandria (the lighthouse that was one of the Seven Wonders of the Ancient World) and the Great Library, but was destined only to return ten years later in a coffin. **PF**

Broken "Camel's Back"

At the Battle of Gaugamela Alexander breaks the Persian Empire for good.

In 331 B.C.E., Alexander rejected the peace terms of the Persian emperor Darius—who offered him the land west of the Euphrates, a large sum of money, and his daughter's hand in marriage—and marched across the Tigris into northern Mesopotamia. Darius assembled an even larger army than the one he had led at Issus. Contemporary accounts claim Darius was in command of up to one million soldiers. Darius was determined to fight on open ground where his large army and 200 formidable scythed chariots would be effective. The ground on which they fought

"Darius, who had already been in a state of fear, was the first to turn and flee."

Arrian (*d.*146 C.E.), *The Anabasis of Alexander*

on October 1 was close to the village of Gaugamela, which means "camel's back."

Despite being heavily outnumbered, Alexander advanced, forcing Darius to attack with his chariots in the center, enabling Alexander to open their ranks and attack them from the sides. At the same time, he lured the Persian army toward the wings before making a wedge-shaped attack on the Persian line, splitting it, and endangering Darius's own position. Darius fled; Alexander remained on the field.

After the battle, Alexander captured the Persian royal train and marched into Babylon. By January 330 B.C.E. he had taken Darius's capital Persepolis and proclaimed himself King of Persia. Darius escaped eastward but was murdered by one of his own satraps, whom Alexander, in turn, had executed. **PF**

Death of Alexander

The conqueror's death in Babylon ignites a succession battle that lasts for decades.

Alexander was full of ambition when he reached Babylon in 323 B.C.E. and was soon making plans to send a fleet to invade Arabia. On May 29, however, he became sick after a long and drunken banquet with his friend Medius. He was already feverish, but kept working, being carried out on his bed when necessary so that he could issue orders to his army. He also continued to carry out religious rituals and duties, but it was to no avail. After a feverish illness of about two weeks, Alexander died. He was just thirty-two years old.

Inevitably, rumors that he had been poisoned began to circulate, and have still not been laid to rest. On balance, though, it seems more likely that Alexander died of natural causes; several sources have since suggested that he might have been suffering from malaria, with the end perhaps hastened by the remedies prescribed by his doctors.

On June 9, the Macedonian veterans had filed past their leader for the last time. As he lay dying, Alexander gave his ring to his general Perdiccas, who asked about his intentions for a successor, since his wife, Roxane, was still pregnant. "To the strongest" was the reply. The day after his death, the generals argued about what to do, and war between them soon became inevitable, leading to a fifty-year struggle in what would come to be called the wars of the *diodochi* ("successors"). In the end, the empire was divided between the Antigonid dynasty in Macedonia and Greece, the Seleucids in Mesopotamia and Persia, and the Ptolemies in Egypt.

Alexander's embalmed body was placed in a lavish sarcophagus and taken to Egypt, where it was placed in Alexandria, his great city at the mouth of the Nile. It remained there through the Roman period but was lost shortly thereafter. **PF**

○ Detail from *Alexander the Great and the Captured Poros* (1673) by Charles le Brun (1619–1690).

◑ *Funeral Lament at the Death of Alexander the Great* from a fifth-century Armenian manuscript.

"You will soon die, and will own as much of this earth as will suffice to bury you."

Indian sage Dandamis, to Alexander

New Power Base

Chandra Gupta Maurya establishes the Mauryan Empire.

In the chaos created by Alexander's sudden death in 323 B.C.E., Chandra Gupta Maurya acquired a power base in the northwest, from where he overthrew Dhana, King of Magadha. Aged just twenty, he set up his own Mauryan dynasty and created a huge army, which he used to conquer many of the Greek satraps in the Punjab. He also extended his power across Afghanistan in 305 B.C.E. in exchange for 500 war elephants in a treaty with Seleucos, one of Alexander's successors, who had sought to reconquer India.

Little is known about the origins of the man who

"A huge wild elephant went to Maurya and took him on his back as if tame."

Junianus Justinus, 3rd century c.e.

set up India's first great unifying empire. Rumors vary from those that say he was born of royal stock in about 340 B.C.E. to those that suggest his parents were peacock-tamers. As a young man, Maurya was encouraged by a Brahmin to create a guerrilla army; it is also claimed that at the age of about sixteen, he met Alexander the Great and tried to persuade him to continue eastward to challenge the Nanda dynasty ruling Magadha, but that Alexander turned back westward.

Within a few years Maurya's rule had stretched to include most of the Indian subcontinent; his capital, Pataliputra, became one of the largest cities of the ancient world. Chandra Gupta abdicated in favor of his son Bindusara in 293 B.C.E., and is said to have ended his days as a Jain ascetic, fasting to death. **PF**

Ptolemy I Takes Egypt

The first Ptolemaic pharaoh seizes control after the death of Alexander.

After Alexander's death, three of his leading generals divided up the empire and fought one another to establish dominance. Ptolemy was a Macedonian, a childhood friend of Alexander's. He took firm control of—perhaps stole—Alexander's corpse in its lavish gold coffin and took it, in a grand procession, to Egypt; the plan was to take it to Memphis, but eventually he took it to Alexandria, where it remained on display for several centuries. Ptolemy took the title of Satrap of Egypt and may have married the daughter of the previous pharaoh, Nectanebo II.

"Collect books on kingship and the exercise of power, and read them."

Advice to Ptolemy from head of Great Library

After several years of jockeying for power in Syria, and the threat of invasion from his rival Perdiccas, Ptolemy took the title of king of Egypt in 305 B.C.E., establishing a dynasty that was to rule for 300 years until the arrival of the Romans. Encouraging the often insular Egypt to open itself to Hellenistic influence, he also created the Great Library at Alexandria, which became one of the glories of the classical world, and the "museum," which became the first university. He was the patron of the geometer Euclid and was also responsible for starting the building of the Pharos, or great lighthouse of Alexandria, one of the wonders of the ancient world. **PF**

○ An undated depiction of Ptolemy I being crowned by the goddesses of South and North Egypt.

A Colossal Tribute to Helios at Rhodes

The enormous statue, known as the Colossus of Rhodes, *is completed by the harbor entrance and becomes one of the Seven Wonders of the Ancient World.*

🔾 An etching of the Colossus of Rhodes from the book *The Seven Wonders of the World* (1792).

> ## "The artist used so much bronze that it seemed likely to create a dearth."
>
> **Philo of Byzantium, first century B.C.E.**

One of the Seven Wonders of the Ancient World, the *Colossus of Rhodes* was built as a result of the internecine warfare between Alexander the Great's generals, Ptolemy and Antigonus. The Rhodians supported Ptolemy, king of Egypt, and were besieged by Demetrios, son of Antigonus, with a force of more than 40,000 men. Demetrios built two huge siege towers but to no avail—the first was destroyed in a storm, and the second stuck in mud after the defenders flooded ditches around the city walls.

After the attackers withdrew, the Rhodians gratefully built a statue, 40 cubits (108 feet, 33 m) high, to their patron god Helios. It stood on a pedestal by the harbor entrance. Designed by Chares of Lindos, who had been involved in the defense of the city, the statue was made of stone and iron, and covered in plates of bronze taken from the abandoned weapons of the attackers. It took twelve years to build, and Chares committed suicide before it was completed in 280 B.C.E., perhaps because someone pointed out a flaw in the construction.

The statue stood for just fifty-six years until, in 224 B.C.E., an earthquake broke it at both knees, toppling it. The huge pieces remained on the ground and became a tourist attraction. Pliny the Elder, in the first century C.E., said, "Few men can clasp the thumb in their arms, and its fingers are larger than most statues. Where the limbs are broken, vast caverns are seen yawning in the interior." The remains were eventually broken up and the bronze was reused by Arab invaders in the seventh century C.E.

Although later illustrations show the statue straddling the harbor entrance, engineers and scientists now claim it is impossible that it could actually have done so. **PF**

Ashoka Finds Peace

Shocked by the carnage of battle in Kalinga, Ashoka embraces Buddhism.

By his own account, 100,000 men were killed and another 150,000 people driven from the land in the terrible violence that Ashoka, third ruler of the Mauryan dynasty of ancient India, unleashed when he invaded the neighboring kingdom of Kalinga. Overcome by remorse, he became a Buddhist, renounced war, and declared his intention to conquer only by dharma (the principles of right life).

Ashoka's edicts were inscribed on thirty-three stone columns, the Ashoka Pillars, that were erected in various parts of his kingdom. The most famous is

"[May all] be provided with the welfare and happiness of this world and of the next."

Edict of Ashoka

the Sarnath column, originally more than 50 feet (15 m) high, which stood at the site where the Buddha preached his first sermon. Its magnificent capital of four lions looking north, south, east, and west was adopted as India's national emblem in 1948. Ashoka's edicts are also found carved on rocks and cave walls as far as the upper Indus Valley, southern Gujarat, and along the Krishna River in the south of India.

The inscriptions describe Ashoka's conversion to Buddhism and his efforts to spread it, his moral and religious precepts, and his respect for animal life. To care for his people, Ashoka ordered hospitals and rest houses to be built and wells to be dug, and sent missionaries as far as Sri Lanka. The empire he established, unparalleled in ancient India, broke up within fifty years of his death in 233 B.C.E. **SK**

400,000 Buried Alive

The Qin army defeat the Zhao in the Battle of Gaoping.

The creation of a unified Chinese state was the achievement of the western kingdom of Qin, which in the third century B.C.E. ruthlessly eliminated its six major rivals in what is known as the Warring States Period. Ultimately Qin, and its king Yíng Zhèng, was unchallenged, and the Chinese empire was established with Yíng Zhèng known as Shi Huangdi, the First Emperor.

The key battle in the Qin ascendancy was that of Gaoping (also known as Changping) in September 260 B.C.E., when the Qin army, led by Wang He, invaded Han, seeking to conquer the strategically important fort of Shangdang. The weakened Han gave Shangdang to the neighboring northerly—and far more powerful—kingdom of Zhao, which defended Shangdang. A two-year siege ensued, followed by what became one of the bloodiest battles in the history of the world. The Qin army, which numbered approximately half a million men, managed to surround Zhao's army and blockade it on a hilltop for forty-five days. When Zhao Kuo, the young defending commander, was killed in a foray that attempted to break the siege, the Zhao army surrendered, whereupon Bai Qi, the Qin commander, had the entire Zhao army of 400,000 men buried alive in the course of a single night to prevent a mass revolt. Just 240 of the youngest soldiers were spared to bring the news back to Zhao.

Zhao never recovered from the defeat and was conquered by the Qin by 228 B.C.E. Bai Qi was forced to commit suicide three years later, as he was thought to be a threat to the Qin prime minister.

In the mid-1990s, archeologists uncovered pits containing large numbers of bones apparently from this battle. **RG**

Eureka!

Archimedes discovers how to measure density while taking a bath.

⬥ A hand-colored woodcut entitled *Archimedes in His Bath* (1547), by an unknown artist.

King Hieron of Sicily, wanting to find out if a crown he had been given was made of solid gold, or whether he had been palmed off with one containing silver, asked Archimedes to solve the problem. But how was he to do so without melting down the metal and destroying the crown? While taking a bath, Archimedes noticed that the water level rose when he got in, and he realized that he could determine the gold density of the crown by weighing it in water. He was so excited by this discovery that he is reputed to have rushed out naked into the street shouting "Eureka!" ("I have found it!").

Archimedes was born in 287 B.C.E. in the Greek city-state of Syracuse, Sicily, and is also credited with inventing the lever and the Archimedes screw—a device for lifting water—and for setting fire to Roman ships using mirrors and the sun's rays during the siege of Syracuse. When the city fell in 212 B.C.E., Archimedes, so it was said, was killed by a Roman soldier because he ignored a command to leave his mathematical diagrams.

Archimedes was held in great respect by the ancient world, both as a practical and a theoretical scientist. He wrote on mechanics, hydrostatics, catoptrics (refraction), and mathematics. Although much of his work was lost, his surviving writings were known to Islamic mathematicians in the Middle Ages. They were rediscovered by Renaissance scholars, which greatly influenced the development of mathematics in medieval Europe. **SK**

China United "For Ten Thousand Generations"

Zheng, king of Qin, conquers the other Chinese states and adopts the title Shi Huangdi.

○ A view of the Terracotta Army in Xian, one of the largest archeological discoveries ever made.

For more than 200 years, during the Warring States Period, China had been divided into rival states. Qin, in the west, had already begun to emerge as the most powerful of them when Zheng became king in 246 B.C.E., at age thirteen. Eight years later, through a combination of surprise attacks, espionage, and bribery, he set about eliminating the six other states one by one. Qi, in the northeast, was the last to fall in 221 B.C.E. For the first time in history, China was united under one ruler and Zheng proclaimed himself Shi Huangdi, the First Emperor. His dynasty, he announced, would last 10,000 generations.

With his new chief minister, Li Si, Shi Huangdi ruthlessly imposed centralized rule. He did away with all regional variations in weights and measures, standardized the laws and the Chinese script, and began to build roads and canals. He constructed an earth barrier to link the frontier fortresses in the north—the beginning of the Great Wall of China.

Shi Huangdi was afraid of one thing only—death—and is supposed to have traveled to the islands of Japan in search of the elixir of life. It took 700,000 men to build his massive tomb complex, said to be a representation of the cosmos. In 1974, men digging a well broke into a large pit containing thousands of life-size clay soldiers. They had stumbled upon the greatest archeological discovery ever made in China—the Terracotta Army of more than 7,000 warriors that had stood guard close to the body of the First Emperor for over 2,000 years. **SK**

Impossible Journey

Carthaginian general Hannibal leads his men across the Alps to attack Rome.

In the fall of 218 B.C.E., an exhausted, demoralized army lay scattered among the rocks, snow, and ice of a high Alpine pass. A force of wild tribesmen from Spain, Libyan foot soldiers, and Numidian horsemen from north Africa had followed twenty-eight-year-old general Hannibal Barca in a bid to cross this apparently impassable mountain barrier.

Hannibal's native city, Carthage, in what is now Tunisia, was engaged in a life-or-death struggle with the Roman Republic for control of the western Mediterranean. In the spring of 218 B.C.E., Hannibal had led his army from Spain to invade Italy. He set out with more than 100,000 men, tens of thousands of horses and mules, and thirty-seven war elephants. A long journey through hostile territory greatly reduced the army even before it reached the Alps. There, advancing up narrow tracks through mountain gorges, Hannibal's soldiers were attacked by the Allobroges and other local tribesmen. It took nine days to reach the top of the pass.

Hannibal, who had shared in all his men's hardships, rallied the cold and hungry troops to undertake the descent into Italy, which, he said, would place Rome in their hands. Walking on snow and ice, the animals and men struggled along the narrow downward track, terrified of falling to their deaths over the slippery edge. At one point they had to spend four days rebuilding the obliterated path. Only around 26,000 men made it to Italy, with a handful of elephants. Nonetheless, Hannibal had achieved an extraordinary feat in crossing the Alps and could now advance upon Rome. **RG**

○ A detail from *Hannibal and His War Elephants Crossing the Alps*, a nineteenth-century English School lithograph.

Roman Massacre

Hannibal inflicts catastrophic losses upon the Roman legions at Cannae.

Despite being fought with only swords and spears, the bloody battle of Cannae in 216 B.C.E. saw the highest death toll in a single day's fighting in the entire history of Europe.

The Roman Republic sent eight legions of citizen soldiers, and allies, to confront the Carthaginian general Hannibal Barca, who had invaded Italy two years previously. Led by the consuls Paullus and Varro, the Roman force of 70,000 infantry and 6,000 cavalry faced Hannibal on a plain between the River Aufidus (now Ofanto) and the hilltop of Cannae. The armies

> *"Some . . . tortured by their wounds . . . were promptly put an end to by the enemy."*
>
> **Livy, *History of Rome*, c.26 C.E.**

positioned their infantry in the center and horsemen on the flanks. Hannibal's foot soldiers—Libyans, Spanish, and Celts—were heavily outnumbered. Hannibal pushed the Celts and Spanish toward the Roman line, inviting an attack, but holding his disciplined Libyan infantry on each side. In swirling dust the two forces clashed. At first, the Romans drove forward, pushing into the Carthaginian center. Then the Libyans attacked from both flanks, crushing the Roman infantry. Hannibal's cavalry drove out the Roman horsemen and charged into the rear. Encircled, the Romans were systematically massacred, their bodies lying in heaps upon the battlefield. More than 48,000 men from the Roman army were killed. Yet Rome refused peace and Hannibal failed to follow up his crushing victory. The war continued. **SK**

From Peasant Bandit to Emperor

Former peasant Liu Bang seizes control of China and establishes the Han dynasty, which goes on to rule for 400 years.

漢高祖

⊙ An eighteenth-century painting of Emperor Liu Bang, a peasant bandit who founded the Han dynasty.

"I know how to use people, so I was able to conquer the lands under heaven."

Liu Bang

When the First Emperor of China, Qin Shi Huangdi, died in 210 B.C.E., his son was unable to rule effectively. In 209 B.C.E., a series of rebellions broke out against the Qin dynasty, and a bandit, Liu Bang, was encouraged to support the prince of the former kingdom of Chu. Liu Bang, a man of peasant stock who had been a police chief in Jiangsu under the Qin, put together a small force and conquered Guanzhong in Shaanxi, the Qin homeland. In 206 B.C.E. he entered Xianyang, the Qin capital. He was rewarded with the principality of Han (modern Sichuan, Chongqing, and southern Shaanxi).

Liu Bang now sought to conquer the whole of China, and, having abandoned the harsher aspects of the Qin regime, won a great deal of popular support for his campaign. Despite his relatively small forces, he used guile to maintain his position against the usually militarily brilliant but politically naïve Xiang Yu, a Chu nobleman. Liu Bang defeated him in 202 B.C.E.—after which Xiang Yu committed suicide.

After his victory, Liu Bang took the title of Gaozu Emperor, restored centralized authority, and from his capital of Chang'an (formerly Xianyang) established the Han dynasty, which went on to rule for almost 400 years.

Liu Bang retained his peasant manners throughout his reign—once famously urinating in a scholar's hat to show his disdain for education—but he ruled according to Confucian principles. He gained popularity when he sought to reduce taxes on peasants, but gained enemies when he executed several of the generals who had helped him to power. In contrast, he bought off the main external threat, that of the Xiongnu nomads in the north, through strategic marriage and bribes. **PF**

Scipio's Revenge

Scipio's legions finally defeat Hannibal and his elephants at the Battle of Zama.

The Roman general Publius Cornelius Scipio was a survivor of the butchery of Rome's army by the Carthaginian Hannibal at Cannae in 216 B.C.E. By 202 B.C.E. Scipio had turned the tables. Leading a Roman invasion of North Africa, he was threatening the city of Carthage, forcing Hannibal to return from his prolonged campaign to defend his home territory. The forces of Scipio and Hannibal met west of Carthage for the mighty Battle of Zama.

Aware that his army was depleted and, by this time, far inferior to the force that had won his earlier

"The Romans fell upon their foes, raising their war-cry and clashing their shields."

Polybius, Greek historian, 205–123 B.C.E.

combats, Hannibal gambled on the use of war elephants, and eighty of the intimidating beasts charged at the Roman legions. Amid the noise of battle, however, many of the elephants took fright and ran amok, charging Hannibal's own cavalry as they fled. The other elephants passed harmlessly through gaps Scipio had organized in the Roman lines. Hannibal's army was doomed, his cavalry driven from the field, and his infantry succumbed to the inexorable advance of Scipio's legionaries. The contest was over.

The victory at Zama forced Carthage to accept defeat and established Rome as the dominant power in the western Mediterranean. Hannibal was eventually driven into exile and, still pursued by his Roman foes, committed suicide twenty years later. **SK**

Rome Triumphs

Macedonian defeat at Pydna ensures Roman conquest of Greece.

Near Pydna in northern Greece, at the foot of Mount Olympus, the mythological home of the gods, two armies clashed in a contest that would decide the future of Mediterranean civilization. On one side was the 40,000-strong army of King Perseus of Macedonia, on the other, 40,000 Roman soldiers led by a sixty-year-old Roman consul, Lucius Aemilius Paullus.

The expansionist Roman Republic had been intermittently at war with Macedonia, the dominant power in Greece, for thirty years. Perseus's men fought in a long-established but antiquated style.

"Who would not want to know how the world came under Rome's sole rule?"

Polybius, Greek historian, 205–123 B.C.E.

The foot soldiers, armed with *sarissas* (pikes) up to 23 feet (7 m) long, formed tight-packed phalanxes—showing only shields and spear points. The Roman legionaries, however, fought with throwing spears and short swords in small units capable of more flexible fighting.

At first, the Romans could not penetrate the wall of Macedonian spears, but when they found gaps in the Macedonian phalanxes, they could fight at close quarters, and the Macedonians became easy meat for the sword-wielding Romans. Some 25,000 were killed, for the loss of only one hundred Roman lives.

Perseus was the last king of Macedonia, which became a Roman province in 146 B.C.E. The once-powerful Greek city-states were reduced to provincial towns within the Roman Empire. **RG**

Carthage Destroyed

Rome exterminates a rival civilization with genocidal thoroughness.

More than 2,000 years before the atom bomb, the Romans demonstrated how to destroy an entire city by military action. Their legions razed to the ground the city of Carthage, in modern-day Tunisia, and either killed or enslaved every single citizen. Not a single building was left standing.

Once Rome's great rival in the western Mediterranean, Carthage had been forced to accept humiliating peace terms after its defeat at Zama in 202 B.C.E. The Carthaginians were stripped of their military power, but many Romans remained suspicious of their old enemies, including the orator Cato the Elder, who frequently declaimed, "Carthage must be destroyed!"

Eventually the Carthaginians were maneuvered into a technical breach of the terms of the peace treaty. On this pretext, in 149 B.C.E., the Romans sent an expeditionary force to besiege the city, but Carthage had imposing fortifications and at first the Roman operation went badly. In 147 B.C.E. command passed to Scipio Aemilianus, grandson of Scipio Africanus, the victor of Zama. Scipio tightened the blockade of the city, which soon faced starvation.

In the spring of 146 B.C.E. Roman troops penetrated the city walls. The Carthaginians put up desperate resistance, but surrender was inevitable. Some 50,000 survivors were marched off into captivity. A final hard core of 900 resisters burned themselves to death in a temple. After a few days of plunder, work began on the systematic destruction of the city, mostly by fire. Scipio is said to have wept, foreseeing that one day the same fate might befall Rome. **RG**

◗ A gruesome engraving depicting the storming of Byrsa and the defeat of the Carthaginians.

Spartacus Defeated

The Romans finally subdue the great slave leader Spartacus and his followers.

Spartacus, leader of the largest internal revolt against the Roman republic, was finally defeated by the Romans in 70 B.C.E. Spartacus was a slave who trained in a gladiators' school near Capua in southern Italy. In 73 B.C.E., seizing knives from the kitchen, he and around seventy others escaped and set up a group of outlaws—some gladiators, others robbers, and yet more runaway slaves—on the slopes of Mt. Vesuvius. Again and again Spartacus defeated forces sent to destroy him and took their weapons. His forces soon swelled to more than 100,000, including women,

> ## "Spartacus . . . was most intelligent and cultured, being more like a Greek."
> **Plutarch (c.46–120 C.E.), *Life of Crassus***

children, and old men. The gladiators trained the less experienced men into a formidable army. According to Roman historians, Spartacus divided the considerable booty he won between his followers.

In early 70 B.C.E., a legion commanded by Crassus threw up defenses that trapped the slave army at Calabria. Although Spartacus managed to break out of the encirclement, his army was finally destroyed near the River Silarus. Spartacus himself was killed, though his body was never found. Crassus rounded up around 6,000 survivors and had them crucified along the Appian Way from Brundisium to Rome. Their bodies remained hanging there for many years as a warning to slaves considering revolt in the future. Spartacus, though, has been remembered as a champion for those fighting slavery and servitude. **PF**

Silla Is Founded

The first Korean kingdom, Silla, is founded by a Son of Heaven.

It was not until 57 B.C.E. that the first Korean state was formed. From at least the eighth century B.C.E., the Koreans had come under the cultural influence of their powerful neighbor, China. Rice cultivation and bronze tools and weapons, both borrowed from the Chinese, propelled the Koreans toward urbanization and the formation of a state. By the fourth century B.C.E., small states had emerged throughout the Korean peninsula, each based on a walled town. Wars and alliances between the cities led to the development of loose confederations under the rulers of the dominant cities. The Chinese began to perceive these confederations as a threat, and from 109–106 B.C.E., the Han dynasty conquered most of northern and central Korea.

In the unconquered parts of Korea, three kingdoms began to develop in the first century B.C.E.: Koguryo, Paekche, and Silla. According to legend, the earliest of these states was Silla, founded in 57 B.C.E. by King Pak Hyokkose, a Son of Heaven, who hatched from a great red egg that had been delivered to earth by a flying horse. The people prayed for an equally remarkable wife for Hyokkose, and a beautiful baby girl was duly delivered from under the rib of a hen dragon. The people were amazed to see that the girl had a beak like a bird, but this fell off when she had her first bath. After reigning for sixty-one years, Hyokkose ascended to heaven, and after seven days his bodily remains fell to earth; they are buried in a tumulus in the grounds of Tamom monastery. The reigns of most of Silla's early kings are similarly shrouded in legend: its first truly historical king was Naemul, who reigned from 356 to 402 C.E. **JH**

◐ Detail of "A Story of Three Kingdoms" on an eight-panel folding screen at the Gahoe Museum, South Korea.

Caesar in Britain

The first Roman military force sets foot upon British soil, only to be driven back.

One summer's morning in 55 B.C.E., a fleet of eighty transport vessels carrying two Roman legions and escorted by warships approached the southern coast of Britain. The expedition—a bold venture, for Britain lay at the farthest extremity of the known world—had set out at midnight from what is now Boulogne in France. The legions' leader, Julius Caesar, knew nothing about the island except that its people were supporting hostile tribes in Gaul, on the European mainland, which he had been trying to subdue. The approach of the Roman fleet was watched by British

> **"All the Britons dye themselves with woad . . . and shave . . . their bodies."**
>
> **Julius Caesar, *The Gallic War*, c.45 B.C.E.**

warriors on the white cliffs around Dubrae (Dover). Instead of risking uphill battle there, Caesar ordered his ships to sail north to a more open beach at Walmer. However, the British warriors had followed to contest the landing. Roman legionaries jumped from their boats only to come under attack in the shallows and on shore. The Britons were driven off only when Caesar's warships subjected them to artillery fire from *ballistae* (large crossbows).

The landing had not been easy, and bad weather stopped Caesar's cavalry from crossing the channel and battered his fleet. Worried that they might be cut off, the Romans sailed back to Gaul. Caesar returned in 54 B.C.E. and advanced north of the Thames, but it was another ninety years before the Romans came to Britain to stay. **RG**

Massacre at Carrhae

A Roman plutocrat leads the legions to defeat by the Parthians.

Marcus Licinius Crassus was the richest man in Rome and controlled the Republic with Julius Caesar and Pompey. However, Crassus sought to match the military glory awarded his two colleagues, and so in 53 B.C.E., he led some 50,000 legionaries to invade Mesopotamia, part of the Parthian Empire. The Parthian king, Orodes II, sent an army to meet them, commanded by an aristocrat known as Surena.

When the two forces clashed in the desert near the town of Carrhae on June 6, it was soon obvious that Crassus had severely misjudged the military situation.

"The enemy who carried the head of Publius rode close up and displayed it."

Plutarch (c.46–120 c.e.), *Life of Crassus*

Whereas most of the Roman army consisted of armored infantry, the Parthians fought on horseback. Their fast-moving, lightly clad horsemen, armed with powerful composite bows, tormented the legionaries, galloping up to fire into their serried ranks and riding off before the Romans could counterattack. Crassus's cavalry—auxiliaries from Gaul commanded by his son Publius—mounted an offensive sortie but were massacred. Publius's head was displayed on a spear, further demoralizing the Roman forces.

During the Roman retreat at nightfall, more were killed, including Crassus, whose head was sent to King Orodes. Some 20,000 Romans were killed and 10,000 captured. The death of Crassus opened the way for a power struggle between Pompey and Caesar, and the end of the Republic. **RG**

No Mercy Shown

Doomed from the start, the Gauls are crushed by Julius Caesar at Alesia.

"Vercingetorix, who was the chief spring of all the war, putting his best armor on, and adorning his horse, rode out of the gates [of Alesia], and made a turn about Caesar as he was sitting, then quitting his horse, threw off his armor, and remained quietly sitting at Caesar's feet until he was led away." Thus the Greek biographer Plutarch describes the surrender of the leader of a doomed revolt against the Roman conquest of Gaul in 52 B.C.E.

The Celtic tribes of Transalpine Gaul—the area of Europe west of the Rhine and north of the Alps and Pyrenees—had proved powerless to resist the campaigns led by Caesar from 58 B.C.E. onward, partly because of their disunity. However, early in 52 B.C.E. Vercingetorix, a young chieftain of the Arverni, formed an alliance between the tribes of western and central Gaul. Their large army took on the Roman legions with a mix of harassing guerrilla tactics and set-piece battles in defense of their hill forts.

In September, Caesar trapped Vercingetorix, besieging his army in the fortified hill town of Alesia. The Romans built a double line of siege fortifications around the town—the inner line to keep Vercingetorix in, the outer line to defend against a counterattack by his Gallic allies. When the Gallic relief force arrived, coordinating its attacks with the Alesia garrison, Roman lines narrowly held out.

For the Gauls, surrender was the only option. The Romans showed no mercy—every legionary was given a Gaul to sell as a slave. Vercingetorix was taken to Rome, and six years later he was displayed in Caesar's triumph and then put to death. **RG**

○ *Alesia Besieged by Julius Caesar* (1533), an oil painting by the little-known artist Melchior Feselen (d.1538).

QVANTA STRA
GE VIRVM SVBLI
MIS ALEXIA CESSIT
CÆSAREIS AQVI
LIS. PICTA TABEL
LA NOTAT

Pompey Decapitated

The fugitive and former Roman general Pompey is assassinated in Egypt.

Once Rome's most successful general and most powerful political leader, Pompey (Gnaeus Pompeius Magnus) had by the late summer of 48 B.C.E. become a desperate fugitive. Defeated at Pharsalus in northern Greece by his rival Julius Caesar, he had fled by sea to Egypt. Here, Pompey sent a message to the country's young king, Ptolemy XII, requesting refuge. But the king's council of advisers, headed by the eunuch Pothinus, were cautious and devious men. They reasoned that Caesar would be enraged if they gave Pompey shelter, but also argued that Pompey

> **"... they cut off Pompey's head and threw his body unclothed out of the boat."**
>
> **Plutarch (c.46–120 c.e.), *Life of Pompey***

could be a future threat if they turned him away. The safest solution, therefore, was to kill him.

A member of the council, Achillas, with two former Roman soldiers, embarked in a small boat to fetch Pompey to shore. Pompey stepped into the boat accompanied by his servant Phillip. As the boat entered the shallows, Pompey was stabbed in the back and beheaded by the assassins. They then abandoned his body, leaving the faithful Phillip to build a meager funeral pyre on the beach.

Caesar arrived four days later. When he was shown Pompey's head, he reportedly turned away in disgust at the murder of a great Roman. Yet the killing opened the way for Caesar to become the undisputed ruler of Rome, as well as the lover of Cleopatra, Ptolemy XII's rival for the Egyptian throne. **RG**

Julian Calendar

Caesar's reforms lay the foundations for our modern calendar.

The daily life of Rome revolved around seasonal festivals and the annual election of magistrates, so it was important to be able to calculate the date accurately. However, the Roman calendar, based on the lunar year of 355 days, was about ten days shorter than the solar year. To adjust the calendar for this discrepancy, the Pontifex Maximus (head of the college of priests) would announce annually the addition of extra days for that year.

By the first century B.C.E., the Pontifex Maximus was often a politician, and sometimes this power

> **"Caesar called in the best philosophers and mathematicians..."**
>
> **Plutarch (c.46–120 c.e.), *Life of Caesar***

was used unscrupulously to extend the magistracy of a political ally, or reduce that of a rival.

Julius Caesar was elected Pontifex Maximus in 63 B.C.E., but it was not until he returned to Rome twenty years later that he reformed the calendar. On the advice of the astronomer Sosigenes, he introduced a Julian calendar based on the solar year of 365 and a quarter days, with an extra day every fourth year. However, Sosigenes had overestimated the length of the solar year by 11 minutes, 14 seconds, so that by the mid-1500s the cumulative effect of this error had shifted seasonal dates, such as Easter, forward by ten days. In 1582, Pope Gregory XIII removed the extra days and reformulated the rule for leap years, thus creating the Gregorian calendar, which is still in use today. **SK**

Death of a Dictator

Julius Caesar is assassinated by conspiratorial senators in Rome, bringing about the beginning of the end for the Republic.

On the day known to Romans as the "Ides" of March, Julius Caesar was scheduled to attend a meeting of the Senate in a hall adjoining the Theater of Pompey. Various omens suggested danger loomed, but Caesar was persuaded to ignore them. This was a fatal error, as there was indeed a plot to kill him.

All-powerful in Rome after defeating Pompey, Caesar had gained great popularity with the people—but he had alienated the aristocracy who dominated the Senate. Cassius Longinus and Marcus Brutus had persuaded some sixty senators to join an assassination plot. The conspiracy was justified as a defense of Republican freedom, since Caesar had declared himself "dictator for life" and was rumored to aspire to kingship.

As Caesar was carried in a litter to the Senate meeting hall, a note detailing the plot was slipped into his hand, but he did not read it. His powerful follower Mark Antony was distracted by one of the conspirators outside the hall while Caesar entered the building. Another conspirator, Tillius Cimber, approached Caesar on a pretext and tugged off his toga. Then, pulling out concealed daggers, senators fell upon him from all sides. Caesar fought back until, according to the historian Suetonius, he recognized Brutus among his assailants. Crying, "You too, my child?" he abandoned resistance and fell dead at the foot of a statue of Pompey.

Faced with popular hostility, the assassins were forced to flee Rome. Mark Antony, one of Caesar's most loyal followers, took control of the city. Within two years Brutus and Cassius were dead. Far from saving the Republic, the assassination precipitated a power struggle that ended in the establishment of the Roman Empire. **RG**

◐ An engraving of Mark Antony's funeral oration over the corpse of Caesar (by an unknown artist).

> ## *"Whichever way he turned he met with the blows of daggers . . . "*
>
> **Plutarch (c.46–120 c.e.), *Life of Caesar***

"O Tempora, O Mores!"

The reconciliation of Mark Antony and Octavian leads to Cicero's murder.

⚫ A fresco of Cicero delivering one of his famous orations, by Cesare Maccari (1840–1919), painted in the Palazzo Madama, Rome.

The great orator Cicero was being carried in a litter to the ship that would take him to safety when the assassins arrived. They included the centurion Herrennius and the tribune Popillius, whom Cicero had defended against a charge of patricide. Cicero looked all of his sixty-four years, his hair disheveled, his face worn. His last words were reported to be "There is nothing proper about what you are doing, soldier, but do try to kill me properly." He is said to have put forth his own neck. By Mark Antony's command, Cicero's hands were also severed.

It was not the sort of death that anyone would have predicted for Marcus Tullius Cicero, a brilliant orator, lawyer, and subtle philosopher, who, though neither noble nor patrician, had become consul in 63 B.C.E. He was said to be a man of discretion, even timidity, disapproving of Caesar's autocracy and yet not taking part in his assassination. But he could not keep silent when he considered Mark Antony a tyrant. In the *Philippics* (his famous speeches) he sought to praise Octavian, Caesar's adopted son, and bury Mark Antony. He very nearly succeeded. Mark Antony was declared an "enemy of the state," but his eventual reconciliation with Octavian spelled Cicero's doom. Mark Antony wanted the tongue that had spoken and the hand that had written against him.

As Mark Antony's slaughter continued, Romans recalled Cicero's words of warning. Octavian later defeated Mark Antony and remembered Cicero as "a learned man who loved his country." **RP**

Antony and Cleopatra Defeated

The future of Rome is decided at the Battle of Actium on the west coast of Greece.

○ *The Battle of Actium* (1600), a mural by Antonio Vassilacchi (1556–1629), in the Villa Barbarigo, near Vicenza, Italy.

In the civil strife that followed the assassination of Julius Caesar in 44 B.C.E., Caesar's adoptive son Octavian and Mark Antony, formerly Caesar's right-hand man, emerged as joint leaders of the Roman world. While Octavian ruled in Rome, Mark Antony based himself in Alexandria, bound both politically and amorously to the Ptolemaic queen of Egypt, Cleopatra VII. Unsurprisingly, the two men eventually came to a showdown to decide who would be the undisputed ruler of Rome.

In summer 31 B.C.E., Mark Antony and Cleopatra, commanding a large army and naval force, were cornered by Octavian at Actium on the west coast of Greece. Octavian's fleet, led by Marcus Vipsanius Agrippa, cut their supply line to Egypt, while some 80,000 Roman soldiers confronted them on land. Facing disaster, Antony and Cleopatra devised a plan to break through Agrippa's naval blockade and escape back to Egypt They packed the most seaworthy of their warships with soldiers and loaded sixty merchant vessels with treasure. Maneuvering inshore of Agrippa's blockade ships, they waited for a favorable wind. The two fleets stumbled into a confused combat, before the wind turned and Cleopatra sailed the merchant vessels into open sea. Antony succeeded in joining her, but his 300 warships were unable to follow and were burned or captured.

Antony and Cleopatra returned to Alexandria, but, facing defeat, both would soon commit suicide, leaving Octavian undisputed ruler of Rome. **RG**

Cleopatra's Suicide

The last pharaoh's demise signals the end of an era in Egypt.

Three thousand years of a unified and independent Egypt ended when—according to Shakespeare, at least—Cleopatra VII held a poisonous snake to her breast. Her actions were prompted by the defeat of her forces—and those of her Roman lover Mark Antony—by Octavian at the battle of Actium, and the subsequent suicide of Mark Antony. She was the last pharaoh. Although Caesarion, her son by Julius Caesar, Octavian's uncle, was briefly proclaimed ruler, he was soon executed and Egypt became a Roman province. Octavian went on to take the title Augustus, thus instituting the Roman Empire.

In 51 B.C.E., Cleopatra, aged seventeen, had ruled jointly with her ten-year-old brother, Ptolemy XIII. However, she was forced to flee Egypt three years later. After Ptolemy enraged Julius Caesar by having his rival Pompey beheaded, Cleopatra won her way into Caesar's affections by being smuggled into his rooms wrapped in a carpet. They became lovers, and Caesar helped restore her to the Egyptian throne.

Following Caesar's assassination in 44 B.C.E., Mark Antony, one of the triumvirs, summoned Cleopatra to assess her loyalty, and she seduced him. They married in 37 B.C.E., and had three children. It was assumed that they were setting up an empire to rival Rome, so Octavian moved against them, leading to their defeat and subsequent deaths.

Judging by her effigies, it is doubtful that Cleopatra was the famous beauty of legend. Nor was she Egyptian—she was the last of the Greek Ptolemaic dynasty that had been set up by Alexander the Great's general Ptolemy I Soter. **PF**

◐ A detail from *The Death of Cleopatra*, painted in 1658 by Italian baroque artist Guido Cagnacci (1601–1663).

An Empire Is Born

Octavian's rule lays the foundations of the Roman Empire.

Gaius Octavianus (Octavian) was the great-nephew and adoptive heir of Julius Caesar. Although only eighteen at Caesar's assassination, he went on to share power with Mark Antony and Lepidus. However, when Antony married Cleopatra and sought to establish an empire in Egypt, Octavian fought and defeated him at Actium, becoming in effect the sole authority in Rome. Yet, whereas Caesar's dictatorial powers had challenged the traditional Roman political system, Octavian was careful to restore the outward appearance of the republican constitution.

"On my own initiative, I raised an army with which I set free the state."

Deeds of the Divine Augustus, Inscription, 14 c.e.

In January, 27 B.C.E., Octavian went to the Senate to lay down his powers. Not permitted to do so, he accepted the command of several provinces and the titles "Princeps" (first citizen, effectively making him a monarch for life) and "Augustus" (illustrious one). He added Caesar to his name in honor of his adoptive father, which over time implied imperial rule. A laurel wreath was placed at the door of his house, making it the effective seat of power. The Senate then took an oath of allegiance to him as Imperator (supreme commander). Over the years he became ever more powerful while maintaining the traditional titles. By controlling the army and the Praetorian Guard, it became impossible for the Senate to challenge him. Octavian was emperor in all but name, and his rule marks the beginning of the Roman Empire. **PF**

City of Trier Established on Sacred Site

Trier, Rome's capital in the north, is instituted and grows into a flourishing city.

◐ A rare surviving fresco from the Villa Rustico in what was Augusta Treverorum; the fresco has been dated to *c.*200 C.E.

When the first Roman emperor, Augustus, ordered the building of the city of Augusta Treverorum in 18 B.C.E., he could not have known how influential it would eventually become. Built on the site of a sacred shrine of the Trevari, an ancient Germanic tribe, on the banks of the Mosel River, it occupied a key strategic position on an established trade route.

Despite what may have been local hostility to this violation of a sanctuary, the new city soon flourished—in the second century C.E., Treveris (as Trier was then known) became the capital of the Belgic division of Roman Gaul before becoming, in the third century, the seat of the Emperor Diocletian's imperial court and capital of the Western Roman Empire. Trier was the birthplace of Saint Ambrose,

the seat of early bishops, and an important focal point for the spread of Christianity.

The city's status as a center of worship survived Frankish invasions and the collapse of the Western Roman Empire. It became an archbishopric in 815, and in the twelfth century the archbishops of Trier became electors of the Holy Roman Emperors.

The city flourished as a trade and cultural center in the Early Modern period, with a university founded there in 1473. Occupied by the French during the revolutionary wars, Trier came under Prussian rule following Napoleon's defeat in 1815. In 1818, Karl Marx was born there. Trier is now part of the Rhineland Palatinate in Germany and celebrated its two thousandth anniversary in 1984. **TB**

The Birth of Jesus Christ

The central figure of Christianity, Jesus of Nazareth, is born.

○ *Adoration of the Baby* (c.1620) by Gerrit van Honthorst (1590–1656; also known as Gherardo delle Notti).

Pinning down the exact date of Jesus Christ's birth is no easy task. The New Testament insists that it happened in the reign of King Herod, who ruled Judaea for more than thirty years, during which time he rebuilt the temple in Jerusalem and created vast palaces and fortresses in the desert outside the city. Unfortunately for the traditional chronology, Herod died in 4 B.C.E., four years before the date commonly accepted for Jesus's birth. There is no other external evidence other than the gospel stories.

The Roman emperor Augustus had a governor called Quirinus in Syria, who decreed that his subjects must be taxed, but this was in about 6 C.E., ten years after Herod's death. And there is no evidence he required people to return to their ancestral homes.

There is no evidence of a visit to Judaea by three wise men or of a massacre of children by Herod (though his reputation for cruelty makes this possible).

None of which is to deny that a child was indeed born around this time who grew up to become a powerful teacher and healer, and whose death some thirty years later led to extraordinary and enduring changes. But the familiar Bible stories—the journey to Bethlehem, the inn, the shepherds, the magi, the flight into Egypt—are more likely mythological accretions. The Gospels give no indication of the month—or even the season—of the birth. Early Christians celebrated it on January 6, but from the fourth century onward, the birth of Christ was celebrated on December 25. **PF**

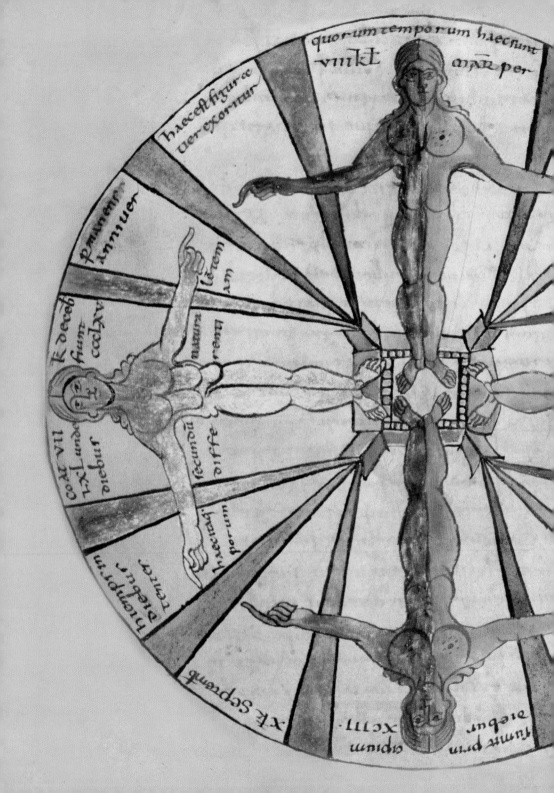

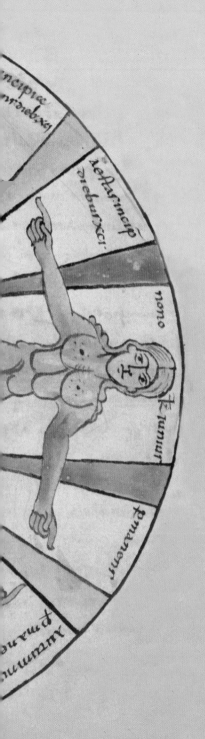

A wheel of the months and seasons from the ninth-century *De Natura Rerum* by St. Isidore of Seville.

1–999

Slaughter in the Forest

Three Roman legions perish in Teutoburg Forest at the hands of German tribesmen.

"In the center of the field were the whitening bones of men … strewn everywhere or piled in heaps. Near lay fragments of weapons and limbs of horses, and also human heads nailed to tree trunks." According to Roman historian Tacitus, this was the scene in the Teutoburg Forest, Germany, in the year 15. Six years earlier, it had been the site of the most comprehensive military disaster in the history of the Roman Empire.

Rome embarked upon the conquest of the area between the Rivers Rhine and Elbe in 12 B.C.E. It seemed that the wild Germanic tribes would soon

"The Roman army … in grief and anger, began to bury the bones of the three legions."

Tacitus (c.56–c.117), *Annals*

succumb to Roman rule. Indeed, when Publius Quinctilius Varus led the seventeenth, eighteenth, and nineteenth legions on operations in the year 9, his legionaries were accompanied by local auxiliaries led by their chief, Arminius, who was also a Roman citizen. But as the legionaries headed toward the Rhine, Arminius and the auxiliaries deserted.

Encumbered by a long baggage train and numerous camp followers, the legions plunged into the forest. Arminius's mounted warriors harassed the slow-moving column until the Roman force was so weakened it was overrun. There were few survivors, and Varus took his own life. The aging emperor, Augustus, never recovered from the shock of losing three legions, and the Rhine continued to divide the Roman and "barbarian" worlds. **RG**

Christ Is Risen

Jesus is buried, and on the third day rises from the dead.

Although no one saw it happen and no more than a score of people claimed to have had any direct evidence afterward, the disappearance of the body of Jesus from his tomb, and his disciples' conviction that he subsequently visited them arguably changed the world. Millions of people have found a direct and personal belief in the literal truth of this apparently impossible event, with dramatic effects on their morality, culture, and ethical and political behavior.

Jesus, a charismatic healer and wandering apocalyptic preacher in the Roman province of Judaea, upset the Jewish religious establishment by deliberately flouting many traditional practices and claiming that his teachings superseded the laws of Moses on which Judaism was founded. His final visit to Jerusalem for the festival of Passover (the date is not certain, but is most likely to have been 30 C.E.) has been interpreted as a deliberate confrontation. The Sanhedrin and High Priest condemned him and sought the assistance of the Roman governor, and Jesus was put to death by crucifixion. Placed in a private tomb by a supporter but guarded by Roman soldiers, his body vanished three days later. That day, and on several occasions over the coming months, his friends were convinced they saw him alive. The first was Mary Magdalene, followed by Peter and the other disciples, both in Jerusalem and elsewhere.

As a result, Jesus's followers reevaluated his teachings and death, seeing in them a uniquely powerful, optimistic, and transformative message from God. To this day, the message continues to be highly attractive to people around the world. **PF**

◑ A resurrected Jesus Christ shines out of a sixteenth-century tapestry woven in Brussels, now in the Vatican museums.

Blinding Light Strikes Saul at Damascus

After a revelation on the road to Damascus, Saul becomes Paul and begins spreading the word of Christ throughout the eastern Mediterranean.

One of the most dramatic stories in the Bible is also one of the most historically significant. According to the Acts of the Apostles, Saul, a tent maker from Tarsus in Asia Minor, had a dramatic experience on his way to Damascus. He later described the event as being struck by a blinding light and hearing the voice of Jesus speaking directly to him.

Temporarily blinded, Saul was taken to Damascus, where he was healed by a Christian believer called Ananias. He was then baptized with the name Paul, and changed from being the most avid persecutor of the Christian church to being its most tireless promoter. As a young man, Saul had taken it upon himself to destroy the young Christian community in the first years after the crucifixion of Jesus. For the rest of his life, though, he traveled throughout the eastern Mediterranean, preaching the faith, visiting nascent Christian communities, and supporting them in their attempts to practice the teachings of Jesus. In the process, he defined the nature of Christianity, taking it beyond the Jewish community and making it palatable to other cultures.

Whereas many of the other leaders of the early Church had known Jesus personally, Paul's experience of him was limited to the revelation on the road to Damascus. Perhaps as a result of this, he stressed the transforming power of faith in the risen Christ, rather than the words and deeds of Jesus during his ministry. Although Paul's letters are the oldest known Christian writings, compiled a generation before the Gospels, they contain strikingly few references to the life and teachings of Jesus. **PF**

◁ *Saint Paul on the Road to Damascus*, by Lodovico Carracci (1555–1619), in the Pinacoteca Nazionale of Bologna.

Britain Falls to Rome

Eleven British tribes submit to the rule of Roman Emperor Claudius.

Late in 43, Roman Emperor Claudius received the surrender of eleven tribes of southern Britain at Camulodunum (modern-day Colchester). It marked the beginning of the Roman occupation of Britain, which was to last for almost 400 years.

The island had long been in contact with the Roman-ruled world on mainland Europe, and a number of British tribes paid tribute to their powerful neighbors. The pretext for the Roman invasion in 43 was a dispute between British tribal chieftains. Verica, leader of the Atrebates and a faithful ally of Rome, had been defeated and exiled by the Catuvellauni, led by Caratacus. Claudius, a distinctly unwarlike emperor looking for an opportunity to demonstrate his military prowess, decided to avenge Verica's eviction.

A large invasion force set off across the English Channel under the command of Aulus Plautius. Owing to the vagueness of the ancient sources, it is not clear where the legionaries came ashore, but Richborough in Kent is a possible site. Despite relying mainly on guerrilla tactics to harry the invaders, the Britons were twice brought to battle and defeated, first at the River Medway and then at a crossing of the Thames. By the time Claudius arrived, reportedly with war elephants among his forces, the Catuvellauni capital at Camulodunum lay undefended and was occupied by the emperor without bloodshed.

Claudius spent just sixteen days in Britain, but on his return to Rome, according to the biographer Suetonius, he "celebrated a triumph of great splendor." In Britain, resistance to the Roman conquest continued, but to little avail. Within four years, the area south of a line from the Humber to the Severn had been "pacified." **RG**

Conversion Rules Set

Apostolic Council decrees that Gentiles can convert straight to Christianity.

The decision of the Apostolic Council in 51 to allow Gentiles to convert to Christianity without first converting to Judaism has been seen as a crucial moment in the mission of the church. It took it from being a sect limited to the Jewish world to one whose teachings have universal relevance.

In the early years of the Christian church, disputes arose about the nature of the new faith. The most important concerned its relationship with Judaism, from which it had sprung. As the apostles began to preach the faith of Christ beyond the bounds of the Jewish community, a difficult question arose. James "the Just," known as the "brother of Jesus" and a strict leader of the church in Jerusalem, believed it was necessary for a Gentile first to convert to Judaism—in particular, to be circumcised—before becoming a Christian. However, Paul taught that a Gentile could convert to Christianity directly.

A council of the apostles convened to resolve the matter in Jerusalem, where a group of converted Pharisees had powerful influence over church affairs. After a long discussion, Peter, the man ordained by Jesus as the head of the church, resolved that circumcision was not necessary for conversion, and finally James agreed. The council resolved, in the Apostolic Decree, that although circumcision was not required, Gentiles would be expected to make certain sacrifices, namely to abstain from "food polluted by idols, from sexual immorality, from the meat of strangled animals, and from blood."

This decree was taken by Paul, Barnabas, and two others to Antioch, where it was read to the young church there and later passed to others. In due course, it became clear that Paul himself took a very lenient line even on these dietary restrictions. **PF**

Nero Watches Rome Burn

The emperor blames the Christians for the fire that ravaged the Eternal City.

○ Nero is alleged to have "fiddled" while Rome was destroyed by fire; he blamed the Christians for the blaze.

"Nero fastened the guilt and inflicted the most exquisite tortures on . . . Christians."

Tacitus (c.56–c.117), Annals

During a hot July night in the year 64, rickety shops near the Circus Maximus in Rome caught fire. The blaze quickly spread through the city and raged for nine days before burning itself out. Although no contemporary accounts of the disaster exist, a later report by the historian Tacitus, who witnessed the fire as a nine-year-old, claimed two-thirds of the Eternal City was destroyed, including thousands of crowded *insulae* (apartment blocks) in which most of the inhabitants made their homes.

Ten of Rome's districts were ruined, and much of the population of two million was made homeless. The ancient Temple of Jupiter Stator and the Atrium Vestae, the hearth of the Vestal Virgins, were also destroyed. Emperor Nero, whose reputation for megalomania and cruelty was unenviable, was said to have watched the flames from a high vantage point, enjoying the fire as an aesthetic drama and playing his lyre to accompany the blaze. Whether true or not, he did allow the stricken citizens into his palace and organized emergency relief. In the aftermath, he had the city rebuilt in stone and organized into blocks, while reserving a vast area of some 350 acres (142 ha), or one-third the total area of the city, for his own lavish palace, Domus Aurea.

The cause of the fire was never clear, and it may well have been accidental. Many citizens believed that Nero himself was responsible—an accusation repeated by the historian Suetonius, who had little good to say about the emperor. Tacitus suggested that, faced with such accusations, the unpopular emperor blamed the Christian sect (which expected the imminent end of the world and saw the materialist Roman Empire as the creation of the devil). As a reprisal, Nero launched a wave of persecution that sent Christians to the lions for the first time. **PF**

Peter Is Crucified Upside Down

The Christian church's "first earthly head" meets his demise in Rome.

In 64 Peter was put to death as one of many Christians scapegoated by Nero for the great fire that had recently destroyed much of the city. He was nailed on the cross upside down, according to the Christian scholar Origen. This was supposed to have been at Peter's own request, to ensure his fate did not mirror too closely that of Jesus himself. Paul was traditionally said to have been beheaded at the same time as his crucifixion—perhaps even on the same day.

The fisherman Simon Peter, who was described in the Bible as the first among the disciples, was given the task of being the *petrus* (rock) upon which the church was to be built. In the years after the death of Jesus, he and Paul competed for dominance in the early Christian community. Peter was instrumental in the decision to spread the news of Jesus's teaching and resurrection beyond the Jewish world, and apparently traveled and preached in Syria and Greece. Peter moved to Rome in about 42 and probably lived there as leader of the nascent Roman church. In the late 40s, Emperor Claudius expelled both Jews and Christians from the city for their disruptive squabbling and they were not allowed to return until 56. Little else is known of Peter's time in Rome, not even where his church may have been.

For the earliest Christians, a martyr's death was not deliberately sought, as may have been the case in the later Roman Empire, nor was it entirely unexpected. But crucifixion offered the consolation of sharing the fate of their master, Jesus. Peter's body was collected and buried by his supporters, and the Basilica of St. Peter in the Vatican was built by Emperor Constantine on the traditional site of his burial. The tomb and his bones were apparently rediscovered in 1950. **PF**

○ *St. Peter's Crucifixion* (1601–1602) by Caravaggio, preserved in the church of Santa Maria del Popolo in Rome.

"Peter, through unjust envy, . . . departed unto the place of glory due to him."

Clement of Rome (died *c*.99), *First Epistle*

balneber

IOPAS

TITVS

Iolephus

Titus Takes Jerusalem

The Romans force the Jewish rebels to surrender in Jerusalem.

The former Jewish kingdom of Judaea had come under direct Roman rule in 4 B.C.E., but the Jews had too strong a religious identity to be assimilated into the Roman Empire. Rebellion broke out in 66 and, in 69, the newly installed Emperor Vespasian, who had defeated the rebels in northern Judaea, sent his son Titus to suppress the revolt in Jerusalem. On September 7, 70, after nearly five months under a Roman siege, the city surrendered.

Jerusalem's population probably numbered around 600,000. Inside the city were approximately 25,000 armed rebels led by Simon bar Giora and John of Gischala. Despite their proficiency in siege warfare, the Romans had struggled to overrun this large city, in part because it was divided into walled districts that had to be penetrated one by one. Early in the siege, food supplies ran out. Tens of thousands died of starvation. Some citizens, crazed by hunger, tried to flee but were captured by the Romans and crucified within sight of the city's defenders.

During August, the Romans fought their way into the Great Temple, the ritual heart of the Jewish religion. It was burned to the ground and its holy vessels were looted. Surviving rebels sought refuge in the sewers of the Old Town, but by September 7 there was no alternative to surrender. John of Gischala was consigned to life imprisonment, and Simon bar Giora was carried back to Rome, where he was made a star exhibit in the triumph staged by Vespasian and Titus and then ritually strangled. An estimated 97,000 Jews were taken captive, many of them used as slave labor in the building of the Colosseum in Rome. **RG**

◑ A manuscript depicting Flavius Josephus brought before Titus at the Siege of Jerusalem in 70.

Massacre at Masada

The Roman siege of a Jewish stronghold ends in slaughter and suicide.

On April 15, 73, in a fortress atop a hill near the Dead Sea, then in the Roman province of Judaea, 960 Jewish men, women, and children met a gruesome death ordered by their leader. They belonged to a group of extremists known as the Sicarii. Led by Eleazar ben Yair, they had continued to defy Roman rule in Judaea after the failure of the Jewish revolt of 66 to 70.

The fortress they occupied at Masada appeared impregnable. Granaries and cisterns provided a reliable supply of food and water, potentially allowing

> ## *"Miserable men indeed were they, whose distress forced them to slay their own wives."*
> **Josephus, *The Jewish War*, (c.75)**

the rebels to survive a siege for years. The only path up the cliffs was precarious and exposed to attack. But through the winter of 72 to 73, Roman legionaries constructed a vast ramp sloping upward from the valley to the hilltop 650 feet (200 m) above. By spring, they were able to haul a siege tower up the ramp, equipped with powerful catapults and a battering ram.

Facing defeat, Eleazar persuaded his followers that suicide was preferable to falling into Roman hands. Ten Sicarii fighters, chosen by lot, were given the task of killing the others, and then each other. According to the Jewish historian Josephus, when the Romans broke through the walls the next day, they were shocked and "could only wonder at their immovable contempt of death." **RG**

Vesuvius Explodes, Incinerating Thousands

The Roman Empire endures one of its worst natural disasters in the Bay of Naples.

○ A depiction of Vesuvius erupting into the Bay of Naples by Jean Baptiste Genillion (1750–1829).

○ A plaster cast of a person buried alive by the hot ash, made by filling hollows in the hardened ash and lava with plaster.

" . . . they fixed pillows to their heads, as protection against the falling stones . . . "

Pliny the Younger, contemporary account

The region had suffered a catastrophic earthquake a mere seventeen years previously, and the earth tremors had returned over recent days. The inhabitants of Pompeii, Herculaneum, and other towns around the Bay of Naples were still taken by surprise by the dramatic explosion of the apparently extinct volcano shortly after midday on August 24, 79. A huge plume of smoke and ash rose 20 miles (30 km) into the sky, then began to fall on the city in a rain that created a layer of pumice 10 feet (3 m) thick.

Naturalist Pliny the Elder, the admiral of the navy in nearby Misenum, organized a relief operation, but then insisted on viewing the cloud from close quarters, and so met his death on the beach the following morning. His nephew, Pliny the Younger, recalled the moment of eruption: "It resembled an umbrella pine tree, shooting up to a great height in the form of a tall trunk and spreading out at the top into branches. It appeared sometimes bright, and sometimes dark and spotted, as it was either more or less impregnated with earth and cinders."

That day a toxic cloud of burning gases poured down the mountain to engulf everyone who remained in Pompeii. Both Pompeii and Herculaneum were buried and forgotten for centuries. The disaster was too great for the Roman state to be able to organize a major recovery operation, although some salvage and/or looting occurred. Up to 20,000 people are thought to have died in two days, most suffering from the inhalation of hot toxic gases.

The remains of Pompeii were rediscovered only in 1748, and archeological work has continued ever since. In the mid-nineteenth century, plaster casts made of hollows found within the lava provided disturbingly vivid images of the inhabitants of the city in their final moments. **PF**

Colosseum Opens

Roman crowds are entertained with one hundred days of games.

The great amphitheater of ancient Rome was ten years in the building. At almost 660 feet (200 m) long and capable of seating more than 50,000 people, it was built on a site that had been devastated by fire in the reign of Nero. The arena was opened during the first year of Emperor Titus's rule, which had begun with huge disasters, including the eruption of Vesuvius, that destroyed Pompeii and Herculaneum and an outbreak of plague in Rome. The inaugural games were therefore seen as an attempt to change the mood of crisis and perhaps to appease the gods.

The games continued for one hundred days. The mornings featured animal shows, in which different species were put in the arena to hunt and fight one another, and the afternoons showcased gladiatorial combats. It is said that more than 9,000 animals were killed during these inaugural games.

At first called the Flavian Amphitheater, it later became known as the Colosseum after the nearby colossal statue of Nero. The first amphitheater to be built in the heart of the city, it was partly paid for with treasures taken from the Temple of Jerusalem that had been sacked in 70. Later, under Emperor Domitian, a top story was added to increase capacity, as well as an underground complex of tunnels and animal cages.

It is often said that many Christians were martyred in the Colosseum, but evidence for this is scanty. It was also said that it could be flooded to allow sea battles to be enacted for the crowds, but many historians also think this is unlikely. The Colosseum remained in use until at least the fifth century. **PF**

◐ A lithograph cutaway of the Colosseum, the amphitheater
   built in the heart of Rome under Emperor Titus.

Hadrian Is Emperor

The new ruler sets about strengthening the empire's frontier.

Hadrian became emperor when Trajan died in August 117 in Cilicia (southern Turkey). Some say Trajan had already named his former ward and protégé Hadrian as his heir, but according to the historian Cassius Dio, it was Empress Plotina who engineered the succession by concealing her husband's death while she sent letters announcing Hadrian's adoption to the senate in Rome. Only when the succession was secure did she reveal that Trajan was dead.

Under Emperor Trajan (r.97–117), the boundaries of the empire reached their farthest extent. Hadrian

> ## "He then set out for Britain, where he put things to rights and was first to build a wall."
>
> **Historia Augusta, Life of Hadrian**

believed that the empire had become too large to govern, and one of his first acts was to abandon Dacia, the land north of the Danube, which Trajan had added to the empire barely fifteen years before. Hadrian also gave up territories recently conquered in the east and pulled Rome's eastern frontier back to the Euphrates. To strengthen its northern defenses, he erected a 300-mile-long (485 km) earth and timber barrier between the Rivers Danube and Rhine in Germany, but it is for Hadrian's Wall that he is best remembered. This impressive stone barrier stretched for 80 miles (128 km) across northern Britain, with turrets at regular intervals to provide look-out posts and garrison forts. Large portions of the wall, which took less than ten years to construct, are still standing today as a monument to Roman engineering. **SK**

Jews Are Slaughtered and Forced to Flee

The Bar Kokhba Revolt sees the Romans drive the Jews out of Jerusalem and Emperor Hadrian ban Judaism.

The Roman province of Judaea had always proved troublesome for the Romans, even after the destruction of Jerusalem in 70. In what was the only major war of his reign, Emperor Hadrian suffered heavy losses during the Bar Kokhba Revolt, but finally retook Jerusalem in 135.

In 130, Hadrian visited the ruins of the city and promised to rebuild them. When the Jews realized he intended to change the name to Aelia Capitolina and to dedicate the main temple to Jupiter, the outraged rebels began a new revolt and for two years established an independent state. Hadrian assembled a large army to suppress the uprising, which is known as the Bar Kokhba Revolt. It is named after the commander Simon bar Kokhba, who was seen by many as the Jewish Messiah. The rebels made a last stand in the fortress of Betar, but they were finally overwhelmed and slaughtered. It is possible that half a million died in the fighting.

Hadrian then outlawed Judaism, banning the Torah law and burning the sacred scroll. He banned Jews from entering Aelia Capitolina and renamed the province of Judaea, which now had just a few impoverished Jewish communities left, as Syria Palestina. Many Jews were sent abroad as slaves. This event has often been seen as the beginning of the dispersal, or diaspora, of the Jews across the Middle East and Mediterranean world, which characterized their situation throughout the Middle Ages until the foundation of the modern state of Israel in 1948. **PF**

◗ A 1927 miniature by Arthur Szyk depicting Simon bar Kokhba in battle against the Romans.
◗ A former underground olive oil storeroom used as an escape tunnel and hiding place by the Bar Kokhba rebels.

Japan Woos China

Queen Himiko establishes diplomatic relations between Japan and China.

In 238, ambassadors from Queen Himiko of Yamatai (or Yamaichi) in the lands of Wa (Japan) arrived at the Chinese court to present gifts of four male slaves, six female slaves, and two lengths of patterned cloth to the Chinese emperor. Such gifts from "barbarian" rulers were always treated as tributes offered as a token of submission to the emperor, and the queen was duly rewarded with suitable baubles: a title and a gold medal. The exchange marked the emergence of Japan from prehistory. Shortly after, in 240, a Chinese embassy was dispatched to visit Queen

"We confer on you, therefore, the title Queen of Wa, Friendly to Wei."

Decree of Emperor Wudi to Queen Himiko

Himiko and learn about her kingdom. Its report forms the earliest detailed written account of Japan.

Himiko was said to have become queen after bewitching her people using sorcery and magic. Although a mature woman, she was unmarried and was rarely seen in public, using her brother as an intermediary with her people. Himiko's kingdom was essentially a confederation of thirty tribes, held together by her religious authority. Japanese historians have argued for the last thousand years about the location of Yamatai/Yamaichi. Most believe that Yamatai can be identified as Yamato, near Osaka in central Honshu, which was the capital by the sixth century. The plains around Yamato are dotted with burial mounds, the largest of which are believed to hold the remains of Japan's earliest rulers. **SK**

Rome's New Age Begins

Spectacular games herald a new dawn, but Rome's future is not bright.

In 248, the *ludi saeculares* (secular games) mounted by Emperor Philip the Arab commemorated the thousandth year since the founding of Rome by Romulus in 753 B.C.E. Traditionally, the start of a *saeculum novum* (new age)—a period of time that approximated to the longest human life in a generation, computed at various times at 90, 100, or 110 years—was celebrated in Rome with games lasting three days. Emperor Augustus had revived the games in 17 B.C.E. with sacrifices, chariot-racing, hunting displays, and theatrical performances.

"When a hundred years and ten are past . . . Romans be sure due offerings to make."

Oracle of Sibyl, Zosimus, *New History*, c.500

It was said by contemporaries that more than 1,000 gladiators, along with hundreds of exotic animals imported from Africa—hippopotami, leopards, lions, giraffes, and even one rhinoceros—were killed before the crowds in the Colosseum in 248.

Despite the *saeculum novum*, Rome's fortunes were at a low ebb. Philip was one of twenty-six emperors between 235 and 285 who ruled, on average, for less than two years each, and only one of whom did not die a violent death. Philip had become emperor in 244 after murdering Gordian III, a teenage emperor for whom he was regent. Even as Rome's millennium was marked, there were uprisings against Philip. In 249 Decius, the trusted senator he had sent to rouse the troops' loyalty, was proclaimed emperor by the army. Philip was killed in battle at Verona. **JH**

A Human Footstool

Roman Emperor Valerian is defeated and captured by the Persians at Edessa.

The times were certainly propitious. The third century was one of the most turbulent in Roman history. A combination of invasions by German barbarians, runaway inflation, and civil war had brought the empire to the brink of collapse. The Romans were down on their luck, and in 260, Roman Emperor Valerian was defeated by Persian King Shapur I at Edessa (modern-day Urfa, Turkey). Valerian was taken prisoner and subjected to various humiliations, including, reputedly, being used as a human footstool. He died in captivity.

After its conquest by Alexander the Great in the fourth century B.C.E., Persia was ruled by foreign dynasties until 224–226, when the Sasanian dynasty came to power. Vigorous and ambitious, the Sasanians aspired to regain for Persia the superpower status it had enjoyed under the Achemenid dynasty (559–330 B.C.E.). This made conflict with Rome inevitable, because Asia Minor, Syria, Palestine, and Egypt—all formerly ruled by Persia—were part of the Roman Empire.

In 258, King Shapur conquered Armenia, a Roman ally, and advanced to the Mediterranean, capturing the Syrian city of Antioch. Roman Emperor Valerian launched a counterattack, recapturing Antioch and driving Shapur back across the Euphrates. Valerian was defeated at Edessa. In the aftermath of the battle, Roman fortunes sank to a new low. Britain and Gaul declared independence, and the "Thirty Tyrants" fought for power in the east. In 261, Shapur was defeated by Odaenathus, the Romanized Arab ruler of Palmyra. The Romans regained control of the area in 274 when they defeated Odaenathus's widow, Zenobia. **JH**

◗ *Emperor Valerian Is Captured and Mistreated by the Persians,*
  a copper engraving by Matthäus Merian the Elder from 1630.

Thrown to the Lions

Diocletian's first edict against Christians unleashes a wave of persecution.

Roman Emperor Diocletian's motives for launching the last great persecution of Christians remain uncertain. In all, he issued four edicts against Christians—the first, in February 303, called for the destruction of all churches throughout the Roman Empire; the last, published in April 304, ordered all Christians to sacrifice to the traditional gods of Rome or face execution. At this time, probably about 10 percent of the population professed Christianity. Terrible punishments were inflicted on those who refused to recant, with thousands being put to the

---

"Many rulers of the churches bore up heroically under horrible torments."

Eusebius of Caesarea, *Ecclesiastical History*, c.320

---

sword, burned, or thrown to the lions. Christians blamed Galerius, Diocletian's caesar (junior emperor), for the ruthless persecution in the Eastern Empire (the West escaped more lightly).

Diocletian had been emperor since 284. A man of huge energy, he had rescued the empire from crisis, strengthened its defenses, and reformed the army and the imperial administration. Realizing it was too big for one man to govern, he had established the Tetrarchy (rule by four), by which he ruled as emperor (Augustus) in the east with Galerius as his caesar, and Maximian ruled as Augustus in the west with Constantius as his caesar. In 305, Diocletian, by now in poor health, took the extraordinary step of abdicating, retiring to the magnificent palace he had built for himself at Split on the Adriatic coast. **SK**

"By This, Conquer"

Constantine is victorious at Milvian Bridge, apparently with the help of God.

◐ A detail from *Battle Between Constantine and Maxentius at the Milvian Bridge* (1613), by Pieter Lastmann (1583–1633).

> ### *"By this saving sign I have delivered your city from the tyrant and restored liberty."*
> **Inscription on the Arch of Constantine, Rome**

By the year 312, there were just two genuine rivals for power in the Western Roman Empire. They were Maxentius, who maintained control of Italy and Africa, and Constantine, who claimed authority in Gaul and Spain. In the spring of 312, Constantine decided to cross the Alps with a relatively small army. He overran north Italy and advanced on Rome. Maxentius initially retreated behind the great city walls, but when he saw Constantine's modest troops approaching, he decided to risk all in open battle. The two armies met at the Milvian Bridge, to the west of Rome. As Constantine's forces pushed forward, the bridge unexpectedly gave way and Maxentius and many of his troops were killed in the ensuing chaos as they tried to swim to safety.

The next day, the triumphant Constantine was acclaimed as the sole Augustus in the west. Soon afterward, he formed an uneasy alliance with Licinius, the Augustus in the east. At a meeting in Milan in spring 313, the two men agreed to divide the empire between them, thus bringing an end to the long-standing and damaging civil wars that had broken out on the abdication of Diocletian in 305. Their uneasy partnership lasted little more than a decade until 324, when Constantine declared himself sole emperor and undisputed master of the Roman world.

Shortly before the Battle of the Milvian Bridge, Constantine is said to have seen at midday a vision of a cross standing in front of the sun, with the words "By this, conquer" inscribed upon it. He was later told in a dream to use the sign he had observed in the heavens in all his battles against his enemies. And so he ordered a cross to be painted on his men's shields. Christian historians did not hesitate to ascribe his victory to God's miraculous help. **SK**

Christianity Is Tolerated—Officially

Constantine and Licinius agree to end the persecution of Christians.

It was in Milan in February 313 that Constantine and Licinius, rulers of the Western and Eastern Roman Empires, reached a momentous decision in the history of the Western world—to end the persecution of Christians everywhere. In a letter sent out under both their names to the governors of every Roman province, they granted all people freedom to worship whatever deity they pleased. They guaranteed full legal rights to all Christians and ordered the immediate return of any property previously confiscated from Christians. The so-called Edict of Milan did not make Christianity the official religion of the Roman Empire—that would not happen until Theodosius I outlawed pagan worship and closed all the pagan temples in 391—but by giving Christians the same rights as pagans and worshippers of other cults, the ruling transformed the status of Christianity and brought "the age of martyrs" to an end.

In a matter of years, Christianity grew from a relatively minor cult to the major religion of the Roman world, thanks in no small part to the patronage of Constantine. He had probably been a Christian for some time before his victory at the Battle of the Milvian Bridge in 312, and although he did not forbid the worship of the old gods (retaining the image of the sun god on his coins until 320), he supported the church financially, built churches, presided over church councils, and promoted Christians to high office. When, in 324, Licinius ordered the arrest and execution of a number of eastern bishops, Constantine seized the opportunity to overthrow his rival, presenting himself as the champion of Christians everywhere. Yet it was only on his deathbed in 337 that he took the final step of receiving Christian baptism. **SK**

○ *Baptism of Constantine* (detail) by Jacopo Vignali (1592–1664), currently in the Galleria Palatina in Florence.

"This regulation is made that we may not seem to detract from any religion."

Edict of Milan, c.315

Bishops Argue over the Nature of Christ

The Council of Nicaea attempts to resolve theological differences.

◯ A late-fifteenth-century Novgorod School icon of Constantine at the Council of Nicaea.

> *"[Constantine] proceeded
> . . . like some heavenly
> messenger of God."*
>
> **Eusebius of Caesarea, *Life of Constantine*, c.320**

On June 19, 325, Emperor Constantine opened the proceedings of the Council of Nicaea, seated upon his imperial throne. Constantine had recently made himself sole Roman emperor after defeating Licinius, his rival in the east, at the Battle of Chrysopolis (September 18, 324). Anxious to impose his authority and to make good his claim to have brought peace, Constantine summoned all the bishops of the Christian church to his palace at Nicaea (Iznik, Turkey). Of the 1,800 invited, 318 bishops attended. Top of the agenda was the "Arian controversy."

It all started when Arius, a presbyter (a type of minister in the early Christian church) at Alexandria in Egypt, claimed that Christ, the Son of God, was not equal with God the Father, but was the highest of all God's creations. Questions of doctrine were matters of urgent and passionate debate in the fourth-century church, and the Arian controversy, as it came to be called, unleashed a storm of bitter argument and recrimination that was felt throughout the Eastern Empire.

Church historians regard the Council of Nicaea as the first ecumenical council of the Christian church, responsible for producing a uniform statement of belief in the shape of the Nicene Creed, with its declaration that the Father and the Son are of the same substance and co-eternal, "begotten, not made." It was an overwhelming defeat for Arius, who received only two votes in support of his views. The council also settled that Easter should be celebrated each year on the first Sunday after the vernal full moon, thus separating it from the Jewish Passover. It set a precedent for the emperor to play an important role in the affairs of the church. But it did not end the Arian controversy, which continued to divide the church for many years to come. **SK**

Constantinople—A New Rome Is Born

Constantine celebrates the inauguration of his new capital city.

The dedication of the city that would after his death be known as Constantinople (City of Constantine) was perhaps the greatest moment of Constantine's reign. It was less than six years since the emperor had first earmarked the small Greek port of Byzantium, standing on a promontory projecting into the Bosporus, the narrow strait of water dividing Europe from Asia, as the site for an entirely new capital for the Roman Empire. Coins struck to honor the dedication celebrated the *Nova Roma* (New Rome), and in many ways his new creation was a conscious copy of the old—it was even built on seven hills and divided into fourteen administrative districts, just like the city on the Tiber. It had its own senate and, as in Rome, a corn dole (free grain allowance) was established, along with other incentives to encourage new settlers.

But there was one all-important difference. From the start, Constantinople was conceived as a Christian city, symbolizing the break with Rome's pagan past, and Constantine embellished his creation with numerous churches and basilicas. Many of these structures—including Hagia Sophia (Divine Wisdom), founded in 325—were built on the sites of pagan temples.

Constantinople quickly eclipsed Rome in wealth, population, and importance. For 1,000 years, under the Byzantine emperors, it was the intellectual, religious, and commercial hub of the Greek-speaking world, before falling in 1453 to the Ottoman Turks, who in turn made it the capital of their empire. They had heard the Greek inhabitants refer familiarly to Constantinople as "*eis ten polin*," meaning "in the city," and in time this phrase was rendered in Turkish as "Istanbul," the name by which Constantine's city is still known today. **SK**

A 1493 woodcut by Hartmann Schedel depicting Constantinople as a fortified city.

> *" . . . he embellished [the city] with large martyr-shrines, and splendid houses."*

Eusebius of Caesarea, *Life of Constantine*, c.320

The Church of the Holy Sepulchre Is Built

Constantine excavates a cliffside to establish a shrine in Jerusalem at the traditional site of Jesus's burial and resurrection.

On Constantine's orders, soldiers cut away the cliffside around the cave-tomb. It was then encased within a small building and later covered by a domed rotunda. Just to the east, Constantine built a large basilica, which was consecrated in 335. According to some, Macarius, bishop of Jerusalem, asked for Constantine's help in restoring the holy places associated by Christians with the life and death of Jesus. Other sources say that in c.326, the emperor's mother, Helena, went on a pilgrimage to the Holy Land, where she built churches in Bethlehem and on the Mount of Olives and collected relics. On being shown the traditional site of Jesus's tomb in Jerusalem, covered by a Roman temple dating from the second century, Helena began to excavate and was miraculously guided to the remains of the cross on which Jesus was crucified.

A holy shrine for Christians, the Church of the Holy Sepulchre survived fire and earthquake before being almost completely destroyed by a Fatimid caliph in 1009. The army of the First Crusade sang a *Te Deum* (a hymn of thanksgiving) within its ruined walls after capturing Jerusalem in 1099, and crusaders later rebuilt the church in Romanesque style, giving it the basic shape it has today. Traces of Constantine's original building remain and, although some experts have doubted the authenticity of the site, a strong body of archeological opinion now accepts the traditional identification of the tomb with the burial place of Jesus. **SK**

◑ Entrance to the Church of the Holy Sepulchre in Jerusalem (1822), by Maxim Nikiforovich Vorobyev (1787–1855).

◐ A nineteenth-century landscape from the English School depicting Jerusalem and the Church of the Holy Sepulchre.

The First Christmas

Jesus Christ's birthday is first recorded as being observed on this day.

A calendar compiled by one Furius Dionysius Filocalus in 354 contains the following entry for the year 336: "*VIII kal. Ian. natus Christus in Betleem Iudeae*" (Eighth day before the kalends of January [December 25], Birth of Christ in Bethlehem in Judea). This is the first definite indication that by the mid-fourth century Christians had fixed December 25 as the date of Jesus's birth. The Gospel writers make no mention of the time of year that he was born.

There are a number of probable explanations for the choice of December 25. It was the date of the

> ## "They call it the 'Birthday of the Unconquered.' Who is so unconquered as Our Lord?"
>
> **John Chrysostom (c.407), *del Solst. Et Æquin***

winter solstice and was already celebrated in Rome as *Sol Invictus* (Unconquered Sun), a popular pagan holiday. It fell exactly nine months after the spring equinox on March 25, which early Christians held to be the fourth day of creation when light-givers such as the sun were brought into being. It was logical to also regard March 25 as the day of Jesus's conception.

The custom of celebrating Christ's birth on December 25 spread from Rome to the rest of the church by the late fourth century, but most regarded Epiphany (January 6) as the more important festival, as millions of Christians still do. It was not until the Middle Ages that the celebration of Christmas Day began to take a form we would recognize today, with the ox and the ass at the manger, and shepherds tending their flocks in the snow. **SK**

Barbarian Triumph

The Goths defeat Roman Emperor Valens at Adrianople.

According to Edward Gibbon, the eighteenth-century chronicler of Rome's decline and fall, "the ninth of August [was] a day that has deserved to be marked among the most inauspicious of the Roman calendar." The battle fought outside Adrianople in 378 revealed the inability of the Roman Empire to control the influx of "barbarian" peoples into its territory.

In 376 some two million Germanic Visigoths and Ostrogoths had crossed the frontier into the empire west of the Black Sea. Unhappy with the treatment they received from the Roman authorities, these immigrants soon went on the rampage. Led by the Visigoth Fritigern, by 378 they were camped 12 miles (20 km) outside Adrianople. The ruler of the eastern half of the Roman Empire, Valens, marched from Constantinople to confront them. Instead of awaiting the arrival of Gratian, the Western Roman Emperor who was bringing an army to join him, Valens set out early on August 9 to attack Fritigern's camp.

Following a hot, dusty march, the Romans found the barbarians camped in a defensive circle of wagons. The formidable Ostrogoth horsemen were away on a foraging expedition. Fritigern called for a parlay, but before negotiations could begin, fighting broke out and Valens ordered his infantry to attack. Thirsty, exhausted, and disorganized, the legionaries might have had problems even without the sudden arrival of the Ostrogoth cavalry. As the horsemen enveloped the Roman foot soldiers, Visigoth warriors rushed out from the wagon camp to join the melee. Encircled and crowded into an ever-smaller space, the Roman foot soldiers were hacked down. Some 40,000 men, approximately two-thirds of the Roman force, were slaughtered. The body of Valens was never recovered. **RG**

Serapeum Destroyed

Part of the great library of Alexandria lost with the destruction of the Serapeum.

In the late-fourth-century Roman Empire, the struggle between Christians and those who adhered to ancient pagan traditions reached a boiling point. In 391, the Serapeum, a building reputed to house part of the great library of Alexandria came under siege.

Throughout the empire, pagans were persecuted and their temples destroyed. The situation worsened when the Christian emperor, Theodosius, issued a decree ordering the destruction of all heathen temples. In Alexandria, the Patriarch Theophilus was only too happy to comply. Under his sanction, attacks on pagans, their property, and their places of worship intensified. Enraged by this violation of sacred temples, the pagans retaliated and attacked the Christians.

What followed was a bloodbath. When the Christian faction fought back, the pagans took hostages and barricaded themselves in the Serapeum, the most imposing of the remaining temples. During the course of the siege, it was reported that some of the pagans plundered the temple while others tortured and sacrificed their helpless captives. Despite the ferocity of the incident, Theodosius spared the pagans but had the Serapeum destroyed, claiming that its pagan imagery had caused all the trouble.

There is some debate about how much of the great library was contained in the Serapeum. If, as is widely believed, the Serapeum did house part of the library, its destruction was a tragedy that would have caused the loss of many ancient texts. However, at the time, this was probably not uppermost in the minds of most. There is no doubt that the violent events of 391 were seen by early Christians as further evidence of the triumph of Christianity over pagan mysticism. **TB**

Roman Empire Divided

The death of Theodosius the Great splits the Roman Empire, hastening its decline.

The death of Theodosius the Great in 395 was greeted with fear by many who lived in the Roman world. Less than one year after Theodosius had brought the empire together after years of civil war, it was divided once again between Theodosius's inexperienced sons, with Honorius ruling in the west and Arcadius ruling in the east. The fears of the populace were well founded. From this point on, the Roman Empire would never again be unified under one emperor.

Honorius was only ten years old when he became emperor, and he relied on the leadership of

"The Roman empire is become the habitation of barbarians."

Zosimus, *New History*, Book IV, c.500

Stilicho, a general who defeated the barbarian Radagasius in 406. But Honorius was plagued by setbacks as the Western Empire slowly collapsed around him. Things became worse when Honorius had Stilicho executed in 408 on charges of conspiracy. On August 24, 410, the Roman world was shaken to its core when Alaric the Goth sacked Rome. By the time Honorius died in 423, his empire was plagued by revolts and usurpers.

In the east, Arcadius did not have to face the calamities of the west. According to ancient texts, he was weak-willed and easily led. He was dominated by his wife and spent his time as a pious Christian rather than attending to matters of state. Arcadius died in 408 barely in control of an empire dominated by court intrigue. **TB**

Rome Is Sacked by Visigoths

Led by Alaric the Goth, the Visigoths lay siege to and invade the former capital of the Roman Empire; it is the first time in 800 years that the city's walls are breached.

By 410 the city of Rome was no longer the capital of a great empire. The center of Roman power had shifted east to Constantinople, and in the west Emperor Honorius had moved his court to Ravenna on Italy's Adriatic coast. Still, Rome remained a rich and populous city, protected by its formidable Aurelian Walls. Its citizens could boast that it had not been overrun by a foreign enemy for some 800 years. But on the night of August 24, Rome was betrayed

The man who ended Rome's record of invincibility was Alaric, chief of the Visigoths. Like many other barbarians, his Germanic warband had been co-opted by the Romans to fight as *foederati* (allies) alongside the dwindling official legions. Alaric believed he had not been adequately rewarded for services rendered. Laying siege to Rome was a method of extorting wealth that he believed his men had earned.

One of the gates in the Aurelian Walls, the Porta Salaria, was opened from the inside, and the Visigoths poured into the sleeping city unopposed. Their "sack of Rome" fell short of unbridled destruction. Most of the Visigoths were Arian Christians, and they respected Rome's churches and the lives of those who took refuge in them. But sites considered pagan were looted and destroyed. Theft, murder, and rape occurred, if on a lesser scale than citizens might have feared. Because of the siege, food supplies in Rome were largely exhausted. After three days, then, the Visigoths left the starving city, heading south toward grain-rich Sicily. Alaric died later in the year at Cosenza. The humbling of Rome was a shock to its citizens and the wider Roman world, pointing forward to even worse humiliations in the years ahead. **RG**

○ An engraving depicting the sacking and pillaging of Rome by the Visigoths in 410.

> ## "The city which took captive the whole world has itself been captured."
>
> **St. Jerome, Letter CXXVII to Principia, 412**

Holy Mission to Ireland

A former slave, St. Patrick is called in a dream to go as a missionary to Ireland.

The date that is traditionally given for St. Patrick's holy mission to Ireland, 432, assumes that he is one and the same as a certain Palladius who was sent by St. Germanus, bishop of Auxerre in Gaul, to found a bishopric in Ireland on this date. Whether or not this is factual, we can be sure that St. Patrick was active in Ireland during the fifth century, and that through his tireless evangelizing he spread the word of Christianity throughout the country.

"We beg you, holy boy, to come and walk again among us."

St. Patrick, *Confessio*, c.450

St. Patrick was born into a Christian Romano-British family in Wales about the end of the fourth century. *Confessio* (Declaration), a text known only from a ninth-century copy but credibly attributed to Patrick, says that Irish raiders captured him and sold him into slavery in Ireland when he was sixteen. Seven years later he escaped, but some time later received a call in a dream to go back to Ireland as a missionary. He was ordained into the priesthood and consecrated as a bishop before returning to Ireland, where, according to his own account, he "baptized thousands of people," from nobles to slaves, ordained priests, and founded Christian communities.

The hymn "St. Patrick's Breastplate" is of a much later date. He did not drive out snakes from Ireland or use the shamrock to illustrate the Trinity—these are just a few of the many legends that grew up around St. Patrick in the centuries after his death. **SK**

Attila the Hun Fails

The Roman general Aetius defeats Attila the Hun at the Catalaunian Plains.

After spending several years terrorizing the Balkan provinces of the Eastern Roman Empire, Attila, king of the Huns (r.434–453), invaded the Western Empire in 451 with a huge army of Huns and allied Germans. Fighting began midafternoon on June 20, and continued well into the midsummer night, but all did not go according to plan. Attila advanced across Gaul, pillaging as he went. He intended to force the Western Emperor Valentinian III to hand over his rebellious sister Honoria, who had sent him a secret proposal of marriage, together with a dowry comprising half of the Western Empire.

Opposing Attila was the Roman master general Aetius. Attila and Aetius knew each other well. Aetius had spent part of his youth as a hostage with the Huns and had since made frequent use of Hun mercenaries in his campaigns against the Germanic invaders who had seized parts of Gaul and Spain.

Attila's invasion was as much a threat to these German settlers as it was to the Romans, enabling Aetius to build an unlikely coalition of his former enemies. Attila advanced as far as Orléans but failed to take the city before Aetius approached with an army of Romans, Visigoths, Franks, Burgundians, Saxons, and Alans. Attila withdrew to the open country of the Catalaunian Plains, between Troyes and Chalons, where he could use his cavalry to best advantage. Casualties were very heavy on both sides, but Attila eventually withdrew. The next day Attila's forces retreated in good order. Aetius did not pursue him. Attila invaded Italy the following year, but this campaign failed too, and he died in 453. **JH**

◗ *Attila and His Army Marching on Paris*, a detail of a fresco depicting the great leader on his rampage.

End of an Empire

Romulus Augustulus, last of the emperors of the West, is deposed.

On August 23, 476, the barbarian general Odovacar began a rebellion against the Western Roman Emperor Romulus Augustulus. On September 4, Odovacar captured Romulus and pensioned him off to a villa near Naples. Odovacar wrote to the Eastern Roman Emperor Zeno, at Constantinople, telling him that it was no longer necessary for the empire to have two emperors, and that he would rule Italy—all that remained of the Western Roman Empire—on his behalf as viceroy. These events are generally seen as marking the fall of the Western Roman Empire.

"Odovacar deposed Augustulus but granted him his life, pitying his infancy."

Chronicle of the Anonymous Valesianus, 550

The young Romulus had been appointed emperor in October 475, by his father, the general Orestes, who had deposed the previous emperor, Julius Nepos, and wanted to rule through his son. When Odovacar captured Orestes on August 28, he had him beheaded, but Romulus was spared because the title of emperor no longer held much status. For historians, the deposing of Romulus marks the end of the Roman Empire and the start of the Dark Ages.

Zeno had always regarded Romulus as a usurper, and he accepted Odovacar's offer to rule as viceroy, which maintained the legal fiction that Italy remained part of the Roman Empire. As Odovacar upheld the Roman administration, life for the vast majority of his subjects went uninterrupted by the watershed that the end of Romulus's reign represented. **JH**

King Clovis Is Baptized

Clovis I embraces Roman Catholicism and is baptized in Rheims Cathedral.

Many bystanders in Rheims in December 496 believed they were breathing the delights of paradise as King Clovis, often known as Chlodovocar, rode to the cathedral to be baptized in his people's religion. It was significant that Clovis was to become a Roman Catholic, rather than following Germanic Arianism. By embracing the popular religion of the old Roman province of Gaul, Clovis would go on to create a united Frankish kingdom, later to become France.

The road to creating a united Frankish kingdom by military conquest was already well under way

"Daily did God cause Chlodovocar's enemies to fall into his hand."

Gregory of Tours (d.594), *History of the Franks*

before Clovis's conversion. However, by adopting Roman Catholicism, Clovis was able to win the hearts and minds of those peoples that he came to lead after his conquests on the battlefield. Also, Clovis indirectly ensured that the united Frankish kingdom would be linked to the papacy and to what remained of the empire, thus retaining much of the old Roman culture and easing the transition for the conquered.

Despite embracing Roman Catholicism, Clovis was unable to conquer Burgundy, although he did restrict the Visigoth influence to Spain. Before his death in 511, Clovis added Aquitaine to his kingdom, with Paris as his capital. Unfortunately, Clovis's united kingdom was divided again at his death between his four sons who ruled the regions of Paris, Orléans, Soissons, and Rheims. **TB**

Influential Work Written in Prison

Boethius, the last Roman philosopher, is convicted of treason and writes
The Consolation of Philosophy *while awaiting execution.*

The Roman philosopher Ancius Boethius (c.480–524) is best known for *The Consolation of Philosophy*, written while he was imprisoned by Theodoric, the Ostrogothic king of Italy, after being convicted of treason. Boethius had tried to combine loyalty to the ideal of a universal Roman Empire with service to the barbarian king who ruled Italy.

The last Roman emperor of the West had been deposed in 476, but, in theory, Italy remained part of the Roman Empire, and Theodoric acknowledged the sovereignty of the Eastern emperor at Constantinople. Yet despite this outward display of amity between the rulers, Theodoric was paranoid about losing power and, to him, Boethius's close relations with the East looked like part of a plot to restore imperial rule. The philosopher was therefore convicted of treason and sentenced to death.

Boethius took his imprisonment and impending execution hard. The senior civil servant was a member of a wealthy patrician family, a lauded scholar, and a consul of Rome. In his despair, he wrote *The Consolation of Philosophy*, which takes the form of a dialogue between Boethius and the personification of Philosophy. It considers the nature of good and evil, happiness, free will, and the twists of fate and fortune, drawing on the doctrines of Plato and Aristotle, the Stoics, and the Neoplatonists. How long he was imprisoned is unknown, but eventually Boethius was tortured and beaten to death.

The Consolation of Philosophy languished in obscurity for centuries, and then became one of the most influential philosophical works of the Middle Ages. It was translated into English by King Alfred the Great in the ninth century to encourage his subjects in their struggles with the Vikings. **JH**

○ *Boethius Bidding Farewell to his Family* by French artist Jean Victor Schnetz (1787–1870).

"Instead of reward for true goodness, punishment for a crime I did not commit."

Boethius, The Consolation of Philosophy

Hermits No More: Monastic Life Is Established

St. Benedict writes a set of rules detailing how monastic communities should live.

The summit of a rocky hill rising steeply above the town of Cassino, between Rome and Naples, was the place to which Benedict (480–547) and a few followers retreated to live a spiritual life. There, in 529, Benedict set about composing a rule, or set of instructions, for communities of monks to follow, laying down times of prayer, work, the need for study, and obedience.

Benedict had been seeking to lead a holy life for many years. The child of wealthy parents, born in Nursia, central Italy, he abandoned his studies in Rome—shocked by the licentiousness he encountered there, so Gregory the Great tells us—and lived as a hermit in a cave at Subiaco, east of Rome. After three years, the fame of his sanctity drew him out into the world again and he became abbot of a nearby monastery. Disciples flocked to him, and he founded twelve further monasteries, each with twelve monks. A disagreement with a neighboring priest persuaded him to move to Monte Cassino.

From early in the history of Christianity, individual men and women had chosen to live as hermits, fasting and praying in the desert, in imitation of Jesus's forty days in the wilderness. Sometimes they came together to live in small communities of monks (a word derived from the Greek *monakhas*, "solitary"), often under the rule of an abbot (from *abba*, the Aramaic word for "father").

In Cassino, Benedict developed the cenobitic tradition of monasticism, which emphasized a communal life and family spirit among monks. This differed from the anchorite tradition of hermits, which he had initially followed. Although the rules he developed there were not the first monastic rules, the Rule of St. Benedict became the basis of monastic life throughout western Christendom. **SK**

◑ *Scenes From the Life of Saint Benedict: The Saint Drives Away the Devil* by Spinello Aretino (c.1332–1410).

◑ *Saint Benedict* by Hans Memling (c.1425–1494), a German-Flemish artist of the Northern Renaissance.

> ## "The holy man wrote a rule for monks remarkable for its clarity of language."
>
> **Gregory the Great, *Dialogues*, 590**

Riot at the Races

Constantinople burns as mob violence threatens the Byzantine throne.

In sixth-century Constantinople, chariot-racing was the chief passion of the populace. Rivalry between the two main racing teams, the Blues and the Greens, ran deep. News spread that some charioteers had been hanged for murder following a recent fracas, and the crowds filling the hippodrome, the city's racetrack, on January 13, 532, were tense and angry. As the day's races proceeded, the partisan chants of "Blue" or "Green" changed to a single cry of "*Nika, nika,*" ("Win, win"), and before long the rival factions had joined in wreaking violence on the government. They poured out of the stadium and during five days of rioting attacked the imperial palace and set fire to buildings throughout the city. When the mob met in the hippodrome to acclaim a usurper, all seemed lost for Emperor Justinian, ruler since 527.

It was his wife, Theodora, who saved the day. The daughter of a circus-bear tamer and herself an actress and former prostitute, or so her enemies said, she was his most trusted adviser. She persuaded him to stand his ground rather than flee the city while the imperial generals, Belisarius and Narses, rallied the army against the mob, leaving thousands dead.

The same generals were behind Justinian's military successes, which included trying to reconquer the Western Roman Empire from the barbarians. In 533 he dispatched an army to destroy the Vandal kingdom in north Africa, and he fought long wars in Italy and Persia. When Justinian died in 567, imperial power had been restored throughout Italy and in southern Spain—gains his successors were not able to retain for long. **SK**

◐ An image of the ancient city of Constantinople, showing monuments erected in the hippodrome.

Heaven on Earth

Justinian attends the consecration of Hagia Sophia in Constantinople.

No one had ever attempted to build a dome on such a scale before. "Solomon, I have outdone you!" Byzantine Emperor Justinian is said to have remarked on entering his recently completed church of Hagia Sophia (Divine Wisdom of God) shortly before its consecration in December 537.

Within a few days of witnessing its predecessor burned to the ground in the riots of January 532, Justinian had ordered the construction of a new basilica, the third to stand on the site since Constantine's original foundation in 325. According to the historian Procopius, more than 10,000 people were employed during the construction, and the engineering ingenuity of architects Isidore of Miletus and Anthemius of Thalles was tested to the full.

Designed to represent the vault of heaven, the dome rose 210 feet (64 m) above the floor and was supported on four round arches springing from four solid pillars, each measuring 1,060 square feet (99 sq m) at the base. The gilded interior of the dome was lit by forty single-arched windows and adorned with rich mosaics and colored marbles—red, green, black, and yellow—all intended to give the worshipper the impression of entering heaven.

For more than 900 years, Hagia Sophia served as the seat of the Patriarch of Constantinople and the visible center of Orthodox Christianity. However, it suffered damage by earthquake and was stripped of its treasures by the army of the Fourth Crusade in 1204. When Constantinople fell to the Ottoman Turks in 1453, Sultan Mehmed II ordered the building to be turned into a mosque and four minarets were added, giving it the familiar outline it has today. In 1935, it was turned into a museum by the secular Turkish government, and remains so to this day. **SK**

Secret of Chinese Silk

Monks smuggle silkworms out of China to win favor with Emperor Justinian.

From 552 onward, the production of silk flourished in the Byzantine Empire thanks to two monks. On learning that Emperor Justinian was unwilling to buy silk from the Persians, the monks told him they had discovered the secret of silk production. They were members of a heretical Christian sect that had been expelled from Constantinople and had settled in a province of the Persian Empire lying on the overland trade route along which silk was carried from China.

The Chinese had made and exported silk for hundreds of years but jealously guarded the

---

"With time and patience the mulberry leaf becomes a silk gown."

Chinese proverb

---

knowledge of how it was produced. Although silk dyeing and weaving was an established industry in Constantinople at this time, protected by the emperor who granted the imperial silk factories a monopoly in 541, the material could be sourced only by importing raw silk.

Justinian was at war with the Persians, the middlemen in the long-distance silk trade. He promised to reward the monks generously if they could bypass the Persians and bring him the secret of how silk was made. Procopius tells us that the monks returned to China, where they got hold of some silk cocoons. They hid them inside hollow bamboo sticks, buried in dung to keep them alive on the long journey back to Constantinople. There they hatched into silk moths and the secret of silk was no more. **SK**

Gregory Becomes Pope

The first monk to be made pope proves an able leader and administrator.

When Pope Pelagius II died in an outbreak of the plague in 590, his secretary, Gregory, was chosen to succeed him—the first monk ever to become pope. Gregory I (540–604) was a Roman, born into a noble family. He probably trained as a lawyer before serving as the chief civil magistrate of Rome. Disenchanted with public life, he became a monk in 574 in the monastery he had founded in the family palace on the Caelian Hill. From 579 to 585 he was Pope Pelagius II's agent in Constantinople, and later his secretary.

These were difficult times for the city and for the papacy, under threat of attack from the Lombards, who had invaded northern Italy in 568. Gregory proved to be an able leader and administrator, planning strategy, leading diplomacy, repairing the city's aqueducts, ensuring the food supply, and eventually negotiating a settlement with the Lombard kings. He reorganized the Church's lands and finances, restored contact with churchmen in Africa, Spain, and Gaul, to whom he wrote hundreds of pastoral letters, and defended the papacy, protesting that the patriarch of Constantinople used the title "Ecumenical (universal) Patriarch." Gregory called himself "the servant of the servants of God," the first pope to do so.

Gregory's writings, especially the *Liber regulae pastoralis* (Book of Pastoral Care) on the office and duties of bishops and priests, were widely studied throughout the Middle Ages, and when he was canonized, he was called "the Great." Among his legacies was the systematization of plainsong, still known today as "Gregorian chant." **SK**

○ Saint Gregory as depicted in a twelfth-century illuminated manuscript, painted by French monks.

Thousands of Britons Convert to Christianity

Augustine baptizes Anglo-Saxons and founds the archdiocese of Canterbury.

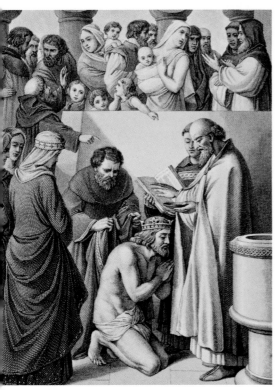

◔ A nineteenth-century engraving entitled *The Baptism of Ethelbert, King of Kent, by Saint Augustine at Canterbury in 597.*

◔ *St. Augustine of Canterbury,* a study for a stained-glass window for Chester Cathedral, UK, glazed by Frederick Charles Eden.

> ### "More than ten thousand Angles have been baptized by our brother Augustine."
> **Gregory I to the Patriarch of Alexandria, 598**

When Pope Gregory sent Augustine, prior of his monastery in Rome, to the former Roman province of Britain, it resulted in the conversion of a king and his people to Christianity. It is recorded that Augustine carried out a mass baptism at Christmas 597 and it is likely the pagan King Ethelbert of Kent had already converted before his people began to be baptized.

According to legend, Gregory saw fair-haired slaves for sale in the market in Rome and asked where they were from. On being told that they were Angles he replied, *"Non anglii sed angeli"* ("Not Angles but angels"), and decided to send a mission to convert their countrymen. Bede repeats this story in his *Ecclesiastical History of the English People,* but it may well be apocryphal—more likely is that news had already reached Gregory's ears that Bertha, a Christian Frankish princess married to Ethelbert, had appealed for priests to convert her husband's people.

Gregory chose Augustine to head the mission and he left for Britain in 596, with forty monks. When they reached southern Gaul, however, their courage failed them, knowing the journey would be a dangerous one, and they returned to Rome. Gregory persuaded them to try again and in 597 the monks landed in what is now Kent. King Ethelbert welcomed the monks at his court and not long afterwards became a Christian.

Augustine made his base at Canterbury, in Kent, and when Gregory sent four more monks to join the mission, in 601, they brought with them a pallium, the woolen stole bestowed by the pope on an archbishop. One of the new monks was Paulinus, who would become the first missionary to the powerful northern Anglo-Saxon kingdom of Northumbria, where he converted King Ethelbert's son-in-law, King Edwin, in 627. **SK**

Muhammad on the Mountain

Archangel Gabriel appears in a vision to Muhammad as he sleeps on Mount Hira and tells him that he is the apostle of God.

In the fortieth year of his life, while sleeping alone in a cave on Mount Hira (in modern-day Saudi Arabia), Muhammad received his first revelation of the archangel Gabriel. In a state of mental turmoil, Muhammad confided in his wife, Khadija, and told her that Gabriel had announced that Muhammad was the apostle of God. Khadija had complete faith in her husband's sincerity, thus becoming the first convert to the new religion of Islam.

Muhammad was born in Mecca in 570. A member of the minor Quraysh clan, Muhammad was orphaned at the age of seven and from then on was brought up in the household of his uncle Abu Talib. Muhammad grew up to become a thoughtful, serious young man. At the age of twenty-five, he married Khadija, a wealthy widow of the Quraysh who was about fifteen years his senior. Despite the age difference, this was a good match for Muhammad, raising his status with the Quraysh and giving him the means and the leisure to indulge his interest in religion. Every year he would spend the month of Ramadan praying and meditating alone on Mount Hira in the desert outside Mecca.

Muhammad's own religious ideas were undoubtedly influenced by the religious diversity of sixth-century Arabia. Although most Arabs were still polytheists, many had converted to Judaism, and smaller numbers to Christianity. Some indigenous cults, such as that of the warrior god Hubal, were also developing in the direction of monotheism. However, when Muhammad began to preach publicly three years after his first vision, he did not claim to be the founder of a new religion, but the restorer of the original monotheistic religion of Abraham, from which Jews and Christians had deviated. **JH**

○ A book illustration showing the moment the archangel Gabriel visited Muhammad.

"Allah sent him as a prophet of mercy to the people of the visible and invisible worlds."

Ibn Ishaq, *The Life of Muhammad*, 12th century

A New Era Begins

The hijra, *Muhammad's migration from Mecca to Medina, begins the Muslim era.*

Muhammad's reputation as a religious visionary spread widely, and in 622, he and his followers secretly left Mecca for Medina, where he had been invited to resolve a dispute between tribes. This event is known as the *hijra* (migration) and marks the beginning of the Muslim calendar. After receiving his first vision in 610, Muhammad had told only his wife, Khadija, and other close family members about his experience. Three years later, Muhammad had another vision in which the archangel Gabriel told him to preach publicly.

Muhammad's emphasis on social justice attracted converts among the poor, but most of the people of his hometown of Mecca were hostile. The Black Stone in Mecca's Ka'bah shrine was an important pilgrimage center for Arab polytheists, and Meccans benefited economically from the visitors. They feared Muhammad's new religion threatened their future and he was mocked and insulted wherever he went, but tribal custom protected him from violence.

By negotiating with the tribes of Medina, Muhammad established the first Muslim *umma* (community). The *umma* was a theocracy in which religious and political authority was exercized by Muhammad acting in the name of God. The Jews of Medina, who were critical of Muhammad's teachings, were ordered to leave. Those who refused were enslaved or massacred. Muhammad made Medina a base from which to spread Islam by diplomacy and force, teaching his followers that it was their religious duty to make war on unbelievers. In 630, he captured Mecca without a fight. Muhammad reconciled the Meccans by declaring the Ka'bah the holiest shrine of Islam. After his victory, Muhammad continued to live at Medina, where he died in 632. **JH**

Umar the Conqueror

The caliph Umar begins the great Arab conquests of Persia and Byzantium.

Umar ibn al-Khattab was the father of one of Muhammad's wives. He was well known for his piety and simple, austere lifestyle, and his accession to caliph in 634 was unopposed, even though Muhammad's cousin and son-in-law Ali believed he had a better claim to the caliphate. Umar's ten-year reign was decisive in the history of Islam.

Muhammad had no sons and had not nominated a successor. When he died in 632, his father-in-law, Abu Bakr, one of the earliest converts to Islam, was chosen as the first *khalifat rasul Allah* (successor of the

> ## "Umar's submission to Islam was a conquest . . . his caliphate was a blessing."
>
> **Abdullah ibn Mas'ud, Muhammad's follower**

Prophet of God or caliph). Reigning for just two years, he completed the political and religious unification of the Arabs that had been begun by Muhammad, by sending armies to raid the Byzantine and Persian Empires. The two empires had just concluded an exhausting war lasting twenty-six years, and their resistance was easily overcome. Abu Bakr's last act in August 634 was to appoint Umar as his successor.

Vigorously following up Abu Bakr's successes, Umar directed (but did not lead in person) the conquest of the Persian Empire and the Byzantine provinces of Egypt, Palestine, and Syria, transforming the caliphate from a purely Arab state into a great empire. In so doing he also transformed Islam from a religion practiced only by Arabs into a phenomenon of global significance. **JH**

Isle of Christianity

Aidan, a monk from Iona, is made bishop of Lindisfarne and founds a monastery.

One of the first acts of Oswald on becoming king of Northumbria was to send for Aidan, an Irish monk from Iona. In 635, the king asked Aidan to be a bishop in Northumbria and gave him the tiny island of Lindisfarne (also known as Holy Island), which lies just off the coast not far from the royal stronghold of Bamburgh, to build a monastery. During the reign of his predecessor Edwin (r.616–33), Oswald had been an exile in the Scottish kingdom of Dalraida, where he was converted to Christianity by the monks of Iona, an island monastery off the west coast of Scotland founded by St. Columba in about 595. It was during Edwin's reign that Paulinus, one of Augustine's missionary companions from Rome, had brought Christianity to Northumbria. Edwin had been baptized in a ceremony in 627, and Paulinus had made many other converts.

In his *Ecclesiastical History,* completed in 731, Bede paints an attractive picture of Aidan's character and behavior, his care for the poor, his readiness to deal equally with kings and with ordinary people, and the simplicity of his life. He made Lindisfarne the base of his evangelizing mission and set up a school there to train future priests and bishops—among them Chad, who became the first bishop of Lichfield. St. Cuthbert (c.634–87), who spent many years as a hermit on the neighboring islet of Farne, was later made bishop of Lindisfarne, and another bishop, Eadfrith, was the probable artist of *The Lindisfarne Gospels*, an illuminated book and masterpiece of religious art, which was completed in the monastery about 715 and is now in the British Museum. **SK**

◯ An illuminated page from *The Lindisfarne Gospels,* which are also known as *The Gospels of Saint Cuthbert.*

Jerusalem Surrenders

Sophronius surrenders Jerusalem to Caliph Umar I and it becomes Muslim.

Caliph Umar I arrived in Jerusalem in January 638 to claim the city for the Arabs. He made a great show of his humility, wearing a patched cloak and walking barefoot while he toured the Temple Mount, the site of Muhammad's "Night Journey" dream.

In the autumn of 637, Sophronius, the patriarch of Jerusalem, had reluctantly opened negotiations with Umar for the surrender of his city to Muslim control. The Arabs had invaded the Byzantine Empire in 634, capturing Damascus the following year. The emperor Heraclius sent an army to recover the city,

> ## "Behold the abomination of desolation spoken of by Daniel the prophet."
>
> **Sophronius, Patriarch of Jerusalem, 638**

but it was destroyed by the Arabs at the battle of the Yarmuk in 636. By autumn 637 the Arabs occupied all of Syria and Palestine except for Jerusalem and Caesarea. The fall of Jerusalem to the Arabs became inevitable. Sophronius's task was made easier by the Muslims' respect for Jerusalem as a holy city, but one of Sophronius's conditions was that he would surrender the city only to Umar in person.

The terms offered by Umar were generous to the city's Christians, who were guaranteed protection on payment of *jizya* (tribute) to their Muslim overlords. Jews, however, were banned from Jerusalem. Most Christians in Palestine belonged to the Monophysite sect, which had been persecuted by the Byzantines, so they regarded the Arabs as liberators. Jerusalem remained under Muslim control until 1099. **JH**

Dagobert Dies

The death of the king hastens the decline of the Merovingian dynasty.

Dagobert I was the last of the Merovingian kings to rule over a united Frankish kingdom and his death, on January 19, 639, was followed by the slow decline of a dynasty that had ruled since Clovis I, more than one hundred years earlier. Dagobert's power was partly a result of his close alliance with Byzantine Emperor Heraclius. Despite defeat at the hands of the Austrasians in 631, Dagobert won important victories against the Gascons and the Bretons, campaigned against the Slavs in the East, and sent an army into Spain to support the Visigothic

---

"King Dagobert, swift, handsome, and famous with no rival."

Dado of Rouen, *The Life of Eligius*, 7th century

---

usurper Swinthila. By 632, Dagobert had become the most powerful Merovingian king in the west.

Dagobert's reign was a prosperous one. Many churches were adorned with golden decorations and tombs dating from this time have been found to contain many rich artifacts. He patronized the arts, revised Frankish law, encouraged learning, and founded the first abbey of Saint Denis.

Dagobert was succeeded by his sons, Sigebert III and Clovis II, who came to be known as the *roi fainéant* ("do nothing") kings because they did little else but father heirs. Real power lay with the nobility, a situation that lasted until 751 when Peppin the Short deposed the last Merovingian king, Childeric III. Peppin the Short was the first Carolingian king and the father of Charlemagne the Great. **TB**

Caliph Umar Murdered

A disgruntled slave, Abu Lulu, fatally stabs the caliph six times.

Early on the morning of November 3, 644, after repeating the Muslim profession of faith, the second caliph Umar died. He was buried next to Muhammad and Abu Bakr, the first of the caliphs to succeed the Prophet as temporal and spiritual leader of the Muslims. A few days earlier as he walked through the streets of Medina, Umar had been approached by Abu Lulu, a Christian slave, who claimed to be mistreated by his master. Umar dismissed his complaint as unreasonable. The next day as Umar attended morning prayers in the mosque, Abu Lulu stabbed the caliph six times before turning his knife on himself.

Before he died, Umar appointed a committee to choose his successor. The leading members were Ali ibn abi Talib, the cousin and son-in-law of Muhammad, and Uthman ibn Affan, also a son-in-law of Muhammad and a member of the rich Umayyad clan. The committee began to fall out almost immediately, and the dying caliph ordered them to suspend their deliberations until after his death.

After Umar's burial, the committee was placed in a room under guard and given three days to reach a decision. Ali and Uthman were the only serious candidates for the caliphate, but when the three days were up, no decision had been reached, so the chairman Abdul Rahman invited the congregation at morning prayers for their opinions. Because he appeared to have the greater support, Abdul Rahman chose Uthman as caliph (r.644–656). A worldly and nepotistic caliph, Uthman's favors to his own clan led ultimately to rebellion, his own murder, and the beginning of the breakdown of Muslim unity. **JH**

◐ A late sixteenth- or early seventeenth-century Turkish illustration of the death of Umar.

Imperial Revolution Transforms Japan

The new emperor, Kotoku, initiates the wide-ranging Taika Reforms, which codify laws and reorganize government administration.

◐ An illustration from the *Tounomine engi emaki* showing the assassination of Soga no Iruka by Prince Naka no Oe.

"In Heaven there are not two suns: in a country there are not two rulers."

Emperor Kotoku, *Taika Reform Edicts*

In 645, Prince Naka no Oe overthrew the powerful Soga clan and, having taken the name Emperor Kotoku, set about reforming the Japanese system of government. He did so in order to consolidate his power and gain control over all of Japan. He instigated land reforms based on the ideas of Confucius and those of T'ang China. These reforms resulted in greater centralized control and the increased power of the imperial court. Kotoku also adopted the Chinese system of naming eras after an emperor's reign, taking the name Taika, or "Great Change," for the first part of his reign.

Before the Taika era, Japan had been controlled by numerous warring clans and the imperial court was dominated by the Soga family, which had maintained its grip on power by strategic use of intrigue and murder. By freeing the court from the domination of the Soga, Kotoku was able to organize an effective, centralized imperial government.

The four key articles of the Taika era brought about a revolution in government. They abolished private ownership of land and people, proclaiming they should be owned by the public—in effect the emperor. In addition, new administrative and military organizations were set up throughout Japan, directly responsible to the emperor; a census was introduced to bring about a fairer distribution of land; and an equitable tax system was created.

Laws were codified and government departments were staffed with officials, many of whom had been trained in China. A network of roads was built to augment centralized control. In effect, the reforms created a feudal system, whereby local magnates held hereditary rights as long as they were loyal to the emperor. **TB**

Sunni and Shi'a Schism

The murder of Caliph Ali divides the Islamic world into Sunni and Shi'a.

The murder of Caliph Ali on January 24, 661, marked the beginning of the schism of Islam into Sunni and Shi'a traditions. Ali, Muhammad's cousin and son-in-law, became caliph in 656, after the murder of Caliph Uthman. The caliphate had expanded under Uthman, but money from conquered territories was not shared equally, creating dissent against him.

For many Muslims the message of Islam was being forgotten as the Arabs argued over the spoils of empire. Because of his close relationship with Muhammad, Ali attracted the support of those

> ## "Ali dead was effective. As a martyr he retrieved more than he lost in a lifetime."
>
> **Philip K. Hitti, *History of the Arabs*, 1937**

Muslims who believed that the purity of Islam would be best served if the caliphate was restricted to members of the Prophet's family. They became known as *shi'atu 'Ali* (the party of Ali), or the Shi'a.

Ali's claim to the caliphate was credible, but the way he had achieved power put his legitimacy in doubt. He soon faced a rebellion by Uthman's cousin, Muawiya, who was outraged by Ali's refusal to punish his kinsman's murderers. For the first time, Muslims fought Muslims. Kharijite members, who rejected the caliphate as an institution, plotted to murder both Ali and Muawiya. But they killed only Ali, leaving Muawiya to become caliph, his followers becoming Sunnis, from the Arabic word *Sunnah* (example of the Prophet). Ali's supporters became loyal to his son Hasan, causing a permanent breach in Islam. **JH**

Vengeance Is Ours

Caliph Muawiya takes control of the Muslim world for Umayyads.

In 661, Caliph Muawiya founded the first Muslim dynasty in the name of his Umayyad family. Muawiya, governor of Syria, rebelled against Caliph Ali in 657, after he failed to punish the murderers of his cousin Caliph Uthman (644–656). In Arab tradition it was Muawiya's duty to seek vengeance on a relative's killers, and he had widespread sympathy for his cause. In 660, Muawiya proclaimed himself caliph in Jerusalem in a bid to drive Ali from power. However, he was not complicit in Ali's murder in January 661. Ali's supporters, known as Shi'ites, transferred their allegiance to his son Hasan, but he resigned his claim to the caliphate. Within seven months of Ali's death, Muawiya had won control of the caliphate supported by his Sunni followers.

Muhammad had made no formal provisions for the succession, and the first four caliphs were all chosen by acclamation. Muawiya established the caliphate as a hereditary office by appointing his son Yazid as his successor during his own lifetime. For this reason, Muawiya is considered to be the founder of the Umayyad dynasty, which became one of the fastest-growing empires in history.

Muawiya's original power base had been in Syria, so he moved his capital from Medina to Damascus, which had better communications with the rest of the caliphate. Arabia had had its brief moment of glory and now became once again the backwater it had been before the time of Muhammad. But the Umayyad expansion, taking Islam with it, meant that Arabic became the common language of this vast region. The Umayyads ruled the entire Muslim world until 750, the empire's sway reaching from Spain to central Asia. They were overthrown by the Abbasids, whose power base lay in modern-day Iraq. **JH**

Rome Versus Ireland

The synod of Whitby chooses between the Irish and the Roman traditions.

In the early 660s, Wilfrid, a Northumbrian churchman who had visited Rome and spent three years at Lyon, in France, was given charge of the monastery at Ripon. This led to the expulsion of the Ionan monks already there, and caused the disagreements between the followers of the Irish and Roman traditions to come to a head. In 664, King Oswy (642–670) summoned a synod to help decide the matter. They met at Whitby in the large double monastery of monks and nuns ruled by the powerful abbess and noblewoman Hilda.

The Irish church had developed its own distinctive usages in the two centuries after St. Patrick introduced Christianity, which Aidan, the first bishop of Lindisfarne, had brought to Northumbria from Iona. The biggest disagreement was over how to calculate the date of the movable feast of Easter—the most important in the Christian year. The Irish monks still used tables that Rome had long considered to be incorrect. Other differences included the shape of the tonsure, the shaved patch of hair worn by monks.

Bede gives an account of the synod in his *Ecclesiastical History* of 731. The main supporters of the Irish tradition were Hilda and Colman, third bishop of Lindisfarne. Wilfrid was the most influential speaker for the Roman tradition, and his views held the day. King Oswy chose Rome and the teaching of St. Peter, who held the keys to heaven and hell. This important decision placed the Northumbrian church directly under the authority of the pope in Rome and brought it closer to Gaul and Italy. **SK**

◐ Engraving of *Bede, Le Venerable,* the celebrated English scholar and Benedictine monk.

Silla Dominates

The kingdom of Silla conquers its rival Koguryo and unifies Korea.

The period of Korean history between the first century B.C.E. and the seventh century C.E. is known as the "Three Kingdoms" period. At this time Korea was divided into four parts. The northwest was under Chinese occupation, and the rest was fought over by three native kingdoms: Koguryo, Paekche, and Silla. In 676 the smaller elite forces of Silla's king, Munmu, finally drove out the larger Chinese armies and Silla became the dominant kingdom.

All three had been militaristic, aristocratic states with a hierarchy of social ranks based on hereditary

> ## "In the year of Tsungchang the king led his army and destroyed Koguryo."
>
> **Ilyon, *Memorabilia of the Three Kingdoms***

bloodlines known as the "Bone Rank" system. Only those of the highest rank, the "Hallowed Bone Rank," were eligible for kingship. For most of the period, the strongest of the three kingdoms was Koguryo, which expanded mainly at the expense of China. To counter its power, China allied with Silla, the second-strongest kingdom. The allies conquered Paekche in 660 and Koguryo in 668, uniting the peninsula under a single ruler for the first time. The Chinese assumed the united Korea would be a vassal state and began to garrison the country. However, Munmu, rebelled and fought for eight years to establish Silla's dominance. Silla retained its dominance until 892 when Paekche regained its independence. In 901, Kungye, a rebel prince, revived the kingdom of Koguryo, which in 918 was renamed Koryo (or Korea) by King Wang Kon. **JH**

Shi'a Martyrdom

Husayn ibn Ali is killed at Karbala by the forces of Caliph Yazid I.

On October 10, 680, Husayn ibn Ali, the grandson of the Prophet Muhammad, was killed in a battle that saw the deaths of male members of the Prophet's family and the capture of women and children.

The Battle of Karbala, as it came to be known, was the result of factionalism that broke out following the succession of Yazid I to the Umayyad caliphate. Sections of the population loyal to the grandson of Muhammad rebelled in the city of Kufah and invited Husayn ibn Ali to join them, promising to proclaim him caliph in Iraq. On hearing this, Husayn set out from Mecca with most of his family, expecting to be received triumphantly by the citizens of Kufah. In the meantime, Yazid had sent Ubayd Allah, governor of Basra, to restore order in the rebellious city. When Husayn reached Karbala, a small town to the west of the Euphrates, he was confronted by an army reputed to number 40,000. Husayn gave battle, expecting to receive aid from his supporters in Kufah. Unfortunately for Husayn, no aid arrived, and he and many members of his family were slain.

When news of the death of Muhammad's grandson reached Kufah, those who had invited him were ashamed at their part in this tragedy. Yazid and his supporters were regarded as murderers, and their name was forevermore cursed by Shi'a Muslims. The violent death of Husayn is one of the most significant events in fueling the spread of Shi'a Islam, and its anniversary is observed as a day of public mourning. To Shi'a Muslims, the tomb in Karbala of the decapitated martyr, Husayn ibn Ali, is one of the holiest places on earth. **TB**

◗ *The Battle of Karbala* painted by Abbas Al-Musavi, now in the Brooklyn Museum of Art, New York.

Japan's First Capital

Empress Gemmei decides that Japan needs a permanent capital city.

In 710 the Empress Gemmei founded the first permanent capital of Japan at Heijo-kyo, west of the modern city of Nara. Before the late seventh century the emperors of Japan did not have a permanent capital. The capital was simply the emperor's palace and the government was composed of members of his household. On the death of the emperor, the palace was burned because of its association with death, and a new one built. However, the growth of an imperial bureaucracy based on that of China made a permanent capital increasingly desirable. In

> ## "Our great sovereign, a goddess, of her sacred will has reared a palace."
>
> **Anonymous, *Man'yōshū* (contemporary poem)**

694 a great palace was built at Fujiwara-kyo (*kyo* means "capital"), which served three emperors before being abandoned in 710 in favor of Heijo.

Heijo was a scaled-down version of the Chinese Tang dynasty capital at Chang'an. Much larger than Fujiwara, Heijo was built on a grid pattern 2.8 miles (4.5 km) east to west and 2.5 miles (4 km) north to south. When completed in *c.*720, Heijo had a population of around 200,000.

The foundation of Heijo began a seventy-year period of political stability known as the Nara Period (710–784), when Japanese government, culture, and law became increasingly modeled on those of China. In this period too, the Chinese writing system was adapted to the Japanese language. The Nara Period also saw the rapid growth of Buddhism in Japan. **JH**

Saracens Invade Spain

Tariq leads a Saracen army in the invasion of the Iberian peninsula.

In April 711, the Arab general Tariq led an army of Arabs and Berbers (Moors), who were referred to in Europe as "Saracens," across the sea from Morocco to invade the Visigothic kingdom of Spain. The place of his landfall became known as *Jebel al-Tariq* (the mountain of Tariq), or Gibraltar.

The Visigothic King Roderic rushed to meet Tariq, but was defeated and killed at the Battle of the Guadalette in July. After a second Saracen army arrived in Spain in 712, organized Visigothic resistance collapsed completely, and within two years Tariq had

"[T]he ruin of Spain [by the Saracens] is beyond human description."

Continuatio Hispana (Mozarabic Chronicle), 754

brought the entire Iberian peninsula under Muslim control, except for the mountainous northwest. This was the beginning of a period of Muslim influence that persisted in Spain for nearly 800 years.

A legend grew up to explain the rapid collapse of the Visigothic kingdom. According to the tale, an ancient king of Spain sealed a secret in a locked chamber, forbidding any of his successors to open it. Twenty-six kings obeyed, but Roderic, against all advice, ordered the chamber opened. He found the walls painted with Arab warriors. At the center of the chamber was a golden table with an urn containing a parchment that read, "Whenever this chamber is violated, and the spell contained in this urn is broken, the people painted on this wall will invade Spain, overthrow its kings and subdue the entire land." **JH**

Mountain Ambush

A Muslim army is defeated at the Battle of Covadonga in Asturias, Spain.

On a hot summer day between 718 and 724, a force of Muslim Arabs and Berbers advanced up a narrow valley in the mountains of northern Spain. At Covadonga, they came under attack from Christian fighters armed with bows and slings, positioned along the sides of the valley. To add to the devastation, the Muslims' own missiles, fired upward at their attackers, fell back upon them. Suddenly, 300 Christian warriors, led by the Visigothic nobleman, Pelayo, burst out from their hiding place in a cave. They attacked the Muslims, who were routed and retreated in disarray. This mountain ambush, although dismissed as a minor skirmish by Muslim writers, took on great importance in Spanish history.

In 711, the Iberian Peninsula had been invaded by Muslim forces from north Africa. The Christian Visigothic kingdom that had ruled Iberia since the sixth century collapsed. Pelayo and other Christians took refuge in the remote Asturian mountains. He urged local villagers to resist the imposition of Muslim rule, encouraging them to carry out guerrilla warfare and thereby provoking the counterinsurgency operation that brought the Muslims to Covadonga.

After the Battle of Covadonga, Pelayo founded the kingdom of Asturias as a center of resistance to the Islamic government. Christian chronicles described the battle as a mighty victory against a Muslim army of 180,000 men, although this number is almost certainly exaggerated. Covadonga came to be seen as the first battle of the *Reconquista*, the struggle to restore Christian rule in Iberia, which took more than seven centuries to complete. **RG**

◗ The statue of San Pelayo in Gijon, Spain, commemorating his victory in battle.

The Fight for the Kingdom of the Franks

Under the leadership of Charles Martel ("The Hammer"), the Franks defeat the Arabs at the Battle of Tours, preventing further northward Muslim expansion.

In 732, on a hilltop between Tours and Poitiers in France, one of the most decisive battles in European history was fought. In the hundred years following the Prophet Muhammad's death, armies inspired by the Islamic faith had pressed forward through north Africa and the Iberian Peninsula to arrive in the heart of Western Europe. In 732, the governor-general of Muslim Spain, Abd ar-Rahman al-Ghafiqi, led an army across the Pyrenees and conquered Aquitaine, laying waste to Bordeaux. He then headed for the kingdom of the Franks, toward the city of Tours.

The Frankish leader Charles Martel placed his 30,000-strong army on high, wooded ground, in their line of advance. He formed his men into a tight infantry square, and waited. Abd ar-Rahman al-Ghafiqi held off from attacking for seven days, although his force may have outnumbered the Franks by two to one. When he finally launched his cavalry, the Frankish infantry stood firm and repelled their charges. After a long fight, most of the Muslim horsemen withdrew to defend their war chests, and, abandoned by his men, Abd ar-Rahman al-Ghafiqi was surrounded and killed.

It is likely that Abd ar-Rahman al-Ghafiqi had not sought to conquer European Christendom, but just to lead a raiding expedition. But if the Frankish warriors had lost, nothing would have stood in the way of a Muslim takeover of western Europe. Charles Martel consolidated the Carolingian Empire, which formed a barrier to the northward expansion of Islam. **RG**

◐ An idealized, nineteenth-century chromolithograph of the Frankish king, Charles Martel.

◐ A detail from *The Battle of Poitiers* (1837)—another name for the Battle of Tours—by Charles Auguste Steuben (1788–1856).

Banquet of Blood

The Umayyad caliphate is overthrown by the Abbasids.

The authority of the Umayyad caliphs who had ruled the whole Muslim world since 661 gradually declined in the eighth century—and came to a bloody end in 750. The Abbasid general Abdullah ibn-Ali invited eighty members of the Umayyad family to a banquet at abu-Futrus near Jaffa on June 25, 750, and during the course of the feast had them all slaughtered. To add insult to injury, dead Umayyads were exhumed and their bodies burned.

One factor in the decline of the Umayyad caliphs had been their failure to resolve the Sunni-Shi'ite schism that had divided Islam. Another was the resentment felt by non-Arab converts to Islam of the way the Arabs treated the caliphate as their private property. Non-Arabs believed the caliphate had been founded to spread the word of Islam, not to advance Arab interests. In 747 a rebellion against Umayyad rule broke out in Persia and spread quickly to Iraq. Abu al-Abbas as-Saffar, a descendant of Muhammad's uncle al-Abbas, was proclaimed caliph by the rebels, so founding the Abbasid dynasty (749–1258). After routing the Umayyads at the Battle of the Zab in January 750, Abdullah ibn-Ali captured Damascus, the capital of the caliphate. The last Umayyad caliph, Marwan II, fled to Egypt, where he was hunted down and killed in August. To destroy any possibility of opposition, Abdullah held his infamous banquet.

The accession of the Abbasids marked a decisive shift of power in the Islamic world away from Arabs in favor of new converts who were now free to advance in government. It also marked the end of the political unity of the Muslim world. Only one significant member of the Umayyad family survived. Abd ar-Rahman escaped to Spain, where he founded a breakaway state. **JH**

The Battle of Talas

Arab victory ends Chinese expansion plans in central Asia.

The Arab victory over the Chinese at the Battle of Talas in 751 established Islam as the dominant religion in central Asia. This precipitated the collapse of China's central Asian empire.

During the reign of Emperor Taizong (628–649), China had extended its power into central Asia. The aim was to control the Silk Road that linked China to the Middle East and the Mediterranean. By the eighth century, the Chinese had conquered a 1,000-mile-long (1,610 km) salient extending to the Hindu Kush mountains. However, newly Islamized Arabs also had

> ## "[Arab] men have high noses, are dark, and bearded. The women are very fair."
>
> **Du Huan (Captured at Talas),** *Jingxingji*

expansion plans of their own, and in 710 they captured the great caravan cities of Bokhara and Samarkand.

In 750, a Chinese army under Gao Xianji captured Tashkent and executed its Turkish ruler. The ruler's son enlisted the aid of the Arabs in expelling the Chinese. In 751 a 40,000-strong Arab-Turk army advanced into Chinese territory and met Gao's army on the Talas River, in modern Kyrgyzstan. The Chinese army was mainly infantry and was outmaneuvered by Arab-Turk cavalry. Only a few thousand Chinese soldiers escaped.

It is said that after the battle, Chinese prisoners were put to work at Samarkand building a paper mill that used the well-guarded Chinese secrets of papermaking. This story may be apocryphal, but at this time the use of paper spread in the Islamic world, and then to Europe in the thirteenth century. **JH**

One Man to Rule *and* Reign

Pope Stephen II confirms the former mayor Peppin III as king of the Franks.

○ A fifteenth-century illuminated manuscript (detail) of Peppin the Short, king of the Franks, on vellum.

"By apostolic authority I bid that you be crowned King of the Franks."

Pope Zacharias's reply to Peppin III, 750

In November 753 Pope Stephen II left Rome and made his way across the Alps in desperate search of military aid from Peppin III (also known as Peppin the Short or Peppin the Younger), the former hereditary mayor of the palace to Childeric III, last of the Merovingian dynasty of kings. By the eighth century, power had slipped significantly from the Merovingians, and the mayors of the palace—in effect, heads of the royal household—acted as kings in all but name. In 750 Peppin had sent two envoys to Pope Zacharias asking, "Is it just to have one man to reign and another to rule?" The pope gave him the answer he was looking for. Peppin swiftly deposed Childeric and in November 751 was anointed king, the first of the Carolingian dynasty, by Archbishop Boniface, the pope's legate.

Now Stephen, Pope Zacharias's successor, was traveling to France in person—the first time any reigning pope had journeyed across the Alps. In Italy, Aistulf, king of the Lombards, had seized the Byzantine Exarchate of Ravenna and was threatening to attack Rome. The Byzantines were powerless to help, and, in desperation, Stephen turned to the Franks. The two men met at Ponthion, south of Paris, on January 6, 754, and Peppin agreed to raise an army to march against the Lombards. In return, Stephen agreed to anoint him with holy oil at the Abbey of St. Denis in Paris in June, at the same time recognizing his sons, Charles (the future Emperor Charlemagne) and Carloman, as heirs to the crown.

Although Peppin did manage to force Aistulf to withdraw his attacks, the cease-fire did not last for long. In a subsequent campaign, the Franks drove the Lombards from Ravenna and gave the Exarchate to the pope, thus creating the territorial basis of the papal state. **SK**

The Fight for Control of Spain

Abd ar-Rahman I founds the Umayyad emirate, overthrowing the Abbasids.

On May 15, 756, Abd ar-Rahman I was proudly proclaimed Umayyad emir of Cordoba and the ruler of Muslim Spain. The event marked the beginning of the breakup of the political unity of the Muslim world. Since the death of the Prophet Muhammad in 632, all Muslims had been united in a single state in which ultimate religious and political authority was exercised by the figure of the caliph. Within two years of Muhammad's death, the caliphate embarked on a spectacular expansion, and by the eighth century it had become a vast empire extending from the River Indus to the Pyrenees. However, the caliphate was riven by a Sunni–Shi'ite schism and tensions between Arab and non-Arab converts to Islam. In 750, the Umayyad dynasty that had ruled the caliphate since 661 was overthrown by the Abbasids.

Despite the best efforts of the Abbasids to exterminate every member of the Umayyad family, Abd ar-Rahman had escaped and made his way in disguise to Spain. Because Spain was so far from the main centers of Abbasid power in Persia and Mesopotamia, the dynasty had still not established effective control there when Abd ar-Rahman arrived in 755. There were many Umayyad sympathizers in Spain, and they welcomed the opportunity to unite under his leadership against the unpopular Abbasid governor Yusuf. On May 14, 756, Abd ar-Rahman defeated Yusuf's forces at Carmona near Cordoba, and the following day entered the city without opposition. Abd ar-Rahman hoped to restore Umayyad control of the caliphate, but rebellions fomented by Abbasid agents tied him down in Spain for most of his reign. However, by the time he died in 788, Umayyad control of Spain was secure, whereas the Abbasids were struggling to maintain control of north Africa. **JH**

○ *Abd ar-Rahman, Sultan of Morocco* by French artist Eugene Delacroix (1798–1863).

"Let us . . . swear to fall like soldiers if victory cannot be ours. We conquer or we die!"

Abd ar-Rahman I before the Battle of Carmona

Baghdad Founded

Caliph al-Mansur chooses a location to build the new Abbasid capital.

The overthrow of the Umayyad dynasty by the Abbasids in 750 represented a shift of power in the Muslim caliphate away from Arab lands toward Persia. Because of this, the first Abbasid caliph, Abu al-Abbas, decided to abandon Damascus and move east to a temporary site on the banks of the Euphrates in Iraq.

In 762 Abu al-Abbas's successor, his brother al-Mansur, selected a small village on the west bank of the Tigris as the site of a new permanent capital. Officially, the new city was to be called Madinat al-Salam ("City of Peace"), but it was popularly known

"Only a place like this can support both the army and the populace."

Caliph al-Mansur, 762

by its Persian name of Baghdad ("God gave it"). Planned as a circular, walled city 1.6 miles (2.6 km) in diameter and divided into four equal quarters, Baghdad was completed in just four years.

Apart from its central location in the caliphate, Baghdad had many other advantages. The city was close to a major east–west caravan route, and the Tigris River gave access to Basra and the Persian Gulf. Baghdad was also surrounded by fertile farmlands so a large urban population could easily be supported. Not surprisingly, Baghdad flourished and soon spread beyond its walls. By the end of the century it had become the world's largest city. The splendid Abbasid court attracted merchants, scholars, and craftsmen from afar, and Baghdad played host to a golden age of Islamic cultural achievements. **JH**

Peppin Legacy Lives On

On Peppin's death, the Frankish kingdom is split between Charles and Carloman.

The achievements of Peppin the Younger, the first Carolingian king of the Franks, have been rather overshadowed by those of his eldest son, Charles, who became known as Charlemagne, but his legacy was a key factor in his son's success. With his military domination of the Frankish magnates and his close alliance with the papacy, Peppin was able to extend his rule over the whole Frankish kingdom, expanding the military and maintaining a large standing army. In addition to setting down the early laws of feudalism that would be the administrative blueprint for most of medieval Europe, Peppin embarked on a policy of Frankish expansion that saw the Moors driven out of Gaul, and the acquisition of Narbonne and Aquitaine. When he died in 768, the dominion of the most powerful king in Europe was divided between his two sons, Charles and Carloman.

Unfortunately, the period of joint rule was dogged by fraternal tensions. When Charles repudiated his first wife, a daughter of King Desiderius of the Lombards, the Lombard king sought an alliance with Carloman to defeat Charles. However, Carloman's death in 771 led to the absorption of his kingdoms by Charles.

Charlemagne built on his father's successes by creating an empire that incorporated much of western and central Europe. He also instigated a series of political and cultural reforms that are referred to as the Carolingian Renaissance. Charlemagne was crowned Imperator Augustus in St. Peter's Basilica in Rome on December 25, 800, by Pope Leo III in an attempt to restore the Western Roman Empire. **TB**

◗ A painting of Charlemagne taking the plate and chalice used at the Last Supper to the cathedral at Aix-la-Chapelle.

The Basques Humble Charlemagne

Charlemagne's rearguard is destroyed by the Basques at Roncesvalles.

⬥ A fourteenth-century French illustration of the Battle of Roncesvalles, from the British Library in London, England.

Although it was a defeat, Roncesvalles is today the most famous battle of Charlemagne's reign. It began after the annual assembly of the kingdom of the Franks in summer 777 was attended by Ibn al-Arabi, the Muslim governor of the Spanish city of Zaragoza. Ibn al-Arabi was in rebellion against his overlord, Abd al-Rahman, and offered to hand over his city to the Frankish king Charlemagne in return for protection. The following summer Charlemagne invaded Spain only to find that Ibn al-Arabi had reneged on the agreement. After besieging Zaragoza and extracting token submission from al-Arabi, Charlemagne retreated across the Pyrenees via the Roncesvalles pass.

On August 15, as the rear guard was beginning to descend from the pass, it was ambushed by the Basques. By the time a rescue party got to the scene, the fighting was over. The Basques had plundered the baggage train and melted away into the mountains. Frankish casualties were heavy and most notably included Roland, count of the Breton March. For many years the true extent of the disaster was covered up, and Charlemagne never campaigned again in person in Spain. However, the defeat was only a temporary setback, and the capture of Barcelona in 802 firmly established Frankish power.

Roncesvalles's fame is due to the *Song of Roland*, a heroic epic poem from circa 1100 celebrating Count Roland's heroism in the battle. The author, Turoldus, gave the battle a makeover, turning Charlemagne's Spanish campaign into a prototype crusade. **JH**

Sumptuous Court Inspires *1001 Nights*

Harun al-Rashid initiates a golden age of Islamic culture.

⬥ *In the Palace of Harun Al-rashid*, an 1895 French School engraving for *The Arabian Nights*.

With the accession of Harun al-Rashid in 786, the Abbasid caliphate entered its most glorious period. While still a youth, Harun was given nominal command of a number of campaigns against the Byzantine Empire, taking the credit for their successes by awarding himself the title "al-Rashid" (the just). On the death of their father in 785, Harun's elder brother al-Hadi succeeded to the caliphate. However, within a year al-Hadi had fallen ill, and when he died on September 14, 786, young Harun was immediately proclaimed caliph.

Al-Hadi's death seemed a little too convenient for many contemporaries, especially because he had quarreled bitterly with his mother over her efforts to influence his government. Rumors quickly began to circulate that he had been suffocated on her orders after a previous attempt to poison him had failed.

A great patron of the arts and learning, Harun had little interest in government. He left the running of the caliphate almost entirely in his vizier's hands while he cultivated a sumptuous court at Baghdad, legendary for its luxury and sophistication. In later times, the court inspired many of the stories of *The Thousand and One Nights,* and King Shayrar, whose wife, Scheherazade, is the narrator, is thought to be based on Harun himself. Though Harun presided over a golden age of Islamic culture, his inattention to government stored up problems for his successors. When, late in his reign, he took control of government, the signs of decline were already apparent. **JH**

Raiders from the Sea

The monastery of Lindisfarne is destroyed in the first Viking raid.

The attack came without warning. The Viking longships, with their cruelly carved prows, appeared from nowhere out of the sea. Suddenly the calm of a summer's day was made terrible by the screams of the monks as the pagan Norsemen struck with their swords before making off with the church's treasure.

News of the destruction of the island monastery of Lindisfarne, burial place of St. Cuthbert, caused widespread horror and alarm. It was the first recorded raid by Viking pirates from Denmark and Norway, who had crossed the North Sea in search of plunder.

" . . . behold the church of St. Cuthbert spattered with the blood of the priests of God."

Alcuin of York, Letter to King Ethelred, c.793

In 794 another monastery in Northumbria was burned, and the monastery of St. Columba on the Scottish island of Iona was attacked a year later. From then on, the Viking longships arrived every summer, raiding around the coasts of England, Scotland, and Ireland before returning to Scandinavia for the winter. By the end of the decade, the ships were venturing as far as western France.

The success of the Vikings was due to their ship-building prowess, navigational skills, and military tactics. Their longships were strong enough to stand ocean buffeting but were shallow-drafted so they could sail deep inland. Monasteries, with their many treasures and jewel-encrusted holy books, were the main target, and many churchmen saw the pagan attacks as a sign of God's anger with his people. **SK**

Dawn of Heian Era

Emperor Kammu founds a new Japanese capital, and then another.

In the eighth century the Japanese capital at Nara was dominated by its many Buddhist monasteries. To escape the influence of the monks, Emperor Kammu decided to move to a new capital. His supervisor of construction, Fujiwara no Tanetsugu, chose a site at Nagaoka, and work began in 784. However, the project was dogged by intrigue and factional rivalries, culminating in Tanetsugu's murder. Kammu decided that the site was ill omened and abandoned construction to start again on a new site in 794.

The new capital was called Heian-kyo ("capital of peace and tranquility"), later to become known as Kyoto. It remained the capital of Japan for more than a thousand years until the emperor Meiji moved the court to Tokyo in 1868. Though larger than the old capital, Heian was built to a nearly identical plan, based, like Nara, on the Chinese capital at Chang'an. The city, including its main palaces and temples, was built almost entirely of wood, and it suffered frequent devastation from fires. Though the old monasteries at Nara were forbidden to relocate, Kammu allowed new monasteries to be founded, and Heian soon became a major religious center.

This was the beginning of the Heian period (794–1185), when an exquisitely refined court culture developed and the arts flourished, but the emperors became increasingly isolated from the everyday running of the country. Government was dominated by members of the aristocratic Fujiwara family, who strengthened their influence via skillful marriage alliances, and amassed vast tax-exempt estates at imperial expense. By the time Minamoto Yoritomo founded the shogunate (military government) in 1185, the emperors had become powerless figureheads. **JH**

Charlemagne's Historic Crowning in Rome

At Christmas Day Mass in St. Peter's Basilica, Pope Leo III unexpectedly proclaims Charlemagne emperor.

In 799, Pope Leo III, who had been forcibly expelled from the papal throne by his enemies, appealed to Charlemagne, the king of the Franks, for help. In response, Charlemagne traveled to Rome and presided over a council that restored Pope Leo to power. On Christmas Day, Charlemagne entered St. Peter's Basilica to attend Mass. As he knelt in prayer, Pope Leo lifted a crown from the altar, placed it on Charlemagne's head, and proclaimed him emperor.

It was an unprecedented act, and Einhard, Charlemagne's biographer, says that Charlemagne was unaware of Leo's intention. This seems unlikely. Yet, there is little evidence to suggest that Charlemagne deliberately sought to revive the Western Roman Empire, as many have argued. At this time, the Eastern Byzantine Empire was ruled by a woman, the empress Irene (r.791–802), whose authority the pope did not recognize. Although Pope Leo had no power to confer the imperial title, he seemingly took advantage of the Frankish king's presence in Rome to create a new Roman Catholic emperor in the west—one who would strengthen papal influence in Italy.

Charlemagne, a devout Christian, was in the thirty-second year of his reign by this date, and had already made himself ruler of most of western Europe. He is often regarded as the first Holy Roman Emperor, but it was in fact the Ottonian emperors of Germany who first used the title a century later. Charlemagne described himself as "the emperor governing the Roman Empire," and he also retained his title "King of the Franks and the Lombards." **SK**

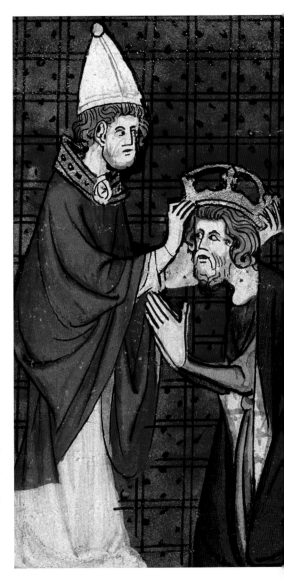

⊙ A sixteenth-century French illumination of Charlemagne being crowned by Pope Leo III, in St. Peter's, Rome.

Saint's Tomb Found

The legend of St. James the Moorslayer inspires the Reconquest of Spain.

According to a Spanish tradition dating back to the seventh century, St. James the apostle ("Sant' Iago" in Spanish) visited Spain during his lifetime to preach the gospel. After his martyrdom in Jerusalem in 44, angels transported the saint's body—miraculously reunited with his severed head—to Spain in a stone boat. It landed at Padrón on the Galician coast. During the reign of Alfonso II (r.791–842) the tomb of St. James was supposedly discovered at the recently reclaimed town of Compostela, in Galicia.

During the eighth century, the kingdom of Asturias, created after Pelayo's victory at Covadonga in 722, consolidated its position as a center of resistance to the Muslims, extending its frontiers little by little into the mountains of northern and western Spain. St. James was believed to have come to the aid of the victorious Christian army at the Battle of Clavijo (844), and from this time on, the saint was given the epithet Matamoros ("Moorslayer"). Those fighting the *Reconquista* ("Reconquest") marched under his banner, and his name was their battle cry.

As St. James's fame spread, more people made their way to his shrine. By the twelfth century, the cathedral of Santiago at Compostela had become the third most important pilgrimage center in western Christendom, after Jerusalem and Rome. Guidebooks were written to help pilgrims find their way along the four main routes through the Pyrenees to Compostela. A vast industry grew up around the shrine, providing food and shelter to pilgrims and selling the cockleshell badges that pilgrims wore to show they had completed the journey. **SK**

◑ A ceramic plate with a picture of St. James of Campostela, probably made as a gift for someone named after the saint.

Baghdad Stargazers

Caliph al-Mamun founds the first Arab astronomical observatory at Baghdad.

After Christianity became the official religion of the Roman Empire in 391, the scientific literature of pagan Greece was left to gather dust on library shelves. The Abbasid caliph al-Mamun (r.813–33) founded the House of Wisdom at Baghdad for the translation of Greek, Persian, and Hindu works into Arabic. Because of the need to fix the direction of Mecca, and to maintain the accuracy of the Islamic lunar calendar, there was a keen interest in astronomy, so al-Mamun founded an astronomical observatory near the Shamsiyah gate at Baghdad.

"al-Mamun wrote to the Byzantine emperor asking [for] old manuscripts."

Ibn al-Nadïm, *Kitab al-Fihrist*, 938

During the ninth century, the Arabs adopted almost wholesale the corpus of ancient Greek science, even sending missions to the Byzantine Empire to collect long-unread manuscripts, which would otherwise have been lost to posterity. When medieval Europeans rediscovered this knowledge in the twelfth century, it was usually from Arabic translations of the original Greek works.

The assimilation of this knowledge was greatly encouraged by al-Mamun. As well as the House of Wisdom and the observatory at Baghdad, he founded another observatory near Damascus. Arab astronomers built on the achievements of the ancient world, improving the accuracy of star catalogues and refining the design of astronomical instruments, including the astrolabe. **JH**

First King of Scotia

Kenneth MacAlpin founds the kingdom later known as Scotland.

For many centuries before Kenneth MacAlpin conquered and appointed himself ruler of a forcibly united people, Scotland did not exist as one entity. At the beginning of the Middle Ages, around 500, the area now known as Scotland was inhabited by four different peoples. The longest established were the Celtic Britons, who inhabited the whole of Britain south of the Forth-Clyde isthmus, and the Picts, who lived in the highlands and islands to the north. The main difference between the two was that the Britons had become Romanized during the Roman occupation of Britain (43–410), whereas the unconquered Picts had not. After the end of Roman rule in 410 Britain was invaded by Anglo-Saxons from northern Germany and by the Irish, who at this time were known as Scots. The Anglo-Saxons occupied southeast Scotland as far north as Edinburgh, and the Scots occupied the west coast district of Argyll, founding the kingdom of Dálriada.

After the Picts had been weakened by Viking attacks in the early ninth century, they were conquered in 843 by Kenneth MacAlpin, the king of Dálriada. It is believed that Sueno's Stone, a contemporary monument to the conquest in northeast Scotland, may show the mass execution of Pictish nobles that followed. Kenneth ruled as king of the Scots and the Picts, but his successors described themselves as kings of Scotia or "Scotland." However, it was only in the eleventh century, with the conquest of Anglo-Saxon and British territory south of the Forth-Clyde isthmus, that Scotland achieved (approximately) its modern borders. As for the Picts, their language, culture, and identity did not long survive their conquest by the Scots, and they are not heard of again after 900. **JH**

An Empire Fractured

Charlemagne's empire is partitioned by the Treaty of Verdun.

It was always Charlemagne's intention that the Frankish Empire would be divided equally between his three sons when he died. In the event, Charlemagne was survived by only one son, Louis the Pious, who inherited the whole empire in 814. A strong believer in the unity of Christendom, Louis decided to abandon the Frankish custom of partible inheritance. In 817 he appointed his eldest son, Lothar, sole heir to the empire. To his two younger sons, Louis the German and Peppin, he gave only dependent sub-kingdoms.

This settlement began to unravel in 823 when Louis the Pious's second wife, Judith, gave birth to a son, Charles the Bald. Judith naturally wanted Charles to inherit a sub-kingdom of his own. Louis's older sons, anxious that this might diminish their inheritances, opposed her. Louis spent the remainder of his reign struggling to find a settlement acceptable to his wife and his increasingly rebellious sons. After Peppin died in 838, followed by Louis in 840, no one expected a smooth succession.

As soon as his father was dead, Lothar attempted to seize the whole empire. Despite their animosity, Louis the German and Charles allied against Lothar and defeated him at the Battle of Fontenay in 841. In 843, the empire was divided into three kingdoms at the Treaty of Verdun: Louis receiving most of Germany, Charles most of West Francia ("France"), and Lothar everything in between. It was from the breakup of Charlemagne's empire, which began at Verdun, that over the next century the kingdoms of France, Germany, and Italy would emerge. **JH**

○ A woodcut circa 1850 of Judith, wife of Louis the Pious, and her son Charles the Bald (mistakenly referred to as Charles I).

Vikings Sack Paris

The decline of the Carolingian Empire is hastened by repeated Viking raids.

The feeble and crumbling Carolingian Empire was dealt a heavy psychological blow in March 845 when one hundred Viking ships managed to sail down the Seine, causing death and destruction as they went. The Vikings met very little resistance from Charles the Bald, king of the Western Frankish Empire, and were able to sail straight into Paris.

Once in Paris, the Viking raiders plundered the city and many churches were either desecrated or destroyed. The ordeal for the people of the city was finally ended when Charles offered a huge ransom. Laden with loot, the Vikings withdrew from the city with many hundreds of prisoners and sailed back to the coast, where they looted, pillaged, and burned many coastal towns.

The Vikings did not stay away for long. This was to be the first of many such attacks on Paris and elsewhere as the Viking threat was felt throughout Europe. For the ailing Carolingian Empire, the most vulnerable areas were in the Low Countries and the regions of Gaul and Germania, where many navigable rivers gave the raiders easy access.

Paris was attacked three times in the 860s, the raiders leaving only when their haul of loot or bribes were considered large enough. Facing almost annual raids, Charles the Bald at last took positive steps to counter the threat. In 864, the Edict of Pistres brought about a development that included the creation of a large force of cavalry and a series of bridges across the Seine that Viking longboats would not be able to pass. These bridges would prove highly effective when the Vikings besieged Paris again in 885. The inability of the Carolingian Empire to stop these recurring calamities was a key factor in its eventual decline from power. **TB**

Zanj Slaves Revolt

Captive Africans rise up against the Abbasid and set up their own capital.

The slave revolt in 868 was inevitable for many years. The trade in slaves between east Africa and Arabia had existed before the rise of Islam, but it expanded vastly with the spread of the Islamic caliphate. Most were taken to work in households, but thousands of Africans—known as Zanj from the Arabic name for the east African coast—were sent to southern Iraq to drain the salt marshes of Shatt al-Arab around Basra. Others fought in the Abbasid armies.

The revolt began under the leadership of Ali bin Muhammad, said to have been a descendant of the

> ## "[The Zanj] are always cheerful, smiling, and devoid of malice."
>
> **Abu Uthman al-Jahiz, *The Essays*, c.860**

fourth caliph Ali (and therefore not an African himself). Although it began with just a few men and no weapons, the revolt grew quickly as some of the Africans in the caliphate's armies began defecting. The rebel forces were familiar with the difficult terrain of southern Iraq and had soon developed into a sophisticated and well-equipped military unit, managing to capture part of the Abbasid fleet. Ali built a well-defended capital at Mokhtara, east of Baghdad. He presented himself as a religious and military leader, offering a purified form of Islam.

The Zanj were defeated in 883 only after an amnesty was offered to defectors. The victorious Abbasid general Muwaffaq refused to return the Zanj to their former masters, instead incorporating them into his own forces. **PF**

Alfred Becomes King of Wessex

The new king fights off the Danes, demonstrating the fierce determination that will characterize his long reign.

Alfred could not have succeeded to the throne at a more critical time, just when the kingdom of Wessex, in southern England, was under fierce attack from a Danish Viking army. He had stood beside his brother, King Ethelred I, as he fought the Danes five times in the winter and spring of 870–871. Then, on April 15, 871 Ethelred died. Although he left two young sons, it was Alfred, then aged twenty-two but already a battle-hardened and experienced leader, who was chosen to succeed him. In the months after his succession, Alfred fought nine more battles with the Vikings before they turned their attention to the neighboring kingdom of Mercia—no doubt deterred by the fierceness of Alfred's resistance. It was five years before they returned to Wessex.

Born in 849, Alfred was the fifth and youngest son of King Ethelwulf of Wessex. The kingdom had recently consolidated its power over all of England south of the Thames, from Cornwall in the west to Kent in the southeast. Since he had four elder brothers, it must have seemed unlikely that Alfred would ever become king, but the education he received befitted his royal birth and shows the close connections between Anglo-Saxon England and the continent at this time. He made two visits to Rome, in 853 and 855, and while there he acquired the taste for learning that would become apparent in his later life—he is known to have translated Gregory the Great's *Pastoral Care* and Boethius's *The Consolation of Philosophy*. Alfred also received military training, which stood him in good stead in his coming struggles with the Danes. **SK**

◗ A nineteenth-century painting evoking the time of Alfred,

A Model for Alfred's Navy (1851) by John Horsley (1817–1903).

The Decline of the Crown

The Holy Roman Emperor Charles the Bald recognizes hereditary fiefdoms.

In what has since been seen as a key stage in the development of European feudalism and of the decline of the power of the crown, Charles the Bald brokered a deal with his magnates with the help of Hincmar, archbishop of Rheims. The deal would replace the old system of lands being granted for a single lifetime with a system whereby the king would grant lands on the basis of hereditary ownership.

Charles was the youngest son of Louis the Pious, and acquired the kingdom of West Francia in 843. He claimed the title of emperor on the death of his nephew Louis II in 875. He had been under extreme pressure in the years immediately preceding his death in October 877. In particular, magnates had refused to support the king in a number of key campaigns, such as his expedition into Italy in 876 to help Pope John VIII fight invading Saracens. Charles's concession to hereditary fiefdoms can therefore be seen as another sign of the weakening authority of the Carolingian dynasty.

The recognition of hereditary rights was significant on two counts. First, it was an important step in the development of feudalism, and granted magnates greater power over their own dominions and enabled them to form local dynasties. Secondly, the power of the king declined as the feudal lords became more independent of the crown and built up small territorial states of their own, which were often at war with each other.

Feudalism of this sort meant that power and the administration of the law became decentralized, and that rather than power being vested in the crown, the crown was to some extent dependent on the local dynasties it had created. With this system, the age of large empires, such as that of the Carolingian emperors, would be difficult to maintain. **TB**

○ Charles the Bald, described as "the first true King of France and Holy Roman Emperor," indicated by his laurel wreath.

○ A medieval illuminated manuscript depicting a scene from the life of Charles the Bald.

"Many, hungry for fame and honors, were incited by the opportunities of the age."

Chronicle of the Counts of Anjou

Alfred Fights Back

The king of Wessex drives back the Danes at the Battle of Edington.

In the 870s Danish invaders looked set to take over England. Arriving by sea from Scandinavia, they had conquered the Anglo-Saxon kingdoms of Mercia, Northumbria, and East Anglia. Only Wessex in southern England remained under Anglo-Saxon rule. By early 878 even the king of Wessex, Alfred, was a fugitive in his own country after being forced to flee from his base at Chippenham, Wiltshire.

In spring 878, however, Alfred emerged from hiding and built a new fortifications at Athelney in Somerset. He called upon the men of Hampshire,

---

"His attack was long and spirited, and finally by divine aid he triumphed."

Bishop Asser, *Life of King Alfred*, 893

Wiltshire, and Somerset to join him at a place called Egbert's Stone. Marching his assembled army toward Chippenham, Alfred was met by the Danes under Guthrum at Edington. According to the contemporary chronicler Bishop Asser, after a hard fight, King Alfred's men drove the Danes from the field.

Guthrum's surviving warriors took refuge at Chippenham, hotly pursued by the Anglo-Saxons, who put them under siege. After fourteen days experiencing, in Asser's words, "the horrors of famine, cold, fear, and at last of despair," the Danes sued for peace. Alfred forced Guthrum to hand over hostages, promise to leave Wessex, and accept conversion to Christianity. The victory at Edington drove the Danes back to "Danelaw"—the north and east of England— while Alfred strengthened his defenses. **RG**

The Danes Contained

Alfred and Guthrum redraw the frontier between Saxon England and Danelaw.

In 885 Guthrum, the leader of the Danes, broke the agreement he had made with Alfred after the Battle of Edington, and invaded Kent with a large force. Alfred responded by capturing London, forcing the Danes to abandon their base in the south. A new agreement, known as the Treaty of Alfred and Guthrum, was reached that gave London to Wessex and redrew the frontier between Saxon England and "Danelaw," the area occupied by the Danes.

A line now divided England into two halves. In the north and the east, the Danes ruled as a military aristocracy and imposed their own laws and customs on the population. Their impact on the land and people was dramatic—literacy appears to have died out as monastic centers disappeared. The concentration of Scandinavian place-names in northern England around York, and in Lincolnshire and East Anglia—together with stone crosses carved with distinctive Scandinavian designs—still bears witness to the Danish presence in the region, although it is not known how far they assimilated with the local population.

South and west of the dividing line, Wessex was now recognized by all as the effective ruling power. Although the Danes would remain a constant threat until his death in 899, Alfred undertook important defensive measures to ensure Wessex's survival, including the building of a chain of fortified strongpoints with permanent garrisons to serve as refuge points for the population in times of war. Known as *burhs* ("boroughs"), these settlements were the origin of many of England's market towns. Alfred also had a number of large ships built to fight off coastal raids, for which he has sometimes been called the founder of the British Navy. **SK**

Cluny Abbey Sparks Monastic Revival

Burgundy becomes home to a center of monastic reform and the most important religious house in western Christendom.

Duke William I of Aquitaine, nicknamed the Pious, founded many religious houses, but the most important was his new abbey at Cluny, in Burgundy. Under a series of intelligent and able abbots, Cluny spearheaded a movement for monastic reform that came to play a large part in the revitalization of the Church and papacy.

By the end of the ninth century, discipline within the Benedictine Order of monks had become lax. In part, this was because the local lords, who gave land for the foundation of new monasteries, tended to interfere too much in their business. Duke William took the novel step of placing his new abbey under the immediate authority of the pope, a highly significant decision, since the pope lived far away in Rome, and so the abbots had greater freedom to carry out reforms, which included a greater emphasis on prayer. The abbey founded a network of subsidiary houses, or priories, that came under the direct supervision of the mother house, and the reforming movement spread ever wider. Wealth flowed to Cluny, and three abbey churches were built in quick succession; the last, begun in 1088, was the largest church in the world until St. Peter's in Rome was completed in the sixteenth century.

It was Cluny's second abbot, St. Odo (d.952), who drove forward its success. Another abbot, St. Hugh the Great (d.1109), famous for his learning, was also canonized. Four Cluniac monks became popes: St. Gregory VII, Urban II, Pascal II, and Urban V. **SK**

◑ Detail of an eighteenth-century engraving of Cluny Abbey; much of the eleventh-century building survives.

◑ A twelfth-century illustration depicting the consecration of Cluny Abbey by Pope Urban III in 1095.

Sergent del.t   Et Sculp.t 1791

ROLLON, SURNOMMÉ RAOUL,

Et nommé, en 912,   lors de son baptême,

Robert, 1.er Duc   de Normandie;

Né vers l'an 856; mort à Rouen en 917.

Rollo the Raider

The Viking leader is granted a parcel of land in France by Charles the Simple.

Legend has it that Rollo was one of the leaders of the Viking fleet that brutally attacked and besieged Paris in 885. The Frankish king had paid them a sum of gold to persuade them to leave, only for them to swiftly attack elsewhere. When, in 911, Rollo led a raid in the Chartres area, the king, Charles the Simple (r.898–929) tried a different approach. He granted Rollo a parcel of land in the north of his kingdom if he and his men would agree to settle there and defend it against subsequent Viking attacks.

Rollo accepted, and the agreement was signed at St. Clair-sur-Epte. In return for land on either side of the Seine estuary (an area equivalent to Upper Normandy today), Rollo recognized the king as his feudal overlord and was baptized. Rollo initially kept his word and dutifully repelled a few invaders.

To his fellow Norsemen the Viking leader was known as *Göngu-Hróflr* (Hrolf the Walker) because no horse was large enough to carry him; it was the French who called him Rollo or Robert (his baptismal name). For more than sixty years, the Vikings under his control had raided the north coast of France and far inland. Within a few years of his agreement with Charles the Simple, he returned to the attack and extended his control westward. By 933 Normandy (the land of the Norsemen) stretched all the way to the Cotentin peninsula and had acquired the geographic boundaries it still has today. The first of Rollo's descendants to use the title Duke of Normandy was Duke Richard II, grandfather of Duke William (c.1028–87), who later became William the Conqueror, the first Norman king of England. **SK**

◐ An eighteenth-century portrait of Rollo by French artist Antoine-François Sergent-Marceau (1751–1847).

King Unites Germany

Henry I is elected king of Franconia and proceeds to unite the German duchies.

As Conrad I, King of Franconia, lay on his deathbed, it was his enemy Henry, duke of Saxony, who received the dying king's blessing, in the hope he would unite the people. Legend has it Henry was laying bird snares when the news reached him. For this reason, he came to be known as Henry the Fowler.

Henry's election was not universally supported by the duchies of the kingdom. Saxony and Franconia, two of the four most important duchies, rallied behind him, but Swabia and Bavaria resisted. Henry desired to control his kingdom as a confederation of

> **"Henry . . . is the ablest ruler in the empire. Elect him king, Germany will have peace."**
>
> **King Conrad I, Henry's predecessor**

duchies rather than ruling absolutely. He permitted Burchard, duke of Swabia, to retain control over the administration of his duchy, but Henry was forced to invade Bavaria in 921, and after two campaigns, Arnulf, duke of Bavaria, agreed to similar terms.

Henry's achievements include the conquest of Lorraine and the region's incorporation into his kingdom as the fifth important duchy. His last campaign—an invasion of Denmark in 934—saw the addition of Schleswig to the German kingdom. By the time Henry died in 936, he had united all the German duchies into a single kingdom. He is widely accepted as the founder of the medieval German state and the founder of what eventually became the first Holy Roman Empire. His son Otto took over a much more unified confederation. **TB**

Spain's New Successor

In a challenge to his Abbasid rulers, Abd ar-Rahman III declares himself a caliph.

On January 16, 929, Abd ar-Rahman III, the emir of Cordoba, proclaimed himself "caliph." The new title had profound implications. *Caliph*, meaning "successor," was usually adopted only by the successors of Muhammad, who exercised both spiritual and political supremacy over the Muslim world. *Emir*, meaning "commander," had no spiritual overtones, and in the early Muslim caliphate had been used by regional governors. When the caliphate began to break up under the Abbasids in the ninth century, the emirs set themselves up as independent rulers. Although this diminished the political authority of the Abbasid caliphs in Baghdad, it did not challenge their spiritual authority, so it paid lip service to the ideal of Muslim unity.

The first challenge to the Abbasids' spiritual authority came from the Fatimid rulers of Egypt, who promoted themselves to the rank of caliph in 910. The Fatimids were Shi'ites, however, and were regarded as heretics by the majority Sunni Muslims. Abd ar-Rahman was the first Sunni ruler explicitly to reject the Abbasid caliphs as both political and religious leaders. His claim to the caliphate was based on his descent from the Umayyads, who had ruled the entire Muslim world as caliphs between 661 and 750. The emirate of Cordoba had been founded by a refugee Umayyad prince after the dynasty's overthrow by the Abbasids in 750.

As the new caliph, Abd ar-Rahman built an extravagant palace complex at Medinat al-Zhara, outside Cordoba, modeled on the former Umayyad palace at Damascus. Under his rule, Muslim power in Spain would reach its peak, although the caliphate would eventually collapse in a civil war that broke out in 1008. **JH**

Magyars Subdued

Otto the Great defeats the marauding nomads at the Battle of Lechfeld.

The Magyars were nomadic horsemen from central Asia who migrated to the area of modern-day Hungary in the late ninth century. For half a century their ferocious raiding parties regularly marauded westward across Germany, penetrating as far as Italy and Spain. The rulers of Christian Europe were too weak and divided to defend themselves. In 955, however, Otto I, duke of Saxony and king of the Germans, succeeded in gathering a substantial force to take on the Magyars. With some 10,000 knights, Otto set out to confront a Magyar horde.

> ### "Never was so bloody a victory gained over so savage an enemy."
> **Widukind of Corvey, *Gesta*, c.955**

Confident and aggressive, the Magyars rode out to meet the Germans on the floodplain of the River Lech. Fast-moving horsemen, they expected to run rings around the slower-moving, armored Christian cavalry, whom they probably outnumbered by five to one. According to German chroniclers, the Magyars were undone by their indiscipline. Having swarmed around the flanks of Otto's army, many dismounted to plunder the German baggage train. Otto's knights first slaughtered the dismounted men and then charged through a volley of arrows into the main body of the Magyars, driving them from the field.

The Battle of Lechfeld ended the Magyar incursions. Otto emerged with great prestige, and in 963 was crowned Holy Roman Emperor. Western Europe took a major step toward security. **RG**

Denmark Is Converted to Christianity

In an ordeal by fire, a German missionary succeeds in converting King Harald Bluetooth to Christianity where all previous missionaries had failed.

King Harald Bluetooth of Denmark challenged Poppo, a missionary from Germany, to prove to him that the Christian faith was true. After Poppo picked up a hot iron, but was unharmed by the searing heat, the king declared that he now believed in the power of the Christian God and immediately demanded the conversion of all the Danes.

That is the story as told by Widukind of Corvey, a German monk writing in circa 967. He adds that Poppo "is now a bishop." We know from other sources that a priest called Poppo became bishop of Würzburg, Germany, in 961, which suggests that Harald's conversion probably took place shortly before this date.

Poppo was not the first missionary to travel to Denmark, but all earlier attempts to persuade the Danes to abandon their pagan gods had failed. It seems likely that Poppo's mission was sponsored by Otto I, king of the Germans and later Holy Roman Emperor, and it is very probable that Harald's conversion was made largely for political reasons—he was an ambitious ruler who built roads, bridges, and forts to create a centralized power structure and defend southern Denmark from incursions by the Germans. Christianity would have provided a further means of consolidating his authority over his people and unifying the country.

Sometime during his reign Harald erected a large carved stone at a place called Jelling. It was sited close to the burial mound of his father, Gorm, who was a pagan. One face of the stone depicts Jesus Christ's Crucifixion, another bears a pagan image of a horned beast entwined with a serpent, and the third carries a long inscription in runes proclaiming Harald's conversion. **SK**

○ A detail from an eleventh-century Danish relief sculpture of King Harald declaring his faith at Jelling.

> ## "[Harald] won for himself all Denmark and Norway, and made the Danes Christian."
>
> **From the inscription on the Jelling stone**

Otto Crowned Emperor

After twenty-six years, Otto I realizes his dream of becoming Holy Roman Emperor.

Otto was widely accepted as the successor to the glories of Charlemagne—he had even been crowned as king in Aachen. It was only a matter of time before Otto would set the seal on his claim to the imperial title by entering Rome himself; however, Otto had to wait twenty-six years before realizing his dream.

His rule had been built on the wealth obtained from the rich silver mines of Saxony, but despite this financial security, it was not a trouble-free time. Otto had been plagued by rebellions from rival duchies in his kingdom. It was only when he defeated his rivals

---

"Otto came to Italy amid a strong following and with his arm extended. . ."

Arnulf of Milan, *Book of Recent Deeds*

---

and placed the troublesome duchies under the control of family members that peace was restored. Yet further problems in southern Germany, and with Magyar raids, meant that it was not until 962 that Otto's position was secure enough for him to come to the aid of the Papal States at the request of Pope John XII. In return for Otto's guarantee of protection for the Papal States, the first such guarantee since the days of Charlemagne, Otto was crowned Holy Roman Emperor. He therefore became the first of a line that would last until abolished by Napoleon in 1806.

Otto's first years as emperor were dogged by papal intrigue and rivalry. Despite this, his reign became known as the Ottonian Renaissance—many new cathedrals were built and a large number of illuminated manuscripts date from this time. **TB**

Greenland Is Settled

Erik the Red leads a group of settlers from Iceland to virgin territory in the west.

Erik the Red, a Norseman whose fiery temper matched the color of his hair, was a murderer and outlaw from Norway who had taken refuge among the Vikings in Iceland. In 980, after killing a number of men, he was banished from Iceland as well. Unable to return to Norway, he decided to sail west in search of an unnamed land that had been sighted some sixty years earlier by a Viking sea captain named Gunnbjorn Ulf-Krakuson, when blown off course by wild storms on his way from Norway to Iceland.

Three years later Erik returned to Iceland, boasting of a land where the meadows were so lush he called it Greenland, and asking for volunteers to help settle it. Good farming land on Iceland was in short supply, and nearly 1,000 men and women decided to join him. Of the twenty-five ships that set out, only fourteen survived the journey to reach the sheltered fjords of southern Greenland in 986. Here, with safe harborage, good fishing, and low rolling hills for pasturage, most of the Vikings decided to settle. Some sailed on and founded a second settlement 430 miles (650 km) farther north.

Enjoying comparatively mild climatic conditions, the Greenland settlers were able to hunt and fish, and grow fodder to support their livestock through the winter—a thirteenth-century account speaks of the "large and fine farms" of Greenland. Churches were built and a bishopric founded, but by the mid-fourteenth century what meteorologists term "the Little Ice Age" had set in, gradually extinguishing life in this most remote of settlements on the edge of the Western world. **SK**

⊙ *Erik the Red from Gronlandia* (1688) by Arngrin Jonas—the first printed account of the Vikings' discovery of America.

EIREKVR Hôß bngd
hinn Ravde/, a Grænlande.
Fyrſte Ladnams madr ANNO
Grænlands. 986t

France Crowns Its First Capetian King

The crowning of Hugh Capet, Duke of France, as king is the beginning of the Capetian royal dynasty and marks the start of the history of modern France.

A new ruling dynasty was desperately needed and it began with Hugh Capet (*c.*940–96). West Francia, an area roughly equivalent to modern-day France, had come under frequent attack from Viking raiders in the late tenth century, and the failure of the Carolingian kings to deal effectively with the menace eroded their authority. They gave away increasing amounts of land to their nobles to garner support, and consequently the kingdom became a patchwork of virtually independent dukedoms. Meanwhile, the royal domains shrank to a tiny pocket of land centered on the Île de France, the area around Paris.

Hugh Capet, Duke of France, who owned land around Orléans, was one of the most powerful nobles. Known as the Robertians from the family's founder, Robert the Strong (*d.*866), three of Hugh's ancestors—his great-uncle Eudes, his grandfather Robert I, and his uncle Raoul—had previously been elected king by the nobles in place of weaker Carolingian candidates. When the last Carolingian king, Louis V, died in May 987 without an heir, Archbishop Adalberon of Rheims had little difficulty in persuading the nobles to elect Hugh as king.

Soon after his coronation, Hugh arranged that his son, Robert, was also crowned; this ensured a smooth succession when Hugh died in 996. The practice of crowning the heir during the king's lifetime continued and was a powerful contributory factor to the longevity of the Capetian dynasty, a line of fourteen kings who ruled France until 1328. Hugh's election as king is thus regarded as marking the beginnings of the history of modern France. **SK**

❍ A portrait of Hugh Capet, king of France from 987 until 996, depicted wearing full royal regalia.

Kiev Is Converted

*Grand Prince Vladimir I is baptized
and his empire adopts Christianity.*

Although it is the reign of Vladimir I that is most often associated with the rise of Christianity in Kiev (now Ukraine) many residents had actually adopted Christianity under Vladimir's predecessor, Yaropolk. When Yaropolk was murdered by his half-brother in 980, however, paganism took hold once more.

The new Grand Prince, Vladimir I, is reputed to have had seven wives and many concubines, to have built new pagan temples and to have taken part in pagan rituals involving human sacrifices. Eventually, though, he came under pressure from his own subjects and from abroad to adopt monotheism. Legend has it Vladimir sent out emissaries to report on various religions so that he could make a choice of faith. It was the richness of the Byzantine churches, not the more somber religion of the German kings, that attracted him most.

Politics also shaped the future direction of Vladimir's faith. In 987 the Byzantine emperor, Basil II, was forced to ask Vladimir for help against usurpers who threatened the imperial throne. Vladimir agreed on condition that he be allowed to marry the emperor's sister, Anne. To strengthen his bargaining position, Vladimir took an army into the area now known as Sebastopol and threatened to attack Constantinople. Basil agreed, providing Vladimir was baptized. So, in order to secure an advantageous marriage, Vladimir was baptized in 988.

Vladimir proceeded to order the tearing down of pagan temples, the destruction of idols, and the baptism of his people in the Greek Byzantine form of Christianity. Vladimir's baptism had decided the future religious direction of the Russian people and halted the spread of Roman Catholicism in the Slavic East. **TB**

A New Emir for Ghazni

*Mahmud—a Turk and a Sunni—plays
an important role in the Muslim world.*

Mahmud is one of the most controversial figures of south Asian history. He was the eldest son of Sebutkigin, a Turkish Mamluk ("slave soldier") who had seized control of the city of Ghazni in southern Afghanistan. Mahmud became emir in 998 and spent most his reign campaigning in Iran, central Asia, and India, building a considerable empire for himself and, through his patronage of the arts—which led to a revival of Persian literature and craftsmanship—turned Ghazni into one of the great cultural centers of the Muslim world.

> ## "[Mahmud was] the lion of the world, the wonder of his time."
>
> **Al-Biruni, Ghaznavid scholar c.1030**

Although the Ghaznavid Empire declined after his death, Mahmud's reign was pivotal in many ways. Mahmud was a Sunni Muslim at a time when the Muslim world was dominated by Shi'ite dynasties, his rise to power proving the first sign of a Sunni recovery. He was the first prominent Turk of the Muslim world, and he firmly established Muslim influence over northern India; it is the latter that is most controversial. Mahmud's campaigns in India destroyed and plundered dozens of Hindu holy places. In Indian historical traditions, Mahmud has come to be seen as a tyrannical oppressor who used his religion to justify wanton destruction and slaughter of Hindus. Conversely, in Pakistan and Afghanistan, Mahmud is regarded as a hero who fought to spread Islam throughout the Indian subcontinent. **JH**

Ã В Г Д Є S Ѕ Z И Ѳ · Т К Λ М N Ѯ О П Ч

© A perpetual calendar from the late eleventh- or early twelfth-century *Breviary of Mont-Cassin*, created by Italian monks.

1000–1499

eua de
uidi ard
tem luce
tante m
mtudm
ut aliqi
mons m

nus & altius e. ' insumitate sua ue
i multas linguas diuisa. Et cota
luce ista quedam multitudo alb
rum hominu stabat. ante quos
lut quoddam uelum tãqm crist
lus plucidu apectore usq; adpec
eorum extensu erat. S; & ante
multitudine ista. quasi iqdã ur
uelut quidã uermis mire mag
tudinis & longitudinis supin ia
bat. ' qui tanti horroris & unsan
uidebat. ultra qua homo effari
test. Adeui sinistra quasi toru e
ubi diuicie hominu atq; delicie
culares & mercatus diuersaru te
apparuert. ' ubi etia quidã homi
multa celeritate currentes. nullu
mercatu faciebant. quidã aute r
pide euntes. & uendicioni & empt
ni ubi insistebant. Uermis aut ill
niger & hirsutus atq; ulcerib' &
stulis plenus erat. qnq; uarietat
acapite puentre suu usq; adpec

Millennium Fears

Signs and portents were thought to tell of the imminent end of the world.

It was widely believed the approaching end of the first millennium after the birth of Christ heralded the imminent end of the world and the coming of the Antichrist. Such apocalyptic ideas have been present throughout the history of Christianity, yet evidence suggests they were particularly intense, especially in France and England, from *c.*950 until *c.*1050. This can be seen from references in chronicles and other documents to portents such as floods and famines, eclipses, comets, and violent storms; although reports of a "panic" that swept through Europe as the year 1000 dawned are probably exaggerated.

The system of dating from the year of Christ's birth—*Anno Domini*, A.D.—was the invention of a monk, Dionysius Exiguus, in 525. Before then, dating was based on the year of the foundation of Rome, or the regnal year of a king, or, for eastern Orthodox Christians, the supposed date of the creation of the world, *Anno Mundi*.

Dionysius reckoned that Christ was born in the year 754 after the founding of Rome, which he thought was year 1 A.D. In fact, he miscalculated, and Christ was probably born four years earlier. But his system was accepted in most of western Europe by the tenth century, but not by the eastern Orthodox church. Nor was January 1 universally accepted as New Year's Day at this time. For many, the year began on March 25, for others December 25. Such matters were questions for monks and churchmen. Most people judged the passage of time by the yearly seasonal cycle of sowing, reaping, and harvesting, as they had always done. **SK**

◯ An illuminated manuscript depicting the kind of apocalyptic horror that some expected with the coming of the millennium.

Vikings Sail to America

Leif Eriksson sails west from Greenland and finds a country he calls Vinland.

Leif Eriksson was the son of Erik the Red, founder of the Viking colony in Greenland. On hearing the story of Bjarni Herjolfsson, a sea captain who claimed to have sighted a long, flat coastline covered in trees far to the west of Greenland, Leif set out to find it. After sailing north up the west coast of Greenland, he crossed what we know today as the Davis Strait to Baffin Island and then turned south. He sighted the coast of Labrador, forested as Bjarni had described it, and sailed on to reach a promontory of land that was covered in grass, which he called Vinland. Although

"There was no lack of salmon there either in the river or in the lake."

Anonymous, *Saga of Erik the Red*, 13th century

the sagas, written some 200 years later, say it was named after the wild grapes growing there, it is at least as probable that the name came from the Old Norse word *vin*, meaning "meadow." Leif spent the winter there before returning to Greenland. The sagas say that later attempts to colonize Vinland failed—probably owing to hostile Native Americans.

Most experts now agree that the site of Leif's landing was L'Anse-aux-Meadows on the northern tip of Newfoundland. Here, in the 1960s, archeologists found evidence of a Viking settlement: foundations of turf-built houses similar to those in Greenland and Iceland, and a bronze pin of unmistakable Norse origin. In 1965, the U.S. Congress resolved that October 9 should be observed as "Leif Eriksson Day" in honor of the first European to reach North America. **SK**

Mahmud Plunders the Punjab

Mahmud of Ghazni launches the first of seventeen invasions of India, and is still remembered for his desecration of Hindu temples.

In 1001 Mahmud, emir of Ghazni in Afghanistan, invaded India, defeated Jaipal, the raja of Lahore, and plundered the Punjab. On his return from the campaign, Mahmud, a militant Muslim, took the title Ghazi ("valiant for the faith"). This was only the first of seventeen great raids he would make into the subcontinent, culminating in 1025 with an attack on the Hindu sanctuary at Somnath in Gujarat in which it was claimed that up to 50,000 people died. Mahmud personally smashed the temple's Shiva lingam (sacred symbol) and took the fragments back to Ghazni to be incorporated into the steps of a mosque to be trampled daily by the believers.

Although Mahmud eventually conquered the Punjab, plunder rather than territory was the main purpose of his raids. Each expeditionary force returned to Ghazni with wagon trains laden with booty and crowds of captives destined for the slave markets of the Muslim world. Mahmud used his plunder to beautify Ghazni, to support scholars and craftsmen, and to finance further campaigns.

In Afghanistan and Pakistan, Mahmud is regarded as a hero; in India he is reviled for destroying so many Hindu holy sites. Historians are divided on the true extent of Mahmud's antipathy toward Hinduism. Some claim that his attacks on Hindu temples were motivated only by the desire to plunder their wealth, but Mahmud's wanton destruction of the lingam at Somnath and other Hindu idols makes this a difficult argument to sustain. **JH**

🔾 The Victory Column built during the reign of Mahmud of Ghazni on the road between Ghazni and Rowza.

🔾 Ruins of the Somnath temple in Gujarat, India, as they appeared in 1899.

Death of Almanzor

Muslim Spain's loss begins the decline of the Caliphate of Cordoba.

On August 8, 1002, the unofficial ruler of Muslim Spain, Abu 'Amir al-Mansur ("Almanzor" to his Christian enemies), died in battle at Calatañazor against the combined armies of the Christian kingdoms of Castile and León. This was the last of no fewer than fifty-seven campaigns that Almanzor had led against the Christian kingdoms of northern Spain. One chronicler wrote that Almanzor "had been seized by the Devil and buried in Hell."

Born Muhammad ibn Abu 'Amir, Almanzor rose to power from humble origins, as the secretary and

---

"Almanzor was like none who has gone before nor will be again."

Historia Silense, Miscellany, 11th century

---

supposed lover of the mother of the young Umayyad Caliph Hisham II (r.976–1009). He overthrew and succeeded the chief minister in 978. Tightening his control over the caliphate, he was exercising supreme power by 981 when he took the title al-Mansur bi Allah ("made victorious by God"). In 994 he adopted the title al-Malik al-Karim ("Noble King"), leaving the caliph as only the nominal head of state.

To pursue his campaigns against the Christians, Almanzor recruited thousands of Berber mercenaries from north Africa. This had the unintentional effect of exacerbating ethnic tensions within the caliphate. Although Almanzor had thrown Christian Spain on the defensive, his usurpation of power undermined respect for the caliph. His death left a power vacuum that led eventually to the fall of the caliphate. **JH**

Holy Tomb Razed

Caliph al-Hakim orders the destruction of the Church of the Holy Sepulchre.

The sixth Fatimid caliph of Egypt, al-Hakim was one of the most eccentric rulers in Islamic history. Unlike his Fatimid predecessors, who had shown great religious tolerance, al-Hakim was a fanatical Shi'ite who actively, and often bloodily, persecuted Christians, Jews, and Sunni Muslims. Some historians believe he suffered from schizophrenia. Christians were forced to wear black hats, and 2-foot (0.5 m) heavy wooden crosses around their necks in public. He was greatly feared for his arbitrary laws, one of which banned chess, another the eating of grapes, and equally arbitrary killings of officials, poets, judges, doctors, generals, cooks, bath attendants, and slaves. In 1005, he ordered the killing of all dogs in Egypt because their barking annoyed him.

Al-Hakim's persecution of Christians reached its peak in 1009 when he ordered the destruction of the Church of the Holy Sepulchre in Jerusalem. The walls of the church were razed, and the Edicule—the tomb of Christ—was vandalized with hammers and pickaxes. The caliph also ordered the destruction of the Church of the Nativity in Bethlehem, but local Muslims refused to carry out his orders.

Al-Hakim disappeared, almost certainly murdered, in mysterious circumstances in 1021 to the great relief of everybody except followers of the Shi'ite Druze sect, who regarded him as an incarnation of Allah. The modern-day Shi'ite Druze believe that al-Hakim will one day return as the prophesied redeemer Mahdi and bring justice to the world.

Though the Church of the Holy Sepulchre was rebuilt in 1048, its destruction led many Christians to believe that Jerusalem had to be brought back under Christian control, contributing directly to the development of the crusading movement. **JH**

Germany's Saintly Emperor

Henry II's quelling of Arduin, a rival for the throne of Italy, paves the way for him to be crowned Holy Roman Emperor.

Henry II was the last of the Saxon Ottonian Holy Roman Emperors, and was the only German king to be canonized (by Pope Eugenius III in 1146). After defeating Arduin of Ivrea in 1014, Henry was crowned Holy Roman Emperor.

Despite his canonization and Henry's strong religious faith, as a king he was far from saintly. His chief legacy is that he worked to strengthen the strong links between church and state started by Otto I, the first German Holy Roman Emperor.

Henry was not universally supported when he succeeded to the throne of Germany, in 1002. He was quick to assert his claim by taking the royal insignia from his cousin Otto III as soon as he was dead and then spent the first two years of his reign consolidating his German throne, and confronting Arduin, a rival for the throne of Italy. Arduin was overcome without much difficulty and Henry was crowned king of Italy at Pavia on May 15, 1004. Arduin rebelled again in 1013, but was quickly defeated. It was this victory that saw Henry become Holy Roman Emperor.

Henry's reign is significant in that the jurisdiction of the bishops was strengthened against the monasteries and their temporal power came to cover large territories. Henry was a champion of ecclesiastical reform and a staunch supporter of clerical celibacy. It is thought he and his wife, Cunigunde of Luxembourg, took a mutual vow of chastity. Certainly, their marriage produced no children, and therefore no heir. Henry was working to have his ecclesiastical reforms enshrined in law when he died suddenly in 1024. **TB**

○ An illuminated manuscript depicting Henry II as a saint, carrying his sword in one hand and Christianity in the other.

East–West Divide

Christianity is divided into Western Catholicism and Eastern Orthodoxy.

One summer afternoon in 1054, just as service was about to begin in the basilica of Santa Sophia in Constantinople, Cardinal Humbert and two other papal legates entered the bastion of Greek Orthodoxy and made their way past the people assembled to hear the divine liturgy. Humbert produced a papal bull of excommunication, uttered the words "Let God look and judge," and placed the document on the altar. Although a deacon beseeched him to withdraw the excommunication, Cardinal Humbert refused and the papal decree fell to the ground. That evening saw riots across the city as news of the excommunication quickly spread.

Although this dramatic event marked the formal split in the Christian church between the Greek Orthodox East and the Latin West, the increasing tensions between Latin and Greek Christendom had developed over many years. The two branches had been drifting apart culturally and linguistically for some time, but the the break was finally caused primarily by disputes over the extent of papal authority. Put simply, Pope Leo IX claimed to hold primary authority over the Eastern patriarchs, and the East claimed that papal authority was only honorary and that the pope did not have power to force decisions upon Eastern ecumenical councils.

Attempts to reunite the churches in 1274 and in 1439 were unsuccessful, and the two halves of Christendom remained firmly divided. Moves to reconcile the differences between the two churches were started in 1965 when mutual decrees of excommunication were withdrawn. Then on December 13, 2006, Archbishop Christodoulos became the first head of the Greek Orthodox Church to make an official visit to the Vatican. **TB**

Turkish Baghdad

The Seljuk Turks make their mark by capturing and taking over Baghdad.

The fortunes of Baghdad rose and fell with those of its founders, the Abbasids. So splendid in the ninth century, Baghdad gradually declined in the tenth century when the Abbasid caliphate fragmented into half a dozen independent emirates. The conquest of Baghdad by the Buwayhids of Persia in 945 finally ended the Abbasids' territorial power but, because of its residual prestige, they retained the caliphate as a purely spiritual office.

Despite this, the Shi'ite Buwayhids treated the Sunni caliphs with undisguised contempt and forced

> ## "Know that Baghdad was great in the past but is now falling into ruins."
>
> **Al Muqqadassi, Arab geographer, c.1000**

them to celebrate Shi'ite festivals. Although the Buwayhids maintained several magnificent palaces in Baghdad, the city lost its preeminence as an Islamic cultural center and by 1000 had been overtaken by Cairo, Cordoba, and Ghazni in this respect.

Liberation, of a kind, came for the caliphate from the rising power of the Seljuk Turks—central Asian nomads who had converted to Sunni Islam around 1000. In 1054 their leader, Toghril Beg, answered a call for help from Caliph al-Qaim and invaded the Buwayhid emirate. On December 18, 1055, the caliph welcomed him into Baghdad as a liberator. Although the caliphate was to be no more independent than it had been under the Buwayhids, at least it now had a sympathetic overlord. The Turks emerged from this event as major players in the Muslim world. **JH**

William Defeats Harold at Battle of Hastings

William, Duke of Normandy, conquers England after Harold is killed in battle.

○ *Coronation of William the Conqueror, from a late fifteenth-century Flemish manuscript illumination.*

▶ *King Harold Being Fatally Wounded by an Arrow (Battle of Hastings 1066) from the eleventh-century Bayeux Tapestry.*

"Here King Harold has been killed and the English have turned to flight."

Bayeux Tapestry, c.1070

In the most decisive battle ever fought on English soil, the mounted knights of William, Duke of Normandy, famously defeated the army of King Harold II, which had hurried south from the Battle of Stamford Bridge on hearing of William's invasion. William claimed to have been promised the throne of England by King Edward the Confessor, but Harold, although he had sworn an oath to support William, had been crowned instead on Edward's death in January 1066. So William sailed to England at the head of an invasion force, having obtained the pope's backing for his enterprise.

The Bayeux Tapestry, an embroidered wall-hanging made around 1070 for William's half-brother Odo, Bishop of Bayeux, shows in a long series of dramatic scenes the events leading up to William's historic invasion and the battle itself. At first, the Norman army of cavalry and archers made little impression against Harold's weary foot soldiers, who appeared to hold firm massed behind a wall of interlocking shields. In the midst of the melee, we see the figure of William turning and raising his helmet to encourage his cavalry to charge. He orders his archers to shoot over the wall of shields, and Harold is killed, apparently by an arrow in his eye. Harold's army is routed, and William proceeds to London, where he is crowned king of England.

Within two years, William, known throughout history as William the Conqueror, had taken control of the entire country, suppressing rebellions in the north and west with brutal force. He rewarded his followers with land, replacing the English nobility with Normans, Bretons, and Flemings. Norman law and feudalism were introduced, and Norman French became the language of the court. England would never be the same again. **SK**

Palermo Falls to Robert Guiscard

The Norman victory is the first step toward the Kingdom of the Two Sicilies.

○ A nineteenth-century image of Robert Guiscard, pointing in the direction of Sicily.

> ## "[The Normans in Italy] are eager and greedy for profit and power. . . ."
>
> **Geoffrey Malaterra, chronicler, c.1100**

A stream of restless, landless adventurers from Normandy made their way south to Italy during the eleventh century, looking for the opportunity to carve out a substantial territory for themselves. The most daring and enterprising of these Viking freebooters was Robert Guiscard, the sixth-born of the twelve sons of Tancred of Hauteville. Robert's nickname Guiscard means "foxlike" or "wily," and he proved himself adept in political diplomacy as well as military cunning. In 1059 he made an alliance with the pope, who agreed to recognize Robert as duke of Apulia and Calabria, and the "future" duke of Sicily, if he could seize and hold these lands for himself, for which he would pay the pope an annual rent of twelve pence per plowland.

It took Robert ten years to oust the Byzantines from Calabria, finally driving them from their last foothold in Bari in April 1071. He next focused his attention on Sicily, which was in Arab hands at the time. With his brother Roger, he swiftly crossed the Straits of Messina and laid siege to Palermo, which fell to them in January 1072. After safely investing his brother as "count of Calabria and Sicily," Robert left him to complete the conquest of the island, which he finally achieved in 1091. Roger's son, Roger II (c.1095–1154), continued with the campaign and later united all the Norman lands in south Italy and Sicily to create the Kingdom of the Two Sicilies, which survived as a separate political entity in Italy until the nineteenth century.

Robert Guiscard's last adventure was to launch an attack on the Byzantine empire in an attempt to have himself crowned emperor in place of the deposed Michael VII. However, he died of fever while besieging the island of Cephalonia on July 17, 1085, at the age of seventy. **SK**

Holy Roman Emperor Left Out in the Cold

Henry IV does penance and submits to Pope Gregory VII at Canossa.

In the early days of his papacy, Pope Gregory VII infuriated the Holy Roman Emperor, Henry IV (1050–1106), by changing the rules by which he could invest bishops so that he would not have to seek the approval of the emperor. What ensued was a clash between the German king and the papacy. Henry retaliated by renouncing Gregory as pope, and Gregory struck back by excommunicating Henry and withdrawing his support for Henry's right to the German throne. Henry had to find a way back into the church and the pope's support.

Crucially, Gregory gave Henry one year in which to seek forgiveness before the excommunication became permanent. For Henry, it could not have come at a worse time; with rebellion breaking out among his nobles. Henry felt it necessary to have the papal decree lifted before he could tackle rebellions at home.

Wearing no shoes and clothed in a hair shirt for penance, Henry set out to cross the Alps in January 1077. On January 25, he reached Canossa, and sought an audience with Pope Gregory. The pope refused to see Henry and the king waited for three days standing barefoot and freezing in the snow. Eventually, Gregory agreed to see the king. When Henry knelt before the pope and begged forgiveness, he was welcomed back into the Church. However, Henry would have the last word. In 1084, he invaded Italy, laid siege to Rome, and deposed Pope Gregory VII

The events surrounding Canossa became significant in later years. In particular, Henry's resistance to papal interference became a rallying cry to supporters of the sixteenth-century Protestant Reformation. Also, for Germans, Canossa is symbolic of their nation's resistance to outside interference from the Roman Catholic Church. **TB**

○ *Emperor Henry IV in Canossa 1077* (1862), by Eduard Schwoiser (1826–1902), depicting the emperor doing penance.

"With his feet bare, [Henry] stood, fasting, from morning until evening."

Lambert of Hersfeld, *Annals*, c.1077

The Domesday Book Is Compiled

William the Conqueror orders a survey of all England to determine who owns what.

○ The original, fragile Domesday Book is kept in the National Archive in London.

> " . . . not an ox, nor a cow, nor a swine was there left, that was not set down in his writ."

Anglo-Saxon Chronicle

It was while he was spending Christmas with his court in Gloucester that William the Conqueror decided to send out teams of clerks all over England to compile information about the land. He wanted to know who owned the land, and what their holdings and livestock were worth. The survey was a huge undertaking—the equivalent of a modern-day government census—and nothing like it had ever been attempted before. The task of gathering the information took place between January and August and the results were then written down in two huge books. In the words of the eighteenth-century philosopher David Hume, these books are "the most valuable piece of antiquity possessed by a nation."

The name "Domesday Book" comes from an Old English word *dom*, meaning "reckoning" or "account." No one is quite sure why William ordered the records to be made. One possible explanation is that he was seeking to raise a tax to defend the country from a threatened Danish invasion—or he may simply have wanted to learn as much as possible about the land he had conquered twenty years before, which he had only recently brought under effective control.

The historic work is organized by counties, and each county entry starts with a list of landholders, beginning with the king and followed by all the tenants-in-chief. The entries provide an amazingly detailed picture of each manor (a village and the surrounding land) in England at the time, down to the numbers of pigs and cattle. The survey reveals just how drastically the country had been affected by the Norman Conquest. Fewer than 250 people controlled most of the land in England, and among all the tenants-in-chief, only two were English. The rest were foreigners, Normans and Flemings, who had come over with William in 1066. **SK**

Bologna Becomes a Student City

Bologna's School of Jurisprudence begins the growth of Europe's first university.

The year 1088 is widely regarded as the date when the University of Bologna came into being as an institution independent of ecclesiastical control. The university is one of the first in the world, and the oldest in western Europe.

One of the university's earliest recorded scholars was Irnerius, who founded the School of Jurisprudence sometime between 1084 and 1088. Irnerius taught at the university and became an expert in the Roman law code, the *Corpus Juris Civilis*, which had been set down between 529 and 534 by order of the Byzantine Emperor Justinian I, and recently rediscovered in the eleventh century. Irnerius's work culminated in his summary of Justinian's laws, the *Summa Codicis*, which was an important stage in the cultural development of European society that laid the foundations for a system of laws that were written, systematic, and rational.

The university gained a reputation as a center of excellence in the fields of science and the humanities. In return for its work on codifying Roman law, and linking its authority to that of the Holy Roman Emperor, the university received a charter in 1158 from Emperor Fredrick I Barbarossa, recognizing its status as a place of learning and research that could develop independent of external pressure. The university was particularly enlightened for the time. It is said that a woman, Bettisia Gozzandini, attended in the late eleventh century. Rumor has it that she went on to teach at the university and gave lectures in front of huge crowds.

After a period of decline in the nineteenth century, the university was honored in 1988 when representatives of the academic community from around the world celebrated Bologna's status as the mother of all universities. **TB**

○ *Teaching Law at the University of Bologna*, from a fifteenth-century Italian manuscript.

"Each university must . . . ensure that its students' freedoms are safeguarded."

Magna Charta Universitatum Europaeum, 1988

"God Wills It!"

Pope Urban II makes an impassioned speech to launch the First Crusade.

◑ *Arrival of Urban II at the Council of Clermont 1095; Urban II calls for the First Crusade,* from a fourteenth-century French illumination.

Seated upon a dais on a hillside outside Clermont in central France, Pope Urban II addressed a throng of bishops, nobles, and citizens and called on the knights of western Christendom to stop fighting each other. Rather, he said, they should turn their swords to God's service by freeing Jerusalem from the Muslims. His words had an electrifying effect, and his speech was interrupted with cries of *"Deus vult!"* ("God wills it!").

Urban was responding to an appeal from the Byzantine emperor Alexius II for military aid from the West. Such an appeal had been made before. Shortly after the Seljuk Turks had destroyed a Byzantine army at Manzikert in 1071 and overrun Anatolia, Pope Gregory VII had called for *milites Christi* ("soldiers of Christ") to go to the aid of their fellow Christians in the East, but without success. Since then reports of Muslim attacks on Christian pilgrims had aroused a new mood of religious fervor in the West, and the pope's call met with enthusiasm. By 1096, thousands of people, mostly from France, the Low Countries, and Germany, had taken a solemn oath to make the long and dangerous journey to the Middle East.

Urban's speech at Clermont signaled the start of the Crusades, the series of wars that would pit Christian against Muslim in the Middle East, Spain, and the Balkans for centuries to come. If some of those who signed up for the First Crusade did so out of worldly ambition and the hope of personal gain, the great majority were moved to join out of spiritual piety and the promise of heavenly reward. **SK**

The People's Crusade

Enthusiastic but inexperienced followers of Peter the Hermit join the Crusade.

○ A detail from *Overseas Voyages* (*Passages fait Outremer*), *c*.1490, by Sebastian Marmoret, showing a battle during the People's Crusade.

Peter the Hermit was a charismatic preacher who took up Pope Urban II's call for a crusade. In summer 1096 he led a disorganized army of knights and peasants, known as "the People's Crusade," through Hungary to the Middle East ahead of the main body of the First Crusade. According to some accounts, they numbered as many as 100,000, including women and children. Having set out before the harvest, they were short of supplies and resorted to stealing. Even before they arrived in Constantinople, news of their unruly progress had reached the Greek emperor Alexius II. Dismayed by the influx of such a large and ill-disciplined force, far more than he had expected when he asked for help, he arranged to ferry the crusaders across the Bosporus, and on August 6 they arrived in Nicomedia (modern Izmir, Turkey). Once in Asia Minor, the crusaders began to quarrel among themselves and Peter returned to Constantinople. While he was away, the inexperienced crusaders were set upon by a Seljuk army and wiped out.

Another group of crusaders inspired by Peter's preaching also failed to make it to Jerusalem. An army of about 10,000 recruits from Germany were persuaded by their leaders that Jews as well as Muslims were the enemies of Christ. They turned on the Jewish communities in several towns along the Rhine, massacring any who refused to convert. Contemporaries reacted with horror to news of the killings, now seen as an early indication of growing anti-Semitism in Western Europe. **SK**

Monks Reject the Easy Life

The Cistercian Order is founded by a small group of monks eager for reform.

🔾 *The Virgin Appearing to St. Bernard*, detail from the polyptych *The Lives of the Saints* (1353–1363), by Giovanni da Milano.

"They appear a little less than the angels, but much more than men."

William of St. Thierry describes Clairvaux, *c.*1143

In 1098, a small band of monks, dissatisfied with what they saw as the easy living of their Abbey of Molesme in Burgundy, left to form a new monastery. The monks wished to follow a stricter adherence to the rules of St. Benedict and were led by their abbot, Robert of Molesme, who had been unsuccessful in reforming the monks at the abbey.

Robert had tried to leave Molesme twice before, but on both occasions the pope had ordered him back. This time, Robert's family connections with the Champagne aristocracy had resulted in a promise of land from Renaud, Viscount of Beaune, and Robert was determined that he and his band of followers would not be returning. The land was little more than a deserted valley, but that did not deter Robert from founding the new monastery of Citeaux. Robert returned to Molesme after only a year when the monks there agreed to follow his stricter interpretation of Benedictine rules.

Under the leadership of two of Robert's followers, Alberic, and later, Stephen Harding, Citeaux became the founding monastery of the Cistercian Order, and Harding's Charter of Charity became the blueprint for Western Monasticism. The Cistercian Order gained influence in the twelfth century when Bernard, abbot of the Cistercian abbey of Clairvaux, intervened in the papal schism of 1130–1138. As Bernard's influence grew, so did that of the Cistercian Order. Then, in 1145, in what was seen as a triumph for the order, the abbot of the Cistercian monastery of Aquae Silviae near Rome was elected Pope Eugene III. Between 1130 and 1145, nearly 100 Cistercian monasteries were founded throughout Europe. Conservative as they were, Cistercian monasteries are credited with playing an important role in the spread of improved farming techniques. **TB**

Jerusalem Falls

Crusaders seize control of Jerusalem, amid scenes of terrible slaughter.

"The slaughter was so great that our men waded in blood up to their ankles." So wrote the anonymous author of the *Gesta Francorum* (*c.*1100–1101) about the events that unfolded once the army of the First Crusade had succeeded in breaking down the walls of Jerusalem and making their way into the city.

It was more than two years since the army—mostly made up of French knights and nobles, with a contingent of Normans from south Italy—had left Constantinople to begin the long march to Jerusalem. Held up for eight months at the city of Antioch, which eventually fell (some said through the miraculous intervention of the Holy Lance) in June 1098, the Crusade was also delayed by disagreements with the Byzantines and quarrels between its own leaders. Bohemund of Taranto was particularly troublesome, yet he succeeded in making himself Prince of Antioch and left the Crusade. All this time the crusaders had been fighting the Seljuk Turks, but now they were making their way into the territory of the Fatimid caliphs of Cairo, who had retaken Jerusalem from the Seljuks in August 1098.

By the time the weary crusaders encamped in front of Jerusalem on June 7, 1099, only 1,200 knights remained of the 7,000-strong army that had initially set out. On July 15, Godfrey of Bouillon's men captured a significant sector of the walls and were able to open the city gates. Over the course of the next two days, the crusaders indiscriminately murdered almost every inhabitant, be they Muslim or Jew, and even some Eastern Christians. Even those who had taken shelter in the Al Aqsa Mosque were ruthlessly slaughtered. Godfrey of Bouillon became the new Christian governor of the city, taking as his title *Advocatus Sancti Sepulchri*, meaning "Protector of the Holy Sepulchre." **SK**

◑ *The Looting of Jerusalem after the Capture by the Christians in 1099*, an illuminated miniature from 1440.

"In five weeks we shall be in Jerusalem, unless we are held up at Antioch."

Stephen of Blois writing to his wife, June 1097

Uncle's Awful Revenge

A love affair with Héloïse has terrible consequences for Peter Abelard, the greatest theologian and philosopher of his day.

Peter Abelard himself tells the story in his *Historia Calamitatum* ("History of My Misfortunes"). As a lecturer in the cathedral school of Notre Dame in Paris, he became tutor to Héloïse, the seventeen-year-old niece of a canon, Fulbert. He was struck by her intelligence and education; they fell in love, had a son, and were secretly married. But Fulbert took terrible revenge and had Abelard castrated.

On Abelard's bidding, Héloïse became a nun, while he entered a monastery. Later he resumed teaching, first in the oratory of the Paraclete, which

> ## "Héloïse . . . was the highest woman by virtue of her wealth of learning."
>
> **Peter Abelard, *Historia Calamitatum*, c.1132**

he founded, then in Paris. Abelard died in 1142 and was buried at the Paraclete. On her death, Héloïse's body was placed in the same tomb. In 1817 they were reinterred in a monumental sepulchre in the newly opened cemetery of Père Lachaise in Paris.

Theirs is one of the most famous love stories of all time. It has inspired poems, novels, paintings, and plays. What is often overlooked is Abelard's very real importance as a teacher and thinker at a time when learning was being revived throughout Europe. He was a poet and musician as well as a theologian, and his thinking had considerable influence on medieval scholars throughout Europe. **SK**

◗ A detail from *Abelard and His Pupil Héloïse* (1882), by Edmund Blair Leighton (1853–1922).

A New Song Era

Gaozong establishes the Southern Song dynasty at Hangzhou.

Under the benign rule of the Song dynasty (960–1279), China became the world's most prosperous and technologically advanced country. The Song, however, were less successful in military affairs and their rule was confined mainly to areas of ethnic Chinese settlement. Their fortunes would be saved in 1127 by Gaozong.

Almost from the dynasty's foundation, the Song faced formidable external enemies whom they tried to control by a "divide and rule" policy. The Khitan empire of Liao, whose southern border lay only a few miles north of Beijing, was a constant threat and the Song had frequently been forced to pay tribute in return for peace. In 1114 the Song Emperor Huizong thought he saw an opportunity to cut the Khitan down to size by supporting a rebellion by their tributaries, the Jürchen people of Manchuria. After years of war, the Jürchen finally overthrew the Khitan in 1124 and founded their own state under the Jin dynasty. This soon became a greater threat to the Song empire than the Khitan had ever been. In 1125, the Jin invaded and Huizong abdicated in favor of his son Qinzong. Qinzong failed to rally the Chinese troops, and in January 1127, the Jin captured the Song capital at Kaifeng, along with Huizong, Qinzong, and 3,000 members of the royal family, who were taken off to a lifetime of captivity.

Gaozong, a younger son of Huizong, managed to escape the mass capture of the royal family and declared himself emperor on June 10, 1127. Though unable to reconquer the north, Gaozong established a new capital in southern China at Hangzhou, beginning the Southern Song period (960–1126 is known as the Northern Song period), which was ended by the Mongol conquest in 1279. **JH**

Birth of the Gothic

Abbot Suger begins work on the rebuilding of the church of St. Denis.

In 1122, Suger, a man of peasant origins, was elected abbot of St. Denis. Suger was an adviser to King Louis VI, and the two had been close friends since childhood, when they had been educated together by the monks of St. Denis. In 1137, Louis VI died, and his successor, Louis VII, rejected Suger as adviser. Thus freed from his former responsibilities, Suger turned his attention to the church of St. Denis, which was attached to the abbey and dated back to 737. For the next five years, Suger concentrated on overseeing the rebuilding of the church.

"We exerted ourselves, vehemently enlarging the body of the church."

Abbot Suger, *Book of Suger*, c.1148

He began with the west front, replacing the original Carolingian stonework with a new design based on the Arch of Constantine in Rome. The new facade now had three large entrances, and a large, stained-glass rose window, one of the first of its kind. Leaving the original nave untouched, Suger had the choir rebuilt using new architectural forms involving pointed arches, ribbed vaults, and clustered columns. The use of flying buttresses allowed for more stained-glass windows. Suger had invented the Gothic style.

The new structure was completed and dedicated on June 11, 1144. One hundred years later, the nave was rebuilt in the same Gothic style. Under the influence of the Angevin kings, the style spread throughout Europe, becoming the blueprint for the design of many churches and cathedrals. **TB**

Debacle at Damascus

The Second Crusade begins a farcical siege of the Muslim city of Damascus.

○ The Siege of Damascus and The Battle of Barada, from a fifteenth-century French illumination by Sebastien Marmoret.

"[They] had been assured that a vast army could be fed on the orchard fruits. . . ."

Archbishop William of Tyre, Historia, c.1175

On July 24 the army of the Second Crusade arrived outside the walls of Damascus to begin an unsuccessful siege that lasted just five days. The crusade had been called because Zangi, the emir of Mosul, had recently captured the eastern crusader stronghold of Edessa (now Urfa in Turkey). The fiery preaching of St. Bernard of Clairvaux whipped up enthusiasm for the expedition, which was led by two of Roman Catholic Europe's most powerful kings, Louis VII of France and Conrad III of Germany. The crusaders attempted to retrace the route of the infamous First Crusade, gathering at Constantinople in autumn 1147 and then crossing the Anatolian plateau to reach the Holy Land.

As they crossed Anatolia, the crusaders were immediately badly mauled by the Seljuk Turks. Because of their substantial losses, Louis and Conrad abandoned the original plan to recapture Edessa and decided to attack Damascus instead. Damascus was a rich and strategically valuable city, but its emir, Unur, was the only Muslim ruler in the region who was not hostile to the crusader kingdom of Jerusalem. It was an act of folly to attack, but having come so far, the crusaders were determined to fight the Muslims—any Muslims—at any cost.

The Damascenes were unprepared for the crusaders' attack, and the city came close to falling on the very first day of the siege. However, the crusaders had been expecting a quick victory, and a lack of food supplies and water made it impossible to sustain the siege. On the morning of July 28, the crusaders packed up their camp and began a humiliating retreat. The Second Crusade was entirely counterproductive, its only notable consequence being to strengthen the drive to restore Muslim unity and destroy the crusader kingdoms. **JH**

Becket Becomes Archbishop

Chancellor's appointment to Canterbury leads to a dangerous rift with Henry II.

Thomas Becket was aware of what King Henry intended to do and warned him against it. The bishopric of Canterbury had been vacant for a year, and Henry saw political advantage to himself if Becket, who was already chancellor of England—that is, head of the royal administration—also became archbishop of Canterbury. Although an archdeacon, Becket was a courtier known for his luxurious lifestyle, rather than a sober churchman. However, the king did not let this fact stand in his way. Thomas was duly consecrated archbishop—an act that was to have great consequences for the lives of both men.

Born in London in 1118, the son of a wealthy Norman merchant, Becket had been educated in Paris and worked as a clerk for the sheriff of London before joining the household of Theobald, the then archbishop of Canterbury. In 1154 Theobald proposed Becket as chancellor to the newly crowned king of England, Henry II. In the role, Thomas showed himself to be devoted to the king's interests; he was efficient and hardworking, especially in the raising of taxes. Henry clearly thought that Thomas would continue to serve him in the same way once he became archbishop, but the king was soon proved wrong.

Once installed as archbishop in 1162, Thomas refused to continue as chancellor. Not only that, he became as zealous in defending the Church's interests as he had been the king's. Henry was eager to impose his authority over the Church. However, when Becket resisted Henry's demands that "criminous clerks" (priests who had broken the law) should no longer enjoy the privilege of being tried only in ecclesiastic courts, the rift between them deepened to such an extent that in 1164 the archbishop fled abroad and all attempts at reconciliation failed. **SK**

○ An early fourteenth-century English manuscript illumination of Henry II of England arguing with Thomas Becket.

"Know that Thomas has been judged . . . to be a wicked and perjured traitor."

Henry II's proclamation against Becket, 1164

Normans Arrive in Ireland

The incursion marks the first significant English involvement in Irish affairs.

● A tympanum above the north door of Cormac's Chapel in Ireland of a Norman centaur killing a Celtic Christian lion.

> " . . . neither winds from east nor west have brought your much-desired presence."

Letter from Mac Murchada to Strongbow, 1170

Two ships carrying seventy heavily armed Norman soldiers and Welsh archers arrived in the calm waters of Bannow Bay, on the southeast coast of Ireland in 1169. The troops on board intended to reinstate Dairmait Mac Murchada to the throne of Leinster from which he had been ousted a few years earlier. Mac Murchada had first fled to Wales and then to France, where he had found that the English king, Henry II, was happy to lend him political and military support. Robert FitzStephen and Richard de Clare, Earl of Pembroke, also known as Strongbow, helped him raise a mercenary army.

The invading force was barely opposed and swiftly took the Viking settlement of Wexford the following day. But after failing to take Tara, seat of the high kings of Ireland, Mac Murchada called for substantial reinforcements. In 1170 Strongbow himself arrived with a larger force and established a strong point in the southeast around Wexford and Waterford, before taking Dublin. Strongbow married Mac Murchada's daughter Aoife and was named heir to the kingdom of Leinster. Mac Murchada died shortly after and, when Strongbow claimed the crown as his own, a general rising occurred that drove Strongbow back to Henry, to whom he surrendered all his land and castles.

The Angevin king himself therefore arrived in Waterford in 1171 at the head of a large army. The king proclaimed Waterford and Dublin royal cities, and toured the whole island. As he did so, he made the rulers of all the Irish kingdoms swear allegiance to him, while his son John (later King John) became lord of Ireland (king of Ireland after Henry's death). In 1175 a treaty was signed at Windsor to confirm the English presence in Ireland, which has remained until modern times. **PF**

"The Holy, Blissful Martyr"

Becket is brutally murdered by four knights in Canterbury Cathedral.

Four knights—Reginald Fitzurse, Hugh de Moreville, William de Tracy, and Richard le Breton—stormed into Canterbury Cathedral and found the archbishop at vespers. They tried to drag him outside to take him prisoner. He refused to leave the cathedral, whereupon they unsheathed their swords and hacked him to death on the spot, slicing off the top of his head with their blows.

Thomas Becket had been back in England from exile for less than a month; fear of a papal interdict had led Henry to allow him to return. Thomas showed no sign of ending his opposition to the king, however, and when Henry, irritated beyond endurance, asked, "Who will rid me of this turbulent priest?" the knights decided to take justice into their own hands and immediately set out for Canterbury to hunt the archbishop down.

Within days of Thomas's death, ordinary people were flocking to pray at his tomb. Visitors reported so many miraculous cures that Pope Alexander III was persuaded to canonize Thomas as a saint within three years of his death. The following year Henry traveled to Canterbury to do penance. Barefoot and wearing sackcloth, he was publicly flogged and spent the night in prayer at the tomb. Thomas became one of the most popular saints of the later Middle Ages—numerous churches were dedicated to him, and his shrine was notorious throughout Europe as a place of pilgrimage. Geoffrey Chaucer's narrative poem *The Canterbury Tales*, one of the first great works of English literature, describes a group of fourteenth-century pilgrims on their way from London to Canterbury, "the holy, blissful martyr for to seek." Thomas's shrine was destroyed in 1540, on the orders of King Henry VIII, and the venerable saint's bones were scattered. **SK**

○ A thirteenth-century illumination of the assassination of Thomas Becket in Canterbury Cathedral by loyalist knights.

" . . . the sword struck . . . and the crown of the head was separated from the rest."

Edward Grim, *Life of St. Thomas*, 1172

Saladin Takes Power

The Kurdish general seizes Damascus and declares himself sultan.

○ A fifteenth-century manuscript illumination from *The Six Ages of the World* showing Saladin holding a scimitar.

> **"This adolescent . . . needs a tutor and a regent, and no one is better placed than me."**
>
> **Saladin, 1174**

A major factor in the success of the First Crusade (1096–1099) was the disunity of the Muslim world. Muslim recovery was begun by Zangi, the emir of Mosul, who recaptured Edessa from the crusaders in 1144 and his son Nur al-Din, who united Syria under his rule in 1154 and conquered Egypt in 1169. The crusader states in the Holy Land were now surrounded on land by territory that was controlled by Nur al-Din. After his victory, Nur al-Din continued to rule from Mosul and sent the Kurdish general Saladin to Egypt as his viceroy. This was a serious error of judgment.

Rich and populous, Egypt provided Saladin with a strong power base from which to pursue his own ambitions. In 1170 and 1172, Saladin deliberately sabotaged Nur al-Din's campaigns against the crusader Kingdom of Jerusalem. Although Saladin shared his ruler's desire to expel the crusaders, he wanted their kingdom to remain intact as a buffer between Egypt and Syria until he was ready to seize power for himself.

Nur al-Din was preparing for war against Saladin when he died at Damascus on May 15, 1174. His eleven-year-old son, al-Salih, was proclaimed his successor under the regency of a eunuch called Gumushtigin. Saladin, however, claimed to be the rightful regent. In late October he seized Damascus and proclaimed himself sultan, reinforcing his authority by marrying Nur al-Din's widow. Saladin's position was finally secured only when al-Salih died suddenly at Aleppo in 1181, probably from poisoning. Saladin was widely regarded as a usurper for his callous actions, but his success in recapturing Jerusalem from the crusaders in 1187 easily counterbalanced this train of thought and made him a hero in the Muslim world. **JH**

Emperor Suffers Humiliating Defeat

The Lombard League defeats Frederick I Barbarossa at the Battle of Legnano.

As dawn broke on May 29, 1176, the army of the Holy Roman Emperor, Frederick Barbarossa, crossed the Olano River and was met by the 3,500-strong army of the Lombard League, a collection of states that remained loyal to the beleaguered Pope Alexander III. Frederick must have been confident of victory as his cavalry force of German knights stared at the infantry of the Lombards.

At first, although the Lombard infantry fought valiantly, it appeared that Frederick would win the day. However, the decisive turn of events was brought about when a relief force of cavalry from Brescia sprang a surprise attack from the rear of Frederick's army. The emperor's forces were thrown into disarray as the Brescians broke through the imperial line and drove straight for Frederick, killing his standard-bearer and personal guards. The emperor was thrown from his horse, and, fearing their great leader dead, the imperial troops panicked and fled. The Lombard cavalry pursued the fleeing imperial forces as Frederick's commanders tried in vain to rally their troops to stand and fight. By the end of the battle the Lombards had taken many prisoners and large amounts of Frederick's gold.

The Lombard victory determined the future political course of Italy. In the resulting Treaty of Venice, Frederick was forced to accept the pope's sovereignty over the Papal States and temporal rights over the city of Rome. Frederick also ended several years of schism in the church by withdrawing his support for the antipope Calixtus III. In addition, a peace treaty was agreed with William II of Sicily, which brought about a period of peace and prosperity for the Sicilian people. After further struggles, Frederick finally gave up his ambition to control the Lombard cities in 1183. **TB**

🔾 A detail of Massimo Taparelli d'Azeglio's 1831 depiction *The Battle of Lagnano in 1176.*

> ## "The emperor ... shall confirm with his own oath ... peace with the church."
>
> **Treaty of Venice, 1177**

Samurai Sunset

Minamoto Yoshitsune defeats the Taira Samurai clan at Dan-no-ura and a military government is formed to displace the emperor.

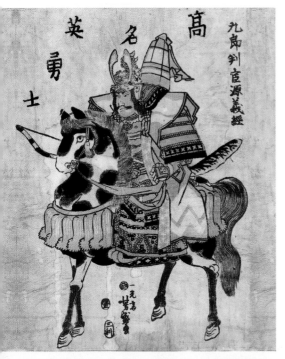

The history of Japan in the twelfth century is dominated by the rivalry between two clans of samurai warriors, the Taira (or Heike) and the Minamoto (or Genji), who vied to control the imperial court at Kyoto. The struggle came to a head in the Genpei War (1180–1185). The Taira had expelled the Minamoto from Kyoto in 1159 and ruled Japan unchallenged until Minamoto Yoritomo led an uprising against them in 1180. Yoritomo concentrated on building support among the *daimyo* (feudal lords) and delegated military leadership of the war to his half-brother, the great samurai warrior Minamoto Yoshitsune.

After they were driven out of Kyoto in 1183, the Taira retreated to the island of Shikoku to plan a counterinvasion. With his own larger fleet, Yoshitsune attacked them in a bay at Dan-no-ura on April 25, 1185. Trapped and outnumbered, the Taira fought bravely. When defeat was inevitable, most of the leaders jumped into the sea and drowned. The fall of the Taira at Dan-no-ura was immortalized in *The Tale of the Heike*, one of the greatest works of medieval Japanese literature.

Yoritomo founded a military government at Kamakura, taking the title shogun ("generalissimo") in 1192. The emperors continued to reign from Kyoto, but in practice Japan would be ruled by shoguns until 1868. Yoritomo became increasingly hostile to Yoshitsune, and excluded him from government. Yoshitsune committed suicide in 1189. **JH**

○ A Japanese depiction of the warrior Minamoto Yoshitsune on horseback, 1886.

○ A woodblock print of Minamoto Yoshitsune in the sea battle at Dan-no-ura.

Germans Rule Sicily

Henry of Hohenstaufen marries Constance of Sicily at Milan.

On January 27, 1186, Henry, the son of the Hohenstaufen Holy Roman Emperor Frederick Barbarossa, married Constance of Sicily. The marriage eventually destroyed Hohenstaufen power, but at the time it seemed to be a diplomatic coup. Henry was heir to the Holy Roman Empire, which included northern Italy. Constance was the aunt and heir of the childless Norman king William II of Sicily, whose kingdom also included most of southern Italy.

A union between the Holy Roman Empire and the Kingdom of Sicily was not welcomed by the pope. It had been less than a century since Pope Gregory VII and Holy Roman Emperor Henry IV had struggled for control over the power to appoint church officials in what is known as the Investiture Contest. The granting of church offices had traditionally been carried out by secular authorities, but Pope Gregory VII reclaimed this authority solely for the church and narrowly won the ensuing power struggle. However, tensions remained between the pope and the emperor for decades, and Henry's marriage to Constance would now leave Rome surrounded by Hohenstaufen territory. The prospect of German rule was not welcomed in Sicily either. When William II died, the Sicilians chose as their king Tancred of Lecce, the illegitimate son of Constance's brother Roger. It was not until Tancred's death in 1194 that Henry and Constance won control of Sicily.

Henry's death from malaria at Messina in 1197 broke the connection between Sicily and the empire. Constance, however, ruled as regent to her young son, the future emperor Frederick II. To the papacy's dismay, Frederick won control of the empire in 1212. However, the papacy ultimately destroyed the Hohenstaufens in both the empire and Sicily. **JH**

Jerusalem Falls

Saladin seizes the moment and defeats the crusaders at the Battle of Hattin.

As the dominant figure of the Muslim world, Saladin, the sultan of Egypt, saw the destruction of the crusader Kingdom of Jerusalem as a religious and political priority. However, Saladin could field a large army only for a few months in summer, when the annual Nile flood released manpower from work on the land. At these times, the crusaders could simply retreat into their castles and wait for Saladin to withdraw again in late August.

Early in 1187, the baron Reynald de Châtillon broke a truce by attacking a Muslim caravan. When

> ## "Since their first assault on Palestine the crusaders had never suffered such a defeat."
>
> **Ibn al-Athir, *The Perfect History*, c.1231**

Saladin responded by laying siege to Tiberias, King Guy of Jerusalem abandoned a strong defensive position near Nazareth and marched to relieve the city. Harried by Muslim forces, the crusaders made slow progress and were forced to stop for the night of July 3. They had run out of water and the Muslims lit grass fires around the hill to torment them. When dawn broke on July 4, the crusaders found themselves surrounded. King Guy was taken prisoner and only a handful of the crusaders escaped. Jerusalem, left defenseless by this entirely avoidable disaster, surrendered on October 2.

The fall of Jerusalem led to the calling of the Third Crusade, but even the combined efforts of the kings of France, England, and Germany failed to restore the holy city to Christian control. **JH**

Death of an Emperor

Emperor Frederick Barbarossa drowns on the road to the Holy Land.

○ The Gotha manuscript of the *Anglo-Saxon Chronicle* (late thirteenth century) showing the drowning of Frederick I Barbarossa.

In the summer of 1190 a vast host of German crusaders, knights, foot soldiers, and camp followers advanced across a plain in southern Anatolia (in modern Turkey), tormented by the glare and heat of a burning sun. At their head rode the Holy Roman Emperor, Frederick I Hohenstaufen, known as Barbarossa—although he was unaware of the fact, this was to be his last campaign.

Frederick was the most powerful ruler in Europe. Aged sixty-seven, he was leading an army to Palestine where hard-pressed crusader states were facing destruction by the Saracen leader Saladin. The army had been traveling for more than a year, yet was still almost intact. They were a disciplined, well-equipped force whose arrival Saladin awaited with trepidation.

Their advance brought the crusaders to the banks of the River Saleph. Its waters were less than waist deep, yet it brought disaster. Frederick may have waded into the current to savor its freshness in the heat or he may have slipped from his horse while fording the river. Either way, he ended up in the water with fatal consequences. His armor was not heavy, but it would have held him underwater if he was stunned by a fall, and he soon drowned.

With their leader dead, the army began to fall apart. So did Frederick's corpse. Although an attempt was made to preserve the emperor's body in vinegar, by the time the crusaders reached Antioch, decay had set in. Saladin, meanwhile, thanked Allah for a miraculous deliverance. **RG**

The Siege and Fall of Acre

The kings of France and England capture a city from the Saracens.

○ *Philip II Lands Outside Acre with His Crusader Army*, a French manuscript illumination, c.1335 from *Les Grandes Chroniques de France*.

In 1190 England's King Richard I (known as "Lionheart") and the French king Philip II Augustus embarked on a crusade to Palestine, where Christians were facing defeat by the great Muslim general Saladin. Thoroughly distrusting one another, they set off together so neither could attack the other's lands in his absence. Philip made better speed, joining Christian forces besieging the Muslim-held city of Acre in April 1191. Richard arrived on June 8.

It was, in effect, a double siege. The city's Muslim defenders were under blockade, their walls bombarded by giant catapults, but in turn the Christians had to defend their backs against Saladin's army farther outside the city. In the unhealthy conditions of the Christian camp, both Richard and Philip fell sick. Nonetheless, the arrival of the English Lionheart, a vigorous military commander with fresh troops, rendered the city's position hopeless. In early July, as breaches opened in the walls, the garrison negotiated surrender terms. They were promised their lives would be spared.

On July 12 the half-starving Muslims walked out of Acre into captivity, impressing the Christian knights with their "gracefulness and dignity." There was little dignity from the crusaders as they occupied the city. Philip swiftly left for France, an act seen by the English as cowardly and treacherous. In a disgraceful coda to the siege, on August 10 Richard massacred the Muslim prisoners—men, women, and children—claiming the surrender terms had not been met. **RG**

Japanese Enlightenment

Monk Myo-an Eisai introduces Zen Buddhism and tea drinking to Japan from China.

🜂 *Zen Monk Near Waterfall with Landscape*, a silk painting by Japanese painter Manotobu.

"Our country is full of sickly looking, skinny persons ... because we do not drink tea."

Myo-an Eisai (1141–1215), *Drinking Tea for Health*

What we think of as the distinctive philosophy of Japan—underlying such cultural forms as the tea ceremony, flower arranging, and the martial arts—arrived from China in 1191 when the Japanese monk Myo-an Eisai, who had lived in China for four years to study the Lin-Chi form of Ch'an Buddhism at Mount T'ien-T'ai, returned home. He brought back a more rigorous form of Buddhism known in Japan as Zen.

In Kyoto, Eisai planted the tea seeds he had also brought back from China, believing that tea both aided meditation and conferred health benefits. He wrote *Kissa Yojoki* ("Drinking Tea for Health"), which advocated tea as a restorative and health aid.

Eisai always referred to himself as a monk of the Tendai school, but his teachings laid the foundations for the practices that came to be known as "Rinzai." He was the first Japanese monk to be recognized as a Zen master, and he strengthened relationships between monasteries in Japan and China. The emperor supported him and offered him the title of Great Master, which he declined.

The practice of Rinzai emphasized gaining *satori* ("sudden enlightenment") as a result of physical shocks, such as shouts or blows, or intellectual ones in the form of *koan* ("paradoxical questions"). By also teaching that Rinzai should include defending the state and taking part in public ceremonies, Eisai attracted many samurai, who used his teachings to inform the practice of the martial arts.

One of his disciples, Dogen, who also studied in China, returned to Japan in 1227 to set up an alternative Soto school of Zen, which emphasized sitting in meditation as the means for achieving and expressing enlightenment. The Soto school acquired a more popular following, and is now the main school of Zen in Japan. **PF**

Royal Fugitive Captured

Richard the Lionheart is taken prisoner by the Duke of Austria.

Shortly before Christmas 1192, a bearded foreigner arrived in the village of Erdberg, outside Vienna, accompanied only by his servant, a German-speaking boy. The traveler found a room at an inn, where he took to his bed, shaking with fever and exhaustion. He was none other than Richard I, King of England, popularly known as "Richard the Lionheart."

Richard was returning to his kingdom after leading a crusader army in Palestine. Shipwrecked on the Croatian coast, he had decided to travel overland to Saxony. Unfortunately his route lay through the territory of his sworn enemy, Duke Leopold of Austria. Riding while discreetly dressed on country roads accompanied by a handful of knights, Richard hoped to pass unnoticed. But observant eyes noted the unusual manner and wealth of these mysterious foreigners. Once the authorities guessed Richard's identity, he became a hunted fugitive, eventually riding day and night, alone but for his servant, until hunger and exhaustion forced him to seek rest.

At Erdberg his anonymity did not last long. His boy, sent to buy food, attracted attention by the silver coins he proffered and the fine gloves lent to him by his master. After three days Leopold's soldiers surrounded the inn and searched it. They found Richard cooking meat in the kitchen, trying to pass himself off as a simple Templar knight. He was seized and taken to meet Leopold on the road to Vienna.

Leopold imprisoned Richard in Durnstein castle above the Danube, and put his captive up for auction to the highest bidder. He was sold to the Holy Roman Emperor Henry VI, who finally released him in February 1194 in return for a huge ransom of 150,000 marks, which his mother, Eleanor of Aquitaine, had to raise by taxing the English. Richard returned to a kingdom much weakened by his long absence. **RG**

○ A later reproduction of a fourteenth-century manuscript showing Richard in prison in Vienna.

> ## "He whom death or prison hides from sight / Of kinsmen and of friends is bereft."

Richard I, poem written in captivity

Miracle at Chartres

The survival of a holy relic in a fire at Chartres Cathedral funds a new church.

As soon as the flames that destroyed much of the cathedral at Chartres in June 1194 had died down, the shock of those who had witnessed the raging inferno soon turned to dismay when they realized that the holy relic of the tunic of the Blessed Virgin Mary had also been destroyed. The tunic was visited by pilgrims and so was a valuable source of revenue.

However, three days after the fire, a group of priests emerged from the smoking ruins carrying the famous holy relic. They had taken shelter in the crypt during the fire and waited until it was safe to venture

"The king gave two hundred pounds of Paris for the building of the church."

Cartulaire de Chartres, 12th century

out. Witnesses to their emergence, including Cardinal Melior of Pisa, proclaimed the priests' survival and that of the relic a miracle. The cardinal, a papal legate, told the people of Chartres that, despite their opposition to the taxes levied to fund a new building, a more splendid cathedral should be built to celebrate the miracle of the survival of the relic. As the story of the miracle spread, contributions poured into the building fund from all over Europe.

Although the events surrounding the fire have the suspicious look of a publicity stunt to rescue an unpopular project, the new cathedral was a triumph of Gothic architecture. With its magnificent flying buttresses and high arches, it pioneered new construction techniques that enabled the cathedral to soar to heights never before attempted. **TB**

Shameful Crusade

Constantinople burns as the army of the Fourth Crusade vents its fury.

The Fourth Crusade, summoned by Pope Innocent III, was not intended to travel to Constantinople. The crusaders had assembled at Venice in June 1202 to attack the Ayyubid dynasty in Egypt, which controlled Jerusalem and most of Syria, but they were unable to raise the money to pay for a fleet. Duped by the Venetians into attacking the port of Zara in Croatia for a share of the booty, they then proceeded to Constantinople, where they joined the Venetian army in attacking the city and restoring Emperor Alexius IV to the throne. But Alexius did not pay the

"They smashed holy images ... and brought horses and mules into church."

Nicetas Choniates, Sack of Constantinople, 1204

reward, and when he was murdered six months later, the crusaders attacked the city again.

For three days they ransacked Constantinople, venting their anger on the Greeks, whom they believed had betrayed them. The crusaders then established a "Latin Empire" based on Constantinople, carving out for themselves feudal estates in Greece and the Balkans, whereas the Byzantine emperors were reduced to ruling a rump around Nicaea in Turkey. The sack of Constantinople permanently embittered relations between the Catholic West and the Orthodox East. It also completely destroyed the credibility of the crusading ideal. **SK**

◗ A detail from a floor mosaic at the Church of St. John the Evangelist showing the Siege of Constantinople.

The First King of France

Philip II Augustus captures Rouen and takes Normandy from the English.

French King Philip II Augustus, who laid siege to the city of Rouen in Normandy in mid-May 1204, was not a heroic figure. He bore little resemblance to the chivalrous ideal of military prowess and noble deeds. But he was a supremely intelligent ruler who thoroughly outwitted the Angevin kings of England.

When Philip came to the throne in 1180, the English king, Henry II, ruled more of France than he did, including Normandy. However, the accession of the unpopular John to the English throne on the death of Richard I in 1199 gave Philip his chance. Cunningly exploiting a twist of feudal law that in some circumstances made John subject to his jurisdiction, Philip summoned him in 1201 to defend the contested legality of his marriage to Isabelle of Angoulême. John understandably declined to attend. Philip responded by declaring most of John's French lands forfeit. When John's young nephew Arthur, a rival claimant to the English crown, was murdered at Rouen in April 1203, much of the French nobility in Angevin-ruled areas turned against him. It was said that John had murdered Arthur, tied a stone to the body, and thrown it in the Seine.

Philip invaded Normandy with 6,000 men and took the English fortress of Chateau-Gaillard after a long siege. The rest of Normandy succumbed without a fight. Rouen, however, had strong trading links with England. At Philip's approach its burghers destroyed the four-arched bridge across the Seine to keep him at bay. Their city was defended by double walls and triple ditches, but morale inside was poor. After a forty-day siege, with no help from John forthcoming, Rouen surrendered on June 24. When Philip entered the city, he for the first time styled himself *rex Franciae* ("king of France") instead of *rex Francorum* ("king of the Franks"). **RG**

○ An illuminated manuscript depicting the French capture of Rouen from the English.

> ## "After King John captured Arthur . . . he slew [him] with his own hand."

Margam Annals, Margam Abbey, 13th century

Genghis Khan Unites the Mongols

Mongol warlord Temujin is proclaimed "Universal Ruler."

In the summer of 1206, the Mongolian nomad tribes gathered near the source of the Onon River for a grand *quriltai* ("assembly") to lay the organizational foundations for the first unified Mongolian state. During the *quriltai* the tribes formally acclaimed Temujin as their supreme leader, giving him the title Genghis Khan ("Universal Ruler").

Born around 1162, Temujin was the son of Yesügei, chief of a minor Mongol clan, who was murdered by the Tatars, the most powerful of the Mongolian tribes, when Temujin was just nine. Temujin was too young to become chief, so the clan expelled his family and seized its property. Without the protection of a clan, the family struggled to survive, forcing Temujin to take up banditry and horse stealing as he grew up. Because of his skill and daring, Temujin soon acquired a loyal following of young warriors, and in 1195 he was accepted as khan of the Mongols. It may also have been at this time that he first used the title Genghis Khan. In 1202 Temujin destroyed the Tatars, and by 1206 he had united all the Mongolian tribes under his rule and conscripted their warriors into his army.

The Chinese usually employed a divide-and-rule strategy against their enemies, and Genghis Khan knew they would try to undermine the unity of the nomads. This should not have been difficult—raiding and feuding were part of the Mongol life and a way for young warriors to win wealth and reputation, just as Temujin had done. But Genghis Khan turned Mongol aggression outward in a series of terrifying campaigns. One of his armies rampaged through the Middle East, and the other conquered Georgia and what is now Russia. The expansion continued after Genghis Khan's death in 1227, creating the largest contiguous land empire in world history. **JH**

⊙ A Persian manuscript of Genghis Khan and his wife Bortei enthroned before courtiers, by Rashid ad-Din (1247–1318).

"They hoisted nine pennants and gave Genghis the title 'Khan.'"

The Secret History of the Mongols, 13th century

Cathar Persecution

The killing of Castelnau precipitates a crusade against the Cathars.

On January 14, 1208, Dominican monk Peter of Castelnau was riding near the River Rhone, north of Arles. Peter was a papal legate entrusted with suppressing heresy in Languedoc, southern France. Suddenly, a horseman rode up to the legate and ran him through with a lance. As his body was brought to the Abbey of St. Gilles for burial, messengers carried the news to Pope Innocent III in Rome.

The pope had long urged action against Languedoc's heretics, known as "Cathars" or "Albigensians." They believed the world was created

"Fill your souls with godly rage to avenge the insult done to the Lord."

Pope Innocent III to the French aristocracy

by a Satan-like entity, practiced vegetarianism, and believed in reincarnation. Although they considered themselves to be Christians, they did not recognize the Church, which had been unable to assert its authority in the Languedoc region.

Before his death, Peter quarreled with Raymond VI, count of Toulouse, the most powerful man in Languedoc, who had been excommunicated for not cracking down on heresy. Peter's assassin was therefore recognized as Raymond's servant, and Raymond was branded the murderer. On March 10, the pope called on the French nobility to launch a crusade against the Cathars and the count of Toulouse. The path was open for those branded as heretics to be massacred and the resulting absorption of Languedoc into the kingdom of France. **RG**

Preaching the Word

Francis hears a message and forms the Franciscan Order of Friars.

On February 24, 1208, Francis was attending mass in the Porziuncola, the chapel he had rebuilt with his own hands near Assisi, when he was struck by Christ's words in the Gospel of St. Matthew, "And as you go, preach the message 'The kingdom is at hand!'... Take no gold, nor silver, nor money in your belts, no bag for your journey, nor two tunics, nor sandals, nor a staff." Francis removed his shoes, put on a rough garment, and took to the road, preaching to the people of central Italy.

He soon had followers who lived simply, in a

"This is what I wish; this is what I am seeking . . . from the bottom of my heart."

St. Francis on hearing the Gospel of St. Matthew

former leper house near Assisi, and devoted their lives to preaching. They were not priests, so they took the name friars, from the Latin *frater* for brother, and as they relied on alms, they were known as beggars or mendicants.

In 1209, Francis traveled to Rome to seek Pope Innocent III's approval for his new order. At first, Innocent was uncertain, but he gave the order his blessing in April 1210 after a dream in which he saw a poor man propping up a crumbling church. Innocent realized that the friars would be a powerful teaching instrument for the Church at a time when heresy was perceived to be on the rise. In 1216, his successor, Pope Honorius III, approved another order of friars, the Dominicans, founded by St. Dominic to preach against the Albigensian heresy. **SK**

Thousands Slaughtered at Béziers

The crusade against the Cathar heresy results in an indiscriminate massacre that kills thousands and causes more than a century of tension.

On July 21, 1209, the forces of Pope Innocent III's Albigensian Crusade against the Cathar heresy surrounded the city of Béziers in southwest France. The commanders, Simon de Montfort and the papal legate Arnaud-Amaury, demanded that the Catholics in the city give up the Cathars who sought refuge there. But the Catholics refused, and some claim that copies of the Old Testament were thrown down in resistance from the city walls.

The people of Béziers attempted to break the siege by sending out a small force, but the crusaders repelled it and forced their way into the city. Everybody in Béziers was slaughtered. Even those who took refuge in churches were massacred. The cathedral of St. Nazaire was set on fire and collapsed, crushing hundreds inside. Ironically, the contemporary accounts place the number of dead between 10,000 and 20,000, with only 200 of them being Cathars.

As news of the fate of Béziers spread across France, many Cathar cities surrendered, and their inhabitants were forced to leave with nothing. Many Cathars chose to return to Catholicism. Those who did not were burned at the stake. However, despite the tactics of the crusade, many Cathar towns later rebelled. As a result, the struggle between the Roman Catholic Church and the Cathars continued for much of the thirteenth century, with the last recorded execution taking place in 1321. The crusade impoverished the region of southwest France and destroyed much of its ancient culture. **TB**

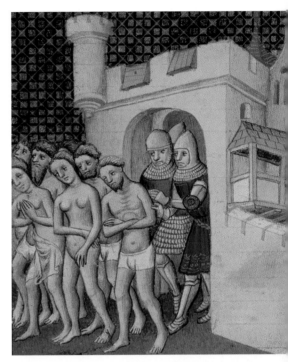

◔ *The Expulsion of Catharist Heretics* (c.1390–1430),
   from *The Chronicles of France*, by Master Boucicaut.

◑ An early fourteenth-century Gothic representation
   of the Albigensian Crusade against the Cathars.

Muslim Spain Falls

A Christian victory at Las Navas de Tolosa breaks Muslim power in Spain.

The Arab and Moorish conquest of Spain of 711–713 fell slightly short of complete victory. A thin strip of territory in the far northwest remained in Christian hands. In Spanish tradition, the Christian victory at Covadonga in 719 marked the beginning of the *Reconquista* ("Reconquest"), although in reality the Christian foothold in Spain remained precarious until the breakup of the Umayyad caliphate in the early eleventh century. Thereafter, the balance of power swung between the Muslim and Christian kingdoms, but the general drift was toward the Christians.

In 1160 Muslim Spain came under the control of the militant Almohad dynasty of Morocco. In 1195 the Almohads won a crushing victory over the Christian king, Alfonso VIII of Castile, at the Battle of Alarcos. By 1211 the Christian position had become so bad that Pope Innocent III proclaimed a crusade against the Almohads. With Pope Innocent's support, Alfonso built a coalition with the kings of Navarre, Portugal, and Aragon, and with the crusading Knights Templar and the Knights of Calatrava. Though the Almohads outnumbered the Christians by at least two to one, Alfonso succeeded in invading Muslim territory undetected. When they fell on the Almohad army at Las Navas de Tolosa, they achieved total surprise, killing or capturing 100,000 Muslim soldiers.

Muslim power in Spain never recovered from the devastating defeat. For the remainder of the century, the Christian kingdoms made steady advances at Muslim expense until by 1294 only Granada remained. That too would fall in 1492, bringing the Reconquest to a triumphant conclusion. **JH**

◐ *Battle of Las Navas de Tolosa in which the kings of Castile defeat the Almohads in 1212, by Francisco de Paula van Halen (d.1887).*

King's Power Restricted

Magna Carta proves a major milestone in the development of democracy.

Even before he had become king of England, John's frequent conspiracies against his brothers, Henry, Richard, and Geoffrey, gave him a reputation for treachery. His reign has generally been labeled as one of the most disastrous in English history.

This reputation is not entirely fair. John was an efficient administrator, a well-informed ruler, and a just judge in the Royal Courts. However, he is chiefly remembered for bringing misfortune on his kingdom through his dispute with the pope and his wars with France, taxing his barons to the point of civil war, and

> ## "John . . . granted the laws and liberties, and confirmed them by his charter."
>
> **Roger of Wendover, *Flowers of History*, c.1215**

being forced to submit to the laws of Magna Carta at Runnymede on June 15, 1215.

Magna Carta attempted to restrict the powers of the king in relation to the barons, and outlawed arbitrary imprisonment. It contained little that was new since it was copied from Henry I's Charter of Liberties, dating back to 1100. However, John was prepared to provoke civil war as he tried to break his word, having signed the charter under duress. John died in October 1216, and was succeeded by his nine-year-old son Henry III. The charter underwent several revisions during Henry's reign, and became enshrined into the laws of England. Magna Carta influenced the United States' Constitution and Bill of Rights, and is considered one of the most important legal documents in the history of democracy. **TB**

Another Holy War

The fourth Lateran Council meets by order of Pope Innocent III.

The Catholic Church held an air of excitement in November 1215, as Pope Innocent III called for a crusade at a council of some 400 bishops, more than seventy patriarchs, and more than 900 abbots and priors. The result of a papal bull of 1213, the General Council of the Lateran also formalized the Seven Sacraments of the Catholic Church.

Innocent's rallying cry to defend the crusader states in Palestine resulted in the ill-fated Fifth Crusade of 1217–1221, which attempted to win back the Holy Land by conquering the Ayyubid state

Crusaders in Egypt

Damietta falls to the Fifth Crusade, but Cairo remains untaken.

The failure of the Third Crusade (1190–1192) to recapture Jerusalem from the Muslims led crusaders to adopt a more sophisticated strategy to taking the Holy Land. It was recognized that Jerusalem could not be held securely while Egypt remained the center of Muslim power. If they had control of Egypt, the crusaders could recapture Jerusalem and hold it.

The first attempt to use this strategy failed when the Fourth Crusade got diverted and sacked Constantinople in 1204. Finally, in May 1218, the ships of the Fifth Crusade arrived at Port Damietta, on the

"Crusaders shall assemble in the kingdom of Sicily on June 1 after next."

Fourth Lateran Council

"Had there been one wise and respected leader, Cairo might have been occupied."

Steven Runciman, *A History of the Crusades*, 1954

of Egypt. The crusaders surrendered following a crushing defeat by the Sultan Al-Kamil.

However, from the Church's perspective, the theological aspects of the council of 1215 were more successful. Innocent had called the council to protect the Catholic Church in Europe by proposing measures to discourage heresy, and to standardize Church doctrine and practice. More than sixty canons were accepted, including the election of Frederick II, King of Germany, as Holy Roman Emperor.

The most significant development was the formalization of the Seven Sacraments: Sacraments of Initiation would be Baptism, Confirmation, and the Eucharist. Sacraments of Healing, Penance, and the Anointing of the Sick were accepted. Sacraments of Vocation would be Holy Orders and Matrimony. **TB**

eastern mouth of the River Nile. The port was to be used to support an attempt to capture Cairo. While the garrison of Damietta held fast against the assaults, the crusaders defeated Egyptian attempts to relieve the city, so a siege began. But in 1219, the crusaders noticed the battlements of Damietta were not being manned, and when they broke into the city the next day, they found the entire garrison sick, dying, or dead from an epidemic.

The Sultan al-Kamil offered to return Jerusalem to Christian control in exchange for Damietta, but the offer was refused. The following spring the crusaders began their planned advance on Cairo, but they moved too slowly and were trapped by the Nile's summer flood. They were forced to surrender Damietta as the price of their release. **JH**

St. Francis Receives the Stigmata

Wounds appear on St. Francis's hands, feet, and side as he meditates on the sufferings of Christ at a mountain retreat near Assisi.

In the autumn of 1224, Francis of Assisi retired to a mountain retreat at La Verna, not far from Assisi. Here, on the morning of September 14, a day devoted to the adoration of the Holy Cross, he is said to have had a vision and received the stigmata—marks on his hands, feet, and side resembling the five wounds on Christ's crucified body. After Francis died, Pope Alexander IV and several others attested they had seen the marks—a clear indication of St. Francis's sanctity and a powerful advertisement for the newly established Franciscan Order of Friars.

St. Francis's is the first documented case of stigmata—the spontaneous appearance of wounds (sometimes bleeding), often accompanied by pain. However, in the century after his death more than twenty cases were reported. One of the most famous is St. Catherine of Siena (1347–1380), a mystic who experienced the pain of the nails in her hands and feet without visible lesions. To date, more than 300 cases of stigmata have been identified by the Roman Catholic Church. In about sixty cases, they have been used as evidence for the recipient being declared a saint or beatified. Stigmata are nearly always associated with religious ecstasy.

Francis lived for two more years after receiving the stigmata, in constant pain and almost totally blind. He begged pardon of his body, "Brother Ass," for having treated it so harshly. Many of the stories about him—his preaching to the birds and taming the wolf—stress his love of the natural world, which is also apparent in his poem *The Canticle of the Sun*, in which he praises all of God's creations. **SK**

○ *Saint Francis Receiving the Stigmata (c.1240–1270),*
  by the Master of the Bardi of St. Francis.

Precious Relic Obtained by Louis IX

King Louis IX of France, later St. Louis, welcomes the crown of thorns to Paris,
and builds the magnificent Sainte-Chapelle as its repository.

At a time when kingdoms and cities, cathedrals and abbeys gained prestige from the possession of saints' relics, King Louis IX of France had secured one of the most precious of all—the supposed crown of thorns that Jesus wore on the Cross. For this, and several other relics, including portions of the Cross, the diapers of the infant Jesus, and a vial of the Virgin's breastmilk, he had paid Baldwin II, the Latin emperor of Constantinople, the enormous sum of 135,000 livres. Now, in a solemn ceremony, he received the crown of thorns from the hands of the two Dominican friars who had brought it to Paris.

Today we may doubt the authenticity of such objects, but for medieval Christians, pilgrimage to the shrine of a holy relic brought great spiritual rewards, and Louis set about creating a setting worthy to hold the relics he had bought. Built between 1242 and 1248 in Paris, and one of the glories of the French Gothic style of architecture, the Sainte-Chapelle, lit by glorious stained-glass windows and with every inch of its interior stonework brightly painted and encrusted with jewels, was designed as a reliquary, the highly decorated container for a relic.

For contemporaries, Louis IX personified the highest ideals of a Christian monarch—the impartial dispenser of justice and the defender of the Church. He personally led two crusades to the east, in 1248 and 1270, dying of dysentery in Tunis while on the second. He was canonized in 1298. Badly damaged in the French Revolution, the Sainte-Chapelle was restored in 1846, and the relics that it was built for are now in the nearby cathedral of Notre Dame. **SK**

◐ Sainte-Chapelle on the Île de la Cité, Paris, photographed
  in the late nineteenth century.

Swedes Repulsed

Prince Alexander defeats the Swedish forces at the Battle of Neva.

In July 1240, a huge Swedish fleet invaded Russia. The ships carried a large army of Swedes, Norwegians, and Tavastians and landed at the confluence of the Izhora and Neva rivers. It was probably the intention of the invaders to seize control of the mouth of the River Neva and the city of Lagoda. If successful, the Swedes would have gained control of a trade route that had long been under Novgorod control.

On hearing the news of the invasion, Prince Alexander Yaroslavich of Novgorod quickly moved his small army to meet the invaders before they

> ## "They had loaded two ships with the bodies ... but the others they cast to a pit."
>
> **Novgorod First Chronicle, 14th century**

could reach Lagoda. On July 15, 1240, Alexander's small army faced the invaders at the River Neva. According to fourteenth-century Russian chronicles, Alexander's army inflicted heavy losses on the invaders. Many nobles were killed and their bodies placed on ships to be returned to Sweden. While Alexander's army buried many more dead in a huge pit, many of the wounded did not wait to be captured but fled into the countryside. Following his famous victory, Prince Alexander was named *Nevsky*, meaning literally "Alexander of Neva."

In contrast, there is little evidence of a battle in Swedish chronicles. Nevsky's political influence was strengthened, and his victory at Neva can be seen as one in a sequence of victories that were significant in the development of Muscovite Russia. **TB**

Mongol Triumph

The defeat of Christian knights leaves Europe open to invasion from the east.

In spring 1241, the Mongols, who had already conquered a vast area of Eurasia from China to the Ukraine, pushed into Hungary and Poland. While Hungary looked to its own defense, King Wenceslaus of Bohemia and Henry II of Silesia assembled armies farther north. Well informed of the movements of the Christian forces, the Mongols in Poland moved to attack Henry before he could join with Wenceslaus.

They found Henry's army at Liegnitz (Legnica in modern Poland). His knights, some belonging to military orders such as the Templars, despised the Mongol horsemen as a "barbarian" horde. But the Mongols's battlefield tactics were breathtakingly sophisticated. Moving swiftly on their sturdy ponies, they harried the Christians, deluging them with arrows fired from the saddle, then withdrawing in feigned flight to tempt the knights into pursuit. The movements of their dispersed bands of riders were coordinated by signal banners and disguised by smoke screens. The heavily armored knights, committed to the mass cavalry charge, were left chasing shadows. Although the knights were protected against arrows by their armor, their horses were not. Once a knight had lost his mount, he was easy meat for Mongols closing in for the kill with lance, sword, and mace. Almost the entire Christian force, perhaps 20,000 men, was massacred. Henry was beheaded and his head paraded on a pole.

The Hungarian army was soon also defeated, leaving western Europe wide open to Mongol invasion. This was prevented by the fortuitous death of the Mongol leader, the Great Khan Ogatai. The Mongols had to journey back to their distant capital, Karakorum, to choose his successor, and were never to mount a full-scale invasion of Europe again. **RG**

Gained and Lost

Jerusalem is permanently removed from Christendom by Khwarizmian Turks.

Jerusalem, taken by Saladin in 1187, was returned to Christian control by the emperor Frederick II in 1229 by negotiation with al-Kamil, the Ayyubid sultan of Egypt. Frederick got little credit for the achievement because he had not gained enough territory to make Jerusalem secure from future Muslim attack.

On August 23, 1244, the inevitable happened, but the attack did not come from the Ayyubids, who were busy having a civil war between rival sultans based in Damascus and Egypt. A few years earlier the Mongols had destroyed the Turkish Khwarizm

"The Khwarizmians burst suddenly into the Christian lands by Safed and Tiberias."

The Rothelin Continuator, c.1250

Shahdom, a province covering much of central Asia and Iran, sending Turkish refugees fleeing west. In June 1244 about 10,000 Khwarizmian horsemen entered the territory of Damascus, plundering their fellow Muslims. Damascus was too strong to take, so the Khwarizmians headed for Jerusalem.

The Christians realized the danger too late. The bulk of their forces was on its way to Egypt in support of the sultan of Damascus. On July 11 the Khwarizmians broke into Jerusalem. The small garrison of Knights Templars and Hospitallers held out until the Khwarizmians promised safe conduct to the coast. On August 23, 6,000 Christians left the city for Jaffa but they were attacked on the way. Only 300 reached their destination. Jerusalem was never regained by the Christians. **JH**

Cologne's Cathedral

The foundation stone is laid for a project that will take over 600 years to complete.

On August 15, 1248, Archbishop Konrad von Hochstaden laid the foundation stone for Cologne's new cathedral to replace the five-aisled construction completed in 818, which had burned down in April 1248. The site had been continuously occupied since a Roman temple stood there in the late second century.

It was important that the new cathedral be of epic proportions since it was to house the famous holy relics of the three kings who brought gifts to the infant Jesus, brought from Milan by the Holy Roman Emperor Frederick Barbarossa in 1142. Archbishop Konrad's plans were thus well suited to a cathedral that would attract pilgrims from all over Europe.

Work on the eastern wing was completed by 1322, and the walls were sealed so that the new cathedral could be used. The huge western front was started in the mid-fourteenth century, but work was halted in 1473, leaving a great crane towering over the incomplete spire. A print dating from the mid-nineteenth century, before the cathedral was completed, clearly shows the old medieval crane still in place after almost 400 years.

Following the discovery of the original plans, construction work began again in 1842. Completed in 1880, the cathedral was a triumph of Gothic architecture and the opening ceremony was attended by Kaiser Wilhelm I. The western front is the largest of any cathedral, and the two spires that became the landmark of Cologne ranked the cathedral as the tallest building in the world until the Washington Monument surpassed them in 1885, closely followed by the Eiffel Tower in 1889. **TB**

▶ A 1493 illustration of Cologne and its cathedral from *Liber Chronicarum* by Hartmann Schedel.

COLONIA·

Baghdad Burns

The Mongols destroy Baghdad and execute the last Abbasid caliph.

On February 13, 1258, the Mongols stormed Baghdad, beginning a week-long orgy of killing, rape, looting, and wanton destruction. The Mongol army under Hulegu had laid siege to the city on January 29, but Caliph al-Musta'sim had made few preparations beyond warning Hulegu that he would face the wrath of Allah if he attacked Baghdad. Hulegu was not deterred, however—the sack of Baghdad and the destruction of the Abbasid caliphate was one of the worst atrocities committed by the Mongols.

The House of Wisdom, a vast library of scientific and philosophical texts built up over 500 years, was destroyed, and tens of thousands of books were flung into the Tigris, turning its waters black with ink. Estimates of the death toll range from 90,000 to 200,000. The caliph was captured and forced to watch while his subjects were massacred. He was then executed. Superstitiously fearing to spill royal blood on the earth, the Mongols rolled the caliph up in a rug and trampled him to death under their horses' hooves. Hulegu is said to have moved his camp upwind of the city to avoid the stench of rotting corpses.

Although the Abbasid caliphate was a mere shadow of its former greatness, the death of the caliph and the destruction of Islam's greatest city sent shockwaves around the Muslim world. However, this appalling atrocity failed to have the desired effect. The Mongols hoped to demoralize and terrify other rulers in the Middle East so much that they would surrender without fighting. The Mamluk rulers of Egypt, however, were not cowed, and it was at their hands that the Mongols suffered a significant defeat, at the battle of Ain Jalut in 1260, which ended their westward rampage across the world. **JH**

Battle of Ain Jalut

Victory at Ain Jalut saves the Muslim Middle East from Mongol conquest.

In 1256 the Mongol leader Great Khan Mongke ordered his brother Hulagu to conquer the Muslim lands to the west of their empire. By 1260 Hulagu had destroyed Baghdad, seat of the Abbasid caliphs, and captured the Syrian capital Damascus. Only Egypt was left, ruled since 1250 by a tough elite of former slave-soldiers, the Mamluks. When Hulagu sent an ambassador demanding his surrender, the Mamluk sultan, Said ad-Din Qutuz, had the envoy killed.

Qutuz boldly took the offensive, advancing through Palestine. Meanwhile, Hulagu was forced to

> ## "'Finish me off as quickly as possible.' Qutuz ordered his head severed from his body."
>
> **Kitbuqa's death, *A History of the Mongols*, c.1300**

return to Mongolia with part of his army. The remainder, led by Kitbuqa Noyen, ran into the Mamluk army at Ain Jalut in eastern Galilee.

The two forces had around 20,000 horsemen each, but the Mamluks proved to be the wilier tacticians. The commander, Baibars, led part of his army into the open with the rest concealed to the rear. Kitbuqa took the bait, riding straight into an ambush—the Mongols were cut to pieces and Kitbuqa was beheaded. Qutuz was assassinated, possibly by Baibars, on the way back to Egypt, and Baibars became sultan in his place.

The battle marked the end of the westward expansion of the Mongol Empire. It also confirmed the ascendancy of the Mamluks. Baibars's successors ruled Egypt until the nineteenth century. **RG**

Simon de Montfort Summons Parliament

Elected citizens represent towns for the first time in English history, signaling the beginning of parliamentary democracy.

The Parliament summoned by Simon de Montfort, Earl of Leicester (1208–1265), which met on January 20, 1265, was an important milestone in the evolution of representative government. Previous parliaments had been limited to members of the nobility. This was the first time that the knights of each county and the burgesses (citizens) of a select number of borough towns were required to send two representatives to Parliament, elected from among their number.

Simon de Montfort owned extensive estates in England and France. He married the sister of King Henry III in 1238 but became increasingly critical of Henry's rule. Simon joined with the barons who were demanding limits to the king's powers and a greater say in government, especially with regard to Henry's ambitious and expensive foreign policies. In 1264, Simon raised a rebellion and defeated the king's army at the Battle of Lewes, taking Henry and his son Edward captive. Now in virtual charge of the country, Simon's arrogance alienated the other great barons, and his support came mostly from the lesser barons, county knights, and burgesses whose representatives he summoned to his Parliament as a means of strengthening his own position.

When Simon's last baronial supporter deserted him, Edward led a large army against him and Simon was killed at the Battle of Evesham in 1265. However, when Edward became king, he made sure that his parliaments included representatives from the towns and counties, the first step in the foundation of modern parliamentary democracy. **SK**

◯ Simon de Montfort's rebellion helped usher in representative parliamentary democracy.

Rudolf Made King

Rudolf of Habsburg is elected king of Germany and Holy Roman emperor.

Legend has it that when riding home one day, Rudolf of Habsburg came across a priest trying to carry the Sacrament to a sick man. The priest, who was on foot, had stopped by a river. Rudolf dismounted, offered his horse to the priest, and led the horse across the river to the house of the sick man. The horse was given to the priest and Rudolf walked home on foot. Years later, the priest, then the archbishop of Mainz, helped secure Rudolf's election as King of Germany.

Rudolf was crowned in Aachen Cathedral on October 24, 1273, and his reign helped consolidate

"His very name spread terror among the barons and joy amongst the people."

Contemporary eulogy

the power of the Habsburg dynasty in Germany and elsewhere. But tensions continued with Ottokar II of Bohemia, Rudolf's main rival for the German throne. In 1274, Ottokar was ordered to cede all imperial lands taken since the reign of Emperor Frederick II back to the German crown. He refused, and the resulting war lasted until he was killed in battle in 1278.

Rudolf spent several years trying to establish his authority in Austria. In 1282, he succeeded in gaining the duchies of Austria and Styria for his two sons, thus laying the foundations for the House of Habsburg, but he was never able to maintain peace in Germany. Before his death in 1291, Rudolf tried to have his son Albert elected as German king, but was unsuccessful, perhaps due to fears in Germany of the rising power of the Habsburg family. **TB**

Beatrice Glimpsed

Beatrice Portinari inspires Dante's greatest works.

Born of a noble Florentine family of noble ancestry, Dante Alighieri came to be known as one of the greatest writers of Renaissance Italy. His output encompassed poetry, literary theory, moral philosophy, and political theory. But some of Dante's greatest works might never have been written but for a chance meeting with Beatrice Portinari, when he was just nine years old.

Dante met Beatrice at the Portinari household for a May Day celebration. He would admire Beatrice for the rest of his life, even though Beatrice married a banker in 1284 and Dante himself married in 1285. Dante's relationship with Beatrice comprised chance meetings, following the standards of medieval "courtly love." Courtly love was a secret, unrequited form of admiration and respect for another person.

When Beatrice died in 1290, Dante took solace in literature and composed a collection of poetic works inspired by his second meeting with Beatrice on the streets of Florence. His sonnets featured Beatrice watching over him, as if divine, and became known as *La Vita Nuova* ("The New Life"). The collection marked the subject of love gaining popularity as a literary theme. Dante's later works were also influenced by the memory of Beatrice: his most famous work, *The Divine Comedy*, features Dante guided on a journey through hell and purgatory by the Latin poet Virgil, and then into paradise by Beatrice, who he describes as "the glorious lady of my mind." *The Divine Comedy* was one of the first works written in Italian, rather than Latin, and established Italian as a language suitable for literary expression. **TB**

◐ A thirteenth-century Italian School manuscript of the meeting between Dante and Beatrice.

The Divine Wind Defeats the Mongols

A powerful typhoon saves Japan from the invading Mongol, Kublai Khan.

○ The Mongol invasion fleet under Kublai Khan is devastated by storms and the Japanese finish off any vessels that survive.

Since the start of the thirteenth century the Mongols had grown from a minor tribe on the Asian steppes to ruling the largest land empire in the history of the world, stretching from Europe across Asia. In 1264, Kublai Khan took Beijing to seize control of northern China and battled the remains of the Sung dynasty in the south. The Sung's ally, the Emperor of Japan, Hojo Tokimune, was Kublai Khan's next target.

In November 1274, a Mongol invasion fleet sailed from Korea and landed at Hakata Bay on Kyushu Island, defeating a Japanese samurai army ranged against it. But the force returned to its boats, which were dispersed in a sudden storm—perhaps 200 ships and 15,000 men were lost in a single night. Having completed the destruction of the Sung in

1279, Kublai Khan returned to Japan, with perhaps 150,000 soldiers, in 1281. He defeated the samurai defenders and sailed south to Takashima. A retired Japanese emperor made a pilgrimage to a Shinto shrine to pray for victory. The following night a violent typhoon sank 4,000 Mongol ships and drowned an estimated 100,000 men. Archeology has suggested that their flat-bottomed boats were for river use, and unsuitable for storms at sea.

The second defeat ended the Mongol aspirations of expansion, and was celebrated in Japan as being the result of a *kami kaze* ("divine wind"). This sense of divine protection for the nation endured until World War II, when the concept of *kami kaze* was revived in very different circumstances. **PF**

Revolt of the Sicilian Vespers

Bells for vespers herald riots as assault on Sicilian women starts war.

○ A late nineteenth-century painting by Erulo Eruli depicting a riot in a church outside Palermo at the hour of vespers.

On Easter Day, 1282, residents of the city of Palermo were holding a festival outside the city walls. The French, who were occupying Sicily at the time in the name of the Angevin king, Charles I, sent soldiers to check that the festival posed no threat. Reports claim that the French handled the Sicilians roughly, and on the pretext of searching for weapons, assaulted Sicilian women. Incensed, the Sicilians began to riot.

At that moment, the bells for vespers began ringing all over Palermo as if signaling the Sicilians to rebel. News of the riot spread across Sicily, and soon there was a full-scale insurrection in which thousands of French were massacred and the French crusader fleet was burned in the port of Messina. The rebellion, which came to be known as the Revolt of the Sicilian Vespers, turned into war when the Sicilians offered Peter III, King of Aragon, the Sicilian throne. However, in response to the rebellion, Charles I landed a force at Messina and besieged the city. But Charles's army was attacked by Peter's Aragonese forces, and they soon abandoned Sicily.

For the next twenty years, the War of the Sicilian Vespers continued to rage throughout the Mediterranean between the Angevin kings of France, their relatives, and the papacy on one side, and the Aragonese kings on the other. The conflict came to an end in 1302 with the Treaty of Caltabellotta, in which the Kingdom of Sicily was partitioned into the island of Sicily and southern Italy, which later came to be known as the Kingdom of Naples. **TB**

A Traveler's Tales

Marco Polo's best-selling Asian account opens up a new world to Europeans.

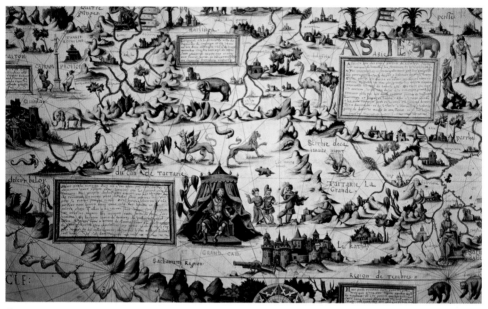

O Marco Polo's account of the Map of Asia, engraved by Jenkinson in 1562, now in the British Library in London.

Three years after Venetian merchant and traveler Marco Polo (1254–1324) returned to Europe following his twenty-five-year journey through Asia, his war galley was captured by the Genoese, and he was thrown into prison. Here he began dictating the wonderful stories of his great adventures to a fellow-prisoner, Rustichello, a writer of romances. *The Travels of Marco Polo* (known in Italian as *Il Milione*) became a best seller. It was translated into more than a dozen languages at a time when printing was not yet known, so every copy had to be written by hand.

What was the fuss about? Simply, Marco Polo told an amazing tale. He claimed to have journeyed across central Asia to the court of the Great Mongol Kublai Khan, in what is now Beijing, and to have been sent by him on various diplomatic missions throughout Cathay (China) as far as Burma, Indochina, and southern India. Marco described life at court, and in the cities and countries he visited.

For centuries—until European travelers began to venture into Asia in the eighteenth and nineteenth centuries—his account remained the most important source of knowledge in the West about the Far East. Christopher Columbus made use of its geographic information to plan his 1492 voyage of discovery. Some questioned whether Marco Polo did travel to China—he could have picked up his information from Arab merchants along the Silk Road—but there is no doubting the immense influence his book had upon the medieval European imagination. **SK**

"Liberty's in Every Blow!"

The execution of William Wallace in London makes him a Scottish legend.

○ A detail from *Portrait of Sir William Wallace*, from the Scottish School, *c.*1870.

The mob knew nothing about the Scot who was dragged naked through the streets on August 23, 1305, except that his death would be good entertainment. A noose was placed around his neck, which meant slow strangulation, but the expert executioner cut the rope before it was complete. Then, amid the cheers of the baying crowd, he sliced off his victim's genitals and made a gash in his torso, plucking out his heart and other organs. The head was severed, dipped in pitch to delay putrefaction, and displayed on London Bridge. What remained of the body was quartered for exhibition in the north as a warning against the example of one William Wallace.

We do not know much about Wallace, except for an account of his death and why Edward I of England had him executed. The son of a minor Ayrshire lord, Wallace refused to accept that Edward "Longshanks" had conquered the Scots in 1296, instead raising an army and winning a famous victory at Stirling Bridge on September 11, 1297, massacring over 5,000 men. A peasant army on foot had defeated the mighty English. Edward eventually captured Wallace in 1305, and he was taken to a show trial in Westminster Hall. He pleaded guilty on all counts except to treason. For how could he be guilty of treason when his allegiance was to the King of Scotland?

The manner of his most gruesome death made William Wallace the supreme Scottish patriot. His potent legend inspired many others to rebellion against the English enemy. **RP**

Pope Moves to Avignon

Clement V decides to move the papal court to luxurious Avignon.

By the beginning of the fourteenth century, factionalism and violence between rival Roman aristocrats had become so dangerous that Pope Clement V moved the entire papal court to Avignon. In addition, residence in Rome could not have been comfortable, given that fire had destroyed the pope's ancient ecclesiastical seat. This move, in 1309, marked the beginning of the period known as the Avignon Papacy, which lasted until 1377.

Perhaps it is no accident that all seven popes who resided at Avignon were French. However,

"I am astounded, as I recall their predecessors, to see these men loaded with gold."

Petrarch 1340–1350

France was not a united nation: the north was under the influence of the French kings, whereas the south was aligned to the Holy Roman Empire. It was not until the papacy of Urban V (1362–1370) that the French crown exerted influence on the papacy. A stronger draw for the papal court may have been the fact that the Roman Curia (church administration) had already moved to Avignon in 1305, to escape the same violence that caused Clement to move in 1309.

However, the Avignon period damaged the pope's prestige—the papal court took on the luxury of a royal court and leading members of the clergy lived like princes. The luxurious living and partisanship of Urban V weakened the church's authority and increased the attraction of religious orders preaching a return to the vows of poverty and humility. **TB**

Last Grand Master

King Philip IV of France brings about the downfall of the Knights Templar.

The brutal execution for heresy of Jacques de Molay, the twenty-third and last Grand Master of the Knights Templar, in front of the cathedral of Notre Dame in Paris, on March 19, 1314, was unjust but politically expedient. The Knights Templar, sworn to defend the Temple in Jerusalem, were one of the most powerful religious-military orders founded after the First Crusade. The order owned extensive property and was run as an efficient business and money-lending organization. When, after the fall of Acre in 1291, it was forced out of Syria and lost its crusading purpose, resentment at its wealth surfaced, and rumors circulated of corruption (or worse) within the order.

Philip IV of France, heavily in debt to the Templars, saw in these stories a way out of his financial difficulties. On October 12, 1307, he ordered the arrest of all of the Templars in France, charging them with performing acts of blasphemy, such as spitting or trampling on the Cross, during their secret initiation rites. Many knights, including Jacques de Molay, confessed under torture to these crimes, and although they later recanted, Philip had dozens of Templars burned at the stake in 1310. The king put increasing pressure on Pope Clement V to disband the order, which he reluctantly did in 1312. The final act was the burning of Jacques de Molay and Geoffrey de Charney, preceptor of Normandy. Both died proclaiming their innocence and de Molay is said to have called from the flames that the pope and the king would soon meet him before God. Clement V died within a month, and Philip IV was dead by the end of the year. **SK**

○ A fourteenth-century French School manuscript of Jacques de Molay being burned at the stake for heresy.

Triumphant Scots

Robert Bruce upholds Scotland's independence by defeating Edward II.

In 1314 the Scots were struggling to escape the domination of the kings of England, led by the fearsome warrior-king Robert Bruce, who was also fighting to maintain his claim to the Scottish throne, which he had seized by force. Bruce usually avoided pitched battles, but in late June at Bannockburn he decided to stand and fight England's armored knights.

Confident of military superiority, the English king Edward II had led an army into Scotland to engage Bruce's men, who were laying siege to the English-held castle of Stirling. Initial skirmishes on June 23

> ## "As long as but a hundred of us stay alive, never will we be brought under English rule."
>
> **The Declaration of Arbroath, to the Pope, 1320**

immediately revealed the Scots' formidable fighting spirit. Bruce led by example, felling the English knight Sir Henry de Bohun with a mighty blow of his ax. The following day the Scottish took up position: they were on foot, pressed together in tight formations known as "schiltroms," with long pikes thrust out, presenting an impenetrable barrier to a cavalry charge. Edward's trump card should have been his archers, but the English knights charged forward in an undisciplined rampage, blocking the archers' line of shot. Many knights were impaled on the pikes. In the confusion, Bruce launched a counterattack that swept the disorganized English from the field.

It took another fourteen years for the English to recognize Scottish independence, but Bannockburn is seen as a key turning point in Scottish history. **RG**

Aztec Capital Is Born

An eagle holding a snake marks the site of the new Aztec city of Tenochtitlan.

In 1325 the Aztecs were wandering along the shores of Lake Texcoco in the Valley of Mexico looking for somewhere to settle. They had migrated into the valley about a century before and had been allowed to settle on land controlled by the city of Culhuacan, but an unfortunate misunderstanding cost them their home: after the Aztecs had acquitted themselves well in a battle, Coxcox, the king of Culhuacan, had given the chief one of his daughters as a wife. The grateful Aztecs promptly sacrificed the girl, believing she would be transmuted into a war goddess.

Imagining that he would be pleased, the Aztecs had invited Coxcox to witness the ceremony. He had come expecting a wedding celebration and was horrified. Driven away from Coxcox's land, the Aztecs eventually found a new home on a marshy island near the western shore of Lake Texcoco. Their chief ordered the construction of a city (named Tenochtitlan after him), the site of which now lies buried beneath Mexico City.

Finding the site fulfilled an ancient prophecy that the Aztecs would build a city where they had seen an eagle sitting on a cactus with a snake in its mouth. The small size of the island allowed little scope for expansion, so the Aztecs began building *chinampas*—artificial islands made from mats of floating water plants. These *chinampas* became the basis of a highly productive system of agriculture capable of supporting a large urban population. This enabled the development of a formidable war machine that went on to conquer much of Central America over the next 150 years. **JH**

❍ The front cover of the *Codex Mendoza*, depicting the founding of Tenochtitlan.

Acacitli Aколнауак

Ocelopa Huitzilhuitl

Tecineuh Tenoch Xomimitl

Xococyotl

tenochtitlan

Xiuhcaqui Acxotl

colhuacan. pueblo. tenayucan. pueblos

Death of Giotto

The great painter, whose innovations help to initiate the Renaissance, dies.

○ Detail of a fifteenth-century portrait of Giotto, attributed to Paolo Uccello (1397–1475).

○ *The Adoration of St. Francis* (c.1320), detail of a Giotto fresco from the Basilica of St. Francis in Assisi, Italy.

"Giotto translated the art of painting from Greek to Latin."

Cennino Cennini, painter, c.1400

Giotto di Bondone was renowned in his lifetime for taking painting beyond the traditional, stylized forms of Byzantine and medieval composition. By the time of his death on January 8, 1337, Giotto was rich and well connected, but documentary evidence concerning his life is meager, and arguments continue to rage about many of the attributions made to him.

Born in a small village outside Florence in 1260, Giotto was apprenticed to the great Florentine painter Cimabue, in whose workshop Giotto acquired a unique reputation for painting in an unusually lifelike manner. In the early years of the fourteenth century he painted a famous cycle of frescoes in the Scrovegni Chapel (also known as the Arena Chapel), Padua. The figures in these religious scenes are particularly noteworthy because they are clearly three-dimensional. They are naturalistic in style and are portrayed interacting and gesturing in a realistic manner. Giotto's work was also greatly admired for his ability to convey human emotions.

After Padua, Giotto traveled around Italy and worked in Assisi (he was said to have painted the life of St. Francis in the town's Upper Church, although this has been disputed and no evidence exists), Florence, Rome, and Naples. In the mid-1330s he returned to Florence, where he designed the *campanile* ("bell tower") beside the cathedral.

A good number of the stories about Giotto's life derive from Giorgio Vasari's *Lives of the Painters*, which was not written until the early 1500s, so relied on history. On his death, Giotto was most probably buried in Florence Cathedral. In the 1970s bones were discovered there that have plausibly been identified as belonging to Giotto. They reveal the skeleton of a man little more than 4 feet (1.2 m) tall, with a large head and a hooked nose. **PF**

Longbow Triumphs at Crécy

English and Welsh archers defeat Philip VI's French army in the first major land battle of the Hundred Years War.

On the afternoon of August 26, 1346, two armies met near the village of Crécy in northern France. English King Edward III had led a cross-Channel rampage to assert his claim to the French throne. To meet him, the French king, Philip VI, had assembled a sizable army—possibly 30,000 to the English 12,000. Unable to avoid battle, Edward took up a defensive position on a hill and awaited the arrival of the French.

After a hard day's march in oppressive heat, Philip's forces reached the battlefield late in the afternoon. The French king advocated resting until the following day, but his hotheaded nobles insisted on an immediate attack. Philip's crossbowmen, Genoese mercenaries, were urged forward in preparation for a charge by armored knights. They soon faltered under a shower of arrows from English and Welsh longbowmen. As the Genoese fell back, the Count d'Alençon, the French king's brother, led his knights up the hill, but the charge was reduced to a shambles under the arrows. The battle broke up into a savage melee, in which dismounted knights engaged in close combat, and English foot soldiers finished off the French wounded.

By the end of the day, the bodies of the French lay thick upon the ground. Those killed included the Count d'Alençon, the Duke of Lorraine, and the Count of Flanders. The battle also signaled a triumph for the English longbow against mounted cavalry. Yet despite the slaughter and his victory, Edward was no nearer seizing the French throne. **RG**

◐ Illustration from *Chronicles of Jean Froissart* (c.1337–1404) depicting the Black Prince's victory at the Battle of Crécy.

◑ A detail from a fifteenth-century illumination of the battle showing the French (on the left) and English (on the right).

Plague Ends Siege

In the siege of Kaffa, victims of the Black Death are used as biological warfare.

For nearly a year, the army of the Khanate of the Golden Horde in Central Asia had laid siege to the Genoese-owned port of Kaffa on the Black Sea. Kaffa stood at one of the western ends of the Silk Road, the great trade route that stretched across Asia to China, and its crowded quays and large slave market were usually bustling. In October 1347, its citizens huddled in terror as the enemy catapulted plague-ridden corpses over the city walls. They had died of a virulent pandemic, known as the Black Death, which had broken out in China a year earlier and swept over Asia.

"No bell tolled and nobody wept . . . people said, 'This is the end of the world.'"

Agnolo di Tura, *The Plague in Siena*, c.1349

Disease spread quickly. Almost no one escaped, and the dead had to be stacked up against the walls like firewood. Some traders managed to get away in four ships, but by the time they reached Messina, in Sicily, most of the people on board were dead.

The disease made its deathly passage along all the main arteries of trade from Asia and the Middle East to northern Europe. Within weeks it had swept through Italy, and by June 1348 had reached France, Spain, and England. By 1351, between one-quarter and two-thirds of the European population had perished. Villages were deserted, towns devastated. The social and economic effects were cataclysmic. During the next 300 years, the Black Death returned regularly, more than a hundred times, before finally dying out in the 1700s. **SK**

Imperial Elections

Charles IV redefines the constitution of the Holy Roman Empire.

On January 10, 1356, Emperor Charles IV of Luxembourg (r.1346–1378) summoned the German princes to a diet to propose new procedures to elect the Holy Roman Emperor. These were then promulgated in a Golden Bull—so named because it carried a golden seal ("*bulla aurea*" in Latin) to stress its importance.

At this time four rival families of German princes (the Wittelsbachs of Bavaria, the Luxemburgs, the Wittenbergs of Saxony, and the Habsburgs of Austria) contested control of the imperial elections among themselves. Subject to papal confirmation, the chosen candidate was formally crowned King of the Romans in Germany before, in theory, proceeding to Rome to be crowned Holy Roman Emperor by the pope, although few emperors had a full imperial coronation.

Charles aimed to bring an end to the damaging dynastic disputes that weakened the authority of the imperial office. He wanted to strengthen the position of his own family by naming seven elector-princes: the archbishops of Mainz, Cologne, and Trier, the King of Bohemia, the Count Palatine (a Wittelsbach), and the dukes of Saxony and Brandenburg (Bohemia and Brandenburg were both Luxembourg possessions). They would elect the Holy Roman Emperor so that the election could not be disputed,

The elections would take place in Frankfurt-am-Main, and the candidate who received a majority of votes would exercise full royal authority straightaway, so ending the pope's role. If they failed to make a choice within thirty days, the electors were to be given only bread and water until they had come to a decision. These arrangements, with the later addition of Bavaria and Hanover to the number of elector-princes, would govern the election of the Holy Roman Emperor for the next four centuries. **SK**

Day of Disaster for France

Edward the Black Prince and his outnumbered army triumph over the French king.

○ A fourteenth-century manuscript illumination of the Battle of Poitiers in which the English defeated the French knights.

"God be praised for it, the enemy was discomfited, and the king was taken...."

Letter of Edward the Black Prince, 1356

At sunrise on September 19, 1356, the quiet of the French countryside outside Poitiers was broken by the sound of trumpets and the clash of metal as the army of King John II prepared for battle. From a wooded slope, the knights and longbowmen of Edward the Black Prince, son of English King Edward III, watched apprehensively. They were a heavily outnumbered raiding party that had done its best to avoid the battle it was now obliged to fight.

The French opened with a mounted charge by 300 chosen knights. The English position was protected by hedges and ditches, which funneled the French horsemen into a lane dominated by Edward's archers. The longbowmen targeted the horses' unprotected flanks, and soon the ground was heaped with flailing mounts and fallen riders.

Through this carnage advanced a battalion of knights on foot, commanded by the nineteen-year-old French Dauphin. Reaching the English line, they engaged in hand-to-hand combat, taking a heavy toll of English knights. But when the Dauphin's men fell back to regroup, their apparent retreat panicked the battalion behind them, which fled the field. King John still commanded a third battalion, untouched by the fighting. Boldly, the English took the offensive. Edward ordered a frontal charge by knights and other men-at-arms, and a separate body of knights rode around to take the French from the rear. John was surrounded. As his bodyguard fell around him, the wounded king accepted a call to surrender.

John and a great many other noble captives were carried off to England and massive ransoms were demanded for their return. Impoverished by war and racked by peasant revolt, France never raised the full money to liberate its king, and John died a prisoner of the English in 1364. **RG**

Merchant Guild Becomes Powerful Force

The first diet of the Hanseatic League is held at Lübeck in 1356.

At the diet of the Hansa in 1356, the Hanseatic League obtained formal structure for the first time. Historians, however, link the origins of the league to the foundation of the northern German town of Lübeck, in 1159, after the area was captured by Henry the Lion, Duke of Saxony. Over the next one hundred years, Lübeck became a thriving town and a base for merchants operating in the Baltic and North Sea.

The Hanseatic League came to dominate the Baltic trade, and as their business expanded, the merchants formed guilds, or "*Hansa,*" to protect their mutual interests and to protect against piracy. Despite gaining formal organization after the diet of 1356, the league never became a single, unified political institution. The diets met regularly, but not all of the cities sent delegates to every meeting. Instead, over time, the league came to form a network of informal alliances involving more than seventy cities and towns. Lübeck remained the most important of the Hansa cities, and was often referred to as "Queen of the Hansa."

In 1368, the Danish king Valdemar IV tried to break the league's hold on the Baltic and North Sea trades. At one of their assemblies, the members of the league decided to raise an army that ultimately led to the defeat of the Danes and the Hanseatic League taking control of Denmark for a short time.

The league's influence was at its greatest in the mid-fourteenth century, but in the fifteenth century, regional differences began to weaken the bonds that held the members together. In the sixteenth century, the rise of the Dutch as trading rivals further weakened the league, and when trade with the New World expanded, the league went into a sharp decline from which it never recovered. The last diet was held in 1669. **TB**

O A fifteenth-century illustration from the Hamburg City Charter showing the importance of ports and merchant trade.

> ## *"Each city shall, to the best of her ability, keep the sea clear of pirates. . . ."*
>
> **Decrees of the Hanseatic League, First Decree**

Ming Dynasty Founded

Peasant Zhu Yuanzhang unites China under his "brilliant" dynasty.

The Mongol Yuan dynasty in China, established by Kublai Khan, apparently suffered the all-too-frequent problems of a degenerate and indulgent leadership: it promoted racial discord, failed to supervise officials, and raised heavy taxes. The need for a new leader led to the successful reign of Zhu Yuanzhang, which began in 1368.

Rebellion had begun in the late 1340s when rebel leaders from the merchant or lower classes seized cities and set themselves up as kings. China was carved up among the rebel warlords, one of whom, in Anhui, appointed peasant Zhu Yuanzhang as general. A scholar told Zhu he would succeed in his ambition to conquer China if he followed three rules: build strong city walls, gather as much grain in storage as possible, and be slow to assume titles.

By 1368, Zhu controlled the whole of southern China and he set up his Ming ("brilliant") empire in Nanjing, restoring the empire to native Han Chinese. He called himself the Hongwu emperor and is considered one of China's greatest emperors. Along with Liu Bang, founder of the Han dynasty, Zhu was one of only two peasants to reach this rank. By 1369 he had driven the Mongols out of China, except for Szechuan and Yünnan.

The Hongwu emperor reasserted the authority of the imperial system, reestablishing the examination system for officials, allowing no dissent from scholars, and abolishing the office of chief minister. Under the Ming, the empire reached its zenith, expanding westward and southward, and undertaking major naval expeditions across the Indian Ocean to Africa. **NJ**

⊙ A portrait of China's first emperor, Zhu Yuanzhang, now on display in Nanjing.

Great Schism Begins

The election of two popes divides the Catholic Church and splits Europe.

In 1377, Pope Gregory XI moved the papal capital back to Rome from Avignon, where it had been established for seventy years. When Gregory died, the Roman people—whose infighting had been the cause of the papal flight from Rome in 1305—took to the streets, demanding an Italian pope. The choice of the conclave fell on the archbishop of Bari, who took the title of Urban VI, but within a short time a majority of the cardinals had second thoughts. The new pope was proving too harsh a disciplinarian for their taste, and on September 20, 1378, they elected another

> ## "They compelled us . . . through violence and fear, to elect an Italian."
>
> **Manifesto of the Revolting Cardinals, 1378**

pope, Clement VII, claiming that the first election had been held under duress.

There were now two popes, one based in Rome and the other at Avignon, where Clement VII set up court. This unprecedented situation caused lasting damage to the reputation of the Church as well as to the papacy. Europe was split into two political camps as its secular rulers were forced to choose between the two popes. Even after the initial claimants had both died, the Papal Schism carried on with the election of successors. In 1409, the Council of Pisa, which had been summoned to end the dispute, elected a third pope, Alexander V (who died soon after, to be succeeded by John XXIII), but as the other popes refused to stand down, this expedient merely prolonged the schism. **SK**

King Confronts Rebels

Richard II persuades the leaders of the Peasants' Revolt to disperse.

○ A dual illustration showing the death of Wat Tyler and the young King Richard II talking to the rebels.

On June 15, 1381, King Richard II, a boy of fourteen, went to meet the leaders of the English Peasants' Revolt at Smithfield. The Peasants' Revolt had begun in Essex with protests against the imposition of a poll tax. As resistance spread, groups of rebels from all over southern England marched on London, where they attacked the property of the rich, including the palace of John of Gaunt, the king's uncle. The government, taken by surprise, began to negotiate with the rebels, but the violence continued, and, on June 14, a mob led by Wat Tyler stormed the Tower of London and beheaded the archbishop of Canterbury and the lord treasurer.

After an angry exchange at Smithfield, the mayor of London struck Tyler down. With great presence of mind, the young king rode forward and, appealing directly to the rebels, persuaded them to disperse.

The Peasants' Revolt drew in urban artisans as well as agricultural laborers. There was a moral edge to their anger, fanned by the egalitarian ideas of the rebel priest John Ball. The clergy were made particular targets of the mob's fury. The grievances that led up to the revolt had their origins in the social upheavals that followed the Black Death. With a much reduced population, there was a shortage of labor, and the Statute of Laborers (1351), which attempted to hold down wages, had been bitterly resented. After the death of Wat Tyler and the arrest of other ringleaders, the rebellion collapsed, and by June 25 the first great popular uprising in English history had ended. **SK**

Vital Victory at Aljubarrota

King João defeats the army of Castile to preserve Portuguese independence.

○ A fifteenth-century illumination of João I of Portugal defeating Juan I of Castile.

The battle at Aljubarrota, central Portugal, on August 14, 1385, is seen by the Portuguese as the most important in their history, for it came at a moment when the very existence of Portugal as an independent kingdom was under threat. Portuguese King Fernando I had died in 1383, leaving his daughter Beatrice as his sole legitimate heir. Beatrice's husband, King Juan of Castile, claimed the right to annex Portugal. Many Portuguese who feared Castilian rule backed a counterclaim to the throne by Fernando's illegitimate brother João, Grand Master of the Knights of Aviz. The struggle became linked to the Hundred Years War: England backed João, France backed Juan.

The Portuguese army included a contingent of English soldiers, among them longbowmen. Since the Castilian army was accompanied by French knights, it is perhaps unsurprising that the course of the battle so closely resembled the Anglo-French encounters at Crécy and Poitiers. João's general Nuno Alvarez Pereira took up a defensive position with knights on foot in the center and archers on the flanks. Ditches dug in front of the line protected against a cavalry charge. The French knights charged nonetheless, with the familiar lack of success. By evening, the tide of battle was flowing in favor of the Portuguese. The Castilian retreat turned into a rout as local peasants set upon the fleeing soldiers, using agricultural implements as weapons. João won the Portuguese crown, founding the house of Aviz that ruled the country for almost 300 years. **RG**

Battle of Kosovo

The defeat of the Serbs by Ottoman Turks results in four centuries of Turkish rule and sows the seeds of Serbian nationalism that still lasts today.

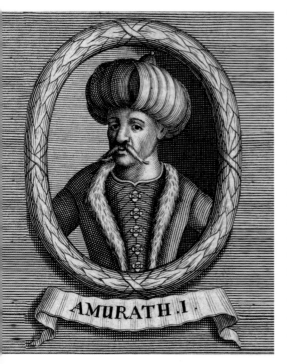

The Battle of Kosovo was fought on St. Vitus's Day (June 28) 1385, at *Kosovo Polje* ("Field of the Blackbirds") between the armies of the expanding Ottoman Turkish empire under Sultan Murad I and a coalition of Christian armies from disparate Balkan states under Serbia's Prince Lazar. Historians estimate that the Ottoman forces greatly outnumbered the Serbs.

The battle opened with a volley of arrows from the Ottoman archers, provoking a general Serb advance, which at first carried all before it. The Turks were demoralized by the death of Murad, assassinated on the eve of battle by a Serb, Milos Obilic, who tricked his way into the Ottoman camp and stabbed the sultan in the stomach. Eventually they rallied under Murad's successor, Bajezid I, and after a fierce fight their superior numbers overwhelmed the Serbs. Lazar was beheaded on the battlefield.

The consequences were dire for the Serbs. Their kingdom was absorbed by the Ottomans, leading to four centuries of Turkish rule. The Serbs, however, preserved their Orthodox Christian culture. Kosovo became a cornerstone of Serb nationalism, and its anniversary was marked down the centuries. It is no accident that the assassination of Archduke Franz Ferdinand of Austria by a Serb nationalist in 1914 (which began World War I), took place on June 28.

Kosovo became the Serbs' spiritual heartland. The Kosovan conflict of the 1990s between Serbs and ethnic Albanians was fueled by the potent issues that Kosovo has come to represent. **NJ**

◐ Sultan Murad I, leader of the Ottoman Turkish army, who was fatally stabbed the night before the Battle of Kosovo.

◐ An eighteenth-century engraving entitled *The Battle at the Field of Blackbirds*.

Towers of Skulls

Timur the Lame sacks Baghdad and massacres its population.

Timur the Lame (or Tamerlane) captured Baghdad on July 10, 1401, after a siege of six weeks. Despite brave resistance, Timur's attack on the city from seven different directions overwhelmed the defenders. Timur is often considered the last great Mongol conqueror, but though he claimed descent from Genghis Khan and was a nomad by birth, he was probably ethnically and culturally a Turk and a Muslim. He had become emir of Samarkand in 1361 and used it as a base to build a short-lived empire that included much of central Asia, Iran, Iraq, and Afghanistan.

"When he had laid waste a great city, in all its gardens he built a palace. ..."

Ibn Arabshah, *Tamerlane of Timur*, c.1420

After the fall of Baghdad, Timur ordered that every soldier should return with at least two severed human heads, which were then piled high around the city. An estimated 90,000 people died in the massacre, making it one of the worst atrocities of Timur's blood-drenched career. Sparing only the mosques, Timur ordered Baghdad to be burned and the ground leveled.

Timur was no simple barbarian, however. He spared the lives of scholars and theologians; many astronomers were sent to Timur's observatory at Samarkand, which became a flourishing cultural center under his rule. However, the city of Baghdad went into a long decline. It was not until 1921, when it became the capital of the British Mandate of Iraq, that it finally began to recover. **JH**

Flying China's Flag

Admiral Zheng He begins to reestablish Chinese maritime power.

In 1405 the eunuch admiral Zheng He set sail from Nanjing at the head of a fleet of sixty-two ships carrying more than 27,000 sailors and soldiers and a vast amount of treasure. Over the next two years, Zheng He visited Vietnam, Siam (Thailand), Malacca, Java, India, and Ceylon (Sri Lanka). Zheng He was not an explorer, or even a sailor, but a diplomat. His mission was a flag-flying exercise to show the "barbarian" kingdoms of Southeast Asia and the Indian Ocean that after a century of Mongol occupation China was a force to be reckoned with.

During the period of the Mongol conquest and occupation (1211–1368), the Chinese economy had been devastated by war and huge demands for tribute. Under the able rule of the first Ming dynasty emperor Hongwu (r.1368–1398), China recovered rapidly, but its prestige and influence in Asia had been severely damaged. Hongwu's son Yongle (r.1403–1424) reaped the rewards of his father's policies. With domestic peace and a full treasury, Yongle used military and naval expeditions to reestablish his country's international prestige.

Zheng He's expedition was considered to be a great success, and he was sent on six more expeditions between 1407 and 1433, extending China's network of tributaries as far as Arabia and east Africa and bringing envoys from dozens of states to pay homage to the emperor. After Zheng's death in 1435, the emperor Zhengtong abruptly ended all maritime enterprises to concentrate his resources on defending China's northern frontier against the resurgent Mongols. It was a disastrous decision that left the Chinese coast undefended against Japanese pirates and the aggressive European merchants who began to arrive in the early sixteenth century. **JH**

Czech Reformer Burned at the Stake

Jan Hus is brought before the Council of Constance and convicted of heresy.

O A dramatic woodcut of Jan Hus being burned at the stake, his expression denoting that he was an innocent man.

> ## "In the truth of the Gospel . . . I will die today with gladness."

Jan Hus refuses a final invitation to recant

Jan Hus, the controversial Czech reformer, was summoned by the Holy Roman Emperor Sigismund of Luxembourg (r.1410–147) to defend his religious views before the church prelates assembled for the Council of Constance. Although Hus had been promised safe conduct by Sigismund, he was arrested soon after arriving at the lakeside town in November 1414 and put on trial as a heretic in June 1415. His accusers denied him an opportunity to explain his views, and Hus refused to recant any belief that he did not preach but that had, he said, been brought against him by false witnesses. The vote of the council went against him, and, as the prescribed death for a heretic was by fire or water, Hus was burned at the stake on July 6, 1415.

A century before the Reformation, Jan Hus anticipated many of the theological arguments of the German reformer Martin Luther. He had made a name for himself as a teacher at the University of Prague in Bohemia (now part of the Czech Republic) in the 1390s, from where he further challenged the power of the church in the years before his death. He was strongly influenced by the writings of the English reformer John Wycliffe (c.1329–1384), and he criticized the wealth of the Church and the abuses of the clergy, especially the granting of indulgences. His championing of the Czech language won him popular support, and he is regarded as a Czech national hero to this day.

Hus's death caused outrage in Bohemia. His followers adopted the name of Hussites and when, in 1419, Sigismund inherited the Bohemian crown from his brother, a long and bitter war broke out. The Hussites resisted attempts to crush them until, by an agreement made in 1436, they won control of the church in Bohemia. **SK**

Victory for Henry V's "Happy Few"

An outnumbered English army trounces the French at Agincourt.

On the morning of St. Crispin's Day, 1415, the scene was set for a great French victory. English King Henry V had embarked upon an ill-judged invasion of Normandy. With his forces ravaged by disease during a prolonged siege of Harfleur, he marched north toward the safety of English-held Calais. But a French army led by Constable Charles d'Albret had maneuvered to block Henry's path, forcing him to a fight. Hungry, exhausted, and heavily outnumbered—with perhaps 6,000 men against 20,000 to 30,000 French—the English faced almost certain defeat.

The key to the unlikely outcome at Agincourt was terrain. The English king drew up his defensive line on a narrow field between thick woods. His 900 knights and other men-at-arms dismounted while his longbowmen massed on the flanks. Forced to fight in this constricted space, the French could not bring their superior numbers to bear. A densely packed mass of French knights floundered forward in heavy armor across soft, muddy ground, harassed by a rain of arrows. The English men-at-arms cut them down in savage close combat, joined by the archers, who discarded their bows to fall upon the enemy with axes and knives. A great English victory was tarnished by the ruthless massacre of the many noble French prisoners taken—ordered by Henry as a precautionary measure when an attack on his baggage train made him fear encirclement.

Agincourt was a military catastrophe for France. About a hundred French noblemen were killed, including three dukes and seven counts. The cowed French king, Charles VI, recognized Henry as the rightful heir to his throne and gave him his daughter, Catherine de Valois, in marriage. Henry's death in 1422, aged thirty-four, undid all these arrangements, denying the battle any long-term consequences. **RG**

○ A detail from a medieval depiction of the Battle of Agincourt, showing the English and French military flags.

> **"In cold blood the nobility of France was beheaded and cut to pieces."**
>
> **Jehan de Wavrin,** *Recueil,* **c.1471**

Great Schism Ends

"Big Tom's" Trinity

The Council of Constance results in the election of a single pope, Martin V.

Florentine artist Masaccio uses perspective to paint in three dimensions.

After three years of deliberation, on November 11, 1417, the Council of Constance finally elected a new pope, a Roman called Oddone Colonna, who took the papal name of Martin V, after the saint whose feast day it was.

The Papal Schism (also known as the Great Schism or Western Schism) had run on for forty years and brought the papacy into ever deepening disrepute. Since 1409 there had been three papal claimants, each with his own college of cardinals, curia, and followers: John XXIII, backed chiefly by the Germans; the Avignon pope Benedict XIII, whose support had dwindled to Scotland, Sicily, Aragon, and Castile; and the Roman pope Gregory XII. In a fresh attempt to end the scandal, Emperor Sigismund put pressure on John XXIII to convene a general council of the Church at Constance in southwest Germany, which opened in November 1414. Declaring the power of a general council to be superior to that of the pope (a decree that later popes ignored), the council recommended that all three popes abdicate the position, leaving the way open for the election of a new pope who would be recognized by and acceptable to the whole of Christendom.

It took lengthy negotiation and intricate diplomacy to bring about the desired result. In March 1415, John XXIII fled from Constance and was presumed to have abdicated. In July, Gregory XII offered his resignation on the understanding that the council would proceed to elect a new pontiff. However, Benedict XIII declined to submit, forcing the council to depose him. An irrepressible Aragonese named Pedro de Luna, he retreated to the island castle of Peñíscola, near Valencia, where he died in 1423, aged ninety five, still claiming to be pope. **SK**

The son of a notary from a village outside Florence, Tommaso Cassai was known as Masaccio, a nickname meaning "Big Tom" to distinguish him from his collaborator Masolino ("Little Tom"). He worked for most of his career in Florence. Little is known of his life, but he died in his twenties, probably in poverty, said to have been poisoned by a rival.

Masaccio's two great achievements were to incorporate classical learning into his art and to develop techniques of architectural perspective and foreshortening to give his paintings real depth. Both

---

"He was absent-minded, whimsical, [and] paid little attention to himself."

Vasari, *Lives of the Artists*, 1550

---

are exemplified in his huge, 25-foot (7.6 m) high *Holy Trinity*, a fresco painted in the mid-1420s in the church of Santa Maria Novella, Florence. Masaccio may have worked with Brunelleschi, the architect of Florence's cathedral, whose knowledge of classical architecture transformed aesthetic ideas at the time.

In the *Holy Trinity*, the figures are framed by a carefully observed classical arch. Beyond is a coffered and barrel-vaulted roof, giving the artist the opportunity to explore perspective. The vanishing point is at the eye level of the viewer, who is drawn into the picture by two flanking figures. The work influenced painters such as Michelangelo. **PF**

◐ Masaccio's *Holy Trinity* (mid-1420s); its use of perspective has influenced generations of artists.

A Domain of Blood

Itzcoatl founds the Aztec Empire in Mexico, and bloody sacrifices are made.

🔾 Aztec leader Itzcoatl, dressed in the skins of animals and birds so he might gain their skills.

"They take out the hearts and entrails and burn them before the idols as sacrifice."

Letters of Hernan Cortés

The Aztec people, who called themselves "Mexica," moved into what is now central Mexico from the north in the thirteenth century; it was on the orders, they believed, of their tribal god, Huitzilopochtli. Around 1325, they founded the city of Tenochtitlan on an island in the marshes of Lake Texcoco—where Mexico City stands today. The city had its own king, but the Aztecs played second fiddle to the city-state of Azcapotzalco, which dominated the whole region and with which they were obediently allied.

In 1426, however, the aged ruler of Azcapotzalco died, which set off complicated intrigues and power struggles between the city-states that led to the murder of the Aztec ruler of Tenochtitlan. His successor, Itzcoatl, with the support of his principal military commander, Moctezuma, saw an opportunity. He gained allies among other peoples of the area, rose in revolt, and in 1428 successfully stormed Azcapotzalco, following a siege that is said to have lasted for 114 days. The defeated ruler of Azcapotzalco was held down on a sacrificial block, his heart was torn out with an obsidian knife, and his blood was scattered to the four directions.

The Aztecs and their allies were now the dominant power in central Mexico. Itzcoatl was succeeded in 1440 by Moctezuma, and the Aztecs went on to build up an empire that, by the time Cortés and the Spaniards arrived in 1519, covered approximately 75,000 square miles (194,000 sq km). Moctezuma ruled a population of between five and six million people.

It seems the Aztec gods had a consuming appetite for human bodies. Victims were sacrificed in the thousands to Huitzilopochtli and the other Aztec deities, and their flesh was eaten as a kind of communion with these deities. **RC**

"Maid of Orléans" Condemned to Death

The English burn Joan of Arc at the stake on a charge of heresy.

Today a church stands on the site in the marketplace at Rouen, France, where a nineteen-year-old girl was tied to a stake and burned in front of a great crowd on May 30, 1431. As the fire took hold, she asked a priest to hold a crucifix high before her eyes and to pray in a voice loud enough for her to hear above the roar of the flames. Once she was dead, the English soldiers raked over the remains of her body and threw her ashes into the River Seine.

The peasant girl from Domrémy, who claimed to have been told by Saints Michael, Catherine, and Margaret to rid her country of the English, and who, wearing white armor and carrying her own standard, led an army to raise the siege of Orléans in 1429, had fallen into the hands of John of Luxembourg, a Burgundian captain, who sold her to the English. They arranged to have her tried as a heretic before a church court under the jurisdiction of Pierre Cauchon, bishop of Beauvais, who was an English sympathizer.

Throughout the spring of 1431 the proceedings dragged on as the court bullied her to try to extract an admission of guilt. The trial records show, "Asked if she knew she was in God's grace, she answered: 'If I am not, may God put me there; and if I am, may God so keep me.'" On May 29, three days after signing a document renouncing her beliefs, she changed her mind and took off the gown she had been forced to wear and put on men's clothes again. The action sealed her fate, and she was handed over to the English. The "Maid of Orléans," who two years before had won a great victory over the English and seen the Dauphin crowned King of France, was publicly executed.

Twenty-four years later, after the English had been driven out of France, Joan's sentence was revoked by the pope. An enduring symbol of French national courage, she was made a saint in 1920. **SK**

○ A book illustration of Joan of Arc being burned at the stake, dating back to just fifty-three years after her death.

> ## *"If I am not [in God's grace], may God put me there; and if I am, may God so keep me."*
>
> **From the record of the trial of Joan of Arc**

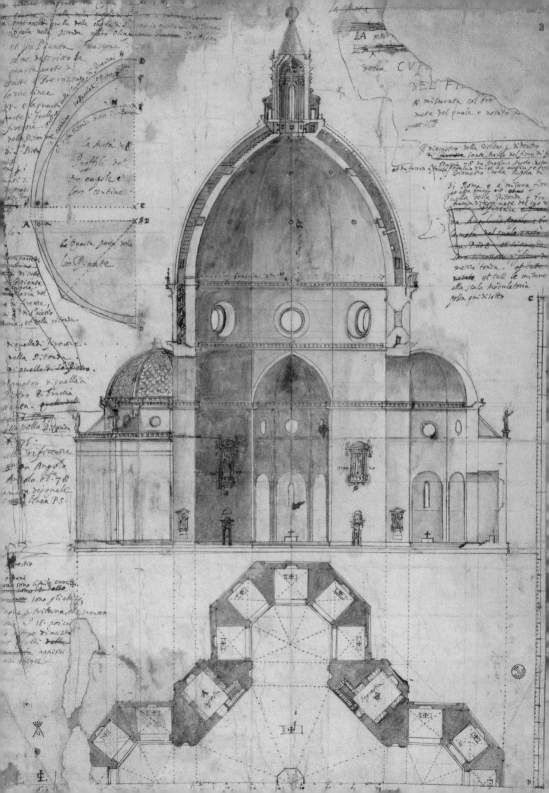

Brunelleschi's Dome

Pope Eugenius IV consecrates the recently completed cathedral in Florence.

It was a challenge to test the most ingenious of brains: how to raise a dome over the east end of the cathedral at Florence in Italy. The building had been begun in Gothic style in 1296, but seventy years later the team in charge decided all new work should be in classical Roman style, to reflect Florence's growing importance. The new plans called for an octagonal dome with a span of 140 feet (42 m). The traditional way of building an arch or vault was to raise it on a wooden framework, but the vast span made this impossible. For more than half a century the dome remained unbuilt—when it was finally finished, it was consecrated by the pope on March 25, 1436.

The man who came up with the solution was Filippo Brunelleschi (1337–1446), a goldsmith and sculptor, who had made several trips to Rome to study the construction of its ancient ruins, particularly the vast domed roof of the Pantheon. He convinced the authorities that he knew how to build the dome. His plan was accepted, and work began in 1420.

Brunelleschi constructed a lightweight, inner dome covered by an outer layer to reduce the weight of the structure, and designed elaborate machines to raise up the building materials. He then laid the bricks and masonry in a herringbone pattern—a technique he had learned from studying ancient Roman buildings. His rivals mocked his scheme and prophesied failure. Yet despite their jeers, the dome rose stage by stage, and by 1436 it stood supreme above Florence's cathedral at 348 feet (106 m) high. It stands today as a monument to the skill and artistry of Renaissance engineering. **SK**

◑ Two drawings of Brunelleschi's dome by Tuscan artist Ludovico Cigoli (1559–1613).

The Warrior Stones

Pachacutec founds the empire of the Incas after defeating the Chanca.

In 1438, the Chanca people were attacking the Inca capital of Cuzco and threatened to take it, but they were fought off by Pachacutec, the principal architect of the empire who ruled from 1438 to 1471, and his men. According to legend, at the crucial moment in the battle, the stones in the fields turned temporarily into warriors and helped Pachacutec destroy the enemy. The stones were collected afterward and placed reverently in shrines.

Pachacutec took power when the Incas were threatened by the Chanca tribe and his father, the elderly Inca Viracocha, had fled. This victory was the springboard for Inca expansion. Pachacutec extended his sway over much of the Peruvian highlands and rebuilt the great temple of the sun in Cuzco. Machu Picchu may originally have been his country retreat. The story of Pachacutec's war with the Chanca was told long afterward, in the sixteenth century, by Juan Betanzos, a Spaniard who married one of Pachacutec's descendants, learned the family traditions, and wrote them down. Pachacutec's fame is still vividly alive in Peru today.

The word *Inca* was originally the title of the chief of a tribe in the central Andes in South America in about the eleventh century. These tribes apparently came from near Lake Titicaca and moved north to establish themselves in and around Cuzco, in what is now Peru. They believed their rulers to be descendants of the sun god and, under their unquestioned authority in the fifteenth century, they built up the largest state in pre-Colombian America, stretching down the western side of the continent from present-day Colombia into Chile and Argentina. The population of the empire is thought to have been as high as ten million. **RC**

Constantinople Falls

Ottoman Sultan Mehmed II seizes
the capital of the Byzantine Empire.

On the afternoon of May 29, 1453, Sultan Mehmed II rode through Constantinople (now Istanbul). Aged twenty, he had conquered one of the world's greatest Christian cities. While the palaces of the rich were looted by Ottoman soldiers, and the streets ran with blood, Mehmed entered the 900-year-old cathedral of Hagia Sophia and gave thanks to Allah for victory.

Once described as "the city of the world's desire," Constantinople was a shadow of its former glory. When Mehmed's army besieged the city in April 1453, it was still shielded by walls that had stood for a

"The blood flowed in the city like rainwater in the gutters after a sudden storm."

Nicolo Barbaro, contemporary diary

thousand years. Yet while Mehmed assembled 80,000 Turks and Serbs and a powerful fleet to attack Constantinople, Byzantine Emperor Constantine XI could muster only 7,000 soldiers to defend it. A Hungarian artillery expert cast a massive cannon for Mehmed to use to batter the walls, a piece of cutting-edge technology the Byzantines could not afford.

In the early hours of May 29, a massed firing of cannon announced the final assault. By dawn the sultan's elite slave soldiers, the Janissaries, were pouring over the fortifications. The last Byzantine emperor died sword in hand. Over the following days, much of the Christian population was enslaved or slaughtered. The fall of Constantinople to Islam shocked the Christian world. For the Ottoman Turks, it was a supreme triumph. **RG**

First Printed Book

Gutenberg's Bible revolutionizes learning
and the communication of ideas.

In 1450 Johann Gutenberg, a craftsman and metalworker from Mainz in Germany, took out a loan from a financier. He had been experimenting with ways of printing from movable type, using his knowledge of metalworking to produce a method of casting metal type in quantity by means of a hand mold. He needed funds to develop further tools and equipment, including a wooden screw press, oil-based printing inks, and paper that could take an impression. With the printing press he created from all these elements he was able to start work on his masterpiece, the *Gutenberg Great Bible*, the printing of which was completed not later than 1455.

Gutenberg's Bible (also known as the *Forty-Two-Line Bible*, because each page had forty-two lines of text) is commonly held to be the first printed book in Europe and marked the beginning of the mass production of books. It probably took a year to produce the first printing of 180 copies of 1,282 pages each. Gutenberg soon had many imitators, and printing presses were set up in city after city to produce Bibles, encyclopedias, theological works, histories, and romances to feed an ever-growing appetite for the printed word.

The invention of movable type has been likened to the birth of the Internet. It was the technological breakthrough that powered the dissemination of ideas during the Renaissance and the humanist explosion of learning of the early sixteenth century. In 1999, *Time* magazine named the Gutenberg printing press the most important invention of the millennium. **SK**

◗ A beautifully illuminated page of *Gutenberg's Great Bible*,
which heralded the beginning of mass book production.

Incipit prologus sancti iheronimi·
presbiteri in parabolas salomonis
iungat epistola quos iungit sacerdoti
um:immo carta non diuidat:quos
xpi nectit amor. Commentarios in ose
e· amos· z zachariā· malachiā· quoq;
poscitis. Scripsisse:si licuisset pre vale
tudine. Mittitis solacia sumptuum·
notarios nros et librarios sustenta
ns:ut vobis potissimu nrm desuder
ingeniu. Et ecce ex latere frequens turba
diuersa poscentiu:quasi aut equu sit me
vobis esurientibz aliis laborare: aut
in ratione dati et accepti·cuisq; preter
vos obnoxi° sim. Itaq; longa egrota
tione fractus·ne penitus hoc anno re
ticerē·z apud vos mutus essem·vidui
opus nomini vro consecraui·interp
tatione videlicet triu salomonis vo
luminu: malloth qd hebrei parabolas·
vulgata editio puerbia vocat: coeleth
que grece ecclesiasten·latine ācionatore
possum° dicere: sirasirim·qd i linguā
nram vertit canticu canticor. Fertur et
panaretos·ihu filii sirach liber: z alius
pseudographus·qui sapientia salo
monis inscribit. Quor priore hebra
icum reperi·nō ecclesiasticu ut apud la
tinos·sed parabolas pnotatu. Cui iuncti
erant ecclesiastes·et canticu canticor: ut
similitudine salomonis·nō solu nu
mero libror·sed etia materiar gene
re coequare. Secundus apud hebreos
nusq; est: quia et ipse stilus grecam
eloquentia redolet: et nonnulli scriptor
veres hunc esse iudei filonis affirmant.
Sicut ergo iudith· z thobie· z macha
beor libros· legit quidē eos ecclesia·sed
inter canonicas scripturas nō recipit:
sic z hec duo volumina legat ad edi
ficatione plebis:nō ad auctoritatem
ecclesiasticor dogmatu firmandam.

Si cui sane septuaginta interpretum
magis editio placet:habet eā a nobis
olim emendata. Atq; eni noua sic cu
dim°:ut vetera destruam°. Et tamē cu
diligentissime legerit:sciat magis nra
scripta intelligi:que nō in terciu vas
transfusa coacuerit:sed statim de prelo
purissime z emendata teste:suū saprē ser
uauerit. Incipiut parabole salomonis

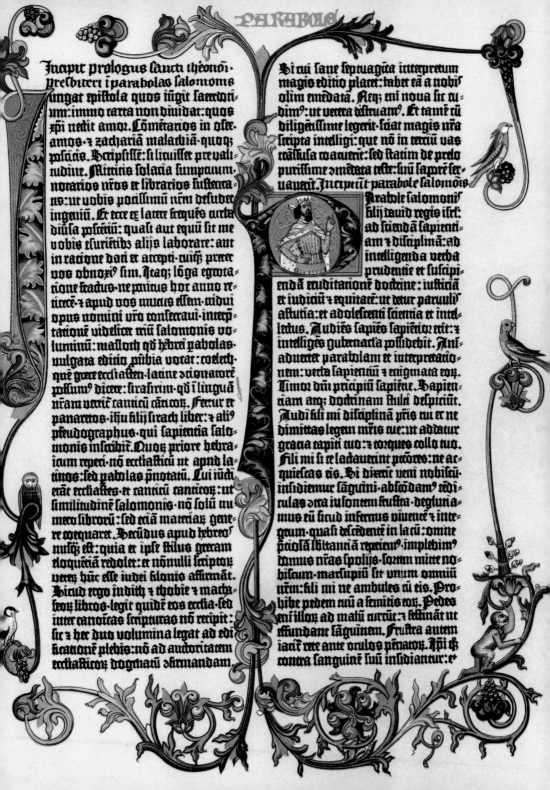

Parabole salomonis
filii dauid regis isrl·
ad sciendā sapienti
am z disciplinā: ad
intelligenda verba
prudentie et suscipi
endā eruditionē doctrine: iusticiā
et iudiciū z equitatē:ut detur paruulis
astutia: et adolescenti sciencia et intel
lectus. Audiens sapiens sapientior erit: z
intelliges gubernacla possidebit. Ani
aduertet parabolam et interpretatio
nem: verba sapientiu z enigmata eor.
Timor dni principiu sapiente. Sapien
tiam atq; doctrinam stulti despiciut.
Audi fili mi disciplinā pris tui et ne
dimittas legem mris tue:ut addatur
gracia capiti tuo:z torques collo tuo.
Fili mi si te lactauerint pctores:ne ac
quiescas eis. Si dixerint veni nobiscu
insidiemur sāguini·abscondam° tendi
culas cōtra insontem frustra·deglutia
mus eū sicut infernus viuente z inte
grum·quasi descendentē in lacu: omnē
preciosā sūbstantiā reperiem°·implebim°
domus nras spoliis·sortem mitte no
biscum·marsupiu sit unum omniu
nrm:fili mi ne ambules cū eis. Pro
hibe pedem tuu a semitis eor. Pedes
eni illor ad malu currūt:z festinant ut
effundant sāguinem. Frustra autem
iacitur rete ante oculos penatos. Ipsi q;
contra sanguinē suū insidiantur:et

Muslim Invaders Repulsed

Peasant crusaders join Hungarian warriors, knights, and priests to defeat the Ottoman forces at Belgrade.

In July 1456, Ottoman Sultan Mehmed II, fresh from the conquest of the Byzantine Empire, led an army north to attack the Christian kingdom of Hungary. The defense of Hungary depended on two men: veteran Hungarian warrior John (János) Hunyadi and seventy-year-old Italian friar Giovanni da Capistrano. A fiery preacher, Capistrano had been stirring up violence against Jews and heretics.

Mehmed's first target was Belgrade, then a Hungarian border fortress. Although its triple walls were formidable, Belgrade was not expected to withstand the sultan who had triumphed over Constantinople. As the Ottomans put Belgrade under siege, Capistrano devoted his oratory to preaching a crusade. Thousands of peasants, armed with scythes and clubs, joined up with Hunyadi's knights and mercenaries to form a relief army. Sailing down the Danube, they broke through the Ottoman blockade to join the defenders inside Belgrade.

On July 21 Ottoman troops broke into the fortress but were repulsed. The next day, some of Capistrano's enthusiastic peasant crusaders charged out of the walls to carry the fight to the Turkish camp. It was an act of undisciplined folly, which Capistrano did his best to prevent, but, miraculously, the Christian sortie gathered an unstoppable momentum. As Hunyadi's seasoned professionals joined in the fight, Sultan Mehmed was wounded and carried unconscious from the field. The Turks were soon in full retreat. Unfortunately, Hunyadi and Capistrano had little time to savor their triumph; both were dead of disease before the year's end. **RG**

◖ A sixteenth-century Turkish engraving showing Mehmed's proud attack on Belgrade—but not his defeat.

Medici Golden Age

Lorenzo de' Medici takes control of the city-state of Florence.

There was no doubting which of the two brothers was the handsome one. Giuliano easily outshone his elder brother in good looks, as he did on the sports field. The nose of the ugly Lorenzo was so severely squashed into his face that he had no sense of smell, and he was constantly plagued by ill health. Yet it was Lorenzo to whom the people of Florence looked for leadership when Piero de' Medici died on December 2, 1469, leaving his two sons as coheirs.

The day after Piero's death, no fewer than 700 Medici supporters visited the young brothers in the Medici Palace in the center of Florence to ask Lorenzo to take control. Under his leadership there began a twenty-four-year period that was commonly regarded as a golden age. Many people soon thought that "Il Magnifico" was not only the ideal Renaissance ruler, which is arguable, but also the prince of Florence, which is quite untrue.

The Medicis had become the wealthiest family in the city, but Lorenzo's Florence was a republic, and executive power lay with the nine-man Signoria, which was still elected by the leading families every two months. Lorenzo had to work very hard and very skillfully to influence the electors and pull the strings of the councilors. Inevitably, there were rival families, and the Tuscan noble family, the Pazzi, managed to assassinate Giuliano in 1478. But Lorenzo lived until 1492 and died peacefully.

By the time of his death, Florence had seen a magnificent efflorescence of artistic production, owing partly to Lorenzo's patronage of scholars, assembled in his Platonic Academy, and artists, including Botticelli and Leonardo da Vinci. The young Michelangelo lived in Lorenzo's palace for several years and was treated as a member of the family. **RP**

Heretics Rooted Out

Ferdinand and Isabella extend the Inquisition throughout Spain.

Isabella of Castile and Ferdinand of Aragon—whose marriage in 1469 had brought together the two kingdoms of medieval Spain—saw it as their divine duty to drive heresy from their lands. Isabella had already obtained the pope's permission to establish the Inquisition in Castile to root out any Jews or Muslims who falsely claimed to be *conversos* ("Catholic converts"), and on October 17, 1483, Pope Sixtus IV issued a bull instituting the Inquisition throughout Ferdinand's territories of Aragon.

Inquisitions had been set up before by the

> ## "Had there been no Inquisition, [we] would be in a lamentable state. . . ."
>
> **King Philip II of Spain, 1569**

medieval papacy to combat heresy (the first was against the Cathars in 1231), but the Spanish Inquisition was a special case. It was constituted as a royal court, its proceedings were kept secret, and it relied heavily on informers. Torture was often used to extract confessions, and condemned heretics were burned in front of huge crowds at the popular *auto-da-fé* ("act of faith") ceremonies. The crown, the Inquisition, and the informers all got a share of the victim's confiscated property.

The Inquisition later moved on to target humanists and Protestants, especially during Philip II's reign. This was used as propaganda by Spain's enemies, particularly in England, and it was at this time that the Spanish Inquisition acquired its, possibly exaggerated, reputation for sadistic cruelty. **SK**

English King Slain by Rebels

Victory at the Battle of Bosworth Field ends the War of the Roses and opens the way for Henry Tudor to found a new dynasty.

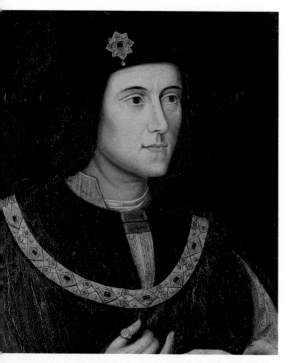

Fifteenth-century England was racked by civil strife as the houses of York and Lancaster asserted their competing claims to the throne. Known as the War of the Roses, these internal struggles came to a decisive close in August 1485 when the Yorkist king, Richard III, was hacked down on the battlefield, a victim of rebellion and betrayal.

The rebel leader was Henry Tudor. An exile living in Brittany, Henry's hereditary claim to the throne was tenuous, but he was the best candidate that Richard's opponents could find. He landed at Milford Haven on August 7 with 2,000 French mercenaries and advanced unopposed into the English Midlands, gathering followers as he went. It was soon clear that Richard had trouble commanding his subjects' loyalty. His own right to the throne was dubious—he was rumored to have murdered his young nephews, Edward V and Richard, Duke of York. The allegiance of the powerful Stanley family was especially in doubt.

In principle Richard's army outnumbered Henry's, but both the Stanleys and the Duke of Northumberland held their men back when battle was joined on August 22. In a furious bid to seize victory with his own hands, Richard led a charge, slashing a path through the bodyguard of knights. At the crucial moment, Sir William Stanley committed his men to the fight—on the rebel side. Richard was felled with an ax blow. Henry Tudor took the throne as Henry VII, and founded a dynasty that reigned for 118 years until the death of Queen Elizabeth I in 1603. **RG**

⚬ A portrait of Richard III, who died at the Battle of Bosworth Field, painted by an unknown artist.

⚬ A nineteenth-century engraving showing the moments before Richard III was slain in battle.

Dias Rounds the Cape

An ocean route to India and its valuable spice trade is opened.

The first time Bartolomeu Dias sailed past the Cape of Good Hope in January 1488, he did not even see it: Africa's famous southern tip was obscured by storms. Dias, a skilled seaman, navigator, and ship designer, had set out from Lisbon in August 1487 with two small caravels and a broader-beamed supply boat. The *Sao Cristivao* and *Sao Pantaleao* carried three commemorative stone pillars bearing the arms of Portugal to mark landfalls and territorial claims. The aim of the expedition was to secure a route to the Indian Ocean and the alluring Asian spice trade.

Leaving the supply ship safely anchored, Dias and his crew beat down the coast of southwest Africa before heading out into deeper water to seek better winds. They picked up the prevailing westerlies that took them southwest, but the wind soon became storm force. When the storm subsided, Dias headed east, hoping for landfall on Africa's west coast, but nothing was sighted. This made Dias suspect he had overshot Africa's tip. He headed northward and reached Africa's southern coast about 250 miles (400 km) east of the Cape of Good Hope, on February 3, 1488.

Dias realized he had discovered the African landmass's southern limits. He continued eastward, but by now the crew were agitated at being so far from their supply ship. After a general meeting it was agreed they should set a return course. On this return leg, they finally reached the great cape that had been hidden from view on the outward journey. Dias erected his final pillar, here naming it Cabo Tormentoso ("Cape of Storms"). However, the king of Portugal, João II, did not approve the name, and renamed the southern promontory of Africa the Cape of Good Hope. **JJH**

Nzinga Converted

Portuguese rulers seek to carve out an empire in Africa.

Nzinga Nkuwu ruled as the fifth hereditary king of the Kongo tribe, which was based in the region of modern-day Congo in western central Africa. The Portuguese explorer Diego Cao made the first contact with the Kongo in 1482, and returned two or three years later bearing gifts from Portugal's King João I. Nzinga welcomed Cao to his capital, Mbanza (later São Salvador), and sent his own emissaries to the Portuguese court with a plea for aid. The Portuguese responded in 1490 when the explorer Rui de Sousa arrived in the Kongo with ships carrying

> **"The one who throws a stone forgets; he who is hit remembers forever."**
>
> **Angolan proverb**

gifts, soldiers, and priests. Nzinga promptly converted to Christianity and was baptized.

The Portuguese troops helped him impose Christianity by putting down a revolt by those opposed to enforced Christianization. Nzinga took the title João I in honor of Portugal's king, and sent his eldest son, Nzinga Mvemba, to Portugal to train as a Christian ruler. He returned ten years later, thoroughly westernized, with the name Afonso. However, tensions between monogamous Christian "modernizers," led by Afonso, and polygamous traditionalists caused Nzinga Nkuwu to exile Afonso and make a second son, Mpanzu u Kitima, his heir. Disillusioned, the king renounced Christianity before he died in 1506. After his death, Afonso took the throne and continued Christianization. **NJ**

Granada's New Era

The capture of the city marks the final act of the Reconquista.

The *Reconquista* ("Reconquest") of Muslim Spain was completed after an 800-year struggle when Moorish ruler Abu Abdullah Muhammad XII (or "Boabdil") placed the keys of the city of Granada in Ferdinand's hand on January 2, 1492. From near-total domination of the Iberian Peninsula, the Moors had been systematically rolled back until, by the 1400s, only the southern province of Granada remained under Muslim rule. Determined to unify Spain under Christian control, Ferdinand II of Aragon and his wife, Isabella of Castile, opened an offensive against

> ## "You do well to weep like a woman for what you could not defend like a man."
>
> **Attributed to Boabdil's mother on son's exile**

Granada in the 1480s. Internal divisions hampered the Moors, and by summer 1490, after his scorched-earth offensive had taken most of the province, Ferdinand had Boabdil bottled up in Granada.

After an exchange of religious insults—the prayer *Ave Maria* ("Hail Mary") was nailed to the door of a mosque; the Moors retaliated by tying it to a donkey's tail—decisive battle was joined in July 1491. The Moors were chased back behind the city walls, leaving 2,000 casualties.

The Spaniards tightened their siege until the Moors faced starvation. Negotiations were opened and in January 1492 Boabdil agreed to capitulate in return for a guarantee of freedom of worship or a paid passage back to north Africa for those Moors unwilling to live under Christian rule. **NJ**

Jews Ordered Out

An edict of Isabella and Ferdinand requires all Jews to leave Spain.

On March 31, 1492, less than three months after the fall of Granada, Isabella and Ferdinand issued the Edict of Alhambra, which ordered the mass expulsion of all Jews from Spain who refused to convert to Christianity. The author of the edict was Tomás de Torquemada, the inquisitor general. There is a story that when a wealthy Jewish financier and scholar, Isaac Abravanel, offered Ferdinand a bribe of 600,000 crowns to revoke it, Torquemada threw down a crucifix before the king and queen and demanded whether, like Judas, they would betray their Lord for money. Abravanel was among the thousands of Jews—figures vary between 165,000 and 800,000—who were forced to flee from Spain. He died, exhausted and penniless, in Venice in 1508.

There had long been a sizable Jewish community on the Iberian Peninsula, and they had generally enjoyed good relations with the Muslim rulers, but their position had worsened with the spread of the Christian *Reconquista*. By 1300 Jews were required to wear a distinctive badge, and there were violent anti-Jewish riots in 1348 and 1391. Thousands of Jews were persuaded to convert to Christianity.

After the Edict of Alhambra, many Jews fled to Portugal or to north Africa. Others settled in the Ottoman Empire, where they were welcomed by the sultan, who sarcastically thanked Ferdinand for sending him some of his most valuable subjects. A very considerable number ended up in northern Europe, particularly the Netherlands, England, and Scandinavia. The expulsion of the Jews was regarded inside Spain as a triumph for the Catholic religion, but the chief effect was to deprive the country of some of its most economically successful and important citizens. **SK**

Death of Lorenzo "The Magnificent"

Lorenzo de' Medici's demise signals the collapse of Florence's golden age and ushers in an era of turmoil and strife.

When Lorenzo de' Medici died on May 9, 1492, at the age of forty-three, his passing marked the last great phase of Florence's cultural leadership of the Italian Renaissance. Since the 1470s, Lorenzo de' Medici had kept a firm grip on Florence's power among Italy's cluster of city-states. A poet, aesthete, banker, and political fixer, he presided over a period of peace and high culture. He encouraged others to employ the city's artists, and both Leonardo da Vinci and Boccaccio enjoyed Lorenzo's largesse. He also opened a school for sculpture in his garden of San

> *"Ah, woe is me! / O grief, o grief! / Lightning has struck / our laurel tree."*
>
> **A. Poliziano, *Lament on Lorenzo's Death*, 1492**

Marco, where a fifteen-year-old pupil was brought up like a son of the family—Michelangelo.

At Lorenzo's deathbed stood Savonarola. This dogmatic monk vehemently opposed what he saw as the Church's obsession with worldly wealth. He thought this had been encouraged by the pragmatic patriarch Lorenzo. After Lorenzo's death, religious orthodoxy soon held sway thanks to Savonarola. Within two years Charles VIII, King of France, had invaded and the Palazzio Medici was sacked. One hundred years of art appreciation was vandalized in a matter of hours. After Lorenzo's death, the Italian states were plunged into fifty years of turmoil. **JJH**

⦿ Lorenzo the Magnificent, a detail from the frescoes (1459–1460) by Benozzo Gozzoli in the Palazzo Medici Riccardi.

Columbus Discovers America

Christopher Columbus does not realize that he has found a new continent.

○ A seventeenth-century republication of Theodor de Bry's *c.*1594 engraving of Christopher Columbus's discovery of America.

On Friday October 12, 1492, Christopher Columbus reached an island in the Bahamas, which he assumed to be part of Asia, and christened it San Salvador ("Holy Savior"). The voyage that led to the European conquest of the New World had begun in the Spanish port of Palos on August 3. Columbus, commissioned by the Spanish regime to "discover and acquire islands and mainlands in the Ocean Sea," had set out with 120 men in a flotilla of three small ships—the *Santa Maria*, the *Pinta*, and the *Niña*—to reach China and the Far East by sailing west.

Giving thanks to God, Columbus took possession of the land for Ferdinand and Isabella of Spain. Presently, natives of the island appeared, bringing gifts of cotton thread, parrots, and tobacco. Columbus traveled on to what are now Cuba and Haiti before returning to Palos the following March, where he was greeted with tremendous acclaim. His second voyage, later in 1493, with a fleet of twenty ships, took in more of the Caribbean.

To begin with, everyone in Europe shared Columbus's assumption that he had reached Asia, and it was not until the great navigator saw mainland Venezuela on the third of his voyages, in 1498 to 1500, that he began to wonder whether he might possibly have discovered a new continent. His last voyage, in 1502, took him to the Gulf of Mexico, but he failed to find a passage through to China and spent his last years in obscure retirement in Spain until his death in 1506 aged fifty-five. **RC**

"New World" Carved Up

The Treaty of Tordesillas divides up the largely undiscovered "New World."

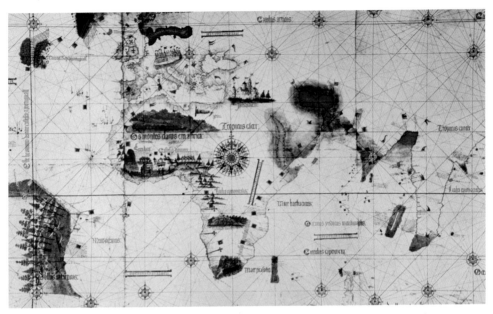

○ The first map showing the papal line of demarcation dividing New World discoveries between Spain and Portugal, 1502.

It was extraordinarily audacious in its scope and presumption: on June 7, 1494, the rights to the "New World" were divided up by an arbitrary line running from pole to pole through the Atlantic Ocean.

The catalyst had been Columbus and his big mouth. With neither tact nor diplomacy, Columbus taunted King João II for letting sponsorship of his epic voyage slip to his rivals Ferdinand and Isabella of Spain. Concerned that Spain might encroach on his African ambitions to secure a route to the Spice Islands, João hastily sent a fleet to the New World.

But he was outmaneuvered by Ferdinand and Isabella when, on May 3, 1493, Pope Alexander VI granted their request to secure Columbus's newly discovered lands and seas. The pope drew an imaginary boundary 100 leagues (300 miles, 480 km) west of the Cape Verde Islands and gave Spain sole rights to the land west of that line. João was furious but retaliated through diplomacy rather than war. He started talks with Ferdinand and Isabella to move the line an extra 270 leagues (810 miles, 1,296 km) west.

At the negotiations in Tordesillas, the Portuguese embassy included sailors and a cartographer, whereas Spain was represented by courtiers with little knowledge of the Atlantic. An agreement was made to tweak the line, which effectively safeguarded Portugal's African interests. Critically, however, the new division handed Brazil to Portugal. The "conspiracy theory" that the Portuguese had already discovered Brazil has never been proved. **JJH**

In Search of New Fishing Grounds

Labrador and Newfoundland are discovered by John Cabot.

○ A detail from *The Departure of John and Sebastian Cabot from Bristol,* by Ernest Board, 1906.

John Cabot sighted land in what is now Canada on June 24, 1497, somewhere near the opening of the Strait of Belle Isle between Labrador and Newfoundland. He claimed the land for England and Christianity. After a careful examination of the coast, Cabot sailed back to Bristol, where he was greeted by a customs official named Richard a Meyric—some Bristolians like to think America was named for him.

John Cabot was an expert sailor who seems to have met Columbus in Spain in 1493 and been inspired with transatlantic ambitions. He arrived in Bristol, England, a year or two later, and met merchants who were interested in transatlantic possibilities, particularly the discovery of new fishing grounds. King Henry VII authorized Cabot to find and conquer lands "of the heathen and infidels," previously "unknown to all Christians." After an abortive first effort, Cabot set out from Bristol on May 20, 1497, in the *Matthew* with a crew of around fifteen sailors.

Cabot had found fishing grounds for the Bristol merchants, but he believed he had reached northeast Asia. He set off on a second voyage in 1498 but was lost at sea and never returned. The memorial tower on top of Bristol's Brandon Hill commemorates him.

The Norwegian adventurer Leif Erikson had discovered North America from Greenland 500 years before and set up a short-lived settlement in Newfoundland, but Cabot's discovery was the first step on England's path to a key role in the history of Canada and North America. **RC**

Vasco da Gama Reaches India

The Portuguese break the lucrative Venetian monopoly on the spice trade.

🔵 *The Arrival of Vasco da Gama in Calcutta, 20th May 1498*, a sixteenth-century tapestry by the Flemish School.

On May 20, 1498, Vasco da Gama anchored at Calicut, a major port on India's southwest coast, having traveled northward from Malandi across the Indian Ocean. Nearly one year before, on July 8, 1497, da Gama had walked in solemn procession to the Lisbon docks with his crew of 170. He had been chosen by Portuguese king Manuel I to galvanize his men for the hardships of a long haul to reach India, establish friendly relations with Eastern rulers, and open the way for Portuguese missionaries and merchants.

St. Gabriel and its sister ship *St. Raphael* had been purpose-built for the expedition under Bartolemeu Dias's supervision. He had already navigated Africa's west coast, so he knew of the dangers. The ships also carried guns to defend against Muslim resistance.

Da Gama chose a wide tack to avoid adverse conditions and to pick up favorable currents. On November 4, 1497, he reached St. Helena Bay, about 160 miles (260 km) north of modern Cape Town. It was a remarkable navigation and by far the longest undertaken by European seamen out of sight of land. Heading up the uncharted east coast of Africa they passed a spot on Christmas Day they named Natal.

Da Gama's ships were then met by Muslim traders in all the harbors they visited. They were greeted variously with surprise, suspicion, and hostility. At Mozambique, gunfire was used to ensure safe passage. At Malandi, 50 miles (80 km) north of Mombasa, the sultan supplied the services of a pilot who showed them the rest of the way to India. **JJH**

Savonarola Pays the Price for His Zeal

Dominican friar and preacher Girolamo Savonarola is burned at the stake in Florence.

In 1497, Savonarola's passionate denunciation of worldly wealth and moral laxity had inspired the people of Florence to make a pile of all the ungodly goods they could lay their hands on—mirrors, pagan books, immoral sculptures, gaming pieces, luxurious robes, musical instruments—and set fire to them in the Piazza della Signoria. On May 23, 1498, it was the Dominican friar's turn to burn. He had sought to establish a Christian Commonwealth in Florence, but was found guilty of false prophecy and heresy. He was hanged in chains from a cross, with two of his closest associates beside him, and an enormous fire was lit beneath them, on the very spot where the "Bonfire of the Vanities" had previously blazed.

Savonarola's hellfire sermons had begun to attract a wide audience soon after his arrival in Florence in 1490. His attacks on corruption struck a chord with many people in the city who resented the political grip of the wealthy Medici family. In 1494, when Piero de' Medici was overthrown by the French, Savonarola became the guiding light behind the establishment of a Christian republic.

The spirit of millennialism was in the air with the approach of the year 1500, and at first the Florentine citizens responded enthusiastically to Savonarola's apocalyptic message of impending doom. They took to fasting and hymn singing, and willingly passed strict laws against vice and frivolity. But by 1497 they had begun to tire of Savonarola. The taverns reopened, and dancing and gambling began again in public. On April 8, 1498, a crowd attacked the friar within his convent of San Marco, and several people were killed. Savonarola surrendered himself to the religious authorities and was put on trial on the orders of Pope Alexander VI, who had been the target of his most vicious attacks. **SK**

○ A fifteenth-century bronze coin depicting Savonarola by Luca (1400–1482) and Ambrogio della Robbia.

○ *Savonarola Being Burnt at the Stake, Piazza della Signoria, Florence*, a sixteenth-century Italian School oil painting.

> ## "He is an infidel, a heretic, and as such has ceased to be pope."
>
> **Girolamo Savonarola about Pope Alexander VI**

Three panels of a series of twelve representing the months, painted in the sixteenth century by the Kano School, Japan.

1500–1699

Cabral Sails to Brazil

Mistaking it for a small island, Cabral claims Brazil for Portugal.

Pedro Alvares Cabral left Lisbon in March 1500 with 13 ships and 1,200 men, but was blown off course to the southwest in the Atlantic Ocean and arrived at the coast of Brazil near what is now known as Porto Seguro on April 23. It has long been suspected that there was more of an element of calculation involved than the Portuguese cared to admit, but there is no evidence of it.

Christopher Columbus had discovered mainland South America in 1498, and a Spanish expedition sailed to explore what is now Venezuela in 1499. In the same year, Vasco da Gama returned to Portugal from his epoch-making voyage to India. A follow-up expedition was mounted under the leadership of Cabral in 1500.

On landing in Brazil, Cabral thought he had arrived at an island, which he named Vera Cruz (True Cross). He dutifully held a religious service, erected a cross, and sent a swift ship back to Portugal to report his find. After staying for ten days, he left a handful of convicted criminals on shore (the ancestors of Brazil's *mestizo* population) and returned across the Atlantic to round the Cape of Good Hope and continue his expedition toward India.

Amerigo Vespucci claimed to have journeyed to South America in 1497, before Columbus, and discovered Brazil. He did go to Brazil on a Portuguese expedition, but not until 1501. The Portuguese government was rather slow to follow up on the discovery, as for a century the main export was hardwood. With the introduction of sugar plantations in the seventeenth century, the Brazilian economy grew and, with it, the importation of slaves from Africa, after which Brazil became a major possession in the New World. **RC**

New World Is Identified

Vespucci writes the earliest account of what lies beyond the Atlantic Ocean.

Amerigo Vespucci had a passion for geography that got him on board a series of Spanish expeditions to the New World between 1499 and 1502. In May 1501, his journey took him along the coast of what we now know as South America. His geographical knowledge was very sound and he surmised that the islands Columbus had seen in 1498 were in fact a continent—the New World—and not part of Asia. He outlined the vast size of the continent and suggested the Indies could be reached by sailing southwestward, pointing the way to a western passage to the East.

> ## "They live together without king, without government, and each is his own master."
> **Amerigo Vespucci**

It is not certain precisely how many voyages Vespucci undertook, but his explorations covered the greater part of the Atlantic coast of South America down to the Patagonian coast. His log and maps were supposedly lost, but a series of letters to friends Piero Soderini and Piero de' Medici describing his voyages were published. The assessment of the places seen from Vespucci's ship fired the imagination of the men of the Renaissance. Authorship of the published missives is disputed, but Vespucci certainly made the voyages and his name was attached to accounts of them—accounts that were later taken up by cartographer Martin Waldseemüller. In 1507, Waldseemüller produced a famous printed planosphere, which for the first time called the new hemisphere "America." **JJH**

Safavid Dynasty Takes Control of Persia

Shi'ite Muslim Ismail I proclaims himself shah of Persia and forces Persians to convert to his faith.

After centuries of conquest and rule by foreign invaders, a native Iranian dynasty, the Safavids, took control of Persia in 1501. The Ottoman Akkoynlu (White Sheep) dynasty was overthrown by the young Shah Ismail I.

Ismail hailed from the Azerbaijani town of Ardabil, but also drew support from the fierce Turkomen tribesmen of eastern Anatolia, known from the color of their turbans as *Qzilbashi* (redheads). After losing both his father and a brother as a child, he proclaimed himself shah in the town of Tabriz in 1501, while still a teenager. By 1510, after adopting the Farsi language, he had conquered all of present-day Iran, later adding modern Azerbaijan, Iraq, much of Afghanistan, and Anatolia to his domains. A devout Shi'ite Muslim, he forcibly converted most Persians to his faith, alarming his Sunni neighbors.

His conquests were checked at the Battle of Chaldiran in eastern Anatolia in 1514 when his Turkomen army was cut down by the Ottoman janissary cavalry and artillery of Sultan Selim I. Despite narrowly escaping capture in the defeat, which lost him Anatolia, Ismail continued his wars with the Ottomans and other Sunnis, defeating the Uzbek ruler Shaybani and converting his skull into a jeweled drinking goblet.

Although Ismael sank into melancholy in his later years, his dynasty continued to prosper. A later Safavid shah, Abbas I, moved the capital to Isfahan in the late sixteenth century. From there Abbas I presided over a magnificent renaissance in Persian Islamic art and architecture. **NJ**

◗ A sixteenth-century Persian painting entitled *A Princely Reception*, now in the Louvre, Paris, France.

Masterwork of Florentine Genius

Michelangelo's David *is displayed on the steps of the Palazzo Vecchio in Florence.*

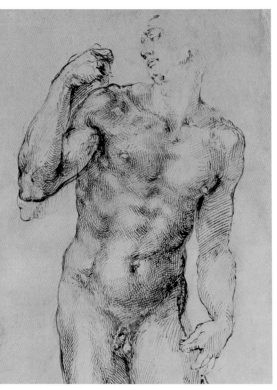

○ Detail from Michelangelo's *Sketch of David with His Sling*, drawn in 1503–1504.

○ Michelangelo's *David* is now housed in the Accademia in Florence; it has become a globally recognized icon.

"After seeing this no one need wish to look at any other sculpture...."

Giorgio Vasari, *Lives of the Artists,* **1550**

By September 8, 1504, Michelangelo had spent three years working on his masterpiece. The colossal statue of the naked David was originally meant for the cathedral in Florence, but it was decided instead to place it on the steps of the Palazzo Vecchio. It took forty men four days to haul the sculpture, on a special framework, from Michelangelo's workshop to this new position. At one point along the way, onlookers threw stones at the statue, presumably protesting against its pagan nudity (this was later hidden by a gilt-bronze belt). While the statue was being set up, Piero Soderini, the *gonfaloniere* (head of state) elected to rule Florence in 1502, told Michelangelo that the nose was too big. The sculptor immediately seized a chisel, climbed the scaffolding, and pretended to trim the offending organ.

Florentines had long regarded David, the biblical hero who slew the giant Goliath, as a symbol of their civic virtue. Michelangelo was only twenty-six years old when, in 1501, cathedral officials selected him over several better known and more experienced sculptors to create the statue. He sculpted it out of a 14-foot (4.2 m) block of Carrara marble that had been standing in the cathedral yard since the 1460s, originally intended for a giant statue for one of the apse buttresses of the cathedral.

What was amazing to contemporaries was that the artist worked without a full-size model as a guide, but drew directly on the face of the block of marble before carving it. He made his measurements purely by eye. The first nude to be carved on such a scale since antiquity, the *David* is simple and graceful despite its monumental size. Now housed inside Florence's Accademia gallery, it is considered to be one of the masterpieces not just of Renaissance art, but of all time. **SK**

Ceiling Designed to Inspire

Pope Julius II commissions Michelangelo to paint the Sistine Chapel ceiling.

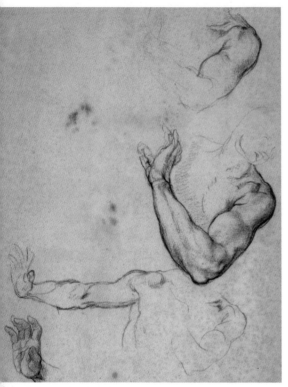

It was a job Michelangelo did not want. He had set his heart on sculpting Pope Julius II's tomb—a commission he had been given in 1505—and in any case he was not experienced in fresco technique. Would not the pope do better to ask another artist to paint the ceiling of the Sistine Chapel? But Pope Julius insisted that Michelangelo should accept the prestigious commission and on May 10, 1508, paid the artist an advance.

The original scheme was for twelve large figures of the Apostles, but Michelangelo complained that this design would be a "poor thing" and got the pope to agree to a more complex design consisting of nine panels along the center of the vault illustrating the Creation and the Fall of Man, and the promise of salvation through the chosen family of Noah. Where the original plan called for the twelve Apostles, Michelangelo inserted twelve prophets and sibyls predicting the arrival of the Messiah. In all, there are more than 300 figures on the completed design.

Michelangelo began the work in the winter of 1508 to 1509 and finished it in 1512. Contrary to popular belief, he did not paint the ceiling lying on his back, but stood on a platform that projected from the walls on brackets. It was cramped, painful work. Although he painted the most important figures himself, he had assistants to grind the colors and prepare the plaster for each day's *giornate* (section). As he became more confident with his painting, the brushwork became freer and more energetic, with bold sweeping outlines. Giorgio Vasari in his *Lives of the Artists* (1550) admiringly tells us that Michelangelo took just a single day to complete the figure of God reaching out to Adam. Today it is the ceiling's most iconic image and is reproduced on mouse pads and fridge magnets the world over. **SK**

○ Michelangelo's studies of Adam for the ceiling of the Sistine Chapel, which he completed in 1512.

○ A general view of the ceiling of the Sistine Chapel before its restoration in the 1980s.

"When it was uncovered everyone ... gazed in silent astonishment."

Giorgio Vasari, *Lives of the Artists*, 1550

Raphael Triumphs

Raphael completes his most famous fresco, The School of Athens.

The years around 1510 were artistically feverish ones in Rome: Donato Bramante, architect of the High Renaissance, was at work on the new basilica of St. Peter's; Michelangelo was busy with the ceiling of the Sistine Chapel; and Raffaello Sanzio—better known as "Raphael"—was decorating a suite of rooms in the Vatican, which included his fresco *The School of Athens*. The artists had been hired by Pope Julius II, who was a great patron of the arts.

Handsome, charming, and ambitious, Raphael had learned his art in Florence, where he was

"Here lies . . . Raphael by whom Nature feared to be outdone while he lived."

Epitaph, Raphael's tomb, The Pantheon, Rome

influenced by Leonardo da Vinci and Michelangelo. It was Bramante, however, who recommended him to Julius in 1508. The commission to decorate a suite of *stanze* (rooms) in the pope's private apartments was a turning point in Raphael's career. For the *stanza della segnatura* (room of the signatura), Julius had chosen the theme of celestial and earthly wisdom, and it is the latter that Raphael depicts in *The School of Athens*, a masterpiece of fresco painting that connects the pagan philosophers of antiquity with the Neoplatonism of Renaissance thought.

At the center of the composition are Plato and Aristotle. Plato is modeled on Leonardo, whom Raphael greatly admired, and he included portraits of himself and Michelangelo among the supporting cast of Greek and Roman philosophers. **TB**

Church Criticized

Humanist scholar Erasmus castigates the Church in Praise of Folly.

The Dutch scholar Desiderius Erasmus wrote the book for which he is most famous in the space of a week in 1509, when he was staying with the English statesman and fellow humanist Sir Thomas More, to whom the book is dedicated. Its Greek title *Moriae Encomium* is a pun on More's name (the Latin version, *Stultitiae Laus*, is usually translated as *Praise of Folly*). Written in Latin, it proved instantly popular on its publication in 1511, going into forty-three editions within Erasmus's lifetime. It is a satirical examination of the corrupt practices of the Roman Catholic Church, which prefigured the criticisms of the German reformer Martin Luther. Erasmus also wittily satirizes the folly of pedants, including himself, and concludes with a statement of his Christian faith.

Erasmus was the leading humanist scholar of his day. A former Augustinian monk, he had left the cloister, disillusioned with the rigid dogmatism of medieval scholasticism, to immerse himself in classical studies. In 1500 he published *Adagia* (Adages), a collection of proverbs and phrases that became a best seller. His growing friendship with More and other English humanists led him to spend several years in England, and it was there that he began work on his famous edition of the *Greek New Testament* (1516). His writings helped prepare the way for Luther's Reformation, and although he was originally sympathetic to Luther's views, describing him to Pope Leo X as "a mighty trumpet of Gospel truth," he regretted the break in Church unity. Later he was very critcal of Luther, and both Catholics and Protestants came to regard him with suspicion. **SK**

◯ An undated portrait by Quentin Metsys (c.1466–1530) entitled *Erasmus of Rotterdam*.

Spain Takes Cuba

Diego Velázquez founds settlements on the new Spanish conquest of Cuba.

By 1510 the Spanish had explored and discovered the Caribbean below Cuba, but the island itself and the Gulf of Mexico were still uncharted, as was the vast amphitheater of Mexico, North America, and Florida. Columbus had first landed on Cuba nearly twenty years before. In 1511 his brother Diego commissioned the conquest of the island.

Led by Diego Velázquez de Cuéllar and Hernán Cortés, a force sailed the 60 miles (100 km) across the Windward Passage from Hispaniola. They settled quickly on Asunción de Baracoa. The conquest proceeded relatively unhindered as the native Tainos' bows, arrows, and slings were no match against Spanish armor, archers, artillery, and lethal, long steel swords. Velázquez moved inland to Bayamo, where around one hundred Taino natives were slaughtered and the tribal leader was executed—thus setting the pattern of ruthless slaughter for conquest on the mainland. Some natives were befriended, but massacre was used as the quickest route to victory.

The formula for empire building was also established in Cuba. Plans for a settlement were drawn and the natives were assigned to the Spanish soldiers and landowners. The Indians were forced to pan for gold and to plant cassava, maize, sweet potatoes, and rice in return for religious instruction. It was slavery by any other name, even though the enslavement of Cuba's Indians was prohibited.

Sheep, pigs, cattle, and black slaves were also brought in, and the settlers sent for their wives. Ranching and mining were developed along with other commercial ventures including turtle farming and tobacco planting. As *adelantado* (governor), Velázquez went on to found Santiago de Cuba in 1514 and Havana in 1515. **JJH**

The Fountain of Youth

Ponce de León officially claims Florida for the Spanish crown.

The first Europeans to explore and colonize what is now the United States of America were the Spaniards, the English, the French, and the Dutch. In early 1513 Juan Ponce de León, a Spanish soldier who had sailed to the New World with Columbus in 1493 and made himself a fortune in Puerto Rico, fitted out three ships and sailed northwest from Puerto Rico. On March 27, he sighted land. He named it La Florida in honor of the day on which he landed—*Pascua de Flores* (the Spanish name for Easter Sunday). On April 2, Ponce de León landed a little north of present-day St. Augustine

> ## "It is cause for merriment, that Ponce de León went . . . to find the River Jordan."
>
> **Hernando Fontaneda, *Memoirs*, 1575**

and took formal possession of the territory for the Spanish crown. He then sailed off to explore part of the west coast, where he was repeatedly attacked by the inhabitants, before returning to Puerto Rico.

It seems that Ponce de León was looking for gold and slaves, but an apocryphal story grew that he had been searching for the fabled River Jordan or Fountain of Youth, which he hoped would cure his sexual impotence and restore his youth. In 1521 he set out for Florida from Puerto Rico again to found a settlement. He landed on the west coast, perhaps near Charlotte Harbor. But while he and his people were building houses, the local Calusa people attacked and Ponce de León was wounded with a poisoned arrow. The Spaniards fled to Havana in Cuba, where Ponce de León died of his wound. **RC**

Cut Down Like Flowers of the Forest

The Battle of Flodden, in which the Scots are routed and their king and many nobles killed, is the bloody climax of Anglo-Scots hostility.

With the loss of some 5,000 lives, the Battle of Flodden was one of the heaviest defeats the Scots ever suffered. It was said that the "Flower of Scotland" died that day in September 1513, including James IV himself and almost the entire Scots nobility.

Chronicler Edward Hall judged that Henry VIII was "ever desirous to serve Mars." Certainly the Scots were alarmed when he insisted on August 11, 1513, that he was "owner of Scotland." Yet Henry's priority was war with France, and he sent troops north as a defensive measure. Nevertheless, James IV took the offensive. A formidable 20,000-man army led by the Scots king forded the River Tweed and brought the English border castles into submission. On the evening of September 8, they took up position on Flodden Edge in Northumberland, overlooking the smaller English forces below. The Scots opened fire the following afternoon, launching stones that passed over the English heads. The smaller but more accurate English weapons caused considerable damage until the Earl of Huntly and Lord Home attacked the English right flank. At that point James joined the battle. Events were going the Scots' way, until Huntly and Home inexplicably withdrew. The battle was harsh and the Scots were trounced.

Henry was too preoccupied to follow up the victory, but he could rest assured that, with James V only eighteen months old and a shortage of nobles to form an opposition, there would be no further Scottish threat to England for a generation. **RP**

◐ This nineteenth-century painting romanticizes the battle, *News of Flodden, 1513* by William Brassey Hole (1846–1917).

◑ A sixteenth-century engraving of James IV of Scotland, who was killed at the Battle of Flodden.

First European Sighting of the Pacific

Balboa's discovery brings hope for a westward sea route to the East.

🜂 *Vasco Nunez de Balboa claiming the South Seas*, a colored copper engraving that dates back to 1513.

At the top of the hill above the thick forest, Vasco Nunez de Balboa surveyed the wide blue expanse of the Gulf of San Miguel. It was ten o'clock in the morning, and Spain's conquistador had just become the first European to set eyes on the Pacific Ocean.

Balboa had no idea of its expanse, but like many adventurers he reckoned it extended the whole length of western America's shores. He also guessed that the land they were on (modern-day Panama) was a thin strip of land and that an all-sea route to the East now lay within Spain's grasp. Wary of several powerful nobles he had upset, Balboa did not wait for official authorization. He set off with 190 Spanish troops in a brigatine and canoes, followed by hundreds of Indians. They landed at Acla, the narrowest part of the isthmus, and then hacked their way inland through humid, dense jungle, across wide river torrents and snake-infested swamps, fighting off tribal attacks as they went. It was an extraordinarily determined and brave trek.

Holding a royal banner and claiming possession of the Mar del Sur (South Sea) for "the mighty and powerful sovereigns Don Ferdinand and Dona Joanna...," Balboa walked knee-deep into the water. The survivors with him built a mound of stones and a makeshift cross, which they inscribed with King Ferdinand's name. A notary drew up a legal certificate of discovery with the names of those present, including an ex-swineherd, who would soon be a conquistador in his own right, Francisco Pizarro. **JJH**

Glory for Young French Monarch

King Francis I defeats the Swiss at the Battle of Marignano.

○ *The Battle of Marignano, 14th September 1515*, by Natale Datti.

When twenty-year-old Francis I acceded to the French throne in 1515, he brought fresh ambition to the court. Francis was a cultured humanist, destined to win renown as a patron of Renaissance artists such as Leonardo da Vinci and Benvenuto Cellini. But the young ruler was also eager to prove his worth on the battlefield. In the first summer of his reign, he led an army into Italy—crossing the Alps with some fifty heavy bronze cannon by a route previously considered impassable—and there, in the second week of September, took on the current champions of European warfare, the Swiss pikemen.

In alliance with Venice, Francis's aim was to wrest the prosperous duchy of Milan from Swiss control. After a long standoff, Swiss forces marched out of Milan and confronted Francis's army at the village of Marignano (or Melegnano). The battle was a savage, close-run affair. Determined charges by Swiss pikemen broke upon the implacable resistance of Francis's German mercenary foot soldiers, the *Landsknechts*, who hated the Swiss as their mortal foes. The French cannon cut down swaths of the enemy, and Francis led his armored knights in medieval-style charges with couched lance. The combat lasted twenty-four grueling hours. The turning point was the arrival, on the second morning, of mercenary cavalry somewhat tardily sent by Venice. Faced with these fresh forces, the Swiss quit the field and Francis basked in the glory of military triumph. **RG**

Charles of Habsburg Comes to Spanish Throne

Spain acquires a new, non-Spanish ruler and a troubled succession begins.

◑ *Charles V on Horseback* (1620) by the workshop of the Baroque master Antony van Dyck (1599–1641).

"So thin one can hardly believe it, pale, melancholy always with his mouth open."

Venetian courtier on Charles, Duke of Burgundy

Shortly after the death of his grandfather Ferdinand II on January 23, 1516, Charles succeeded to the Spanish throne. He had an impressive pedigree, and three years later he became Holy Roman Emperor. Charles, duke of Burgundy, was grandson of the Holy Roman Emperor Maximilian I and of the "Catholic kings" Ferdinand and Isabella I. He was pious, pale, and lanky, but nonetheless out-jousted a fellow duke over accusations that he liked effeminate music.

In 1504 the death of Isabella stripped Ferdinand of his joint ruler's title and Castile passed to Juana, their daughter. She was married to Archduke Philip of Burgundy, thus connecting the fate of Spain to the court of Burgundy. Courtly intrigue over rights of succession ensured negotiations between Philip and his father-in-law were tense. However, Ferdinand stepped down in favor of his "most beloved children." This might have been the end of it had Philip not suddenly died, leaving Juana as sole heir to the Spanish throne. Concerns over her mental health ensured her eldest son, Charles, was entitled to act as regent—although because he was a child, power was actually exercised by the archbishop Cisneros.

The young regent became a pawn in the hands of his Grand Chamberlain Chievres, who wrote to Cisneros when Ferdinand died, saying his services were no longer required. Not having any knowledge of Spanish affairs, Charles's accession hardly augured well and his government was little better than foreign rule. The courtiers lined their own pockets, giving rise to the witticism "Congratulations, double doubloon, on not falling into Chievres hands."

In 1518 Charles I became Holy Roman Emperor Charles V. His realms stretched from the Philippines to Peru and much of central and western Europe, but the troubled succession had only just started. **JJH**

Ottoman Empire Doubles in Size

Selim I takes control of the Arab world and enlarges the Ottoman Empire.

When the last Mamluk sharif of Mecca handed control over to the Ottoman sultan Selim I in July 1517, the size of the Ottoman Empire was doubled at a stroke. The acquisition of all of the lands of the old Islamic caliphate, with the exception of Iran and Mesopotamia, was of immense benefit to the Ottomans. By giving the Arab world an efficient administration, Istanbul was able to draw on wealth and resources that would solve the financial crises of the fifteenth century and enable the Ottomans to develop their empire into one of the richest and most powerful states of the sixteenth century.

In addition, by gaining control of the holy places of Islam such as Mecca, Selim I and his successors were able to promote the sultan as the most important ruler of the Islamic world and thereby gain access to the intellectual, artistic, and administrative legacy of the Islamic civilization. Furthermore, by taking control of territory previously under the control of the Mamluks, the Ottomans now controlled the old trade routes between Europe and the Far East.

With the power vacuum in the Middle East that had followed the demise of the Abbasid Empire filled, and the revenues of the Ottoman treasury doubled, it was Selim's successor, Suleiman I, who would reap the benefits of Selim's conquests. Suleiman came to be known as "the Magnificent," and during his reign, the Ottoman Empire was recognized as a major European power, entering into an alliance with France, England, and the Netherlands against the power of Habsburg Spain and Austria. However, after Suleiman's death in 1566, the Ottoman Empire came under pressure from the increasing naval superiority of Spain, culminating in defeat at the Battle of Lepanto in 1571. **TB**

○ *The Faithful Before the Kaaba in Mecca*, a sixteenth-century painting now in the Topkapi Palace, Istanbul, Turkey.

"God's might and Muhammad's miracles are my companions."

Suleiman the Magnificent, Inscription, 1538

Nailed to the Door at Wittenberg

Martin Luther's ninety-five theses spark the start of the Protestant Reformation.

○ A 1543 portrait of Martin Luther by Lucas Cranach the Elder (1472–1553), now in the Galleria degli Uffizi, Florence.

"We are looking forward to a new heaven and a new earth where justice will reign."

Martin Luther to Philipp Melanchthon, 1521

In 1517 Johann Tetzel, a Dominican friar, was on a fund-raising tour of Germany. The papacy needed money to pay for the rebuilding of St. Peter's, and Tetzel was using the well-tried device of selling indulgences—certificates that granted remission of time in purgatory for sins already forgiven. Martin Luther, an Augustinian monk and lecturer in the theology faculty of Wittenberg University, Saxony, was so enraged that he wrote to the archbishop of Mainz, Tetzel's superior, listing his objections. That same day, October 31, Luther is said to have posted the ninety-five theses, or statements, on the door of the castle church in Wittenberg for everyone to read. What particularly angered Luther was Tetzel's claim that "as soon as the coin in the coffer rings, the soul from purgatory springs."

Luther had previously given little indication of his growing disillusion with Church authority. He was a diligent scholar whose translation of the Bible helped to develop a standard version of German. His objections to indulgences seem to have formed during a visit he made to Rome in 1511. Here he was shocked to the core by the worldly depravity of the papal court. It is likely, though, that he was already formulating his ideas on "justification by faith" and the "priesthood of all believers" that would form the platform of his later theology.

Once his protest was made, Luther was quick to mobilize the comparatively new technology of the printing press. Within two weeks, printed copies of the *Ninety-Five Theses* were circulating throughout Germany and within two months throughout Europe. For Luther, and for the Church, there was no turning back. On May 25, 1521, the Emperor Charles V issued the Edict of Worms, which declared Martin Luther an outlaw. **SK**

Trade in Slaves Given Royal Seal of Approval

Holy Roman Emperor Charles V grants the first Asiento.

The official granting of the first *Asiento* in 1518 (the Spanish term means "agreement" or royal "assent") to license and approve the slave trade was one of the first major acts of the youthful Holy Roman Emperor Charles V upon coming to the Spanish throne. The *Asiento* gave monopoly powers to licensed merchants to abduct slaves in Africa and transport them across the south Atlantic to the labor-hungry Spanish colonies in Latin America and the Caribbean. The agreement marked the beginning of the inhumane transatlantic slave trade, and it did not take long for the merchants to set off to sea. The first recorded cargo of black slaves from Africa landed in the West Indies in the same year that the first *Asiento* was granted.

Charles V later withdrew his approval of the slave trade, passing laws banning it in 1542. He was influenced by Catholic missionary Bartolome de las Casas (1474–1566), who wrote vividly about the suffering of enslaved Indians in Spanish territories. However, the slave trade continued unabated.

Portuguese merchants bought slaves from dealers in the Upper Guinea and Sierra Leone regions of West Africa and shipped them to the Americas. After the Portuguese colony of Angola was established in 1575, the Portuguese governor, Benta Banha Cardoso, became notorious for profiting personally from his alliance with slavers—a practice that was continued by his successors. By the early seventeenth century, some 85 percent of slaves arriving in Spanish ports in the Americas were from Angola, shipped by the Portuguese.

The Portuguese resisted attempts by the Spanish to take direct control of the slave trade, but as Iberian power waned in the later seventeenth century, the trade became dominated by the new maritime powers, Britain and Holland. **NJ**

◐ A portrait of Charles V, the Holy Roman Emperor who fully sanctioned the slave trade—although he tried later to ban it.

> *"Each day the traders are kidnapping our people— children of this country."*
>
> **King Alfonso of Kongo to King João III, 1526**

Death of a Great Artist

Leonardo da Vinci, genius of the Renaissance, dies in the arms of King Francis I.

○ A contemplative self-portrait of Leonardo da Vinci as an elderly man (c.1515), drawn in red chalk.

○ A page from one of Leonardo's notebooks showing a design for a flying machine, with his notes in mirror-image script.

> ## "His spirit . . . passed away in the king's arms in the seventy-fifth year of his age."
>
> **Giorgio Vasari, *Lives of the Artists*, 1550**

At the end of his life Leonardo da Vinci became court painter to King Francis I of France, and it was in his residence, Clos Lucé, close to the king's summer palace at Amboise on the River Loire, that the greatest artist of the Renaissance period died on May 2, 1519. According to the story told by Giorgio Vasari in his *Lives of the Artists* (1550), the king himself supported the dying Leonardo in his arms.

Born in 1452 not far from Florence, Leonardo had been apprenticed at the age of eighteen to the Florentine artist Andrea del Verrocchio, from whom he received a well-rounded training in painting, sculpture, architecture, and design. From the beginning, Leonardo was deeply interested in technical matters, and in 1482 he wrote offering his services as a military engineer to Ludovic Sforza, duke of Milan. Only at the end of his letter did he mention that he also sculpted and painted. He remained in the duke's household until 1499 and painted his masterpiece mural of the *Last Supper* during this period. When Ludovic was expelled from Milan, Leonardo returned to Florence and completed his most famous easel painting, *Mona Lisa* (c.1504). He worked successfully for a time in Milan and Rome, and in 1515 he was commissioned to make a centerpiece in the shape of a mechanical lion for Francis I, whose service he entered the next year.

Vasari tells us that sixty beggars followed Leonardo's coffin to his final resting place in the chapel of Amboise. Leonardo's reputation was immense during his lifetime and has remained undiminished to this day. His restlessly inquiring mind and quest for understanding illuminated everything he drew and studied—from the articulation of his hands or the whorls of a flower to crossbows, cannon, and flying machines. **SK**

Luther in Debate

A disputation with Johann Eck helps transform Luther into a Protestant.

On June 26, 1519, in Leipzig, at the request of Pope Leo X, Dr. Johann Eck, professor of theology at the University of Ingolstadt, began a marathon, eighteen-day public debate with Martin Luther. Schism had to be prevented at all costs, and that meant Martin Luther had to be dealt with. Admittedly some humanists had dubbed Eck a "garrulous sophist," but few doubted his intelligence or debating skills. Had he not successfully defended the practice of money lending, much to the satisfaction of the Fugger banking dynasty, in 1514?

"He is learned. . . . A perfect forest of words and ideas stands at his command."

An observer at Leipzig describing Luther

The disputation ranged widely, from indulgences to grace, penance, purgatory, and the papacy. Eck was in no doubt that he had the better of the exchanges. He forced Luther to take his ideas to their logical conclusion and then branded him a heretic.

Luther's protests against indulgences, in his *Ninety-Five Theses* (1517), had been unwelcome. Many Catholics sympathized with the view that salvation could be earned only by penitence rather than by buying remission of sin. Luther was not beyond the doctrinal pale. He simply lacked the virtue of obedience. Yet the disputation with Eck helped to crystallize his ideas, especially that salvation was a matter of faith alone. The pope was convinced that Luther was a threat and in June 1520 issued a bull of excommunication. The Reformation had begun. **RP**

A Warm Welcome

Cortés and the Spaniards enter Tenochtitlan and meet Moctezuma.

The Spanish conquistador Hernan Cortés first met Aztec ruler Moctezuma at Tenochtitlan on November 8, 1519. The Spaniards had rapidly opened up the New World after Columbus's discoveries. They settled in the Caribbean and Panama and, from 1517, explored the shores of Yucatan. They were coming closer to the realm of the Aztecs, among whom it seems that word had spread that the long-departed god-king Quetzalcoatl, the Plumed Serpent, was making his return with a band of white-skinned companions to reclaim his throne. In 1519 a white conqueror did indeed arrive, from Cuba.

Cortés landed on the Mexican coast with a force of 500 soldiers and scuttled his ships to keep any of his followers from sailing away. The Aztec ruler Moctezuma sent offerings of gold and silver disks with jeweled and feathered ritual costumes appropriate for gods. Marching toward the Aztec capital, the intruders found a welcome among the Aztec peoples. Cortés got down from his horse to greet Moctezuma, but the Aztec nobles intervened before he could embrace the emperor. The Spaniard took off a necklace of pearls and fine Venetian glass and put it around Moctezuma's neck. The emperor responded by bestowing gold necklaces on Cortés. Then they walked together along the street to a palace that had been prepared for the Spaniards.

According to the Spanish account, Cortés told Moctezuma that he came in the name of the One True God and served a powerful king who ruled much of the world, and Moctezuma told Cortés that he was ready to be this king's vassal. However, Moctezuma was given little choice in the matter. His welcoming treatment of the Spaniard would soon lead to his death and the destruction of his empire. **RC**

Revolt of the Comuneros

Castile rebels against heavy taxation and declares a new type of government, setting the stage for popular revolutions to come.

In April 1520 the communities of Castile rose in rebellion against the heavy taxation being imposed on Spain by Charles V, the Holy Roman Emperor. The high expense of Charles's European adventures could not have come at a worse time for Castile. The area was suffering from poor harvests and the nobles were trying to reassert their influence after the reign of Queen Isabella I of Castile.

In 1520 Charles V left Spain to further his ambitions in Europe, leaving the country to be ruled under the regency of Charles's ally, Adrian of Utrecht, the future Pope Adrian VI. However, the high levels of taxation needed to fund Charles's campaigns incited a popular rebellion in Toledo. Other cities soon followed and a revolutionary *Cortes* (assembly) was set up as the legitimate government, thus deposing the Royal Council. The Castilian War of the Communities had started, a period often referred to as the "Revolt of the Comuneros." Attempts by Adrian to put down the revolution failed; as the unrest spread and the peasants began to join the rebellion, Adrian's army fell apart.

Charles was forced to take action in 1521 by appointing a co-regent who enjoyed the loyalty of the nobility. Despite a defeat by the Comuneros at Torrelobaton, Charles's army was victorious at the Battle of Villalar, and some of the revolutionary leaders were executed. One by one, the towns surrendered to the Imperial Army; the last to hold out was Toledo, where the revolution had started. **TB**

◐ Detail of a portrait of Pope Adrian VI painted in 1650. The original was by Jan van Scorel (1495–1562).

◖ *The Execution of Padilla and His Comuneros in Madrid 1521* (1860) by Antonio Gisbert Perez (1834–1901).

End of the Aztec Empire

The death of Moctezuma heralds the birth of the "New Spain."

○ *An Eagle Taking Moctezuma* by Theodor de Bry (1528–1598); it became very popular as an engraving in the seventeenth century.

Within a year of the arrival of Cortés in Tenochtitlan, the Aztec emperor Moctezuma was dead. The Spaniards took him prisoner soon after their arrival and persuaded him to declare himself a vassal of the king of Spain. He tried to calm the rising anger of many Aztec lords, but his palace was attacked. Moctezuma went up to the palace roof and called for calm. His brother Cuitlahuac was chosen as the new emperor, but the attack was renewed. Moctezuma went to the roof again, but this time he was greeted with volleys of stones and arrows. He was taken inside but died on May 30, 1520, whether as a result of the attack or killed by the Spaniards is uncertain.

Fearing repercussions, Cortés and his men crept away from Tenochtitlan in the dead of night. The Aztecs followed them and killed many, but Cortés was not a man easily daunted. He and his remaining men reached safety in the town of Tlaxcala, where he recruited willing allies among the subject peoples of the Aztec Empire and led thousands of their warriors to besiege Tenochtitlan. His allies did not realize that they were aiding in their own eventual subjection to the Spaniards, and after three months, in August 1521, the defenders of Tenochtitlan surrendered.

The whole Aztec Empire collapsed into Spanish hands and in the following year Cortés was appointed governor of New Spain. Immigrants flocked in from the Caribbean and from Spain itself to make Mexico the leading Spanish center in the New World, subsequently joined by Peru. **RC**

Luther Accused of Heresy by Charles V

Martin Luther stands by the contents of his writings at the Diet of Worms.

○ *Luther at the Diet of Worms* (1872) painted by German artist Paul Thumann (1834–1908).

The confrontation between Holy Roman Emperor Charles V, only twenty-one years old but already aware of his responsibilities as the leading Catholic monarch of Europe, and Luther was inevitable once the reforming monk had taken the irrevocable step of burning the pope's bull of excommunication in December 1520. Luther was ordered to appear before the imperial diet (general assembly) at Worms to answer charges of heresy, under promise of safe conduct from the elector Frederick III of Saxony.

April 17, 1521, saw Luther standing before a table spread with copies of his writings. He was asked if the books were his and whether he stood by their contents. He confirmed he was the author but asked for time to reflect upon his answer to the second question. Next day he said he could retract nothing, "since it is neither safe nor honorable to act against conscience," but there is some doubt as to whether he actually uttered the famous statement: "Here I stand. I can do no other. God help me. Amen."

Charles V formally declared Luther an outlaw and ordered his arrest "as a notorious heretic." It was the opening shot in his war on Protestantism. Frederick of Saxony arranged that Luther should be seized and hidden, for his own protection, in his castle of Wartburg at Eisenach. Luther remained there in secret for nearly a year, during which time he began the work of translating the New Testament into German so that the message of the Bible would be available to all. **SK**

Magellan Killed

Portuguese explorer Ferdinand Magellan is killed in battle in the Philippines.

Although he is often credited with the feat, Ferdinand Magellan was not the first person to circumnavigate the globe. He actually died halfway around.

Magellan did not intend to circle the earth when his five ships and 250 men set sail from Spain on September 20, 1520; the mission entrusted to him by the king of Spain was to find a closer western trade route to the profitable Spice Islands in what is now Indonesia. But after rounding Cape Horn, Magellan's men found themselves in the vast expanse of the Pacific. Arriving in the Philippines with his crew

"They killed our mirror, our light, our comforter and our true guide."

Antonio Pigafetta, contemporary journal

reduced to 150, the forceful mariner persuaded a local ruler, Rajah Huambon, to adopt Christianity and become a subject of Spain. In return Magellan agreed to lead an attack on Huambon's enemy Lapu-Lapu, ruler of the neighboring island of Mactan.

Coral reefs prevented Magellan from bringing his cannons to bear, and when he led fifty of his men through the shallows, they came under attack from an army of 1,500 armed with bamboo spears and poisoned arrows. Losing his helmet, Magellan was speared and hacked to death.

With Magellan dead, Juan Sebastian Elcano assumed command and, losing more men to storms and starvation, rounded the Cape of Good Hope with only rice to eat, returning with just eighteen men to Spain two years after their departure. **NJ**

Chivalrous Ending

The Knights of St. John are politely driven out of Rhodes by Suleiman.

On the evening of New Year's Day, 1523, some 163 Knights of the Order of St. John, led by their Grand Master Philippe Villiers de L'Isle-Adam, marched out of their fortress at Rhodes in full armor, banners flying and drums beating. Watching them were Ottoman Sultan Suleiman I and his army, who had fought for five hard months to evict the Christian soldiers from their Mediterranean island base. Accompanied by ordinary soldiers and by civilians who preferred exile to Turkish rule, the knights embarked on fifty ships provided by the sultan and sailed for Crete.

The Knights of St. John (or Hospitallers) were one of the military monastic orders established in Palestine during the Crusades, dedicated to holy war against Islam. They had made Rhodes their home after Palestine fell to the Muslims in 1291 and had held out on the island for more than 200 years. But in 1522 Suleiman decided their presence in his home waters could no longer be tolerated. He landed on the island in late July with an army of more than 100,000 men. His cannons battered the walls; his sappers tunneled underneath them and blew them up; his janissaries stormed any breaches. By December the defenders were still fighting, whereas Suleiman's forces groaned with wounds and disease.

The siege ended not in an orgy of violence, but in an outbreak of chivalry and good sense. The sultan and the Grand Master established a relationship of trust and negotiated a deal for the surrender of the fortress that left Christian lives, property, and honor intact. Suleiman would live to regret his generosity to the Hospitallers, who, following a period of political uncertainty, established a new base in Malta in 1530 and went on to inflict a major defeat upon his besieging forces there in 1565, late in his reign. **RG**

Sweden Elects New King

Gustav Eriksson becomes King Gustav I of Sweden and swiftly unifies the country, laying the foundations of both Swedish Protestantism and the modern state.

Gustav Eriksson finally managed to eject the Danes from his country in 1521. In return, he was proclaimed regent and on June 6, 1523 he was elected king. On June 24, the relatively unknown King Gustav I marched into Stockholm in triumph.

Legend has it that while leading the Swedish campaign against Denmark, the young Gustav hid on a farm from Danish soldiers. Fearing the Swede might be discovered, the lady of the house managed to divert the attention of the Danes by beating Gustav with a bakery spade as if scolding a useless farmhand. The Danish soldiers were so diverted by the spectacle that they failed to recognize the cowering farmhand as the man they were seeking.

Scholars later referred to Gustav as Gustavus Vasa, with the second part of his name being that of his family. Some have labeled Gustav a tyrant, but others see him as a liberator. However, there is general agreement that, as the first truly authoritative ruler of Sweden, Gustav laid the foundations for a stable, centralized Swedish state, and that by forming Sweden's first professional army Gustav created the conditions that would enable Sweden to become a regional power in the seventeenth century.

Gustav's legacy does not end there. The king soon came into conflict with the papacy over his intention to select his own archbishop, since Gustav Trolle, the papal choice, was thought to be a Danish sympathizer. Despite the protests of Rome, Gustav appointed Laurentius Petri, the brother of a Lutheran scholar. Gustav had therefore set in motion the events by which Sweden would adopt Protestantism. **TB**

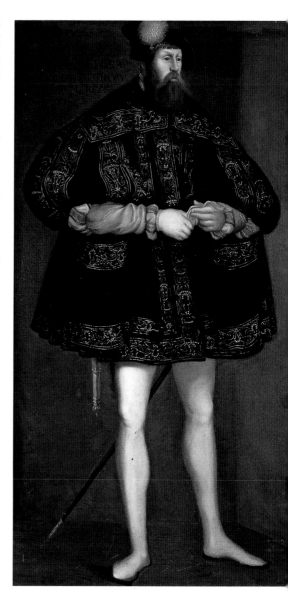

○ A portrait of Gustav I, painted in 1542 by an unknown artist, now in Kalmer Castle in Sweden.

Disaster for France at Pavia

Francis I is taken prisoner as his army succumbs to the forces of Charles V.

◐ A detail from an imperial tapestry from Brussels showing Francis I's Swiss mercenaries trying to flee the battle (c.1530).

> ## "All is lost to me save honor and life, which is safe...."
>
> **King Francis I to his mother, Louise of Savoy**

French King Francis I returned from Italy bathed in glory after a military victory at Marignano in 1515. Ten years later, on February 24, another Italian battlefield at Pavia was the scene of his defeat and humiliation. Between those dates, the power balance in Europe had shifted decisively when the Habsburg king Charles I of Spain had linked the impressive resources of his realm to those of the Holy Roman Empire, which he ruled from 1519 as Emperor Charles V.

In October 1524, at war with the empire, Francis laid siege to Pavia. The emperor sent an army to relieve the siege and the opposing forces dug in outside the city, facing one another across a stream. On the night of February 23, 1525, the imperial army crossed the stream under cover of darkness. After daybreak, a chaotic combat was joined. Early morning fog added to the confusion as the French struggled to organize a response to the unexpected onslaught. Francis led mounted charges by his armored knights, even though this blocked his artillery's field of fire. German *Landsknecht* mercenary foot soldiers fought on both sides, laying into one another with exceptional ferocity. The French nobility suffered severe losses, including the veteran knight Louis II de la Trémouille, killed by a ball from an arquebus—a primitive handgun. After four hours the French were beaten, although their *Landsknecht* "Black Band" fought on until virtually exterminated.

King Francis was surrounded and taken prisoner on the battlefield. He was carried off to Madrid, where the hardships of captivity brought him close to death. The emperor released him in January 1526 after Francis signed a treaty ceding large amounts of territory. Francis renounced the treaty once free, and the struggle between France and the Holy Roman Empire was resumed. **RG**

German Revolt Put Down

The popular uprising known as the Peasants' War ends with a crushing defeat.

On May 15, 1525, the Peasants' War suffered a huge defeat at Frankenhausen, resulting in the capture and execution of Anabaptist leader Thomas Muntzer. The revolt came to an end as cities and nobles brokered their own separate peace terms with the Holy Roman Emperor, Charles V.

In 1524, rebellion had broken out in Germany and spread into parts of what is now Switzerland and Austria. The revolt was the largest popular uprising until the French Revolution of 1789 and involved all sections of society from the nobility to the peasantry. Known as the Peasants' War, it involved an estimated 300,000 people and resulted in 100,000 deaths. Thomas Muntzer became one of its leaders as economic distress and religious fervor quickly developed into a revolt against feudalism, aligned behind a list of grievances called the Twelve Articles of the Black Forest.

The causes of the revolt were rooted in the social, religious, and economic factors affecting the steadily rising population. The favorable living conditions of the peasantry at the end of the fifteenth century were gradually eroded by the rising prices of food and wool during the early sixteenth century and by a drop in incomes. In addition, the harsh living conditions were made even worse when landlords increased rents to preserve their living standards.

However, religious factors may also have played a part, particularly the challenge to religious authority posed by a group known as the Anabaptists. Crucially, Muntzer, a leader of the Anabaptist movement, had traveled widely during 1524, proclaiming his radical doctrines with growing success among the lower orders of society. Muntzer's challenge to the authority of the Church and State even attracted the criticism of the Protestant reformer Martin Luther. **TB**

◐ A chalk lithograph depicting a scene from the Battle of Frankenhausen, created *c.*1861.

"[R]emember that nothing can be more poisonous . . . or devilish than a rebel."

Martin Luther, May 1525

Mughals Defeat the Lodi Sultanate

Babur's victory at the Battle of Panipat founds the Mughal Empire.

○ *Battle of Panipat 1526 (c.1590) by Deo Gujurati (fl.1590), a book illumination now housed at the British Library, London.*

"[Khalifas found] Ibrahim's body amid many corpses and brought me his head."

Babur, *Journal of Emperor Babur*

In April 1526, the Mughal leader, Babur, advanced on Delhi with a 15,000-strong army, including nomad horse archers and Ottoman Turk artillerymen with about twenty cannons (unknown in India at the time). To oppose him, Sultan Ibrahim Shah Lodi fielded an army of 40,000 and 100 war elephants, but no artillery.

Driven from their homeland in Ferghana, Central Asia, by the Uzbeks in 1501, the Mughals (so-called because they claimed Mongol descent) had migrated east under the leadership of Babur and founded a new principality at Kabul in 1504. In 1515, Babur began a series of raids into northern India, then under the rule of the Lodi sultanate of Delhi. When the Punjab rebelled against Sultan Ibrahim, Babur took the opportunity to seize Lahore. He was soon driven out, but in 1525 returned in greater strength and conquered the whole Punjab.

Babur was outnumbered and prepared a defensive position at Panipat, north of Delhi, using his baggage carts. In gaps between the carts, Babur placed his Ottoman cannons, stretching chains between them so they could not easily be overrun by a cavalry charge. After a standoff lasting several days, Ibrahim, leading from the front, attacked at dawn on April 20. Babur's cannons proved decisive— they panicked Ibrahim's elephants into flight, trampling and disorganizing his army as they ran. Babur's cavalry then attacked from the flanks, winning a complete victory. Ibrahim and more than 15,000 of his soldiers died in the battle. Although Mughal losses were also heavy, Babur managed to capture Delhi a week later, thereby founding the Mughal Empire that would dominate India for 200 years. Babur celebrated his victory at Agra, where he was presented with the famous Koh-i-noor diamond, which is now part of the British crown jewels. **JH**

Hungary Loses Independence

King Louis II is defeated by Sultan Suleiman at the Battle of Mohacs.

On August 29, 1526, a small town just 115 miles (185 km) from Budapest was the site of a battle between the forces of King Louis II and the Ottoman Sultan Suleiman the Magnificent. At stake was the independence of Hungary and, arguably, the future direction of Europe. The battle was bitterly fought and, despite early successes in which the Hungarian archers nearly killed the sultan, the Hungarian forces were steadily worn down by a counterattack of the Sultan's elite soldiers, the janissaries. By twilight, what was left of the Hungarian army was surrounded and captured. As King Louis fled the battlefield, he was thrown from his horse and killed. After the battle, the sultan ordered that all 2,000 of the Hungarian prisoners be killed. Among the prisoners who died were many members of the Hungarian nobility.

Defeat was a disaster for Hungary and resulted in the country's partition and the effective end of Hungary as an independent kingdom. The immediate aftermath of the battle was the division of Hungary between the Ottoman Empire, the Habsburgs of Austria, and the principality of Transylvania. Over the decades that followed, this division of Hungary between the eastern-aligned Ottoman Empire and the western-aligned Austrian monarchy saw many battles. Bohemia and Croatia fell to Austria, but the Ottoman Empire managed to retain control over central Hungary and Transylvania. However, the wars between the Habsburg and Ottoman empires continued for more than two centuries, devastating the Hungarian countryside and population.

Mohacs is seen by Hungarians as a national trauma and the lowest point of their nation's history. The defeat is so deep-rooted that, in moments of personal tragedy, many Hungarians still refer to it, in such ways as "more was lost at Mohacs." **TB**

◆ A sixteenth-century illuminated manuscript depicting Suleiman the Magnificent at the battle of Mohacs.

> ## *"I am Suleiman . . . I seized the Hungarian crown and gave it to the least of my slaves . . . "*
>
> **Suleiman the Magnificent, inscription**

Sack of Rome Brings Shame on Charles V

Soldiers show no mercy as they pillage and murder during a three-day rampage.

○ *The Sack of Rome in 1527* by Dutch painter Johannes Lingelbach (1622–1674).

The capture and sacking of Rome in 1527 by a mutinous imperial army, with Pope Clement VII fleeing for his life down a secret Vatican passage to take refuge in the Castel Sant'Angelo, was an event that shocked Europe and shamed Emperor Charles V.

The duke of Bourbon led the German, Spanish, and Italian army, which was in Italy to see off the League of Cognac, an anti-imperial alliance led by France and the papacy. In April 1527, with their pay in arrears, the troops mutinied and advanced on Rome. The German *Landsknechts* (mercenary foot soldiers) led the attack, many of them Lutherans who relished the thought of plundering the corrupt papal city.

It was the Swiss Guards, the pope's personal bodyguards, who enabled Pope Clement to escape—only forty-two out of nearly 200 guards survived as the imperial troops stormed the Vatican on May 6. Churches, monasteries, and palaces were pillaged, cardinals and prelates attacked, and nuns raped during three days of rampage and murder. The troops did not withdraw until June 6, when Pope Clement agreed to pay a ransom of 400,000 ducats.

Although the sack was condemned by Charles V and beyond his control, few lamented the predicament of the weak Clement VII, the last Renaissance prince-pope. He remained Charles's prisoner for some months and, once free, ceased all opposition to the empire. In 1530, he crowned Charles in Bologna, the last time in history a pope crowned the Holy Roman Emperor. **SK**

Siege of Vienna Is Broken

Austrian resistance marks the end of the Ottoman expansion into Europe.

⬤ A detail of the frescoes (c.1540) attributed to Marcello Fogolino depicting the siege of Vienna by Turkish troops.

The siege of Vienna ended in 1529 and was the climax of Ottoman incursions into Europe. Rivalry between King Francis I of France and Holy Roman Emperor Charles V had weakened sixteenth-century Europe. Ottoman Sultan Suleiman I "the Magnificent" had taken advantage of the divisions to capture Buda and make Hungary a vassal state. Alarmed, Archduke Ferdinand of Austria encouraged a Hungarian revolt in 1528, while Suleiman was in Persia.

In 1529 Suleiman led his armies from Constantinople to Ferdinand's capital, Vienna, where commander Graf Nicholas zu Salm-Reifferscheidt hastily repaired the city's walls. The Austrians had a force of 22,000 infantry, 2,000 cavalry, and 72 cannons. The Ottomans numbering some 350,000 men arrived at Vienna on September 26, but abandoned their siege guns, bogged down along the muddy roads. The Turks laid mines under the walls and Austrian pikemen beat back the attacks of the janissaries—Turkish cavalry composed of Christian converts sold into slavery and trained as a sacrificial warrior elite. On October 14, having lost 20,000 troops, Suleiman ordered a final push. But a massive mine collapsed the wall outward, blocking the attackers' path. The assault was over. Graf Salm was wounded (dying the following year); the Turks burned all they could, including captives, and left.

The Ottomans failed to invade Vienna again in a siege of 1683, after which their empire entered its long and inexorable decline. **NJ**

Henry VIII Remarries

King of England marries Anne Boleyn in defiance of the pope and Rome.

The marriage of Henry VIII to Anne Boleyn in 1533, the maid of honor who had first caught his eye at a masquerade ball, took place six years after Henry had appealed to Pope Clement VII to annul his 1509 marriage to Catherine of Aragon. Henry claimed that their relationship was contrary to divine law. In truth, he was tired of the forty-year-old Catherine, who would never bear him a son and heir (their only child, Mary, had been born in 1516). It was Henry's misfortune that his request to the pope was just after the sack of Rome. Clement VII did not dare offend

"My Mistress and Friend ... the pang of absence is already too great."

Henry VIII, Letter to Anne Boleyn, 1528

Charles V—Catherine of Aragon's nephew. The answer was no. For three years Henry fruitlessly pursued legal ways of achieving "the King's great matter" as the divorce became known, growing determined to marry Anne. Finally, Henry tried a new tack—if Rome would not give him what he wanted, the Church of England should separate from Rome.

Thus he married Anne, in open defiance of the pope, and in May Archbishop Cranmer declared his first marriage null and void. Anne was crowned queen, also in May, and in September bore Henry a daughter, Elizabeth. In 1534 the Act of Supremacy declared that the king was "the only Supreme Head on Earth of the Church of England." The consequences of Henry divorcing Catherine of Aragon had proved more revolutionary than originally intended. **SK**

Atahualpa Is Executed

The removal of the Inca king leaves South America open for Spain.

The Inca emperor Atahualpa would have been burned alive as a heretic in 1533, but a last-minute conversion to Christianity had him throttled instead. Atahualpa had succeeded his father in 1525 to the vast, and vastly wealthy, Inca empire, which dominated Peru, after fighting a war against his half-brother Huascar. He then had all of Huascar's family killed. In 1532 his nemesis appeared in the form of the Spanish adventurer Francisco Pizarro and his men. Although he had a huge army, Atahualpa did not attack the small Spanish force. Instead he sent them gifts and

"He kept repeating, 'Why are they killing me? ... What have I done ... ?'"

Pedro Cieza de Leon, *Chronicles of Peru*, 1553

let them take possession of the town of Cajamarca. He then accepted Pizarro's invitation to visit Cajamarca. Most of Pizarro's men, armed to the teeth, were concealed in ambush. A Spanish priest there told the Inca his people must convert to Christianity and gave him a Bible, which Atahualpa threw away.

At this heretic act, Pizzaro's men sprang from their hiding places, killing many and taking Atahualpa himself prisoner. The Inca army did nothing, and Pizarro demanded an enormous ransom from his captive, who ordered a room to be filled once with gold and twice with silver for the Spaniards. The treasure duly arrived, but Pizarro still had Atahualpa executed. The way was now open for the entire Inca Empire and much of South America to be brought under Spanish control. **RC**

Society of Jesus Is Founded

Ignatius Loyola and six companions take vows in Paris that will lead to the establishment of the Jesuits, a weapon of the Counter-Reformation.

Seven friends, students of theology at the University of Paris, founded the Company of Jesus, soon to be called the Society of Jesus, in August 1534 while on a retreat. Their leader, Ignatius Loyola, was a Basque and former soldier who had experienced a religious conversion while recovering from a battle wound. After a year's retirement at Manresa, near Barcelona, he had devoted himself to a life of study and teaching, which had brought him to Paris. Praying together, the friends took solemn vows of poverty and celibacy, in imitation of Christ, and pledged to go to Jerusalem to convert the Muslim infidels. But in Venice they were unable to find a ship to take them to Palestine, so they went to Rome and placed themselves in obedience to the pope.

Ignatius drafted a constitution in Rome in 1539 for the religious order, and it was approved by Pope Paul III on September 27, 1540, although he stipulated that members should not exceed sixty in number. The Society of Jesus was established as a missionary order, ready to go wherever the pope demanded "among the Turks, to the New Worlds, to the Lutherans or any manner or believers or unbelievers," as Ignatius wrote.

In 1548, Ignatius opened a school in Messina in Sicily for lay students, and education became one of the order's most important activities. Its emphasis on dedication and obedience made it effective in training young minds for Catholicism, and Jesuit schools would come to play a key role in the Counter-Reformation's recovery of ground lost to Protestantism, especially in the Low Countries and Poland. **SK**

⊙ *Saint Ignatius of Loyola Receiving the Bull of the Order of Jesuits from Pope Paul III* (detail), by Juan de Valdes Leal (1622–1690).

Ex-Papal Powers Conferred on Henry VIII

The Act of Supremacy confirms the monarch as head of the Church of England.

○ *Henry VIII Introducing Anne Boleyn at Court*, by William Hogarth (1697–1764).

"The king ... shall be taken, ... the only supreme head of the Church of England."

Act of Supremacy, 1534

How should the vacuum left by the removal from England of the pope (now merely "the bishop of Rome") be filled? Should the new Church of England govern itself? Certainly many clergy thought that laymen could not possibly exercise control. But Henry VIII had other ideas. There was only one place for ex-papal powers to reside and that was with the Crown. The Act of Supremacy, passed in November 1534, made it clear that the monarch was the "supreme head" of the English Church.

There was a potential problem, however, for what parliament gave, parliament could surely take away. Would the means Henry used to establish his supremacy actually undermine it, so that in effect it was shared with the House of Lords and the House of Commons? Henry was aware of the pitfall. The Act insisted that the king was "justly and rightly" the supreme head of the Church, so that by implication the position was God-given—all the new law did was "corroborate and confirm" what was already the case. Henry would brook no rival.

In 1521, Leo X had conferred on Henry the title "defender of the faith," and he might well have remained loyal to the papacy if Pope Clement VII had been able to grant him a divorce. It was "the King's great matter" that led to the breach with Rome and the declaration of royal supremacy. That further change occurred was not what Henry intended.

Henry was no Protestant, but his uncoupling of the English Church from Rome undoubtedly boosted the chances of the reformers. After his death, his son officially made England a Protestant nation. Similarly his extensive use of the "Reformation Parliament" made that institution far more important, though not yet dominant, in English politics—despite the repealing of the Act by Mary in 1554. **RP**

"New Jerusalem" Is No More

The bloody defeat of the Anabaptists of Münster spells the end of their regime.

After eighteen months in control of the city of Münster, Westphalia, the Anabaptists—radical believers who held that only confessing adults could be baptized—were ousted on June 24, 1535.

A number of Anabaptist groups had emerged in Germany and Switzerland in the 1520s and faced frequent persecution. Melchior Hoffman was a fanatical Anabaptist preacher whose prophetic message proclaiming the speedy approach of the Day of Judgment attracted large numbers of followers, two of whom—Jan Matthys, a baker from Amsterdam, and Jan Bockelson (John of Leyden)—spread his ideas to Münster, which they declared to be the New Jerusalem. Under their influence, the council there ordered that no unbaptized adults should remain in the city, leading to mass baptisms in the marketplace. Meanwhile, a combined army of Catholics and Lutherans, led by the expelled bishop, laid siege to the city.

On Easter Sunday 1534, Matthys, believing himself to be a second Gideon sent to slay the enemies of Israel, led a sally outside the city walls but was immediately cut down, whereupon Bockelson proclaimed himself king. He legalized polygamy and declared all goods to be held in common—a necessary step, as food was running short. The end of his reign, a year later, was sudden and savage. The city was overtaken by treachery and virtually no man escaped the slaughter. Bockelson and other leaders were executed—the iron cages in which their corpses were displayed to the public are still hanging on the tower of St. Lambert's church. Accounts of the uprising caused a wave of horror throughout Europe, and it has been estimated that no fewer than 30,000 Anabaptists in the Netherlands alone were put to death in the ten years after the fall of Münster. **SK**

◐ An 1890 print of Jan Bockelson being led through Münster in an iron cage before his execution.

> *"That infant baptism is a silly, blasphemous outrage, contrary to all Scripture."*
>
> **Conrad Grebel, leader of Zürich Anabaptists**

Thomas More Executed at Tower of London

Thomas More chooses death over Henry VIII's new religious dispensation.

O A late sixteenth-century copy of the 1527 portrait
of Thomas More by Hans Holbein the Younger.

> **"We would rather have lost the best city . . . than such a worthy councillor."**
>
> **Emperor Charles V, on More's execution**

He was one of the most distinguished men of his age and had been one of the most powerful in England. Now, stripped of high office and of his freedom, Thomas More had little left beside high principles and unusual courage. On Monday July 5, 1535, he wrote to his daughter that he longed "to go to God." The following morning, mounting the rickety scaffold outside the Tower of London just before 9 A.M., he joked that the master lieutenant should see him safely up, but "for my coming down let me shift for myself." Then he urged the executioner to "pluck up" his spirits and to do his work without fear, although he should "strike not awry" for his neck was "very short." The king had urged him not to use many words at his execution and he refrained from doing so. His last wry words, as he pulled aside his beard before putting his head on the block were, "This hath not offended the king." Like Shakespeare's Thane of Cawdor, Thomas More seemed to "throw away the dearest thing he owed as 'twere a careless trifle."

As well as being a successful lawyer, renowned humanist, and learned theologian, More had been in royal service since 1518, becoming lord chancellor in 1529. He resigned in May 1532, unable to accept or endorse Henry's resolve to divorce Catherine of Aragon. But it was his refusal to swear an oath accepting the royal, rather than the papal, supremacy of the Church that sealed his fate. Henry VIII's determination to govern the Church of England soon opened the way to the Protestantism that he, and of course More, had found anathema. As for More, he became the archetypal martyr for his conscience. In 1935 he was canonized.

The story of Thomas More is told in *A Man for All Seasons*, a play by Robert Bolt that has been filmed twice, in 1966 and 1988. **JJH**

Anne Boleyn Executed

Henry VIII's queen Anne Boleyn goes to the scaffold on trumped-up charges.

Wearing a red petticoat under a loose, dark-gray damask gown, Anne Boleyn made her way to the scaffold on Tower Green. When she was informed that Henry VIII had commuted her sentence from burning to beheading with a sword, she is supposed to have joked that the executioner would not have much trouble, "for I have a little neck." The execution was swift, accomplished with a single stroke.

On January 29, three years almost to the day after her marriage to Henry VIII, Anne had miscarried a son—one of several unsuccessful pregnancies she is known to have endured. Henry's affections had already turned to Jane Seymour, Anne's lady-in-waiting, and from then on he engineered Anne's downfall. At the end of April, a Flemish musician, Mark Smeaton, was arrested and confessed under torture to being Anne's lover. Other arrests followed, including Anne's brother George Boleyn, and on May 2, Anne herself was seized and taken prisoner to the Tower of London, charged with adultery, incest, witchcraft, and high treason. Eleven days after her execution, Henry married Jane Seymour.

Opinion is still greatly divided about Anne Boleyn. For many people she is an innocent and simply the victim of a king's inconstancy. But many others argue that, even before her marriage, she was a secret supporter of Protestantism, in touch with many English radical reformers in Europe, and was the guiding force behind Henry's break with Rome. Her daughter Elizabeth, brought up in the Protestant faith, survived a precarious childhood and the reign of her Catholic half-sister Mary I to become England's greatest queen. Jane Seymour, undoubtedly Henry's favorite wife, died giving birth to his only son, Edward VI, in 1537. As is well known, Henry married three times more. **SK**

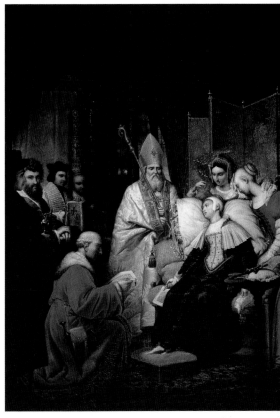

◆ Pierre-Nolasque Bergeret's c.1814 painting of Anne Boleyn being condemned to death.

"I am come hither to die . . . I pray God save the king and send him long to reign."

From Anne Boleyn's speech on the scaffold

Sikh Founder Dies

The first of the Sikh gurus, Guru Nanak, dies at the age of sixty-nine.

When the death of Guru Nanak drew near, a dispute broke out between the Guru's Hindu and Muslim followers. The Hindus saw Nanak as their Rama and wished to cremate him, whereas the Muslims saw him as the avatar of Allah and, as such, wanted to bury him. Nanak's last act was to intervene by offering a compromise whereby the two groups should both place a garland of flowers next to his body. The group whose garland had wilted the least after three days would be allowed to choose the method of disposal. When both groups went to check their garlands, all that was left was the flowers; Guru Nanak's body had disappeared. The Hindus proceeded to cremate their garland and the Muslims buried theirs.

Nanak became interested in religious issues at an early age and would compose hymns with Mardana, a Muslim servant at the household in which Nanak worked as an accountant. Nanak founded a canteen where Muslims, as well as Hindus of different castes, could eat together and listen to the hymns. Nanak is believed to have received a vision from God at Sultanpur, in which he was ordered to preach to mankind. Nanak is reputed to have traveled widely spreading his faith but spent the last years of his life in Kartarpur, in present-day Pakistan.

The nine Gurus who followed Nanak further developed the Sikh religion in the face of often brutal persecution by the Mughal leaders of India. The final Guru, Guru Gobind Singh, died in 1708. He was succeeded by the Sikh Holy Scripture, the Guru Granth Sahib, which had been set down in his lifetime and became the perpetual Guru of Sikhism. **TB**

◯ Guru Nanak and Mardana with King Shivanabh, after c.1500 (artist unknown).

Mississippi Sighted

Spanish scouts in search of gold and silver discover the "great river."

Commissioned to explore the country north of Mexico, Hernando de Soto sailed from Cuba in 1539 to the west coast of Florida. He then led his force of around 600 men northward to the neighborhood of present-day Tallahassee. From here they moved on through Georgia into the Carolinas, fighting some hard battles against the inhabitants on the way. After winter camp they carried on northwest until, on May 8, 1541, de Soto's scouts came in sight of the Mississippi River. The name means "great river" in Algonquin, but de Soto named it Río de Espiritu Santo (River of the

---

"Many of the conquistadors said that this river was larger than the Danube."

Rodrigo Rangel, contemporary account

Holy Spirit). It was wide, deep, muddy, and fast flowing, with debris swirling past in the current.

The Spaniards crossed over and moved on to the Ozarks, but they failed to find the hoped-for gold or silver and returned to the Mississippi for the next winter. By this time, de Soto had spread the idea among the local natives that he was divine. However, in the spring of 1542, he died of a fever, still only in his early forties. In order to continue the ruse of de Soto's divinity, his body was secretly sunk in the Mississippi in the middle of the night. The first Spanish exploration of the American Southeast now complete, the expedition built boats and sailed down the Mississippi to Mexico. Despite their efforts, the territory would be taken over by the French in the seventeenth century. **RC**

Pizarro Is Brutally Murdered

The revenge killing of Francisco Pizarro in his palace in Lima prompts Spain to take a more hands-on role in South America.

Francisco Pizarro lost his life in a revenge attack on his palace in Lima on June 26, 1541. He killed two of his attackers and ran a third through with his sword, but he was stabbed in the throat and fell to the floor, where he was stabbed repeatedly. He was said to have drawn a cross on the floor with his blood, in death calling on Jesus Christ.

While holding the Inca Atahualpa captive in Cajamarca, Francisco Pizarro had had long, friendly conversations with him and learned about the political situation, rivalries, and factions in the empire. The shrewd Spaniard was able to use this information after Atahualpa's execution, and he found some of the Inca nobility ready to help him. This situation, mixed with guile, superior weaponry, and a ruthlessness that Pizarro and his men justified as necessary to bring the people the blessings of Christianity, was crucial in helping Pizarro gain control of many Inca provinces.

He seized Cuzco, installed a puppet Inca, and founded Lima as his headquarters, but he fell out with his right-hand man Diego de Almagro, who took Cuzco in 1537. Pizarro told his three brothers, Hernando, Juan, and Gonzalo, to bring Almagro to heel. They defeated him in a battle at Las Salinas in 1538, and Hernando Pizarro had him executed in Cuzco's main square. Almagro's son, another Diego, and his followers took revenge three years later by forcing their way into Pizarro's palace and killing him.

The younger Almagro was executed in 1542 as the Spanish government began to take a firmer grip on its South American empire. **RC**

◐ *Francisco Pizarro Assassinated by an Army of Conspirators,* a 1541 engraving by Theodore de Bry (1528–1598).

Apocalyptic Vision

Michelangelo completes The Last Judgment *for the Sistine Chapel.*

In 1534, Michelangelo was invited by Pope Clement VII to return to Rome to paint a fresco for the large end wall of the Sistine Chapel. Clement died shortly afterward, and it was his successor, Pope Paul III, a great admirer of Michelangelo, who urged the artist to begin the project. It was said that when Paul III first saw the finished fresco in 1541, he fell on his knees begging God to forget his sins at the Day of Judgment, so terrible did he deem the despair of those damned to hell and the emotional intensity of the composition.

In the quarter of a century that had passed since Michelangelo had painted the chapel's ceiling, the papacy had been shaken by challenges to its authority from Martin Luther and from rulers such as Henry VIII. The new pope, who is often regarded as the guiding spirit behind the Counter-Reformation, was determined to reassert the Church's authority. To contemporaries, the fresco's theme, The Last Judgment, would have made the point that salvation comes only through the Church of Rome.

In the center of the fresco, which takes up the whole wall, is the figure of Christ, right arm raised to point the souls of the saved to heaven, the left dropped, directing the damned to hell. The figures are heavy and fleshy, their limbs contorted—even the martyrs holding the implements of their tortures seem fearful and apprehensive. Some were outraged by the fresco's depiction of nudity, which they considered sacrilegious. Paul loyally defended Michelangelo from these attacks, but a later pope ordered Daniele da Volterra, a former pupil of Michelangelo, to paint draperies over the offending parts, earning the unfortunate artist the shameful name of *Il Braghettone* (breeches-maker). **SK**

Book of Bartolome

The priest champions the cause of the Native Americans in the New World.

The arrival of the Spaniards in the Americas from 1492 onward brought catastrophe to the Native Americans. Smallpox ravaged the population from Mexico to Peru, native religions and traditions were extirpated, and entire populations were massacred or enslaved by their colonial conquerors and forced to work in gold and silver mines. In 1542, Fra Bartolome wrote *A Brief Account of the Destruction of the Indies*, in which he set out the genocidal atrocities of the conquistadors. The book was dedicated to Philip II of Spain and published ten years later. It was widely translated and proved influential across Europe.

Fra Bartolome de Las Casas was a boy from Castile who emigrated to the Caribbean in 1504, aged eighteen. In 1511 he heard a sermon by Father Antonio de Montesinos denouncing Spanish behavior in the Americas. Soon after, in 1512, he became the first man to be ordained a priest in the New World, traveling as a missionary to Cuba where he witnessed murderous atrocities by the Spaniards. He returned to Spain in 1515 to plead the Indians' case before King Charles I (Holy Roman Emperor Charles V).

In the early 1520s, with the king's support, he attempted to construct an racially egalitarian community in Venezuela, but it failed after his neighbors incited opposition to him among the natives. He now joined the Dominican order, and in 1530 returned to Spain once more to campaign against slavery in Peru. Later he became bishop of Chiapas in Guatemala, where he protested against the *encomienda* system of forced labor. He left the New World in the 1540s, and in 1550 took part in a famous debate with Juan Ginés de Sepúlveda over whether the Native Americans were capable of self-government. **PF**

Inquisition in Rome

Pope Paul III hopes to combat rising
heresy with the Roman Inquisition.

Faced with what were seen as increasing acts of heresy against the Roman Catholic Church, Pope Paul III established a permanent tribunal of cardinals in Rome to defend the integrity of the faith. On July 21, 1542, he sanctioned what became known as the Roman Inquisition. The tribunals prosecuted those who were accused of crimes such as sorcery, witchcraft, and blasphemy, and covered much of Italy as well as other areas where the pope held jurisdiction, such as Avignon.

The pope appointed the cardinals who presided over its meetings and, in addition, a team of consultants. These consultants were experienced scholars who advised the cardinals on complex issues of canon law. The inquisition was primarily put in place to combat the spread of Protestant ideas in Italy, but because of the influence of the Papal States it lasted until the eighteenth century, when the Italian states began to suppress its meetings.

The team of consultants was asked to assess Copernicus's claim that the sun was immobile and that the Earth revolved around it. The theologians argued that such ideas were absurd and ordered that his book De Revolutionibus Orbium Coelestium be placed on the index of forbidden books. The most famous case tried by the cardinals of the Roman inquisition was that of Galileo Galilei in 1633. Galileo was imprisoned for suspicion of grave heresy and for refusing to denounce his heliocentrism—the belief that the sun is at the center of the solar system. The inquisitor, Cardinal Bellarmine, quoted psalms and passages of the Bible that "proved" that this could not be so. Although Galileo believed his evidence of tidal movements proved heliocentrism, he eventually recanted, but died under house arrest in 1642. **TB**

Key Book Published

Copernicus reveals that the Earth
and planets revolve around the sun.

It is said that Nicolaus Copernicus (Mikolaj Kopernik), the Polish mathematician and astronomer, died on May 24, 1543, within a few hours of being handed a printed copy of the work he had waited so long to publish. In 1530, he had begun to write De Revolutionibus Orbium Coelestium (The Revolutions of the Heavenly Orbs), in which he set out his theory that the sun is the center of the universe, around which the Earth and other planets orbit. But he had first developed his views even earlier, between 1508 and 1512, in the Commentariolus (Brief Commentary).

> ## "In the middle of everything is the Sun . . . as though seated on a royal throne . . ."
>
> **Copernicus, De Revolutionibus Orbium, 1543**

The Church held that the Earth was the fixed center of the universe, accepting the geocentric model of the Greek astronomer Ptolemy (c.83–161), who had followed in Aristotle's steps. Copernicus developed his system while seeking to find solutions to the mathematical difficulties presented by Ptolemy's model, and it has been argued that he hesitated to make his findings public because of possible religious controversy and the fear of ridicule from his fellow mathematicians.

In 1539, astronomer Georg Joachim Rheticus visited Copernicus and persuaded him to publish his work. Few people realized the world-shaking implications of Copernicus's findings. Controversy over the heliocentric universe would wait until the work of Kepler and Galileo seventy years later. **SK**

Mary Rose Capsizes Off British Coast

The Tudor warship, one of the most powerful vessels of England's Navy Royal, capsizes and sinks as King Henry VIII watches from shore.

The *Mary Rose* was part of a fleet of eighty warships that sailed out of Portsmouth to engage a French invasion fleet of 200 galleys in the Solent. King Henry VIII had taken up a position in nearby Southsea Castle to watch the battle, but the lack of wind on July 19, 1545, left the English fleet becalmed, whereas the French galleys, driven by oars, were able to bring their guns close. In the afternoon, the wind picked up and the English fleet moved forward in pursuit of the French. The *Mary Rose* then capsized, and, as water poured in through her open gun ports, she sank within minutes, taking some 400 men with her.

Built in 1509, she was a large sailing warship with high castles at the bow and stern, and was the first to have gun ports cut into her hull. The loss of a powerful warship, in sight of the shore and without visible damage from the enemy, caused consternation at the time. But the *Mary Rose* is best remembered for what happened to her some 430 years later, when a team of marine archeologists began to excavate the site of the wreck, exposed after a severe gale uncovered a few structural timbers. Thousands of artifacts, from bronze cannon to gaming boards and cooking utensils, were brought to the surface, and on October 11, 1982, before a television audience of some 60 million people, the hull of the ship itself was lifted from the water. Since then, analysis of the remains of 200 or so individuals found on the wreck and study of their possessions have provided unrivaled insight into conditions on board a Tudor warship. **SK**

⊙ A detail from the twentieth-century painting *Mary Rose, Henry VIII's Ship*, by artist Richard Willis.

⊙ A photograph of the raising of the hull of the *Mary Rose* on October 11, 1982; it is now in Portsmouth, England.

Mission in the East

Jesuit Francis Xavier arrives in Kagoshima, Japan, aboard a Portuguese ship.

The spread of Christianity into Asia went hand in hand with the expansion of Portuguese trade into the Indian and Pacific Oceans. In 1542 Francis Xavier, one of Ignatius Loyola's original group of Jesuit companions, traveled to the Portuguese trading settlement at Goa in India at the invitation of King João III of Portugal, where he spent three years and made many converts before sailing on to found missions in Malacca and the Spice Islands. It was in Malacca in 1548 that he met Anjiro, a Japanese trader from Kyushu, who persuaded Francis that Japan would prove a fertile ground for conversion. Thus it was that on August 15, 1549, a Portuguese ship bearing Francis, the newly baptized Anjiro, and several companions sailed into Kagoshima harbor.

At this time Europeans knew virtually nothing of Japan—the first Portuguese ship had arrived there only seven years before. Francis spent almost a year in Kagoshima learning Japanese and translating the catechism and scriptures, and later visited Kyoto and Yamaguchi. He found the Japanese unimpressed by the simple attire of a Jesuit priest and much less receptive to his preaching than Anjiro had suggested. All the same, when he returned to Goa in 1551, he left 2,000 converts in the charge of his companions.

Francis was on a new mission, this time to China, when he died of fever off the Chinese coast on November 21, 1552. Other men were to follow in his footsteps in ensuing decades. Thirty years later, Matteo Ricci, an Italian Jesuit and a man of considerable learning, traveled to Macao. During several visits to China he conversed with scholars on mathematics and astronomy and mastered classical Chinese script. In 1601 he became the first Westerner to be invited into the Forbidden City in Beijing. **SK**

Peace of Augsburg

Charles V snubs the Diet, held to settle Germany's religious divisions.

The imperial Diet that assembled in Augsburg, Bavaria, in February 1555 had one purpose—to end the bitter wars of religion that had brought such destruction to Germany. In 1552 the elector Maurice of Saxony had led a Protestant alliance against the emperor. In the negotiations that followed, Catholics and Protestants wanted a lasting settlement, but Charles V granted a peace only until the next imperial Diet, at Augsburg.

Disgusted at the compromises that would follow, Charles refused to attend the Diet and sent his brother Ferdinand in his stead. Ferdinand was far

> ### *"Let neither . . . Majesty nor Electors, do any . . . harm to any estate of the Empire."*
> **Peace of Augsburg**

more realistic in his appraisal of the religious situation than Charles. When the Peace of Augsburg was promulgated, it provided that, until the Catholic-Lutheran rift was healed, the German states were not to make war on each other for religious reasons. Meanwhile, the religion of each state was to be decided by its ruler—summed up in the Latin formula, *cuius regio, eius religio* (to whom the kingdom, to him the religion). Any subject who rejected his ruler's choice could migrate elsewhere.

The peace applied to Catholics and Lutherans but Calvinists, Zwinglians, Anabaptists, and Mennonites were not mentioned. The agreement kept the Holy Roman Empire free of civil war for more than fifty years. The greatest winners were the German princes, whose independence increased. **SK**

King of Spain Surrenders Power

Charles V resigns as king of Spain in favor of his son, Philip, and divests himself of office in preparation for a secluded retirement.

No monarch had ever held so much power. As king of Spain, Charles's rule extended over the growing Spanish Empire in the New World; in addition, as Holy Roman Emperor, he controlled the Habsburg possessions in Europe. His extraordinary decision to hand over the crown of Spain to his son, Philip II, in January 1556 directly followed his resignation of the Netherlands and the Duchy of Burgundy to Philip. This had taken place in a ceremony at the Hall of the Golden Fleece in Brussels in the previous year, 1555.

Why did Charles voluntarily give up power? His health was failing and he was often in severe pain from gout, but this was not the only reason for his decision. A devout Catholic, he regarded the spread of Protestantism during his stewardship as his greatest failure. Unhappy with events in Germany, he had placed the running of the Holy Roman Empire in the hands of his brother Ferdinand after the religious compromise with the Protestant princes at Augsburg in 1555, and now, no longer king of Spain, all that remained for him was to make peace with God.

He formally abdicated as Holy Roman Emperor to make his home at the monastery of Yuste in the remote hills of Extremadura in Spain, the country in which he had spent only sixteen of his forty years as king. There, among his books and pictures, he tended his garden until his death in 1558. The empire of Charles V had proved too big for one man, and from now on the Habsburg dynasty would remain split between its Austrian and Spanish branches. Nine members of the Austrian Habsburgs were elected Holy Roman Emperor from 1558 until 1740. **SK**

○ *Portrait of Philip II of Spain*, painted by Titian and assistants in 1548–1550, currently in the Pitti Palace, Florence.

Revenge of a Catholic Queen

Thomas Cranmer, the first Protestant archbishop of Canterbury, is burned at the stake as Queen Mary I reintroduces Catholicism to England.

Thomas Cranmer—former archbishop of Canterbury, now a condemned heretic—was paraded to St. Mary's Church in Oxford on March 21, 1556. Kept in prison for more than two years, stripped of his offices, and publicly humiliated, he had been forced to sign six documents admitting his heresy and was now required to make his recantation public. To the amazement of his listeners, he took back his words and declared that as his right hand had offended "in writing contrary to my heart," he would thrust it first into the flames. And that is what he did when he was taken out and burned at the stake, holding it there "so the people might see it burnt to a coal."

By training and inclination a scholar who was in close touch with reformers on the Continent, Cranmer had been thrust unwillingly into the office of archbishop by Henry VIII. He had overseen the translation of the Bible into English, but it was as archbishop to Henry VIII's sickly son Edward VI that he had established the basic liturgy of the Church of England, being largely responsible for drawing up the Book of Common Prayer (1552).

Queen Mary I had not forgiven Cranmer for his part in arranging Henry's divorce from her mother, Catherine of Aragon. A devout Catholic, she saw it as her divine duty to return England to the true faith and had reintroduced the laws against heretics. Far from winning back souls, her brutal policies created more martyrs, and more than 300 Protestants were burned in the last years of "Bloody" Mary's reign. **SK**

◗ Engraving of Thomas Cranmer, who was archbishop of Canterbury from 1533 to 1556.

◖ Cranmer burning at the stake, from John Foxe's *Actes and Monuments of these Latter and Perillous Dayes* (1563).

A Boy Emperor

Thirteen-year-old Jalaluddin Muhammad Akbar becomes Mughal emperor.

On February 12, 1556, the claimant to the Mughal throne, Humayun, was descending the stairs of his library when the call to prayer sounded. Trying to bow in reverence, Humayun fell down the stairs and died. This unfortunate event brought his son, thirteen-year-old Akbar, to the Mughal throne. He was not crowned until October 15, though, because his father had been engaged in a war with the Afghan Sikandar Shah for the contested Mughal throne.

The day after his father's death, Akbar donned a golden robe and placed a tiara on his head and

" . . . like Alexander of Macedon, he was always ready to risk his life."

Abul Fazal, *Book of Akbar*, 1590s

proclaimed himself "King of Kings." During his long, nearly fifty-year reign, Akbar proved to be a wise, benevolent ruler and a man of new ideas. He eliminated the military threat from Afghanistan and secured rule over Hindustan. He gained the support of non-Muslims by repealing taxes that were imposed only on them. His religious tolerance led to the preservation of Hindu temples, and his court held debates between Muslim scholars and representatives of Sikhs, Hindus, and Jesuits. A special building, the *Ibadat Khana* (House of Worship), was built for religious debates.

Perhaps Akbar's greatest legacy was in the arts. He commissioned works of literature, adorned his palaces with works of art from around the world, and constructed many fine buildings. **SK**

Mughals Saved

Akbar the Great's victory at Panipat is a turning point for the Mughal Empire.

With Bairam Khan, a Persian noble at the Mughal court, at his side, Mughal Emperor Akbar went into battle at Panipat, north of Delhi, in November 1556. Akbar was thirteen years old and had been crowned emperor only the month before. Now he was faced with an Afghan army led by a Hindi general, Hemu.

The previous February, when Humayun, second ruler of the Mughal dynasty, fell to his death, the future of Mughal rule in India had never been in greater doubt. During Humuyan's reign, the conquests of his father, Babur, had mostly been

"His majesty . . . secures by these ties of harmony the peace of the world."

Abul Fazal, *Book of Akbar*, 1590s

swept away, leaving a rump around Kabul and the Punjab. Victory in the battle at Panipat was crucial.

It seemed that Hemu's greater forces would win, but a stray arrow struck Hemu in the eye and he was brought before Bairam Khan and Akbar and beheaded. Coming thirty years after Babur's defeat of Ibrahim Lodi, the last sultan of Delhi, it was the second pivotal Mughal victory at Panipat. Within two years, Akbar controlled the western part of the Ganges plain, the rich Mughal heartlands, and by his death in 1605 he had extended his empire's borders east to Bengal and south into the Deccan.

Akbar the Great consolidated Mughal power through centralized taxation, formed alliances with Hindu Rajput princes, and encouraged theological debate at his capital at Fatehpur Sikri. **SK**

France Wins Back Calais

Mary I loses "the brightest jewel in the English crown" after two centuries.

◯ A detail from *The Taking of Calais by Francis, 2nd Duke of Guise (1519–1563)* by Francois Edouard Picot.

Calais fell to a French army led by the duke of Guise in January 1558. When reports reached Queen Mary, she is reputed to have said, "When I am dead and opened, you shall find 'Philip' and 'Calais' lying in my heart." The port of Calais on the northern coast of France had been an English possession since its capture by King Edward III in 1347—he had been so angered by the town's lengthy resistance that he agreed to spare its citizens only on condition that the six leading burghers surrendered themselves to him, bareheaded and with ropes around their neck. It was only through the pleading of Queen Philippa that he pardoned them. The king then settled the town with English merchants, and it became a "staple" port for the export of wool, cloth, tin, and lead, sending its own representatives to the English Parliament. After the end of the Hundred Years' War in 1453, Calais remained the only English possession in France.

Mary I's marriage to Philip II of Spain in 1554 was a failure. She was ten years his senior and too old to bear him a child, and he spent very little time in England. Most damaging of all, in 1557 the marriage dragged England into a highly unpopular war against France in support of Spain. Protestant pamphleteers inflamed opinion against the alliance with the Catholic enemy, and when the war went badly for England, resulting in the loss of Calais, anger against Mary increased to such a pitch that the news of her death on November 17, 1558, was greeted with bonfires and the ringing of church bells. **SK**

French King Dies in Freak Accident

Henry II dies ten days after being wounded in a peace tournament held in Paris.

O Depiction of the tournament in rue St. Antoine, Paris, during which Henry II was fatally wounded.

A tournament was held in Paris to celebrate the end of France's war with Spain and the marriage of French king Henry II's daughter Elisabeth to Philip II of Spain. During the tournament, a splinter from the shattered lance of Gabriel, captain of the king's Scottish guard, penetrated Henry's left eye and entered his brain. He died ten days later on July 10, 1559.

Henry II had succeeded his father, Francis I, in 1547, at the age of twenty-eight. He had married Catherine de Médicis in 1533, when they were both fourteen, and although they had eight children, including three future kings of France (Francis II, Charles IX, and Henry III), it was Henry's mistress, Diane de Poitiers, who wielded influence at court. By 1559 it was clear that neither France nor Spain could continue the war that Henry had started in 1551, and by the terms of the Peace of Cateau-Cambrésis, signed on April 3, Henry renounced any further claims in Italy.

Henry wanted to end all military commitments so that he could concentrate his efforts on the battle against Protestantism, which had spread rapidly in France through the writings of the French-born Genevan reformer John Calvin. Henry persecuted Protestants relentlessly, setting up a special court, the *Chambre Ardente* (Burning Court), to try heretics. On June 2, 1559, he published the Edict of Ecouen, declaring war on Protestants. He did not live to see it enacted, but it opened the way to the Wars of Religion that would divide France for forty years. **SK**

Birth of a Royal Capital

Philip II establishes his court at Madrid, in the center of the Iberian peninsula.

O *A View of the Calle de Alcala, Madrid*, painted by Antonio Joli c.1750.

In 1559 Philip II returned to Spain from the Netherlands, never to leave again. Two years later he decided to base his court at Madrid, in the very center of the Iberian peninsula. Before this date, the court moved wherever the monarch happened to be, in Castile, or Aragon, or Naples, but the growth of the royal court, which in 1561 numbered around 15,000 people, made this increasingly impractical.

With a harsh climate and few natural resources, Madrid was an unpromising site for a capital. By choosing an obscure town far from Spain's populated centers, such as Seville, Cadiz, or Barcelona, Philip removed himself from the public gaze of his subjects. A workaholic who hated delegating any decision, great or small, he spent hours at his desk worrying over minutiae and perfecting a bureaucratic system of government that was secretive, cumbersome, and slow, while keeping the court nobles at a distance by giving them diplomatic or military posts abroad.

One day, while on a hunting trip, Philip discovered, about 25 miles (40 km) north of Madrid, the site for the greatest memorial of his reign, the monastery-palace of the Escorial. This huge complex of buildings took twenty years to complete, from 1563 to 1584, and included rooms to house Philip's vast collections of books, manuscripts, and holy relics, as well as a mausoleum for the kings of Spain, beginning with Charles V. Philip spent much time here until dying in 1598. It was left to his son Philip III to transform Madrid into a Baroque capital. **SK**

Council Clarifies Roman Catholicism

The Council of Trent spends eighteen years spearheading the Counter-Reformation.

○ *The Council of Trent* (1563) is attributed to Titian and can be seen in the Musée du Louvre, Paris.

The Council was convened three times between 1545 and December 1563, in the city of Trento (Trent) on the Adige River in Italy, by three different popes—Paul III, Julius III, and Pius IV. It issued seventeen decrees, signed by 255 members, including four papal legates, two cardinals, three patriarchs, twenty-five archbishops, and 168 bishops. By clarifying Catholic doctrine, condemning Protestant teachings, and reforming Church discipline, the Council of Trent became a powerful instrument of the Counter-Reformation—the movement of the Roman Catholic Church in response to Protestantism.

The Council took an uncompromising stand on transubstantiation—the doctrine that Christ is present in the consecrated bread and wine at the Eucharist, and upheld the teaching that salvation comes by grace through faith and works, which Luther and others disputed. It introduced a standardized form of the Mass, which came to be known as the "Tridentine Mass" (from *Tridentum*, the Latin name for Trent), and established a *catechism* (manual of instruction). Practices such as indulgences, pilgrimages, and the veneration of saints and relics, and of the Virgin Mary were reaffirmed.

The Council's pronouncements strengthened papal authority and the absolutist tendencies of Catholic monarchs. New self-confidence took form in grand Baroque churches, and renewed missionary zeal found expression in the spread of new religious orders such as the Jesuits and the Capuchins. **SK**

Turks Forced to Lift Siege

The Knights of St. John resist an Ottoman onslaught to seize control of Malta.

⬭ Depiction of the attack on the Post of Castille during the Great Siege of Malta, 1565.

The siege of Malta was faltering when, on September 7, 1565, a Christian relief force arrived from Sicily. "I do not believe that ever did music sound so sweet to human beings. It was three months since we had ever heard a bell which did not summon us to arms against the enemy." Thus Spanish soldier Francisco Balbi described hearing the summons to Mass, after the Ottomans finally fled on September 8.

Malta had been home to the Knights Hospitaller of St. John since 1530. Lying across sea routes between the Ottoman capital, Constantinople, and north African ports, this Christian stronghold was an inevitable target for Ottoman attack. The force that General Mustafa Pasha landed on Malta in 1565 probably numbered around 30,000 men. Facing

them were 550 knights, supported by 8,000 assorted soldiers, commanded by the order's grand master, Jean de la Valette. In May, Ottoman cannons bombarded Fort St. Elmo, by the island's harbor. The walls were soon reduced to rubble, but 600 men held out for almost a month, fighting to the death. Next the Ottomans turned their attention to the harbor's inner fortifications. Hassan, the pasha of Algiers, mounted an assault on the seaward defenses in a flotilla of small boats, which was repulsed with heavy losses. Mining and bombardment opened up land walls, but they were not successfully stormed.

The failure of the siege blocked Ottoman expansion into the western Mediterranean. The knights remained in control of the island until 1798. **RG**

Struck Down Before the Queen

The murder of David Rizzio begins the downfall of Mary, Queen of Scots.

○ *The Murder of Rizzio*, painted in 1787 by John Opie, is held in the Guildhall Art Gallery collection in London.

The young queen was at supper in Holyrood Palace, Edinburgh, on March 9, 1566, when a group of armed men broke in and fatally stabbed her private secretary and confidante, David Rizzio. It was the start of a bizarre chain of events in the life of Mary, Queen of Scots, which was already marked by drama and tragedy.

Queen at only six days old after the death of her father, James V of Scotland, from 1542 Mary was brought up at the French court. In 1558, she was married to the Dauphin, a sickly boy of fourteen, and when Henry II died the following year, Mary suddenly found herself Queen of France. Within months, her husband, Francis II, was also dead and Mary returned to Scotland in August 1561, where she was soon at odds with her Protestant subjects.

In July 1565, she married (for love) the Earl of Darnley, but the marriage soon turned sour and Darnley joined a number of Protestant nobles to kill Rizzio, who was suspected of encouraging Mary's Catholic sympathies. Mary was pregnant and in June 1566 gave birth to a son, the future James VI (James I of England), and then Darnley was found dead in mysterious circumstances. Mary's next, disastrous step was to marry the Earl of Bothwell, who had been implicated in Darnley's death. It was a fatal move—the Scottish nobility raised an army against them, and in July 1567 Mary was forced to surrender and was formally deposed. She later escaped from prison in Loch Leven and fled to England, to spend the rest of her life in exile. **SK**

Dutch Rebels Quell Spanish Force

Victory over the Spanish army gives temporary hope of Dutch independence.

○ *Persecution by the Duke of Alba* (1568) is part of a collection owned by Cheltenham Art Gallery & Museums, England.

The 1568 victory over a Spanish force at Heiligerlee in the Gronigen Province is regarded as the start of the Eighty Years' War, the long struggle for Dutch independence that would end in 1648 when the Spanish formally recognized the Dutch Republic at the Peace of Westphalia. Resistance to Spanish rule in the Netherlands had been mounting for a long time, fueled by the spread of Calvinism, economic hardship, and high taxation, and the opposition of the local nobility to the erosion of their privileges by the Spanish government. When, in 1566, in an outbreak of violence against the Catholic religion, mobs stormed churches and smashed statues, Philip II sent in an army of 10,000 troops under the duke of Alba to stem the rising tide of rebellion.

Alba's brutal policies caused outrage. The special court he set up to try the rebels quickly gained the name of the Council of Blood for its number of executions. No one was spared—even the loyal Catholic nobles, the counts of Horne and Egmont, were arrested for high treason and beheaded. William the Silent, Prince of Orange, the most powerful of the Dutch *stadholders* (hereditary magistrates), had fled the Netherlands on Alba's arrival. He now returned with a Protestant army, but after success at Heiligerlee, a lack of funds ran his military campaign into the ground, and William stayed at large. As Alba's grip tightened, only the Geuzen (Sea Beggars)—pirates who attacked Spanish shipping—kept Dutch hopes alive. **SK**

The Gun Is Mightier than the Sword

Oda Nobunaga captures Kyoto and begins the unification of Japan.

⬤ This silk portrait of Oda Nobunaga by an unknown artist can be seen in the Kobe Municipal Museum, Japan.

In 1568 Oda Nobunaga, the lord of Owari, seized control of the imperial capital at Kyoto, so starting the reunification in Japan. This ambition was not realized in Nobunaga's lifetime, but by his death in 1582 he had control of around half the country.

In the early sixteenth century, power in Japan had devolved into the hands of the local *daimyo* (feudal lords), with neither the emperor nor the military shoguns exercising real authority. The more powerful *daimyo* fought one another, to achieve a regional dominance to start the reunification of the country.

The first to achieve this position was Nobunaga. He rose to prominence after defeating and capturing Imagawa Yoshimo, the most powerful lord of eastern Japan, at the battle of Okehazama in 1566. The secret of Nobunaga's success was his adoption of muskets, which had been introduced to Japan in 1542 by the Portuguese. Training and equipping a samurai was expensive and time-consuming, and it was a career open only to men of noble birth. In contrast, almost anyone could be trained as a musketeer in a matter of weeks. Musket brigades of 3,000 men were rotated in three ranks, making it possible to fire a volley every ten seconds. Opponents who still relied on samurai cavalry and pikemen were easily crushed by such tactics. Nobunaga also consolidated his power by building a new type of castle at Azuchi, near Kyoto. Azuchi was built to control the rice fields, villages, and roads of the plain and to prevent peasant uprisings. **JH**

Holy Battle at Lepanto

The Holy League defeats the Ottomans in the last battle of oared galleys.

○ The sixteenth-century Mannerist painting *The Battle of Lepanto* is the work of Paolo Caliari Veronese.

"... you have only shaved our beard ... [it] will grow all the better for the razor."

Grand Vizier Sokullu Mehmed Pasha

On a Sunday morning in October 1571, in the Gulf of Corinth, Greece, 100,000 men prepared for a battle not only of fleets, but of religions. Advancing westward from Lepanto (now Navpaktos), the commander of the galleys of the Ottoman Empire, Pasha Ali Mouezinzade, flew a banner inscribed 28,900 times with the name of Allah. His adversary Don John of Austria, illegitimate son of Emperor Charles V, sailed under an image of the crucified Christ, which had been blessed by the pope.

By combining in a Holy League, the Christians had assembled 220 oared warships, chiefly from Spain, Venice, and Genoa. They included six Venetian galleasses, twice the size of ordinary galleys, heavily armed with cannons. The Ottomans had 280 ships, although of a mostly smaller size. Both sides' galleys were packed with oarsmen and soldiers. Their aim was to get close enough to fire handguns and bows, then board to fight hand to hand. Don John's galleasses punched into the enemy center, supported to the left and right by Venetian commander Agostino Barbarigo and the Genoan Andrea Doria. In the gigantic melee, slaughter was vast. Commanders were not spared: Barbarigo died of a head wound, whereas Pasha Ali was beheaded after Spanish soldiers boarded his flagship. In five hours' fighting, the Ottomans lost 30,000 men and most of their ships. The Christian dead are estimated at 8,000.

Christendom was triumphant, yet the victory was far from decisive. The Holy League had been set up to stop the Ottomans taking Cyprus and to stop their slave trade in the Mediterranean, but in these aims it failed. The Ottoman Empire had the resources to rebuild its fleet the following year. Lepanto stands out above all as the last great example of a style of naval warfare that had lasted for 2,000 years. **RG**

Paris Runs with Blood

Thousands killed in the streets as Catholics turn on the Huguenots.

Shortly before dawn on St. Bartholomew's Day, 1572, a church bell tolled to signal the start of the killing. A horrific wave of violence was unleashed across Paris—Protestants were hunted down and killed in their houses, shops were pillaged, whole families slaughtered. The cream of Huguenot (French Protestant) aristocracy was still in Paris, having attended the wedding, a few days before, of Henry of Navarre, a Protestant prince, to Marguerite of Valois, sister of the French king, Charles IX. The feeling in the city was tense. The marriage, arranged by the king's mother, Catherine de Médicis, in an effort to heal the wounds between Catholics and Protestants, had been widely denounced by Catholic preachers, and anti-Huguenot feeling was running high in Paris.

The day before, an attempt had been made on the life of the Huguenot leader, Admiral de Coligny. Accounts of the events of the next twenty-four hours are very confused, but it seems that on the evening of August 23, Catherine, fearing anti-Catholic reprisals, persuaded the weak king she dominated to get rid of all the leading Huguenots in the city. Coligny was roused from his sickbed and run through with a sword. Other nobles soon died. The newly wed Henry of Navarre escaped by pretending to convert. Too late, the king tried to stop the massacre, but it had spread to other cities. By October, when the killing ceased, some 3,000 Huguenots had died in Paris, and up to 30,000 elsewhere in France.

Philip II of Spain welcomed the news of the massacre. Pope Gregory XIII had a celebratory medal struck, and commissioned the artist Giorgio Vasari to paint a picture of the massacre. But, far from stifling Huguenot opposition, the massacre plunged France into another civil war as Huguenots prepared to take up arms against the state. **SK**

◑ Detail from *An Eyewitness Account of the Saint Bartholomew's Day Massacre* (1572) by François Dubois.

> ## "I was seized with horror at the sight of furies bawling 'massacre the Huguenots!'"

Mémoires of the Duc de Sully, published 1638

Plague Kills Titian

The leader of the famed Venetian School of the Italian Renaissance dies in Venice.

When Titian succumbed to the plague in Venice in 1576, he was famous for not only his great works of art, but also his great age, which has been the subject of much debate. Although Titian claimed his birth date to be 1477, and some contemporaries claimed an improbable date of 1473, scholarship suggests a date nearer to 1490. As a sign of reverence, Titian was the only victim of the plague to be buried. He was interred in the Santa Maria Gloriosa dei Frari church. However, reverence for the artist was not enough to deter looters from plundering his luxurious mansion.

"The Sun amidst small stars, not only among the Italians but all the painters. . . ."

Giovanni Lomazzo, 1590

Titian was a versatile artist, excelling in mythological and religious subjects and gaining fame in the two genres of portrait and landscape. Titian's style continually changed, although his early and later works share the same subtle use of color, something that had no precedent at the time.

Titian's early career is highlighted by the great fresco of *Assunta* (Assumption of the Virgin), in which his use of color established him as the greatest painter north of Rome. In 1548, Titian's portrait of Charles V on horseback established the genre of equestrian portraiture, and, in 1562, elements of the *Rape of Europa* anticipated the Baroque style. Titian continued to accept commissions right up to the year of his death. His last work, *Pieta*, was finished by Palma the Younger. **TB**

Antwerp Massacre

Rioting Spanish troops end all chances of reconciliation with Dutch rebels.

An English observer compared the aftermath of the Antwerp massacre begun on November 4, 1576, to Michelangelo's *Last Judgment*. The cruelty and destruction inflicted by the Spanish army became known as the "Spanish Fury" and turned many against the Spanish Habsburg monarchy. The ten southern provinces accepted Spanish rule, but the seven northern provinces resolved to fight for independence—later to become the Dutch Republic in the north and the Spanish Netherlands in the south. From these would grow the Holland and Belgium we know today.

In the sixteenth century, Antwerp was the commercial and financial hub of Europe. It traded in English wool, Moluccan spices, and Spanish silver, and its bustling industry carried commodities and products from the Baltic to Brazil. It flourished, until Habsburg troops killed around 8,000 inhabitants and set fire to the port. After that, foreign traders were forced to seek out new commercial links.

Antwerp was one of many towns and states of Flemish- and French-speaking Catholics federated into seventeen provinces under the Spanish Habsburgs and ruler Philip II. The disaffected voices of nobles, Protestants, and merchants angry at Habsburg taxes spilled over into revolt. Philip needed to pacify the rebels, but this could work only if the army were kept under control. In the 1570s, recession hit Seville's trade with the Americas, and Philip could not make regular payments to his discontented troops in the Netherlands. They decided to pay themselves by sacking Antwerp. **JJH**

○ Detail from *The Spanish Fury in Antwerp on 4th November 1576*, painted by an unknown artist.

Sebastião Disappears

The king of Portugal is presumed dead at the catastrophic Battle of Alcazarquivir.

King Sebastião I of Portugal was twenty-four years old when he embarked on the conquest of the Muslim kingdom of Morocco. It was not a wise move, because on August 4, 1578, he disappeared amid the carnage of battle and his body was never found.

A deposed Moroccan ruler, Muhammad Al-Muttakawil, had appealed to Sebastião to reinstate him to the throne. This fired the young king with visions of leading a major assault on Islam. Reality should have taken hold once King Philip II of Spain made it clear he would not join a Portuguese-led crusade, but Sebastião refused to be deterred. Enlisting mercenaries from Spain, Germany, and Ireland, he sailed from Lisbon on June 25, with an 18,000-strong army.

Landing at Tangier, the Christian army struggled across Morocco in the burning summer heat. The superior forces of Moroccan Sultan Abd al-Malik, amply provided with firearms, awaited them at Alcazarquivir (Ksar el-Kebir). Any chance of survival the exhausted Christians might have had was ruined by the indisciplined impetuosity of the Portuguese knights, for whom Sebastião set the example, charging forward into the thick of the enemy. Almost the entire Christian force was killed or captured.

The loss of Sebastião was significant. In 1580 Philip inherited the Portuguese throne. Absorbed into the Spanish kingdom for the next eighty years, Portugal ceased to exist. Many Portuguese clung to the belief that Sebastião would return to claim his throne. "Sebastianism," the myth of the return of the lost king, remained a mystical strand in Portuguese thinking well into the twentieth century. **RG**

◗ Print of *King Sebastian in the Battle of Alkassar*, made in 1578; the king falls from his horse wounded and exhausted.

Dutch Rebellion

The United Provinces of the Netherlands assert independence from Spanish rule.

The Union of Utrecht, signed on January 23, 1579, was limited to the seven northern provinces of the Netherlands and declared their independence from Spanish rule. The southern provinces had concluded a reconciliation with Philip II, known as the Union of Arras, earlier in the month.

When the Holy Roman Emperor Charles V had handed over his title in 1555 to his son, Philip II, his Netherlands possessions were the richest, most industrious, and most urbanized of their time. Within just a few years, however, the seventeen provinces,

> ## "[The provinces are] for all time as if they were a single province."
>
> **Union of Utrecht**

which included Holland, Zeeland, and Utrecht, and important towns such as Antwerp, Ghent, and Bruges, were in revolt against the rule of Spain. The rebellion was sparked by Philip II's bureaucratic, centralized rule, the activities of the Spanish Inquisition, and a clampdown by the duke of Alba's Spanish troops. However, without effective aid from England or France, the rebels hardly posed a military challenge to Spain. The Union of Utrecht was really a holding operation designed to present a united front to the outside world and foster support.

As the tension escalated, the revolt's leader, William the Silent, issued the Oath of Abjuration. The oath was effectively a "Declaration of Independence" since the Union of Utrecht had stopped short of renouncing the king of Spain. **JJH**

Spain Takes Control of Portugal

At Alcântara, Portugal is defeated by Spain, leading to the union of the two countries.

🔾 Portrait of Fernando Alvarez de Toledo, Duke of Alba, painted in 1549 by Antonis Mor.

> ## "The cause of religion must take precedence over everything."
>
> **Philip II, 1591**

After Spain's decisive victory over the Portuguese at the Battle of Alcântara in August 1580, Portugal was added to Philip II's impressive list of lands, which for a while stretched from Peru to the Philippines and from Patagonia to the North Sea.

In 1578 King Sebastião of Portugal was killed during a misguided crusade against the Muslims of Morocco, leaving no heir. His much older uncle Henry took the throne, but several other claimants challenged his legitimacy, including Philip II. Philip tried court lobbying and intrigue to support his cause, but this only served to harden Portuguese opposition. With the sudden death of Henry, Philip unleashed the formidable duke of Alba to win by battle what he had failed to achieve by bribery.

On June 27, a powerful army of 23,000 men set off from Badajoz to march toward Lisbon, while a Spanish fleet of 157 boats was dispatched from Cadiz to block any retreat along the Tagus. Alba's army and navy met little effective resistance. Indeed the duke had got within 6 miles (10 km) of Lisbon before he was finally challenged just west of the small Alcântara River by Dom António, prior of Crato, another contender for the throne, with an army including 5,000 Lisbon burghers. In the subsequent battle, the Portuguese forces were decisively defeated, losing 4,000 men, including 1,000 dead, against Spanish losses of just 500 men. Two days later, the duke of Alba captured Lisbon, and with it a convoy loaded with goods and spices from India. The prior of Crato managed to escape, but by the end of 1580 most of Portugal was in Spanish hands. On March 25, 1581, Philip II was crowned king of Portugal, but the union of the two countries, which would last for the next sixty years, served only to increase rather than reduce the antipathy between Castile and Portugal. **JJH**

English Explorer Circumnavigates the Globe

Francis Drake is welcomed on his return from an epic voyage around the world.

When Drake anchored at Deptford, London, in September 1580 after a three-year epic voyage, Elizabeth I came aboard his ship, *The Golden Hind*, to welcome him. The gesture was a calculated snub directed at the Catholic enemy, Spain. When Drake had proposed his expedition to the queen, Elizabeth had verbally encouraged him to seize and harass Spanish ships and outposts en route.

At the helm of his small 100-ton flagship *Golden Hind* (formerly *Pelican*), with four other ships and 164 men, Drake set sail from Plymouth on November 15, 1577. He followed Magellan's route to South America and entered the straits that would bear Magellan's name on August 21, 1578. Drake sailed through in just sixteen days—a record that lasted the century.

Drake's original plan was to cross the Pacific and reach the Moluccas (formerly the Spice Islands), where he could muscle in on the lucrative spice trade, but he now realized that at this latitude the plan was impossible. So he set a new course north, hugging the Chilean and Peruvian shorelines and plundering Spanish shipping and ports. The Spanish were completely unprepared, having never encountered a hostile ship in these waters before. Drake's great prize was the capture of the *Cacafuego* with her treasure of Peruvian silver, gold, and jewels. Heavily laden with booty, Drake sailed on as far as modern-day Vancouver (becoming the first European to see the west coast of Canada) before anchoring in northern California.

From here he picked up the trade winds across the Pacific to the Moluccas, where he loaded up with cloves donated by a sultan then at war with Portugal. Following the Portuguese route back to Europe via the Cape of Good Hope, Drake completed his remarkable voyage with fifty-six men. **JJH**

○ Detail of a portrait of Sir Francis Drake, painted by Samuel Lane (1780–1859).

> *"... we found ... fowl which could not fly ... we killed in less than one day 3,000."*
>
> **Contemporary account of penguins**

Calendar Reset

The Gregorian calendar is adopted in the Catholic countries of Europe.

In Catholic Europe (Italy, Spain, Portugal, and Poland) people going to bed on the night of October 4, 1582, woke up on October 15. Overnight, ten days had been removed from the calendar. The change had been instituted by Pope Gregory XIII's Gregorian Calendar, now used in most of the world.

The purpose of the Gregorian reform was to correct the date of Easter, the Church's most important festival. According to a ruling of the Council of Nicaea in 325, the date of Easter was the Sunday closest to the full moon after the vernal

"... We approve this calendar, now reformed and made perfect."

Pope Gregory VIII, *Inter Gravissimas*, 1582

(spring) equinox, which at this time fell on March 21 but by the sixteenth century was falling on March 11. The Julian Calendar, established by Julius Caesar in 46 B.C.E., had miscalculated the length of the solar year (365.25 days rather than a more precise 365.2422 days), causing the dates to "drift" by about one day every century, despite a "leap day" every four years. The Gregorian Calendar solved the problem by dropping ten days from 1582 and establishing that, in future no century year should be a leap year unless divisible by 400 (such as 1600 and 2000).

The new calendar was first recognized only in Catholic Europe, but gradually Protestant countries came to accept it too. But the calendar's 1752 introduction into Britain and the American colonies is reported to have caused public outrage. **SK**

Cossack Invasion

Ermak enters Siberia and his Cossacks defeat the Tatar Khan Kuchum.

The Cossack leader Ermak entered Siberia in 1580 with the financial and military support of the wealthy merchant Semyon Stroganov. Ermak took about 1,600 men and proceeded along the Tagil and Tura rivers. In 1582 he laid siege to Isker, the capital of the Siberian khanate, and sacked the city. Tsar Ivan the Terrible rewarded the Stroganovs for their success with tracts of land.

The primary intention had been to conquer the Siberian Khanate, allowing Russian expansion into the region, which was under the leadership of Khan

"... the festival was a joyful one for the Tsar, and he held a great feast to celebrate."

Siberian Chronicle, mid-seventeenth century

Kuchum. The expedition was also partly defensive, since the Tatars had been launching sporadic raids against Stroganov's territories in the Urals. Trade was also an issue because forays into Siberian territory often returned with large amounts of valuable fur.

However, Kuchum regrouped his forces. In 1584, he killed Ermak and regained control of his ruined capital. But rival noble factions prevented him from reestablishing his rule. As a result, Kuchum relocated his khanate south, into the Russian steppe.

The dislocation of Kuchum's domain caused conflict with Russian governors. In 1586 he attempted to return to his lands but failed. In 1598 he was finally defeated at the Battle of Urmin. The Siberian khanate was gone. Isker was never rebuilt because instead the Russians founded a new city, Tobolsk. **TB**

Ivan the Terrible Dies

The death of the first Russian ruler to use the title tsar was as mysterious and outlandish as the rest of his ambiguous, tumultuous reign.

Ivan the Terrible was possibly poisoned by his closest advisers, Belsky and Godunov, after a violent quarrel over accusations that Ivan had attempted to rape Godunov's sister. Three days after the quarrel, the tsar "called for a chess-board and set out the pieces, all saving the king, which by no means could he make stand in his place with the rest." This provoked a final, fatal seizure on March 18, 1584.

A strong ruler, in a tradition later followed by Peter the Great and Stalin, Ivan had brought stability and a brutal order to Russia. He opened his country up to trade with the West, introduced printing, set up his own secret police, reduced the power of the noble Boyars, and expanded his realm into Siberia and Tartary. But he was also—especially late in his reign—cruel, dissolute, and unpredictable.

Always suspicious of threats to his power, Ivan became increasingly paranoid after a serious illness in 1553. Following the death of his beloved first wife, Anastasia, in 1560, his behavior—veering between bouts of manic piety and dissolute, drunken orgies—began to suggest serious mental instability. In 1581, his insanity led him to beat his daughter-in-law, causing a miscarriage, and then to kill his own son, Ivan, by striking him with a pointed staff. An analysis of Ivan's remains in the 1960s found high levels of mercury—suggesting that he had been poisoned. Alternatively, he may have taken treatments containing mercury for syphilis, a condition that may have contributed to his mental instability. **NJ**

◑ This twentieth-century portrait painting of Ivan the Terrible is held in a private collection.

◐ *The Oprichnina at the Court of Ivan IV (1530–84)* is the work of Nikolai Vasilievich Nevrev (1830–1904).

William the Silent Assassinated in Delft

Philip II deals the Counter-Reformation a powerful—but not fatal—blow.

◐ A wood engraving made in 1890 from *Assassination of William of Orange in Delft* painted by Wilhelm von Lindenschmit.

> ## "My God, have pity on my soul. May God have pity on this poor people."

William's words on being fatally shot

In response to William's signing the Oath of Abjuration proclaiming Dutch freedom from Spain, the Spanish Inquisition declared him a heretic, and in 1581, Philip II of Spain allocated 25,000 crowns for his assassination. An assassin succeeded in July 1584.

William the Silent—so called because of his discreet diplomacy—properly William of Nassau, Prince of Orange, was the champion of Europe's Protestantism at the height of the Counter-Reformation. The first attempt on his life was made in 1582 by a Portuguese clerk who overpacked his pistol with powder. William was wounded, and his hair set on fire, but he was not killed. Further attempts prompted William to shift his court from Antwerp to the less populated Delft. But the relentless assassins followed. In April 1584 Hans Hanzoom was executed for trying to blow up the prince with explosives.

Balthazar Gerard, a fanatical young Catholic, appeared at Delft posing as a dispossessed French Huguenot. William gave him twelve crowns, which he used to buy pistols—ironically from William's own guards. On July 10, in William's palace, the Prinsenhof, Gerard shot the prince through his lungs and stomach, and tore chunks out of the plaster wall. William died minutes after answering "Yes" to his sister's anxious question, "Do you die reconciled with your Savior, Jesus Christ?"

Gerard was caught and tortured—including having the flesh ripped from his body in strips with red-hot pincers—before being executed. Philip II paid his reward to Gerard's parents after raising the sum by holding William's son hostage—ensuring the Dutch paid a ransom that paid off their prince's killer. Gerard's head was preserved for half a century by sympathizers who unsuccessfully petitioned to have him canonized. **NJ**

Martyr or Conspirator?

Mary, Queen of Scots, is beheaded for high treason against Elizabeth I of England.

The execution took place in the great hall of Fotheringhay Castle in Northamptonshire, England, in 1587. The executioner is said to have bungled the job and it took two strokes of the ax to separate the head of Mary, Queen of Scots, from her body. Mary was then forty-four years old and had proved a romantic and tragic figure to the last. One of the stories told of her death was that her pet lapdog, which had crept beneath her skirts, could not be persuaded to leave the dead queen's corpse.

Ever since her impetuous flight to England twenty years before, Mary had been a thorn in Queen Elizabeth's side. As a descendant of King Henry VII through his daughter Margaret Tudor, Mary was next in line to the English throne. For the Catholic minority in England she was the rightful queen, and so long as she remained at liberty would be the focus of plots to restore England to Catholic rule. Elizabeth therefore used the excuse of Mary's implication in the Earl of Darnley's murder to confine her in a series of prisons.

It was the discovery in 1586 of a plot by an English Catholic, Anthony Babington, that sealed Mary's fate. Elizabeth's secretary of state, Sir Francis Walsingham, claimed to have evidence that Mary knew of the plan to murder the queen, and she was tried and sentenced to death. Elizabeth's ministers contended that "so long as there is life in her, there is hope; so as they live in hope, we live in fear." Her son, James VI of Scotland, did not prevent the execution of the mother he had not seen since infancy, but after he had succeeded Elizabeth as King James I of England, he had Mary's body removed from Peterborough Cathedral in 1612 and placed in the vault of King Henry VII's Chapel in Westminster Abbey, not far from the tomb of Elizabeth, the cousin and rival for the throne whom she never met in life. **SK**

○ Robert Beale's *The Execution of Mary, Queen of Scots* (1587) is held in a collection at the British Library in London.

"She endured two strokes ... with an axe ... making very small noise or none at all."

A contemporary account of Mary's execution

Raid on Cadiz

Francis Drake attacks Spanish fleet and delays plans for an English invasion.

Francis Drake sailed boldly into Cadiz harbor in broad daylight on April 19, 1587, and proceeded to wreak destruction on the ships that were thronging the crowded port. King Philip II of Spain had made no secret of his "enterprise of England"—his assembling of a great armada to carry an invading army to extirpate Elizabethan England and the Protestant heresy it harbored. In response, Queen Elizabeth had despatched Drake, her boldest seadog, to disrupt the invasion preparations in his flagship the *Elizabeth Bonaventure*.

"The like preparation was never heard of . . . Spain hath to invade England."

Francis Drake, in his journal

For one and a half days he boarded, bootied, and burned—sinking, torching, or capturing some thirty-seven vessels. Laden with spices, wines, oils, and precious metals, Drake sailed out the way he had come. He paused to destroy the supposedly impregnable fortress of Sarges—against the advice of his lieutenant, William Borough, who was court-martialed on his return for opposing Drake.

Drake's destruction on the voyage home of a single Spanish ship laden with new staves to make wine and food barrels was probably his greatest single contribution to delaying and eventually destroying the Spanish Armada. Historians claim that the action forced the Spaniards to use old and inferior barrels, leading to the rotting of much of the armada's food and drink. **NJ**

Armada Defeated

Maritime victory signals England's emergence as a naval superpower.

The Spanish Armada was first sighted off Cornwall in July 1588. By August 25, the English had won a decisive naval victory. In May 1588, the Spanish force of 128 ships (comprising 20 galleon warships and 108 converted trading vessels), 8,000 men, and 19,000 troops had set off to rendezvous with the Spanish army based in the Spanish Netherlands. The English fleet was larger with 197 ships and 16,000 experienced sailors under the command of Charles Howard.

After a near-disastrous escape across the bows of the Spanish ships at Portsmouth, the English fleet

"Thou didst blow with Thy winds and [the Spanish ships] were scattered."

Bishop of Salisbury, after the English victory

harassed the Spanish along the English Channel with their longer-distance, broadside-firing weaponry. But the damage inflicted was light, and the armada's formation remained intact.

On August 6 the armada reached the Straits of Dover and anchored off Calais for the vital rendezvous. But the troops were not ready for boarding. The armada was effectively trapped. The next day Drake sent six fireships into Calais harbor; the result was catastrophic. The Spanish ships cut loose their anchors and lost their defensive formation. Strong winds, sandbanks, and English ships left only a northward retreat. The English fleet now attacked the Spanish ships as they dispersed northward. Only seventy-six ships survived, whereas England lost no ships and only 100 men during the fighting. **JJH**

Hideyoshi Unifies Japan

Toyotomi Hideyoshi's victory at the siege of Odawara finally brings to a conclusion Japan's "Warring States Period."

Hideyoshi's political unification of Japan was complete when the castle at Odawara eventually capitulated in August 1590. Once disparagingly called "monkey" by Oda Nobunaga, the peasant foot soldier Hideyoshi not only succeeded his warlord master but also completed the unification that Nobunaga had left unfinished when he was assassinated in 1582.

Previously, Hideyoshi had conducted a series of swift campaigns against virtually all the *daimyos* (regional warlords), making them his vassals. He did not take the title of shogun but effectively became the supreme commander with the emperor's blessing. However, the northern lords on the main island remained a threat. The Hojo clan persisted in viewing Hideyoshi as a lowly servant. He bided his time in Kyoto, consolidating his position until 1590, when he made a move on the Hojo fortified castle of Odawara. A massive army of more than 100,000 laid siege. Little actual fighting took place, as Hideyoshi starved his enemy into submission rather than launch an all-out attack. While the army waited, the siege came to resemble a town fair, with prostitutes, singers, and circus-style entertainments provided for the troops.

Hideyoshi later became bogged down in a campaign to secure Korea as a gateway for an attack on China. The stalemate that ensued is said to have driven Hideyoshi to a mental breakdown. The once skillful general failed to understand the nature of Korea, her navy, and the residual power of Ming China. He died leaving a weak son in charge of powerful warlords, paving the way for the third great unifier of Japan, Tokugawa Ieyasu. **JJH**

○ *Hideyoshi Blowing a Conch Shell* from "100 Phases of the Moon" is by nineteenth-century artist Tsukioka Yoshitoshi.

Freedom of Worship

King Henry IV grants religious liberties to the French Huguenots.

Henry IV issued the Edict of Nantes, introducing religious toleration, on April 13, 1598. Pope Clement VIII is reported to have said, "This crucifies me," but most French Catholics were content to see social harmony and peace in place of religious division.

In 1589 King Henry of Navarre, leader of the French Huguenots (Protestants), had become King Henry IV of France when Henry III was murdered, leaving no direct heir. Henry IV, whose claim to the throne came through his father, Antoine de Bourbon, founded the Bourbon line of kings. But at the time,

"We are all French and fellow-citizens of the same country."

Henry IV appeals for unity after his conversion

his succession was in no way assured. France was still in the throes of the Religious Wars, and opposing him was the powerful Catholic League, backed by Philip II of Spain. Henry had to win his kingdom by force, and by 1593 only Paris was unconquered. Declaring that *"Paris vaut bien une messe"* ("Paris is well worth a Mass"), Henry permanently renounced Protestantism. The next year he was king.

By 1598, the Catholic League was defeated. Henry confirmed Roman Catholicism as the state church while giving some religious liberties to Protestants. They were allowed to worship in public in twenty designated "free" cities, were granted full civil rights, had their pastors paid by the state, and could keep certain strongholds, such as La Rochelle, as places of safety. **SK**

Death of Philip II

"Champion of the Counter-Reformation" dies with the Spanish Empire at its zenith.

The man who had ruled an empire, Philip II, died on September 13, 1598, in his modest apartment surrounded by his devotional books and small Flemish masterpieces. For Philip, the quill was as mighty as the sword. He had been left copious notes of guidance and instructions by his father, Charles V, and continued to make all his decisions in written memoranda. From one study in the gloomy magnificence of the high-vaulted monastic mausoleum of El Escorial, this solitary, hunched figure issued decrees and read reports from across the

"[Philip's] smile and his dagger were very close."

Cabrera de Cordoba, official court historian

globe that he ruled for forty years, controlling every action his agents and advisers undertook. Philip trusted no one; his suspicions even led him to sanction the murder of one secretary.

His international legacy was mixed. He had tried and failed to subdue England with the ill-fated armada, whereas his religious bigotry had made him the "demon of the south" for the people of the Netherlands, who revolted against his policies. Philip in turn had channeled the Spanish-Atlantic economy into financing his aggressive imperialism, leaving an empty treasury and an exhausted nation. However, the Battle of Lepanto had halted the Ottoman offensive in the Mediterranean, he had unified Spain, and the spread of heresy was prevented in southern Europe and the southern Netherlands. **JJH**

Akbar Threatens Southern India

In a final act of empire building, Akbar marches on Asirgarh, which opens the way for future Mughal encroachments into southern India.

Akbar, whose name means literally "very great," extended the Mughal Empire farther than it had ever been before—from Kashmir in the north and Afghanistan in the northwest to Bengal in the east and the Deccan Plateau in the south. The fort at Asirgarh protected the only easily accessible route from northern India to the Deccan in the southwest. After a long and historic siege, Akbar achieved his final conquest in 1599 and went on to install a governor over this province, under his authority.

It had been more than forty years since Akbar, aged thirteen, had first ruled with a regent, Bairam Khan, and together they had extended Mughal influence over northern India in the region bounded by the Indus and Ganges rivers. The empire was well protected by palace fortresses at Agra, Allahabad, Ajmer, and Lahore. When Akbar came of age in 1560, he began a series of military campaigns against the military threat of the Afghan descendants of Sher Shah (who had ousted Akbar's father, Humayun), and also defeated the Hindu leader Hemu.

The splendor of Akbar's court became world renowned, even though he shifted it between Agra and his new walled capital Fatehpur Sikri (Fortress of Victory). But it was his centralized system of government, dynamic religious tolerance, and fostering of Indian arts and culture that was to bind the 100 million Hindus, Muslims, and other faiths under his rule. Akbar even founded his own religion and certainly had a sense of his own worth, as every morning at dawn he would stand at an open window to be seen and revered by his people. **JJH**

⊙ From the illustrated text *Akbarnama* (*c.*1590), Akbar is seen hunting tigers.

Globe Theatre Opens in London

An open-air, circular playhouse provides a venue for the plays of William Shakespeare.

O This watercolor of the Globe Theatre, Southwark, London, is held in a private collection.

"Within this wooden O . . . 'tis your thoughts that now must deck our kings."

William Shakespeare, *Henry V*, c.1599

The Globe opened in 1599 and was the biggest and most sensational playhouse in Elizabethan London. The open-air, circular building stood on the south bank of the River Thames, in a busy area crowded with bear- and bull-baiting rings, gaming houses, and taverns, and was capable of holding up to 3,000 spectators, who flooded to see the plays of William Shakespeare. Works such as *Hamlet, Othello, King Lear,* and *Macbeth* were performed here for the first time and are still enthralling audiences around the world today.

Shakespeare had arrived in London from the Warwickshire town of Stratford-on-Avon more than ten years before. He had joined the "Chamberlain's Men" (later the "King's Men"), a company of actors that performed regularly at court, and began to make a name for himself as the author of popular comedies and history plays. Following a disagreement over the lease of their theater in Shoreditch, east London, the players dismantled the old building and shipped the timbers across the Thames to build the Globe. Along with six other actors in the company, Shakespeare became a partner in the new theater.

The London crowds flocked to the Globe to see Shakespeare's latest dramatic successes, many of them standing as "groundlings" in the unroofed "yard" in front of the stage, while those prepared to pay for seats filled the three tiers of galleries. In 1613, the original Globe burned to the ground after a cannon used during a play set fire to the thatched roof during a performance of *Henry VIII.* The theater was immediately rebuilt but was closed down by the Puritans in 1642 and never reopened. Today a replica of the Globe, built close to the site of the Elizabethan theater, attracts large audiences for its performances of Shakespeare's plays. **SK**

Bruno Becomes the First "Martyr for Science"

Giordano Bruno is burned as a heretic in Rome for his philosophical beliefs.

"Perhaps your fear in passing judgment on me is greater than mine in receiving it"—with these words Giordano Bruno addressed his judges after hearing the death sentence formally read out to him. A few days later, on February 17, 1600, he was taken, with his tongue locked in a gag, to the Campo de' Fiori in Rome and burned to death at the stake as a heretic.

Born in 1548 in Nola, near Naples in southern Italy, Bruno became a Dominican friar, but before long grew increasingly critical of orthodox theology and was excommunicated in 1576. He left the order and fled to Geneva, where he embraced Calvinism for a time, but finding that the Reformed Church was no more tolerant of his ideas than the Catholic, he adopted the life of a wandering scholar, settling at different times in Paris, Oxford, and Frankfurt, and writing treatises on a vast range of topics, including mathematics, magic, and the occult. His philosophical theories, influenced by pantheistic mysticism, led him to reject the Aristotelian cosmology that put the Earth at the center of the universe. Although he was influenced by the heliocentric theory of Copernicus, he went further, arguing that the universe is infinite, and contains multiple worlds—an idea that anticipated modern science.

In 1591 he journeyed to Venice, and was denounced to the Venetian Inquisition for heresy. The trap was closing around him, and in 1593 he was handed over to the Roman Inquisition. Throughout his seven-year trial, Bruno disclaimed any interest in theological matters, while holding firm to his philosophical beliefs. He appealed to Pope Clement VIII, but refused to make an unconditional retraction and was condemned to death. Bruno's tenacious defense of his unorthodox ideas led many to regard him as the first "martyr for science." **SK**

◐ A late-nineteenth-century engraving of Giordano Bruno shows him being burned at the stake for scientific heresy.

"... if the earth rotates on its axis, what do we mean by rising and setting?"

From the Vatican records of Bruno's trial

Treachery on the Battlefield

The Battle of Sekigahara paves the way to a united Japan.

○ A Japanese popular print of Tokugawa Ieyasu after he overthrew the Toyotomi at the Battle of Sekigahara.

"The summer grasses / All that remain / Of brave soldiers' dreams."

Matsuo Basho, haiku, 1689

The battle of Sekigahara was the most decisive event in early modern Japanese history, establishing the "eastern" Tokugawa clan as the country's effective rulers and inaugurating a long period of peace, stability, and isolation from the outside world, which lasted until the 1860s.

Seeking to seize the strategic Sawayama castle of the rival "western" Toyotomi clan after decades of brutal civil war, Tokugawa Ieyasu made a rapid forced march westward with an army of 80,000 in the autumn of 1600. His move forced the head of the "western" Toyotomi clan, Ishida Mitsunari, to intercept him with a numerically roughly equal force. They met in a drizzly October dawn at the small mountain village of Sekigahara on Honshu Island. Although Mitsunari held the higher ground, this advantage was offset by the secret prior decision of one of his principal commanders, Kobayakawa Hideaki, to betray him. Some 25,000 men of the Mori and Chosokabe clans stood idly by until the outcome of the battle became clear.

Hideaki made his treacherous move and turned his coat around noon after fierce but inconclusive fighting had gone on for some hours. This treason turned the tide of battle, and the western forces retreated in disorder. Some 60,000 were slain, including Ishida, who was captured and executed.

The Battle of Sekigahara put an end to the "western" Toyotomi clan's claims to supremacy, although fifteen years later the Tokugawa clan were to march on their Osaka stronghold and destroy it. Meanwhile, two years after the battle, in 1603, Tokugawa Ieyasu accepted the shogunate of a united Japan, establishing its capital at Edo. Apart from the action against the Toyotomi, the following 250 years of the Edo period were politically stable. **NJ**

Elizabeth's Golden Speech

The sixty-eight-year-old queen of England addresses Parliament for the last time.

The end of Elizabeth I's reign was a time of melancholy decline. As she visibly aged, the main topic of interest at court, spoken behind her back, was who would succeed her. Increasingly isolated since the death of her chief adviser, Lord Burghley, in 1598—for she never established a similar relationship of trust with his son and successor, Robert Cecil—she appeared to have lost her political touch. In 1599 she despatched her favorite, Robert Devereux, Earl of Essex, to put down a rebellion in Ireland. He failed miserably and, returning to England without the queen's permission, insulted her in public. Banished from court, he then attempted to lead an uprising against her and was executed for treason on February 25, 1601.

Later that year, Elizabeth summoned what was to be her last Parliament. The session was a bad-tempered one, with Parliament demanding an end to her use of monopolies—the granting of an exclusive right to trade in certain commodities was a useful way of rewarding servants, and one she was reluctant to abandon. On the afternoon of November 30, the Speaker and 140 Members of Parliament gathered to hear Elizabeth's closing speech. Instead of the rebuke they were expecting to hear, she delivered an uplifting speech on the relationship between a monarch and her subjects. Elizabeth, conscious as ever of creating and maintaining her regal image, had lost none of her ability to flatter her listeners.

Elizabeth's words have since become known to history as "The Golden Speech." It was delivered by a queen so frail that she could barely support the weight of her royal robes, yet she was lauded for her "usual dignity and grace." Less than two years later, on March 24, 1603, she died. The succession passed to her cousin, King James VI of Scotland, son of her old rival, Mary, Queen of Scots. **SK**

⬥ Elizabeth I, by the Italian Federico Zuccari, who traveled to England in 1574 to paint her and members of her court.

> **" . . . this I count the glory of my crown—that I have reigned with your loves."**
>
> **Elizabeth I, "The Golden Speech," 1601**

Japan Is Unified

Tokugawa Ieyasu unifies Japan and founds the Tokugawa shogunate.

○ A Japanese School portrait of Tokugawa Ieyasu (1543–1616) from the seventeenth century.

"To come to know your enemy, first you must become his friend . . ."

Tokugawa Ieyasu

In 1603 Tokugawa Ieyasu was appointed shogun by the emperor Go-yozei; this was the foundation of the Tokugawa shogunate that would rule Japan until 1868. The shogunate had been a long time coming. Lord of a small clan of eastern Honshu, Ieyasu had first become influential as an ally of Oda Nobunaga, who began the unification of Japan in 1568. After Nobunaga's death in 1568 he had initially opposed his successor, Toyotomi Hideyoshi, but switched sides in 1584. In 1590, Ieyasu joined Hideyoshi in crushing Hojo Ujimasa, the last independent feudal lord of Japan. Hideyoshi gave Ieyasu the Hojo lands in exchange for his more centrally situated family lands. Establishing himself at the castle town of Edo, later to be called Tokyo, Ieyasu won the loyalty of the local population through his economic reforms, and the relative isolation of Edo from Kyoto helped him to maintain a high degree of autonomy.

Shortly before his death in 1598, Hideyoshi appointed Ieyasu as head of the regency council on behalf of his young son Hideyori. In 1599 Ieyasu occupied Osaka castle, Hideyori's residence, splitting the regency council and causing a civil war to break out. At the battle of Sekigahara on October 21, 1600, Ieyasu decisively routed his opponents, leaving him in unchallenged control of Japan. Ieyasu's appointment to the shogunate, which had been vacant for forty years, was the final recognition and legitimization of the power he had long held.

Ieyasu's palatial castle at Edo became the administrative capital of Japan. Ieyasu formally abdicated in favor of his son Tokugawa Hidetada in 1605, but nevertheless remained the effective ruler of Japan as "Cloistered Shogun" until his death in 1616. The final challenge to Japan's unity, a rebellion by Hideyori, was crushed in 1615. **JH**

Tilting at Windmills

Don Quixote, *one of the greatest works of European literature, is published.*

According to one tradition, Miguel de Cervantes (1547–1616) wrote *Don Quixote* while he was in prison for debt. This may explain the carelessness with which some of it is written, but the humorous story of the impoverished *hidalgo* (noble) from La Mancha—who reads too many books on chivalry and dons a rusty suit of armor to set out in search of adventure with his dull-witted squire Sancho Panza and his skinny horse Rocinante—proved an instant success. Within weeks of publication, pirated editions were on sale throughout Spain, and within seven years it had been translated into French, German, Italian, and English. The popularity of Cervantes's creation has never diminished, and it has entered deep into the Western imagination—the idiom "tilting at windmills," (to fight futile battles) recalls the episode in which Don Quixote attacks a row of windmills, believing them to be ferocious giants.

A former soldier, Cervantes lost the use of his left hand as a result of a wound received fighting the Ottoman navy at the Battle of Lepanto in 1571. After the battle he was seized by Barbary corsairs, spending five years as a captive in Algiers before being ransomed by his family. Returning to Spain, he struggled to make a life for himself by writing plays while serving intermittently as a tax collector. After publishing *Don Quixote* he went on to write a number of other works that were to add to his reputation as the greatest writer of Spain's "Golden Age."

In 1615 Cervantes was prompted to write a sequel to *Don Quixote* by the appearance of a rival sequel published pseudonymously by Alonso Fernandez de Avellaneda the previous year. He died on the same date (though not the same day because England was using the Julian Calendar) as William Shakespeare, April 23, 1616. **JJH**

○ This first edition of Cervantes's *The Ingenious Gentleman Don Quixote of La Mancha* is in the National Library of Catalonia.

> ***" . . . who keeps a lance in the lance-rack, an ancient shield, a skinny old horse."***
>
> **Opening words of *Don Quixote***

Plot to Blow Up Parliament Is Averted

Guy Fawkes is prevented from blowing up the English Parliament and King James I.

⊙ An engraving of Guy Fawkes and the other conspirators who plotted to blow up Parliament.

At midnight, a party of armed men burst into a cellar beneath the Houses of Parliament and discovered the cowering figure of Guy Fawkes. Not far away were thirty barrels of gunpowder. In a few hours' time, King James I, the royal family, and all the chief officers of state were due to assemble for the State Opening of Parliament. A plot to blow up Parliament, murder the king and his entire government, and start a rebellion had been averted in the nick of time.

Although the plot is forever associated with his name, Guy Fawkes was not a principal conspirator but had been drawn in because of his knowledge of explosives. The chief plotters, led by Robert Catesby, were Catholic gentry who had been disappointed in their hopes of seeing Catholicism restored, or at least tolerated, by James I. They had been hatching their plan for months, and the gunpowder had been placed in the rented cellar in July, in time for the State Opening, which was planned for October 3. But an outbreak of plague delayed the opening, and during this time one of the conspirators, Francis Tresham, warned his brother-in-law, Lord Monteagle, a prominent Catholic, to stay away from the rescheduled opening on November 5. Monteagle passed the warning on to the government.

People in the United Kingdom still remember the failure of the plot every November 5, Guy Fawkes Night, with fireworks and bonfires and the burning of the "guy," but the political significance of the celebration has largely been forgotten. **SK**

A Foothold in Virginia

Jamestown, the first permanent British settlement in the New World, is founded.

○ A steel engraving (c.1850) of John Smith founding Jamestown, the basis for the colony of Virginia.

The first British settlers in the New World intended to "dig, mine, and search for all manner of mines of gold, silver, and copper," and convert "the infidels and savages" of the region to Christianity and civilization. Three ships, the *Susan Constant*, the *Discovery*, and the *Godspeed*, carrying around 100 colonists, reached the Chesapeake Bay area of Virginia in May. From there they sailed up the James River to a spot far enough inland to be safe from a Spanish surprise attack. The colony was called Jamestown in honor of King James I, but unfortunately it had been built on swampy ground and was plagued with malaria. It was also undermined by the incompetence and interminable quarreling and plotting of the colonists. Half of them died during the first winter.

Much time was wasted looking for nonexistent gold mines and a route to China. Jamestown was eventually saved from ruin by one of the colonists, a seasoned soldier and adventurer named John Smith, who traded with the Native Americans of the area for supplies of food. He was presently brought before the principal local chief, Powhatan, and initiated into the tribe in a ceremony that was a mystery to him.

In 1608 Smith was made president of the colony's council and rapidly started persuading his fellow colonists to clear the ground, plant crops, and work together sensibly. He returned to England a year later, but he had kept Jamestown alive. He later explored the American northeast coast and was responsible for naming that area New England. **RC**

The Making of New France

The fortified outpost of Quebec is founded by Samuel de Champlain.

○ A nineteenth-century illustration of the first house erected in Quebec, begun during Samuel de Champlain's founding of Quebec.

Early French interest in the New World focused on the north. In 1524 an expedition discovered the Hudson River and sailed to Nova Scotia, into an area that would come to be called Acadia. In 1535, Jacques Cartier penetrated the St. Lawrence River to the future location of Montreal. A French colony in Florida in the 1560s was wiped out by the Spaniards, but from 1603, French expeditions explored around the St. Lawrence region and two abortive colonies were established in Acadia.

Samuel de Champlain was one of those involved, and made useful contacts with the Native Americans, explored and mapped the Acadian and New England coasts, and penetrated into the interior hoping to find a route to China. It was Champlain who in 1608 founded a trading post at Quebec to control the fur trade. It was the first permanent French settlement in Canada and capital of New France. There were three buildings, defended with a moat, but only eight of the twenty-eight inhabitants survived the winter. Undaunted, Champlain organized a trading network and allied the French with the Algonquins and Hurons against their enemies, the Iroquois. In 1615 he brought the first Christian missionaries to Quebec, and the Jesuits arrived ten years later. Cardinal Richelieu sent more colonists in 1627, but they were captured by the British, who besieged Quebec and starved Champlain into surrender in 1629. The French colony was restored in 1632, and French is still the official language of the Quebec Province. **RC**

Moriscos Expelled from Spain

The Spanish government orders the Moriscos to leave Spain.

⊙ A nineteenth-century Spanish School engraving of the expulsion of the Moriscos from Spain, beginning in 1609.

Philip III of Spain (1598–1621) was content to leave the business of government to his favorite and chief minister, the duke of Lerma, who decided to expel the Moriscos—Muslim descendants who had converted to Christianity after the fall of Granada in 1492—from Spain. It is estimated that as many as 300,000 (about 4 percent of the Spanish population) were forced to leave, between 1609 and 1614, using ships that had been released from the war in the Netherlands. Many Moriscos who remained Catholic settled in Italy and France, but most settled in Morocco and the Ottoman Empire.

Most Spaniards greeted this ruthless act of ethnic cleansing with enthusiasm. In the early years of the sixteenth century, the Moriscos, though ostensibly Catholic, had been tolerated—because the majority were productive and hardworking agricultural laborers, they were protected from persecution by local landowners. But as Spain's war against the Ottoman Empire intensified in the 1560s, suspicion grew that the Moriscos were in league with Spain's Muslim enemies, especially the Barbary pirates who attacked Spanish shipping in the Mediterranean. The banning of Muslim dress and use of the Arabic language by Philip II led in 1569–1571 to an uprising among the Moriscos of Andalusia, as a result of which they were forcibly resettled in other parts of the peninsula. Forty years later Lerma deported them altogether, thus eradicating the last traces of Spain's 900-year-old Islamic culture. **SK**

Who Was "The Onlie Begetter"?

The publication of Shakespeare's Sonnets *raises puzzling questions.*

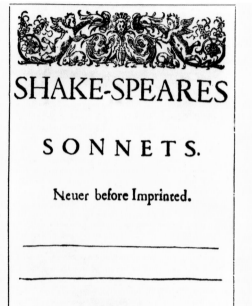

SHAKE-SPEARES

SONNETS.

Neuer before Imprinted.

AT LONDON

By *G. Eld* for *T. T.* and are
to be folde by *Iohn Wright*, dwelling
at Chrift Church gate.
1609.

○ The title page of the first edition of Shakespeare's *Sonnets*,
published in London in 1609.

○ The Chandos portrait (*c.*1610), attributed to John Taylor and
alleged to be of Shakespeare, though never fully proven.

"Let me not to the marriage of true minds / Admit impediments . . ."

William Shakespeare, Sonnet 116

We shall never know whether William Shakespeare authorized the printer Thomas Thorpe to publish the only edition of his sonnets (poems of fourteen lines each) that appeared during his lifetime. The sequence of poems, on themes such as love's ecstasy and despair, the passing of time, separation and betrayal, fame and death, had been written several years before—probably between 1592 and 1598. Most of the 154 sonnets are addressed to an unnamed young man, whom the poet admires in loving and intimate language. This has invited speculation that Shakespeare was romantically involved with the unidentified figure of the printer's dedication, "To the onlie begetter of these insuing sonnets Mr. W. H. . . ."

The initials (in reverse) could apply to Henry Wriothesley, Third Earl of Southampton, to whom Shakespeare dedicated two longer poems, "Venus and Adonis" and "The Rape of Lucrece." Other scholars have suggested William Herbert, Earl of Pembroke, but many theories abound—including the possibility that they are an unfortunate misprint of William Shakespeare's own initials—W. S.

The speculation does not end there. Some twenty-seven of the sonnets are addressed to a woman, commonly referred to as the "Dark Lady," with whom the poet is painfully and jealously in love. Many attempts have been made to identify her, but it is probably a mistake to look for too many autobiographical clues in the poems—it is not even certain that the order in which Shakespeare wrote them is reflected in the book. What the sonnets reveal, as do his plays, is his extraordinary genius and ability to expose the psychology of the human heart, with all its sorrows and passions, in language that still thrills and resonates with readers today. **SK**

Astronomical Breakthrough

Using a homemade telescope, Galileo discovers the four moons of Jupiter.

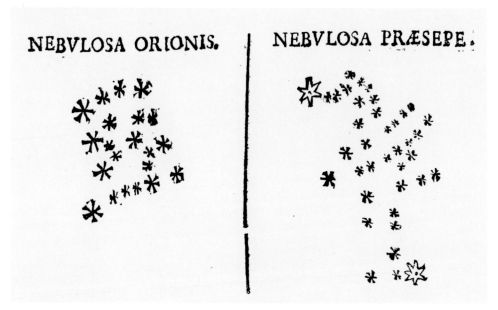

NEBVLOSA ORIONIS.　　NEBVLOSA PRÆSEPE.

◐ A seventeenth-century print of Galileo's observation of the star cluster in Orion and of the Praesepe cluster in 1610.

In 1609 reports reached Galileo Galilei that a Flemish spectacle maker, Hans Lipperhey, had invented an instrument that greatly magnified distant objects. Galileo, then professor of mathematics at the University of Padua, was famous for his contributions to the study of motion—he is said to have demonstrated by dropping balls from the leaning Tower of Pisa that the speed of falling bodies is not proportional to their weight. He now set out to make a telescope, grinding his own lenses, and perfected one that could magnify objects twenty times.

Galileo turned his telescope to the moon and showed its surface was "rough and uneven, and just like the surface of the Earth," rather than the smooth, perfect sphere described by Aristotle and Ptolemy.

Between January 7 and 13, 1610, Galileo observed the changing positions of four celestial bodies in the vicinity of Jupiter and concluded that they were moons orbiting the planet. He published his startling findings—which turned on its head the Aristotelian model of the universe, in which everything orbited in orderly fashion around the Earth—in a short treatise, *The Starry Messenger*, in March.

In 1611 Galileo demonstrated his telescope to the mathematicians of the Jesuit College in Rome and was elected a member of the Accademia dei Lincei, Italy's foremost scientific institute. However, his championing of the Copernican system, which maintained that the planets move around the sun, was making him enemies within the Church. **SK**

Act of a Madman

An assassin strikes down Henry IV while he is being driven through Paris.

⊙ An engraving shows Ravaillac rushing at King Henry IV's carriage brandishing a long knife.

François Ravaillac was waiting on the king's route where the street narrowed, forcing the royal coach to stop. He leaped on board and attacked and stabbed Henry IV, who died immediately.

Ravaillac was a fanatical Catholic, obsessed by religion—he had been rejected for the Jesuit priesthood because he was "prey to visions." Despite being tortured, he denied having accomplices, but it is possible he was part of a wider plot. It was well known in Paris that Henry was planning to send an army to north Germany to intervene on behalf of a Calvinist prince against the emperor, and others may have worked on Ravaillac's unbalanced mind to persuade him to carry out the murder. Condemned as a regicide, he was taken to the Place de Greve, scalded to death with molten lead and boiling oil, mutilated, then pulled apart by four horses.

Henry IV, practical, energetic, and good-humored, had been popular—he is best known for saying that every French laborer should have *une poule au pot* (chicken) to eat on Sunday. With his minister, the Duc de Sully, he began to mend France's shattered economy after years of civil war by encouraging trade and industry. The Pont Neuf, the bridge built by Henry across the Seine, still stands today. In 1600, he married his second wife, Marie de Médicis, mother of the future King Louis XIII. But his greatest love was his mistress, Gabrielle d'Estrées, and his many other love affairs won him the fond nickname of *le vert galant* (gay old spark). **SK**

Death of Caravaggio

The greatest painter of his age dies aged thirty-eight, but his body is never found.

○ Caravaggio's *Ailing Bacchus*, c.1593, which some believe to be a self-portrait.

◔ *The Martyrdom of St. Matthew* (detail), painted 1599 to 1600, shocked people with its realistic depiction of the saint.

"He lacked any preconceived distinction between the beautiful and the ugly."

Cardinal del Monte, 1610

Michelangelo Merisi da Caravaggio was born in 1571 in Milan. After a painting apprenticeship, he went to Rome in 1592 and within a couple of years, although living virtually destitute on the street, he began a remarkable career, first by producing paintings of low life (such as *The Card-Sharps*, 1594) and then, from 1597, of religious scenes. Many of the latter had radical compositions, stripped bare of the supernatural trappings of the late Renaissance and the Counter-Reformation.

His remarkable *Calling of St. Matthew* and its companion piece the *Martyrdom of St. Matthew* (both 1600) caused a sensation and led him to be described as the most renowned artist in Rome. Religious figures had never before been painted with a realistic touch that treated them as ordinary citizens. But despite a string of commissions, his work continued to shock both his patrons and the general public—particularly for the everyday detail and flawed humanity applied to the loftiest themes, and his capture of the most dramatic moment in a story.

From his arrival in Rome he had been involved in a violent, perhaps homoerotic subculture. In 1606 he killed a man in a brawl and fled to Naples and then Malta. After a few years he was arrested and expelled to Sicily, where he worked intensively while displaying increasing symptoms of paranoia. He then returned to Naples, where his face was severely wounded in another brawl. In Naples he twice painted this disfigurement, in *Salome with the Head of John the Baptist* and *David with the Head of Goliath*. His final journey was as a stowaway on a boat to Rome, to seek a pardon from the pope for the man he had killed. He died alone after collapsing and catching a fever while desperately running along the beach to catch the boat and retrieve his belongings. **PF**

Pocahontas Weds

Daughter of Powhatan marries Jamestown colonist John Rolfe.

The winter of 1609 to 1610 saw the colonists who had founded Jamestown penned in their fort by the hostile local people and reduced to eating dogs and cats. One man even ate his dead wife.

In 1613 Pocahontas, the daughter of Powhatan, the local chief, was then about seventeen. She had been friendly and helpful to the newcomers—and enjoyed cheerfully turning cartwheels around the fort stark naked—but was taken hostage by the colonists, who tried to ransom her to her father. He refused, but the colonists liked Pocahontas. They gave her Bible lessons and baptized her as Rebecca, naming her for the brave and resourceful wife of Isaac. The following year in Jamestown's chapel she married an English colonist, John Rolfe. Powhatan was not at the wedding but he did not object, and the marriage, as was probably intended, helped to bring about a reconciliation between the colonists and their Native American neighbors, who had both tired of the feud. The English hoped that Pocahontas might lead the way for all her people to become Christians, and in 1616 she and her husband arrived in England with their new baby, Thomas, to raise money and support. The English found *la belle sauvage* delightful, but she fell seriously ill as she was starting on the return voyage to Virginia. The ship landed at Gravesend, where she died, and her grave can be seen at the church of St. George to this day.

Her father, Powhatan, died a year later and the future English colonists of Virginia proved to be bent more on conquest than peaceful coexistence. Pocahontas's son, Thomas Rolfe, was brought up in England and emigrated to Virginia in 1640. Through him, Pocahontas's bloodline was to descend to thousands of white Americans. **RC**

Trouble in Prague

Two Catholic regents thrown from a Prague window spark Thirty Years' War.

The local Estates met in Prague on May 23, its noble members determined to protest about recent developments. Not only had Archduke Ferdinand of Styria, the new Bohemian king and also the Holy Roman Emperor designate, banned non-Catholics from holding office, but also the Protestant church in Klostergrab had been pulled down and the one in Braunau closed. The authorities ordered the Estates to disperse, but instead they took their cue from Count Thurm and marched to the Nradschin Palace. Here they seized two Catholic regents, Martinitz and Slavata, hastily tried them on charges of ignoring the Letters of Majesty that had granted Bohemia freedom of religion in 1609, and found them guilty. Their summary punishment was to be thrown out of a high window—the men survived, a sign of divine intervention, according to the Catholics, although the Protestants noted that they landed on a dung heap. The word "defenestration" was thus coined.

Probably three-quarters of Germany had become Protestant by the end of the sixteenth century. Many felt that the old religion would be swept away, until the Counter-Reformation gathered pace.

The events of May 23 unleashed a conflict lasting for three decades. If it began as a religious war, the enormously complicated Thirty Years' War became more political as the contest in Bohemia became linked with the war between the Spanish Habsburgs and the Dutch. The war ended in 1648 with the Treaty of Westphalia. Germany had become a collection of absolute monarchies, with the Habsburg Holy Roman Emperor ruling Austria. **RP**

○ *The Defenestration of Prague*, an oil painting depicting the events that began the Thirty Years' War.

Slaves Stolen and Sold in North America

In Jamestown, Virginia, human beings from Africa are sold as indentured servants to the highest bidder.

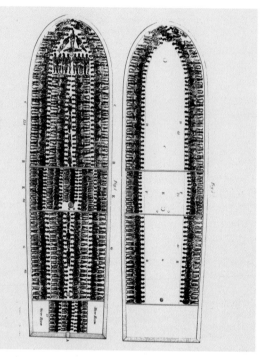

A MAP of the most INHABITED part of VIRGINIA containing the whole PROVINCE of MARYLAND with Part of PENSILVANIA, NEW JERSEY and NORTH CAROLINA. Drawn by Joshua Fry & Peter Jefferson in 1775.

The English settlement at Jamestown grew quickly following its foundation in 1607, and by 1620 almost 1,000 people had emigrated to Virginia. Although the hoped-for gold did not materialize, the valuable alternative tobacco took its place, finding a ready and profitable market back in England despite the strictures of James I (the king's *Counterblaste to Tobacco* had been published, to little effect, in 1604). But the tobacco crops flourished and the industry soon required more labor than the colonists themselves could provide.

In August 1619 the *San Juan Bautista*, a Portuguese vessel carrying 350 slaves from Luanda in Angola to Mexico, was attacked and seized by two ships, the *Treasurer* and the *White Lion*, one flying a Dutch flag, the other flying an English one. Fifty Africans were taken ashore to Jamestown, and "twenty and odd" were sold as indentured servants to the colonists.

Under the terms of an indenture, the Africans were obliged to give their labor to an employer for seven years in return for accommodation and food. This was the first recorded arrival of Africans in British North America, although thirty other Africans were mentioned in a census of Virginia earlier in the year. The first clear evidence for slavery dates from 1640, when John Punch, a runaway indentured servant, is recorded as being sentenced to serve his master for the rest of his life, and in 1662, slavery was recorded within the colony's statutory law. **PF**

◆ A plan of the hold of a slave ship; ships like these brought thousands of Africans into a life of misery in the New World.

◆ Detail from *A Map of the Most Inhabited Part of Virginia . . .* drawn by Joshua Fry and Peter Jefferson, 1775.

Mayflower Sails

A sea voyage becomes one of the founding myths of the United States.

The 160-ton *Mayflower* carried a crew of about thirty. Traveling with them were approximately 102 Puritans—men, women, and children—who were mainly younger members of an exiled separatist Puritan congregation that had broken away from the Church of England in Nottinghamshire and sought sanctuary from state persecution at Leiden in the Netherlands. Fearing absorption into Dutch culture, the community raised money in London and chartered two ships to take them to a new colony in Virginia.

"They blessed God who had brought them over the vast and furious ocean."

William Bradford, Pilgrim Father

After two false starts, one ship, the smaller *Speedwell*, was abandoned and its passengers crammed into the *Mayflower*. The sixty-six-day voyage of 2,750 miles (4,425 km) was stormy, and one passenger, William Butten, and one crew member died. Another passenger, Elizabeth Hopkins, gave birth to a son during the voyage and baptized him Oceanus.

Blown off course, the *Mayflower* made landfall at Cape Cod (in current-day Massachusetts) on November 11. A permanent colony was established on December 21. The successful voyage gave the early English settlements in New England their strongly Puritanical flavor, a sense of sturdy independence from central authority, and the idea that they were uniquely favored by God. **NJ**

First Thanksgiving

The Pilgrim Fathers celebrate their first year in the New World.

The men, women, and children who sailed from Plymouth in England on board the *Mayflower* in 1620 were dominated by Puritan dissidents looking for freedom to practice their brand of Calvinist Christianity. They were bound for Virginia, but after a traumatic voyage they dropped anchor in Cape Cod harbor in November and found a sheltered site they called New Plymouth. There they built houses and a protective palisade.

The colonists were helped by the local American Indian tribe—who welcomed them to the settlement as potential allies against their neighbors—and managed to survive a fierce winter. By the summer, half of the colonists were dead, but in the autumn their leader, William Bradford, invited the local chief and his braves to a harvest feast to thank God for the colony's abundant crop of corn, beans, squash, and barley. He wanted to celebrate the conclusion of their first year in the New World, a year characterized by struggle, sorrow, heartbreak, and fortitude. His men went out to hunt fowl for meat, and the locals brought five deer as a contribution as well as something the colonists called "popped corn." They feasted on wild turkey, goose, duck, venison, and possibly fish, cooked outdoors and eaten with knives and their fingers (forks had not yet been invented) in a celebration that lasted for several days. One of the colonists is reputed to have said, "We have found the Indians very faithful in their covenant of peace with us, very loving . . . "

The celebration is now commemorated as Thanksgiving Day, which has become an annual day of thanksgiving in the United States. Traditionally it is a family-oriented celebration held on the fourth Thursday in November. **RC**

Dutch West India Company Seizes Bahia

The city of Bahia changes colonial hands and becomes a slave-port.

○ *Capture of the City of Salvador (Bahia) by the Dutch Fleet*, a 1624 painting by Andries van Eertvelt (1590–1652).

After the discovery of Brazil in 1500, the Portuguese took their time creating a colony. Their first founded settlement was Bahia, now Salvador da Bahia, where 400 settlers, including both priests and prostitutes, arrived in 1549. It became Brazil's leading port. But both the French and the Dutch wanted a new empire. The French took control of Rio de Janeiro harbor in 1555, but were pushed out by the Portuguese in 1567, and Dutch ships were either attacking Spanish settlements in the Caribbean or surreptitiously trading with them.

In May 1624, the recently formed Dutch West India Company sent an expedition that seized Bahia. The following year a Spanish-Portuguese force (Spain and Portugal shared a monarchy from 1580 to 1640),

expelled them, but in 1630 they returned to grab the Pernambuco region. Prince Maurice of Nassau, of the House of Orange, was governor from 1637 to 1644, when the Dutch founded the provincial capital of Recife. Many Dutch Jews came to settle there and sugar plantations were established. A battle between the Dutch and Spanish-Portuguese fleet in 1640 was inconclusive, but after a long struggle with the Pernambuco landowners, the Dutch were driven out in 1654 and the Portuguese returned.

Slaves were imported from Africa in substantial numbers, and Salvador de Bahia, which was Brazil's principal slave-trading port, is today a center of Brazilian-African culture and traditions, including the voodoo-style religious cult called Candomblé. **RC**

Peter Minuit Purchases Manhattan

The Dutch buy the island of Manhattan from local Native Americans.

○ *The Purchase of Manhattan Island*, an illustration by Alfred Frederick, c.1892.

The first exploration of what is now New York State was carried out by English navigator Henry Hudson, who traveled up the river to which he left his name when searching for a northwest passage to Asia in 1609. He was working for the Dutch, who in 1624 established bases in New Netherland, including a fur-trading post among the Mohawks at Fort Orange and a farming settlement on Manhattan Island, which the Dutch director-general, a Walloon called Peter Minuit, bought from the local Delaware chieftains. According to the apocryphal story, he swindled them out of the land for a mere $24 worth of beads, but historians dismiss this. One surviving contemporary document says that he "purchased the Island of Manhattes from the Indians for the value of 60 guilders." When he bought Staten Island, Minuit paid in cloth, kettles, axes, hoes, awls, wampum, and Jews' harps, and presumably Manhattan was purchased similarly. Whether the Delaware *sachems* (kings) had any right to sell the land, or any concept of permanent land ownership, is doubtful.

Minuit made what became New Amsterdam the center of Dutch operations in the region. He maintained friendly relations with the Delaware and the Mohawks, and in 1627 sent letters to Governor William Bradford in New Plymouth that opened up trade between the Dutch and English colonies in North America. He also helped establish the colony of New Sweden, now Wilmington, Delaware, in 1637 to 1638. It was annexed by the Dutch in 1655. **RC**

Greatest Church in Christendom

Pope Urban VIII dedicates the new basilica of St. Peter's in Rome.

○ A painting from the Roman School, 1665, showing a view of St. Peter's in Rome, with Bernini's colonnade.

◑ *Longitudinal Cross Section of St. Peter's in Rome*, from a nineteenth-century Italian School engraving.

> **"Upon this rock I will build my church . . . I will give you the keys . . . of heaven."**
>
> **Matthew 16:18–19, inscribed on the dome**

Towering over the city of Rome and crowned by its magnificent dome, the new basilica of St. Peter's symbolized all the might and splendor of the Counter-Reformation papacy. For 120 years, since construction began in 1506 under Pope Julius II, generations of Romans had observed the work in progress. In 1626, even as Pope Urban VIII solemnly dedicated the building, there was still a long way to go before completion. The piazza in front of St. Peter's, designed by Gianlorenzo Bernini, would not be finished until 1667.

The new building replaced the fourth-century basilica that Emperor Constantine constructed to mark the site where the apostle St. Peter is traditionally said to be buried. By the end of the fifteenth century, the basilica was dilapidated, and it was decided to erect a more worthy building. It was the selling of indulgences to pay for this new church that led Luther to make his stand at Wittenberg in 1517.

Bramante, the great architect of the High Renaissance, won the commission to design the new basilica. He was succeeded by Raphael and Giuliano da Sangallo, who modified the original Greek-cross plan to a Latin cross with an extended nave. In 1547, Pope Paul III persuaded Michelangelo to take over the work. He was then in his seventies and reluctant to take it on, but he is regarded as the principal designer of a large part of the building. Incorporating the previous designs, he redrew the body of the church. He also began work on the dome, which was completed by Giacomo della Porta. With an interior diameter of 139 feet (42 m), this amazing structure rises a stupendous 394 feet (120 m) above the high altar, beneath which the remains of St. Peter are believed to lie. **SK**

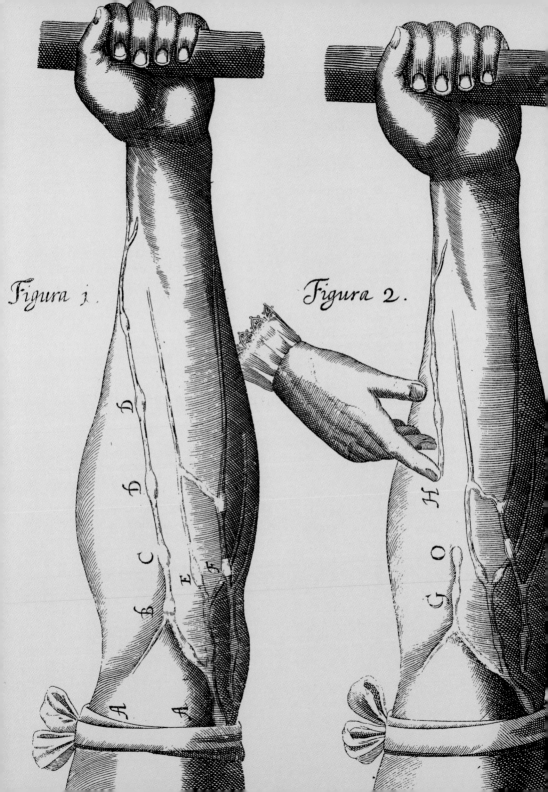

Figura 1.

Figura 2.

The Heart Explained

William Harvey shows that blood is pumped around the body by the heart.

We take the function of the heart so much for granted that it is difficult to grasp the magnitude of William Harvey's discovery, published in his work *Exercitatio Anatomica de Motu Cordis et Sanguinis in Animalibus* (*An Anatomical Exercise on the Motion of the Heart and Blood in Animals*), that it is a pump, circulating the blood around the body and back to the heart.

Born in 1578 in Folkestone, Kent, Harvey had studied medicine at the University of Padua, reputed to have the best medical school in Europe (Italy was regarded as the center of anatomical study), where he had sat at the feet of Hieronymus Fabricius (Girolamo Fabrici), the leading anatomist of the day. On returning to England in 1602, he married the daughter of a physician to the royal household, and it may have been through her family's influence that he obtained the post of physician to St. Bartholomew's Hospital in London.

Harvey's great passion was for anatomy. Determined to discover how blood passes through the heart, he dissected every kind of creature from earthworms and insects to mammals, eventually arriving at a correct description of the circulatory system. His book made him famous throughout Europe, although traditionalists, especially in France, ridiculed his findings, which contradicted the long-established writings of Galen (*c.*129–216). A few years after Harvey's death in 1657, Marcello Malpighi was able to confirm with a microscope that he had correctly assumed the existence of capillaries, too small to be identified with the human eye, linking the arterial to the venous system. **SK**

◐ A 1628 diagram shows the existence of valves in veins from Harvey's *Anatomical Exercise on the Motion of the Heart.*

A City Upon a Hill

John Winthrop and the Massachusetts Bay Company found Boston.

After the Pilgrim Fathers settled in New Plymouth, they started founding other small settlements nearby, fueled by the arrival of more immigrants from England. In 1628, the Massachusetts Bay Company was founded in England.

On the face of it, it was a commercial venture, but this cloaked an intention to create another center for dissident Puritans. One of the leaders was John Winthrop, squire of Groton, who disapproved of the Church of England and viewed King Charles I as a tyrant. Winthrop was chosen governor of the company

> ## "Ye are the light of the world. A city that is set on an hill cannot be hid."
>
> **Matthew 5:14**

and the settlers crossed the Atlantic in eleven ships in 1630, with Winthrop aboard the *Arbella*. He picked a site with a fine harbor on the Charles River, which they named Boston after the Lincolnshire town in England. In a sermon preached on the *Arbella*, Winthrop told the settlers, "We shall be as a city upon a hill. The eyes of all people are upon us."

Only the godly, the "saints," were allowed to vote or form the colony's government. Church attendance was compulsory and Winthrop issued edicts against gambling, blasphemy, sexual misbehavior, and excessive drinking, although he rejected a demand for all women to be veiled. Through the 1630s, the flow of immigrants increased, and by 1643 more than 20,000 Englishmen had reached Massachusetts Bay. Boston became the area's leading port and city. **RC**

Magdeburg Stormed

Sweden's King Gustavus Adolphus fails to reinforce the Protestant city of Magdeburg, allowing it to be sacked by forces of the Holy Roman Empire.

The first major battle of the Thirty Years' War was fought in 1620 when forces of the Holy Roman Emperor Ferdinand II's Catholic League defeated Frederick V, head of the Protestant Union of Princes, at the Battle of the White Mountain outside Prague. The Protestant cause, though, was saved by the intervention of Sweden's King Gustavus Adolphus, who wished to preserve a bulwark of Protestant states in Germany against the imperial advance from the south.

In 1630, Magdeburg, a strategic Protestant town on the River Elbe, was besieged by imperial general Count Gottfried von Pappenheim. The city withstood a winter siege while awaiting relief from Gustavus. Aware that the Swedish army was approaching, imperial commander Count Johann Tilly and 26,000 men joined Pappenheim in April 1631.

Gustavus was unable to march swiftly to the city's relief owing to the vacillations of the Lutheran electors of Saxony and Brandenburg, who were torn between imperial rule and their reluctance to depend on the Swedish invaders. Eventually, Pappenheim and Tilly stormed Magdeburg's walls.

For two days the mainly mercenary imperial soldiers killed and looted until the city caught fire. Shocked by the soldiers' excesses, Tilly remained immobile in Magdeburg's smouldering ruins for the rest of the summer, allowing the electors of Saxony and Brandenburg to finally ally with Gustavus against further imperial attacks. Magdeburg remains a byword for the atrocious slaughter of the Thirty Years' War and retarded Germany's development for centuries to come. **NJ**

◑ The Imperial army under general Tilly storming the town of Magdeburg on May 20, 1631.

Monument to Love

The Taj Mahal is erected to commemorate Mumtaz Mahal, wife of Shah Jahan I.

Mumtaz Mahal—the name was bestowed on her by her doting husband and means "beloved ornament of the palace"—was the third and favorite wife of Shah Jahan I, fifth of the Mughal emperors to rule over most of India. His grief at her death in childbirth with their fourteenth child moved him to order the building of the Taj Mahal mausoleum at Agra. It is considered the jewel of India's Islamic architecture and one of the wonders of the world.

Mumtaz Mahal was born in April 1593 in Agra, the daughter of a Persian noble, and was betrothed

"A teardrop that glistens spotlessly bright on the cheek of time."

Rabindranath Tagore (1861–1941)

to Jahan, then called Prince Khurram, aged fourteen. They married on May 10, 1612, when she was nineteen, and Jahan succeeded his father as emperor in 1627. Poets extolled her beauty and virtue and praised her honesty and lack of political ambition. Her husband loved and trusted her, took her on his travels and military campaigns, and even entrusted her with the imperial seal, the Muhr Uzah, as regent.

The Taj Mahal, an exquisite domed structure standing 180 feet (55 m) tall, was commissioned by Shah Jahan after he emerged from a year of official mourning for his wife—his hair reputedly turned prematurely white with grief. Twenty thousand workers toiled for twenty-two years to complete the structure in 1653. On his death in 1666, Jahan was buried beside his beloved wife in the Taj Mahal. **NJ**

Lion of the North Dies

The death of Gustavus Adolphus sobers triumphant Protestants at Lützen.

Swedish King Gustav II Adolf, Latinized as "Gustavus Adolphus," earned the nickname "Lion of the North" as a tribute to his military leadership. In 1630, he had led the Swedish army into Germany and transformed the Thirty Years' War, reviving Protestant resistance to the Habsburg Empire and the Catholic League. His hallmarks were aggression and mobility, maximizing firepower, and leading his cavalry in charges.

At Lützen in Saxony in 1632, Gustavus's opponent was imperial commander Wallenstein, an arrogant general with a string of victories to his credit.

"I am ready to risk my life and to shed my blood with you."

Gustavus Adolphus to his troops at Lützen

Wallenstein was withdrawing to winter quarters in nearby Leipzig when Gustavus saw this as an opportunity to attack, forcing Wallenstein to turn and give battle. In an impenetrable smog of gunpowder smoke and mist, almost 40,000 men clashed. The Swedish infantry suffered grievously, advancing into the fire of entrenched imperial soldiers and a battery of heavy cannon. In the heat of battle, Gustavus's death went unnoticed.

Despite Gustavus's demise, the Swedes won the battle. Around half of the imperial forces were killed in the bloodbath, and Wallenstein was forced to withdraw from Saxony. But victory brought more grief than joy to Sweden. The Battle of Lützen will always be remembered for the loss of the king and the 6,000 men who fell on the battlefield. **RG**

Galileo Recants His Views Under Torture

The Inquisition summons Galileo to Rome to stand trial on charges of heresy.

○ *Galileo Galilei Before Members of the Holy Office in the Vatican in 1633*, an 1847 painting by Joseph-Nicolas Robert-Fleury.

It was one of the most famous trials in history: on the one side, the Inquisition, insisting on the literal truth of the Bible—that God had set the Earth on its unmovable foundations—on the other, Galileo, with his belief in the Copernican theory that the Earth and the other planets moved around the sun. Ordered on pain of torture to recant his views, Galileo did so. He supposedly muttered, "*Eppur si muove*" (And yet it does move) as he rose from his knees, but there is no evidence to support this.

Galileo, a Roman Catholic, had been told not to "hold or defend" Copernican ideas by Cardinal Bellarmine in 1616. However, the Church had never formally condemned Copernicanism, and when, in 1623, Cardinal Maffeo Barberini, a longtime supporter of Galileo, was elected Pope Urban VIII, he permitted Galileo to write about theories of the universe on condition that he treated Copernican ideas "hypothetically." The book, *Dialogue Concerning the Two Principal Systems of the World*, was published in 1632. It took the form of a witty exchange between Salviatus (representing Galileo) and Simplicius (the dyed-in-the-wool Aristotelian). Naturally, Salviatus has a better argument and Simplicius looks a fool.

Galileo was summoned to Rome and ordered to stand trial on charges of heresy. His sentence of life imprisonment was later transmuted to house arrest in his villa at Arcetri, near Florence, where he continued working and writing, even after going blind. He died on January 8, 1642. **SK**

Japan Chooses Isolation

The Tokugawa Iemitsu shogunate forbids all contact outside of Japan.

○ *Sueyoshi's Junk*, color on wood, a votive tablet from 1633; before the closing of Japan in 1635, boats such as this traded regularly.

During the sixteenth century, Japan had warmly welcomed its growing trade with the outside world, with innovations and certain imports such as clocks and firearms proving popular with the ruling elite. Christianity, too, made inroads into the traditional Japanese religion, and by the end of the century, there were an estimated 500,000 Japanese converts in the country. From 1600 onward, however, under the Tokugawa shogunate, a reaction set in: Christianity began to be persecuted, thousands of Catholic missionaries and converts were crucified, and the religion's practice was forbidden to the Japanese.

In a series of decrees culminating in the so-called *Sakoku* (Closed Country) edict of 1635, the Tokugawa Iemitsu shogunate finally forbade all contact with the outside world. Japanese citizens, on pain of death, were forbidden to travel or trade abroad; and foreigners were only allowed to land on the cordoned-off island of Deshima off Nagasaki, the southwestern port that had previously been a center of Japanese Christianity and foreign enclaves. Two Portuguese who traveled to Japan to plead for a relaxation of the edict were executed.

Although Japanese culture, such as martial arts, the tea ceremony, and its Shinto religion, flourished under these xenophobic laws, its technology and economy were held back until U.S. Admiral Perry and the Meiji dynasty enforced a relaxation of relations and a limited opening to the world and international trade in the 1850s. **NJ**

Académie Française Is Founded

The official guardian of the French language, the Académie Française continues to fulfill its original role almost 400 years later.

The Académie Française is a uniquely French institution. Created by King Louis XIII on the urging of Cardinal Richelieu, his first minister and architect of the absolutist French monarchy, it regulated French grammar and spelling during the classical age of French literature. An official French dictionary was published in 1698, and seven editions followed.

Royal patronage molded public taste in seventeenth-century France, and Louis XIV's finance minister, Jean-Baptiste Colbert, established similar academies for painting and sculpture (1648), inscriptions and medals (1663), sciences (1666), and architecture (1671). Abolished during the Revolution, the academies were reestablished by Napoleon Bonaparte as the Institut de France. The Académie Française remains France's authority on the usage, grammar, and vocabulary of the French language. It polices the infiltration of foreign loanwords—insisting on using French words, for example, *ordinateur* (computer), *logiciel* (software), and *courriel* (e-mail) instead of using English for these words as most other languages do.

Members of the Académie are known as *les immortels* (the immortals). Their numbers are always limited to forty, and they are self-electing. Since Napoleon's day, they have worn an embroidered uniform and carry swords on ceremonial occasions. Most académiciens are writers, although distinguished politicians, diplomats, lawyers, and clergy may be elected. There have been 700 immortals since the creation of the Académie Française, though only four females among them. **SK**

⬡ *Portrait of Armand-Jean du Plessis, Cardinal Richelieu,* oil on canvas by Philippe de Champaigne, c.1639.

Catalonia Rises

Catalonia goes it alone and a Catalan Republic is declared.

Catalonia had long found rule from Castile oppressive. The county of Barcelona had become part of the kingdom of Aragon in the twelfth century, although it retained its distinct rights and became a flourishing center of culture, maritime power, and trade in the high Middle Ages. The region, with its Mediterranean orientation, missed out on much of the boom created by Spain's New World empire, and social and political problems emerged during the reign of Philip II, who sought to break down the region's remaining autonomy. Tensions with Madrid revived during the Thirty Years' War, when the chief government minister, the Count de Olivares, taxed the region heavily and when conflict with France over Roussillon, a Catalan county in the eastern Pyrenees, required the region to support the large Spanish armies.

Unrest broke out on "Bloody Corpus," Corpus Christi Day, June 7, 1640. The spontaneous peasant uprising led by a militia known as the Miquelets marched into Barcelona. Several royal officials were killed and their houses sacked. Faced with the threat of a Castilian invasion, in January the following year Pau Claris, the president of the Generalitat or ruling council, declared a Catalan Republic under French protection; this was confirmed in a military victory over the Spanish crown at Montjuic in January 1641. Claris died shortly thereafter, and, with the Castilian army close to taking Barcelona, Louis XIII of France was proclaimed Luis I of Barcelona. The guerrilla conflict that ensued over the next twelve years is known as the Reapers' Wars and ended in the Treaty of the Pyrenees in 1659, which resulted in Roussillon being incorporated into France but confirmed Madrid's hold over Barcelona. **PF**

Portugal Freed

The eighth duke of Bragança is acclaimed King João IV of Portugal.

Being subsumed into the Spanish Empire for sixty years—after Philip II invaded in 1581—hurt Portuguese pride but little else. A few Spanish garrisons were established, but it was never a military occupation. The Portuguese were not required to contribute to the Spanish treasury, and the Spanish crown bolstered Portugal's seaboard defenses and the Atlantic route to Brazil. Access to the Spanish-American economy made many Portuguese wealthy. As long as the pro-Habsburg Portuguese nobility received titles, offices, and financial benefit from the merger of the two crowns, an independent nation was not on the agenda.

What changed was Philip IV's attempts to introduce more Castilians to offices in Portugal to lessen their hardships as the Spanish-American economy declined and the Habsburg monarchy becoming embroiled in foreign wars. Portuguese interests were jettisoned and, to add insult to injury, they were forced to pay taxes to sustain these wars.

Popular revolt followed in 1637, which was swiftly put down by Castilian troops. Fearing greater Spanish incursions, the aristocratic ringleaders planned a coup. The catalyst came in 1640, when the count-duke of Olivares pressured Dom João of Bragança—the greatest landholder in Portugal—to enlist thousands of Portuguese troops to counter the revolt in Catalonia. The conspirators—Antonio Vaz de Almada, Miguel de Almeida, and João Pinto Ribeiro—had Secretary of State Miguel de Vasconcelos assassinated and Margaret of Savoy, governor of Portugal, imprisoned. Dom João was proclaimed king, and the Spanish garrisons were driven out. Spain, with her troops tied up fighting the Dutch and French, could only look on. **JJH**

Great Work Completed

Rembrandt finishes The Night Watch, *his largest and most famous painting.*

Critics have long regarded Rembrandt's *The Night Watch* as one of the greatest works of northern European art. Commissioned to hang in the grand new headquarters of Amsterdam's town militia, it is a busy group portrait of the company of Captain Frans Banning Cocq and shows a number of well-dressed, armed citizen soldiers marching down a street. The picture acquired its name in the eighteenth century, when darkened varnish falsely suggested a night scene.

When he completed the painting, Rembrandt Harmensz van Rijn, to give him his full name, was at the height of his fame. Born in Leiden in 1609, he had settled in Amsterdam, establishing a reputation as a prodigiously talented painter of historic and biblical subjects and portraits. Always searching for new effects, in *The Night Watch* he turned all the conventional rules of group portraiture on their head—instead of the usual formal lineup, he created a vast and complex action scene, which shows a group of men, armed with muskets and pikes, streaming out through a dark arch. A man beats a drum, the standard-bearer unfurls his flag, while at the front the dominating figure of Banning Cocq is seen urging his men forward. In its dynamism, the painting seems to encapsulate the independent spirit and civic pride of Amsterdam, the mercantile center driving the prosperity of the new Dutch Republic.

The Night Watch proved the high point in Rembrandt's career; after it, commissions began to dry up. He died at sixty-three in 1669. **SK**

◐ A detail from Rembrandt's *Night Watch* (1642), a group image of the civic guards of Captain Frans Banning Cocq.

Civil War Begins

Charles Stuart raises his standard and triggers civil war in Britain.

Toward the end of a stormy summer's day, the diminutive, aloof, and unpopular king of England and Scotland, Charles I, accompanied by a group of noblemen, raised the royal standard from the top of the highest tower of Nottingham Castle. He called on his loyal subjects to join him in the fight against those who opposed the royal prerogative. It was a traditional call to arms.

Each of the regiments with him presented their colors, but only a few men came forward to join him. The Parliamentarians had begun to assemble their

> ## "No man in England is a better friend to liberty than myself."
>
> **Charles I, on the scaffold, January 30, 1649**

own army a few weeks earlier. The "war without an enemy" had begun, sometimes called the English Civil War, a part of the rather longer War of the Three Kingdoms (they were fought in Scotland and Ireland as well). Having shown his resolution, Charles briefly and halfheartedly tried to reopen peace negotiations with the Parliamentarians in London. He was no soldier but believed in his divine right to challenge those who opposed him. As London was a hotbed of popular hostility, he established his new capital at Oxford for the duration of the fighting. Two months later, on October 23, the first major engagement of the war was fought indecisively, at Edgehill in Warwickshire. Subsequent events culminated in the unprecedented public execution of the king outside his palace of Whitehall, in January 1649. **PF**

Europeans Discover New Zealand

After discovering the island that would eventually be named Tasmania in his honor, the Dutch explorer Abel Tasman sights a new and greater landmass.

Born in 1603, Abel Tasman spent his career in the service of VOC, the Dutch East Indies Company, when the Netherlands was Europe's preeminent sea-trading power. In 1634 he was second-in-command of an expedition that reached Formosa (now Taiwan). He also made voyages to Japan in 1641 and to Sumatra in 1642. Later that year, Tasman commanded an expedition to find a fabled "southern land" in the Pacific whose existence had never been verified.

Tasman sighted the west coast of Tasmania on November 24, which he named after Anthony Van Diemen, governor of the Dutch East Indies. Intending to sail north, Tasman was blown east by the prevailing winds, and on December 13, he became the first European to see New Zealand's South Island, which he named Staten Land on the mistaken assumption that it was linked to Argentina's Staten Island. Sailing north, one of his ships was attacked by the island's Maori inhabitants, and four of his sailors were killed. Tasman named the spot Murderers' Bay (now Golden Bay). On his return voyage he spotted a third island group, the Tongan Archipelago.

In 1644, Tasman mapped Australia's northern coast. He settled in Batavia and became a wealthy leader of the Dutch community—his later life marred only when he was fined and demoted for hanging a sailor without trial. He died in 1659. Tasman's voyages did not lead to a major expansion in Dutch trade, and Tasmania and New Zealand were not visited again by Europeans for around a hundred years. However, Tasman remains one of the greatest figures in maritime exploration and discovery. **NJ**

◗ A seventeenth-century Dutch School portrait of Abel Janszoon Tasman (1603–c.1659).

Spain Is Quelled

France overwhelms Spain at Rocroi and consolidates power in Europe.

An invading Spanish army of 27,000 men commanded by Francisco de Melo, count of Fuentes, struck into France from Spanish-ruled Flanders via the Ardennes and besieged Rocroi. The twenty-one-year-old Duc d'Enghien marched to raise the siege with a force of 23,000. Hearing from a deserter that 6,000 Spanish reinforcements were on their way, d'Enghien ordered a dawn attack through a narrow defile bordered by impenetrable woods and marshes, taking up position on a ridge overlooking the town. The Spaniards reacted quickly, drawing up their army in its

"[Spain's kings seem to have] tried to destroy the realm rather than to preserve it."

Louis XIV

traditional square formation. French attacks in the center and on the left were beaten back, but by exploiting his cavalry's success on the right, d'Enghien managed to encircle the Spanish soldiers, sweeping around and attacking them from the rear. The Spanish cavalry were routed, but the infantry squares hung on grimly, blasted by the French guns. A misinterpreted attempt to surrender only served to increase the carnage. The Spanish suffered 15,000 casualties, the French 4,000.

Rocroi was the first major land defeat for a Spanish army in a century. It marked the arrival of France as a major power and the start of a glittering military career for d'Enghien, later known as Le Grand Condé. In 1659, the Treaty of the Pyrenees ended the war and recognized France's new position. **NJ**

Ming Dynasty Falls

Emperor Ming Chongzhen commits suicide as rebels capture Beijing.

Taking the throne in 1628, the last Ming emperor of China, Chongzhen, inherited a corrupt and inefficient administration, a treasury bankrupted by the costs of rebuilding the Great Wall, and famine. China slid into anarchy as a result of widespread banditry and peasant rebellions.

In 1644, the Manchus broke through the Great Wall and sacked forty cities. In April the rebel leader Li Zicheng, known as the "Dashing General," swept unopposed into Beijing. Chongzhen got drunk and ran through the palace ordering everyone to commit

". . . the rebels have seized my capital. . . . Ashamed to face my ancestors, I die."

Chongzhen's final message written on his robe

suicide. The empress killed herself, and Chongzhen killed their daughter and his concubines. As dawn broke on April 25, he climbed a hill behind the palace. He then took off his robes and hanged himself from a tree. Li proclaimed himself the first emperor of the Shun dynasty.

Dismayed by Li's seizure of his favorite concubine and the chaos into which China had fallen, the Ming general Wu Sangui enlisted the Manchu emperor Dorghon to overthrow the rebels. The gates of the Great Wall at Shanhai Pass were opened to the Manchus, who defeated Li and occupied Beijing in June. Li then committed suicide. Dorghon crowned his teenage nephew Fu-lin as Shunzhi, first emperor of the Qing dynasty, which continued to rule China until 1911. **JH**

Royalists Routed at Naseby

The New Model Army under the command of Sir Thomas Fairfax inflicts defeat upon the army of King Charles I at Naseby, England.

The battle fought at Naseby in Northamptonshire in June 1645 was a decisive moment in the English Civil War. The New Model Army, recently established by Parliament under the command of Sir Thomas Fairfax, advanced north from Oxford to meet Royalist forces heading south after the sack of Leicester. The Royalists were outnumbered by 9,000 to 14,000.

The armies drew up with musket and pike infantry in the center and cavalry on the flanks. King Charles I's military commander, Prince Rupert, led a cavalry charge that swept away the left of the Parliamentarian line. The Royalist infantry rushed forward, and after a single volley of musket fire the foot soldiers closed to "push of pike." Had Rupert's horsemen rounded on the Parliamentarian infantry he would have won the day. But instead his men continued in a charge far to the rear. On the other flank, Fairfax's Lieutenant-General of Horse, Oliver Cromwell, advanced with a steady and determined advance trot, then turned to attack the Royalist infantry. As his foot soldiers were slaughtered, the king was restrained from leading his reserves into a losing battle and fled the field to safety.

The New Model Army soldiers did not show restraint in victory. They cut down Royalist soldiers and female camp followers, or lingered to plunder the dead and dying. Thousands deserted after the battle, hurrying to hide their booty. Militarily, the Royalist cause was lost, although it would be some time before Charles would realize it. **RG**

◐ General Thomas Fairfax, third Baron Fairfax of Cameron, c.1645, from a 1754 illustration.

◐ An illustration of a scene during the Battle of Naseby in the English Civil War, 1645.

Debates at Putney

A first step is taken along England's road to parliamentary democracy.

The Putney Debates took place in the parish church of Putney, London, from October 28 to November 11, 1647, in the wake of the parliamentary victory in the First Civil War. Represented were the two main factions in Parliament's victorious New Model Army: the ruling "Grandees," whose chief spokesman was Oliver Cromwell's son-in-law Henry Ireton, and the radical "Levellers," four of whose spokesmen attended the debates: Colonel Thomas Rainsborough and his brother William, John Wildman, and Edward Sexby. Cromwell himself chaired the discussions.

"I think that the poorest he that is in England hath a life to lead as the greatest he."

Col. Thomas Rainsborough, Putney Debates

Basing their arguments on the pamphlets *The Agreement of the People* and *The Case of the Army Truly Stated*, the Levellers put forward radical demands: that the authority of Parliament replace the king's rule, full male suffrage irrespective of property, biennial parliaments, and equal constituencies.

After a fortnight's wrangling, the debates were interrupted by the news that King Charles I had escaped from Hampton Court and fled to the Isle of Wight. Later, Leveller elements in the army mutinied—outbreaks that were swiftly crushed by Fairfax, Cromwell, and Ireton. Thomas Rainsborough was murdered by mysterious assailants, and the steam went out of the Leveller cause. However, Leveller ideals were remembered by radicals fighting for democratic rights for centuries. **NJ**

The First Fronde

An ongoing struggle in France is heightened by two revolts.

When news of the royal French army's victory under Louis II de Bourbon, known as le Grand Condé, over the Spanish at Lens on August 20 reached Paris, France's effective ruler Cardinal Jules Mazarin felt strong enough to act. He arrested the leaders of the French *Parlement*—not a parliament in the modern sense, but an assembly protecting the ancient rights of the nobility—who had been resisting the taxes Mazarin had raised to finance France's part in the Thirty Years' War. The nobles reacted by inciting the Paris mob to revolt, igniting the so-called "Fronde of

"It's too bad that decent people like us are cutting our throats for a scoundrel."

Condé to Marshal Turenne of Cardinal Mazarin

the Parliament," the name deriving from the slingshots used to break Mazarin's windows. The cardinal was forced to back down.

Mazarin reasserted royal authority after successfully negotiating the Peace of Westphalia, which ended the burden of the Thirty Years' War in October 1648. The second Fronde, the "Fronde of the Nobles," which ended in 1653, was a much more prolonged, bloody, and confused affair, pitting rival royal and noble factions against each other, led by the great generals Condé and Turenne. It ended with the royal army taking Paris and a reinforcement of royal authority, culminating in the long absolutist reign of Louis XIV. Mazarin controlled the government until his death in 1661, and the memory of Fronde stiffened Louis XIV's horror of anarchy. **NJ**

Treaty of Westphalia Ratified

Treaty ends the Thirty Years' War and sets a benchmark for international relations.

 A detail of *The Swearing of the Oath of Ratification of the Treaty of Münster, 1648*, by Gerard Terborch (1617–1681).

The war had begun as a conflict over religious and political liberty between the Catholic Holy Roman Emperor Ferdinand III and German Protestant princes and electors in Bohemia, Saxony, and the Rhineland Palatinate. The inconclusive struggle gradually drew in other powers, principally Spain, Sweden, and finally France. The treaty restored the right of German rulers to decide the religion of their states and guaranteed religious freedom to minorities within states, recognizing Calvinism as well as Lutheranism. It made it difficult for outside powers to interfere in the internal affairs of other countries and gave France territory in the Alsace-Lorraine borderlands and Sweden control of the north German ports. Bavaria, Bohemia, and Austria remained in imperial Catholic hands.

The diplomatic mastermind behind the treaty was Cardinal Mazarin, Regent ruler of France for the boy-king Louis XIV. The treaty itself comprised two elements, signed five months apart: the Treaty of Osnabruck (May 15) and Münster (October 24), following a long diplomatic congress, which had to be held in the two towns, as the Protestant and Catholic delegations were unwilling to come face to face. Representatives of Spain, France, Sweden, and the Holy Roman Empire were present as well as many German princes, the United Provinces (e.g. the Netherlands), and the Swiss confederacy. It was the first such Europe-wide diplomatic conference, and the first attempt to produce a comprehensive settlement to long-running disputes. **NJ**

Charles Stuart Loses His Head

England's king is beheaded for treason and the monarchy becomes a republic.

🔹 *The Execution of King Charles I of England at Whitehall in 1649*, an engraving from 1730 by Bernard Picart.

On a cold January morning, wearing an extra silk shirt to keep himself from shivering, King Charles I was escorted through the great Banqueting Hall of his Whitehall Palace, to a hastily built wooden scaffold outside. Faced with a vast crowd, he made a dignified speech, forgave the masked executioner—whose identity is still disputed—and placed his head on the scaffold. As it was cut off with a single clean stroke, so contemporary reports relate, the crowd groaned. Some people are said to have dipped their handkerchiefs into the pools of blood. With that stroke, England became a republic, yet for those faithful to the idea of monarchy, Charles became a martyr.

The previous week had seen the unprecedented trial of the king for treason before a specially constituted court in Westminster Hall. Though Charles, a believer in the divine right of kings, refused to accept the legality of the proceedings or the right of any humanly constituted court to judge him, he was found guilty after seven days and condemned to death, with his warrant signed by fifty-nine people, later known as the regicides. The first to sign was John Bradshaw, president of the court; third was Oliver Cromwell.

Ten days after his death a spiritual memoir, purportedly written by the dead king, entitled *Eikon Basilike*, began to circulate. Its popularity did much to maintain the concept of monarchy through the republic, and to bring back the Stuarts in the form of Charles's son Charles II in 1660. **PF**

Royal Art Sold Off

Charles I's art collection is disposed of to raise funds for the new government.

King Charles I of England, for all his manifest faults, had a genuine love and appreciation of fine art—coupled with a collector's eye for a bargain. His hunger for art was ignited in 1623 in Madrid during his long and unsuccessful wooing of the Spanish Infanta. He was distracted by the Spaniards who teasingly showed, lent, and sold him several sumptuous works by the Italian master Titian, many showing ample female forms scantily clad in furs or silks. Charles returned, brideless, to England but with the foundation of his collection.

"[The art collection is] sinful, idolatrous, and abominable."

Puritan preacher William Prynne, 1649

By the time of the Civil War, Charles had collected well over 1,200 items, including works by Leonardo, Veronese, Rubens, and his own court painter, Anthony Van Dyck. In 1649, soon after the king's execution, the entire collection was hastily sold by the new, cash-strapped Commonwealth. Some works were presented as compensation to widows of those who had fallen in the parliamentary cause, and others were given away as joke gifts to unwanted royal servants: the court draper got some tapestries, and a plumber was presented with Bassano's *The Flood*. After the Restoration in 1660, Charles II did his best to reassemble his father's collection, largely succeeding with the help of a thuggish repossession team. In the end, all but 300 pictures were recovered, which form the core of the Royal Collection today. **NJ**

Drogheda Sacked

Oliver Cromwell presides over the sack of a Catholic Irish town.

In 1649 Drogheda in Ireland was held by Irish Confederates—Catholics in revolt against English rule—and their allies, the English Royalists. Oliver Cromwell and the New Model Army were sent by the English Parliament to suppress the Catholic uprising.

Standing on the River Boyne, Drogheda was ringed by an imposing wall. When Cromwell's forces appeared, the town's Royalist governor Sir Arthur Aston rejected a call to surrender. Cromwell brought his heavy guns to bear upon the walls and ordered his soldiers to storm. Cromwell's men butchered the

"I am persuaded that this is a righteous judgment of God on the barbarous wretches."

Oliver Cromwell at Drogheda

Irish and Royalist troops. One group took refuge in a church, but the building was burned down with them inside. Aston was allegedly battered to death with his own wooden leg.

All but a few hundred of the 3,000 garrison were killed. The rest were taken prisoner and shipped off to Barbados. How many civilians died is not known. Cromwell justified the killings as revenge for previous massacres of Protestants by Catholics, and as a means of instilling terror that would shorten the war. Cromwell's fist of iron did succeed in reducing Ireland to subjection. But the sack of Drogheda—and Cromwell's continuing adoption of fiercely anti-Catholic policies—entered Irish folk memory as an atrocity that would justify future resistance to English rule. **RG**

René Descartes Dies

The eminent philosopher leaves a vast legacy of learning that paves the way for the great leaps of The Enlightenment.

The French philosopher and scientist René Descartes, founder of Continental rationalism and Cartesian mathematics, died in Stockholm, Sweden, in the bitter winter of 1650. He had been invited to the Swedish capital the previous year after a lifetime of travel because the young Queen Christina was eager to learn mathematics, particularly geometry. She insisted that her distinguished tutor match her own penchant for early rising, and Descartes was forced to abandon his lifelong habit of working in bed until noon. Instead, the fifty-four-year-old thinker found himself walking through the dark and freezing streets at 5 A.M. to begin lessons with his royal pupil.

The unfamiliar hours and bleak northern climate undermined the philosopher's always indifferent health, and he fell ill with pneumonia and died. An alternative explanation for the cause of his fatal illness has him catching it from the French ambassador, whom he had successfully nursed through a bout of the same disease. Descartes's influence on science and philosophy has been vast. Claiming "I think; therefore, I am," he argued that reason, rather than faith, could be used as a foundation of knowledge, and arguing that a clear divide should be made between the rationally knowable material world and the unknowable spiritual one.

Descartes's body was buried in Stockholm, but later his remains were reinterred in the Panthéon in Paris during the French Revolution, and then moved to the church of St.-Germain-des-Prés. **NJ**

◐ *Portrait of Descartes*, a copy after the lost original by Frans Hals (1582–1666), *c*.1649.

◑ Descartes depicted with Queen Christina of Sweden in a painting by Pierre-Louis Dumesnil the Younger (1698–1781).

Cape Town Settled

Jan de Riebeeck founds Cape Town and puts down roots.

Although South Africa's cape had been investigated—notably by the Portuguese trio Bartholomeu Dias in 1486, Vasco da Gama in 1497, and Antonio da Saldanha, who named it Table Mountain, in 1503—no sustained attempt had been made to settle the area until the arrival of the Dutchman Jan de Riebeeck in 1652. His foundation of the region's first European colony, coupled with the importation of Asian slaves, gave the European settlement an overwhelmingly Dutch character and contributed to fomenting its subsequent troubled racial history.

De Riebeeck was tasked with establishing a settlement to act as a staging post to supply vessels on their way to and from the Dutch East Indies with fresh food and water. His flagship, *Dromadaris*, made landfall on April 7. De Riebeeck's party, including his wife, Maria de la Quellerie, built wooden shelters and cultivated vegetable patches. The colony prospered by bartering with the indigenous Khoi people to obtain supplies, including sheep and cattle. The Anglo-Dutch wars of the 1650s and 1660s impelled De Riebeeck to build a mud-walled fort, Fort Djinhoep, protected by a thorny almond hedge, which survives in Cape Town's Botanical Gardens.

In 1657 free farming land was granted to settlers to increase food production, and the following year saw the first armed clash with the Khoi, who were alarmed at the European encroachment. In 1679, De Riebeeck's successor, Simon van der Stel, imported the first vines into the Cape, laying the foundations for South Africa's current booming wine industry. Cape Town's European population was further increased in 1688 by the arrival of French Protestant Huguenots fleeing religious persecution. The scene was set for the growth of the city of Cape Town. **NJ**

A Work of Genius

Bernini completes his great sculpture The Ecstasy of St. Teresa.

The saint, clothed from head to foot in a loose, hooded garment, is swooning backward in ecstasy as above her a winged youth stands holding an arrow pointed at her heart. A sunburst of gilded rays falling from the window above bathes both figures in the light of the Holy Ghost. Gianlorenzo Bernini's intensely theatrical and wonderfully composed sculpture, designed for the Cornaro Chapel of the Church of Santa Maria della Vittoria in Rome, is a masterpiece of Baroque art. It depicts a vision that St. Teresa of Avila, a Spanish nun and mystic, describes in her autobiography, where she speaks of an angel piercing her heart with the spear of divine love.

Bernini, an accomplished architect and painter as well as an outstanding sculptor, was the creative genius behind the transformation of Rome into a Baroque city. Born in Naples in 1598, he came to Rome at the age of eight, and by the time he was in his teens was working at the papal court for cardinals and wealthy patrons. Apart from a brief, unhappy visit to Paris in 1665, Bernini worked all his life in Rome, building and embellishing its churches and palaces. The many works he created for St. Peter's include the magnificent marble, bronze, and gilt *baldacchino* (canopy) above the high altar as well as the colonnades that enclose St. Peter's Square.

However, it is for the elaborate fountains he designed for the city's streets and squares—especially the Triton Fountain in the Piazza Barberini and the Four Rivers Fountain in the Piazza Navona—that Bernini, who died in 1680, is best remembered by the people of Rome. **SK**

◐ The Cornaro Chapel of Santa Maria della Vittoria in Rome: a detail of the altar with Bernini's *The Ecstasy of St. Teresa.*

Queen Abdicates

Christina of Sweden converts to Roman Catholicism and abdicates.

Born in 1626, Christina was the only surviving child of Sweden's Protestant king Gustavus Adolphus. On her militaristic father's orders, Christina was brought up as a boy. She was always dressed in male attire and taught to behave in "unfeminine" ways. Few concessions were made to her gender when she came to the throne after the death of her father fighting for the Protestant cause at the Battle of Lützen in 1632. Following her father's orders, she was crowned with the title "king." At first, advised by her father's wise chancellor, Axel Oxenstierna, Christina's greatest interest was reserved for her learning, which led her to invite the philosopher Descartes to be her personal tutor.

After 1651, however, she took progressively less interest in affairs of state and more in her secret attraction to Catholicism. Her new religion, her extravagance, and her foreign favorites made her abdication a popular topic of discussion. Christina finally abdicated and left Sweden for Rome, under the pseudonym Count Dohna, where she was welcomed and treated as a star convert by Pope Alexander VII.

Bankrupted by her extravagances, she turned to a life in France, but lost favor there when she had a treacherous courtier, Monaldeschi, murdered while she was in an adjoining room. She attempted to return to Sweden but died en route in Hamburg in 1689. Christina is one of only four women accorded the honor of burial in St. Peter's Basilica in the Vatican. Adopted as a popular lesbian icon and a heroine of transgender people, it seems more likely that she was a nonpracticing heterosexual, who, like Elizabeth I before her, was never tempted to share power and attention with a consort. **NJ**

An Enigmatic Scene

Velázquez's Las Meninas *captures the ambiguities of the Spanish court.*

Diego Velázquez, a remarkably skillful painter born in Seville to Portuguese parents, was the image-maker-in-chief to the court of King Philip IV during Spain's golden age in the mid-seventeenth century. Having won the favor of the king early in his time at court, he successfully survived the fall of his chief supporter, the count of Olivares, in 1643.

Velázquez executed several famous portraits of the king and queen and scenes of Spanish triumphs such as the *Surrender of Breda* (1634–1635). However, it is *Las Meninas,* an inspired painting of the king's

---

> *". . . it was [Velázquez's] duty to satisfy his royal master with a correct record."*
>
> **Kenneth Clark,** *Looking at Pictures,* **1960**

---

young daughter and her entourage, that has become emblematic of that age. It is an enigmatic, crowded painting centered on the five-year-old Infanta Margarita and two *meninas* (ladies-in-waiting), two dwarfs, a chaperone, and a dog. On the left is the painter (the only known self-portrait of Velázquez), standing in front of an easel (of which the viewer can see only the reverse). On the back wall is a mirror in which the reflections of King Philip IV and Queen Mariana (of Austria), can be seen. Often called "a painting about painting," the ambiguities of the scene have fascinated artists and critics for centuries. **PF**

⟳ Velazquez's famous *Las Meninas* (1656), showing the family of Philip IV, now in the Museo del Prado in Madrid.

Brothers Fight for Imperial Crown

In a war of succession, Aurangzeb succeeds his father to the Mughal throne after eliminating his older and younger brothers.

In 1657, the Mughal Emperor Shah Jahan fell ill and word quickly spread that he had died. The rumors triggered a war of succession in which the emperor's sons fought for the crown of the Mughal Empire. After a series of victories in the name of his younger brother Murad, Aurangzeb declared that his elder brother Dara had usurped the throne. In response, Shah Jahan handed control of his empire to Dara, determined that his eldest son should succeed him.

Bloody battles followed, culminating in the Battle of Samurgah, where Dara's forces were defeated by Aurangzeb. The emperor found himself surrounded by Aurangzeb's forces at Agra and surrendered. Aurangzeb then withdrew his support for Murad and executed him. Murad's supporters defected to Aurangzeb, proclaiming him emperor in July 1658.

It took Aurangzeb another year before he overcame resistance from his elder brothers, Dara and Shuja. He was finally crowned emperor in 1659. Aurangzeb went on to rule until 1707 before dying at the age of eighty-eight and is regarded as the last great Mughal emperor. Although he built the empire up to its greatest point during his reign, he is charged with overextending and ultimately losing much of the northwest to the rising Maratha Empire.

Aurangzeb is revered by many Muslims for his Sunni interpretation of Islam and his attempt to institute Sharia law throughout the empire. He abandoned the religious tolerance of his predecessors and instigated a period of repression against Hindus. Aurangzeb's critics blame his divisive policies for the decline of the Mughal Empire following his death. **TB**

◑ An eighteenth-century Indian miniature from the Mughal School of Dara and his army.

Charles II Restored

Charles Stuart is invited by Parliament to return and reclaim his crown.

Charles Stuart had a great thirtieth birthday present—the restoration of his kingdom. A teenager during the English Civil War, he was sent to France for his own safety, but after his father's execution in 1649 he was proclaimed king of Scotland and arrived there in 1650 to claim his crown. In September 1651, his army was defeated at Worcester, and Charles had to flee in disguise, at times reportedly escaping his pursuers by hiding in trees. He settled in Breda, Holland, where he and his followers waited for times to change.

In 1660, eighteen months after the death of

> ## "Parliament ordered . . . the king's birthday to be kept as a day of thanksgiving."
>
> **Samuel Pepys's diary**

Oliver Cromwell, when general disillusionment had set in at the rule of his hapless son, Richard, Charles's time finally came. General George Monck, commander of the army in Scotland, in a bid to end the political confusion, called a new parliament to which many Royalists were elected. Parliament invited Charles to return, and he set sail in the third week of May. He arrived in Dover on May 25. He processed through Kent and entered London at the head of a large parade on May 29, his birthday.

Charles executed twelve of the surviving thirty-one men who had signed his father's death warrant, and the bodies of Cromwell and two other regicides were dug up and hanged. He spent the rest of his reign ensuring that, whatever his political troubles, he would not be forced into exile again. **PF**

Fouquet Arrested

Fouquet's great fireworks spectacular sparks the ire of Louis XIV of France.

Louis XIV ascended to the throne aged five and ruled for seventy-two years from 1638 to 1715. Early in his reign, Louis's court was beset by political unrest and financial instability. For money he came to rely on Nicholas Fouquet, a wealthy man who from 1653 was superintendent of finances.

Fouquet had great personal charm and many talents: he was handsome, well informed, and a brilliant raconteur. He was also politically shrewd, supporting Cardinal Mazarin, Charles's chief minister, even when Mazarin was exiled. He spent a small fortune rebuilding his family chateau of Vaux-le-Vicomte and furnishing it magnificently. In contrast, the cash-strapped young Louis had to sleep between torn sheets and wear old clothes. After Mazarin's death in March 1661, the king had growing concerns that Fouquet was fleecing him, and he gave orders that a close watch be kept on the financier.

On August 17, 1661, Fouquet aroused the king's jealousy by offering him a magnificent entertainment at Vaux. The king arrived at 6 P.M. and, after a rest, visited the garden and had a meal to a musical accompaniment provided by twenty-four violins. This was followed by an homage to Louis and a performance of a comedy-ballet. At 1 A.M. Louis was offered a fireworks display over the canal and, as he retraced his steps to the château, was greeted by a shower of rockets fired from its dome.

Three weeks later, Fouquet was arrested. Louis set up a new tribunal to prosecute financiers suspected of corruption. Fouquet skillfully defended himself but, after a trial lasting three years, was found guilty and sentenced to banishment and confiscation of his property. Fouquet spent the last fifteen years of his life in prison. **PF**

Colony Capitulates

New Amsterdam surrenders to the English without a shot being fired.

New Amsterdam failed to prosper, despite the efforts of wooden-legged Peter Stuyvesant, governor from 1647. He built a defensive wall—on the site of today's Wall Street—and the little town attracted immigrants from England, France, and Scandinavia, and imported African slaves. Nonetheless, by 1660, the place had only around 1,500 inhabitants. In that year, the Stuart dynasty was restored in England under Charles II, and it was decided that the English colonies in New England and the south should be linked by taking over the Dutch New Netherland settlements that lay between them.

In 1664, the king bestowed massive tracts of land in North America, including the Dutch land, on his brother, James Duke of York (the future King James II). Four English ships with 300 troops on board sailed into New Amsterdam harbor and aimed their cannon at the crumbling fort. They were commanded by Colonel Richard Nicolls, a shrewd Royalist veteran of the English Civil War and a trusted associate of the duke of York. He demanded the colony's capitulation while promising to protect the citizens' lives and property and ensure that trade with Holland would continue. Governor Stuyvesant did his best to rally resistance, but the townspeople would have none of it. They begged him to spare their lives and surrender, which, after some days, reluctantly he did. The English took over without firing a shot.

Nicolls kept his promises. The Dutch garrison was accorded the honors of war and sailed for home. Stuyvesant lived quietly on his Manhattan farm until his death in 1672. England now had a chain of colonies down the East Coast from Maine to Virginia, and in June 1665, New Amsterdam was renamed New York City. **RC**

London's Burning

The "Great Fire" rages for days, ravaging the city of London.

The crowded, jumbled, wooden city of London, home to about 250,000 people, began to burn on Sunday, September 2, 1666, when a baker's shop in Pudding Lane, near London Bridge, caught fire. The strong east wind soon spread the fire to neighboring houses, many of them thatched, and within hours the fire was out of control. Despite desperate efforts to douse the flames, the fire raged for five days.

About four-fifths of the city, some 13,000 houses and 88 churches, including the medieval cathedral of St. Paul's, were lost. Thousands of people fled, taking

> ## "The churches, houses, and all on fire and flaming at once, and a horrid noise . . ."
> **Samuel Pepys's diary**

refuge in Moorfields to the north of the city. Despite the destruction, there were only a handful of recorded deaths and the fire did at least provide an opportunity to rebuild the city in brick. Several schemes were proposed with a regular street plan, but the legal claims to plots of land were too strong, and the old street layout was mostly retained. Christopher Wren became the architect of post-fire London, rebuilding St. Paul's and fifty-three churches.

In 1677, a monument was erected on the site of the first outbreak of the fire—its original inscription attributed the blaze to the Roman Catholics, but this was later removed. The monument still stands. **PF**

○ A seventeenth-century English School woodcut (colored later) of the Great Fire of London in 1666.

Paradise Lost Published

John Milton receives the princely sum of five pounds on publication of the epic poem that is now regarded as one of the greatest works in the English language.

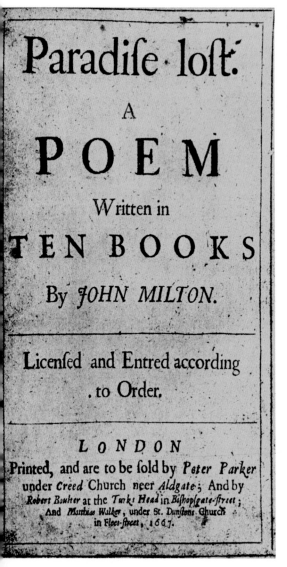

He was the greatest prose propagandist of Oliver Cromwell's Puritan revolution, yet events conspired to drive John Milton back to his first love, poetry. Writing tracts and letters for the Commonwealth caused him to go blind, one wife died and then another, and in 1660 the monarchy was restored. It was as if the Israelites suddenly decided to leave the promised land and return to captivity in Egypt. There was nothing for Milton now in public affairs. Instead, the poem he had first planned in 1639 could now be completed. It was finished in 1663 and printed in 1667.

Milton's subject matter was the Old Testament: his aim, "to justify the ways of God to men"; his means, an epic poem in the manner of Homer and Virgil. *Paradise Lost* was a dramatic representation of the fall of man, beginning with the fallen angel Lucifer (Satan) taking over hell, proceeding to the temptation and the expulsion of Adam and Eve from the Garden of Eden, and ending with the coming of the Messiah, and an assurance that a "Paradise Within" is possible. The essence of the poem is its attempt to see the fall from God's perspective, though, in fact, some critics see Satan as the real hero.

Milton mixed Bible stories with classical and pagan myths to expound his radical Protestant views on subjects such as idolatry—which, for Milton, included kings ruling by divine right. The work thus enabled Milton to criticize the Royalist regime under which he lived during his later years. *Paradise Lost* is regarded as one of the greatest works in the English language, and became a source of inspiration for many writers and artists such as William Blake. **RP**

○ The title page from the first edition of Milton's *Paradise Lost*, published in London in 1667.

First Modern Bank

A centrally managed Swedish bank is set up to take deposits and issue loans.

In 1661 the world's first paper banknotes were printed by Stockholms Banco, a private bank that had been founded by a Dutch merchant called Johan Palmstruch four years earlier. Half the bank's profits were promised to the Swedish crown, in return for a thirty-year monopoly on banking in Sweden. Palmstruch began using short-term deposits to finance long-term loans, but ran into trouble when depositors demanded repayment. To improve the bank's liquidity he introduced credit notes in various denominations. These proved extremely—in fact overly—popular. Too many were produced, and in 1664 the bank ceased operating. It was closed three years later, and Palmstruch was imprisoned.

In September 1668 the privilege to run a bank in Sweden was transferred to a new institution, Riksens Ständers Bank (Bank of the Estates of the Realm). The new bank was managed by civil servants under the direct control of the *Riksdag* (parliament) of the Estates. As a result, banking issues became a key aspect of Swedish domestic politics until the mid-nineteenth century. Initially, the bank took deposits and offered loans to individuals, but with the outbreak of the Great Northern War in the early eighteenth century, this function was mainly replaced by the need to make large loans to the government.

Although it was not initially permitted to issue banknotes, the bank began issuing "transport bills" from 1701 and set up a paper mill at Tumba Bruk to reduce forgery. It also licenced commercial banks to issue notes, while the Bank of Sweden held deposits covering the value of the notes issued. In 1866, the name of the bank was changed to Sveriges Riksbank. It became a central bank in 1897 and is now the world's oldest surviving national bank. **PF**

French Claim Louisiana

La Salle claims territory in Mississippi, but Louis XIV is unimpressed.

René-Robert Cavelier, Sieur de La Salle (1643–1687), a onetime priest from a wealthy Rouen family, traveled to Canada in 1666 and set up a fortified village near Montreal. In the late 1660s he made several journeys to the south and west, discovering the Ohio River and exploring the Great Lakes in the name of the king of France, seeking routes first to the Pacific and then to the Caribbean through the unknown lands west of the English colonies of the eastern seaboard.

Traveling down Lake Michigan and along the frozen Illinois River on sleds, in February 1682 he reached the Mississippi and traveled down it on canoes; on April 9 his party reached the Gulf of Mexico, where he erected a cross and a wooden post on which he fastened a coat of arms—cast from a cooking pot—of the king of France. La Salle claimed the entire Mississippi basin for France, naming it La Louisiane. After a fraught journey northward, he returned to France, where Louis XIV reportedly described La Salle's discoveries as "utterly useless."

La Salle set off for the New World once again in July 1684 with a small fleet and 200 men, intending to establish a colony near the mouth of the river. They landed well to the west of the Mississippi delta, in Texas, at Matagorda Bay, and their colony of Fort St. Louis struggled. In March 1687 an expedition led by La Salle set out in search of the Mississippi in the hope of linking up with the French colonies in Canada, but mutineers killed La Salle before the journey was completed.

Louisiana developed slowly, as the appearance of the French caused a renewal of Spanish activity along the north coast of the Gulf of Mexico, and conflict with the English colonies was endemic. Napoleon sold the entire territory to the United States in 1803. **PF**

Penn's Constitution

William Penn establishes the principle of freedom of conscience in Pennsylvania.

O Allan Stewart's nineteenth-century depiction of William Penn receiving the Charter of Pennsylvania from King Charles II.

"No one can be . . . subjected to the political view of another, without his consent."

Frame of Government, April 25, 1682

In 1681 England's Charles II gave a vast tract of land—almost as large as England—to the Quaker William Penn in settlement for a debt he owed to Penn's father, the Admiral Sir William Penn. The younger man named it in memory of his father and established the colony of Pennsylvania for his fellow Quakers and other religious dissenters who were persecuted in England at the time. The main settlement was to be at Philadelphia, which he laid out on the grid pattern that was to become familiar in many North American cities. A year later, a fleet of some two thousand emigrants arrived from England, followed by groups from Germany, France, and elsewhere.

To ensure the colony developed according to the tolerant principles of Quakerism, Penn wrote the "Frame of Government of Pennsylvania." This document defined the rights of landowners and other citizens, confirmed the rule of law, set up an elected council, and determined its role and the role of Penn himself as governor. It also established—for the first time anywhere in the Western world—the principle of freedom of conscience for all those who believed in a supreme god, whatever their form of belief or practice. The death penalty was reserved for murderers and traitors only.

The signing of the "Frame of Government" took place on April 25, 1682. As the first constitution in the world to provide for the possibility of peaceful change through being amended—as indeed happened several times over the next ten years—it was supplemented by a "Charter of Privileges to the Inhabitants" in 1701, which reduced the authority of the governor. In time, it demonstrated the benefits of a written constitution and became a model for the Founding Fathers of the new United States a century later. **PF**

Court of the Sun King

King Louis XIV establishes the French court at the Palace of Versailles.

The French court's official move to the magnificent new palace that Louis XIV had designed and built for himself in the forested countryside southwest of Paris marked the apotheosis of French absolute monarchy. As a young boy, Louis had witnessed the Fronde revolts, when warring factions of nobles had fought for control of the machinery of state. From the day, in 1661, that he personally assumed the reins of government, Louis directed all his considerable energies to asserting his royal authority over the nobility. He most probably did not make the famous statement often attributed to him, *"L'état, c'est moi"* ("I am the state"), but the remark nevertheless sums up the core of his royal program—to elevate the monarchy far above the nobility and out of the reach of the Paris mob.

And so, at Versailles, Louis employed the greatest artists of the day, the architect Louis Le Vau, the painter Charles Le Brun, and the garden designer André Le Nôtre, to create a backdrop for the ostentatious display of absolute royal power that was not just a palace, but the nerve center of royal government. The spectacular balls and ballets held in Versailles's gilded and mirrored chambers, as well as the outdoor fetes and fireworks that celebrated Louis's military victories, had one purpose only—the self-glorification of the king.

Louis's personal symbol of the sun—hence his well-known soubriquet *le Roi Soleil* (the Sun King)—was everywhere to be seen, and his personality cult came to dominate the everyday life of the palace so completely that courtiers competed quite seriously to attend the daily ritual of the king's *lever* (getting up) and *coucher* (going to bed), even to the extent of jostling each other for the honor of holding the royal shirt. **SK**

◊ A detail of *Louis XIV, King of France, Promenading in the Gardens of Château de Versailles, c.*1688 by Etienne Allegrain.

"He [the king] loved splendor, magnificence, and profusion in all things."

Duc de Saint-Simon, *Memoirs 1691–1723*

Vienna Saved from the Turks

Polish King Jan Sobieski's rescue of the Habsburg capital ends the Ottoman advance in Europe.

In September 1683, Vienna, Austrian capital of the Habsburg Holy Roman Empire, was in peril. Since mid-July, the city had been under siege, ringed by 200,000 soldiers of the Turkish Ottoman Empire. Most of the Viennese population, along with Emperor Leopold I, had fled, leaving a garrison of 12,000 troops. Short of food and sleep, the defenders were mocked by the spectacle of the Ottoman camp with its silken tents, presided over by Kara Mustafa Pasha.

By September 10, the fall of the city seemed imminent. But the following day a Christian relief

> ## "It is a victory as nobody ever knew, the enemy completely ruined. . . ."
>
> **Jan Sobieski in a letter to his wife, 1682**

army appeared on the hills, led by Jan III Sobieski, King of Poland and Grand Duke of Lithuania. At dawn on September 12, battle was joined on two fronts. As Sobieski attacked the Ottomans from the rear, Kara Mustafa launched a final assault on Vienna's weakened defenses. A final charge spearheaded by Polish hussars—glittering figures with eagle-feather wings on their backs—broke through to menace the Turkish encampment. The Ottoman army panicked and fled, leaving a treasure trove of booty behind.

In hindsight, the defeat at Vienna marked the end of the Muslim threat to Christian Europe and the beginning of the decline of Ottoman power. **RG**

● *The Battle of Kahlenberg at the Second Siege of Vienna*, by Franz Geffels (late seventeenth century).

Huguenots Flee France

Louis XIV revokes Huguenot privileges sparking an exodus of skilled craftsmen.

Under the influence, so it was said, of the pious Madame de Maintenon, his second wife, Louis XIV declared Protestantism illegal in France. The Edict of Fontainebleau revoked all the privileges that Louis's grandfather Henry IV had granted to Protestants (Huguenots) in the Edict of Nantes in 1598. It ordered Huguenot ministers to be banished, schools closed, places of worship destroyed, and children born to Huguenot parents baptized as Catholics.

The revocation of the Edict of Nantes was the culmination of a sustained policy of repression. To

---

"They . . . brought their horses into the shop and used the books as litter."

Thomas Bureau (Huguenot bookseller), 1685

Louis XIV, the Huguenots represented a threat to national unity and strong government. Huguenot resistance was strongest in the Cévennes mountains of southern France, where a rebellion among the so-called Camisards was not suppressed until 1705.

Although the Edict of Fontainebleau formally denied Huguenots permission to leave France, between 200,000 and 500,000 (about half the total number of Protestants) fled the country. Huguenots were among France's most skilled artisans, working in crafts such as silk-weaving, glass-making, cabinetmaking, and silversmithing, and they took their expertise elsewhere to the benefit of France's commercial competitors in Protestant countries such as England, the Netherlands, and Denmark. It was a brain drain that would cost France dearly. **SK**

Bijapur Annexed

Expanding the Mughal Empire reaches a high point and sows the seeds of decline.

The son of Shah Jahan and Mumtaz Mahal, Aurangzeb, was given military and political responsibilities when young, but fell out with his father and fought a bitter war of succession with three of his brothers. Having executed two of the brothers, Dara and Murad, and forced the third, Shuja, into exile, Aurangzeb took the throne in 1659 and immured his father in Agra's Red Fort until the old man's death in 1666.

Aurangzeb's long reign was distinguished by his forceful rule, his personal piety as a Sunni Muslim, and his strict application of Muslim Sharia law. He discouraged music, dancing, and art, destroyed Hindu temples, and executed the Sikhs' spiritual leader Guru Bahadur for refusing to convert to Islam. He spent almost his entire reign engaged in warfare, both in attempting to expand his domains and in putting down constant rebellions by groups offended by his rigid policies.

Given the official title Alamgir I (world conqueror), Aurangzeb battled Sikhs, Rajputs, the Hindu Marathas, and above all, the rival realm of the Deccan. He spent the last half of his reign on constant but largely futile campaigns, but his annexation of Bijapur in 1686 when he deposed the Adil Shahi dynasty was a high point. He campaigned with a mobile city 30 miles (48 km) in circumference, inhabited by 500,000 soldiers and followers, 50,000 camels, and 30,000 elephants.

The cost was huge and left his treasury destitute. Despite apparently repenting of his excesses and advising his sons on his deathbed in 1707 not to follow his example, they too fought wars against each other and continued the conflicts with the Deccan and the Marathas, which eventually fatally weakened the Mughal Empire. **NJ**

Newton's Laws

Isaac Newton publishes his great work Principia Mathematica.

Isaac Newton's *Philosophiae Naturalis Principia Mathematica* (The Mathematical Principles of Natural Philosophy) was published by the Royal Society in London. Its appearance had been in doubt until the very last moment, as rival Robert Hooke did his utmost to prevent publication. Nonetheless, it seemed unlikely to be a work that would have much impact. It was written in classical Latin as a series of propositions, each building on the previous one, so that the book could not be dipped into. Its author remarked privately that he had deliberately made it unreadable so that only the elite could follow it.

The professor of mathematics at Cambridge was soon pointed out as the man who wrote the book nobody understood. Not surprisingly, only a few hundred copies were sold within a decade. And yet eventually it ran to more than one hundred editions and would be translated into virtually every language. It was probably the most important scientific work ever written. *Principia* is a highly sophisticated and complex description of the mechanisms at work in the universe, based upon essentially simple propositions. Newton established three laws of motion that govern the movement of bodies on Earth and in space. His theory of universal gravity explained both the fall of an apple and the motion—and wobbles—of the planets.

Newton was elected president of the Royal Society in 1703, and two years later became the first scientist to be knighted. His work exerted a profound influence on scientific method and changed the physical as well as the intellectual world. **RP**

⦿ Gottfried Kneller's 1710 painting, one of several portraits of Newton in Trinity College's collection in Cambridge.

Carnage at Glencoe

The brutal massacre at Glencoe helps keep Scots nationalism alive.

At 5 A.M. on Saturday, February 13, 1692, soldiers rapped on the door of John Maclain's house. They were leaving Glencoe after enjoying its hospitality. As Maclain hastily pulled on his trousers and called for a dram of whisky to see them on their way, he was shot in the head and the back. Two others in the house were also killed. In total, thirty-eight people were slaughtered in the village of Glencoe, the youngest being a boy of four or five. The soldiers had been ordered to kill all the villagers—of those who escaped, most perished in the bitter cold.

"The soldiers . . . had all been receiv'd as Friends by those poor People."

Gallienus Redivivus or Murther Will Out, 1695

The massacre stemmed from what, in England, was called the "Glorious Revolution," the replacement of the Catholic James II by the Protestant William III in 1689. In Scotland the Jacobites (supporters of James II) were stronger, and they rose against the Williamites. The government became determined to impose its will on the troublemakers, and so all clan chiefs were ordered to take an oath of allegiance by New Year's Day, 1692. When the chief of the MacDonald clan was delayed by a snowstorm and missed the deadline, the Scottish secretary, Sir John Dalrymple, sent a force to Glencoe composed largely of Campbells, who were traditional enemies of the MacDonalds.

An enquiry exonerated the king, but not Dalrymple, and the Jacobites never forgot the most emotive incident in Scottish history. **RP**

Six Witches Executed in Salem

Witchcraft hysteria sweeps through Massachusetts, with fatal consequences.

○ *The Trial of George Jacobs, August 5, 1692*, by Tompkins H. Matteson (1813–1884).

The early New England Puritans believed in the malign power of Satan and the dark power of magic, and five people were executed as witches between 1630 and 1690. However, the events in Salem were on an altogether different scale.

Beginning in February 1692, two girls, the daughter and the niece of the local minister, Samuel Parris, began throwing hysterical fits. The doctors decided they had been bewitched and suspicion focused on Parris's black slave girl, Tituba, who had apparently been using folk charms to foretell whom the girls would marry. Other girls had fits and blamed not only Tituba but five other women, and then many more people, including several men. A special court tried the accused in a frenzy of wild assertions of flying on broomsticks and worshipping Satan.

In summer 1692, the hysteria reached a climax. On August 19, Martha Carrier, George Jacobs Sr., George Burroughs, John Willard, and John Procter were hanged. At his execution, Burroughs, Salem's ex-minister, recited the Lord's Prayer perfectly—something supposedly impossible for a wizard—but he was hanged despite the crowd's protests.

By October more than a hundred people had been indicted, nineteen hanged, and one man pressed to death. The tide turned when leading members of the establishment were accused. By early in 1693, the special court refused to hear any more cases. In time, the Salem farrago contributed to the decline of belief in the whole phenomenon. **RC**

Peter the Great's Great Embassy

In his quest to modernize Russia, Peter seeks knowledge, a navy, and armaments.

○ *Peter the Great at Deptford Dock*, a painting by Daniel Maclise (1806–1870).

Having a navy in Tsar Peter I's time was like having nuclear capability today, and the new tsar wanted Russia to join the elite club. This urgency to build a fleet set the wheels of his "Great Embassy" in motion. Officially, he was seeking a European alliance against Russia's nemesis, Turkey. Such an outcome would be a diplomatic coup because Russia was not then a serious player in European politics.

The embassy took the form of a European tour. It represented a dramatic break with the Muscovite past, so much so that Peter traveled under an alias to bypass any hostile, conservative reaction. In Saardam, Holland, he worked for four months at the massive dockyards of the Dutch East India Company. Then on January 9, 1698, he sailed to England, where he was warmly welcomed by the new king, William of Orange, and given a twenty-four-gun ship, *Royal Transport*. Its designer, Peregrine Osborne, marquis of Carmarthen, befriended Peter and "showed him the ropes" of English shipbuilding at the Royal Navy's dockyard in Deptford, London.

The tsar's thirst for technical know-how had been truly whetted. For the Europeans, their hospitality was a shrewd gamble to gain access to Russia's potentially lucrative markets. Peter eventually secured 750 skilled shipbuilders, mast and sail makers, captains, pilots, gunners, and engineers. This foreign workforce was crucial in building a Russian navy and armaments, so that within twenty-five years, Peter had acquired his "shock and awe." **JJH**

1700–1899

St. Petersburg Arises

Peter the Great creates a new capital for Russia on an unpromising site.

○ An eighteenth-century engraving shows Peter the Great supervising the building of St. Petersburg.

In May 1703, the Russian army reached the mouth of the River Neva. Peter the Great's twin obsessions of warfare and Westernization now complemented each other perfectly. What better place for building a new city and port, and providing Russia with the "Window on Europe" he had long cherished? On May 27, Peter personally laid the foundation stones for a new fortress on Zayachy Island and began plans for a shipyard opposite. St. Petersburg was born.

Yet many were incredulous. Could there be a worse place to build a city? Russia's war against Sweden was still raging, which meant that Sweden's Charles XII might still win back the area, if indeed he thought it worth fighting for an island-studded marshland. Strong southwesterlies periodically flooded the islands; the area was generally ice-bound between November and April; and at the height of winter there were only a few hours of daylight.

Some 25,000 peasants lost their lives during the construction of the city, and the pace was so brutal that the first ships were able to dock in November 1703. Tolls were set at half the Swedish level, and soon Russian trade was being diverted from the northerly port of Archangel. But Peter did not just want a port, he wanted a great city. He enlisted the architect Domenico Trezzini, who provided St. Petersburg with its distinctively ornate Baroque style. People were ordered to migrate at their own expense. In 1712, St. Petersburg became the capital of Russia and by 1725 had 40,000 inhabitants. **RP**

Slaughter at Blenheim

The Grand Alliance triumphs in a key battle of the War of the Spanish Succession.

◯ The Battle of Blenheim—also called Blindheim—saved the city of Vienna from French domination.

In summer 1704, the armies of French King Louis XIV dominated Europe. Britain, the Dutch Republic, and the Austrian Holy Roman Empire formed a Grand Alliance to take on the Sun King but, with their Bavarian allies, the French were menacing the Austrian capital, Vienna. The English Duke of Marlborough and Austrian Prince Eugene of Savoy went on the offensive and led their 56,000-strong army to invade Bavaria. Early on August 13, French lookouts were startled when lifting fog revealed dense columns of troops advancing across the plain.

The Franco-Bavarian force was slightly larger than the Grand Alliance army and was led by Marshal Count Camille de Tallard. Tallard had not expected Marlborough and Eugene to attack outnumbered and outgunned. Their infantry and cavalry had to cross a marshy stream under fire and then assault fortified villages—Blindheim, Oberglau, and Lutzingen. These attacks were driven back with heavy casualties. Marlborough struggled to steady his men, but, with many of Tallard's men pinned down in the villages, Marlborough's cavalry routed the enemy horses on the open plain. Their headlong flight left the French infantry exposed to slaughter. By evening, even those valiantly defending Blindheim had surrendered.

The Franco-Bavarian army lost almost 40,000 men. Bavaria was knocked out of the war, and Vienna was saved. Queen Anne rewarded Marlborough with a country house in Oxfordshire, which he named after the site of his famous victory. **RG**

Union of England and Scotland

The Act of Union joins the two countries into the single state of Great Britain.

⬥ The Articles of Union between England and Scotland, signed in 1707 are housed in the Houses of Parliament in London, England.

Although the two countries had shared the same monarch since 1603 when James VI of Scotland succeeded Elizabeth I of England to become James I, England and Scotland remained separate states. The Act of Union, signed on May 1, 1707, was driven by England's keen desire to secure the "auld enemy" against the threat that Scotland would choose a Scottish Stuart Catholic monarch in preference to England's Protestant one, Queen Anne.

Scottish motives were rather more venal. Scottish investors had lost heavily in the Darien scheme—a grossly mismanaged bid to found a Scots colony in Central America—and compensation for their considerable losses was one provision of the act. In addition, several members of the Scottish elite,

including the Earl of Glasgow and the queen's commissioner James Douglas, Second Duke of Queensberry, were paid large cash sums to distribute as bribes to ensure the smooth passage of the act.

The writer Daniel Defoe, who was sent by England's chief minister, Robert Harley, to report on Scottish opinion, claimed, "For every Scot in favor there is ninety-nine against." Despite a remaining degree of bitterness caused by the failed Scottish Jacobite risings of 1715 and 1745 to 1746, by the nineteenth century increasing prosperity had reconciled most of Scotland to the Union. It was a consensus that lasted until the rise of Scottish nationalism and the foundation of a Scottish parliament in Edinburgh at the end of the twentieth century. **NJ**

Battle of Poltava

Sweden's defeat is a turning point in the struggle for dominance in northeast Europe.

○ An illustration of the Battle of Poltava, in which Peter the Great of Russia defeated Charles XII of Sweden.

The Battle of Poltava on June 28, 1709, marked the eclipse of Sweden as a European military power by Peter the Great's Russia. Sweden's young king Charles XII was a military genius, but despite victories against Poland, Denmark, Norway, and Russia, he had failed to end the Great Northern War, begun in 1700. In 1707, therefore, he invaded Russia with 32,000 men, hoping to seize Moscow. However, lack of supplies and inclement weather forced him to turn south to the Ukraine in search of grain. Here, disabled by a wound in the foot, he was unable to take personal command of the coming battle, instead directing operations from a litter. His subordinate commanders quarreled among themselves and, in so doing, failed to fill the gap left by Charles's forceful personality.

Charles ordered an attack on the fortress of Poltava, hoping that Swedish discipline would make up for his depleted numbers and his lack of artillery. Some 18,000 Swedes flung themselves against a Russian force of twice that number in well-fortified positions and supported by one hundred cannon. The guns tore great gaps in the Swedish lines, and repeated assaults failed to make an impact. By 11 A.M. the battle was over. Some 7,000 Swedes had fallen for the loss of just 1,400 Russians. Charles retreated to Ottoman-ruled Moldavia, where he languished for five years before limping home. Swedes taken prisoner in the battle were forced to help construct St. Petersburg, Peter's new capital and an apt symbol of the new power on the Baltic. **NJ**

London's New Cathedral

Parliament declares Sir Christopher Wren's St. Paul's Cathedral to be complete.

◑ The lavishly decorated choir and high altar of St. Paul's
Cathedral, designed by architect Christopher Wren.

◑ A nineteenth-century cross section of the cathedral as it
would have been if Wren's original plans had been followed.

"Reader, if you seek his monument, look around you."

Wren's epitaph, St. Paul's Cathedral

Christopher Wren was one of the great "Renaissance men" of the Restoration and a contemporary of Isaac Newton, Robert Hooke, Robert Boyle, Thomas Hobbes, and Henry Purcell. A scientist, mathematician, and astronomer, his greatest glory was achieved in architecture in 1711, when his masterpiece—London's St. Paul's Cathedral—was completed.

The son of a churchman, Wren studied at Wadham College, Oxford. After a trip to Paris where he was much influenced by the work of Bernini, he took up architecture, designing the chapel of Pembroke College, Cambridge, and the Sheldonian Theatre in Oxford. He also carried out repairs on the decayed fabric of the old St. Paul's Cathedral from 1661.

A week after submitting plans for rebuilding the cathedral in August 1666, the Great Fire destroyed St. Paul's and most of the rest of the city. Within days, Wren was in the smoldering ruins making plans for reconstruction. In 1669, he was appointed surveyor of works by Charles II, and work began on the new cathedral the following year. Construction went on for thirty-six years—much of it personally supervised by Wren. Impatient at delays, Parliament withheld half his salary for fourteen years, and the clergy quibbled with the three versions of his new building that he submitted for their consideration. Nevertheless, Wren persisted and, in 1697, the first service was held in the new cathedral. In 1710, Wren's son Christopher, also an architect, supervised the "topping out" ceremony. The following year Parliament declared the building finished.

Wren survived until 1723—among his later work, carried out for William and Mary, were designs for Kensington Palace and an extension of Hampton Court. His last major project was Greenwich Hospital. He died at age ninety from a chill. **NJ**

Signing of the Treaty of Utrecht

The Treaty of Utrecht concludes the long War of the Spanish Succession.

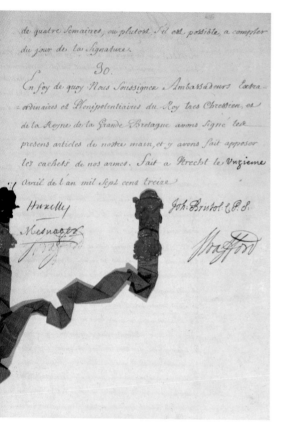

🔾 The Treaty of Utrecht signed by Queen Anne's ambassadors, Thomas Wentworth and John Robinson.

"Europe could by no means bear the Union of . . . France and Spain under one . . . King."

Treaty of Utrecht

The war had broken out originally between the French Louis XIV and the Austrian Holy Roman Empire over the competing claims of the Bourbon and Habsburg dynasties to the throne of Spain in 1701. More than a decade later, the war was ongoing and its eventual conclusion was the Treaty of Utrecht, signed on April 11, 1713.

Austria had objected to the succession of Louis XIV's grandson as Philip V of Spain, fearing that this would augment France's already extensive power and even unite Spain and France against her. Gradually other nations—Britain, the Dutch provinces, Savoy, and Denmark—joined together to form a grand anti-French coalition. A destructive war ensued, marked by the great, but increasingly costly, military victories of the Duke of Marlborough in alliance with Prince Eugene of Savoy over France at Blenheim, Ramillies, Oudenarde, and Malplaquet.

The escalating cost of the war, in both financial and humanitarian terms (400,000 died), for no real strategic gain led to the British "war party," the Whigs, being replaced with a pro-peace Tory administration led by the rival earls of Oxford and Bolingbroke, who began secret negotiations with France in 1710 to end the war. Within the terms of the treaty, Philip V remained in possession of the Spanish throne, but France and Spain were never to be united. Austria gained the Spanish-ruled Netherlands (which corresponded roughly to today's Belgium). France recognized the right of the Protestant House of Hanover to succeed Britain's Queen Anne, officially dropping its support for the rival Catholic Stuarts, and ceded Hudson Bay and Newfoundland in Canada to Britain. Spain ceded Gibraltar, Minorca, and the profitable Spanish trans-Atlantic slave-trading monopoly, the *Asiento*, to Britain. **JJH**

Jacobites Incite Trouble in Northern Britain

Prince James claims the throne and the Earl of Mar starts the 1715 Jacobite Rebellion.

Although the 1745–1746 rebellion led by Bonnie Prince Charlie is better known thanks to its tragic outcome and romantic overtones, the rising by Charles's father, Prince James Edward Stuart, launched in September 1715, was a far more serious threat to Hanoverian rule in Britain because it attracted English as well as Scottish support.

Expelled from the throne by the Protestant "Glorious Revolution" of 1689, James II and his son James Edward languished in exile in France, their hopes of a restoration kept alive by the backing of high-placed, usually Catholic, supporters—known as "Jacobites"—in Scotland and England. The accession of the unpopular Hanoverian George I, in 1714, gave them their chance. A rebellion was planned involving English and Scottish Jacobites. John Erskine, Earl of Mar, made a formal declaration of Prince James's sovereignty on September 9, raised 12,000 men and took Perth on September 14, and sent a detachment of 1,500 Scots to support northern English Jacobites.

Advancing into Catholic Lancashire, the Jacobites attracted little support and got trapped in Preston. After a desultory, two-day battle, they surrendered to a superior Hanoverian force. Meanwhile Mar—whose indecisive nature earned him the nickname "Bobbin' John"—had failed to secure Scotland. After a bloody but indecisive battle at Sherrifmuir on November 13 against an inferior Hanoverian force commanded by the Duke of Argyll, his support melted away. Even the belated arrival of James Edward in December failed to rally the Jacobites. Threatened by an advance on Perth by Argyll and beset by bitter winter weather, James and Mar sailed back to France, leaving their supporters to fend for themselves. Subsequently, several Scottish Jacobite leaders were imprisoned in the Tower of London and executed. **JJH**

○ *The Order of Release, 1746*, (1852–1853) by John Everett Millais, depicts a Jacobite soldier being returned to his family.

"Now is the time for all good men to show their zeal for His Majesty's service...."

Declaration of the Earl of Mar, September 9, 1715

Turks Repelled from the Balkans

Prince Eugene of Savoy captures Belgrade after an unsuccessful countersiege.

○ An eighteenth-century portrait of Prince Eugene of Savoy, the globe and atlas signifying his victorious career.

"An Austrian army awfully arrayed / Boldly by battery besieged Belgrade."

Anonymous poem in *The Trifler*, 1817

The siege of Belgrade led by Prince Eugene of Savoy and concluded on August 17, 1717, was the beginning of the end of Ottoman influence in the Balkans. Eugene's victory ensured the power of the Ottomans would never again menace European states.

The Ottoman Turks had been thirsting for revenge against Austria since the defeat they had suffered in their second great siege of Vienna in 1683. The Ottomans' chance came in 1716 and they declared war against an Austria, which had been weakened by the debilitating War of the Spanish Succession (1701–1713). The Ottoman grand vizier (prime minister) Damad Ali gathered a vast force of 150,000 troops at Belgrade from where he advanced north. Eugene, however, had fortified his already strong defenses at the fortress of Petrovardina on the Danube. From this vantage point, he defeated and killed Damad.

The Turks swiftly retreated to Belgrade, where, in June 1717, a 30,000-strong defense force led by Mustapha Pasha was besieged by Eugene with 100,000 men. But on August 5, the besiegers were themselves besieged when a vast Ottoman relief force, 200,000 strong, surrounded them. By this time, Eugene's force had been depleted to around 60,000 men, but he resolved on a bold breakout. Helped by a thick morning mist, his forces inflicted a piecemeal defeat on the Turks. Soon after, the besieged city of Belgrade capitulated, and the following year Turkey sued for peace.

Prince Eugene of Savoy is often perceived as the junior partner to his great military colleague, John Churchill, Duke of Marlborough. Yet in his decisive defeat of the Ottoman Turkish armies, Eugene proved himself to be at least Marlborough's equal, and he certainly gave Europe a more lasting legacy. **JJH**

Bach's Baroque Brilliance

Bach's Brandenburg Concertos *set new standards in orchestral and chamber music.*

Was the Margrave of Brandenburg pleased to receive a manuscript of six *"Concerts avec plusiers instruments,"* together with the composer's dedication of March 24, 1721? History records no answer, although we do know that he had too few musicians to perform the works and that the scores grew dusty in his library. Yet Johann Sebastian Bach did not trouble himself over the matter. He often seemed a humorless, bad-tempered man, but the concertos were written during one of the happiest periods in his life, when he was court organist at Cöthen in Germany, where Prince Leopold was a real music lover. The prince was a Calvinist, and so music did not figure greatly in Cöthen's worship. This was a bonus, though, since Bach had lost several posts thanks to his "undue elaborations" of simple church music. Instead, Leopold encouraged him to write for secular entertainment. The *Brandenburg Concertos* are indeed superbly entertaining—elegant, vigorous, ebullient, and humorous—as well as startlingly innovatory.

Bach was influenced by the orchestral concertos of Vivaldi and other Italian composers, but he used a much greater variety of instruments for solos, including the recorder and trumpet, often in combination with each other, and his textures were richer and more contrapuntal. Among his innovations was the use of the harpsichord as a solo instrument, making the *Fifth* the world's first keyboard concerto, whereas in the *Sixth,* there are no violins at all. Bach broke all the rules. Or perhaps we should say, he devised new and better ones.

Bach had wonderful technical expertise and a superb harmonic sense. He was the greatest figure of the Baroque, which saw the emergence of modern music, and in the *Brandenburg Concertos* he created the Baroque's most accessible masterpieces. **RP**

◔ A portrait of Bach with a piece of manuscript, painted in 1746 by renowned portraitist Elias Gottlob Haussmann (1695–1774).

"The aim and final end of all music should be none other than the glory of God."

Johann Sebastian Bach (1685–1750)

The Table of Ranks Established

Peter the Great attempts to bring Russia into the modern age by overhauling the military system and making promotion a matter of merit.

Peter the Great's entire reign became one long, desperate rush to reform Russia. However, it was his introduction of a Table of Ranks in January 1722 that was perhaps his most radical attempt to settle accounts with the reactionary old nobility—the Boyars—and ensure that future promotion in Russia's armed and civil service was a matter of merit, not one of inherited privilege.

Influenced by a wide-ranging tour he had made of Western Europe early in his reign, he had been inspired to create a new navy and modernize the army. He devised a table of fourteen ranks for all officials—each with its own uniform—and he decreed that anyone who reached the eighth rank—even if he was the son of a serf—automatically joined the hereditary nobility.

This final attempt to modernize Russia was only partially successful. Its long-term effect was to create a new class of hereditary bureaucrats who suppressed all initiative in the lower ranks of the hierarchy. This state of affairs continued until the abdication of Nicholas II in 1917. Peter was proud of his achievements and reputedly said on his deathbed, "I hope God will forgive me my many sins because of the good I have tried to do for my people." Peter also built a new capital city—St. Petersburg—to act as a window to the West; defeated Russia's rivals, Sweden and Turkey; reformed local and central government; created a senate and cabinet; abolished beards for the aristocracy; and enforced Western dress and customs. He also emancipated women from segregated lives and encouraged their attendance at social events. **NJ**

◐ A grand manner portrait of Peter the Great, who spent his reign trying to modernize the vast territory of Russia.

Island in the Pacific

Jakob Roggeveen sets out to find Australasia and discovers Easter Island.

Jakob Roggeveen was sixty-two when he began his quest to discover Australasia, but it was an ambition fired in his childhood by his father, an astronomer, who had taken out a patent for an expedition to find the fabled *Terra Australis.* The Dutch West Indies Company commissioned Roggeveen to take three ships—the *Arend,* the *Thienhoven,* and the *Afrikaansche Galey*—to find Australasia. He set sail in August 1721. After rounding the southern tip of South America into the Pacific, Roggeveen came across the island of Rapa Nui on Easter Sunday, April 5, 1722.

"That primitive head So ambitiously vast Yet so rude in its art . . . "

Robert Frost, "The Bad Island—Easter"

He renamed it Easter Island. Although impressed by the Moai—giant heads of volcanic stone— Roggeveen made no detailed exploration of the island. He noted the population was between 2,000 and 3,000, and had been up to 10,000 a few years earlier, before a population crash caused by deforestation and other ecological issues. When Roggeveen reached Batavia, he was jailed by the Dutch East Indies Company for breaking its monopoly in the region. After being freed he returned to the Netherlands and wrote an account of his voyage.

Easter Island's population continued to decline because of epidemics such as smallpox and the raids of Spanish slavers. It reached a low of around 100 before the island was annexed by Chile in 1888. Since then tourism has helped it slowly to recover. **NJ**

Fall of Isfahan

Afghan forces inflict a gruesome siege and topple the Persian Empire.

In 1719, the fierce Afghan ruler Mir Mahmud invaded Persia. In March 1722, he defeated a Persian army more than double the size of his own at the Battle of Gulnabad. Mahmud seized the city of Farahabad and laid siege to Isfahan itself, boosting the city's population of 600,000 by laying waste to the surrounding area and driving the inhabitants into the city, where they starved. After a seven-month siege, the defenders had been reduced to cannibalism, and Isfahan capitulated on October 12.

From the sixteenth to the eighteenth century, under the rule of the native shahs of the Safavid dynasty, who forcibly converted their subjects to Shi'ism, Persia (modern Iran) had enjoyed a stability and prosperity unknown since the days of Darius and Xerxes in the ancient world. The jewel in the Safavid crown was the city of Isfahan, which, with its mosques, minarets, palaces, bridges, and shaded streets, was a masterpiece of Shi'ite Islamic art and architecture.

Following a catastrophic invasion of Afghanistan in 1709, however, after which only 1,000 Persian troops returned from Kandahar, the Safavid dynasty rapidly declined, particularly under Shah Sultan Hussein, who deserted Isfahan and spent much of his time in his harem. When the city fell to the Afghans in 1722, Shah Hussein was captured and compelled to abdicate. His son, however, escaped to Tabriz and proclaimed himself Shah Tahmasp II, gaining support from Russia's Peter the Great and the Ottoman Turks. In 1725, Mir Mahmud went mad and was mysteriously murdered, and by 1729 Tahmasp had regained control of most of Persia, only to be deposed and murdered himself by a new ruler and military genius, Nader Shah, who proclaimed himself shah in 1736. The rule of the Safavids was over. **JJH**

The Flying Shuttle

John Kay patents the invention that will revolutionize textile manufacturing.

John Kay was born in 1704 near Bury in the heart of the Lancashire cotton industry. By 1730, the young innovator had applied to patent a machine for cording and twisting worsted. Three years later came his revolutionary invention of the "flying shuttle," a mechanical device that sped the arrival of the Industrial Revolution.

Until Kay's discovery, producing cotton cloth on a handloom was a slow and cumbersome process. A shuttle containing the cloth's weft had to pass through a "shed" formed by lifting alternate warp threads, effectively limiting the width of cloth that could be woven to the length of the weaver's arm as they passed the shuttle through.

Kay's innovation was to increase both the speed of the shuttle as it passed across the loom and the distance that it traveled. He installed two "shuttle boxes" on either side of the loom linked by a wooden track or "shuttle race." The shuttle was propelled rapidly back and forth along the race by a "picking peg" that the weaver jerked from side to side.

The success of Kay's invention transformed the cotton industry by hugely increasing demand for spun cotton and paved the way for later inventors such as James Hargreaves and Samuel Crompton to further mechanize the industry. Sadly, though, Kay himself did not profit from his work. Greedy manufacturers refused to pay him royalties for the use of his shuttle, and in 1753 a mob of Luddite machine wreckers, fearful that mechanization would put them out of work, chased him from his home. He fled to France and died in poverty. His son Robert, who remained in England, inherited the innovative gene and invented the "drop box," a device for weaving complex, colored cloth. **NJ**

Classifying Nature

The publication of Systema Naturae *begins the science of taxonomy.*

It was only eleven pages long, published in Latin in 1735, and bore the formidable title *Systema Naturae per regna tria naturae, secundum classes, ordines, genera, species, cum characteribus, differentiis, synonymis, locis,* but this work by Carolus Linnaeus—an alias of Carl von Linné—was a seminal classification of the natural world into the "animal kingdom," the "plant kingdom," and the "mineral kingdom."

Linnaeus liked to see himself as a new Adam. In the Garden of Eden, the first man had given names to animals and plants, and now this Swedish botanist, who had collected hundreds of new species of plants, provided new scientific names that recognized the relationships between different groups and orders of living things. He classified plants according to their number of stamens, and, controversially, placed Homo sapiens among the apes.

The work was immediately popular, and Linnaeus revised and expanded it regularly. In 1770, his thirteenth and final edition classified 4,400 species of animals and 7,700 of plants and used the binomial system he had invented in 1749. Each organism had a two-part name, the first being that of the genus, the second that of the species. It has been used ever since as the standard taxonomy. Linnaeus was also able to correct mistakes—whales, for instance, became mammals rather than fish.

Linnaeus's work was immensely influential. Although he was interested in classifying living things, rather than explaining their differences, his work proved very useful for later evolutionists. Today, there are far too many identified species to be confined within the cover of even the largest book, but his hierarchical classification and binomial system, though modified, are still indispensable. **RP**

Wesley Preaches Methodism

John Wesley preaches his first outdoor sermon, in Bristol, England, then travels the country to deliver some 40,000 sermons, converting tens of thousands to Methodism.

Methodism's founder, John Wesley, gave his first open-air sermon on April 2, 1739. From then on he tirelessly traveled England, preaching the message of salvation and justification by faith, and converted more than 150,000 people. When he died in 1791, Methodism had become the leading force in the Church of England, although it was destined, against Wesley's wishes, to break away from the established church.

Wesley was an unlikely revolutionary. A gentle man steeped in rural Anglicanism, he nevertheless shared Luther's propensity for interpreting direct personal experience as the touch of God's hand—when he was a child of five he was rescued from a blazing house and claimed he felt like "a brand plucked from the burning." At Oxford University he founded a "Holy Club" with his brother Charles and the radical Calvinist George Whitefield. Ordained, he served as a parish priest in Savannah, Georgia, and was deeply impressed on an Atlantic crossing by the calm faith of a group of German Moravians when threatened with shipwreck. On moving to London, he attended a Moravian meeting and felt personally called by Christ. Whitefield invited him to Bristol, and there he gave his first open-air sermon.

The great wave of Methodism that swept England and the wider Christian world in the late eighteenth century was a religious revival comparable to the Reformation and Puritanism. It revitalized Protestantism, restoring it to early Christian simplicities, with effects that are still felt today. **JJH**

○ John Wesley, who took his message of Methodism directly to the people, preaching to huge crowds all over the country.

○ An engraving of a famed event: John Wesley preaching beside his father's tombstone at Epworth churchyard.

Frederick the Great Annexes Silesia

The campaign announces the arrival of Prussia as a formidable military power.

○ *King Frederick II the Great of Prussia* (1746) by Antoine Pesne (1683–1747) depicts the king as a military overlord.

"I begin by taking. I shall find scholars later to demonstrate my perfect right."

Frederick the Great (1712–1786)

Touching off the Europe-wide War of Austrian Succession (1740–1748), the seizure of the Austrian-ruled German province of Silesia in December 1740 by the new king of Prussia, Frederick II (the Great), was an act of naked opportunism. It was designed to add both land and a population of 1.5 million mainly fellow-Protestant Silesians to Frederick's poverty-stricken and sparsely populated realm. Taking advantage of the accession of the equally inexperienced Empress Maria-Theresa to the Austrian imperial throne, Frederick seized the province with 27,000 of his well-trained troops in a daring winter campaign. But the garrisons of Neisse and Glogau held out against him, and in the spring of 1741 an Austrian army under Marshal Adam Niepperg counterattacked and relieved Neisse (Glogau having already fallen to Frederick).

Inexperienced as a commander, Frederick allowed himself to be outmaneuvered into his first pitched battle at Mollwitz on April 10. The armies were numerically roughly equal, with around 20,000 men each, and at first the Austrians were victorious. They routed the Prussian cavalry and forced Frederick himself from the field. But the superbly well-disciplined Prussian infantry rallied under Frederick's Swedish military tutor Kurt von Schwerin and won a narrow victory. It marked Frederick's apprenticeship as one of the great commanders of history. Mollwitz saved Frederick's Silesian conquests, and although a coalition of European powers lined up against him, the rest of his reign consisted of an almost uninterrupted string of victories against Austria and France. This greatly enhanced the tradition of Prussian militarism and revolutionized military tactics in Europe for half a century or so until the advent of Napoleon. **NJ**

Sir Robert Walpole Resigns

It is the end of the road for one of the most controversial of Britain's prime ministers.

Robert Walpole built his career on a network of family relationships and the shared interests of the Whig squirearchy. It was the corrupt nature of his regime that forced him to resign in February 1742.

A spell in the Tower of London, engineered by his Tory enemies at the end of Queen Anne's reign, had not impeded his progress and from 1721, after skillfully smoothing the aftermath of the South Sea Bubble scandal, he became the pre-eminent member of the government, or "prime minister." (Although the term was not used in his lifetime, historians refer to Walpole as the first prime minister, and he was the first to live at 10 Downing Street.)

The twin pillars of his power were an unashamedly corrupt manipulation of ambition and greed—encapsulated in his famous aphorism, "Every man has his price"—and prosperity brought about by economic stability with low taxes at home and the avoidance of war abroad. Walpole's decline began in the 1730s when an increase in the tax on gin led to riots, and his peace policy broke down with the "War of Jenkins's Ear." In 1731, Robert Jenkins, who captained the ship *Rebecca*, was intercepted by the Spanish coast guard near Havana, and claimed they severed his ear. In 1738, Jenkins appeared before the House of Commons with his pickled ear in a jar. The furor drummed up bellicose feelings against Spain. Reluctantly, Walpole declared war on October 23, 1739.

The issue that triggered his fall, however, was a rigged by-election that Walpole turned into a House of Commons motion of No Confidence, which he lost. George II elevated him to the House of Lords as Earl of Orford and Walpole retired to his magnificent home, Houghton Hall, furnished with the not entirely legitimate fruits of his long tenure in office. **NJ**

○ *Robert Walpole* by John Heins (1732–1771), wearing the robes of an earl and painted in 1743, a year after his resignation.

"My Lord Bath, you and I are now as insignificant men as any in England."

Walpole to the Earl of Bath on becoming lords

Battle of Culloden

The Duke of Cumberland quells the final Jacobite rebellion against Hanoverian rule in a decisive victory at Culloden, Scotland.

The Battle of Culloden was fought on April 16, 1746, between the depleted Jacobite army of Prince Charles Edward Stuart (Bonnie Prince Charlie) and the numerically superior, better armed, and better fed Hanoverian force, led by the Duke of Cumberland. The battle lasted for less than an hour.

Prince Charles Edward had landed in Scotland in August 1745 with a handful of followers. Supported by the mainly Catholic Highland clans, he seized Edinburgh and defeated the English at Prestonpans before marching south to Derby. Here his failure to raise the English Jacobites saw him retire to Scotland, where he defeated another English army at Falkirk.

By mid-April 1746, the Jacobite army had been forced back to Inverness. The prince ordered a dangerous night attack, but his forces lost their way on the moor and returned to their original position exhausted. The Battle of Culloden opened with a huge Hanoverian cannonade. After the prince hesitated, his most capable commander, Lord George Murray, ordered a cavalry charge, which was joined by the claymore sword–wielding Jacobite Highland foot soldiers—but the momentum was lost in the boggy ground and the Hanoverians closed in for the kill. As mounted Hanoverian dragoons appeared, Prince Charles Edward fled the field. The Hanoverians' aggression was matched by the "scorched earth" reprisals led by Cumberland, which broke the Highland clan system and led to lasting bitterness. Culloden finally killed the Jacobite cause. **NJ**

◗ William, Duke of Cumberland—also called the Butcher of Cumberland—with a view of the bloody battlefield.

◗ Bonnie Prince Charlie in hiding after Culloden—those watching over him include Flora Macdonald.

Excavating Pompeii

Charles III orders a full-scale excavation of the buried city of Pompeii.

In 1738, a peasant digging a well near Herculaneum rediscovered the buried city of Pompeii, and ten years later the Bourbon King of Naples, Charles III, ordered a full-scale excavation under the direction of the Swiss-born military engineer Karl Weber.

Pompeii was a prosperous Roman port city near Naples with a population of some 20,000 in the first century c.e. when, on August 24, 79, it was dramatically destroyed and buried by the eruption of the nearby volcano, Vesuvius. Layers of ash and pumice 12 feet (3.7 m) deep covered the town and those inhabitants

"My host, I've wet the bed. My sins I bare. Why? you ask, no chamberpot was there."

Graffiti on a Pompeii bedroom wall

who had been unable to escape. Gradually Pompeii and its sister city Herculaneum, which had been submerged under a sea of mud, faded from memory, despite surviving in contemporary accounts of the disaster by Pliny the Younger and other writers.

Excavations have continued sporadically since 1748, gradually revealing the remains of the most complete Roman town ever found. Among the finds have been an amphitheater, two theaters, a Forum, streets of shops and houses laid out in a grid pattern, restaurants, bars, a large hotel, wine jars, frescoes, numerous examples of graffiti—including erotic art—and votive objects associated with phallic worship. Most poignant are the many casts of bodies of Pompeii's citizens whose lives had come to an abrupt end almost 2,000 years previously. **NJ**

Enlightened Work

Diderot's massive work becomes the "Bible of the European Enlightenment."

Rejecting religion after a Jesuit education, disinherited by his father for his radical views, and determined to become a writer, Diderot endured impecunious years as a Bohemian author until Empress Catherine the Great of Russia appointed him as her librarian. Diderot's *Encyclopedie* of 1751 originated as a commission to translate Ephraim Chambers's *Universal Cyclopedia*, published in 1728, from English. Diderot persuaded the publisher, Le Breton, to finance a much more ambitious project—to gather together in one work all the new knowledge and speculation

"Man will never be free until the last king is strangled with the guts of the last priest."

Traditionally attributed to Diderot

in the arts and sciences that was fermenting in minds of the writers of the Enlightenment, including Montesquieu, Rousseau, and Diderot himself. Volume 1 was issued to a delighted public.

The path to continued publication was not smooth. After completing Volume 2 in 1752, Diderot was accused of sedition, detained, and had his house searched. Ironically, the official in charge of the search was a secret admirer of Diderot who had hidden the offending manuscripts in his own home. Steering his project to completion in 1775 cost Diderot dearly: his eyesight was ruined, and he was continually harassed by the authorities and deserted by his collaborators. Diderot was forced to employ inferior contributors and the final volume was censored by the publisher, who found some of its judgments too dangerous. **NJ**

Franklin Becomes a Lightning Conductor

Benjamin Franklin experiments with electricity in a thunderstorm in Philadelphia.

O *Benjamin Franklin Drawing Electricity from the Sky* (c.1816) by the great history painter Benjamin West (1738–1820).

"He seized the lightning from the Gods and the scepter from the Tyrants."

Jacques Turgot after Franklin's death in 1790

Born in Boston, Massachusetts, in 1706 into a huge family of no fewer than seventeen children, Benjamin Franklin left school at the age of ten and grew up to enjoy phenomenal success as a journalist, publisher, postal official, diplomat, inventor, and scientist. He made remarkable contributions to both the creation of the United States of America and the understanding of electricity, and was especially celebrated for his innovative work on lightning and his invention of the lightning conductor. In June 1752, he conducted his most famous and most dramatic experiment.

Franklin drew electricity from a thundercloud down to a metal key attached to the string of a kite. The whole procedure was described years later by his close friend and fellow scientific pioneer Joseph Priestley. Franklin had been waiting for the steeple of Christ Church in Philadelphia, where he was living, to be completed so that he could test his theory that lightning was electrical, when it occurred to him that a kite would give him "readier and better access to the regions of thunder" than any spire.

Franklin and his son waited impatiently for a thunderstorm to approach and launched their kite. The handmade kite consisted of a large silk handkerchief fastened to two wooden cross-sticks and attached to a long hempen string. Nothing seemed to happen at first. Franklin then noticed that, as a thundercloud passed overhead, some of the loose threads of the string stood erect. When he put his knuckle to the metal key on the string, there was an evident electric spark.

Franklin published a brief account decribing the experiment in October 1752. It helped him to provide the world with badly needed information and protection against lightning and made him one of the most famous men of his day. **RC**

Fast Forward in Time

England adopts the Gregorian Calendar by advancing eleven days overnight.

England (and its North American colonies) finally fell into line with most of Europe when it passed The Calendar (New Style) Act in 1750. In addition to adopting the new calendar, New Year's Day was decreed to be January 1, not March 25 as before. The year 1751 became a short year of only 282 days running from March 25 to December 31, and in 1752, the year was advanced by eleven days—September 2 was followed by September 14.

Until then, England followed the old Julian calendar, first introduced by Julius Caesar in 45 B.C.E., which calculated the length of a year to be, on average, 365.25 days long. This was slightly longer than the actual length of a tropical year. After centuries, the calendar had run ahead by several days, and Easter no longer fell around the spring equinox. In 1582, Pope Gregory XIII imposed a new calendar that dropped ten days and had a more complicated rule for leap years to adjust for drift. Most Continental European countries adopted the Gregorian calendar in the sixteenth century, but England kept to the Julian calendar. By 1750, however, Parliament agreed that the old calendar was "attended with divers inconveniences, not only as it differs from the usage of neighboring nations, but also from the legal method of computation in Scotland, and from the common usage throughout the kingdom, and thereby frequent mistakes are occasioned, . . . and disputes arise therefrom."

The changes gave rise to some discontent, immortalized in a painting by William Hogarth in which the Whig candidate, the Earl of Macclesfield, a supporter of the calendar change, was castigated for robbing the country of eleven days, thus cheating those who paid their rent quarterly of the opportunity to earn their usual wages. **NJ**

⊙ From an engraving in William Hogarth's *Election* series, making reference to people wanting their eleven days back.

> **"The top of yr paper was Thursday Sept 14 . . . have I slept 11 days in 7 hours?"**
>
> **Gentleman's Magazine, September 1752**

Toward Union and Confederation

Benjamin Franklin puts forward a plan for a union of Britain's American colonies.

○ Portrait of Benjamin Franklin in middle age, painted in 1767 by the English artist Joseph Wright of Derby (1734–1797).

"Our enemies have the very great advantage of being under one direction."

Franklin, *The Pennsylvania Gazette*, May 1754

Besides inventing the lightning rod, bifocal spectacles, and an odometer, Benjamin Franklin also made major contributions to the developing cause of American nationhood. In June 1754, he drew up a plan for a union of the British colonies under one general government. However, the terms were too ambitious for either the British government or the individual colonies, both of whom feared a loss of authority.

By the 1750s, the British colonies down the eastern seaboard had found their way west blocked by the French. The situation was further complicated by rivalries between some of the colonies. The government in England urged the colonies to "enter into articles of union and confederation with each other" for their mutual defense and to ensure Native American support. This could be paid for from a common war fund.

The matter was considered at a conference at Albany by representatives from New York, Massachusetts, Connecticut, New Hampshire, Rhode Island, Pennsylvania, and Maryland. It has been described as "a landmark in colonial cooperation," and the delegates discussed the plan drawn up by Franklin. There would be a president-general, who would be appointed by the British Crown, with a grand council of forty-eight delegates from the colonies that would meet at least once every year. It would have power to pass laws, raise its own army, and levy taxes. The number of members from each colony would depend on the colony's population. The grand council was to be responsible for defense, relations with the Native Americans, and all land outside the colonies' boundaries. It would be financed by charges levied on grants of land in the new areas. The plan was ahead of its time, though, and proved to be too farsighted as an initiative. **RC**

Authoritative English Dictionary Published

Samuel Johnson's dictionary is a milestone in the history of the English language.

He was a huge shambling figure, almost blind in one eye and with poor hearing, from childhood scrofula, often twitching uncontrollably and sometimes, in James Boswell's words, "clucking like a hen" because of Tourette's syndrome. Strangers often mistook Samuel Johnson for a lunatic. Even friends thought he was mad to attempt single-handedly to write a dictionary. Nevertheless, on April 15, 1755, his massive undertaking was complete. Two thousand copies of *A Dictionary of the English Language* were published in two huge folio volumes, comprising 2,300 pages and 42,773 definitions, together with more than 100,000 quotations. It was not the first English dictionary, but it was the most thorough and influential, as well as the most idiosyncratic. The English language would never be the same again.

The idea of an authoritative English dictionary originated with a group of booksellers who, in 1746, paid Johnson £1,575 to complete the work in three years. No matter that the Académie française employed forty scholars for forty years to complete a similar project! Johnson recruited a team of amanuenses and began work at 40 Gough Square, London, now the Johnson Museum. In fact the work took nine years, but then Johnson insisted not only upon defining words, but on tracing their etymologies and including illustrative quotations from literature to demonstrate their usages.

Johnson had been determined to fix the meaning of words, and thus bring order to the chaos of language. Yet he soon realized that language was a living thing—it could be cataloged but not controlled. He undertook four revised editions in his lifetime. The first edition of the *Oxford English Dictionary*, in 1928, was a revision of Johnson, and the latest OED contains 1,700 of his definitions. **RP**

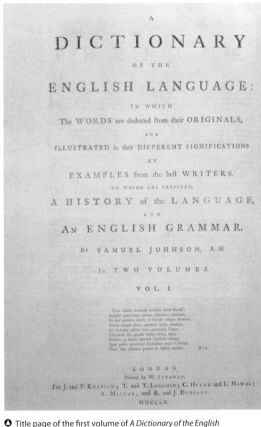

○ Title page of the first volume of *A Dictionary of the English Language* by Dr. Samuel Johnson, published in 1755.

> ## "Dictionaries are like watches ... the best cannot be expected to go quite true."

Samuel Johnson, 1784

Earthquake Destroys Lisbon

The giant tremor, one of the worst ever recorded, decisively influences the thinking of key figures in the European Enlightenment.

The quake struck Lisbon at 9:40 A.M. on November 1, 1755, All Saints' Day. The initial tremor lasted about five minutes, destroying a large number of the city's buildings. Modern scientists estimate that the quake may have registered up to 9 on the Richter scale, with an epicenter 200 miles (320 km) away, under the Atlantic near the Cape Verde islands. The earthquake was followed forty minutes later by a tsunami that swept up the River Tagus, causing even more death and destruction. (The wave also spread across the Atlantic seaboard of Europe, affecting Galway in Ireland and much of the coast of England.) In areas that were not inundated, fires raged for five days.

Out of a population of 275,000, between 60,000 and 90,000 people are estimated to have died as a result of the two natural disasters. In addition, a devastating 85 percent of Lisbon's buildings were destroyed, including the royal palace, which took down with it the magnificent library, containing 70,000 volumes, as well as paintings by Titian, Peter Paul Rubens, and Caravaggio.

The quake caused considerable consternation right across Europe. It prompted Voltaire to write his powerful satire on the intellectual complacency of his day, *Candide*; Rousseau to advocate a return to the rural "simple life"; and Kant to initiate the modern science of seismology—the study of earthquakes. After escaping the quake unharmed, Portugal's King Joseph II and his court slept in tents for the rest of his reign, but within a year his energetic prime minister, the Marquis of Pombal, had begun the reconstruction of Lisbon. **NJ**

◐ Lisbon's buildings collapsing to the ground in a dramatic illustration by Georg Ludwig Hartwig (1813–1880).

Cruelty in Calcutta

The atrocity marks a grim milestone in the building of the British Raj in India.

As part of its drive to colonize Bengal and drive out its French rivals, the British East India Company built Fort William to defend Calcutta and continued to fortify it despite orders from the *Nawab* ("ruler") of Bengal, Siraj ud-Daulah, to desist. In response, Siraj's army besieged the fort, taking it on June 20, 1756, and locked its acting commander, John Holwell, and the surviving soldiers and civilians in a small cell, known as the Black Hole.

In the sole narrative by an eyewitness, Holwell claimed that the cell measured just 14 feet by 18 feet

"Like one agitated wave impelling another, we were obliged to . . . enter."

John Holwell (1711–1798)

(4.3 m by 5.5 m) and had only two small barred windows. He said that 146 people were crammed inside for the night. In the confined space and suffocating heat, those inside begged for release or water—two hatfuls of water were passed in, but most was spilled. Holwell survived by elbowing his way to a window and sucking sweat from his sleeve.

The cell door was finally opened at 6 A.M.. Holwell, supported by other survivors, claimed that 123 people died of heat exhaustion, thirst, or crushing. Subsequent historians have suggested this estimate was deliberately exaggerated and that the true death toll was forty-three. Robert Clive used the atrocity as justification for his defeat of Siraj and conquest of Bengal for Britain the following year. Holwell later became governor of Bengal. **NJ**

Battle of the Bribes

The Battle of Plassey is largely won in advance by bribery and with little fighting.

Robert Clive, commander of the East India Company's army in Bengal, was advancing north after capturing Calcutta en route for Murashidabad, capital of the *Nawab* ("ruler") of Bengal, Siraj ud-Daulah, who, in an alliance with the French, was at war with the company. When Clive's force of 800 British and 2,200 Indians, accompanied by nine cannon, arrived at the small village and mango grove of Plassey, it was vastly outnumbered by Siraj's 50,000-strong army, which had eleven guns and some forty French gunners. Even though he had bribed Siraj's uncle

"By God . . . I stand astonished at my own moderation."

Robert Clive, accused of corruption

and military commander Mir Jafar to quit without fighting, Clive was reluctant to attack.

He was persuaded to change his mind by the urging of his main lieutenant, Sir Eyre Coote, after a torrential monsoon downpour disabled the Indian guns (they had not covered their powder from the rain) and Siraj's army, as prearranged, fled the field. Clive had "won" at the cost of some fifty casualties. Mir Jafar duly deposed Siraj and had him killed, and Bengal was secured by the company. Clive helped himself to the vast sum of £160,000 from Siraj's treasury as his personal plunder from Plassey.

The conquest of India proved highly profitable to the East India Company; its major product was opium, which it shipped in vast quantities to China, where it had a monopoly on the illegal trade. **NJ**

Wolfe Killed as French Troops Defeated

General Wolfe dies as the British triumph at Quebec and claim Canada for their own.

🔾 In a detail of *The Death of General Wolfe* by Benjamin West (1738–1820), the hero succumbs to his mortal wound.

"Don't grieve for me. I shall be happy in a few minutes."

General James Wolfe as he lay dying

The victory at Quebec secured Canada for the British under the terms of the peace treaty of 1763 and a hero's reputation for General James Wolfe. The Seven Years' War of 1756–1763 (sometimes called the first true World War) pitted the British forces against the French across three continents: in Europe, India, and North America.

Wolfe arrived at Louisburg on Cape Breton Island in May 1759 to take command of the British invasion of Canada. A soldier from the age of thirteen, Wolfe was considered an odd fish—sensitive, nervous, hyperactive, and unpredictable. King George III, when told that Wolfe was mad, famously remarked that, in that case, he wished Wolfe would bite some of his other generals.

The expedition sailed up the St. Lawrence and landed north of Quebec late in June. The city stood high on a promontory above the river, and the French commander, the Marquis de Montcalm, had thrown up fortifications on the river's north bank. He had assessed his position, and the north bank seemed the only possible line of approach. After much delay, which his subordinates put down to Wolfe's chronic dithering, the British landed troops on the opposite bank. However, their repeated attacks failed so dismally that, on August 19, Wolfe's nerves gave way and he decided to retreat to bed. He recovered his wits and his health by early September and by personal reconnaissance found a place, the Anse de Foulon, where by night his men could haul themselves up a steep, narrow, ill-guarded road through the woods onto the Plains of Abraham, the heights south-west of Quebec. It was there that the French were brought to battle at last and swiftly routed. Wolfe himself was shot in the chest and died, five days before Quebec was surrendered. **RC**

Catherine Proclaimed Empress of Russia

An obscure German princess, Catherine rises to be one of Russia's greatest rulers.

Born in Stettin (today's Polish Szczecin) as Princess Sophie of Anhalt-Zerbst, Catherine was betrothed to the heir to the Russian throne, Prince Peter, and won the support of her powerful mother-in-law, the Empress Elizabeth, despite the failure of her marriage to the headstrong and inexperienced Peter. She rapidly learned Russian and converted to the Orthodox Church

On his accession in January 1762, Peter alienated the Russian army by making peace with Prussia, attempting to force his officers to adopt Prussian customs and uniforms, and generally favoring foreigners. Catherine agreed to support a plot hatched by the brothers Alexei and Gregory Orlov to depose her husband and make her empress. The plot was put into effect in July while Peter was absent from St. Petersburg.

Securing the support of the crack Ismailovsky regiment by a personal appeal for their protection, Catherine issued a proclamation alleging that Peter's policies were endangering Russia, and set off from the capital in uniform at the head of her army. Peter abdicated, and a few days later was murdered in the custody of Alexei Orlov.

Despite seizing power in this manner, Catherine proved one of Russia's greatest rulers, expanding the empire southward to the Black Sea and enriching its prestige with an exceptional collection of art. This came, however, at the expense of the majority of the population. At one point, Catherine had considered freeing the serfs, but she soon saw that it was more politically expedient to tighten their bonds and the peasants' forced servitude enabled her to fund her cultural and imperial ambitions. She never remarried, taking a string of young lovers, yet maintained a close working relationship with Prince Potemkin. **NJ**

○ *Portrait of Catherine II in the Guise of a Legislator in the Temple of Justice*, by Dimitri Levitzky (1735–1822).

"I shall be an autocrat; that's my trade, and the good Lord will forgive me—that's his."

Catherine the Great

Gibbon Conceives a Masterpiece

Edward Gibbon is inspired to write The Decline and Fall of the Roman Empire *among the ruins of the ancient Capitol.*

He was finding the Grand Tour agreeable enough, but had to admit that the architecture of Turin was "tame and tiresome," and that the marble palaces of Genoa were less than amusing. And who could be impressed by Milan after London? Edward Gibbon's temper, he admitted in a classic understatement, was "not very susceptible of enthusiasm." Yet emotions were strong as he approached the Eternal City. Nor was he disappointed. He experienced "several days of intoxication," particularly among the ruins of Rome's Capitol. Especially vivid was his sense of a living past: the spots where Romulus stood, where Tully spoke, and where Caesar fell were "at once present to my eye." Here, on October 15, 1764, he conceived of writing a history of the city, which later would be a history of the whole Roman Empire.

Little in his own history seemed to fit Gibbon for the task. He described himself as a "puny child, neglected by my Mother, starved by my nurse," while his time at Oxford was "the most idle and unprofitable of my life." He got on badly with his father, who thwarted the one romance of his life, and his main intellectual stimulation had been theological disputation. He might have been written off as a dilettante, if he did not, with immense and unaccustomed dedication, realize his dream.

The Decline and Fall of the Roman Empire was published in six volumes between 1776 and 1788. It was a remarkable achievement, a landmark work of scholarship and, with the grandeur of its scope, the vividness of its detail, and the wit of its style, perhaps the finest work of history ever written. **RP**

◐ A series of portraits by Henry Cook of Roman emperors, from *The History of the Decline and Fall of the Roman Empire.*

Tax Causes Uproar

The Stamp Act ignites resentment and the first fires of the American Revolution.

In Britain, stamp duty was levied on newspapers, pamphlets, playing cards, property conveyances, and legal and business documents, and government favored it as a cheaply collectible tax. Britain needed money to pay for the Seven Years' War, and in 1764 Prime Minister George Grenville suggested that stamp duty be applied in the American and West Indian colonies. The House of Commons agreed and the Stamp Act became law in March 1765.

The effect was electric. The act set light to a giant bonfire of resentment that had been building up

"America is almost in open rebellion. I rejoice that America has resisted."

William Pitt the Elder, January 1766

among the Americans. They were aggrieved at not being treated like British citizens and having no parliamentary members. It was summed up in the slogan "No taxation without representation."

There were riots in Boston and elsewhere, some led by self-styled "Sons of Liberty." Town meetings railed against the act, and newspapers and pamphlets bristled with articles against those who had "invited despotism to cross the ocean and fix her abode in this once happy land." Patrick Henry harangued the Virginia assembly ("Give me liberty or give me death!") to the point of it declaring legislative independence, and Rhode Island declared the act unconstitutional. Delegates from nine colonies denied Parliament's right to tax them. The act was repealed in 1766, but the damage was done. **RC**

Venus Observed

Captain Cook arrives on the island of Tahiti to observe the transit of Venus.

Eight months after leaving England, Lieutenant James Cook, in command of the naval bark *Endeavour*, sighted the cloud-covered peaks of Tahiti. As he made anchor in Matuvai Bayon on April 13, 1769, canoes of curious but friendly islanders paddled out. Earlier contacts with Europeans—Samuel Wallis, sailing in HMS *Dolphin*, had claimed the Pacific island for Britain two years before, followed a year later by Louis de Bougainville, who claimed it for France—had given the Tahitians a taste for iron (they had only shell, stone, and shark's-tooth tools), and their thieving

"... whose faces at least gave evident signs that we were not unwelcome guests."

Captain Cook, April 13, 1769

of nails and fishhooks would prove an irritant to Cook and his men. The Englishmen did not question by what right any European could claim to own Tahiti.

The object of *Endeavour*'s visit was to observe the transit of the planet Venus across the sun, on June 3, in order to measure its distance from Earth. Sponsoring the expedition was the Royal Society, and the ship also carried a team of naturalists and artists to collect and study fauna and flora. Cook, a navigator of genius, measured sea temperature, wind strength, and ocean currents and depths, charting the coasts he visited with a care that places him among the pioneers of modern oceanography.

Soon after observing the eclipse, the explorers put to sea on the next stage of their voyage, southward into the uncharted Pacific. **SK**

Terra Australis Comes into View

Captain Cook sights Australia and charts the eastern coast for the British crown.

○ Detail from an oil painting by Algernon Talmadge showing Cook raising the Union Jack on the shores of Australia.

◑ Copper engraving of a map of Botany Bay, taken from an original map produced by Cook.

> ## "The eastern coast . . . was never seen or visited by any European before us."
>
> James Cook, August 21, 1770

James Cook had been given sealed instructions by the Admiralty that, after visiting the island of Tahiti, he should continue his first voyage of exploration in the Pacific to search for the fabled giant southern continent, *Terra Australis*. He was ordered to take possession of any lands he might discover in the name of King George III. On April 19, 1770, the *Endeavour* came in sight of the eastern coast of Australia, the first European ship ever to do so (although the western seaboard, named New Holland by the Dutch, had been known for more than a century).

Cook had left Tahiti on July 13, 1769, setting a course to sail south and southwest. On October 7, he reached the east coast of New Zealand, previously visited by the Dutch seaman Abel Tasman in 1642. He stayed in New Zealand for six months, charting the entire coastline of the two islands in some detail, before sailing due west on March 31, 1770. Two and a half weeks later, Cook caught his first glimpse of Australia and decided to follow the shoreline to the north to explore.

On April 29, the ship entered a wide inlet, where Joseph Banks and other naturalists collected so many plants that Cook named the place Botany Bay. Here the crew had its first encounter with a group of local Aboriginals, who refused their gifts and threw spears. The explorers were forced to chase them off with musket fire. On June 11, the *Endeavour* accidentally struck the Great Barrier Reef and was forced to beach for almost seven weeks to make the necessary repairs. Finally, on August 21, Cook rounded Cape York Peninsula and landed on Possession Island in the Torres Strait, where he claimed for the British crown the whole of the 3,000-mile (5,000 km) coastline he had just charted. **SK**

German Seizes Danish Rule

Physician Johann Friedrich Struensee becomes dictator in Denmark.

○ A portrait of Johann Friedrich Graf von dän Struensee, engraved by Joseph Friedrich Rein (1720–1785).

> *". . . I would have liked to have saved them both . . ."*
>
> **King Christian VII of Denmark**

The extraordinary career of Struensee—the German doctor who in December 1770 made himself master of a country whose language he did not speak and whose people and customs he despised in order to enact the reforms of fashionable Enlightenment—is a classic tale of unbridled ambition and a ruthless lust for power that brought its own inevitable nemesis.

Son of a theologian and pastor from Halle in Germany, Struensee embraced the egalitarian and atheist ideas of Rousseau at an early age. After becoming a physician, he was brought to Denmark by an exiled political faction eager to regain their dominance over the schizophrenic young king, Christian VII, by appointing Struensee the king's personal physician. Struensee treated the monarch's malady with some success, establishing a dominance over the mad king that was cemented when he became the lover of the young queen, Caroline Matilda, sister of England's King George III.

At first ruling through puppet politicians, Struensee became dictator of Denmark in December 1770, propounding thousands of radical reforms, some progressive (the establishment of orphan hospitals; the curtailing of capital punishment, the abolition of torture); others eccentric (slashing the salaries of officials to pay for balls and masquerades).

Struensee's rule deeply offended the conservative Danish aristocracy, and a plot was hatched to arrest him, the queen, and the king's keeper, Brandt, an ally of Struensee. The palace coup was triggered by the birth of a daughter, Louisa Augusta, to the queen, universally believed to be Struensee's child. In January 1771 the trio were arrested. Despite having outlawed torture and the death penalty, Struensee and Brandt were sentenced to have their right hands cut off, followed by beheading. **NJ**

Powers Partition Poland

Russia, Prussia, and Austria agree to split the country between them.

By the mid-eighteenth century, the once mighty Polish-Lithuanian Commonwealth was in a state of political paralysis, at least in part because of the law of *liberum veto*, which enabled any single Polish nobleman to prevent the passage of any law that failed to meet his approval. Taking advantage of the situation, the three neighboring powers of Russia, Prussia, and Austria divided up the confederation's territories between them. The partition agreement—known as the "alliance of the three black eagles" from the national symbol of all three powers—was signed in Vienna on February 19, 1772.

The Russians had put down a rising of an association of Polish noblemen (called the Confederation of Bar) against growing interference in the affairs of the Polish-Lithuanian Commonwealth. The nobles had tried to gain international support for their cause, but lost much of when it became clear that they had become independent of their king. Troops of the three powers entered Poland in August, and although Polish resistance was fierce, it ended with the fall of Krakow in April 1773 to the Russian General Suvorov, who deported the entire surviving garrison to Siberia. Some 100,000 Poles died resisting the occupation.

Under a treaty ratified that September, Austria took the southern Polish province of Galicia and the area around Krakow, including the rich salt mines. Frederick the Great's Prussia seized the northern coast around the port of Gdansk (Danzig), plus Ermland and Thorn, and Catherine the Great's Russia took Livonia and Belarus. Poland had lost 30 percent of its territory and some four million people—but the partition sparked a revival in Polish national patriotism that would cause problems for the conquerors for centuries to come. **NJ**

○ *The Troelfth Cake*, engraved by Noel Le Mire, shows Catherina of Russia, Frederick of Prussia, and Joseph II of Austria.

> ## *"The Empress Catherine and I are simple robbers ... she wept when she stole."*
>
> **Frederick the Great on the partition**

A Slave Is Freed

Lord Mansfield helps the emancipation movement in England.

In May 1772, James Somersett, a slave brought in bondage from Virginia to England by his master, a Mr. Stewart, sued to win his freedom. Somersett had run away and after recapture had been forcibly put on a ship bound for Jamaica, but he was rescued when his godparents acquired a writ of habeas corpus. Giving judgment in Somersett's favor on June 22, Lord Mansfield, the greatest judge of his day, approvingly quoted an Elizabethan saying that originated in a similar case: "The air of England is too pure for a slave to breathe."

"Fiat justitia ruat coelum (Let justice be done, though the heavens fall)."

Lord Mansfield, quoting Lucius Calpurnius

Mansfield found that slavery was "so odious" an institution that Somersett, even though he was "owned" by Mr. Stewart in his native Virginia, had become a free man by the very act of entering England. Arguing logically, he concluded that "Therefore the black must be discharged."

The case had aroused huge popular interest, as Britain's commercial wealth at the time was built on slavery and the slave trade, and the emancipation movement was beginning to gather pace. Mansfield was well aware that his judgment would unleash a social and political avalanche, but the case was an important milestone on the road toward the eventual abolition of the slave trade, enacted in 1807, and the complete abolition of slavery throughout the British Empire, enacted in 1833. **NJ**

Boston Tea Party

The Bostonians' rejection of the Tea Act shows deep opposition to the British.

One of the most famous events in U.S. history was the Boston Tea Party on December 16, 1773. After the Stamp Act, the British regime's every action was automatically suspect and the American colonies became ungovernable. Boston had a strong tradition of independence, and the British government's attempts to siphon off money from the city's port and trade were resented and resisted. In 1770, British customs house guards had fired on a mob of attackers and killed five of them in what became the "Boston massacre."

Three years later, on November 5, a town meeting in Boston passed resolutions against the new Tea Act, which gave the East India Company the exclusive right to sell tea in America. The first tea ships arrived on November 28, and at a mass protest meeting on December 16, a man named John Rowe asked, "Who knows how tea will mingle with salt water?" From a group who had come prepared in disguise as Native Americans the cry went up, "Boston Harbor a teapot tonight!" Shouting war cries and armed with pistols, hatchets, and axes, they led hundreds of Bostonians to the three British merchant ships anchored in the harbor. Swarming on board the *Dartmouth*, they hacked the tea chests open and threw all the tea into the water. They did the same on the *Eleanor* and the *Beaver*. By 9 P.M. the harbor was heaving with tea leaves. No one was hurt, and the triumphant Bostonians went on a victory march through the city. News of the "tea party" spread swiftly through the colonies, inspiring resistance to the British. New York had a tea party of its own in April. **RC**

❍ Rebellious Bostonians empty tea chests into Boston Harbor in an eighteenth-century engraving of the 1773 event.

Inventor Receives Royal Recognition

King George III rewards John Harrison for his invention of the marine chronometer.

⦿ Detail of a formal portrait of horologist John Harrison, including a reminder of his profession in the background.

> ## "Our faithful guide through all the vicissitudes of climates."
>
> **Captain Cook, on Harrison's chronometer**

John Harrison (1693–1776) was the English clockmaker who revolutionized sea transport in 1773 by inventing the marine chronometer (a device that accurately measured the east-west position of ships), thereby solving a problem that had bewildered some of the best minds in Europe for centuries.

Late in his life, his invention bought Harrison some—but not all—of the massive £20,000 ($12 million [£6 m] by today's value) monetary reward offered by the British Parliament to anyone who solved the longitude conundrum. Harrison worked on the problem for thirty years, producing three highly original designs, before producing a prototype chronometer called H4, which lost just five seconds on its first transatlantic trial and thirty-nine seconds on a subsequent trial. Precision of this order would allow far more accurate navigation than had ever been possible before.

Harrison encountered much skepticism and opposition to his invention. Although he was grudgingly paid £10,000 for the H4, Nevil Maskelyne, the astronomer royal, who himself proposed an alternative solution to the longitude problem, based on careful observation of the planets, opposed Harrison. In particular, he mistakenly claimed that the "drift rate," the natural slippage in time caused by the Earth's rotation, was an intrinsic fault of the chronometer. Harrison made a personal plea to King George III, who, after testing the device himself, in 1773 persuaded Parliament to grant Harrison a further £8,750 in prize money, which he received at the age of eighty—three years before his death. The worth of Harrison's invention was widely recognized after Captain James Cook took the device on his voyages of exploration, and by the nineteenth century no ship would set sail without it. **NJ**

Goethe Becomes a Literary Celebrity

Goethe's celebrated The Sorrows of Young Werther *creates "Werther Fever".*

In 1774, the publication of *The Sorrows of Young Werther* caused such a sensation that it turned its author, Johann Wolfgang von Goethe, into a major literary celebrity almost overnight. The loosely autobiographical novel is a story of unrequited love in which Werther falls for the beautiful Lotte, who is engaged to Albert, a man eleven years her senior. Lotte is thought to be based on Charlotte Buff, whom Goethe met in 1772. Goethe pursued Charlotte for some time but she was engaged to a man older than her, Johann Christian Kestner, whom she married.

In the novel, when Lotte and Albert marry, Lotte informs Werther that they must meet less frequently, but on his last visit, they are overcome and kiss. As a man of honor, Werther realizes that the situation must not continue and decides to commit suicide, using two pistols sent to him by Lotte.

The novel is an important example of the *Sturm und Drang* (Storm and Stress) movement in German literature, in which emotional extremes were given free expression in response to the rational confines of the Enlightenment. *The Sorrows of Young Werther* was a runaway success, and many men were so influenced by it that it triggered a phenomenon called "Werther Fever," in which thousands dressed in clothing described for Werther, and as many as 2,000 copycat suicides took place.

Although Goethe himself later described his distaste for the book, the role it played in developing the career of the writer cannot be underestimated. Goethe came to be known as one of the greatest literary figures Germany has ever produced, and a man described as the last of those who were master of many different subject areas. His body of work includes poetry, memoirs, criticism, and scientific treatises on botany, anatomy, and color. **TB**

◔ A poster advertising a performance of *Werther* by Jules Massenet at the Théatre National de L'Opéra-Comique, Paris.

> ## "I was oppressed with the sensations I then felt; I sunk under the weight of them."

Johann Goethe, *The Sorrows of Young Werther*

The Man for the Moment

Nominated by John Adams, George Washington is made Commander-in-chief of the Continental Army to oust the British.

After the opening skirmishes at Lexington and Concord in the American War of Independence, the British were besieged in Boston, where the redcoats under General Howe attacked the rebel Americans on Bunker Hill. The British won, but so atrocious was the total of casualties that a few more such "victories" would have destroyed them. The Continental Congress in Philadelphia created its own army and put George Washington in command of it in June 1775. He expected the war to be over by Christmas and accepted the post without pay.

As it turned out, there could not have been a better choice. Washington was a career soldier and former British army officer who had seen action against the French. He was a big, impressive man standing some 6 feet 3 inches (1.9 m) tall. Straightforward and reassuringly calm, Washington was a man of few words and sound judgment. His greatest political asset, one of his contemporaries said, was his "gift of silence." He went north to Boston, took a grip on the siege and brought in reinforcements from other states, with which he made the British situation completely untenable. They finally withdrew in March.

There was still a long way to go. The next British threat was to New York, where Washington occupied Manhattan and Brooklyn. The British arrived early in July with an army more than 30,000 strong and a massive fleet, both of which forced Washington to retreat. Washington was almost captured, and his men were losing heart as the army retired into New Jersey and then Pennsylvania. **RC**

◗ George Washington steps up to the mark and proudly leads forward his Continental Army against the British.

Life and Liberty

Congress signs the American Declaration of Independence.

The most famous document in American history was signed on July 4, 1776, after anxiety over whether the colonies should declare independence or compromise with the British. The case for independence was put forward by English ex-schoolmaster and intellectual Tom Paine's *Common Sense* pamphlet, which called George III "the Royal Brute of Great Britain."

The Declaration itself was eventually approved by the Continental Congress in Philadelphia, but only after its original denunciation of slavery had been cut out, not only to appease the South but because

"The God who gave us life gave us liberty at the same time . . ."

Thomas Jefferson, 1774

many in the North were not enthusiastic about it. Drawn up principally by Thomas Jefferson of Virginia, in words that have echoed down the centuries, the document pronounced the "self-evident truth" that "all men are created equal, that they are endowed by their Creator with certain unalienable Rights, that among these are Life, Liberty, and the pursuit of Happiness." All the colonies' wrongs were blamed on King George III, entirely unrealistically, with no mention whatever of the British parliament.

The document ended with the statement that the united colonies "are absolved from all allegiance to the British Crown." Although it was harder to make the declaration stick and the war still had years to run, it had a profound effect on American ideals and American life that has continued to this day. **RC**

"The Fox" Attacks

Washington crosses the Delaware and turns defeat into rebel victory.

The British were calling Washington "the fox," because he had taken refuge for the winter. On Christmas night, 1776, however, Washington came out of hiding and led his men to victory.

Washington had been "wearied almost to death" and feared that the game was up. But the British commander Sir William Howe, who disapproved of British policy in the American colonies, wanted peace by persuading Americans they could not win. Many of the Continental Army's militiamen deserted to accept an amnesty that Howe offered, and bands of

". . . hurry, fright, and confusion . . . will be when the last trump shall sound."

Major-General Henry Knox

armed American loyalists challenged rebel groups successfully in fierce struggles across New Jersey.

Washington rallied his men and led them across the Delaware River into New Jersey. In a hailstorm, they attacked and swiftly defeated a force of German mercenaries at Trenton. Washington had hoped the Germans would be relaxed after their Christmas celebrations, and the story is that their commander was drunk and snoring in his bed. On January 3, Washington crossed the Delaware again and drove the British from Princeton and most of New Jersey.

Rebel morale was restored and in New Jersey the rebels recovered control from the loyalists. Meanwhile Benjamin Franklin was sent to Paris to lure the French, who had been secretly supporting the rebels, openly into the war. **RC**

Americans Gain the Advantage

General Burgoyne's surrender at Saratoga turns the war in the rebels' favor.

○ A postcard commemorating the surrender of Burgoyne, from a painting by John Trumbull.

The surrender at Saratoga on October 17, 1777, was the war's turning point. It could no longer be assumed that the superior British strength would defeat the Americans, now openly allied with France.

In a new strategy for 1777, dictated from an impatient London, an army under the brave, but rash, and dubiously competent General "Champagne Johnny" Burgoyne was to move south to secure New England and join General Howe. Howe, however, ignored the plan and went south by sea from New York to seize Philadelphia on September 17. Burgoyne's army of British, Germans, Canadians, American loyalists, and Native Americans moved south at a snail's pace, harried by rebel sharpshooters. In October, Burgoyne built a fortified camp at Saratoga, but was heavily outnumbered by an American army under Horatio Gates. One story has an Irish private in Burgoyne's army and a rebel waving at each other across a stream and plunging into it to embrace— they were brothers. Two fierce battles left Burgoyne with heavy casualties, short of men and supplies, and his retreat cut off. He ignominiously surrendered.

In 1778, the British evacuated Philadelphia and sent a delegation to negotiate peace with Congress. The settlement did not offer full independence and was rejected. Gates's triumph caused some to suggest that he should replace Washington, to no avail. In February, France signed a military alliance with the United States to bring about American independence. Spain followed suit. **RC**

Pottery Making Enters a New Age

Josiah Wedgwood embraces mass-production at his Etruria ceramic works.

○ Engraving of Wedgwood at work in his Etruria factory near Hanley in Staffordshire.

Josiah Wedgwood was the first tycoon. Wedgwood insisted on quality, smashing inferior products, exclaiming, "This will not do for Josiah Wedgwood." Born to artisan potters in Staffordshire, England, his work transformed small-time English earthenware manufacturer into a mass-production industry.

The Wedgwoods were religious dissenters, and Josiah inaugurated the tradition of the paternalist, philanthropic employer taken up by the Quaker Cadbury, Rowntree, and Fry families who saw care of their workforce as a social duty. Although he enjoyed royal patronage—from as far afield as Catherine the Great in Russia—Wedgwood was a progressive in politics, campaigning for the abolition of the slave trade and distributing ceramic cameos depicting a slave casting off his chains that became the abolitionist movement's logo. Wedgwood opened his Etruria factory in 1769 with profits from the digging of the Manchester Ship Canal. However, it was the installation in 1779 of his friend Erasmus Darwin's horizontal windmill that ensured increased production rates. Mass-production was given another boost in 1782 with the installation—also at Darwin's instigation—of steam-powered engines.

The Wedgwoods and Darwins intermarried, forging a powerful two-family dynasty whose members included Charles Darwin. The works made pottery for 180 years, until mining subsidence forced the firm to move. Wedgwood died in 1795 at Etruria Hall, across from the factory he had created. **NJ**

Stabbed to Death on the Beach

Captain Cook is killed after a violent dispute with islanders in Hawaii.

○ *The Death of Cook* (1779) painted by John Webber, shows the explorer surrounded and outnumbered.

The tension had begun the day before over the theft of tools from a forge on the beach where repairs were being made to *Resolution*'s foremast. That night a large cutter, one of the ship's boats, was stolen. It was a severe loss, and the next day Captain Cook went ashore to remonstrate. Tempers flared, and the Hawaiians crowding around him began throwing stones. As Cook hurried to embark from the beach, marines in the boats standing offshore fired a volley of shots. He shouted to them to stop, but was clubbed down by his assailants. As he lay with his face in the surf, an islander armed with a dagger stabbed him to death.

Cook, on his third Pacific voyage of exploration, had returned to Hawaii after a yearlong voyage exploring the North American coast from California to Alaska in an attempt to find an Arctic passage to the Atlantic, and he may have been worn down by his lack of success and the months of poor diet at sea, as there are signs of unusual irritability toward his crew. But the behavior of the Hawaiians is also difficult to explain if we are to believe that not long before, the islanders had received him as a god.

Cook's extraordinary achievements were recognized in his own lifetime. Even though the American colonies were at war with Britain in 1779, Benjamin Franklin had written to captains of American warships asking that they treat "Captain Cook and his people with all civility and kindness . . . as common friends to mankind." **SK**

Inaugural Race of the Derby

The Earl of Derby's famous horse race is held for the first time.

○ The winner of the 1781 Derby was the racehorse Eclipse, pictured here with its jockey.

Edward Smith Stanley, the twelfth Earl of Derby, loved racehorses, fighting cocks, and gambling. In 1779 he organized a race on Epsom Downs, Surrey, for himself and his friends to race their three-year-old fillies over 1.5 miles (2.4 km). He named it "The Oaks" after his local estate. The next year he introduced a race for colts and fillies, held on May 4, 1780, in search of the best racehorse of the year. The name of the race was decided after the Earl and Sir Charles Bunbury, a leading racing figure of the day and a friend of the Earl, flipped a coin, and Derby won.

The inaugural race was won by Bunbury's horse, Diomed, and two of his other horses won over the next few years. Derby himself claimed victory in 1787, with his horse Sir Peter Teazle.

The early Derbies were run on a Thursday over a mile (1.6 km), with the starting point in a straight line beyond the current five-furlong marker. The sharp bend of Tattenham Corner was introduced in 1784 when the course was extended to its current distance of 1.5 miles (2.4 km). The horseshoe-shaped course and strong gradients make the race an unusual test of a young horse's stamina.

The Derby became the most popular, and richest, flat race in the world. In the nineteenth century, Derby Day moved to a Wednesday, and became a great day out for all Londoners, usually attended by the monarch. The race carried on through both wars, and its prize money is one of the highest in the sport. Today the vast majority of entrants are colts. **PF**

London Torchings in the Gordon Riots

The relaxing of anti-Catholic discriminatory laws sparks the ire of the Protestant mob.

○ A mob of rioters sets fire to the King's Bench prison.

On June 2, 1780, a demonstration in St. George's Fields of 50,000 Protestants carrying slogans of "No Popery!" turned into an orgy of violence in which drunken crowds burned Catholic churches and also torched the Bank of England and London's three chief prisons. They were protesting about the king's refusal to repeal the Catholic Relief Act, which removed most of the disqualifications placed on Britain's Catholics in 1689 under William III. In 1778, impelled by a severe shortage of troops to fight the U.S. War of Independence, the British government had passed the act to boost Catholic recruitment into the armed forces and it was given assent by King George III.

Lord George Gordon, a minor Scottish peer, drew up a Protestant Association petition to repeal the act, attracting widespread support. The petition was so large that a strong man was unable to lift it. But when Gordon tried to present the petition to Parliament, he was refused. He was also rejected during personal audiences with the king. His failure to be heard unleashed a week of violence in which London was given over to anarchy and the rule of "King Mob."

On June 7 the king ordered the military to put down the rioters. Between 285 and 850 people lost their lives in the riots, and twenty-one rioters were later executed. Gordon was imprisoned and eventually converted to Judaism. The Gordon Riots form the background to Charles Dickens's novel *Barnaby Rudge.* **NJ**

World's First Iron Bridge Opens

Erected in Shropshire, the Iron Bridge demonstrates new construction techniques.

○ Pen, ink, and watercolor plan showing a cross section of the Iron Bridge.

The completed iron bridge first opened on New Year's Day 1781. The bridge spanning the River Severn Gorge near Coalbrookdale, England, was the idea of young architect Thomas Pritchard. He commissioned Abraham Darby III, just twenty-nine at the time and a Quaker ironmaster—whose grandfather Abraham Darby I had triggered the Industrial Revolution by inventing the smelting of coke powder to make iron—to build the pioneering design for a single-span, 120-foot (37 m), 378-ton bridge, using massive parts, the largest of which was 70 feet (21 m) long.

The bridge used iron to mimic traditional woodcarving techniques—such as mortise and tenon, dovetails, and wedges—to fit joints together. Although Pritchard died in 1777, work on the bridge continued, financed by another local ironmaster, John Wilkinson. It was completed in 1779, although the approach roads took another two years. No records were kept of the construction, and exact details remained a mystery until 2002, when a watercolor by Elias Martin was discovered in Sweden showing how it was made. The bridge became so celebrated that a new town, Ironbridge, grew up around it.

Darby overspent and was in debt for the rest of his life, but the bridge, although over-heavy and subject to cracks around its foundations, survived and is now recognized as a milestone in the world's industrialization. In 1987, Ironbridge was declared a World Heritage Site, attracting a tourist industry that celebrates the Industrial Revolution. **NJ**

Spanish Execute Tupac Amaru II

In Peru the rebel leader who revolted against oppressive rule in the name of the Incas meets a grisly end as the Spanish reassert their authority.

Jose Gabriel Condorcanqui, a Jesuit-educated great-grandson of the last Inca king, was executed on May 18, 1781. After Spain's destruction of the Inca Empire in Peru and the virtual enslavement of the native Indians, the old aristocracy was still kept on in some regions to maintain control. Condorcanqui inherited the lordship of Tinta province, and adopted the Inca name of Tupac Amaru II.

On November 4, 1780, he launched a major revolt in the Cuzco area, executing the Spanish governor. On November 16 he issued a Proclamation of Liberty, declaring all slaves to be free. He trapped 600 soldiers in a church at Sangara, which he burned down, killing all but twenty-eight, and this, plus his demand for tax reform and vision of harmony between Indians, mestizos, and Creoles, attracted thousands to his revolt. He besieged Cuzco in January 1781, but in April was betrayed and captured. He and his family had their tongues torn out. He was then forced to watch the execution of his family before his own death. Sentenced initially to being torn apart limb from limb by horses, he was eventually hanged, drawn, and quartered before a crowd in the main square in Cuzco.

His brother continued the revolt for two years until his own surrender and execution. The shaken Spanish authorities now attempted to root out of existence entirely the Inca identity and to eliminate any remaining descendants of the Inca royal family. The revolt remained a major inspiration for many South American liberationists and Marxists well into the late twentieth century. **PF**

◖ Twentieth-century painting of Tupac Amaru II by Augusto Diaz Mori.

Defeat at Yorktown

Cornwallis's surrender marks the last battle for the United States.

If not yet the end of the war, the surrender at Yorktown in October 1781 proved to be the end of any significant land fighting.

The British had replaced General Howe with Sir Henry Clinton as their commander-in-chief in the American War of Independence. The fighting continued. A British force under Lord Cornwallis invaded Georgia and the Carolinas. With him were the former rebel general Benedict Arnold and a cavalryman, Banastre Tarleton, leader of the British Legion of Loyalist Americans, whose name was a byword for savagery, as Arnold's was for treachery.

As Cornwallis moved farther north, Washington saw an opportunity and marched south with his army, boosted substantially by French reinforcements. Cornwallis saw his danger and dug in at Yorktown on the York River in Virginia, where he waited to be rescued by the Royal Navy. However, the French admiral, the Comte de Grasse, who had brought a strong fleet from the Caribbean, was able to block Chesapeake Bay and prevent the British navy from reaching the Yorktown garrison.

Cornwallis found himself trapped, besieged, bombarded, and heavily outnumbered. He tried to get his troops away across the river by boat on the night of October 16, but a severe storm made it impossible. On October 17, a redcoat drummer appeared on the British rampart, beating for a parley, and a British officer emerged with a white handkerchief. Terms were discussed and Cornwallis formally surrendered two days later. As the British marched out of their camp at 2 o'clock that afternoon between the watching lines of the Americans, the story has it that their band was playing "The World Turned Upside Down." **RC**

British Seek Peace

The British parliament vote to begin peace negotiations with Congress.

British naval victories in the American War of Independence after Cornwallis's surrender gave them a stronger hand in the peace negotiations, but the British had had enough. In 1783 representatives of the City of London petitioned the House of Commons to prevent the continuance of the war. On March 4 a motion in the Commons against the prosecution of the war was carried without a division, so all that remained was to negotiate the peace.

Congress had appointed Benjamin Franklin, who was respected in both London and Paris, as the

---

"I congratulate you, as the friend of America; I trust as not the enemy of England."

Edmund Burke to Benjamin Franklin, 1782

---

principal American representative in the negotiations. France and Spain both had interests in North America, and Franklin had to ensure the Americans did not lose out. In separate negotiations with the British he played on their suspicion of the French to get them to agree to wider boundaries for the United States than the French and the Spanish wanted. The French were then persuaded to accept this preliminary Anglo-American agreement on the grounds that the Americans and French must not show the British any differences between them. In the treaty signed on September 3, 1783, in Paris, American independence was recognized and the boundaries of the United States were agreed to stretch from the Atlantic to the Mississippi, but Britain kept Canada. The treaty was then ratified by Congress on January 14, 1784. **RC**

First Balloon Flight

The Montgolfier brothers' second balloon takes to the skies over France.

The first successful hot-air balloon flight was made in June 1783 in a vessel invented by the brothers Joseph and Jacques Montgolfier, scions of a wealthy paper-making family from France. The balloon was conceived by the older Joseph, a reclusive inventor, after he noticed laundry billowing as it dried over a fire, but it was built by Jacques, an entrepreneur who ran the family firm. Both brothers believed, erroneously, that smoke contained a gas causing levitation.

Their first balloon was destroyed by frightened peasants after a test flight in December 1782, but the following June another balloon, made of sackcloth lined with paper, weighing 500 pounds (225 kg) and containing 2,800 cubic feet (79 cu m) of air, was ready for a demonstration in Annonay, France. It traveled 1.2 miles (2 km) and ascended to 600 feet (180 m).

The brothers built bigger and better balloons, one of which, gaudily decorated with the signs of the zodiac in blue and gold, flew in Versailles before the Court, including Louis XVI and Queen Marie-Antoinette. The king had suggested sending convicted criminals aloft, but the humane Montgolfiers sent a sheep, a duck, and a cockerel. All the animals survived. The first free manned flight came on November 21 when Pilatre de Rozier, a twenty-six-year-old physicist, and an army officer, the Marquis d'Arlandes, took off from the Bois de Boulogne. They flew 5.5 miles (9 km) across Paris at 3,000 feet (900 m), before scorching of the balloon's fabric forced them down. Of the brothers, only Joseph Montgolfier dared go up in his own balloon, once, when it was tethered to the ground. **NJ**

⬥ Detail from an etching of an original work by Claude Louis Desrais, capturing the launch of the Montgolfiers's balloon.

A Single Nation

The Constitution of the United States of America is finally signed.

The United States had won its independence. Now it needed to decide how to govern the new nation. A constitutional convention assembled in May 1787 in Philadelphia, with representatives from every state except Rhode Island. Agreement was reached only after months of argument, bargaining, and compromise, before the Constitution was signed on September 17, 1787, by George Washington and thirty-eight others.

Washington was unanimously chosen to preside over the convention, but unanimity was otherwise in

"Every word . . . decides a question between power and liberty."

James Madison

short supply. There was disagreement between those who wanted to see a strong central government and the defenders of state rights. It was accepted that the federal legislative, executive, and judicial functions should be separated and safeguarded against the electorate's whims.

It was agreed there should be an executive branch headed by a president, a two-chamber legislature, and a federal judiciary headed by a supreme court. Procedures for elections and amending the Constitution were agreed upon. Deciding each state's voting strength was complicated by whether slaves counted and regulation of interstate commerce was another issue. There was much dispute before all the states ratified the Constitution. The last state to accept it was Vermont in 1791. **RC**

Scandal Sheet

The Times *of London begins its long journey to journalistic distinction.*

It was not the first British daily newspaper—that was the single-sheet *Daily Courant*, which survived for thirty-three years from 1702—but *The Times* is the world's oldest surviving daily. When first founded, its forerunner was *The Daily Universal Register*, published by John Walter in 1785, as a two-and-a-half-page broadsheet whose aim was to publicize a system of typography—with fonts comprising words or portions of words rather than single letters—whose patent Walter had acquired. It failed miserably, so Walter tried to make money from the newspaper itself. On New Year's Day, 1788, he renamed the paper *The Times* and began to specialize in scandal, which

"The weekday Bible, as The Times *is* sometimes called."

Elizabeth Gaskell, 1864

he found good for business—the public wanted to read it, and the rich and famous were sometimes prepared to pay to suppress it. But libel suits from the royal family and two years in prison persuaded Walter to focus on real news, from Europe and Britain.

Its reputation grew under the editorship of Thomas Barnes from 1817 to 1841. Nicknamed the "Thunderer," it was the favorite of the British upper classes. In 1854, during the Crimean War, William Howard Russell reported Russian peace proposals before the British government had heard them. The only period when it was not printed was during a strike in 1984–1985, after the magnate Rupert Murdoch had acquired the paper in 1981. **RP**

Botany Bay Bound

The First Fleet, carrying convicts from Britain, founds penal colony in Australia.

Today Sydney stands on the site where, on January 26, 1788 (celebrated as Australia Day), Captain Arthur Phillip proclaimed the settlement of the colony of New South Wales. In May 1787, he had commanded eleven ships to sail from England. On board were 750 convicts—568 men, 191 women, and 19 children—with 250 sailors, soldiers, and marines. They were bound for Australia, where the British government, desperate to relieve overcrowded jails, planned to found a penal settlement. Sir Joseph Banks, Cook's botanist and now distinguished president of the Royal Society, told Parliament that Botany Bay would be an ideal site.

" . . . Singing too-rall, li-oo-rall, li-addity / Oh we are bound for Botany Bay."

Popular song

The fleet finally reached Botany Bay in January 1788, but Phillip was not at all impressed—the place was flat and scrubby, and offered poor anchorage. Some 5 miles (8 km) to the north he entered Port Jackson and discovered "one of the finest harbors in the world."

For those convicts who survived the horrors of the "hell ships," conditions in the Port Jackson penal colony were brutally hard. In all, between 1788 and 1868, some 160,000 convicts deemed by the British government as suitable for deportation were forcibly shipped to "Botany Bay," the place that had become synonymous with Australia, despite the fact that no penal colony ever stood there. **SK**

First in War, First in Peace

George Washington is unanimously elected president of the United States, a post he accepts more from a sense of duty than from personal enthusiasm.

There could not have been a more suitable first president of the United States than the fifty-six-year-old who had led his country to victory. Now the most trusted figure in the land, he viewed the prospect with gloom (he said it was "the greatest personal sacrifice" he had ever been called upon to make), but no one ran against him, and on February 4 he received every single vote in the electoral college. The procedure for each state to ratify the election was complicated, and it was not until April 14 that Washington was officially told that the matter was settled. On his way from his home in Virginia north to New York he was saluted by crowds that gathered to cheer him on his way, with tributes in verse and troops of maidens showering him with flowers.

On the balcony of the Senate chamber in New York City, tall and bewigged in his black suit, made of American-woven cloth, his sword sheathed at his side, Washington took the oath "to preserve, protect, and defend the Constitution of the United States," to an enormous roar from a huge throng of New Yorkers assembled outside. The federal flag was raised above the building, the church bells began to ring, and a thirteen-gun salute sounded.

The new president's speech was studiously noncommittal and left the feeling that he would rather be somewhere else. Calling down "the propitious smiles of Heaven" on "the wise measures on which the success of this Government must depend," he refrained from indicating exactly what the measures might be. After all, as he said afterward, he was walking on untrodden ground. **RC**

◐ *George Washington at Princeton* (1779) by Charles Willson Peale, painted before he became president.

Rebels Storm the Bastille

A sudden entry of the ordinary people into Paris ignites the French Revolution.

○ *The Bastille Prison, 14th July 1789* by Jean Dubois (1789–1849) marks the beginning of the French Revolution.

"Is this a revolt? No sire, this is not a rebellion, it is a revolution."

Louis XVI and La Rochefoucauld-Liancourt

One of the most famous events in history was the shocking entry of ordinary Parisians into the existing political turmoil of France on July 14, 1789, which led to the tumultuous, sometimes chaotic overthrow of the monarchy and establishment of a republic supposedly based on principles of natural rights and "liberty, equality, and fraternity." Tensions had been high for a year since the bankrupt monarch Louis XVI had recalled France's Estates General (parliament) for the first time in a century. On June 20, 1789, representatives of the Third Estate—all those who were not aristocrats or clergy—vowed to maintain their own political organization, the National Assembly, against government attempts to close it down.

On July 12, alarmed by the king's sacking of the relatively sympathetic finance minister Jacques Necker, and fearing a conservative backlash against the growing unrest, the *sans-culottes* (ordinary people, literally "without breeches") burst onto the streets of Paris. Tensions arose with the Gardes Français who were tasked with maintaining order, and on July 14 the demonstrators broke into the Hotel des Invalides, where they found firearms but no ammunition.

Around 1,000 then marched to the castle known as the Bastille, the traditional place of detention of political prisoners, although on this day it contained just seven men, mainly forgers and "lunatics." The garrison numbered around sixty and was led by the Marquis de Launay. Around 1:30 P.M. the crowd broke down the gates, and as they entered the outer courtyard, firing began. Four hours later, with scores of attackers dead, artillery arrived for use against castle, and the governor surrendered. De Launay was lynched, and the crowd threw up barricades in the streets. The Bastille, symbol of tyranny, was swiftly demolished. The Revolution had begun. **PF**

French Declare the Rights of Man

The historic declaration proves to be a key moment in the French Revolution.

Drafted by, among others, the Marquis de Lafayette, a veteran of the American Revolution, and overseen by Thomas Jefferson, one of the most distinguished makers of that revolution (who was acting as American ambassador to Paris and who had drafted the United States Declaration of Independence a decade before), the Declaration of the Rights of Man and of the Citizen was made quickly. It was adopted by the French National Assembly on August 26, 1789, just over a month after the storming of the Bastille prison inaugurated the French Revolution.

The basis for a new constitution (and an inspiration for subsequent constitutions), the Declaration repudiated feudalism and royal absolutism in favor of universal equality and the indivisibility of rights. Its philosophical background came from such writers as England's Tom Paine, a participant in both the American and the French revolutions, and the Frenchman Jean-Jacques Rousseau, whose dictum "Man is born free but everywhere is in chains" was echoed in the Declaration's First Article. The Second Article proclaimed that the rights of "Liberty, Property, Safety, and Resistance to Oppression" were to be preserved as the "aim of every political association."

Radical critics charged that the Declaration made no mention of the rights of women or slaves, and it was spectacularly breached within months of its appearance as the Jacobins established their arbitrary dictatorship of terror.

Further than this, the Declaration asserted that these universal rights were applicable in every country. By doing so, the revolutionaries instantly aroused the hostility of all existing monarchies in Europe, which feared the spread of such radical notions within their own borders. **NJ**

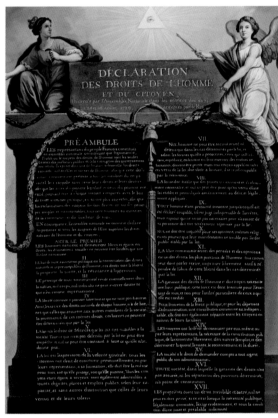

○ *Declaration of the Rights of Man and Citizen, made in 1789; it remains the basis of French law today.*

"Men are born free and remain free and equal in rights."

First Article of the Rights of Man

Art and Reality Meet in Death

Musical genius Mozart dies at the age of thirty-five and is buried anonymously.

○ A watercolor by Louis Carrogis (1717–1806) shows Leopold Mozart, with the young Wolfgang on piano.

○ An eighteenth-century portrait of Wolfgang Amadeus Mozart as an older man by an unknown Austrian artist.

> ## "The last thing he did was to try to mouth the sound of the timpani in his Requiem."

Sophie Weber, Mozart's sister-in-law

Did he muse that his life had been downhill all the way from the age of eight? Back then he had already been busy performing to the accolades of huge admiring audiences in Europe's concert halls. Brilliant and famous, he was the child prodigy to beat all other child prodigies. Now, at the age of thirty-five, he may still have been an adult prodigy (for who else could transcribe a complex piece of music while inventing another in his head?), but his last few concerts had been financially disastrous. Today's musicologists consider everything he wrote after 1780 to be brilliant masterpieces; however, his contemporaries were not in agreement. "Too beautiful for our ears," noted Emperor Joseph II of one work, adding, not so tactfully, "and far too many notes, my dear Mozart." Confined to bed in his Vienna home from mid-November 1791 with a chill that soon gave signs of turning into rheumatic fever, Wolfgang Amadeus Mozart may well have been prey to gloomy thoughts, especially since he was finding it hard to complete his *Requiem*. He was stuck on the *Dies Irae* ("Day of Wrath"). Did he have a premonition that he too would soon be bidding farewell to life? Some later said so, although before his illness his fortunes had been improving marginally, with even his great rival Salieri applauding *The Magic Flute*.

On the afternoon of December 4, Mozart and four singers around his bedside rehearsed part of the *Requiem*. They reached the *Dies Irae* but could get no further than the verse "*Lacrymosa dies illa*" before Mozart put aside the score and wept. Later that day a priest administered the last rites. Soon he slipped into a coma, though occasionally his lips could be observed moving. At 12:55 A.M. on Monday, December 5, 1791, Mozart died. He was buried in an unmarked, multiple grave. **RP**

Crimea Annexed

Under the Treaty of Jassy, the Ottomans cede control of the Crimea to Russia.

The Crimea, the rugged, diamond-shaped peninsula jutting into the Black Sea from southern Ukraine, had always been a coveted territory because of its mild climate and warm-water ports. By defeating the Ottoman Empire in the first Russo-Turkish War (1768–1774), Russia was able to take control of the Crimea. The Ottomans again had to concede defeat in the second Russo-Turkish War (1787–1792), and the Crimea was formally annexed to the Russian Empire under the terms of the Treaty of Jassy. It was a humiliating treaty for the Ottoman Empire because it

"Power without a nation's confidence is nothing . . ."

Attributed to Catherine the Great

was forced to exchange the Crimea for the withdrawal of Russian troops from the Balkans.

For Empress Catherine II (Catherine the Great) of Russia, the annexation of the Crimea was part of her plan to expand the Russian Empire as far south as Constantinople. To this end, she instigated a policy of ethnically cleansing the native Crimean Tatars, who were Turkic Muslims, and replacing them with imported populations, including Swiss and German Christians. The population of Crimean Tatars fell from 5,000,000 to 300,000.

The aim of the Crimean War (1853–1856) was to prevent Russia from reaching the Balkans, and during the nineteenth century, the Crimea continued to be the stage on which various European powers tried to block Russian plans to expand its empire. **NJ**

Tippoo Defeated

The Sultan of Mysore yields to Cornwallis in a milestone victory for the British.

Tippoo succeeded his father, Haider Ali, as Sultan of Mysore in 1782, and acquired the soubriquet "Tiger of Mysore" for his fierce resistance to the British East India Company's spreading conquests. He had taken part in the First and Second Mysore wars against them and their Indian allies, and in 1789, allying with the French, he invaded Travacore, a British protectorate, provoking the Third Mysore War.

His opponent was Lord Charles Cornwallis, governor-general of India, who had surrendered Yorktown in the American War of Independence.

"The faith that Tippoo Sahib keeps / No earthly judge may scan."

Sir Henry Newbolt, *Seringapatam*, 1898

Cornwallis defeated Tippoo in 1792, seized the city of Bangalore, and compelled Tippoo to sue for peace. The resulting treaty stripped Tippoo of half his territory, and he was forced to place his two sons in British care as security against his future behavior.

Despite this, the Sultan of Mysore formed a new alliance with Napoleon's France, giving Lord Arthur Wellesley, who had replaced Cornwallis as governor, an ideal excuse to fight the Fourth Mysore War. This war ended with the siege and capture of Tippoo's capital, Seringapatam, in 1799, and Tippoo's own heroic death defending the city's walls. A mechanical model of a Tiger eating a British soldier that was recovered from his palace appeared, even at the time, to be an apt symbol of this Indian hero's defiant resistance to his country's colonizers. **NJ**

Mob Storms the Tuileries Palace

The French Revolution loses its last vestiges of constitutional legitimacy and comes under the control of violent extremists.

Orchestrated by the extreme Jacobin Club, and summoned by the tocsin bells, a 20,000-strong crowd from the poorer quarters of Paris marched on the Tuileries to demand the abdication of King Louis XVI. The palace was defended by some 900 Swiss Guards and 2,000 National Guardsmen—although the loyalty of the latter to the crown was strongly suspect. Dressed in a purple suit and with his hair powdered, the king inspected the National Guard in a bid to stiffen its resolve, but when the mob approached the palace, they immediately declared their allegiance to the Revolutionary Commune, which had been declared the previous night.

After much dithering, the king and his family fled to the apparent safety of the elected National Assembly, where they sat at the back of the press box while the Assembly debated. Back at the palace, a section of Swiss Guards had fired at the mob, sparking a massacre. Some 600 Guards were killed and their bodies mutilated by the mob, who lost around 260 of their own men in the fighting. As the mob embarked on an orgy of plunder and vandalism, the royal family were taken to the Temple, a medieval tower used as a prison, where they were confined in separate cells.

Exemplifying the new political and moral reality, Maximilien Robespierre, a lawyer and the leading Jacobin, defended Daubigny, a man charged with looting the Tuileries, saying, "Whoever helped France on August 10, is no thief." The stage was set for the September massacres to begin. **NJ**

◀ Eighteenth-century portrait of revolutionary leader Robespierre, known by his followers as "the Incorruptible."

▶ A contemporary illustration of the taking of the Tuileries gives an idea of the mayhem and violence that ensued.

King Louis XVI Goes to the Guillotine

The French king's execution causes an irreparable breach between France and a horrified Europe, and inaugurates the bloodiest phase of the Revolution.

Louis, aged thirty-eight, who had been imprisoned in the Temple tower with his family since the previous August, was summoned before the ruling Convention on December 11, 1792, to answer charges that he had planned to "re-erect tyranny on the ruins of liberty." Louis and his three lawyers ably rebutted the charges, but the Convention was determined on a guilty verdict, and he was unanimously convicted.

Divisions emerged over punishment, with the divided, moderate Girondin faction advocating imprisonment or banishment, or at least a stay of execution while a referendum was organized to decide Louis's fate. The extreme Jacobins, strong in the poor Paris sections of the *sans-culotte* militants, called for the death penalty, which was passed by 361 votes to 319. Those voting for death were cheered by the spectators; those choosing a lesser penalty were loudly abused by the intimidating crowd.

On January 21, the king arose at 5 A.M. and prayed with his Irish priest, Edgeworth de Firmont, who accompanied him to the scaffold in a carriage. Arriving at the guillotine erected on the large Place de la Revolution (now the Place de la Concorde), the king, his hands bound behind his back and his neck shaved, attempted to address the crowd, forgiving those who had condemned him, but his words were deliberately muffled under a drum roll. After the blade fell, the revolutionary Georges Danton declared that France had dared to throw down, as a challenge to the rest of Europe, the head of a king. **NJ**

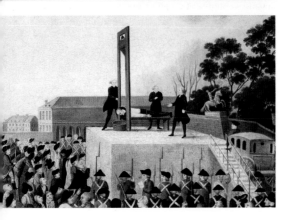

◑ *Farewell to Louis XVI by his Family in the Temple, 20th January 1793*, a painting by Jean-Jacques Hauer (1751–1829).

◑ Engraving by an unknown artist shows the execution of Louis XVI by guillotine, a device made infamous by the Revolution.

Fugitive Slave Act

The U.S. government decides to punish those helping slaves to escape.

The U.S. Constitution had implicitly enshrined the right to own slaves, and to repossess any slave who had escaped to another state. But there was no established mechanism for doing this, and slaves could be helped to escape with impunity. The Fugitive Slave Act closed this loophole.

In colonial times, agreements had been made between states for the return of runaway slaves. Then in the early 1790s a dispute arose concerning John Davis, a fugitive from slave-holding Virginia to abolitionist Pennsylvania. After three Virginians had

" . . . or protect in their states, criminal fugitives, servants, or slaves."

Article 4, Fugitive Slave Act, 1793

arrived and returned him, Pennsylvania's governor, Thomas Mifflin, demanded their extradition on ground of kidnap; the Virginian governor refused.

Under the act, which President George Washington signed on February 12, 1793, a federal district or circuit judge or a state magistrate could decide the status of a suspected fugitive. The act made it a crime to assist escaped slaves, and gave rise to a slave-catching industry. Enshrining the rights of the slave owner in federal law prompted opposition in the northern states, where local laws were passed to hamper the act's operation, giving additional legal rights to those accused. The "Underground Railroad" networks—secret routes to freedom—were set up in response to the act, and help escaped slaves reach the northern states and Canada. **PF**

Terror Committee

Robespierre's Jacobins try to retake control of the French Revolution.

The Committee of Public Safety (CPS) formed by the National Convention was one of many committees, but it became the driving force and war cabinet of the French Revolution. It stopped invasion and directed the bloodiest phase of the Reign of Terror.

The CPS came into being at a moment of crisis for the Revolution. Threatened with foreign invasion and internal counterrevolution, food shortages, and a feud between Jacobin and Girondin factions in the Convention, the Revolution's survival was in doubt.

Meeting constantly in the former palace of the

"I have been able to perceive crimes which are committed daily."

Robespierre on joining the CPS, July 1793

Tuileries, the CPS assumed dictatorial powers to ensure its own survival. It introduced conscription—creating revolutionary armies to repel the Austrian invaders—and sent commissioners, such as St. Just, Fouché, and Carrier, to stiffen the army's officer corps and quell the counterrevolution rising up in Vendée, Normandy, and Lyons. It also conducted bloody purges, sending thousands to the guillotine.

Factions were purged and condemned, including the Girondins, the Hébertists, and the Dantonists, until Robespierre's Jacobins reigned supreme. However, in July 1794, Jacobins organized by Fouché and Tallien, fearing an increasingly paranoid Robespierre, staged a palace coup. Robespierre and his faction were guillotined, and the Reign of Terror was over. Soon after, the CPS was dissolved. **NJ**

First French Republican Constitution

France's Directory declares, "Men are born and remain free and equal in rights."

○ *Celebrating the Acceptance of the Constitution, 10th August 1793*, an engraving by Jonnard after H. de la Charlerie.

The French constitution of 1793 is also known as the "Montagnard Constitution," after the "Mountain," the dominant and extreme Jacobin faction of the ruling French National Convention that pushed it into law. The constitution was the legal framework of the first French Republic, which was created by, and a result of, the French Revolution after the execution of King Louis XVI and the abolition of the monarchy.

Informed by the 1789 Declaration of the Rights of Man—proclaimed by the National Assembly in the early days of the Revolution—which had been inspired, in turn, by the egalitarian ideas of the radical thinkers Jean-Jacques Rousseau and Thomas Paine, the constitution proclaimed the supremacy of popular sovereignty. It insisted that certain human rights were inalienable, including those to personal freedom, free assembly, employment, and education, and the right to revolt against unjust tyranny.

Born in the furnace of the fierce in-fighting between the different factions of the Revolution, the constitution lasted barely two years before it was replaced by a new constitution in 1795. This constitution was proclaimed by the Directory, the ruling body set up by the more moderate Jacobins who had overthrown Robespierre's dictatorship and ended the bloody Reign of Terror. Nevertheless, the ideals of liberty, equality, and fraternity that had inspired the 1793 constitution remained the guiding lights of subsequent French republics and inspired later imitations abroad. **NJ**

France Enters the Reign of Terror

The noble idealism of the French Revolution slips into totalitarian persecution.

🔵 Victims of the Reign of Terror await their fate at the Conciergerie in a poignant painting by Charles-Louis Müller (1815–1892).

The law gave unlimited power to the revolutionary committees set up the previous March to arrest, try, condemn, and kill anyone remotely suspected of opposing the Revolution, no matter how scanty or even nonexistent the evidence against them. The aim was to intimidate all actual or potential foes of "patriotism" into paralysis, and to take revenge on all who did not share the policies and prejudices of the dominant Jacobin revolutionary faction.

The immediate result was an orgy of killing in the fall of 1793 that swept away not only Marie Antoinette, Queen of France, but also twenty-one leaders of the defeated Girondin faction (one of these, Valaze, cheated the guillotine by stabbing himself, but his corpse was guillotined all the same). Other victims included Jean-Sylvain Bailly, the former mayor of Paris, Madame du Barry, a former royal mistress of Louis XV, and Madame Roland, the high-spirited and intelligent inspiration of the Girondins.

By the end of the year, some 3,000 had been guillotined in Paris, and a further 14,000 in the French provinces. But soon after, the Revolution began to devour its own children. In the outbreak of mass sadism, the revolutionary ideals of liberty, equality, and fraternity had been irretrievably lost. As Madame Roland remarked, "The time has come which was foretold when the people would ask for bread and be given corpses." At her execution, she uttered her most famous words, "Oh Liberty, what crimes are committed in thy name!" **NJ**

Queen Marie Antoinette Is Executed

The Queen of France pays the ultimate price for the alleged excesses of her former life.

○ Portrait of Marie Antoinette by Jacques-Fabien Gautier d'Agoty (1710–1781) during the early years of her reign.

◐ After her execution, the French queen's head is paraded before a jubilant crowd in a painting by an unknown artist.

"My blood alone remains: take it, but do not make me suffer long."

Marie Antoinette before her execution

After the mob attacked the Tuileries and captured the royal family in August 1792, Marie Antoinette's life of privilege was turned into one of deprivation and suffering. During her imprisonment she was kept isolated and separate from her husband, and after the king's execution she was parted from her son, the eight-year-old Louis Charles, who was forced to mock and insult his mother, and to accuse her of a variety of vile abuses.

Moved from the Temple to the damp Conciergerie prison on an island in the Seine River, she was accused in court of a range of crimes, from the political—of conspiring with her brother, the Austrian emperor, to invade France—to the personal—particularly, of having an incestuous relationship with her son. She refused to answer the latter charge, declaring that "Because nature itself refuses to accept such an accusation brought against a mother, I appeal to all the mothers here present." When the court inevitably sentenced the queen to death for the crime of treason, she left "with no trace of emotion appearing on her face."

On October 16, Marie Antoinette dressed in a white dress and bonnet, along with black stockings and red shoes. The executioner's son, Henri Sanson, tied her hands behind her back and cut her hair, which had turned white. Trembling with fear at the sight of the tumbril, she relieved herself in a corner of the jail courtyard, but composed herself before she was placed in the cart and trundled to the guillotine where her husband had died ten months before. The artist Jacques-Louis David, an eminent Jacobin and ally of Robespierre, sketched her on her last journey. Her final words were an apology to the executioner, Charles Sanson, for accidentally treading on his foot as she mounted the scaffold. **NJ**

Thomas Jefferson Resigns

A strong opponent of federal power resigns as American Secretary of State.

○ Thomas Jefferson, painted during his presidency by the eminent portraitist Gilbert Stuart (1755–1828).

"The spirit of resistance to government is so valuable. . . . It will often be."

Thomas Jefferson to Abigail Adams, 1787

George Washington was an experienced delegator and, as president of the United States, recruited talent that included Alexander Hamilton at the Treasury, Thomas Jefferson as secretary of state for foreign affairs, and James Madison as leader of the House of Representatives. Jefferson, a Virginia aristocrat like Washington, accepted the foreign affairs portfolio with misgivings. He admired Washington, but there were differences between them.

As minister in Paris, Jefferson had witnessed the beginning of the French Revolution, which he believed might bring the American Revolution's libertarian ideals to Europe and should be supported. Washington was more cautious and isolationist. He believed that the purpose of American foreign policy should be the promotion of American interests. Jefferson was alarmed by the extent to which Alexander Hamilton and his supporters, who believed in a powerful central federal government, seemed to want to turn the presidency almost into an American monarchy. Jefferson strongly disapproved of Hamilton's creation of a national bank, which he regarded as "adverse to liberty," and tried unsuccessfully to persuade Washington to veto it.

Two political parties were now developing in America: the Federalists, who followed Hamilton, and the Republicans (or Democratic-Republicans), who believed in states' rights, wanted federal power held in check, and found a spokesman in Jefferson. Jefferson's supporters are considered the ancestors of today's Democratic Party (the modern Republican Party was not founded until years afterward). Finding himself in a minority in the cabinet, Jefferson resigned and went home to his estate at Monticello in Virginia, from where he would before long emerge to become vice president and then president. **RC**

Robespierre Is Executed

The architect of The Terror of the French Revolution is guillotined without trial.

Maximilien Robespierre, the "sea-green incorruptible" (in the words of Scottish historian Thomas Carlyle) had been a provincial lawyer who rose to prominence during the early years of the French Revolution by adopting a fierce radical and democratic stance, denouncing those who backslid from the revolutionary principles of the Jacobin Club. When, following the proclamation of a republic in France and the execution of Louis XVI in January 1793, the Revolution appeared to be in mortal danger from the armies of Austria and other monarchical states, Robespierre focused on the enemy within.

In June 1793, the working-class revolutionaries, the *sans-culottes*, overthrew the government and the Committee of Public Safety was formed, with Robespierre as its most influential figure. In September, the committee enacted a "Law of Suspects," giving the government a widespread right of arrest, and passed an emergency decree suspending civil rights. Terror became a tool of government policy, and over the next six months more than 16,000 people were executed, including several of Robespierre's former friends and colleagues, notably Georges Danton and Camille Desmoulins.

Robespierre's steely and cold-blooded assertion of the value of terror made him the chief focus of those who sought to end the committee. On July 27, 1794 (known as Thermidor 8 in the revolutionary calendar), Robespierre's opponents barred him from speaking in the National Convention and his arrest was ordered. Robespierre was declared an outlaw. He withdrew to the Hôtel de Ville, where he was seized in the morning, having apparently shot himself in the jaw. The next day he and twenty-one of his associates were guillotined without trial in the Place de la Revolution (now the Place de la Concorde). **PF**

○ Robespierre becomes a victim of the policy of terror he promulgated at his execution in the Place de la Revolution.

> *"Terror is nought but prompt justice; it is therefore an emanation of virtue."*
>
> **Robespierre to the National Convention, 1794**

Hastings Acquitted

Warren Hastings's impeachment ends with his acquittal by the House of Lords.

The impeachment of Warren Hastings, the first governor-general of British India, became an eighteenth-century *cause célèbre* because of politics and personal clashes, rather than his record in India.

Born in 1732, Hastings was an able administrator who rose from clerk in the East India Company under the patronage of Robert Clive to governor-general for twelve years (1773–85). His rule was characterized by respect for Indian traditions and religions: he founded a religious Muslim madrassa while governor of Bengal, and left the Hindu caste system in place.

"An event has happened, on which it is difficult to speak, and impossible to be silent."

Edmund Burke, on Hastings's impeachment

He made native Indians, not Europeans, responsible for tax collection, and scored military successes against the French and the Dutch.

However, he was opposed by Sir Philip Francis, an influential and ambitious company councillor, who goaded Hastings into a duel, where he was wounded, and returned to England to plot Hastings's downfall. Francis persuaded Edmund Burke that Hastings was corrupt, which led to formal impeachment proceedings in Parliament. After seven years Hastings was eventually acquitted. He had spent nearly £80,000 on defending his reputation, but the East India Company purchased his family's former country estate, Daylesford in Worcestershire, for his own use. Hastings died in 1818, having been made a privy councillor in 1814. **NJ**

The Third Partition

Reduced by two previous partitions, the third ends Polish independence.

The first Polish Republic—ended after the first partition of the country in 1772—had been forced into an alliance with its western enemy, Prussia, to protect itself against the incursions of its eastern enemy, Russia. Emboldened by the Polish-Prussian Pact of 1790, the *Sejm* ("parliament") repealed the pro-Russian Repnin reforms. Frightened of imminent revolution, Poland's noblemen formed the Confederation of Targowica, inviting Russia to intervene. Catherine the Great sent a 100,000-strong army in 1793, which, with Prussia, defeated the Poles

"There is a time when you have to sacrifice everything to save everything."

Tadeusz Kosciuszko

and created a second partition, dividing Poland between the Confederation and radical nationalists.

The following year, Polish patriots rose against Russian rule under the inspired leadership of Tadeusz Kosciuszko, a national hero and former general in George Washington's army. The rising collapsed under the weight of Russian numerical superiority ,and Kosciuszko was imprisoned in Russia along with 20,000 of his soldiers. The third partition of Poland, proclaimed on October 24, 1795, gave Russia 46,000 square miles (120,000 sq km), 1.2 million of its people, and the city of Wilno (Vilnius). Prussia got 21,000 square miles (55,000 sq km), 1 million people, and the city of Warsaw, and Austria received 18,000 square miles (47,000 sq km), 1.2 million people, and the cities of Krakow and Lublin. **NJ**

Smallpox Vaccination Invented

English doctor Edward Jenner discovers that inoculating patients with cowpox provides immunity from the deadly smallpox virus.

In 1796, Edward Jenner was a country doctor practicing near his birthplace in Berkeley, Gloucestershire. Most of his patients were rural farmworkers, and he noticed that those who contracted the common, harmless disease cowpox from the cows they milked never fell ill with the deadly, disfiguring scourge smallpox.

On May 14, during a local smallpox epidemic, a milkmaid, Sarah Nelmes, came to Jenner complaining of cowpox blisters on her hands. Jenner lanced the blisters and preserved the fluid. He then persuaded a local farmer named Phipps to allow him to "vaccinate" (Jenner coined the word from the Latin term for cowpox, *vaccinia*) his young son, James. He made two small incisions on James Phipps's arm, dripped in the cowpox pus, and bandaged the wounds. James duly developed cowpox. Six weeks later Jenner daringly injected James with the smallpox "virus" (another word he coined). As Jenner had anticipated, the boy remained immune to the deadly disease. Jenner had stumbled upon the fact that cowpox is a virus related to smallpox, so vaccination with cowpox provides immunity to smallpox.

After further tests, Jenner published his findings in 1798, and despite intense and sometimes hysterical opposition (satirized in James Gillray's famous cartoon of Jenner's patients sprouting cows from all parts of their anatomy), by 1800 vaccination against smallpox was being practiced all over Europe. In acknowledgment of his discovery, Jenner was awarded £30,000 ($150,000) by Parliament. He died on January 26, 1823, aged seventy-four. **NJ**

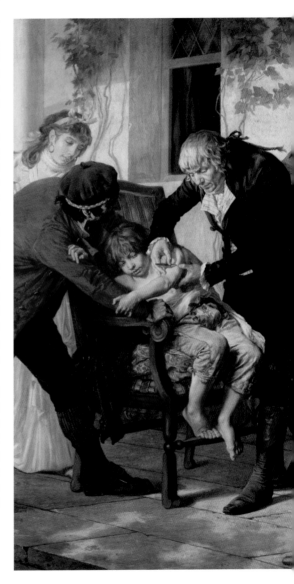

○ Jenner performs the first vaccination against smallpox in 1796 in an oil painting by Gaston Melingue (1840–1914).

River Niger Traced

Scottish doctor and botanist Mungo Park becomes the first European to discover the River Niger on an expedition for the African Association.

After a voyage to Sumatra as ship's surgeon, in 1795, Mungo Park offered to the African Association to explore the River Niger. Park traveled up the Gambia River to a British trading station at Pisania before setting out into the unknown interior in December. He traveled through upper Senegal and the Kaata desert before being captured and held prisoner for four months by a Moorish chieftain. On July 1, he escaped on a horse, and guided only by his pocket compass, reached the Niger at Segu on July 21. Park followed the river for 80 miles (130 km) before turning back at Silla and returning to Pisania.

Park's return with news of his discovery caused a sensation. He published the journal of his expedition, married, started a family, and settled in Peebles, where he learned Arabic from a native speaker in preparation for a return to the Niger. On his second, government-sponsored expedition in 1806, Park tried to trace the course of the Niger, which he thought joined the Congo River. Park and a group of Europeans followed the Niger for several hundred miles. But many members of the expedition died of disease or were killed by hostile tribesmen, and Park himself drowned in rapids on his beloved river during an attack. Park's fate was related by the sole survivor of his expedition, an African guide, and confirmed in 1825 by the explorers Richard Lander and Hugh Clapperton—the latter died of disease during this expedition, as did one of Park's sons who had traveled to the region to discover his father's fate. **NJ**

○ Illustration showing Mungo Park receiving refreshment by African natives during his expedition of the Niger River basin.

◑ Mungo Park's own sketch of himself (bottom far right) drawing the bridge on the Bafing River in Senegal.

Farewell Address

George Washington publishes his last thoughts to the American nation.

George Washington was reluctantly persuaded to stand for a second term as American president in 1793. But he refused to run for a third term, thereby setting a precedent that would last until Franklin D. Roosevelt in 1940. He was sick of partisan politics, and his false teeth were a nuisance.

In 1796, the president issued a final letter to the nation. He called for everyone to work together for the common good. He hated faction, self-promotion, and party politicking, and his letter deplored "the baleful effects of the spirit of party" and warned

"Observe good faith and justice towards all Nations; cultivate peace . . . with all."

George Washington's farewell speech

Americans against "a small but artful, enterprising minority" of politicians who put their own ambitions above American interests. He denounced "the insidious wiles of foreign influence" and politicians who wanted involvement in European warfare. Europe he thought of as a sideshow.

The security, prosperity, and happiness of Americans, he believed, depended on pursuing the interests of America and steering clear of "permanent alliances." Washington also believed in a strong presidency. "The very idea of the power and right of the People to establish Government presupposes the duty of every Individual to obey the established government." It is one of history's ironies that in the land of the free, American presidents exercise more extensive powers than constitutional monarchs. **RC**

Napoleon Goes to Egypt

Though a military failure, the expedition is a success for scholarship and science.

When Napoleon left for Egypt from the southern French port of Toulon on May 19, he had with him 35,000 men in 400 ships, including five of the officers he would later make into Marshals. Napoleon dreamed of becoming a second Alexander, carving out an empire in the east by bringing it the technology of modern Europe, and learning the ancient wisdom of the Orient. To this end, his troops were joined by 167 artists, scientists, scholars, and savants. These learned men would return from Egypt with treasures—including the Rosetta Stone, whose

"We must go to the Orient—all great glory resides there."

Napoleon

hieroglyphs would be translated by Jean-François Champollion—and would be the campaign's real winners. They would distill their knowledge into the twenty-two-volume *Description of Egypt*, triggering Europe's lasting love affair with the Near East.

Militarily, however, Napoleon's campaign was a muted triumph. After scattering Egypt's ruling elite, the Mamluks, at the Battle of the Pyramids in July, Napoleon's fleet was annihilated by Nelson at the Battle of the Nile. Napoleon went to Palestine, sacking Jaffa and besieging Acre, before disease ravaged his forces. He slipped back to France in 1799 in a single ship. When remnants of his army surrendered to the British three years later, Napoleon had crowned himself emperor—but only one in three of the men he took with him to Egypt survived. **NJ**

The United Irishmen Are Defeated

British authorities take on the society of United Irishmen and the French forces that support them, eventually defeating the rebel forces in Ireland.

The United Irishmen was a liberal debating and propaganda society set up under the influence of the American and French revolutions. Its aim was parliamentary reform to encourage Catholic and Protestant Irish people to break the Anglican ascendancy and establish a union of Irishmen of all denominations within an independent Ireland free of British rule.

Fearful of the French Revolution being exported to Ireland, the British authorities cracked down on the society, compelling its leaders to launch a premature revolt in Dublin after the failure of a large French force under General Hoche and the United Irishmen leader Theobald Wolfe Tone to land at Bantry Bay in 1796. Defeated in Dublin, the rebels—known as "Croppies" from their cropped hair—managed to seize control of large areas of rural Ireland, particularly in Ulster and Wexford, where rebels established a revolutionary government for three weeks. In the north, the largely Presbyterian rebel leadership inflicted defeats on the British before being overwhelmed. The last major rebel force of 20,000 men was defeated at Vinegar Hill, north of Wexford, on June 21.

In August and October, French forces landed in counties Mayo and Donegal but were defeated, and Wolfe Tone committed suicide in prison before he could be executed. The rebellion and its suppression were characterized by atrocities on both sides, resulting in up to 30,000 deaths. **NJ**

○ Illustration depicting the Battle of Vinegar Hill, which took place on June 21, 1798, outside Enniscorthy in Wexford.

○ James Gillray's caricature of the United Irishmen in Training (1798) was meant to encourage English recruits to the army.

Battle of the Nile

Nelson destroys the French fleet that escorted Bonaparte to Egypt.

The French fleet, which had escorted Napoleon Bonaparte's army to Egypt, had anchored at Aboukir Bay near Alexandria in shallow water. To protect itself from attack the ships were joined by chains so that their line could not be broken.

Horatio Nelson, commander of the British fleet in the Mediterranean, had been searching for the French ever since they had left Toulon. He was convinced that Egypt had been their target, and on the evening of August 1 he found their fleet. He moved to engage the French immediately, and his

"I had the happiness to command a band of brothers."

Horatio Nelson of his ship's captains

lead ship, HMS *Goliath*, saw that she could sail over the chain line and engage the French from the landward side. Good British seamanship and initiative negated the defensive strategy of the French admiral. Although the opposing fleet were equally matched in numbers, the French were unable to maneuver and the British could move down the line firing into the French ships from both sides. By dawn the French fleet was annihilated—1,700 French sailors died and 3,000 were taken prisoner. The British had 200 killed and 700 wounded. No British ship was sunk.

Such an overwhelming victory ensured the failure of French designs on Egypt, established the moral superiority of the British Navy over its enemies, and confirmed Nelson's personal reputation throughout Europe. **NK**

A New Poetry

Lyrical Ballads marks the beginning of the romantic movement in literature.

With *Lyrical Ballads* William Wordsworth and his collaborator Samuel Taylor Coleridge consciously stood apart from mainstream poetry—replete with what Wordsworth called its "gaudiness and inane phraseology"—and wrote about the lowly and the downtrodden, about human equality and fraternity, about ordinary life with all its extraordinary aspects; and they did so in a language that, by the standards of the day, was remarkably simple and unaffected. Most critics howled, but soon it was apparent that *Lyrical Ballads* marked the beginning of a new era in

"Poetry is the spontaneous overflow of powerful feelings."

Preface to *Lyrical Ballads*, 1802 edition

literature. According to William Hazlitt, it was the literary equivalent of the political revolution in France.

Wordsworth first met Coleridge in 1797, and their creative relationship soon grew. They jokingly called themselves "the Concern," as though they were a manufacturing company for the production of verse. Coleridge penned "The Rime of the Ancient Mariner" and three shorter poems, and Wordsworth wrote the bulk of the book's material, including the ineffable "Lines written a few miles above Tintern Abbey."

The book was not a financial success, though further editions followed in 1801 and 1802. Coleridge's output thereafter was limited, as he became addicted to opium. Wordsworth's was prodigious but uneven in quality. Yet the romantic movement in poetry remains as their legacy. **RP**

Income Tax Introduced

The unheard-of imposition is introduced to pay for the costly Napoleonic wars.

Income tax first appeared in Britain in William Pitt the Younger's annual budget in December 1798, and passed into law the following January 9. Pitt proposed a graduated tax of less than 1 percent on incomes of less than £60 ($280) a year, rising to 10 percent on incomes over £200 ($950). In doing so, he followed the concept of progressive taxation that Adam Smith had advocated in *The Wealth of Nations* twenty years earlier. He hoped to raise £10 million by the measure, but the actual tax receipts for 1799 amounted to just over £6 million.

"Poverty of course is no disgrace, but it is damned annoying."

William Pitt the Younger

The revenue was needed to pay for numerous military measures: for the fleet guarding Britain's global interests; for coastal defenses, such as the Martello Towers, against the threat of French invasion; to finance Pitt's extensive spy service; and to prop up Britain's allies against France in mainland Europe.

The tax proved so unpopular that it was abolished by the short-lived administration of Henry Addington during the equally brief Peace of Amiens between France and Britain in 1802. The renewal of war brought its—and Pitt's—return in 1803, but it was again abolished after the end of the Napoleonic wars in 1816. It was reintroduced—this time for good—by Sir Robert Peel's government in 1842, though unlike Pitt, Peel did not tax incomes of less than £150 a year. **NJ**

Key to the Code

The Rosetta Stone is found, unlocking the secrets of ancient Egyptian writing.

When Napoleon invaded Egypt in 1798, hoping to find a way to break the British stranglehold on India, he sent along with his army a team of 167 savants—scholars and artists who could excavate, record, and study the inscrutable remains of the great ancient civilization of the Nile. Key to any kind of genuine understanding was the decipherment of the mysterious hieroglyphic script.

On July 19, 1799, a unit of army engineers was digging the foundations of a fort on the west bank of the Nile in the port of Rashid, or Rosetta, and found a basalt stele, or engraved stone, more than 3 feet (1 m) long and inscribed in three languages—Greek, Egyptian hieroglyphs, and demotic Egyptian. The Greek text revealed that it dated from 196 B.C.E. The stone's importance was soon recognized and it was taken to Cairo, where it was placed with General Jacques de Menou. Copies of the inscription were made and circulated to scholars across Europe.

Two years later, a British army swept the French out of Egypt. General de Menou attempted to hide the stone, but the British seized it and had it transported to London. It was presented to the Society of Antiquaries, and lodged in the British Museum, where it is still housed today.

Scholars came to realize that the three texts were all versions of the same passage. The stone records a series of decrees issued by the Hellenistic Ptolemaic dynasty of Egypt, which ruled from 305 B.C.E. to 30 B.C.E. With this knowledge in mind, Jean-François Champollion was able to announce, in 1822, that he had successfully translated the hieroglyphs. **PF**

◗ The Rosetta Stone, deciphered between 1822 and 1824, is key to the modern understanding of hieroglyphic writing.

Napoleon in Power

The coup d'etat that brings Napoleon to power in France is a botched affair.

After his ignominious return from Egypt in September 1799, Napoleon's fortunes were at a low ebb. However, one of the five members of the Directory, the body ruling postrevolutionary France, was the Abbé Sieyès, a survivor of the Terror and an inveterate plotter. He was determined to use Napoleon as a puppet to defeat his fellow directors and stage a Jacobin revival.

On November 9, Sieyès and two non-Jacobin director colleagues, Duclos and Barras, resigned. But the two Jacobin directors, Gohier and Moulin, refused to follow suit, and Napoleon was heckled when he stormed into the Council of Ancients with a military escort and attempted to browbeat them into giving him power. He met an even stormier reception in the Council of 500, where he was physically assaulted. His younger brother Lucien, the council president and a former Jacobin, saved the day by melodramatically seizing a sword and threatening to run Napoleon through should he betray the Revolution's principles. Napoleon's grenadiers, under the future Marshal Murat, then cleared the Orangerie of delegates and a new body—a three-man consulate—with Napoleon as First Consul and Sieyès as Second Consul, took over. This is known as the "coup of 18 Brumaire" (18 Brumaire being the date in the revolutionary calendar when this took place).

After Napoleon proclaimed himself emperor, Lucien went into exile while the outwitted Sieyès retired into private life, although both rallied to the emperor in 1815 during his 100 days' restoration that ended at Waterloo. **NJ**

◐ The best-known representation of the coup that brought Napoleon to power is by artist François Bouchot (1800–1842).

Shock of the New

Goya's Los Caprichos *series shows art's capacity to shock and surprise.*

Born in Zaragoza in 1746, Francisco Goya was a gilder's son who became a court painter in the 1780s, and by the 1790s was Spanish king Charles IV's favorite artist. In 1792, a serious illness left Goya permanently deaf, and, in his isolation, he increasingly worked on his own imaginative works. *Los Caprichos* ("the caprices") comprise a series of etchings and drawings that offer musings on the age, and satirical insights into the human condition. The Catholic Church, especially the Inquisition, are favorite themes, as well as witchcraft, and the failings of human nature.

"[Los Caprichos *depicts*] the ... *follies to be found in any civilized society.*"

Goya describes *Los Caprichos*, 1799

The series also explored the new aesthetic possibilities of prints, with the aquatint technique allowing for a softer, more painterly effect than conventional etching. Some 300 copies of the series were printed. Goya sold twenty-seven sets in two days before withdrawing the remaining copies from the market, although it is not clear whether this was because the public reaction was hostile, or for fear of prosecution by the Inquisition.

With the Napoleonic invasion of Spain in 1808 and the subsequent Peninsular War, Goya produced his *Disasters of War* series of etchings, though these were not published until long after his death, and from 1819 to 1823 he made a famous set of fourteen *Black Paintings*, exploring similarly dark themes that he painted on the walls of his house. **PF**

Laughing Gas

Humphrey Davy demonstrates the properties of nitrous oxide.

Although Joseph Priestley had discovered nitrous oxide—a colorless oxide of nitrogen (N_2O)—by heating iron filings in 1793, no practical use had been made of the gas until the British chemist Humphrey Davy demonstrated its properties six years later.

The Cornish-born Davy, after working as a surgeon's assistant, joined the Pneumatic Institute in Bristol, where he experimented with gases. Davy gave laboratory vistors whiffs of the gas, and so demonstrated its pleasant properties, remarking that it had "all the benefits bestowed by alcohol but none

"I am sure the air in heaven must be this wonder-working gas of delight."

Robert Southey, on laughing gas, July 1799

of its flaws." He named the substance "laughing gas," and foretold its use as an anesthetic. "As it appears capable of destroying physical pain, it may probably be used with advantage during surgical operations in which no great effusion of blood takes place," he wrote in his *Researches, Chemical and Physical* (1800).

Davy later became a professor at London's Royal Institution, and president of the Royal Society. He invented the "Davy" safety lamp, which shielded the lamp flame with a gauze mesh, thus preventing explosions. In 1813, Davy and assistant Michael Faraday journeyed to France and Italy, and isolated iodine as an element and showed diamonds to be pure carbon. Davy damaged his eyes in a laboratory explosion, and the chemicals he inhaled contributed to his death in Geneva in 1829. **NJ**

New Capital

Despite protests, the American capital city is moved to Washington, D.C.

The move from Philadelphia to Washington, D.C. had been decided ten years earlier, but many regretted it. Heavy snowfalls made traveling along the east coast difficult, and representatives were often late. Nor were all the new government buildings completed. The cornerstone of the White House had been laid in 1792, and the president's residence was ready but not the Capitol building. Senators complained that the new environment compared unfavorably with the "convenient and elegant accommodations" of Philadelphia. Only the north wing of the Capitol was

" . . . accommodations are not now so complete as might be wished . . . ."

President Adams, addressing the Congress

complete, and this had to house the Senate, the House of Representatives, the Supreme Court, the Library of Congress, and the district courts. Nevertheless, it was here that Congress met on November 17, 1800, and five days later there were enough members present for President John Adams to enter the Senate chamber to congratulate the politicians on their new seat of government.

The new capital was named after President George Washington, who chose the site, although he referred to it as "the Federal City." Progress in building the capital was slow, but Washington flourished, growing to 5,000,000 inhabitants by the end of the twentieth century. Today it is the home of the president, Congress, the World Bank, and the International Monetary Fund. **RP**

United Kingdom Is Established

The Act of Union between Britain and Ireland fails to promote harmony, and instead serves to strengthen religious and political divides.

On January 1, 1801, the Act of Union established the "United Kingdom of Great Britain and Ireland." The Irish parliament in Dublin disappeared, and Ireland elected one hundred Members of Parliament to the House of Commons, while two Irish Lords Spiritual and twenty-eight Lords Temporal sat in the House of Lords. It was hoped that this was an end to the perennial problems between the two countries.

The Union had been born from rebellion in 1798, as the Society of United Irishmen looked to revolutionary France to help sever "the never-failing source of all our political evils"—the political connection with England. This "Year of Liberation" convinced both sides that the old order had to be replaced. Prime Minister William Pitt insisted that Union would promote Irish prosperity and English security, and that Irish Protestants would feel so secure in a Protestant-majority United Kingdom that they would grant equal rights to fellow Catholics. Pitt had promised to include Catholic emancipation— the right of Catholics to sit in Parliament and hold public office—in the act, but King George III would not entertain the idea. In the end, passage of the bill turned on votes in the Irish Parliament, which the government acquired through bribery.

Nothing seemed to change as a result of the act, with the viceroy in Dublin Castle and the Protestants still dominating Ireland. The Catholics were left feeling betrayed, and the national and religious divide was strengthened. Trouble lay ahead. **RP**

○ William Pitt the Younger (c.1785), second son of William Pitt the Elder, and Britain's youngest prime minister.

○ *End of the Irish Farce of Catholic Emancipation* (caricature), an etching and aquatint by James Gillray (1757–1815).

Assassination of Tsar Paul I

Tsar Paul I's assassination ensures that Romanov strife continues to scar Russia.

◊ *Portrait as Grand Master of the Maltese Order* (1800), by Vladimir Lukich Borovikovsky (1757–1825).

"My father has no plan; he orders today what a month later will be countermands."

Grand Duke Alexander to his tutor in 1797

Tsar Paul I was assassinated in the night on March 23, 1801, but life had never been easy for him. When he was only eight years old, his mother had his weak-minded father, Tsar Peter III, murdered. She then ruled as Catherine the Great and had little time or love for her son, whom she gave every sign of detesting. She virtually exiled him to an estate in Gatchina and later took charge of his only son, Alexander, as her preferred successor. Paul did eventually become tsar in 1796, but his inconsistency and incompetence were to make it a brief reign.

Conspiracies against Paul had failed in the past, but in 1801 the ringleader was the governor-general of St. Petersburg, Count Peter van Pahlen, and he had enlisted the support of none other than Paul's own son, the Grand Duke Alexander. The grim deed took place on a cold Monday night at the Mikhailovsky Palace in St. Petersburg. After dinner, the tsar retired to his private apartments, where the conspirators overpowered two valets, battered down the door to his bedroom, and strangled him with a scarf. They may not have intended to kill him, however, since they were holding a document of abdication for him to sign.

Paul had begun his rule liberally, releasing political prisoners, lightening the burden on the serfs, and diminishing the power of the nobility. But he was rarely consistent, and in his foreign policy had a fatal knack of alienating other great powers. His mood could veer quickly from gentle to overpoweringly brutal. Some believed he was mad. All felt insecure, and from this it was but a short step to conspiracy. His successor, Alexander I, never recovered from the sense of guilt attendant upon his father's assassination, and he followed a similar path, from liberal reform to repression. **RP**

The Slave Republic

Toussaint L'Ouverture writes a new constitution for Saint-Dominique.

Toussaint L'Ouverture was the black leader who briefly established Haiti as a state freed by its former slaves, and, in the wake of the French and American revolutions, led the first successful revolt by blacks against whites in the Western Hemisphere. In 1801 he took the last Spanish province, Santo Domingo, and on July 7 granted the island an egalitarian constitution modeled on the revolutionary French constitution framed by the Jacobins.

Toussaint and his ancestors were slaves. He was born a slave at Breda plantation, Haiti (then called Sainte Dominique), and grew up speaking the African dialect of his forebears who had been brought to the island in bondage from the African Gold Coast (now Ghana). Intelligent, literate, and a natural leader, he was both a Catholic and a Mason, and, following a slave rebellion in 1791, had his first command of 4,000 black troops in the Spanish army. When the revolutionary French Assembly granted full equality to Haiti's blacks, he switched loyalty to France, whose revolutionary ideals much influenced him and his fellow rebels, and fought the British and Spanish, who were contending with the French for control of Haiti. Spain officially ceded Haiti to France in 1795.

Toussaint's ability swiftly won him the leadership of the rebellious slave army, and he adopted his nickname L'Ouverture ("the opening," for his ability to spot a gap in opposing armies) as his official surname. He beat the British, who had occupied Haiti's coastal cities, and compelled their withdrawal in 1798, winning seven engagements in as many days. In 1802, the French Revolution having run its course, Napoleon sent an expedition to retake Haiti. A peace treaty was drawn up, but during negotiations Toussaint was abducted to France, where he died in a dungeon in the Jura mountains in April 1803. **NJ**

◐ Toussaint L'Ouverture, dubbed the "black Napoleon," portrayed in a French colored engraving of 1797.

"Thy friends are exultations, agonies, / And love, and man's unconquerable mind."

Wordsworth, *Sonnet on Toussaint*, 1803

Convention
Entre les Etats unis d'Amérique et la République Française.

———

Le Président des Etats unis d'Amérique, et le Premier Consul de la République française au nom du peuple français, par suite du traité de cession de la Louisiane, qui à été signé aujourd'hui, et voulant régler définitivement tout ce qui est relatif à cette affaire, ont autorisé à cet effet, des Plénipotentiaires

Savoir :

Le Président des Etats unis, par et avec l'avis et le consentement du Sénat des dits Etats, a nommé pour leurs plénipotentiaire Robert R. Livingston, Ministre plénipotentiaire des Etats unis et James Monroe, Ministre plénipotentiaire et envoyé extraordinaire des dits Etats-unis, auprès du Gouvernement de la République française; et Le Premier Consul de la République française, au nom du peuple français, a nommé pour plénipotentiaire de la dite République le Citoyen François Barbé-Marbois Ministre du Trésor public; lesquels en vertu de leurs pleins pouvoirs, dont l'échange a été fait aujourd'hui, sont convenus des articles suivans :

Art. 1er

Le Gouvernement des Etats unis S'engage à payer au Gouvernem.t français de la manière qui sera spécifiée en l'article suivant, la somme de Soixante millions de francs, indépendemment de ce qui sera fixé par une autre convention, pour le paiement des Sommes dues par la france à des Citoyens des Etats unis

Art. 2.

Le paiement des Soixante millions de francs mentionnés au

R.R.L.   J. M.

U.S. Expansion

The Louisiana Purchase from the French doubles the size of the United States.

The Louisiana land purchase of April 1803 opened the way for the United States to expand to the Pacific Ocean. It included the states of Arkansas, Iowa, Kansas, Louisiana, Missouri, Nebraska, and Oklahoma, and parts of Colorado, North and South Dakota, Minnesota, Montana, Texas, and Wyoming. The land was a bargain at a little over $23 million.

Thomas Jefferson was the first U.S. president to be inaugurated, in 1801, in the country's new capital of Washington, D.C. The land purchase was his most famous single achievement. Ironically, for a man who had proclaimed his disapproval of a strong federal government, it involved an unprecedented exercise of presidential power for which the Constitution gave him no warrant.

The peace treaty of 1783, which recognized the independence of the United States, had set its western boundary at the Mississippi River, but Napoleon Bonaparte was considering building a French empire in North America and had compelled Spain to surrender New Orleans and Louisiana west of the Mississippi. Complications in Europe changed his mind, and Jefferson's envoys in Paris were offered a huge area stretching from the Mississippi to the Rocky Mountains, and from the Gulf of Mexico to Canada, covering more than 820,000 square miles (2.1 million sq km) and doubling the size of the United States.

The Constitution made no provision for the acquisition of more territory, but President Jefferson considered the deal essential to the national interest and, despite opposition in Congress, ordered his emissaries to sign. **RC**

◗ Document authorizing the payment of sixty million francs to France for the Louisiana Purchase.

Emmet's Legacy

The execution of Robert Emmet creates a martyr for the Irish nationalist cause.

Every hero needs a cause; every cause needs a hero. The death of Robert Emmet on September 20 created a new Irish hero. His cause was Irish independence. But Emmet was an unlikely protagonist—he was overshadowed by his brother, Thomas Addis Emmet, who took part in the United Irishmen's failed rising of 1798, which brought about the 1801 Act of Union (the act that abolished the Irish parliament). Robert Emmet's own rising on July 23, 1803, was more street riot than rebellion.

In 1803 Emmet was waiting, storing weapons, and hoping for support from revolutionary France, when an explosion at an arms depot forced his hand.

"The most memorable words ever uttered by an Irishman."

Patrick Pearse on Emmet's speech at his trial

He led a small force of rebels toward Dublin Castle, hoping for reinforcements. All they achieved was the murder of the chief justice, Lord Kilwarden, and his nephew. Emmet was captured and hanged for treason, at the age of twenty-five.

At his ten-hour trial, Emmet made one of the greatest speeches in Irish nationalist history. He asked that no one write his epitaph, for no one who knew his motives would dare to utter them. "When my country takes her place among the nations of the earth, then and only then, let my epitaph be written." At that moment a legend was born, one that would inspire future nationalists including Patrick Pearse, who masterminded the Easter Rising of 1916. **RP**

Railway Locomotive

The first steam-powered locomotive prepares the way for railway expansion.

Richard Trevithick had little education but many engineering feats to his credit. All stemmed from a fascination with the winding gear and steam engines he had observed as a boy at Illogan, Cornwall, where his father was the manager of a tin mine. As a mining engineer himself, he improved on James Watt's condensing steam engine by the use of "strong steam," which generated extra power. In 1801, he produced a prototype locomotive, the world's first self-propelled vehicle to carry passengers. It overturned on the rough roads, but he made another version. His crowning achievement was the first railway locomotive, unveiled on February 21, 1804.

"We carry'd ten tons of iron, five waggons, and 70 men riding on them."

Letter from Richard Trevithick, 1804

Homfray's ironworks were already building engines to his design, and Trevithick built a locomotive for the Pen-y-darren tramway in Wales. It could pull a load weighing 10 tons (9 tonnes) and transport seventy people for almost 10 miles (14 km). The features of the steam locomotive now existed, thanks to Trevithick: the engine gripped the rails by weight, the piston connected to the wheels, and the exhaust created a draft, making the fire hotter.

However, there was no commercial interest in Trevithick's invention, and he was reduced to giving novelty rides in London. He left for Peru in 1816, to return a decade later to expanding steam transport in Britain. Trevithick died in poverty in 1833. **RP**

Napoleon's Law

The Code Napoleon, a mixture of legal systems, comes into force in France.

The new Civil Code of March 1804 contained more than 2,281 articles and represented the first codification of any country's civil laws. It was the work of French lawyers, debated by the Council of State under Napoleon's chairmanship, and finally bearing the name of the French emperor. It was a compromise between the ideas of the revolution and the *ancien régime*, blending revolutionary rationalism with authoritarian principles. It confirmed the recent abolition of feudalism and gave a fixed deed of entitlement to those with property. It also followed the revolutionary principle of dividing estates among male heirs rather than the eldest son

"The husband owes protection to his wife, the wife obedience to [him]."

Article 213 of the Civil Code, 1804

inheriting everything. But it also gave women the status of minors, allowed parents to keep children from marrying until they were in their twenties, banned trade unions, reintroduced slavery into the French colonies, and subjected workers to police surveillance.

Before the revolution, there had been no uniform legal system in France. Customary laws were predominant in the north, Roman law in the south. The revolution had introduced a massive 14,400 new decrees, making a recodification essential. The new Civil Code meant that France was governed by clear laws. Further commercial and criminal codes followed, but it was the Code Napoleon that had the most influence—across all of Europe. **RP**

The Coronation of Napoleon

Napoleon's magnificent and ostentatious coronation spares no expense to portray the little general as a towering, semidivine emperor.

Nothing was left to chance. Expense was no object for the coronation of Napoleon on December 2, 1804. The church of the Hotel des Invalides was too small, so Notre-Dame was commandeered. Any surrounding buildings not up to standard were demolished. The cathedral was not magnificent enough, so the west front was covered with a pseudo-Gothic annex, whereas inside the choir screen and two altars were replaced with an imposing central theater. New carriages and costumes were made and the finest regalia acquired, including the sword of Charlemagne from Aix-la-Chapelle.

Admittedly, there were hitches. Pope Pius VII insisted that Napoleon and Josephine marry in church before the ceremony, and Napoleon balked at receiving the crown from the pope, at swearing an oath that emphasized his dependency on the papacy, and at taking communion during the Mass. He would not be "made a good Catholic." But the ceremony, culminating in Napoleon placing the crown on his own head, was solemn and magnificent. Thus did France's First Consul become her emperor.

It was a wonderful propaganda coup. Napoleon commissioned Jacques-Louis David to produce enhanced paintings of the coronation, in which Napoleon appears taller than he was; is seen placing a second crown on the head of Josephine, which never happened; and the pope's right hand is raised in a blessing he never gave. The Corsican was now a superhuman figure, and power had clearly gone to his head. Pride undoubtedly came before Napoleon's fall and destruction a decade later. **RP**

○ *Napoleon in Coronation Robes* (1804) by François Gerard can be seen in the Musée du Louvre, Paris, France.

A New Style of Music

Beethoven's Eroica *symphony is performed for the first time to a mixed response.*

O The cover of the first edition of *Sinfonia Eroica* includes a dedication to Franz Joseph Max Prince Lobkowitz.

"So he is no more than a common mortal! ... now he will ... become a tyrant!"

Beethoven on Napoleon becoming emperor

Twenty-first-century people familiar with Ludwig van Beethoven's *Eroica* symphony (Symphony No. 3 in E Flat) will find it difficult to imagine the impact it had at its first public performance on April 7, 1805, at the Theater-an-der-Wien in Vienna. However, in 1805, its length, structure, emotional directness, and dynamism were unprecedented. Compared to the symphonic works of Haydn, it was longer by more than half, and, although it followed the structure of earlier symphonies, it had many new elements. In particular, there was the energy of the third movement, an energetic scherzo replacing the traditionally quieter and more controlled minuet, and an extended fourth movement of a theme and variations. But ultimately the movement that made the greatest impact was the second, an extended funeral march such as had never previously been included in any symphonic music to date. Beethoven, who himself conducted this first public performance, had consciously set out to create a brand new style.

The *Eroica* was originally to be dedicated to Napoleon Bonaparte, First Consul of France, who had won the admiration of the composer as the agent of reform and change in Europe. However, Napoleon's self-elevation to emperor so angered Beethoven, he is said to have torn out the title page with the dedication and rededicated the symphony to the "memory of a great man." He had the work published as *Sinfonia Eroica*.

The reaction of the Viennese musical public to this original and powerful work was mixed. Some hailed it, whereas others thought it bombastic nonsense. It was soon regarded a masterpiece and seen as part of the new Romantic Movement in the arts, which reflected the political and social turbulence after the French Revolution. **NK**

Battle of Trafalgar

The British Navy reinforces its dominance over all other European navies.

Since the 1803 resumption of hostilities between Britain and France, the British Navy had sought to assert its dominance, especially as an alliance between France and Spain had given their fleets a numerical advantage. It was feared that the combined fleets could concentrate in the English Channel and launch a French invasion of British soil. The victory at Trafalgar on October 21, 1805, marked the recognition of British domination of the seas for the next century.

The British and the combined fleets finally met off Cape Trafalgar near the harbor of Cadiz on the Atlantic coast of southern Spain. Horatio Nelson, the British admiral, had planned for this encounter. He had tactics to bring about a decisive result, although his ships would be under fire while making their approach without the possibility of firing back. He had briefed his captains before the battle, "In case signals can neither be seen nor perfectly understood, no captain can do very wrong if he places his ship alongside that of the enemy," to allow them to break formation, if necessary. Nelson knew that the superiority of his ships in handling and gunnery would enable them to inflict great damage close up, despite the greater number of enemy vessels.

The plan succeeded. At the day's end his fleet had destroyed one ship and captured twenty-one, and no British ship had been lost. But on his flagship HMS *Victory* and loath to take off his dress uniform, Nelson was made easily recognizable by his stars and decorations, and was shot by a marksman from the French ship *Redoutable*. Taken below decks, he lived long enough to learn that his sailors had been victorious. The survivors of the French and Spanish fleets returned to Cadiz, and Villeneuve, the French admiral, died in mysterious circumstances on his way to Paris to report to Emperor Napoleon. **NK**

○ The sinking of Admiral Villeneuve's flagship was just one of the losses suffered by the French.

"Kiss me Hardy. Now I am satisfied. Thank God I have done my duty."

Nelson's last words before dying

Expedition to the West Coast of America

The Lewis and Clark expedition travels through the Rockies and reaches the Pacific.

○ Thomas Mickell Burnham's painting shows Captain Meriwether Lewis and William Clark on their transcontinental expedition.

One of the first results of the Louisiana Purchase in 1803 was that President Jefferson commissioned Meriwether Lewis to lead an expedition through the Rocky Mountains to the Pacific with William Clark. On November 7, 1805, Lewis first glimpsed the Pacific and noted in his journal, "Ocian in view! O! the joy."

The "corps of discovery" had wintered near St. Louis and in May 1804, some forty men, mostly soldiers, with Clark's black servant and Lewis's dog, Seaman, set off up the Missouri River, in what Clark called "a jentle brease." After a winter with the Mandan Indians in what is now North Dakota, they built themselves dug-out canoes and with a Shoshone woman as guide pressed through the Rockies and along the Clearwater, Snake, and Columbia rivers to Oregon and the Pacific, where they built a fort near today's Astoria and spent the next winter. Setting back in March 1806, they were greeted as heroes in St. Louis.

Jefferson had instructed Lewis and Clark to record everything they could about the territory they traveled. This they did (although their spelling was wondrously awful), and they brought back information about the Native Americans, geography, minerals, and wildlife. The expedition discovered the grizzly bear ("a most tremendious looking anamal") and paved the way for the U.S. conquest of the West. Lewis died at age thirty-five in 1809, probably having taken his own life. Clark became governor of Missouri and died at age sixty-eight in 1838. **RC**

Battle of Austerlitz

Emperor Napoleon Bonaparte defeats the emperors of Austria and Russia.

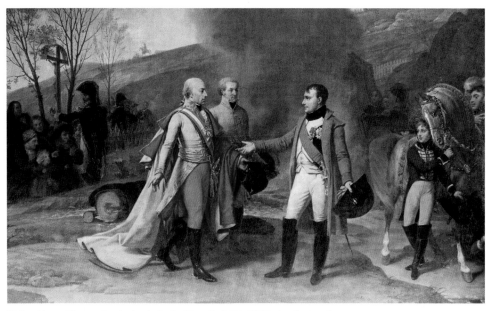

⊙ *Napoléon and Emperor Francis after the Battle of Austerlitz (1806–1812) by Antoine Jean Gros.*

In the morning sun over Austerlitz, on December 2, 1805, Napoleon's infantry under the command of Nicolas Soult stormed the Pratzen heights, from which they could dominate the battlefield. Since dawn, the outnumbered French had stubbornly resisted the armies of the Austrian and Russian empires, but now, firing from the heights, the battle turned. More than 20,000 Russians and Austrians died, a further 20,000 made prisoner. The emperors of Russia and Austria had to come to terms with Napoleon, who now dominated Europe politically and militarily. Only the nervous king of Prussia remained unconquered, with the British triumphant at sea but powerless without allies. The anti-French coalition organized by British Prime Minister William Pitt collapsed. On December 26, Austria signed a humiliating peace treaty at Pressburg and the Russians left Austrian territory and marched home.

In one of the most outstanding modern military campaigns, Napoleon had marched his Grande Armée from the Channel coast, where it had been prepared for an invasion of England, to southern Germany, capturing an Austrian army of 30,000 men at Ulm, and invading Austria before finally overcoming the larger armies of the combined empires. This military virtuosity bewitched Europe. Napoleon was the true master of the Continent and his army the most admired. He started remodeling the map of Europe, creating new kingdoms in Italy, Germany, and the Netherlands for his brothers. **NK**

Charter of Freedom

Britain outlaws the slave trade in its empire, although slavery itself remains legal.

○ A procession was held at Wootton Bassett, Wiltshire, England, after the transatlantic slave trade was declared illegal.

It seemed imminent, as there was a groundswell of opinion in Britain. Two years earlier a bill had passed through the House of Commons, but was blocked by the Lords. Now, in 1807, Prime Minister Lord Grenville called the slave trade "contrary to the principles of justice, humanity, and sound policy"—and the measure was passed by forty-one votes to twenty. The Abolition of the Slave Trade Act became law on March 25, making illegal the slave trade, although not slavery itself, throughout the British Empire. A fine of £100 was to be levied for every slave found aboard a British ship. A moral crusade had been rewarded, although other motives were at work. It was the ideal opportunity to show Britain's moral superiority to Napoleon, who had revived the French slave trade.

In 1771, Britain had effectively abolished slavery at home. Abolitionists then targeted the slave trade itself, reformers inventing the art of political lobbying in the process. William Wilberforce continually raised the issue in Parliament, until his success with the 1807 act—although it had some unforeseen ramifications, such as quadrupling the price of an able-bodied male slave in the United States in the early nineteenth century. As a result, some British captains were tempted to defy the law. If their ships were in danger of being searched, they threw the slaves overboard. Hence, in 1827, slave trading was declared tantamount to piracy and so punishable by death. Then in 1833, slavery itself was made illegal throughout the British Empire. **RP**

Napoleon, the Master of Europe

Alexander of Russia meets the all-powerful Napoleon to determine Europe's future.

○ A nineteenth-century engraving of *The Meeting between Napoleon I and Tsar Alexander I at Niemen.*

The meeting of Napoleon and Emperor Alexander I of Russia on a raft in the middle of the River Nemunas (Niemen) at Tilsit (Lithuania) in June 1807 marks the peak of the French ruler's power in Europe.

Napoleon had defeated the Austrians at Austerlitz in 1805, the Prussians at Jena in 1806, and now he had just humiliated the Russian army at the battle of Friedland. He was master of Europe, from the Pyrenees and Italy to the Baltic, from the Channel and the North Sea to the Russian frontier. So in a pavilion on a raft in the Niemen, accompanied by their guards in dress uniforms, the two emperors met to determine the future of the continent. Alexander agreed to the French remodeling of the states of Europe and agreed to join Napoleon's economic

blockade of Britain. In return Napoleon would support Russian dealings with the Ottoman Empire.

Two days later a further treaty was signed with Prussia, stripping her of half her territory and restricting her to an army of 100,000 men. Napoleon did not get all he wanted. To cement his friendship with Russia, he proposed to divorce his empress, Josephine, and marry Alexander's sister. But this was more than Alexander and his court could accept. In this success lay the roots of future trouble. By humiliating Prussia, Napoleon created an implacable enemy. The economic blockade of Britain did not truly suit the Russians. Good relations did not last, and in 1812, Napoleon decided the only way to deal with Russia was through invasion and conquest. **NK**

French Troops Enter Madrid

Napoleon forces the abdications of King Charles IV and King Ferdinand VII in favor of his brother, Joseph Bonaparte.

Spain was in turmoil. Formally Spain and France were allies, but Napoleon did not trust King Charles IV of Spain, nor his minister Godoy. During the winter of 1807–1808 more French formations moved into northern Spain, nominally to support the troops in Portugal, but there they stayed. A palace coup removed Charles and Godoy on March 19, and Charles's son Ferdinand was proclaimed king. Napoleon ordered his brother-in-law Murat to enter Madrid, and he arrived with his troops on March 23.

Charles and Ferdinand were summoned to France and told they had to abdicate in favor of Joseph Bonaparte, Napoleon's elder brother. Ferdinand refused. On May 2, the population of Madrid rose against the French. Marshal Murat knew how to deal with civil disturbance; the rising was suppressed with violence, episodes vividly depicted in the paintings of Goya. King Ferdinand VII succumbed to Napoleon's threats and abdicated. Joseph Bonaparte was proclaimed king of Spain.

On May 25, the Principality of the Asturias, a Spanish province in the remote northwest, declared war against the French invader, followed by provinces Galicia, Estremadura, Castile, Aragon, and Andalusia. Some 17,000 French troops surrendered to the insurgents at Baylen. King Joseph lost his nerve and fled from Madrid. The French reestablished control of Madrid and the major cities, but the Spanish people never accepted the domination of Napoleon and his French soldiers. **NK**

◗ Detail from *Insurrection de Madrid*, a woodcut from a drawing by Paul Girardet (1819–1880).

◗ *Execution of the Defenders of Madrid, 3rd May, 1808* painted in 1814 by Francisco Goya.

Mamluks Murdered

Mehmet Ali consolidates his rule by slaughtering the competition.

After Napoleon's defeat of the Mamluks, the resulting power vacuum in Egypt gave Mehmet Ali—an Albanian-born soldier in the service of the Ottoman Empire—the opportunity to gain supreme power. Responsible for evacuating the remnants of the French army, his power was officially recognized by the Ottoman court, the Supreme Porte, and he was named viceroy of Egypt in 1805. Declaring a truce with the Mamluks, Ali invited the Mamluk Amirs to a feast in Arabia on March 1, 1811, and had them slaughtered. The killings were condemned, but succeeded in making Ali the ruler of the state and marked the transition from one dynasty to another.

"In truth, the confusion and horrors of that day are indescribable."

The Life and Adventure of Giovanni Finati, 1830

The rest of Ali's long reign was spent in extending his rule. He made Egypt's staple produce, cotton, a personal monopoly, built roads and shipyards, introduced state-run schools and hospitals, and conscripted Egypt's peasant population. His sons conquered Syria and threatened the Ottoman Caliphate until the London Convention of 1839 brought peace by granting Ali hereditary rule over Egypt. Ali's last years were marked by growing senility and paranoia, which led to financial chaos. Ali was succeeded upon his death on August 2, 1849, by his nephew Abbas. Under British protection, the dynasty that Ali founded ruled Egypt for a further century, until the 1953 Nasserist republican revolution. **NJ**

The Final Gamble

Napoleon invades Russia, but withdraws with a heavily depleted army.

With the 1807 Tilsit agreements breaking down, Napoleon decided that defeat of the Russian Empire would ensure that it worked with him in his economic warfare against his most enduring enemy, Britain. On June 24, 1812, Napoleon's army crossed the River Niemen, the frontier with Russia, heading for Moscow.

It was Napoleon's largest army, comprising some 690,000 men. The soldiers were mainly French, with other Europeans, such as the 90,000 Poles commanded by Marshal-Prince Poniatowski and the 35,000 Austrian soldiers under Prince Schwarzenberg. With him, the French emperor had some of his

" . . . the grenadiers glanced at him . . . 'Caesar, they who are about to die salute you.'"

Heinrich Heine, *Pictures of Travel*, 1826–1831

most successful and battle-experienced generals, including the Marshals Davout, Ney, and Soult.

The Russian armies, commanded by Barclay de Tolly and Mikhail Kutusov, initially retreated before the French onslaught. They understood that keeping the Russian army intact was vital, and that distance, lack of supplies, and weather would defeat the French. The Battle of Borodino in September proved indecisive, and Napoleon's entry into Moscow brought no offer of surrender or negotiation from the Russians. As Moscow burned, Napoleon was compelled by lack of supplies, sickness, and worsening weather to withdraw. Only 22,000 of his men left Russia in good order in December. **NK**

Battle of Borodino

Napoleon fails to destroy the Russian army at the bloody but indecisive battle.

○ Franz Roubaud's *Battle of Borodino* (1913) is part of a collection in the State Central Artillery Museum, St. Petersburg, Russia.

The Russian army, under the command of General Mikhail Kutusov, finally gave battle to the French invaders on the road to Moscow in 1812. The Russians had evaded engagement, but at the village of Borodino, they had good natural defenses and strengthened them with redoubts to shelter artillery and infantry.

Napoleon's battle plan was not subtle. All day he committed his troops against the Russian defenses in frontal assaults supported by artillery. The fights for the redoubts, made famous by Leo Tolstoy's *War and Peace*, caused huge French and Russian casualties, with the positions changing hands many times. In the morning as the sun broke through the clouds, Napoleon exclaimed, "It is the sun of Austerlitz," recalling his great victory over the Austrians in 1805.

But it was not to be. He had not won the victory he sought. The Russian army left the field of battle to the French. Kutusov's forces had suffered 52,000 casualties, including 22 generals dead or wounded. Some 29 French generals and 28,000 soldiers were casualties, so the French were in no condition to pursue the Russian army. The French army calculated they had fired 60,000 artillery rounds and 2 million musket balls, and that each minute 140 men, from both sides, had become casualties.

The bloodiest battle of Napoleon's career brought no decisive result, and the French continued their way to Moscow before beginning their retreat back to Germany along the road down which they had advanced four months previously. **NK**

Battle of Vittoria

Wellington gives chase and crushes Napoleon's army retreating through Spain.

○ *The Battle of Vittoria* by John Augustus Atkinson is held in a private collection.

The Battle of Vittoria marked the end of the Peninsula War. The victory was celebrated all over Europe. In Vittoria's main square, a commemorative monument was inscribed "The independence of Spain." Beethoven in Vienna was moved to compose an orchestral piece, *Wellington's Victory*.

Napoleon's empire had come under increasing strain, and as he retreated from Russia in 1813, he could no longer commit resources in Spain against the British. After five years, the British were moving to push the French out of the country. Spain's King Joseph, Napoleon's brother, with an army under the command of Marshal Jourdan, left Madrid with looted artwork and treasure and marched north toward the French frontier.

Pursued by Wellington, Joseph fought outside Vittoria, on the road to the Pyrenees and France, positioning his soldiers in an arc on the hills outside the city. Wellington attacked in three columns and broke through his enemy's center. Joseph's army collapsed and fled, leaving behind 151 guns and accumulated treasure, furniture, pictures, coins, and jewelry—valued then at more than £1 million. The British army plundered whatever it could find. (To this day the soldiers of one British cavalry regiment drink from a bowl they call "The Emperor," looted after the battle—in reality King Joseph's silver chamber pot.) Order restored, Wellington moved north to the French frontier, and British soldiers moved onto the soil of France itself. **NK**

The End for Napoleon

Allied armies enter the city of Paris after Napoleon is betrayed by an old friend.

○ *Passage of Allied Sovereigns in Front of the Porte Saint-Denis* shows the Russian emperor and Austrian commander center stage.

Russian Emperor Alexander I, King Frederick William III of Prussia, and Austrian commander Prince Schwarzenberg, and their respective armies, marched unopposed into the French capital on March 31, 1814. The keys were surrendered by Prince Talleyrand, once Napoleon's foreign minister.

The defenses of the city, commanded by Napoleon's brother Joseph from the heights of Montmartre, had been unlocked by Marshal Marmont. Napoleon's oldest comrade in arms and a friend from military academy, Marmont had arranged, after secret contacts with the Allied commanders, to move his troops to positions where they could be easily surrounded and obliged to surrender. Despite a brilliant campaign against the invaders, Napoleon

was unable to prevent the Russians, Prussians, and Austrians from marching directly on his capital while he was organizing further operations from the chateau at Fontainebleau, south of Paris. Realizing his commanders were no longer all with him, Napoleon bade farewell to his guard and abdicated his throne on April 6. He wanted his son, the king of Rome, to succeed him, but the Allied governments agreed to restore the Bourbon dynasty, and the younger brother of the king guillotined in 1793 ascended his throne as Louis XVIII.

The Prussian commander Prince Blücher wanted revenge on the French capital and to destroy the Pont d'Iéna, celebrating Napoleon's 1807 victory over the Prussians, but he was dissuaded. **NK**

The British Invade America

The British attacks on Washington and Baltimore inspire "The Star-Spangled Banner."

○ The White House is engulfed in flames in the background as the British attack Washington.

The 1812 Anglo-American War, set off by the Royal Navy's interference with U.S. commerce, seizure of U.S. ships, and pressing of seamen, was an offshoot of the Napoleonic Wars engulfing Europe. In 1813, the Americans invaded Canada and burned Toronto's public buildings. In retaliation the British sailed into Chesapeake Bay in 1814 and landed a 4,000-strong force, bent on destroying Washington, the U.S. capital, then a town of around 8,000 inhabitants. The few defenders were scattered at Bladensburg outside the city and included President Madison, who had to send a hasty message to his wife, Dolley, to flee the President's House (later called the White House). She took the Gilbert Stuart portrait of George Washington with her, but the arriving redcoats found the table set for a grand dinner, with joints roasting and fine wines ready. They sat down happily to enjoy it before setting the house on fire.

The British went on to reduce the Capitol building, the Treasury, and other public buildings to charred ruins. Witness George Gleig described "the blazing of houses, ships, and stores, the report of exploding magazines and the crash of falling roofs." The British failed to inflict a blow to U.S. morale. British commander General Robert Ross was killed in action at Baltimore soon afterward, and the successful U.S. defense of the fort there inspired Francis Scott Key to write "The Star-Spangled Banner." The end of the war in 1815 left the Union more securely established than ever. **RC**

Napoleon Escapes from Elba

The emperor evades his guards on the island and returns to France.

○ *Napoleon's Return from the Island of Elba (Landing in Cannes on 1 March 1815)*, an 1818 painting by Carl von Steuben (1788–1856).

When Napoleon abdicated in April of 1814, the Allied governments exiled him to the island of Elba. He retained his title of "emperor" and, closely watched by the Austrians and French, governed his tiny state. Nevertheless, organizing schools and hospitals and improving the water supply for a population of 12,000 did not satisfy either his intellect or his energy. Knowing that France was unsettled under the restored Bourbon monarchy, he resolved to return to France. On February 26, he avoided his guards, boarded a ship, slipped past the British Navy, and made the passage to the coast of France, landing at Fréjus.

His landing was unopposed. The first soldiers sent to arrest him joined him, and as he moved north through France, more and more supporters rallied to his side. Marshal Michel Ney, one of the foremost of the imperial soldiers now serving the returned Bourbon monarch Louis XVIII, promised to bring Napoleon back to Paris in a cage. When he realized that his troops preferred the deposed emperor to the restored king, he too joined his former master. On March 20, Emperor Napoleon slept in the Palace of the Tuileries, King Louis having fled to Belgium.

For one hundred days, the emperor governed France again, until defeated at Waterloo by the Duke of Wellington. He gave himself up to the British, hoping to be kept in England, but found instead that it had been decided that he would spend the rest of his life on a remote, inhospitable, and inaccessible island in the South Atlantic, St. Helena. **NK**

The Congress of Vienna Ends

Napoleon's conquerors settle the future structure of postwar Europe.

❶ *The Fox and the Goose or Boney Broke Loose*, an 1815 cartoon of the Congress of Vienna and Napoleon's escape from Elba.

When the Congress of Vienna began, in November 1814, Napoleon was in exile in Elba and the French armies were driven from the other countries of Europe. The heads of the great powers, Great Britain, Russia, Austria, and Prussia, came together in Vienna to settle the future structure of the continent and to decide how to prevent a repetition of the disturbances that had rocked it since 1793.

Their solutions, agreed on June 8, 1815, by which time Napoleon was back in France, were deeply conservative. France was reduced to its frontiers of 1792. All Napoleon's new European states—the kingdom of Italy, the Confederation of the Rhine, and the Grand Duchy of Warsaw—were swept aside. Austria, Prussia, and Russia regained those regions in central Europe and Italy that Napoleon had taken from them. But a residual fear of France and the need for stronger countries on the French borders led them to create a single kingdom in the Low Countries uniting the Austrian Low Countries to the Netherlands under the king of Holland. They also reduced the number of states in Germany from 300 to thirty-eight and formed a new German Confederation under the chairmanship of Austria and Prussia. Prussia gained more territory in Rhineland and Westphalia.

This settlement guaranteed the peace of Europe for forty years. Nevertheless, in its emphasis on conservatism and political legitimacy, it ignored all the revolutionary and liberal impulses expressed during the turbulent years since the Revolution. **NK**

Napoleon Defeated at Waterloo

Emperor Napoleon is finally crushed by the armies of Wellington and Marshal Blücher.

On June 18, 1815, Arthur Wellesley, Duke of Wellington, deployed his multinational army of British, Belgian, Dutch, and Hanoverian troops along the ridge of Mont St. Jean, south of the village of Waterloo, to stop the advance of Napoleon on Brussels and his conquest of the Low Countries. Wellington was outnumbered, and the quality of some of his soldiers doubtful, but on this ridge, which he had identified earlier as the terrain where he could hold the armies of the emperor, he waited for the French assault.

On Napoleon's return from Elba, the majority of his former army and their commanders had once more rallied to their powerful commander. Moving quickly toward Brussels, he had pushed back Wellington's army at Quatre Bras and the Prussian army on Wellington's left flank at the Battle of Ligny.

All night before the battle it rained heavily, and Napoleon held back from attacking until mid-morning to allow the ground to dry. He started the fight with a heavy artillery bombardment, then with infantry attacks, before finally launching massed cavalry at the British positions. All day the British, supported by their allies, absorbed these fierce assaults, holding their line and two crucial farms, Hougoumont and La Haye Sainte. Late in the day, La Haye Sainte fell when its defenders ran out of ammunition, and it seemed as if Wellington's line would break. But time was not with the emperor. On his left flank he was being attacked by the Prussians under Marshal Blücher, who had maneuvered to aid Wellington. In a final attempt to drive his adversary from the field, Napoleon launched the Imperial Guard, his most experienced soldiers and his final reserve, at the Allied position. But in the face of British musketry, the Imperial Guard turned and fled. Napoleon had lost his final battle. **NK**

◐ *A Plan of the Glorious Battle of Waterloo*, a nineteenth-century English engraving of the allied map of the front line.

◑ The right panel of *The Battle of Waterloo, 18th June 1815*, a painting by Denis Dighton (1792–1827).

"It has been a damned nice thing—the closest run thing you ever saw in your life."

Wellington to his brother June 19, 1815

Medusa Horror

Théodore Géricault paints The Raft of the Medusa *after the disaster at sea.*

The *Medusa* was a converted French frigate leading four vessels to take possession of the port of St. Louis, Senegal, in 1816. Napoleon's defeat at Waterloo had restored the Bourbon monarchy, and the *Medusa*'s master, Hugues de Chaumarys, was an old royalist who had never commanded a vessel. On July 2, Chaumarys ran aground on a sandbank.

Privileged passengers were placed in lifeboats, but 150 others were put on a raft of lashed-together spars. Chaumarys promised to tow the raft, but cut it adrift—his party went on to make landfall and was rescued from the Sahara. The unfortunates crowded on the raft were forced to eat leather, fabric, and each

"From the delirium of joy we fell into profound despondency and grief."

Survivor Alexandre Corréard

other. Cannibalism and slaughter of the weak became the norm in a terrifying two-week ordeal before fifteen survivors were picked up by the *Argus*. Three survivors were found on the *Medusa* itself.

Impressed by accounts of the horror by two survivors, Alexandre Corréard and Henri Savigny, Géricault set to work on his picture, using corpses and body parts from a morgue as his models. Géricault's enormous picture, with its horrific scenes in the style of romantic realism, caused a sensation when it was exhibited at the Paris Salon in 1819. Géricault saw the wreck as both an indictment of the reactionary, incompetent nature of Bourbon rule and a grim comment on human barbarity. **NJ**

Peterloo Massacre

Britain's "Peterloo" becomes a symbol of working-class resistance.

On that Monday, more than 60,000 people marched with banners to the protest meeting at St. Peter's Field, Manchester. They expected a rousing message from Henry "Orator" Hunt, a man who wrote that the authorities "thought of nothing but oppressing the people, and subsisting on the plunder wrung from their miseries." Similar meetings had ended violently, so the magistrates sent the Yeomanry to arrest Hunt, but they got into trouble, so cavalry carrying sabers were sent to rescue them. In the fighting, eleven people were killed and more than 400 wounded.

This was the climax of four years' discontent in Britain, after the Napoleonic wars, which brought

"The cavalry were in confusion . . . and chopped limbs . . . were seen."

Samuel Bamford, *Passages in the Life of a Radical*

economic depression, high unemployment, and low wages. Prime Minister Lord Liverpool was worried about revolutionary ideas spreading from across the Channel. The jittery government did not authorize the massacre, but it reflected its determination to clamp down on radical agitation. Ministers congratulated the magistrates on their action. Hunt was imprisoned for two years and the government restricted public meetings. But the press decided that, whereas Wellington had a glorious victory at Waterloo in 1815, Liverpool's government had won an inglorious victory against unarmed citizens at "Peterloo" in 1819. The massacre boosted the cause of radical reform for many decades. **RP**

The Liberator's South American Crusade

Simon Bolivar defeats the Spanish and loyalists in Colombia and proclaims the Republic of Great Colombia.

In 1800, most of South America was ruled by Spain and Portugal. Burgeoning movements for political and economic independence were stimulated by Napoleon's conquest of both countries, which cut them off from their South American colonies. After Napoleon fell, the restored Spanish regime was determined to reassert control of its South American empire. The result was the wars of liberation, in which the major figure was Simon Bolivar.

"The Liberator" was a wealthy Venezuelan Creole aristocrat of Spanish descent, who was educated abroad and returned to South America in his twenties in 1807 to launch a crusade against Spanish rule. He made himself dictator of Venezuela, but was driven out and fled to the Caribbean. He returned in 1819 with an army to inflict defeat on the Spaniards and loyalists in Colombia. He appointed himself dictator of his new republic of Great Colombia, which was a federation including Colombia, Venezuela, and Ecuador (the fact that Venezuela and Ecuador were still under Spanish rule was considered a technicality). In 1820, Bolivar and second-in-command Antonio José de Sucre defeated the loyalists and took control of Venezuela and Ecuador. He and Sucre went on to secure the independence of both Peru and Bolivia.

Later, Bolivar's tyrannical dictatorship of Great Colombia and Peru roused opposition, and in 1828, he escaped an assassination attempt. Sucre was assassinated in 1830. Bolivar's health weakened, his South American federation plan failed, and Venezuela and Ecuador split off from Colombia. He died in 1830 of tuberculosis, at the age of forty-seven. **RC**

○ A portrait of Simon Bolivar (1783–1830) in military dress by Arturo Michelena (1868–1898).

Missouri Joins the Union as a Slave State

The Missouri Compromise stops the issue of slavery from tearing the Union apart, though only for another generation.

Slavery was a thorny issue in the United States from the beginning. The Louisiana Purchase of 1803, which opened up huge areas west of the Mississippi to U.S. settlement, raised the divisive question of whether slavery should be permitted in territories that joined the Union as new states. There was fierce feeling against slavery in the North, whereas the South wanted slavery, partly because it would make it more difficult to amend the constitution to eradicate slavery from the Union altogether. By 1819, slavery was legal in half of the twenty-two states of the Union.

In that year, Missouri applied for admission to the Union as a slave state, to the fury of the abolitionists in the North. Congressman James Tallmadge of New York proposed that Missouri should be admitted only if it accepted a program of gradual emancipation. Congress was torn by violent arguments, but thanks to Henry Clay, Speaker of the House of Representatives, a compromise was reached. Missouri's admission as a slave state was balanced by making the northern part of Massachusetts the new nonslave state of Maine. It was also agreed that slavery would be permitted only in new states south of a line of latitude set at 36° 30′ north. This was not a long-term solution, but it kept the peace for the time being.

President James Monroe had doubts about the compromise, but approved it to stop the Union division. In 1857, the Supreme Court declared the Missouri compromise unconstitutional, which helped make the Civil War inevitable. **RC**

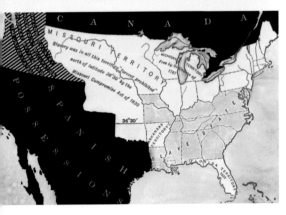

◯ An 1834 portrait of Henry Clay (1777–1852) by Samuel Osgood (1808–1885).

◯ A nineteenth-century illustration of a U.S. map showing the extension of slavery resulting from the Missouri Compromise.

The White South

Nathaniel Palmer, among others, claims the discovery of Antarctica.

Palmer Land is named after one of several claimants to the first sighting of mainland Antarctica. In 1819, the British ship the *Williams*, under William Smith, was blown south from Cape Horn and sighted what is now known as the South Shetland Islands, north of the Antarctic mainland. This land attracted the attention of sealing captains, who had already hunted fur seals close to extinction in Patagonia and the Falklands and needed fresh killing grounds. U.S. and British ships prowled the South Shetlands waters, slaughtering thousands of seals for their pelts.

Meanwhile, the British Admiralty sent Edward Bransfield and William Smith to carry out a survey of

"You, sir, have discovered new territory so let it be named Palmer Land."

Admiral Bellingshausen, on meeting Palmer

the area, and they were reported to have seen the mountainous Antarctic Peninsula in January 1820. The tsar of Russia sent two ships commanded by Thaddeus Bellingshausen, which made claims to have first sighted the Antarctic mainland in January 1821. In February, off the Antarctic Peninsula coast, the Russians encountered U.S. sealing captain Nathaniel Palmer, who maintained he had first sighted the mainland the previous November. Probably the first people to set foot on the mainland, landing briefly in 1821, were from the U.S. sealer *Cecilia*, commanded by John Davis. But it is Nathaniel Palmer's claim to the first sighting that has gone down in history. **RC**

Greece Resurrected

The proclamation of Greek independence begins a ten-year war.

The revolt began not in Greece, but among Greeks in the wider Ottoman Empire. When Archbishop Germanós of Patras raised a banner of the Virgin Mary in the church of Hagia Lávra (today's Romania), it was a legendary call for all Greeks to rebel against their Turkish overlords. Action had already started. On February 22, Alexander Ypsilantis, of the secret society *Philiki Etaireia* (Friendly Brotherhood) in southern Russia, had crossed the River Pruth with 3,000 men—to be defeated by the Ottoman forces. Greek nationalists had little chance of success without more numbers. The revolt then spread to the Peloponnese, and after massacres by both sides

"The world is weary of the past / O might it die or rest at last!"

Percy Bysshe Shelley, *Hellas*, 1822

the Turks retreated to their coastal fortresses. The war for Greek independence had started in earnest.

Grievances had multiplied since the Ottomans took control in 1453. Yet the call for independence had been influenced by the American and French revolutions. It was a cause not just for Greek people, but for its friends throughout Europe. In 1824 the sultan appealed to Mehmet Ali, the pasha of Egypt, whose son Ibrahim subsequently won great victories. The Greeks might have been crushed had not a massacre of Christians caused the intervention of the Great Powers. In 1832, Crete and Thessaly were under Ottoman rule, but the rest of Greece was independent. The age of nationalism had begun. **RP**

The Sun Sets on Bonaparte

Napoleon dies on the island of St. Helena, leaving a powerful legacy to France.

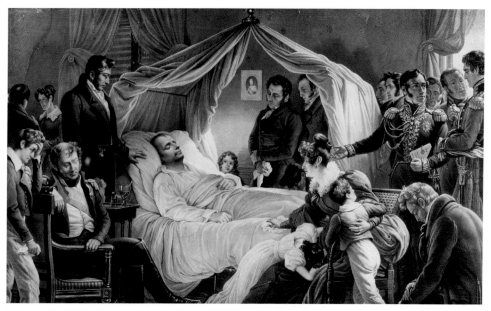

○ *Death of Napoleon Bonaparte (1769–1821), Emperor of France*, an engraving after Carl von Steuben (1788–1856).

For so long, the cries of "Vive L'Empereur!" had filled the air, and even in exile on St. Helena Napoleon had insisted that others address him as "Emperor" and stand in his presence. Despite exile, he had remarked that "the whole world is looking at us; we are martyrs in an immortal cause." But by May 5, 1821, it was clear that Napoleon had only hours to live. He had made a will and updated it with several bequests, including £500 to a would-be assassin of the Duke of Wellington. On May 1, the last rites were administered, and four days later he was reported to be like a corpse. At 5:49 P.M., he sighed four times and died.

The five-year exile on St. Helena was a wretched anticlimax to Napoleon's life. The island was too good a prison, being 1,200 miles (1,930 km) from

Africa and 1,800 (2,895 km) from South America, to allow escape. There were memoirs to compose; he was now the "People's Emperor," fighting reactionary regimes and seeking peace via a United States of Europe, but as time went on, he stayed longer in bed, bored, tired, and ill.

Arguments raged about what killed him, with the French and the English blaming each other, although neither diagnosed the gastric ulcer that had turned malignant. His body lay in state for two days and was buried on May 9 in the Valley of the Geranium. It was predictable that his corpse would be returned to France for several more interments. It was also predictable that the image of Bonaparte would haunt France for a long time to come. **RP**

A New Era for Peru

Peruvian independence is proclaimed, although fighting continues for three years.

○ *José de San Martin Proclaims Independence of Peru, 28 July 1821, Plaza de Armas, Lima, Peru* (artist unknown).

José de San Martin was the Spanish-trained Argentinean general who liberated Argentina from Spain in 1816 and then led his army over the Andes to join his Chilean ally Bernardo O'Higgins in liberating Chile. To secure these gains, he took his 4,500-strong army of blacks and mixed-race mestizos north in 1820 to dislodge the Spaniards from Peru.

San Martin landed at Pisco and marched north to besiege Lima, the Peruvian capital, but he had little support from the European-descended Creoles of Peru, who were accustomed to Spanish sovereignty. He opened discussions with Spanish commander José de la Serna, but they failed to agree on creating a constitutional Peruvian monarchy, and La Serna left Lima for headquarters in Cuzco.

San Martin was now able to occupy Lima, and Peru's independence was solemnly proclaimed in a ceremony in the central plaza. The anniversary has been celebrated as Independence Day in Peru ever since, but there were three years of fighting before Peruvian independence was finally established, largely in the teeth of the Creole ruling class, by Simon Bolivar and his right-hand man, Antonio José de Sucre, who won a succession of victories against the Spanish loyalists. The liberators' attempts to improve the lot of the black and Indian population foundered on Creole resistance, but Peruvian independence was symbolically important because Peru had historically been the heart of Spanish imperialism in South America. **RC**

Pedro I Defies Lisbon

Pedro I is crowned emperor of an independent and nationally proud Brazil.

⊙ A nineteenth-century lithograph after *Acclamation for King Pedro I in the Countryside of Santa Ana* by Jean-Baptiste Debret.

Events in Brazil took a different course from those in Spanish South America. When Napoleon invaded Spain and Portugal, the Portuguese ruler was effectively the future João VI of the Braganza dynasty, acting as regent for his mentally disturbed mother, Queen Maria. He and his family left Portugal in 1807 and were ferried to their colony of Brazil, where they settled in Rio de Janeiro. They took the royal treasury, valued at £22 million (more than £1 billion today), and Rio de Janeiro became a thriving cosmopolitan city.

Brazilian national pride was shrewdly encouraged by Dom João, who furthered the growth of a Brazilian national culture, introduced swimming in the ocean, and in 1815, declared a new united kingdom of Portugal and Brazil. Queen Maria died in 1816, and in

1821 João returned to Portugal to be crowned king, leaving his son Pedro as regent. The Portuguese parliament in Lisbon voted to return Brazil to colonial status, but Pedro declined to return to Portugal as Lisbon demanded. Waving his sword dramatically, he bellowed "*Independencia ou morte*" (Independence or death!), and he was soon crowned emperor.

However, the womanizing Pedro was not popular, and in 1831 he had to abdicate in favor of his five-year-old son, Pedro II, who nine years later, after a succession of regencies, was declared emperor and Perpetual Defender of Brazil. He presided over one of the most prosperous periods in Brazilian history, but opinion turned against the monarchy, and the country became a republic in 1889. **RC**

Separation of New and Old Worlds

The Monroe Doctrine becomes a defining statement of U.S. foreign policy.

○ A 1912 painting by Clyde De Land of the creators of the Monroe Doctrine.

James Monroe was president of the United States from 1817 to 1825. He worked closely with his secretary of state, John Quincy Adams, and both men were sympathetic toward independence movements in South America. In 1823, the British government, with commercial interests to protect in South America, suggested an Anglo-American declaration to warn the European powers against interfering in South America, but Adams persuaded Monroe to act alone rather than "come in as a cock-boat in the wake of the British man-of-war."

In his annual message addressed to Congress, President Monroe declared that, "the American continents, by the free and independent condition which they have assumed and maintained, are henceforth not to be considered as subjects for future colonization by any European powers."

He said that the political system in the Old World was different from that in the New and that the United States would regard any attempt by European powers to extend their system to the Americas as "dangerous to our peace and safety." At the same time, the United States would not interfere with any existing European colonies or dependencies, nor would it intervene in affairs in Europe. The Monroe Doctrine had little importance until later in the century. It was the British navy, not the United States, that kept South America independent. All the same, the doctrine held the seed of the United States' ambitions for hegemony in the New World. **RC**

Death of Lord Byron

Ostracized from Britain, Byron dies in Greece, leaving behind unrealized dreams of ousting the Turks and initiating Greek independence.

He was without honor in his own country, where a reputation for being "mad, bad, and dangerous to know" superseded his fame as the poet who had written *Childe Harold's Pilgrimage*. Byron left Britain for good in 1816, after one failed marriage and accusations of incest. On the Continent, he was loved by those seeking their freedom, and it was to a hero's welcome that he arrived in Missolonghi, Greece, in January 1824. He formed the "Byron Brigade" and planned to attack the Lepanto fortress and drive out the Turks. This would be a fitting culmination to his obsession, from the time he swam the Hellespont in 1810, that Greece should be free.

The reality fell far short of the romance. The hero's welcome had largely been by sailors, cheering the fact that Byron had brought their wages with him. Furthermore, the locals would not stop bickering long enough to unite against the Turks. It also seemed to rain endlessly, and Byron's health deteriorated. He began to feel unwell, probably because of malaria, and was then afflicted with spasms of coughing and vomiting. The doctors bled him, as the only way to preserve his sanity, but soon he was delirious. On April 19, with blood let by leeches trickling down his skull, Byron died.

Permission to bury him in St. Paul's or Westminster Abbey in London was refused, but this romantically tragic end to his life, at least as reported by fellow Romantics, could not fail to enhance the Byronic legend and the cause of Greek independence. **RP**

⬤ An 1813 portrait of George Gordon Byron, the sixth Baron Byron, by Richard Westall (1765–1836).

⬤ *Death of Lord Byron (Missolonghi, 19th April, 1824),* painted in 1826 by Joseph-Denis Odevaer (1778–1830).

Animal Rights

The world's first organization to prevent cruelty to animals formed in Britain.

Richard Martin, known as "Humanity Dick," was concerned that working animals were being abused and then slaughtered in appalling conditions. He also condemned the use of animals in entertainments, such as cockfighting. Martin had enough wealth, including 200,000 acres (80,940 ha) in Ireland, and political clout, being a member of Parliament and friend of George IV, to do something about it. Although early bills to regulate conditions had been defeated, in 1822, Richard Martin's Cattle Cruelty Bill was passed. The Reverend Arthur Broome then

"The question is not, 'Can they reason?' nor, 'Can they talk?' but 'Can they suffer?'"

Jeremy Bentham, 1789

gathered supporters to enforce the Act by calling for prosecutions and issuing propaganda, and on June 17, 1824, this group, which included the slavery abolitionist William Wilberforce, formed the Society for the Prevention of Cruelty to Animals.

Soon the society was reporting and prosecuting offenders. In the next decade, they employed inspectors, and in 1835 they induced Parliament to pass a more extensive Act. In 1840 Queen Victoria provided patronage, and the influence of the Royal Society for the Prevention of Cruelty to Animals spread across the Commonwealth. Anti-cruelty bills were passed in the United States in the 1830s, and in 1866, Henry Berg founded the American Society for the Prevention of Cruelty to Animals. Such organizations were landmarks in recognizing animal rights. **RP**

Bolivia Independent

After numerous uprisings, an independent Bolivia is declared.

Simon Bolivar's name was perpetuated in a country he would have preferred not to exist. Bolivia was ruled by the Incas and then conquered by the Spaniards, who drew huge wealth from the silver of its Potosi mines. The area, part of the Spanish colony of Peru, was called Upper Peru. In the 1800s a drive for independence began, and in 1809, a revolution in Upper Peru was crushed by the Spanish and the rebel leader, Pedro Domingo Murillo, was hanged.

Over the next decade, numerous local uprisings established short-lived, independent republics in

"I may die, but the torch of liberty that I left burning can never be extinguished."

Pedro Domingo Murillo, 1809

Upper Peru. In the 1820s, Simon Bolivar and Lieutenant Antonio José de Sucre won Peru's independence. Sucre told Bolivar that Upper Peru wanted self-government. But Bolivar wanted a South American federation. In 1825, Sucre summoned an assembly to decide Upper Peru's future.

The guerrilla leader Miguel Lanza presided over the discussions to consider three possibilities: independence, union with Peru, or union with Argentina. There were forty-five votes for independence, two for union with Peru, and none for union with Argentina. The delegates signed the Declaration of Independence, calling the new state Bolivia after Bolivar, hoping to ensure the country's survival. But since 1825, Bolivia's neighbors have reduced its original area by more than half. **RC**

Railway Mania Begins

George Stephenson's Stockton to Darlington line becomes the first successful railway.

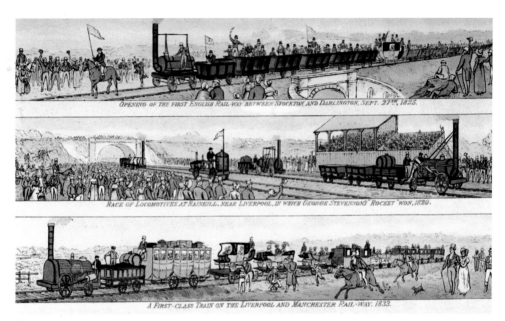

⚓ Nineteenth-century English School lithographs of the opening of the Stockton and Darlington railway and early locomotives.

Horses and stationary steam engines would pull wagons along a track from coal mines near Darlington, in northeast England, to the port of Stockton-on-Tees, 25 miles (40 km) away, providing a cheaper alternative to canals. This was the brainchild of businessmen, who hired engineer George Stephenson to make it happen. Stephenson advised them to carry passengers as well as freight, and when the line opened in 1825, he was driving his own steam engine, *Locomotion*, which pulled 75 tons at 5 miles (8 km) per hour. Downhill it could travel more than twice as fast, much to the terror of its passengers. Fares were one-third less than traveling by canal. There were frequent breakdowns, so horses were not entirely redundant, but Stephenson's steam

engines were in use for twenty-five years, making Stockton to Darlington the first commercial railway.

Stephenson was the archetypal self-made man, a hard worker since the age of eight, with an intuitive grasp of engineering. By 1812 he was "Enginewright," in charge of the machinery at a group of collieries. He invented a safety lamp for mines and then produced his first steam locomotive. On the Stockton to Darlington railway, assisted by his son Robert, he built tracks using wrought iron instead of the more brittle cast iron and fixed the gauge for tracks at 4 feet, 8 inches (1.43 m), which soon became the standard. All over Britain, canal companies cut their prices, as did the stagecoaches, but in vain. The age of railway mania was about to begin. **RP**

Ex-Presidents Die on Independence Day

American ex-presidents John Adams and Thomas Jefferson die on the same day.

○ A detail of American signatories from *Declaration of Independence, 4 July, 1776* by John Trumbull (1756–1843).

By a remarkable coincidence, the second and third presidents of the United States both died on the fiftieth anniversary of the Declaration of Independence. John Adams of Massachusetts, a leading stalwart in the creation of the United States, was vice president to George Washington and president from 1797 to 1801. Thomas Jefferson was fiercely critical of President Adams, but after both men retired, they became good friends again. Adams remained in vigorous health into his eighties. He saw his son John Quincy Adams become president, and he died at the age of ninety, on July 4, 1826. His last words were "Thomas Jefferson survives."

Jefferson did, but only just. He had retired to Monticello, his beloved Virginia estate, in 1809. His wife, Martha (Patty), had died in 1782 and on her deathbed had asked him not to marry again. He made the promise and kept it, and their daughter Martha (Patsy) ran the household for him. His last years were darkened by an enlarged prostate and possibly cancer of the colon, and by debt. He tried to save Monticello by organizing a lottery.

On July 1, Jefferson fell unconscious, but surfaced several times to ask if it was yet Independence Day. He spent most of July 3 asleep, but in the evening asked his doctor, "Is it the Fourth?" The doctor brought him his usual dose of laudanum to make him sleep, but he said, "No, doctor. Nothing more." He woke a few times more, but stopped breathing shortly before 1 P.M. the next day. He was eighty-three. **RC**

The First Photograph

Niépce takes the first photograph after searching for years for an image fixative.

○ A reproduction of the world's first photograph, taken by Niépce out the window of his family home in Burgundy, France.

Photography, one of the great inventions of the early nineteenth century, was created by a Frenchman, sixty-two-year-old Joseph Nicephore Niépce. He and his brother were inventors, developing a boat driven by an internal-combustion engine, the *Pyrelophore*, in 1798. From 1816, Niépce tried to "fix" an image produced by a camera obscura, which projects a scene onto a surface using the principle of a pinhole camera, sometimes with mirrors and lenses. He experimented with silver halide–coated paper and produced an image of a window view, but the negative image vanished when exposed in daylight.

He sought a way of producing a positive image, and in 1822 succeeded in making a contact print of an engraving onto a sheet of paper through the action of light on a glass plate coated with Judea bitumen. Two years later he made the first permanent images from the camera obscura, although these required an exposure time of many hours. He experimented with materials for the photographic plate and in 1827 visited England to demonstrate his pewter technique to the Royal Society at Kew. He did not win a prize because he would not reveal the chemicals used in this process. Around the same time, he produced a successful image—a view from his window exposed over eight hours—etched onto a tin plate, now regarded as the world's first true photograph. From 1829, he worked with Louis Daguerre; Niépce died in July 1833, leaving Daguerre to create the daguerreotype in 1839. **PF**

Battle of Navarino

Allied naval victory over the Ottoman fleet ensures independence for Greece.

❍ A depiction of the Battle of Navarino, October 20, 1827, part of the Greek War of Independence.

The mood of European statesmen after the defeat of Napoleon was for stability, legitimacy, and order, both in relations between states and in their internal affairs. But one national independence movement caught the imagination of the peoples of Europe: the fight of the Greeks for their independence from the Turkish Ottoman Empire. Britain would not intervene, but Russian emperor Nicolas I wanted to be involved with his fellow Orthodox Christians.

The Greek struggle against Ottoman rule started in 1821, but by 1827 their movement was on the point of collapse. The Ottoman sultan had persuaded Egyptian ruler Mehmet Ali Pasha, with the promise of a principality for his son, to send his army to Greece to crush the insurgents. As Russian involvement increased, the British and French governments judged they would have more influence if they worked alongside the Russians.

On October 20, 1827, a combined British, Russian, and French squadron, commanded by Admiral Codrington, entered Navarino Bay on the coast of Greece, where the larger Turkish Ottoman fleet was anchored. The battle soon started when Turkish ships opened fire. Although outnumbered both in ships and guns, Codrington's squadrons, confident in their superiority, destroyed the enemy fleet and cut the Egyptian forces from further reinforcement or supply. Within five years, Greece was accepted as an independent country by the European powers and the Ottoman Empire. **NK**

King Shaka Murdered

The assassination of their king, Shaka, heralds a period of decline for the Zulus.

○ *Chaka King of the Zoolus*, an 1836 depiction of the Zulu leader by British artist William Bagg.

"He is Shaka the unshakeable, Thunderer-while-sitting, son of Menzi."

Traditional Zulu praise song

Few have ever been so admired, hated, and feared. Admired because he was King Shaka, the man who transformed the unimportant Zulu clan into a powerful fighting nation of 250,000 people ruling large swathes of southern Africa; hated because of his love of power, destruction, and cruelty. Those who but murmured protest were likely to have their skulls split open. When his mother died in 1827 and was buried alongside ten living women, Shaka ordered that 7,000 people be clubbed to death. Shaka was feared as a matter of course, even by his half-brothers Dingane and Mhlangana. They decided to confront him the following year, waiting until September, when the tribal warriors were engaged in the north and security was low. Shaka was in the royal *kraal* (livestock enclosure) as sunset approached, awaiting a deputation from the Tswanas. Shaka was a big man—his strength was legendary, as was his physique—but they had the advantage of surprise. An accomplice created a diversion, and the two brothers stabbed their other brother to death.

Shaka had been about thirty years old when he became king in 1816 and embarked on his glorious but sanguinary reign. Only military genius enabled him to devise the new weapons and battle tactics that made the Zulus such a formidable fighting force, although historians have had recourse to his troubled childhood to explain his insensate cruelty. So far as we know, he was unmourned by the nation he had created. His body was wrapped in ox hide and thrown into an empty pit.

The glory days were soon over for the Zulus. Shaka's successor, Dingane, challenged the Boers during the Great Trek but was defeated at Blood River in 1838, and his nephew, Cetawayo, was decisively beaten by the British at Ulundi in 1879. **RP**

Bobbies on the Beat

Home Secretary Sir Robert Peel creates Britain's first professional police force.

In the 1820s it was easy to find lawlessness and the inadequacy of law enforcement. Home Secretary Robert Peel pointed to the burgeoning borough of Kensington, where "three drunken beadles" (parish constables) could not prevent increases in housebreaking and thieving. Indeed, "three angels, under such circumstances, would be sorry protection." However, the home secretary's first attempt to create a new police force, in 1822, had been defeated by Parliament concerned for civil liberties. Finally, in 1829, Robert Peel's Metropolitan Police Improvement Bill was passed, leading to the creation of the Metropolitan Police Force for Greater London, the first professional, uniformed, disciplined police force in Britain. Officers received a regular salary but, unlike previous organizations, no extras for solving crimes or recovering stolen property. Two Metropolitan Police Commissioners were responsible for 1,000 "Peelers," whose recruitment should depend "exclusively upon the character, qualifications and service of the persons selected."

Under the previous system, the Thames River Police, created in 1798, combated crime only in the Port of London, whereas the Bow Street Runners, set up in 1748 to patrol the main highways, were poorly paid and corrupt. The main burden fell on parish officials (including beadles) and unpaid constables. Peel's reforms as home secretary were momentous. He removed obsolete laws from the statute book and abolished the death penalty for nearly one hundred crimes. But "the Met" was his major monument.

The new "Bobbies" on the beat were jeered by the public, but it became a model for new police forces in Britain. It led to a fall in the crime rate and, in 1848, when much of Europe was engulfed in revolution, helped to quell the riots in Britain. **RP**

○ *Pierce The Peeler* (c.1850): Mr. Pierce, the last of the "peelers," a name acquired by English policemen in honor of Robert Peel.

"Liberty does not consist in having your home robbed by organized gangs of thieves."

Robert Peel to the Duke of Wellington, 1829

The *Rocket* Steams into History

Stephenson's Rocket *wins the Rainhill Trials, setting new standards for locomotives and spurring the growth of the railways.*

The success of the Stockton to Darlington line in 1825 showed entrepreneurs that railways were viable. Liverpool and Manchester businessmen decided that the Bridgewater Canal, linking their two cities, was too expensive, with tolls of 15 shillings ($3.50) a ton, and too slow, the 35 miles (56 km) from the port of Liverpool to "Cottonopolis" reputedly taking as long as the transatlantic journey from the United States. George Stephenson completed the railway's route in 1829, and a competition would decide which locomotives to use. The winner would be awarded £500 and a contract to supply the line's engines. More than 10,000 people came to Rainhill to watch.

Each locomotive would have to pull three times its own weight, averaging 10 miles (16 km) per hour, over the short stretch of track at Rainhill, enough times to equal the 70 miles (112 km) from Liverpool to Manchester and back. Most competitors were weeded out until four remained. *Perseverance* failed to reach the requisite speed, *Novelty* broke down twice, and *Sans Pareil* proved too heavy. Stephenson's *Rocket* had the best design; its boiler contained twenty-five separate tubes enabling the generation of twice as much steam as Trevithick's standard engine. It won easily. On October 8, it averaged 14 miles (22 km) per hour and achieved a maximum of almost double that.

Stephenson drove *Rocket* himself at the official opening of the railway in September 1830. It was the first line to be run entirely by steam engines, and its success heralded the age of the railway. **RP**

◑ An 1860 photograph of George Stephenson's *Rocket*, which won the Rainhill Trials and the contract for the new rail line.

◑ A nineteenth-century engraving titled *The Rainhill Competition*, showing *Rocket* competing against *Sans Pareil*.

Smith's New Church

Joseph Smith establishes the Church of Jesus Christ of Latter-day Saints.

"This is the work of God," said Joseph Smith in New York, announcing the new Church of Jesus Christ of Latter-day Saints. Smith was now prophet and first elder of the Mormon Church. Thus began the "marvelous work" of bringing souls to knowledge of the Savior. The five men assembled received "glorious manifestations of the power of the Priesthood."

Joseph Smith was the fourth child of a poor farming family. His mother, Lucy, recalled that he was "a remarkably quiet, well-disposed child." Not satisfied with orthodox Christianity, Smith had a conversion

"Let every man, woman, and child realize the importance of the work."

Joseph Smith, *History of the Church*, 1839–1856

experience (the "First Vision") at the age of fourteen, when he claimed God and Jesus Christ appeared to him. Christ told him his sins were forgiven, whereas God told him all Christian denominations taught incorrect doctrines and to await further instructions. These arrived in the 1820s, when the angel Moroni revealed the secret golden plates that contained the ancient Book of Mormon, telling of Christ's post-resurrection appearance in the United States and correct doctrine. In 1844 Smith was arrested for treason in Illinois and killed in prison by a mob. Schisms followed, over the leadership and doubts about polygamy, introduced after a revelation in 1843. Brigham Young became church president, leading the Mormons to Utah, where Salt Lake City was founded in 1847. In 2007, there were thirteen million Mormons worldwide. **RP**

Charles X Deposed

French King Charles X proves too reactionary and is forced to abdicate.

Thursday July 29 was the third day of what the French referred to as "Les Trois Glorieuses," although it was not glorious for around 1,000 people who lay dead. Dozens had been killed on the Tuesday, when rioters attacked Paris's armed guard. The second day had been quieter, as liberals presented a petition to the obdurate Charles X, and most had been killed on this day of barricades, rioting, and fierce violence. One key part of the city after another fell, until the administrative center, the Hôtel de Ville, was taken. Almost at once the politicians set up a provisional

" . . . the sound of cannon and gunfire is becoming ever louder."

Juste Olivier, *Paris Journal*, July 28, 1830

government. It was all over except the abdication of the king, a formality that occurred the following day.

Charles X, who had reigned from 1824, had been ultra-royalist. He had a traditional coronation at Reims, introduced the death penalty for blasphemy, and seemed to believe in "the divine right of kings." It was almost as if the Revolution of 1789 and Napoleon had never happened. After elections in 1830 had reinforced the liberal majority in the Chamber of Deputies, Charles muzzled the press and reduced the number of deputies and voters, thus making the situation worse. The Bourbon dynasty was at an end. Some favored a Bonapartist autocracy or a republic to replace it. In the end, the Duc d'Orléans, Louis-Philippe, became king, although of a decidedly bourgeois, constitutional type. **RP**

The World's First Dynamo

Faraday's electromagnetic discovery is a breakthrough in understanding electricity.

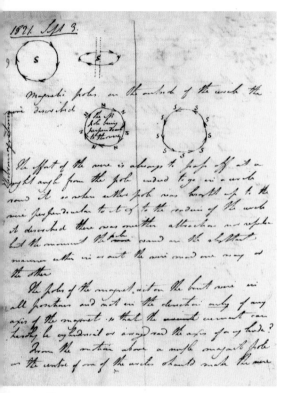

○ Page 74 from Faraday's notebook, on the "Rotation of Current Experiment," September 3, 1821.

◑ A c.1860 photograph of Michael Faraday, who discovered the laws of electrolysis and electromagnetic induction.

> ## "... but still try, for who knows what is possible."
>
> **Attributed to Michael Faraday**

A year earlier he had been earning the staggering sum of £1,000 a year as a scientific consultant. Now Michael Faraday was devoting himself exclusively to research and was living off less than a tenth of that sum. But the cut in pay was worth it. He had long been convinced that magnetism and electricity were closely related. Already he knew that an electric current could produce magnetism, and on August 24, 1831, during an epoch-making period of nine days of brilliant experimentation at the Royal Society in London, he proved that magnetism could produce electricity. Using very simple equipment (a magnet, a copper coil, and a basic ammeter), he demonstrated that moving a wire through a magnetic field induces an electric current whose voltage is proportional to the speed of the movement. Here was, in effect, the world's first dynamo. The principle that he had discovered underlies the fundamental operation of most modern-day electrical machines. Faraday was not only a brilliant experimental scientist, but also one of the most practical.

Born in 1791, the son of a poor Yorkshire blacksmith, amazingly, Faraday had little formal education. He was apprentice to a bookbinder before attracting the attention of Sir Humphrey Davy and becoming a dedicated chemist and physicist, and a superb lecturer. He discovered benzene, invented the system of oxidation numbers, devised an early form of the Bunsen burner, developed the laws of electrolysis, and helped along the birth of nanoscience, as well as giving us the "Faraday cage," the "Faraday constant," and the "Faraday effect."

More than any other man, Michael Faraday made possible the generation of electricity. It took another generation before his discoveries found full practical expression, but humankind is in his debt. **RP**

Revolutionary Evolutionist

Darwin discovers his true calling on the voyage of the Beagle, where his discoveries lay the foundations for the theory of evolution.

ON

THE ORIGIN OF SPECIES

BY MEANS OF NATURAL SELECTION,

OR THE

PRESERVATION OF FAVOURED RACES IN THE STRUGGLE
FOR LIFE.

By CHARLES DARWIN, M.A.,

FELLOW OF THE ROYAL, GEOLOGICAL, LINNÆAN, ETC., SOCIETIES;
AUTHOR OF 'JOURNAL OF RESEARCHES DURING H. M. S. BEAGLE'S VOYAGE
ROUND THE WORLD.'

LONDON:
JOHN MURRAY, ALBEMARLE STREET.
1859.
P. X.

The right of Translation is reserved.

HMS *Beagle*, a ten-gun brig under Captain Robert Fitzroy, successfully sailed from Devonport, England, on December 27, 1831. Her five-year mission was to chart the coasts of South America and the South Sea Islands. No new lands were found, but it still proved to be a voyage of discovery because of the presence of the ship's botanist, Charles Darwin. So far Darwin had failed to find his niche in life. First he studied medicine, and then he entered the church. Yet his real interest lay in collecting sea creatures and insects.

Darwin suffered continually from seasickness but took advantage of his adventure. He hunted and fished, rode a giant tortoise, scaled peaks, and encountered hostile natives. But the voyage was also serious. Darwin improved his powers of observation, acquired "the habit of energetic industry and of concentrated attention to whatever I was engaged in," and collected the data and specimens he would use to develop his ideas. Science took over his life.

Reading the works of Alfred Lyell led him to accept the theory that the land had been shaped gradually. Now his own observations compelled him to believe that animals and birds somehow evolved. How else could he explain that fossil remains differed from their modern equivalents or that four types of finches existed on separate Galapagos islands?

There was no theory to explain his observations, and *The Voyage of the Beagle* (1839) is marked by a wealth of information rather than explanation. It was only a beginning, but a vitally significant one. **RP**

◗ The title page of Charles Darwin's revolutionary book, *On the Origin of Species*, published in London in 1859.

◖ A colored engraving of Darwin's ship, HMS *Beagle*, off the coast of South America.

Factories Regulated

The Factory Act is an attempt to limit the more unsavory workings of capitalism.

The factory owners considered the proposals a disgrace. Power looms meant progress, and the government should let the new textile factories continue to spearhead Britain's industrial and commercial growth. Yet others, including the Tory philanthropist Antony Ashley Cooper, insisted that the disgrace was the exploitative factory system that forced children to work excessive hours for low wages. The Factory Bill was enacted. It became illegal for a textile factory to employ any child under nine. Those aged nine to thirteen could work for a

" . . . children suffer these injuries from the labor they undergo."

Commission of Enquiry into Factories, 1833

maximum of eight hours a day; those aged thirteen to eighteen for twelve hours. Workers under thirteen would be given two hours of education a day at factory schools.

Since an ineffective 1819 Factory Act, the employment of children in the textile mills had boomed. In 1832, a report had passed off extreme conditions as typical, and another insisted factories in Britain were no worse than elsewhere. It was decided that the free market would fix adults' hours and conditions, but that children required protection. Legislation in 1844, 1847, and 1867 further reduced children's hours, increased their educational provision, limited women's hours, and affected other places of work as well. The humanitarian regulation of capitalism was becoming unstoppable. **RP**

Human Trade Ban

The Slavery Abolition Act makes slavery illegal within the British Empire.

It was the end of what some called the "Triangular Trade" between West Africa, the Americas, and Britain, a massive undertaking that had transported more than ten million Africans across the Atlantic, which most knew as the slave trade. The Slavery Abolition Act proclaimed that all slaves in the British Empire should be "manumitted and set free, and that a reasonable Compensation should be made to the Persons hitherto entitled to the Services of such Slaves." As many as 668,000 slaves were freed in the Caribbean, and a sum of £20 million was paid out.

"England is willing to give twenty millions sterling for the Abolition of Slavery."

William Wilberforce in 1833

The end had been a long time coming. In 1787 William Wilberforce and Thomas Clarkson had formed the Society for the Abolition of the Slave Trade, and two years later Wilberforce had made an impassioned, four-hour critique of the slave trade in the House of Commons. But it was only in 1807 that the trade was made illegal for British ships, and even then merchants often circumvented the legislation. So it was decided that slavery itself should be made illegal to stamp the trade out. Wilberforce died three days after the vote that made the bill a certainty.

The consequences of Britain's act were profound. In 1862, the United States abolished slavery. Later the Chartists, the suffragettes, and the civil rights campaigners were inspired by it. It has been called the start of the world's human rights movement. **RP**

Houses of Parliament Ablaze

Most of the Palace of Westminster in England is destroyed by fire.

○ *Fire at the Houses of Parliament, 16th October 1834*, a contemporary painting by P. T. Cameron (fl. 1834).

They had been unharmed by the Gunpowder Plot of 1605 and by the Great Fire of London of 1666, but Britain's Houses of Parliament could not survive an attempt to burn a stack of old tally sticks. According to an eyewitness, Anne Rickman, the flames were first visible at 6:20 P.M. from an upper floor on the west side of the House of Lords. Soon crowds were thronging the nearby bridges and embankments of the Thames to see the awesome spectacle. Most gazed in incredulity, although the artist J. M. W. Turner was inspired to begin a series of watercolors. In the early hours, the fire was brought under control.

All that remained of the Palace of Westminster was the crypt of St. Stephen's Chapel, the Jewel Tower, and Westminster Hall, the latter saved by Prime Minister Lord Melbourne, who arranged for several fire engines to be brought into the hall itself.

A new Palace of Westminster, comprising 1,200 rooms, 100 staircases, 11 courtyards, and approximately 2 miles (3.2 km) of corridors and passages, was built between 1840, when the cornerstone was laid, and 1860. It was predominantly the work of Charles Barry, whose design in the Gothic style was selected out of ninety-seven submitted. His buildings perfectly complemented the surviving Westminster Hall and the nearby Westminster Abbey. Much of the interior was the work of his assistant, Augustus Pugin. Their masterpiece survives to this day, although the chamber of the House of Commons had to be rebuilt after bomb damage in 1941. **RP**

Fall of the Alamo

The legendary siege becomes a milestone in American history.

○ *Battle of the Alamo*, an illustration of the siege at San Antonio, Texas, in which nearly all male American settlers were killed.

Texas was a sparsely populated territory of the Mexican republic in 1835 when an influx of American settlers called for local autonomous rights for Texas under the Mexican constitution. Mexico responded to the demand with military force, and an army of some 6,000 commanded by General Santa Anna besieged around 200 Texans in the Alamo, a derelict mission station turned fortress at St. Antonio. The leading figures among the defenders were William Travis, Jim Bowie—inventor of the eponymous knife—and Davy Crockett, the coonskin-capped son of Tennessee later immortalized in song and on screen. The siege of the Alamo lasted a fortnight, and when the defenders were eventually overwhelmed in a final hour-long assault by nearly 2,000 Mexicans, almost all were slaughtered, apart from a few slaves, women, and children.

One or two days before the final assault, William Travis drew a line in the sand and asked all those who were prepared to fight to the end to step across it. All but one is said to have done so; that man became the only Texan to survive, and he later published his account of the siege.

Mexico's capture of the Alamo proved a Pyrrhic victory, however, winning time for the leader of the Texan rebels, General Sam Houston, to gather troops in preparation for his later victory over Mexico at the battle of San Jacinto. The "Lone Star" state thus established its independence, but soon joined the United States. **NJ**

Dickens's Novel Published in Parts

The serialization of Pickwick Papers *changes literature and reading habits.*

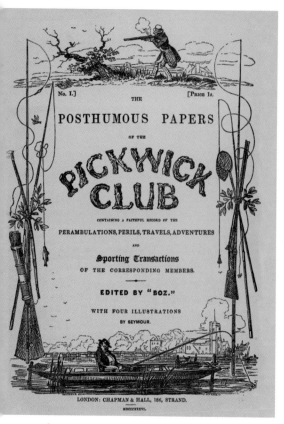

○ The front cover of the first issue of the *Pickwick Papers*, with engravings from the original illustrator, Seymour.

"If I were to live a hundred years . . . I should never be as proud as I am of Pickwick."

Charles Dickens to his publisher, 1836

The first installment of *The Posthumous Papers of the Pickwick Club* appeared on March 31, 1836. It consisted of thirty-two pages and four engravings, enclosed in green wrappers, published at a shilling. Chapman and Hall cautiously published around 400 copies to begin with. Famous books had been circulated successfully in shilling monthly parts, but this work was still being written, and by an unknown author. They had wanted Dickens to provide text to support sporting drawings, but he had insisted that the drawings illustrate his stories. The 400 copies did not sell well, and it seemed the venture might flop, particularly after the suicide of the work's original illustrator after the second installment.

Twenty-four-year-old Charles Dickens accepted the commission because he needed the money, which amounted to just over £14 ($67) for 12,000 words. He began on February 18 and finished the installment within a day. On the strength of this he was able to get married, but there was no let-up with the writing. Despite initial poor sales, news of the work's brilliance, aided by the illustrations of the replacement artist, "Phiz," soon spread far and wide. *Pickwick Papers* eventually ran to twenty parts, the last in November 1837 selling 40,000 copies. Dickens's first biographer described twenty illiterate people avidly listening while a workman read from a copy borrowed for tuppence from a circulating library. The installments appeared in book form in 1837.

Pickwick Papers was exuberant, farcical, and heartwarming, one of the funniest books of the century. It showed Dickens's social concerns, as he wrote of poverty and the need for play in children's lives. Dickens was able to resign as a journalist and devote himself to his art. Neither Dickens, the reading public, nor literature would be the same again. **RP**

Duel Kills Russian Literary Star

Alexander Pushkin's early death robs Russian literature of its first exponent.

The leeches applied to his stomach gave some relief, opium a little more, but it was clear to the doctors that Alexander Pushkin, author of the novel in verse *Eugene Onegin* and the drama *Boris Godunov*, and undoubtedly Russia's greatest poet, was dying in agony. He asked for pistols, that he might shoot himself, but instead was offered the sacraments. Hastily he made a will, leaving everything to his wife, Natalya, and their four children. During his final night he had wretched convulsions, and in the morning he found it hard to recognize Natalya. He waited for death stretched out on a sofa, with one knee raised, his hands behind his head, the position in which he had created so many poems. He seemed to be sleeping when suddenly he called for cloudberries. Shortly afterward he whispered, "Life is done," and at 2:45 P.M. on February 10, 1837, he breathed his last.

Two days earlier he had fought a duel with his brother-in-law Georges d'Anthes, who was alleged to be having an affair with the beautiful Natalya. Pushkin had been hit first but pushed his seconds away and insisted on firing back. D'Anthes was only shot in the arm, but Pushkin was not so lucky.

Pushkin's achievement was to write poetry and prose in his native Russian tongue, thus creating a modern Russian literary tradition. Until then, the Russian nobility used French as their first language. Pushkin had learned Russian from the servants in his childhood home, and his use of the language in a poetic form was revolutionary in its day. After his death, in recognition of his contribution to Russian literature, Tsar Nicholas I paid off Pushkin's debts, gave Natalya a pension, and exiled Georges d'Anthes. Death at the age of thirty-nine in such a dramatic fashion preserved Pushkin's monument as the romantic founder of modern Russian literature. **RP**

Portrait of Alexander Pushkin by Vasili Andreevich Tropinin (1776–1857), in the State Russian Museum, St. Petersburg.

"And where will fate send death to me? / In battle, in my travels, or on the seas?"

Alexander Pushkin, untitled poem, 1829

Victoria Becomes Queen

Victoria's accession to the throne begins the longest reign in British history.

❶ Victoria receives the news that she has become queen in an atmospheric nineteenth-century rendering.

"I shall do my utmost to fulfill my duty toward my country."

Victoria, in her journal, June 20, 1837

On June 20, 1837, she was woken by her mother's kiss at six o'clock in the morning and told that the Archbishop of Canterbury and the Lord Chamberlain wished to see her. She went in slippers and a dressing gown to her sitting room, where the two men told her that King William IV, her uncle, had died at exactly twelve minutes past two that morning in a "perfectly happy, quiet state of mind . . . quite prepared for his death," and that consequently she was queen. The Lord Chamberlain knelt down and kissed the hand of eighteen-year-old Victoria. She was young and inexperienced, she confided honestly to her diary. But she did not lack confidence. She had been heir to the throne since 1830 and had awaited this day with studied patience.

So began the longest reign in British history and one that saw truly momentous changes. It was a period of rapid technological advancement, of improvement in the conditions of ordinary people, of massive growth for the British Empire, and of democratization, as more people were given the right to vote and the monarchy lost almost all its political powers. What did it matter that Victoria had no interest in machinery or in the welfare of the masses, or that she was determined to retain, not relinquish, political power? She also hated pregnancy and disliked children, but nevertheless had nine babies. She gave her name to the age, and some people, however fancifully, came to believe that she embodied it.

Yet in one important respect, her accession was crucial. The fortunes of the monarchy under her "wicked uncles" had been at a very low ebb. The accession of a graceful young woman, who was neither depraved nor corrupt, boosted an institution whose days had seemed numbered. **RP**

Morse Demonstrates Telegraphic Code

Samuel Morse begins the world's electronic communications revolution.

Few people have a genuine vocation, but some, like Samuel Finley Breese Morse, manage to have two. He studied painting in Washington and London, where he exhibited at the Royal Academy. Soon he was a successful and innovative portrait painter, and in 1835 he became a professor of art in New York. Morse, however, had another passion—electricity and the possibility of electrical communication. His work in this field finally came to fruition on January 6, 1838, when he demonstrated his eponymous telegraphic code.

The urgent need for faster communications was brought home to Morse in 1825 when his wife, Lucretia, died before he even knew she was ill. A few years later he conceived the idea of using newly discovered electromagnetism to build an electric telegraph. Morse and Leonard Gale had already devised a telegraph whose signals could travel short distances. In 1836, they had a breakthrough when they used a relay of circuits—one battery sending signals to another, and that one to another, and so on—so that a cable could carry signals over long distances. Morse then perfected a code made up of short marks (dots) and long marks (dashes) to represent letters, numbers, and punctuation, sent as either short or long electrical pulses. Collaborator Albert Vail invented a device to press the dots and dashes into a moving paper tape.

Morse could not patent his telegraph, as he was beaten to it by Europeans, but he patented Morse Code in October 1837 and successfully demonstrated it in New York in January 1838, at a speed of ten words per minute. The world stood on the verge of a communications revolution, although it would be several years before people could fully appreciate the importance of this innovation. **RP**

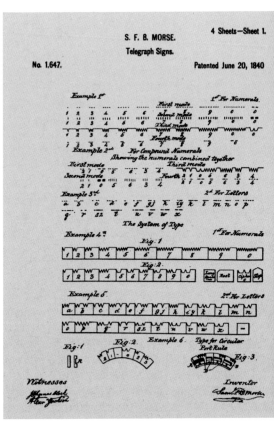

O A chart depicting Morse Code signs; Morse Code was patented in this form in 1840.

> ## "My ambition is to be enlisted in the constellation of genius now rising in this country."
>
> **Samuel Morse to his parents, May 2, 1815**

Retief Murdered in Southern Africa

The Voortrekkers' Great Trek to negotiate new lands ends in bloodshed and the loss of thousands of lives in battle.

On February 6, 1838, Boer leader Pieter Retief and his party of *Voortrekkers* (pioneers) were killed by the Zulus. The *Voortrekkers* had left the Cape Colony in South Africa and wanted to acquire land by treaty; to this end, Retief and a band of his followers had attempted to negotiate with the Zulus. In retaliation for Retief's murder, the Dutch Boers, with their wagons lashed together into circular *laagers* (defense formations), killed thousands of Zulus at the battle of Blood River. But after the massacre the rival British claimed Natal as a colony and moved the Boers on.

Retief and his group of *Voortrekkers* had started out from the Winterberg District with thirty-two bullock carts, heading for the distant mountains as part of the Great Trek. Retief may have thought that he was leading a new "chosen people" to the "promised land," but his followers were just looking for a peaceful existence away from the British government. As Retief wrote in his manifesto, "We will not molest any people, nor deprive them of the smallest property, but if attacked we shall consider ourselves justified in defending our persons and effects to the utmost of our ability."

Before coming to the Zulus, the *Voortrekkers* had met other convoys, and Retief had been briefly elected governor of "New Holland in South East Africa." After Retief's death, the Boers founded two other republics, the Orange Free State and the Transvaal. However, the beleaguered *Voortrekkers* did not find peace, but a sword; a tragedy with historic repercussions. **RP**

◗ A depiction of Pieter (more commonly referred to as Piet) Retief, the leader of Boer pioneers in southern Africa.

◖ The *Voortrekkers*, Boer farmers seeking to escape British rule, emigrate northward to the Transvaal.

Atlantic Record

Great Western, the first transatlantic steamship, sails from Bristol to New York.

He was only 5 feet, 4 inches (1.62 m) tall, but Isambard Kingdom Brunel was a veritable "Little Giant." He had built the Great Western Railway from Bristol to London. Why not extend the line westward, across the Atlantic to New York, via steamboat? Until then, sailing ships dominated because steamships needed so much coal that there was little room for cargo or passengers. But Brunel intended to build big.

At 212 feet (64.6 m) long, the *Great Western* was the largest, heaviest steamship at 1,320 tons (1,341 tonnes). It had a 450-horsepower, two-cylinder, four-

"Why not make it longer, and have a steamboat go from Bristol to New York?"

Isambard Kingdom Brunel, October 1835

boiler engine. The oak bottom was reinforced with iron bolts, and its hull was sheathed in copper.

A fire broke out in the engine room at the end of March, in which Brunel himself was injured. Only fifty-seven passengers had signed up, and now fifty hastily demanded their money back. Perhaps the 702-ton (713 tonne) *Sirius* would make the journey faster. She had begun a shorter voyage, from Cork rather than Bristol, four days earlier.

The *Great Western* steamed from Bristol on April 8, 1838. Coal was shoveled at a rate of a hundredweight (50 kg) a minute. She docked fifteen days later, a few hours after her competitor, which had run aground. The record crossing was twice as fast as that of sailing ships. Henceforth, there were regular, steam-powered voyages across the Atlantic. **RP**

Seeds of Democracy

The working class agitate for greater representation in a democratic system.

It was drawn up by William Lovett and Francis Place and published without publicity. Even at the "monster meeting" on Glasgow Green, Scotland, when Arthur Wade waved a copy to cheers, declaring that he held "a charter—the people's charter," there were no copies made for distribution. The political culture of Chartism was oral not literary, and most knew its six points: universal male suffrage, no property qualifications for Members of Parliament, annual parliaments, constituencies of equal size, payment of MPs, and election by secret ballot.

"[Chartism was a] knife and fork, a bread and cheese question."

Joseph Rayner Stephens, Methodist minister

The origins of Chartism can be traced back to the late eighteenth century, but three factors explained its burgeoning growth at this time. The first was disappointment with the 1832 Reform Act—working men had campaigned tirelessly and yet only the middle class was enfranchised. The second factor was economic depression, and the third was a raft of unsympathetic government legislation, including the "Starvation Law" of 1834. The only remedy, it seemed, was for working people to unite and agitate. Some 1.3 million people signed a national petition, and a national convention was called for February 1839.

The petition was rejected. Chartism petered out in the 1850s, but within a century all of its demands, except that for annual general elections, had become recognized as indispensable to democracy. **RP**

First Photographic "Negative" Created

Daguerre unveils the world's first practical photographic process to the public.

◑ The earliest existing daguerreotype, dates back to 1837; this innovation was a huge step forward in photography.

Louis Jacques Mande Daguerre explained that a twenty-minute exposure onto a polished, iodized silver plate would give a lasting image if exposed to fumes of mercury and then "fixed" by a solution of common salt or sodium thiosulphate. The images on the glass-fronted plates, or "daguerreotypes," were crystal clear. There was the moon through a telescope, a spider through a microscope, and images of shells, fossils, and plaster casts. Daguerre's breakthrough had been signaled at the French Académie des Sciences in January 1839, and now, in August, it was presented to the admiring world.

Daguerre's work as a stage designer led him to buy a camera obscura. He was introduced to Joseph Nicephore Niépce, who had captured images on pewter plates coated with bitumen of Judea, with an exposure time of up to eight hours. The two men became obsessed with how to capture images on light-sensitive materials more quickly. Niépce died in 1833, but Daguerre soldiered on alone.

Success in 1839 brought Daguerre an annual pension of 6,000 francs and international honors. The daguerreotype was particularly suitable for portrait photography, but its big drawbacks were that light and shade were reversed in his images, and a mirrored surface was needed to reflect the correct image. By treating the daguerreotype as a "negative" to be placed on a sheet of sensitive paper, the Briton William Talbot solved both problems and took photography a stage further. **RP**

The Poppy War

China's expulsion of the British leads to the outbreak of the first Opium War.

○ A colored lithograph by F. J. White shows the storming of the forts and entrenchments of Chuenpee during the Opium Wars.

Lin Tse-hsu was the strong man of Qing China. He made his name as governor-general of Hunan and Hupeh, where he destroyed massive amounts of opium. Now, the emperor gave him the task of cleaning up Canton. He forced foreign merchants to sign agreements not to trade in opium, and Captain Charles Elliot, the British crown official, handed over 20,282 chests of opium for destruction. But when a local was killed by foreign sailors and Elliot refused to hand over the culprits, Lin expelled the British, who took refuge on Hong Kong island.

Fighting broke out after Lin refused to let the British buy supplies in Kowloon, and in November, British vessels clashed with the Qing navy. The first Opium War had begun. The British protested that trade should be free, and that once it was free and the world became economically interdependent, there would be no war. It was almost coincidental that the export of opium from Bengal contributed to British revenue. To the Chinese, that was imperialistic claptrap. The Qings had evidence that opium was addictive and wanted it stamped out.

Prime Minister Lord Palmerston sent in steamships and troops. It was an unequal contest, and in the 1842 Treaty of Nanking, five "treaty ports" were opened to unrestricted foreign trade, and Britain took Hong Kong as a colony. Another war in 1856 to 1860 further benefited British traders. Many assumed that a weakened China would be partitioned between the western powers. **RP**

New British Colony

By the Treaty of Waitangi, the British take control of New Zealand.

Captain William Hobson reached North Island, one of the islands of New Zealand, on January 29, 1840. Immediately he invited the *rangatira* (Maori chiefs) to a conference and prepared a treaty for them to sign. It was ready within a few days, and missionary Henry Williams and his son Edward had it rapidly translated into Maori by February 4. Two days later, forty chiefs signed the Maori version at Waitangi, in the Bay of Islands. By it, the Maori were guaranteed control over their land and other property, but in return they ceded sovereignty to Queen Victoria. Over the next few months another 500 chiefs signed copies of the treaty, and the British proclaimed that it applied even to those who had not signed. A new colony had been added to the British Empire.

The first Europeans visited the islands of Aotearoa in 1642, but until 1830, only small numbers of Britons lived there, under Maori sufferance. But then things changed. The numbers of settlers increased, causing disputes about land ownership, and the Maori population declined because of infectious European diseases. There were rumors that France might annex the islands. It was time for Britain to act.

Waitangi Day is celebrated as a public holiday in New Zealand, and the treaty is generally considered to be the founding document of New Zealand. However, the meaning of the treaty has long been highly controversial. The Maori protested by means of five indecisive wars between 1845 and 1872 that the treaty was being ignored, to little effect. By the mid-twentieth century, their protests began to be heard with more seriousness. From 1975, they were able to use the tribunal, set up by the Waitangi Act of 1975, to claim compensation for breaches of the terms of the original treaty. **RP**

Penny Post

The Penny Black becomes the world's first adhesive postage stamp.

A few years earlier the postmaster had mocked Rowland Hill's "wild and visionary schemes," and the secretary to the post office added that his plans were "preposterous." Yet such were the failings of the postal service in Britain, and so vigorous was the call for reform from businessmen, that Hill was given the job of reforming it. Now, on May 1, 1840, the world's first adhesive postage stamp was issued. A standard letter, weighing half an ounce or less, could be sent with the new Penny Black, a small piece of paper stating the sum paid and bearing the image of Queen Victoria. On the back was "glutinous paste." The modern postal system had arrived.

Charles I had made postal deliveries a royal monopoly in the seventeenth century, and by the late eighteenth century improved roads allowed rapid delivery to Britain's main towns. But costs depended on the distance traveled and the number of sheets sent, and receivers had to pay, that is, unless they refused to accept delivery of a letter, each one of which had to be logged. The system was cumbersome and expensive. When educationalist Rowland Hill suggested how to improve the system, in his pamphlet of 1837, *Post Office Reform*, he attracted widespread attention.

His reforms—prepayment by the sender and a low, uniform cost depending on weight, not distance traveled—quadrupled the number of letters sent within a decade and rapidly expanded the postal services. The Penny Black was replaced after one year by the Penny Red, across which cancellation franking could more easily be seen. **RP**

○ A Penny Black, the first adhesive postage stamp, with cancellation stamp, 1840.

Defeat for Britain

The first Anglo-Afghan War reaches a climax in a massacre of British forces.

The British never accepted that they had "invaded" in 1839, or were "occupying" Afghanistan. In their view they had merely helped Shah Shuja retake what was rightfully his, even after his rival, the pro-Russian Dost Mohammad, had been exiled to India. Yet the local people did not believe them and rose up in revolt. Even now, when General Elphinstone had negotiated a safe exit and withdrew his unarmed Kabul garrison on January 6, 1842, the Afghans were hostile. Warriors began to attack as the contingent of 4,500 Indian and British soldiers and around 10,000 wives, children,

"Brydon ... reached this place ... alone, has arrived to tell the fearful tale."

Captain Julius Brockman

and civil servants traveled through the passes and gorges along the Kabul River. At the Gandamak Pass, on January 13, the attacks became a massacre. Only forty men survived, and their chances were slim. The snow was deep, shelter nonexistent, and food scarce. A single survivor, Dr. William Brydon, made his way to Jalalabad.

British prestige in the East had been dealt a blow—until then British soldiers were considered invulnerable. Shah Shuja was assassinated in 1842, and Dost Mohammad took over. This Anglo-Afghan War was part of the "Great Game," to secure Britain's hold on India, using Afghanistan as a buffer against Russian encroachments. Britain invaded again in 1879 and 1919. Afghanistan was easy to defeat; conquering it was something different. **RP**

Ether as Anesthetic

Sulfuric ether is used as an anesthetic in surgery for the first time.

The search for pain relief during surgery and dentistry goes back many centuries. Alcohol, opium, and marijuana were all tried with limited success, and hypnosis was used later, but the modern history of anesthetic drugs begins with the friends of a Georgia physician and surgeon, Crawford Williamson Long, and their desire to have a good time at parties. Long was in general practice in Jefferson, Georgia, where friends asked him for nitrous oxide because they enjoyed its effects. He suggested inhaling sulfuric ether, instead, and noticed that his friends felt no pain, literally, even when severely bruised.

In March 1842, Long decided to try sulfuric ether as an anesthetic when removing a cystic tumor from the neck of a patient named James M. Venable. It worked, and he used it several times in the following years, for amputations and childbirth, including when his wife delivered their second child in 1845. He did not publish his results until he delivered a lecture at the Medical College of Georgia in 1848. The next year his account of his work was published in the *Southern Medical and Surgical Journal*.

Long's delay in making his work known caused confusion and ill feeling when others claimed to have been first in the field. Horace Wells, a Connecticut dentist, claimed to have used nitrous oxide successfully in 1844. A partner of his, William T. G. Morton of Boston, laid claim to pioneering ether, and John C. Warren claimed to have employed ether in an operation at Massachusetts General Hospital in 1846. It is now considered clear, however, that Long was the first to use ether anesthesia during surgery. A statue of Long stands in the crypt of the United States Capitol, one of two statues representing the state of Georgia. **RC**

China Forced to Sign Treaty of Nanking

The first of "the unequal treaties" forced on the decaying Chinese Qing Empire by European powers leaves China subservient to the West.

The treaty followed China's defeat in the First Opium War, which broke out in 1839 as a result of Britain's exporting of the highly addictive opium and imperial China's ineffective efforts to stop the spread of the drug. Opium importation had been banned by China since 1729, but the ban was flouted by Britain, whose opium cultivation in its Indian empire was an official—and very profitable—monopoly of the East India Company. When in 1839, China confiscated opium in the port of Canton, war broke out. The conflict was one-sided, with the British bombarding Canton, seizing Hong Kong, and occupying Shanghai.

The Chinese were forced to sue for peace, and the treaty was negotiated between Sir Henry Pottinger and Qi Ying on board the British warship HMS *Cornwallis* in Nanking Harbor. Under the thirteen articles of the treaty, signed on August 29, 1842, China was compelled to open up five ports—Canton, Shanghai, Amoy, Foochow, and Ningpo—to foreign trade, including opium. The Chinese empire surrendered its imperial monopoly on trade and agreed to free trade between Britain and China. China was forced to pay $21 million in war indemnities and as compensation for opium that it had confiscated. Finally, China ceded the port of Hong Kong to Britain as an entrepot for British exports—primarily opium. The opening of the so-called "treaty ports" initiated a period of jostling by the Western powers for influence along the Chinese coast and inland along rail lines. **NJ**

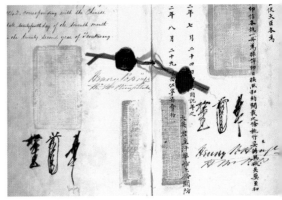

◐ An engraving of the bombardment of Canton by the English under Captain Charles Elliott, 1841.

◑ A two-page spread from the Nanking Treaty of peace, friendship, commerce, and indemnity, August 29, 1842.

The First Self-Styled "Cartoon"

Punch *provides satirical drawings on the theme of social injustice with an indispensable new name and purpose.*

USEFUL SUNDAY LITERATURE FOR THE MASSES ;
OR, MURDER MADE FAMILIAR.

Father of a Family (reads). "The wretched Murderer is supposed to have cut the throats of his three eldest Children, and then to have killed the Baby by beating it repeatedly with a Poker. * * * * In person he is of a rather bloated appearance, with a bull neck, small eyes, broad large nose, and coarse vulgar mouth. His dress was a light blue coat, with brass buttons, elegant yellow summer vest, and pepper-and-salt trowsers. When at the Station House he expressed himself as being rather 'peckish,' and said he should like a Black Pudding, which, with a Cup of Coffee, was immediately procured for him."

○ *Useful Sunday Literature For The Masses; Or Murder Made Familiar, a cartoon from an 1849 issue of* Punch.

"The poor ask for bread, and the philanthropy of the State accords—an exhibition."

Punch, July 15, 1843

Who drew the first cartoon? It depends on how the term is defined. Originally "cartoon" denoted a preliminary sketch for a later, and of course fuller, painting, tapestry, or mosaic. Leonardo left several sketches that could be considered cartoons. The lexicographer Dr. Johnson defined the term in 1755 as "a painting or drawing upon large paper." Cartoons in the modern sense of humorous and satirical drawings may be found in the eighteenth century, particularly in the work of William Hogarth. But the first drawing that called itself a cartoon was "Cartoon no. 1: Substance and Shadow" published in the British weekly magazine *Punch* on July 15, 1843, and drawn by John Leech.

The theme of the drawing was an exhibition of fresco designs at Westminster Hall in London to decide which ones should adorn the walls of the new Houses of Parliament, then under construction. The government even arranged a "free day" when the poor could view them. The editors of *Punch* decided that, at a time of widespread poverty, the whole project was a waste of public money, and Leech illustrated this argument to perfection. He depicted a variety of shabbily dressed, emaciated, and disabled individuals staring disconsolately at depictions of well-fed personages. The government, insisted the *Punch* commentary, had "determined that as they cannot afford to give hungry nakedness the substance which is covets, at least it shall have the shadow."

This was the first of six self-styled "cartoon" attacks in *Punch* on social injustice. The term soon became so familiar that there seemed no other word for such concentrated pictorial satires. **RP**

First Telegraph Message

Morse begins the first telegraph service; a new world of communication is born.

The first stabs at inventing an electric telegraph were made in Europe in the early 1800s, but the father of modern telegraphy was American Samuel Morse. At Yale he was fascinated by lectures on electricity. He began a career as a painter, but failed to make an adequate living, and in his forties turned his attention to the possibilities of electrical communication. By 1837, he had patented an efficient system and in 1844, he started a telegraph service between Baltimore and Washington, D.C. His first message was "What hath God wrought!" The system was extended

"I have sacrificed my profession [as an artist] to establish an invention . . ."

Samuel Morse, January 20, 1864

to New Jersey and attracted financial customers who appreciated instantaneous communication.

Rival inventors involved Morse in legal battles, but the system grew rapidly and by 1852 the eastern states had more than 18,000 miles (29,000 km) of telegraph wires. In 1861 the telegraph was extended to California, with messages costing senders $1 per word. The spread of railroads across the country (and railroads' rights of way) provided the opportunity for erecting telegraph poles and wires.

By 1858, an underwater cable line was laid across the Atlantic by the British ship HMS *Agamemnon*, but it did not last, and in 1866, a British-made transatlantic cable was laid by Isambard Kingdom Brunel's *Great Eastern* steamer, and a reliable telegraphic link between Europe and America was established. **RP**

Annexation of Texas

The Lone Star state joins the Union; it became the twenty-eighth state.

Although the declining power of the Spanish empire brought Mexico independence in 1821, the country remained weak beside its northern neighbor. From the 1830s onward, American pressure to expand westward and southward made it inevitable the two would clash. American settlers moving into the northern Mexican province of Texas, swamping the existing Spanish population, and a demand by the Mexican dictator Santa Anna in 1834 for the northern (Anglo) settlers to leave, sparked war.

Despite the famous defeat and massacre at the Alamo, in March 1836, the Texans seceded to proclaim the independent republic of Texas. The following month they defeated Santa Anna at the battle of San Jacinto. The new republic was recognized by the United States and Britain, but not Mexico. In 1837, a proposed annexation was rejected by President Martin Van Buren, who feared war with Mexico over the issue.

In February 1845, the U.S. Congress passed a resolution to allow Texas to join the Union, and the Texans approved the new constitution, which specifically allowed slavery. The annexation was ratified by Congress in December, making Texas the twenty-eighth state (and included parts of New Mexico and Colorado). The ceremony for the official transfer of authority was held February 19, 1846.

The following spring, President James K. Polk invaded a portion of Texas still claimed by Mexico, thus initiating the Mexican-American War, which ended in 1848 with further land transfers from Mexico to the United States. The enthusiasm surrounding the annexation in Washington led to the assertion of the United States's "manifest destiny to overspread the continent," in the words of journalist John O'Sullivan. **PF**

U.K. Parliament Abolishes the Corn Laws

Repeal of the Corn Laws boosts the Liberals in Parliament, but destroys Peel's career.

Peel's Cheap Bread Shop, Opened January 22, 1846, a cartoon from *Punch* magazine, c.1846.

"I shall leave a name execrated by every monopolist."

Robert Peel, House of Commons, June 29, 1846

A Member of Parliament at the age of twenty-one, a minister at twenty-four, prime minister at forty-six, and now six years into his second premiership, Sir Robert Peel stood head and shoulders above fellow Conservatives in terms of both experience and ability. He knew what was right, and he would do it. The Corn Laws must be abolished. Why should the price of wheat be kept artificially high when there was famine in Ireland? Why should farmers' incomes be boosted to the detriment of ordinary people, who had to buy expensive food, and of manufacturers, who had to pay inflated wages? The debates were prolonged and bitter, but Peel won the key vote with a majority of ninety-seven. Yet two-thirds of Conservatives voted against him, and repeal was won only with opposition support.

The Corn Laws, protective tariffs against imported grain, had made sense in 1815. Production had expanded significantly during the Napoleonic Wars, and free trade might lead to agricultural collapse. Yet this rationale soon wore thin. The laws seemed to many to be a conspiracy by landowners against industrialists and the masses. Peel lowered duties in 1842, and now, with the potato blight affecting Ireland, abolished them altogether. The son of a Bury cotton manufacturer, he had never been exactly popular in his party. Some mocked his Lancashire accent, others found him rather aloof and humorless ("an iceberg with a slight thaw on the surface"). Now, the knives were unsheathed.

The abolition of the Corn Laws led to cheaper food in Britain, boosted industry, and heralded free trade, but Peel was defeated and ejected from office. He died in 1850. Many "Peelites" moved over to the Liberals, and it was thirty years before the Conservatives again held a majority. **RP**

Latter-Day Saints Found City

Brigham Young and his followers, the Mormons, found Salt Lake City.

The founder and prophet of the Mormons, Joseph Smith, made several attempts to find a place for his followers to settle while they were awaiting Christ's return to America, but they encountered fierce hostility, and Smith was killed by a mob at Nauvoo, Illinois, in 1844. Under his successor as leader, the formidably efficient Brigham Young, the Mormons traveled west in ox-drawn wagons, with a brass band to play for dancing in the evenings, to make a new home for themselves in Utah, in theoretically Mexican territory. There the Latter-day Saints founded their new capital and created a strictly disciplined society where for a little while they could live in isolation from the outside world.

The journey was planned in two stages, the first of which during the winter of 1846–1847 was spent near today's Omaha, Nebraska, in temporary log huts at Winter Quarters. In the spring the travelers headed on across the Rocky Mountains to the Great Salt Lake (the largest salt lake in the Western hemisphere) in the area now known as Utah. There were suggestions that it might be better to continue migrating on to California, but when they had reached the site of today's Salt Lake City on July 24, 1847, Young declared "This is the place."

The whole episode was an astonishing feat of organization. The settlers worked hard digging irrigation canals and planting crops in what was then a desert, building a fort and laying out their new city. More immigrants arrived in what they called Deseret as the new temple rose at the city's heart. Parties soon went out to explore and create fresh settlements, and Young was appointed governor of the new Utah Territory by President Fillmore in 1850. With twenty or more wives and a host of children to continue his legacy, he died in 1877. **RC**

○ The founding of Salt Lake City in Utah with the beginnings of a settlement by the Mormon sect evident, *c.*1850.

> ## *"I honor and revere the name of Joseph Smith. I delight to hear it; I love it."*

Discourses of Brigham Young

Freedom in Africa

Troubled Liberia is proclaimed an independent state.

Liberia, in sub-Saharan Africa, was a country set up for former slaves returning to Africa from the United States. Liberia originated in 1821 when an American warship, the USS *Alligator*, captained by Richard Field Stockton, sailed for west Africa on behalf of the American Colonization Society (ACS), an organization established by white idealists who wanted to return former slaves to their African homeland. Stockton persuaded tribal leaders to sell him a thirty-six-mile (60 km) stretch of coastline around Providence Island, site of the future Liberian capital Monrovia.

" . . . may we not hope that a happy day is soon to dawn on that long-abused people."

H. L. Ellsworth to the ACS, May 8, 1842

From the beginning there were clashes between the colonists and the indigenous peoples. Deadly diseases, including Yellow Fever, regularly ravaged new arrivals. Only half of an estimated 4,500 immigrants survived the colony's first twenty years. Renamed the Commonwealth of Liberia in 1839, its founding whites handed control to the blacks. Joseph Jenkins Roberts became its first black governor, and encouraged by the ACS—facing bankruptcy subsidizing the colony—proclaimed Liberia an independent state in 1847. The state's survival was guaranteed when it was recognized by Britain (in 1848) and France (in 1852). Tensions between minority African-Americans and the majority ethnic Africans continued, contributing to civil wars and ongoing violent instability. **NJ**

Gold in the West!

The California gold rush begins, as does the state's population growth.

Captain John A. Sutter, as he called himself, was a Swiss draper who had emigrated to America in 1834 to escape from both his creditors and his wife. In California the Mexican authorities gave him a site for a ranch and agricultural colony called New Helvetia near today's Sacramento. He built a fortress, garrisoned by Native Americans in secondhand Russian uniforms, as well as assorted whites. To Sutter's dismay, traces of gold were discovered on his settlement and, although he tried to keep it secret, word leaked out and his colony was soon destroyed.

"What a great misfortune was this sudden gold discovery for me!"

John A. Sutter, *California Magazine*, 1857

Over the next few years gold-seekers, known as "forty-niners," after the year 1849, came swarming in to pan every stream and mine every piece of land.

The first prospectors were Americans from the east. Mexicans and other Latin Americans came, as did Hawaiians, Chinese, Australians, New Zealanders, and Europeans. Traders, businessmen, and con artists followed, and often did better from the rush than the gold-seekers. Levi Strauss's first trousers, for instance, were sold to miners. From 1850, California flourished. By 1860, the population increased from 14,000 to 380,000. Cities were founded, and roads and railroads were built. The gold rush opened up the American West, and discoveries of gold and silver similarly influenced the settlement of Nevada, Colorado, Oregon, Montana, and the Dakotas. **RC**

United States Expands into Mexico

The Treaty of Guadalupe Hidalgo allows the United States to annex more than half of Mexico, creating a future anti-treaty backlash.

President James Knox Polk called the expansion of the United States "manifest destiny." The territory gained in the Mexican-American War of 1846–48 increased the size and wealth of the Union. The treaty ending the war was signed in the village of Guadalupe Hidalgo, outside Mexico City, on February 2. It established the border between the United States and Mexico at the Rio Grande and the Gila River, giving the U.S. more than 525,000 square miles (1,356,000 sq km) of new territory, around 55 percent of Mexico's prewar land. The United States acquired the whole of present-day California, Nevada, and Utah, and parts of Colorado, New Mexico, Arizona, and Wyoming. The Mexicans received $15 million and had debts of $3.25 million canceled. The war also ended the dispute over the possession of Texas.

The conflict began as a dispute over the U.S. annexation of Texas. In January 1846, President Polk ordered Zachary Taylor to advance south, and he won a series of victories. Most of Mexico's cities were occupied, and with the capture of Mexico City on September 14, 1847, the fighting subsided. The settlement was then dictated by the Americans.

The United States now stretched from the Atlantic to the Pacific, and trade with the East was boosted by possession of east coast ports. In 1853, the Gadsden Purchase provided the U.S. with the remaining parts of Arizona and New Mexico. The loss of so much territory, however, undoubtedly harmed Mexico. After Benito Juarez came to power in the 1850s as part of an anti-treaty backlash, the settlement bedeviled Mexican-American relations. **RP**

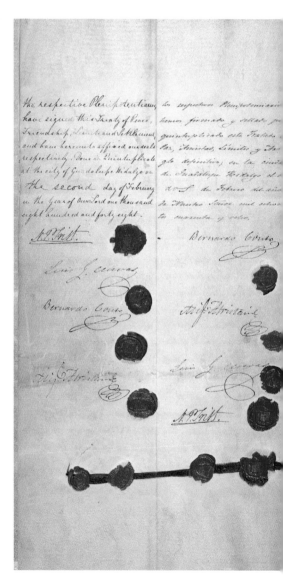

⊙ A page from the Treaty of Guadalupe Hidalgo, which ended the Mexican-American War.

Marx and Engels Redefine History

The publication of The Communist Manifesto *lays the seeds for future revolutionary movements.*

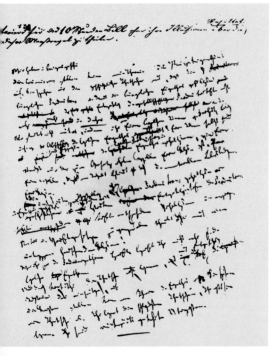

"The history of all hitherto existing society is the history of class struggles." The opening sentence of *The Communist Manifesto* was breathtaking in its scope, its novelty, and its political implications. History had seen the owners of the means of production pitted against those who worked for them. The means of one class's dominance over another was, essentially, the state—the armed forces, the police, and the legal system, allied to schools that controlled by indoctrination, and churches that maintained inequality by promising rewards in the next life. Yet no system was stable. Feudalism had given way to capitalism, and the capitalists were digging their own graves by exploiting workers until they would rise up in a bloody revolution and usher in a new phase of human history—communism.

The manifesto was drafted by Friedrich Engels in 1847, and revised by his compatriot Karl Marx. Then it was presented to the obscure League of Communists in London, and published in German in February 1848, in time for Europe's wave of revolutions that year, though it had little influence on them.

The manifesto was a sociological analysis of capitalist society, and a political call for revolution. It was also easy to read. Analysts soon exposed its shortcomings—its underestimation of the importance of national identity, for instance, and its neglect of tensions within classes. Yet it became the most important revolutionary text of the nineteenth century and, for Marxist believers, a new holy writ. **RP**

◐ A manuscript of the last page of the first draft of
   The Communist Manifesto (1848).

◐ A photo of Karl Marx (right) with his daughters Jenny,
   Laura, and Eleanor, and Friedrich Engels, c.1865.

Surprise Revolt

Mass protests unleash an unintended revolution in France in 1848.

Coming to power during the 1830 revolution, King Louis-Philippe II was determined not to perish in one. He became the "Citizen-King," the bourgeois monarch who reduced censorship, extended the franchise, and allowed the elected assembly to initiate laws. On February 22, crowds clashed with soldiers, overturning omnibuses and erecting barricades. The following morning, the mob was even larger, and many of the 80,000-strong National Guard refused to obey orders. That afternoon, the prime minister, François Guizot, resigned, and that

"We are sleeping on a volcano. A wind of revolution blows."

Alexis de Tocqueville, Chamber of Deputies, 1848

evening troops panicked and shot fifty-two people on the Boulevard des Capucines. On February 24, 1,500 barricades were erected. The king tried to appoint opposition leaders to the government, but they would not have it. After abdicating, Louis-Philippe fled France in disguise.

Despite political problems in the 1840s, what really transformed the situation was economic discontent, with bad harvests, high food prices, and rising unemployment. Louis-Philippe's abdication fueled revolutionary aspirations in the rest of Europe, and in France it made things worse. During the "June Days," more than 1,500 people were killed in Paris. Small wonder that in the 1848 elections a massive majority of voters turned to the nephew of Napoleon Bonaparte, Louis Napoleon. **RP**

Unrest in Austria

The resignation of Metternich gives hope of liberal and nationalist success.

Students were demonstrating in Herrenstrasse, Vienna, calling for a new constitution and liberal freedoms. Troops under the command of Archduke Albrecht had been brought in as a precautionary measure, but shots rang out and four people were killed. The demonstration became a riot. Vienna citizens demanded that the troops withdraw and that leading minister Prince Clemens von Metternich be dismissed, which feeble-minded Emperor Ferdinand, did, bowing before his Council of State's advice.

"We cannot . . . undertake great internal changes without danger."

Clemens von Metternich, February 29, 1848

News of a revolution in France made the ruling elite distinctly jittery, and calls for reform seemed unstoppable. Metternich, foreign minister since 1809, was thrown to the wolves. Perhaps now the revolutionary sting would be drawn and the multi-national Austrian empire would survive.

A strong figure soon emerged in Austria. It was not another revolutionary and not another Metternich but Sophie of Bavaria. She gave the lead that culminated in the restoration of imperial power in Italy, Prague, and Hungary, as well as Vienna itself. She had her son crowned as Emperor Franz Joseph in December 1848. Yet the dynastic Habsburg Empire, a source of stability in Metternich's heyday, was to be a cause of conflict in European affairs up to the outbreak of World War I. **RP**

Revolutionary Dress Rehearsal

An uprising in Milan against Austrian rule achieves a quick but illusory victory.

◑ *Episodes from the Cinque Giornate: The Insurgents Assault Porta Tosa (March 22, 1848),* a Romantic painting in the Museum of Milan.

Revolution was in the air. The French king had fled in February, and now it was the turn of the Italian states. Liberals were calling for political freedoms, and nationalists for independence from Austria. The liberals in Milan, in Austrian-controlled Lombardy, were already heartened by successes elsewhere on the Italian peninsula, and on March 17 came the amazing news that Vienna itself had risen. At once the mayor of Milan, Count Gabrio Casati, arranged for a demonstration, and soon some 10,000 armed men were surging around the government buildings. When two guards were killed, Count O'Donnell, the vice governor, gave way to protesters' demands.

This was just the first of the famous "Five Days" in Milan, for the octogenarian Austrian general Radetzky

was determined to fight and retook several key points in the city. Yet, on March 22, even he decided to withdraw. A provisional government was set up, which appealed to Charles Albert of Piedmont to drive the remaining Austrians out of northern Italy. At the end of May they achieved a famous victory.

It was all too good to last. Radetzky had withdrawn because he was needed at home, not because he was defeated, and in July he returned with reinforcements, winning a major victory at Custozza. Two lessons were apparent: that success required the involvement of the masses, not just the elites, and that a Great Power ally was needed to defeat Austria. The way was thus prepared for the successful unification of Italy by 1861. **RP**

The Battle of Gujarat

British victory at Gujarat leads to the incorporation of the Sikhs into British India.

○ *The Battle of Goojerat on 21st February 1849*, a colored engraving by John Harris from 1850, after Henry Martens.

The Battle of Gujarat, on February 21, 1849, proved decisive in the Second Anglo-Sikh War. The Sikhs under Ranjit Singh had carved out a powerful kingdom in the Punjab, and his successors, alarmed at the British East India Company's expansion, launched an attack in 1845. The first Anglo-Sikh war was a British victory, but the powerful *Khalsa* ("Sikh army") was kept intact. War resumed in 1848, and the Battle of Chillianwala, in January 1849, was a draw, with heavy casualties on both sides.

The British forces under General Gough had 23,000 men to the Sikhs' 60,000. This time head-on bayonet charges would not work. Gough would play to his strengths: ninety-six field guns and sixty-seven siege guns, including ten 18-pounders (8 kg) and six

8-inch (20 cm) howitzers. His men advanced and the Sikhs opened fire, but this only disclosed their positions. Gough halted his divisions and ordered all artillery to fire. Their sustained cannonade continued for two devastating hours, after which the infantry advanced, capturing Sikh positions. The battle was over within three hours. Sikh losses were estimated at between 3,000 and 5,000 men, while ninety-six British were killed and 682 wounded.

After the rout at Gujarat, hostilities ended on March 11, 1849. Three days later, the Sikh army formally surrendered to Major-General Gilbert. Then the Punjab was annexed and its infant ruler, Duleep Singh, deposed. Yet the Sikhs became loyal subjects, and a fearsome fighting force, under the Raj. **RP**

Domestic Sewing Machine Launched

Singer unveils his new sewing machine, the first to be commercially successful.

○ An undated print advertisement for Singer sewing machines from *Harper's Bazar* (as the magazine was then spelled).

"Instead of the shuttle going around in a circle, I would have it move to and fro."

Isaac Singer, on a proto-sewing machine, 1850

The name Singer is now almost synonymous with the sewing machine, but there were other pioneers in the field before Isaac Singer made the first effective machine that people bought to use in their own homes. In 1755, a German called Charles Wiesenthal patented a double-pointed needle—an essential development. A Frenchman, Barthélemy Thimonnier, started to manufacture machines in 1830, but his factory was destroyed by mobs of tailors who made their living sewing by hand. In 1846, an American named Elias Howe patented a machine that was used by a London corset manufacturer.

Isaac Merrit Singer came from a German family, originally called Reisinger, who emigrated to the United States in the 1760s. Young Isaac, who grew up with almost no education, loved the theater and tried to make his way as an actor-manager, with little success. Greater rewards would come from his abilities as mechanic and inventor. He produced machines for rock-drilling and carving type before moving from New York City to Boston and turning his attention to the sewing machine.

In 1850, Singer produced an efficient, practical machine powered by a foot treadle with a needle that moved up and down instead of side to side, but he was soon entangled in legal actions for breach of patent by Elias Howe and other inventors. The "sewing machine wars" were finally settled in 1856, and Singer, who was a ruthless businessman, built up a dominating and hugely lucrative position in the sewing machine market. Singer also had an astonishingly complicated love life. It was rumored that he had fathered more than twenty-eight children. When he died in his sixties in 1875, he was worth more than $13 million. His company went on to make the first electric sewing machines in 1889. **RC**

The First World's Fair

The Great Exhibition is a showpiece for British technology and design.

It was "The Great Exhibition of the Works of Industry of All Nations," and it did indeed contain exhibits from all around the world, but few Britons doubted which nation exceled above all others and would dominate the huge display that opened in Hyde Park, London, at 11 A.M. on that warm spring morning. Their expectations were duly confirmed, for there were 7,381 exhibits of British origin, and 6,556 from the rest of the world. But the centerpiece was the exhibition hall itself, which was dubbed "Crystal Palace" by the satirical journal *Punch*. It was 1,848 feet (563 m) long, 408 feet (124 m) wide, and 66 feet (20 m) high, and covered four times the area of St. Peter's in Rome.

Designed by Joseph Paxton, a former head gardener at Chatsworth in Derbyshire, it was the world's first prefabricated building. Based on the huge greenhouses at Chatsworth, it had an iron frame as its load-bearing structure, was clad in dazzling glass panels, and encompassed three large elm trees. More than 6 million people, one-third of Britain's population, came to see the exhibition between May 1 and October 15, many on new railway excursion trains. It was a hugely successful celebration of modern technology and design, and the team that organized it, led by Queen Victoria's husband, Prince Albert, were rightly proud of their achievement. It was soon followed by other world fairs.

With the profits of the Great Exhibition totaling £186,437, land was bought in South Kensington, London, for permanent educational institutions to be built, including the Victoria & Albert Museum, the Natural History Museum, and the Science Museum. In 1854, the Crystal Palace was reassembled at Sydenham Hill (then in the county of Kent), where it remained until it was destroyed by fire in 1936. The Sydenham Hill area is now called Crystal Palace. **RP**

⊙ The Great Exhibition in Hyde Park: an interior view of the main avenue showing galleries supported by iron columns.

"This day is one of the greatest and most glorious in our lives."

Queen Victoria's diary, May 1, 1851

Publication of *Moby-Dick*

Melville's classic tale of a whaling ship's adventures fails to excite the public.

🔵 An illustration for Melville's *Moby-Dick*, by A. Burnham Shute, from *c.*1851.

"Who would have looked for philosophy in whales, or for poetry in blubber..."

London Magazine, 1851

Moby-Dick is today considered an epic of American literature, by an august author, Herman Melville. However, such recognition seemed unlikely when *The Whale* was first published in three volumes in London by Richard Bentley and, then on November 14, 1851, in New York as the single volume *Moby-Dick* by Harper & Brothers. It seems that, as far as popular tastes were concerned, Melville did not so much interweave his philosophical musings into the harpooning action-adventure as bludgeon them onto the plotline. The tale of Ishmael and his South Sea Islander friend Queequeg, whaling together on a Nantucket whale ship *Pequod* under the command of the sinister Captain Ahab, sank along with its biblical references and accelerated the decline of Melville's literary reputation.

The ex-teacher's literary standing had been built on the back of a series of adventure narratives, including *Typee* (1846), *Omoo* (1847), and *White Jacket* (1850). Like *Moby-Dick*, these tales were based on Melville's experiences in the South Seas as a harpooner, cannibal-observer, and naval deckhand. The years of acclaim brought enough money to buy a farm at Arrowhead in Pittsfield, Massachusetts, where he lived for thirteen years, immersing himself in Shakespeare and developing a friendship with his neighbor, the novelist Nathaniel Hawthorne. But with mounting debts, Melville was eventually forced to sell up and become a customs inspector in New York. The carefree rover and writer who had voyaged around the globe now tied himself to a desk job that paid $4 a day for the next twenty years.

The influence of *Moby-Dick* is perhaps lost on those people who frequent a U.S. chain of coffee shops, named for the coffee-loving first mate of *Moby-Dick*, Starbuck. **JJH**

Louis Napoleon Masterminds a Coup

Louis Napoleon's coup in December 1851 undermines French democracy.

Government printers in Paris had no choice but to work overnight on December 1, 1851, and the police were ordered to shoot anyone leaving early. They were printing a proclamation so secret that no one was allowed to typeset more than a few sentences. Their work was finished by 5 A.M. and copies were then distributed, under the direction of the Prefect of Police, de Maupas. Within a few hours the whole city had been placarded. Parisians read that the assembly had been dissolved and that martial law was in operation, but also that universal suffrage was restored and that they would soon vote on a new constitution. The mastermind behind this coup on December 2, the anniversary of Napoleon's victory at Austerlitz, was none other than Louis Napoleon, the nephew of Bonaparte. He had been elected president in December 1848, for a period of four years, and he had no intention of standing down. By the time the placards appeared, he had rounded up seventy-eight leading political figures, including royalists, generals, radical leaders, and other undesirables. Soon 500 dissidents were killed.

The coup went remarkably smoothly, but then, it had been well planned. Louis Napoleon had worked hard to bolster his image and win supporters within and outside of the assembly. Most important of all, he had 50,000 loyal troops in the city. He was now president for ten years, a position endorsed by 91 percent of the voters in a referendum. The following year he elevated himself to Emperor Napoleon III.

Europe would never be quite the same again, partly because Louis Napoleon's inexpert meddling in foreign affairs helped to unify both Italy and Germany, and undermine France, and partly because his career showed the way to later dictators. **RP**

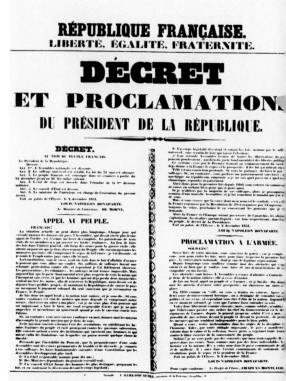

🔼 An engraving of Louis Napoleon's December 2, 1851, Decree and Proclamations, which made him dictator.

"My duty is to maintain the Republic and to save the country."

Louis Napoleon's Proclamation, 1851

提督ペルリ省像

寅六十戈

Opening Up Japan

Commodore Perry arrives in Tokyo Bay to force a treaty upon the Japanese.

Before Commodore Perry's squadron of four warships, including two paddle steamers, menacingly entered Tokyo Bay, with the steamships pouring out such volumes of black smoke that frightened Japanese on shore thought they looked like floating volcanoes, the government of Japan had kept the country firmly closed to foreigners. But the United States under President Fillmore had other ideas, and Perry was sent to demand a treaty that would open up commercial and political relations with America.

Matthew Calbraith Perry, known to his friends as Calbraith and to the Navy as "Old Bruin," was fifty-seven, had enjoyed a distinguished career, and was a believer in expansionist American imperialism. In 1852, Perry accepted command of the expedition to Japan. He embarked with a naval band playing "Hail Columbia," but the Japanese would not accept a treaty, and Perry withdrew with a promise to return.

He kept the promise, returning the following February with a larger squadron of warships. This time when he landed his naval bands played "The Star-Spangled Banner." The Japanese authorities, overawed and divided, signed the Treaty of Kanagawa in March 1854, which gave the United States most-favored status as a trading nation, opened two ports as coaling stations, and guaranteed the safe return of shipwrecked American seamen. Similar treaties were soon concluded with the British, the Russians, and the Dutch. Perry received the thanks of Congress and publicly urged Americans to "extend their dominion and their power across the Atlantic" and the Pacific. He died in New York in 1858. **RC**

◗ A colored woodblock print of Commodore Perry, published in Miki Kosai's *Ikoku Ochiba Kage* (*c.*1854).

New Party Formed

Opposition to slavery leads to the formation of The Republican Party.

The Republican Party was born of hostility to slavery after the Missouri Compromise, which had kept a balance between slave and nonslave states, was shattered by the 1854 Kansas-Nebraska Act. This Act allowed the settlers of the new territories of Kansas and Nebraska the freedom to decide if they wanted to allow slavery within their borders. Opponents of "the slavocracy" of the South created a party in the North to uphold the principle that every man should be free to make himself a good life. It also called for the opening up of the West for small homesteaders.

"No man is good enough to govern another man without that other's consent."

Abraham Lincoln, Peoria, Illinois, 1854

In 1854, the Republican Party was formally founded in Jackson, Michigan, at a meeting of 10,000 people, and the word quickly spread. A leading figure was Abraham Lincoln, who denounced slavery as a breach of the Declaration of Independence.

In the 1854 congressional elections, the Republicans won a majority in the House of Representatives. In 1856, the Republican presidential candidate John C. Frémont carried eleven states. In 1860, the party picked Lincoln to run for president, whereas the Democratic Party, split between its Northern and Southern factions, ran two rival candidates. Lincoln won all of the Northern states' electoral votes, but only 40 percent of the popular vote. The Democratic and Republican parties would dominate U.S. politics from then on. **RC**

Charge of the Light Brigade

A routed cavalry charge at Balaclava highlights the failings of the British army.

O An illustration of the famed "Charge of the Light Brigade" at the Battle of Balaclava.

"It is magnificent, but it is not war. It is madness."

General Pierre Bosquet, French officer, witness

The Crimean War saw Britain and France attacking Russia to restrain the Russian advance into the Balkans; the war degenerated into a long siege of Sebastopol and occasional bloody battles in the vicinity. On October 25, 1854, General Cardigan, commanding the brigade of five regiments of British Light Cavalry at the Battle of Balaclava, received the order to attack a battery of Russian guns at the end of a valley. Putting himself at the head of the formation, he led 673 Light Dragoons, Lancers, and Hussars down the valley toward the guns more than a mile away. First at the walk, then the trot, the canter, and finally at the charge, they broke into the battery and drove the artillerymen from their guns. Their task done, they turned and retired down the valley. On their way down the valley and on their return, they were blighted by fire from guns on both flanks and a battery ahead of them.

When the Light Brigade remustered after the charge, there were just 195 cavalrymen still mounted. Of the remainder, 118 had died and 127 were wounded. The rest returned on foot. Cardigan rode from the field, retired to his yacht, and sat down for his usual lavish dinner.

The heroism of the officers and men of the Light Brigade won widespread admiration. But through misunderstandings and unclear orders, they charged the wrong guns and achieved little. In the words of Lord Tennyson's famous poem, *The Charge of the Light Brigade*, "Someone had blundered."

The charge demonstrated all the strengths and weaknesses of the British army of the time—aging commanders and officers who had acquired promotion through money, influence, and class. The British military establishment was in urgent need of reform. **NK**

Nursing Pioneer

Florence Nightingale organizes care for British soldiers in the Crimean War.

Conditions in the grim, vermin-infested army barracks at Scutari, Turkey, converted to a military hospital for British soldiers wounded in the war against Russia in the Crimea, were far beyond anything Florence Nightingale or her team of thirty-eight nurses had anticipated: sick and dying soldiers, most of them suffering from cholera or dysentery, lay everywhere—in Scutari, war wounds accounted for only one death in six. Also, the military doctors were not particularly pleased to see them, especially when Nightingale set her nurses to thoroughly clean the hospital and reorganized patient care—a slight, they felt, on their own professionalism.

Born into a wealthy, upper-class family in 1820 in Italy, Nightingale—who had had to overcome her parents' opposition to be allowed to take up nursing—considered an occupation for lower-class women—was every inch a fighter. She also had *The Times* newspaper, which had first alerted people in Britain to the cholera epidemic, on her side. Dubbing her "the lady with the lamp," the newspaper took up Nightingale's cause and raised a public fund to help her carry out her work.

With improved sanitation, death rates at Scutari soon began to fall, and when Nightingale returned to England in 1856, she was welcomed as a national heroine and granted an interview with Queen Victoria—unlike Jamaican-born Creole Mary Seacole, who had nursed men with cholera at the battlefront in Crimea itself, but whose name was unknown to the public. At home, Nightingale used her influence to fight for reform of military hospitals and improve the standards of nursing, founding the Nightingale School for Nurses at St. Thomas's Hospital, London, in 1860. In 1907, she became the first woman to receive the Order of Merit. **NK**

◐ A portrait of Florence Nightingale, who used her experiences in the Crimean War to found modern nursing.

> *" . . . she may be observed, with a lamp in her hand, making her solitary rounds."*

The Times, 1854

Outbreak of the Indian Mutiny

Indian soldiers rise in revolt against their commanding British officers.

○ After their capture of Delhi, the Indian mutineers lost the city to British forces, who extracted swift reprisals by hanging the leaders.

On May 9, at the cantonment of Meerut north of Delhi, the commanding officer of the 3rd Bengal Light Cavalry sentenced eighty-five Indian troopers to ten years' hard labor for refusing to perform their firing drills. The next day the Indian native regiments in Meerut mutinied, released the condemned men, and started killing their British officers. They then marched to Delhi to restore Bahadur Shah, the retired Mughal emperor, to his traditional position as the ruler of India. The Delhi native regiments joined the mutiny, which spread across north India.

The immediate cause of the unrest was the introduction of the new Enfield rifle, which required the user to bite a greased cartridge. Hindu soldiers believed they would be defiled because the grease was beef fat, Muslim regiments because it contained pork. This distrust of the British by Indian soldiers was a symptom of the growing distance between the ruling elite and its subjects. The respect for the cultures of India shown earlier by British soldiers and administrators was being overtaken by a more reforming, overtly Christian view of their role. Traditional social structures were interfered with.

Not all Indian regiments mutinied. Nevertheless, the violent suppression of the mutineers and the reimposition of British control, the atrocities, real or imagined, committed by both sides only furthered the growing separation of the two communities and the dangerous illusion of superiority felt by the rulers over their Indian subjects. **NK**

Our Lady of Lourdes

Bernadette Soubirous's visions turn Lourdes into a place of Christian pilgrimage.

○ Crowds gather to watch Soubirous experience one of her visions of the Virgin Mary in the grotto of Massabielle in Lourdes.

It was the sort of weather that would aggravate her asthma, but fourteen-year-old Bernadette Soubirous insisted on going outside to collect firewood. She needed a break from "the Gaol," the single, scarcely habitable room in a disused prison in Lourdes in which she, her parents, and her siblings were living. She wandered to the rocky cliff with a grotto carved out at the bottom and there she "heard a noise something like a gust of wind." Turning, she saw a "gentle light" and then a beautiful woman dressed in white opening her hands in a welcoming gesture. Bernadette tried to make the sign of the cross but had lost control of her hands. The vision made the sign of the cross, then disappeared. Despite her parents' disapproval, Bernadette felt drawn to return and saw more apparitions, although her companions saw nothing. On March 25, the vision revealed herself as "the Immaculate Conception."

Bernadette was accused of being a fantasist, a charlatan, or perhaps just mentally ill. But in 1862, the pope declared her visions authentic, the cult of Our Lady of Lourdes was authorized, and the underground spring was declared to have miraculous properties. Lourdes soon became a site of pilgrimage, with three million annual visitors, many of them sick or disabled.

In 1958, a 20,000-seater underground church was built. As for Bernadette, she became a nun, passing her remaining years in prayer and seclusion, well loved for her wit, kindliness, and stoicism in the face of pain. She died in 1879 and was canonized in 1933. **RP**

Origins of Germ Theory

Louis Pasteur disproves the theory of spontaneous generation.

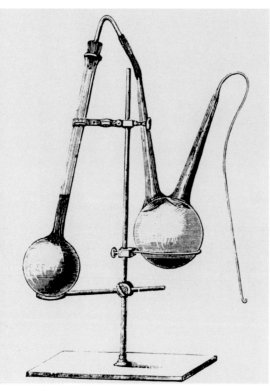

○ An engraving of the apparatus used by Louis Pasteur in an early experiment in the production of a disease-free beer.

○ Chemist Louis Pasteur performs a scientific experiment in his laboratory.

> *"The wine is a sea of organisms. By some it lives, by some it decays."*

Louis Pasteur

Everyone knew that milk or wine left in a flask would go "sour" and that micro-organisms would appear on its surface. But what caused this change? Louis Pasteur, newly appointed professor at the École Normale Supérieure in Paris, was convinced that the generally accepted view, formulated by Félix Pouchet, was wrong. Pouchet believed in "spontaneous generation," the idea that fermentation was a chemical process, and hence life (if only that of tiny organisms) could be generated from mere matter. Pasteur was confident that he could disprove this idea by experiments in the laboratory. He passed air through a plug of guncotton in a test tube and then dissolved the guncotton. He identified in the residue exactly the same microscopic organisms found in fermenting liquids. On the other hand, if the air were heated sufficiently, the micro-organisms would not be found in the residue. Pasteur argued that organisms in the air produced fermentation or putrefaction, and heat killed them. It was a momentous discovery.

After this initial breakthrough, Pasteur continued to develop his findings. He found that the organism *Mycoderma aceti* caused wine to sour, but that heating to a high temperature solved the problem. Heating substances to particular temperatures, or "pasteurization," was a major breakthrough in purifying foods.

Pasteur had shown that there was a fundamental divide between chemical phenomena and living organisms. Now that it was acknowledged that the air was teeming with bacteria, the way was clear to tackle diseases and develop immunization. Pasteur himself created a vaccine for anthrax in 1881, before tackling rabies. He was buried in the Pasteur Institute in Paris in 1895. **RP**

A Star Above Niagara

French acrobat Charles Blondin crosses the Niagara Falls on a tightrope.

○ Charles Blondin, the French acrobat, performs a tightrope walk high above the Niagara River (1859).

"The Great Blondin" was the most celebrated of all tightrope walkers. Born Jean-François Gravelet in France in 1824, he was fascinated by a circus he once saw and started practicing with a rope, using his father's fishing rod as a pole. His parents had him trained as an acrobat, and he made his first public appearance at the age of five. He called himself "Blondin" because of his fair hair.

His most famous feat was his first crossing of Niagara Falls, when he was thirty-five. The rope was pulled across the river by a rowing boat. The distance was just over 1,000 feet (305 m), and the rope's weight made it sag by some 60 feet (18 m) in the middle, which gave it a steep slope. The event was publicized in newspapers, posters, and handbills. Local hotels raised their prices, and a huge crowd of spectators gathered excitedly to watch Blondin make his crossing dressed in a purple vest, white pantaloons, and a cap. He started across at 5:15 P.M. after offering to carry a volunteer across on his back, but there were no volunteers. He took his time over what he privately considered an easy task, with a rope more than 3 inches (7.5 cm) thick. The crowds cheered as he completed the crossing in precisely 17.5 minutes.

Blondin crossed again on July 4, and lay down on the rope for a brief snooze. He later crossed with other variations—blindfolded, carrying his top-hatted manager, pushing a wheelbarrow, even on stilts. He went on performing almost until his death at age seventy-two in London in 1897. **RC**

His Soul Goes Marching On

John Brown's raid on Harpers Ferry, Virginia, fails to ignite a mass slave insurrection.

○ The musket factory of the United States Armory at Harpers Ferry was raided for weapons by John Brown and his followers.

The Kansas-Nebraska Act of 1854 allowed the inhabitants of the two new territories to decide whether to allow slavery. Slave owners from neighboring Missouri moved into Kansas, but other incomers—farmers from Kentucky, Tennessee, and elsewhere—had no slaves and no use for them, and virtual civil war broke out. The situation attracted the attention of John Brown, a devout abolitionist in his mid-fifties, who believed that slavery in the United States was delaying the second coming of Christ. Five of his sons had moved to Kansas, and in 1855 their father joined them with a supply of weapons. The next year, he led a massacre of supposed "slave hounds" at a settlement at Pottawatomie Creek, for which neither he nor anyone else was ever prosecuted.

Brown hoped to stir up a slave insurrection. He would supply slaves with weapons and lead them to a retreat in the Appalachian Mountains where, so he believed, all the slaves in the South would join him and slavery would collapse. It was in pursuit of this scheme that, with a band of fifteen whites and five blacks, he led a raid on the United States Armory at Harpers Ferry in Virginia. At the armory Brown took many local slave owners prisoner and armed their slaves. However, the next day the armory was stormed by a force of U.S. Marines, commanded by the future General Robert E. Lee. Brown was wounded, and two of his sons and eight others were killed. Taken prisoner, he was hanged, achieving immortality as an abolitionist martyr. **RC**

Natural Selection

Darwin publishes The Origin of Species, *producing an intellectual ferment.*

It was bound in green cloth, 502 pages long, and expensive at fourteen shillings. It was published by John Murray in London, with the title *On the Origin of Species by Means of Natural Selection, or the Preservation of Favoured Races in the Struggle for Life*. Only 1,250 copies were printed, and they sold out on the day of publication. Charles Darwin had written a best seller that would spark an intellectual revolution.

Darwin realized the need to explain the variations over time that occurred in animals and birds. Yet he was at his happiest doing detailed research and was

---

"I fully admit that there are very many difficulties not satisfactorily explained . . ."

Charles Darwin, on *The Origin of the Species*

---

reluctant to commit his theories to paper because he knew they would constitute intellectual dynamite.

Darwin argued that there was an intense struggle between creatures for existence. Those possessing natural advantage, making them better adapted to the environment, would be more likely to survive and breed, and pass on their advantages to offspring, which would eventually evolve into new species. To critics, he was attacking God, destroying the concept of a creator, and reducing humankind to the level of beasts. There was intense opposition to the book as well as distinguished support, prompting many acrimonious debates. Soon the evidence for evolution was steadily accumulating, but not for the mechanism of natural selection. It took modern genetics to explain how this may have worked. **RP**

Garibaldi's Italy

Garibaldi reaches Sicily on a mission to extend Italian unification.

The unification of Italy was Garibaldi's greatest venture but it almost did not take place. He originally had his heart set on wresting his hometown of Nice from the French but the architects of unity in northern Italy, Victor Emmanuel and Cavour, were discouraging. They could not stop him and might assist if he was successful, but they advised extreme caution. Nevertheless, Giuseppe Garibaldi sailed to Sicily, where a revolt against the king of Naples had broken out. On May 6, 1860, he left Genoa, with his men on board two old paddle steamers, the *Lombardo* and the *Piedmonte*. They reached Marsala on May 11. Even now the mission could have ended, for the two steamers were opposed by stronger Neapolitan vessels. Fortunately, the local commander hesitated, thinking Garibaldi was under the protection of two British warships at anchor. By the time he did fire, most of the men had been evacuated. Garibaldi's casualties comprised one man wounded in the shoulder and one dog wounded in the leg. The scene was now set for an amazing climax to the whole process of Italian unification.

Palermo fell to Garibaldi's red-shirted "Thousand"—actually there had been around 1,200 on the two vessels—and with success they gained support. Soon Sicily was his. Naples went the same way, and in October, Garibaldi transferred the territories to King Victor Emmanuel, who was crowned king of Italy the following year. As for Italy's national hero, he retired to the island of Caprera with a year's supply of macaroni and very little else. No one could be allowed to outshine the king. **RP**

◐ *Garibaldi before Capua*, a painting by Domenico Induno (1815–1878), now in Milan.

Iron Leviathan

Brunel's Great Western, *the world's largest ship, crosses the Atlantic.*

The *Great Western* had crossed the Atlantic in just fifteen days, but this success was not enough for Isambard Kingdom Brunel, and he would not rest. The north Atlantic route was now his, but what about Australia? Brunel resolved to construct a bigger, better, and faster ship. At 620 feet (189 m) long and 8,915 tons, the *Great Eastern* was just that, even if she did look like a railway station. She was powered by paddle wheels and a steel screw. Her iron hull was double-skinned, so she would surely be unsinkable.

According to the *New York Times*, "The whole career of this gigantic ship seems to have been one gigantic blunder." It was no exaggeration. There were endless financial problems. The launch was a fiasco: first the ship lurched forward, killing a man, then refused to move at all. Only several months later did she take to the water. Then, on September 9, 1859, an engine room explosion killed five men. The ship was not wrecked, as another vessel would have been, but it was the last straw for Brunel. He had already suffered a stroke, and now he died.

The *Great Eastern* left Southampton on June 17, 1860. What else would go wrong? Intrepid journalists were on board to find out. In the event, the voyage to New York was uneventful. There was a half gale in the mid-Atlantic, but only three people were reported seasick. On June 27, the docking was successful, even though the ship struck the wharf and dented it to a depth of 5 feet (1.5 m).

The *Great Eastern* did not live up to expectations, and was never a success as a passenger ship. From 1866, she was used to lay cables across the Indian and Atlantic oceans. Nevertheless, she was the world's biggest ship before the *Lusitania* (launched in 1906), and the prototype for all modern liners. **RP**

Italy Is Reunited

The first Parliament representing the whole of reunited Italy is called.

Italian reunification was principally the work of four very different men: Giuseppi Mazzini, the icy, ascetic idealist, who provided the ideology; Giuseppi Garibaldi, the charismatic patriot, who provided the military muscle; Victor Emmanuel, the king of provincial Piedmont, who became the national rallying royal figurehead; and his prime minister, Count Camillo Cavour, the wily politician, whose action toward an approved end was often devious.

The dormant cause of Italian nationalism was a country divided between Austrian occupation in the northeast, the papal states around Rome, and the Bourbons in Naples and Sicily. It was reignited by Napoleon III's conquests of Austrian territory and his encouragement of Italy's cause. In cahoots with Cavour, the French invaded northern Italy and fought the Austrians to a stalemate. They disappointed the Italians, though, by making a peace that fell short of unifying all north and central Italy.

In 1860, Garibaldi invaded Sicily with his tiny army of 1,000 "Redshirts" and liberated both the island and Naples from the Bourbons. The former republican linked up with King Victor Emmanuel outside Rome, acknowledging Piedmont's monarch as king of a united nation—with only the papal states and Venice remaining outside the new Italian polity. A parliament with representatives from all parts of Italy was called in February, and ratified the new union in March. Garibaldi led Italian troops in expelling the Austrians from Venice in 1866, and in 1871, the papal states surrendered to the new Italian national army. Italy was no longer, in the words of Austrian Chancellor Klemens Metternich "a geographical expression," but—with a little help from her friends—had made herself a nation. **NJ**

Russian Feudalism Abolished

Despite the opposition of the nobility, Tsar Alexander II signs the law emancipating the serfs in a drive toward the modernization of Russia.

Tsar Alexander II was a man of contradictions. Best remembered for his sweeping reforms—primarily the abolition of the feudal system of serfdom—his determination to cling to his autocratic power resulted in the bloody suppression of the 1863–1864 uprising in Poland, and culminated in his own assassination by revolutionaries.

Coming to the throne in the middle of the Crimean War, Alexander's determination to reform the system resulted in his bold decision to abolish serfdom outright. Alexander considered the medieval system, that made millions of Russia's peasants the literal private property of their landlords, a barrier in the path of modernization. Alexander's manifesto that abolished the system came into force on the sixth anniversary of his accession.

The other side of his mercurial personality, though, was seen two years later in his iron-fisted crushing of a Polish uprising aimed at national liberation from Russian rule, after which thousands of Poles were exiled to Siberia. The tsar's modernization of his vast realm—building railways and introducing capitalist enterprises—only served to encourage revolutionaries dissatisfied by his mild reforms. After surviving several assassination attempts—including a bomb that destroyed one whole floor of his Winter Palace—the tsar fell victim to a multiple bomb attack in St. Petersburg in March 1881, carried out by a group of young revolutionaries called "The People's Will." The fatal attack came exactly twenty years after he had signed the decree that won him the accolade "the liberator." His son Alexander III, who witnessed his father's painfully protracted death, resolved that iron reaction and repression were the only ways to deal with the revolutionary threat. **NJ**

O Alexander II, Tsar of Russia, was an active promoter of reform and was responsible for the abolition of serfdom in 1861.

"It is better to abolish serfdom from above than wait for it to abolish itself from below."

Alexander II on his manifesto

Confederates Attack Fort Sumter

The Union-held garrison at Fort Sumter falls to the new Confederacy.

O This composite of two photographs taken in April 1861 by a Confederate photographer shows damage to Fort Sumter.

> ## "Future years will never know the seething hell of the Secession war . . . "
>
> **Walt Whitman,** *Prose Works,* **1892**

Civil war in the United States probably became inevitable in 1860 when Abraham Lincoln was elected president and South Carolina seceded from the Union, followed by other Southern states the following year. A new Confederate States of America was created at a convention in Montgomery, Alabama, in February 1861, with Jefferson Davis of Mississippi as president.

For the moment, what stuck in Confederate throats was Fort Sumter in the harbor of Charleston, South Carolina, which was held for the Union government in Washington. With a garrison of around seventy soldiers commanded by Major Robert Anderson, it was not remotely a military threat to the new Confederacy, but it was a challenge to southern pride. The Charleston authorities refused to sell the fort any more food and on March 5, the day after his inauguration in Washington, President Lincoln was told that the garrison would starve unless supplies arrived not later than April 15. He responded by sending an expedition to carry food and supplies to the fort by sea.

Jefferson Davis now ordered the fort to surrender, but Anderson refused. At 4:30 A.M., April 12, Confederate forces began bombarding the fort. After thirty-four hours—with his ammunition and food supplies almost exhausted—Anderson surrendered. The Stars and Stripes banner was hauled down, and the garrison marched out with the honors of war. No lives were lost on either side.

Neither Lincoln nor Davis had wanted to be the first to strike, but Lincoln now called for 75,000 volunteers to put down the "insurrection" in the South, and on May 6, the Confederate Congress declared a state of war. The "War Between the States" had begun. **RC**

Michaux Introduces the Velocipede

A Parisian blacksmith develops the most efficient form of transport known to humans.

The two-wheeled hobbyhorse or *draisienne* (named after its inventor Baron Karl von Drais), astride which riders sat and propelled themselves by pushing their feet along on the ground, had been known since the late 1810s, but by the middle of the century remained a novelty item. In 1839, a Scottish blacksmith called Kirkpatrick Macmillan designed a revolutionary system with pedals driving the rear wheel, but his invention did not catch on.

Then, in 1861, Pierre Michaux—or, it is sometimes claimed, Pierre Lallemont in Nancy, eastern France—added pedals to allow the rider to turn the front wheel directly. He called the machine the "velocipede," and it is generally considered to be the first true bicycle. In Michaux's original design, the frame was made of cast iron. Lallemont, who worked for Michaux briefly, preferred wrought iron, which proved stronger and more effective. He emigrated to the United States in 1865, and took out a patent for the velocipede in November 1866, but failed to find a manufacturer to take on the invention. He returned to France two years later.

The velocipede's invention led to the first brief craze for cycling across Europe, and Michaux mass-produced machines to meet the demand, producing 200 a day at one stage. The new machines came to be popularly known as "boneshakers." This nickname came about as riding them was extremely uncomfortable because of their iron and wood construction and lack of springs. Cycle races were held, including, in 1869, one over the 75 miles (120 km) from Paris to Rouen, which was won in less than eleven hours. But the craze soon passed. The Franco-Prussian War of 1870 set other priorities for continental ironworkers, including Michaux, and the focus for cycle design moved to Britain. **PF**

○ An 1869 watercolor of the Michaux velocipede, made of cast iron and with pedals that turned the front wheel directly.

> ## *"Even the fleas would desert [the coyote] for a velocipede."*
>
> **Mark Twain, *Roughing It*, 1871**

Royal Typhoid Tragedy

The death of Prince Albert begins a forty-year mourning period for Queen Victoria.

On December 1, 1861, Prince Albert, husband of Britain's Queen Victoria, felt unwell and complained of being so weak that he could hardly hold a pen. The following day, the royal physician Dr. William Jenner, although insisting there was "no cause for alarm," said he expected a fever to break out soon.

The fever duly began, but there was every cause for alarm. Typhoid fever, caused by contaminated water, was no respecter of persons, and in the prince consort it claimed its most august victim. Saturday December 14 was for Victoria the "dreadful day." In the morning, she was alarmed that Albert's eyes were so bright and his breathing was so rapid. In the afternoon, aware the end was close, she bent over him and whispered, in German, "It is your little wife." She asked him to kiss her and he could scarcely do so. By the evening, his breathing was less labored but his hands were cold. Victoria was kneeling beside him, holding his left hand, while members of the family and doctors were clustered around the bed. Albert took two or three long breaths and it was all over.

He died at age forty-two and had been married to Queen Victoria for twenty-one years. Some had feared that, as prince of tiny Saxe-Coburg, he had married Victoria for her money. But he proved himself intelligent and industrious, a good administrator and a discriminating patron of the arts. He was undoubtedly a devoted family man, and Victoria doted on him. She said, "It is like losing half of one's body and soul, torn forcibly away."

Politicians were quick to repackage the queen as the glorious symbol of British imperial majesty, but Victoria never got over the death of her beloved Albert and dressed in mourning black for the rest of her long life. **RP**

Home Sweet Home

The Homestead Act prompts a mass migration to the Midwest.

In the 1840s and 1850s, growing numbers of pioneers and their families moved west of the Missouri River, creating small farms and living in sod huts, made of turf, until they could build themselves log cabins. Senator Thomas Hart Benton of Missouri campaigned year in and year out for cheap land grants for small homesteaders. The idea was taken up by a leading Democrat, Stephen A. Douglas, but it foundered on the opposition of the southern states. Small farmers did not need slaves, and the South saw new nonslave states in the West as an unwelcome threat to the whole institution.

The Republican Party appropriated the initiative and after the North and South had gone to war, Congress in Washington passed the Homestead Act. The act offered any U.S. citizen 160 acres (65 ha) of land from the public domain, free or virtually free, after five years of continuous residence. It also allowed them to buy the land on the cheap at $1.25 an acre after only six months, which meant that speculators could buy up huge acreages through hirelings pretending to be farmers. Congress also passed acts that provided 130 million acres (52 million ha) for transcontinental railroads.

These measures stimulated mass migration into the heart of the country and the development of the modern Midwest, as farms and towns rapidly multiplied from the Missouri to the Rockies. The effect on the Native Americans would be drastic, but between 1870 and 1920, the number of U.S. farms swelled from 2.7 million to 6.5 million, and the average acreage remained small at around 150 acres (60 ha). The 1860s measures also helped to give the Republican Party a dominant position in U.S. politics for fifty years. **RC**

Massive Casualties on Northern Soil

The Battle of Antietam sees the largest loss of life in the American Civil War and the worst losses for a day's fighting in U.S. military history.

In the summer of 1862, the Confederacy launched an offensive from Virginia under the command of General Robert E. Lee, who moved north to cross the Potomac River into Maryland. He intended to invade Pennsylvania, but his advance ended with the bloodiest battle of the entire war.

Lee took up a defensive position on a low ridge behind Antietam Creek at Sharpsburg, close to the Pennsylvania border. The Union army under General George B. McClellan arrived in the afternoon and evening of September 15, but McClellan, who was a cautious man, did not realize how heavily he outnumbered his opponent. He hesitated, and the battle did not begin in earnest until dawn two days later. If McClellan had hurled his strength against the Confederates in a mass attack, he might well have carried the day, but his attacks were piecemeal and the Confederates stood them off.

There were some 4,000 dead and another 17,000 wounded. The Union casualties were greater, but because the Confederates were outnumbered, their losses were proportionally more serious. Dead, dying, and wounded bodies were strewn over the ground the next day. Lee expected another Unionist attack, but it did not come and he withdrew back into Virginia. McClellan was so slow to pursue that President Lincoln dismissed him in November. Although apparently inconclusive, Antietam led Lincoln to announce the end of slavery, and averted European recognition of the Confederacy. **RC**

◕ President Lincoln meets with Major Allan Pinkerton and General McClellan at the Union camp at Antietam.

◑ Slain soldiers of the Louisiana Brigade, who had defended the fence along Hagerstown Road during the battle.

Freeing the South's Slaves

President Lincoln issues his emancipation proclamation.

○ The meeting of Lincoln's Cabinet in 1862 at which he announced his preliminary emancipation proclamation.

The U.S. Civil War was fought to preserve the Union, but the fundamental bone of contention between the North and the South had long been slavery. In July 1862, the Congress in Washington passed an act automatically freeing the slaves of anyone supporting the Southern "rebellion." There was no way in which the legislation could be enforced. Although there was strong abolitionist feeling in the North, blacks were still widely looked down on and feared as potential cheap labor competing with whites for jobs. President Lincoln took his time, but a few days after the Confederacy's failure at Antietam, he issued a preliminary emancipation proclamation, which stated that unless the Confederate states abandoned their rebellion, on the first day of 1863, he would declare that "all persons held as slaves" in Confederate territory "are and henceforward shall be free."

The proclamation in 1863 began the process that would abolish slavery in the United States. It also authorized the enrollment of black troops into the Union forces. Fleeing black slaves were already useful to the Union armies as laborers, drivers, cooks, and nurses, and a few blacks were already serving as soldiers. From 1863, however, blacks joined the Union army and navy in large numbers. Black soldiers were organized into segregated black units, nearly always officered by whites, and were paid less than whites. The courage and efficiency they showed in some fiercely contested battles began to change Northern attitudes. **RC**

Trains Under the Ground

The first underground passenger railway marks the heyday of Victorian engineering.

🔘 A group of people make a trial trip on the world's first underground railway, the Metropolitan Railway in London.

An underground train service for London was first suggested in 1851, after the opening of the Great Northern Railway's terminus at King's Cross. But, after Great Northern showed no interest in the subterranean service, the task went to a newly formed company, the North Metropolitan Railway, and the new line was licensed in 1854.

It took a further ten years to iron out the technical hitches and to build and dig the first section of track, which ran from Farringdon to Paddington, the terminus of Isambard K. Brunel's Great Western Railway. The new track was designed to incorporate Brunel's broad-gauge trains and the narrower gauge of other London trains. Public excitement was intense and, on January 10, the new track carried 41,000 passengers on trains running every ten minutes. A new section of line, to Moorgate, was swiftly opened, and within twenty years the Metropolitan Railway—today part of the Hammersmith & City Line—was carrying a staggering 40 million passengers a year. By 1884, a "round London" ring line, the Circle, had been completed.

The earliest trains were open carriages, pulled by steam locomotives, and among the first passengers was the prime minister, William Gladstone. The first deep-level track, now part of the Northern Line, opened in 1890. London's Underground—known as "The Tube"—was soon copied in other capitals, notably Moscow and Paris, and a new era of speed and mobility in urban transportation was born. **NJ**

The Shock of the New

The "losers' exhibition" liberated French art and boosted the Impressionists.

○ A detail of *Le Déjeuner sur l'Herbe*, 1863, by Édouard Manet, at the Musée d'Orsay in Paris.

The French artistic world had long been dominated by the annual *Salon* in Paris, set up by the French Academy of Fine Arts in 1667. To have one's work exhibited there was a hallmark of artistic success and a guarantee of financial reward. Such an institution would weed out unworthy works, and yet, at the same time, might well act as a break on innovation.

In 1863, more than half of the 5,000 works submitted were rejected by the jury. Emperor Napoleon III, who liked to appear liberal, paid a visit to the *Salon*, and pronounced the rejected works as good as those that had been accepted. He ordered that they be exhibited in the nearby Palais de l'Industrie, as the *Salon des Refusés*. Many rejected artists feared the wrath of the jury or the ridicule of the public, but others took up the challenge. Entry was via a turnstile from the official *Salon*, as if, noted one commentator, "one was entering the chamber of horrors at Madame Tussaud's."

More than 7,000 visitors turned up on the first day of the exhibition. They were able to see works by Manet, Whistler, Pissarro, Cézanne, and others. The most controversial was Manet's *Le Déjeuner sur l'Herbe*, a scene of liberated bohemian life. Some critics loathed it, seeing its realism as the opposite of art and a threat to the moral order. Others championed its freshness. The exhibition delivered a blow to the authority of the *Salon*, and set a precedent for more exhibitions, including eight by the Impressionists. Art was liberated to take new directions. **RP**

Turning Point in the Civil War

The Union army stops the Confederacy heading north at the Battle of Gettysburg.

○ John Richards's painting *The Battle of Gettysburg, July 1–3, 1863*.

In late spring 1863, the Confederacy launched a formidable attack on the North. Robert E. Lee's army of northern Virginia defeated the invading army of the Potomac in thick forest at Chancellorsville, Virginia—but Lee lost his right-hand man, Stonewall Jackson, shot by mistake by his own sentries. Lee moved on north into western Pennsylvania, intending to seize the crucial railroad junction at Harrisburg (to disrupt Union supply lines) and perhaps go on to take Philadelphia or even Washington, D.C., itself. The opposing Union army was commanded by General George D. Meade. Neither army knew exactly where the other was until they bumped into each other at Gettysburg, not far from the site of the Battle of Antietam. The Confederates drove the Union soldiers out of town, but unfortunately drove them south to an excellent defensive position along a ridge.

The Confederates were outnumbered by about 90,000 to 75,000. The situation was the reverse of Antietam as Lee launched a series of attacks uphill, which the Union army withstood for two days. Both sides fought with courage, and the casualties were appalling. Altogether some 8,000 were killed and 27,000 wounded, roughly equally divided between the two sides. In pouring rain, with both sides exhausted, Lee led his army away, back to the South.

The battle is considered a crucial turning point in the war, but that was not at all obvious at the time. There were many more battles to come and many more lives to be lost. **RC**

"Four Score and Seven Years Ago . . ."

President Lincoln delivers the Gettysburg Address, one of history's greatest (and shortest) speeches.

Despite victories, weariness with the war was growing in the North, and there was fierce resentment of conscription. In mid-July, hundreds of people were killed in rioting in New York City, largely by Irish working men. It was set off by anger over the draft system, but focused mainly on blacks, who were hanged from lampposts, and an orphanage for black children was burned to the ground.

President Lincoln had this in mind when he was invited to speak at the dedication of the Gettysburg battleground as a memorial to the dead. The program included music, hymns, and prayers, and the main speech was made by Edward Everett, a former governor of Massachusetts. He spoke for two hours, but was overshadowed by Lincoln, who delivered one of the greatest orations in history in less than two minutes and in fewer than 300 words. Beginning, "Four score and seven years ago," the speech briefly stated what the war was being fought for and defined the fundamental purpose of the United States.

The founders of the Union, Lincoln said, "brought forth a new nation, conceived in Liberty, and dedicated to the proposition that all men are created equal." The brave men who died at Gettysburg "gave their lives that that nation might live." He concluded, "that we here highly resolve that these dead shall not have died in vain; that this nation, under God, shall have a new birth of freedom; and that government of the people, by the people, for the people, shall not perish from the earth." **RC**

◐ A manuscript of the first page of Lincoln's famous Gettysburg Address in his own handwriting.

◐ A distant photograph of Lincoln attending the dedication of Gettysburg National Cemetery, where he gave his address.

"Chinese Gordon"

The defeat of the Taiping rebellion secures Qing rule in China.

The loss of life in Nanjing was enormous, but then the whole rebellion, begun fourteen years earlier, had seen around 20 million people slaughtered. By the third and final day, some 100,000 had been killed in vicious street-by-street fighting. The original rebel leader, Hong Xiuquan, the self-styled brother of Jesus Christ, charged with establishing Taiping (the "Heavenly Kingdom of Great Peace") at the expense of the ineffectual Qing dynasty and the rapacious foreigners, had held Nanjing as his capital for a decade, but had died of food poisoning the previous month. The victorious imperial forces owed a good deal to the British who fought on their side, especially to the successes achieved by Charles Gordon and the "Ever Victorious Army."

The rebels had been on the defensive from 1860, when imperial forces were reorganized by Zeng Guofan and Li Hongzhang. Now they had help from the Europeans wishing to protect their financial stake in the country. Gordon had volunteered to join British forces in China in 1860, and when the U.S. creator of the "Ever Victorious Army" died, Li persuaded the British that Gordon should take command in March 1863. He imposed harsh discipline, with the death penalty for drunkenness. Leading his men from the front, brandishing a rattan cane, he won a series of victories that, in turn, made possible imperial success in Nanjing. He was awarded the Order of the Yellow Jacket, and dubbed "Chinese Gordon".

One of the most bloody conflicts in human history was not entirely over, for more than 250,000 Taiping warriors were still at large. The success of the Imperial dynasty, however, was assured. Qing domination of China, plus the continuing influence of the Europeans, was secure for decades to come. **RP**

Help the Wounded

The Geneva Convention of 1864 aids the work of the International Red Cross.

In 1864, the Swiss government was host to delegates from sixteen countries. They met in Geneva, and on August 22, a dozen of them adopted the Geneva Convention "for the Amelioration of the Condition of the Wounded in Armies in the Field." Now, for the first time, there was a statement of rules, legally binding on the signatories, guaranteeing neutrality and protection for wounded soldiers and medical personnel on the battlefield. A white flag with a red cross would identify the neutrality of hospitals, ambulances, and evacuation centers. For the Swiss businessman Henri Dunant, it was a dream come true.

In June 1859, Dunant had witnessed the aftermath of the Battle of Solferino between France and Austria. No medical help was available, and thousands lay maimed on the battlefield. For several days he did what he could to help the wounded. Back home in Geneva, he wrote *A Memory of Solferino*, advocating the formation of voluntary relief organizations to nurse wounded soldiers in wars. In 1863, he helped set up the International Committee of the Red Cross to achieve this aim. He also lobbied for international treaties to agree to guarantee the protection of noncombatants, a proposal the Swiss government took up successfully the following year.

Dunant so neglected his business affairs that he was declared bankrupt in 1867, and thereafter he lived in great poverty. Yet he was awarded the Nobel Peace Prize in 1901, and in the twentieth century his work bore remarkable fruit. By its close, the International Movement of the Red Cross and the Red Crescent was a flourishing institution, helping to prevent human suffering in peace as well as war, and the fourth Geneva Convention had been signed by more than 190 states. **RP**

International Brotherhood

The First International is founded to hasten the communist revolution.

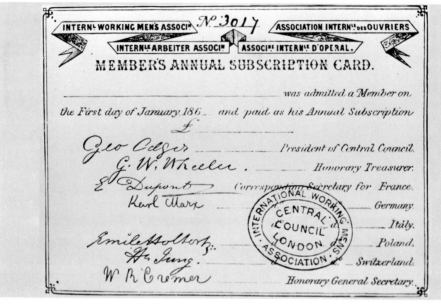

⊘ A membership card of the International Workingmen's Association (also known as the First International) founded by Karl Marx.

Karl Marx was convinced that the days of capitalism were numbered. Proletarians, once they had nothing to lose but their chains, would rise up in a bloody revolution. With this in view, Marx attended a meeting of Europe's socialists and communists at St. Martin's Hall in Covent Garden, London, the city he had made his home since 1849. Working men had to unite, but so too did left-wing intellectuals. Hence he approved of a speech by Professor Edward Spencer Beesley advocating a union of the world's workers.

Trade unionists spoke in favor, and the meeting unanimously decided to found the International Workingmen's Association, or First International, with its center in London. The committee had twenty-one elected members, including Marx himself, who also became a member of the sub-committee charged with drafting the program and membership rules of the new body. They met at his home, and it was soon clear that he was the dominant figure. He wrote the *Address to the Working Classes* that set out the International's raison d'être, and he was elected to every succeeding General Council.

To found the First International was easy. To make it work effectively, as groups representing different doctrinal positons clashed and argued, was extremely difficult. Eventually, after personally clashing again and again with the anarchist Mikhail Bakunin, Marx recognized that it was impossible. The International came to an end in 1876. A Second International was formed in 1889, but fared little better. **RP**

Lee Accepts Defeat

Robert E. Lee surrenders at Appomattox, bringing to a close the American Civil War.

○ Soldiers camp in front of the Appomattox County Courthouse in the town where General Lee surrendered to General Grant.

At the end of March 1865, the Union army of the Potomac under Ulysses S. Grant began an offensive against Robert E. Lee's Confederate army at Petersburg in Virginia. Lee tried to dodge away to the West, but Grant prevented him. Lee's army was short of men, ammunition, and equipment, and another Union army was rapidly advancing from the south. On April 7, Grant sent Lee a message suggesting he surrender to avoid further bloodshed. The two commanders met in the McLean House in the village of Appomattox Courthouse, at about 1:00 P.M. Surprisingly, they took to each other and talked pleasantly before getting down to business. Grant's terms were generous. He did not want to humiliate his opponents, but to bring the South back into the Union fold. Lee's soldiers were to lay down their arms and return to their homes. No further action would be taken against them. They could keep their horses, and the Union army shared its rations with them.

After accepting the terms, Lee stepped out on to the porch and mounted his horse. Grant raised his hat to him. Lee returned the salute and rode to break the news to his men. The other Confederate armies soon surrendered. About 360,000 Union soldiers and some 260,000 Confederate soldiers had been killed, but the North's far larger population had given it a crucial advantage. The more industrialized North was far better equipped than the South. Inevitably, the longer the conflict lasted, the less chance the Confederacy had of winning it. **RC**

Death to the Chief

President Lincoln is assassinated after the North achieves victory in the Civil War.

Five days after the Confederate surrender at Appomattox, President Abraham Lincoln, the chief architect of the North's victory, was murdered. The president had endured a nightmare some nights previously in which he saw a shrouded corpse in the White House and was told that the president was dead. He shrugged it off and later told his wife, Mary, "We must both be more cheerful in future." On Good Friday evening, they were due to attend a performance of a comedy, *The American Cousin,* at Ford's Theater. Mary was reluctant to go, but Lincoln persuaded her, saying he needed a good laugh.

Meanwhile, the actor John Wilkes Booth, a fanatical Southern supporter, had organized a conspiracy to kill the president and other leading members of the administration. The Lincolns arrived at the theater to a standing ovation and the strains of "Hail to the Chief." They took their places in a box, but their bodyguard slipped away to watch the play. Booth sneaked up to the box, went in, and fired a single shot into Lincoln's head. He then jumped down onto the stage and shouted the motto of the state of Virginia, *"Sic semper tyrannis"* ("Thus ever to tyrants!"), before escaping from the theater.

The unconscious president was taken to a boardinghouse across the street. He never regained consciousness and died hours later at 7:22 A.M. on April 15. There was a huge outpouring of grief and vengeful fury in the North. Booth was immediately hunted down and shot while resisting arrest. His fellow conspirators were mostly rounded up and hanged. Lincoln was succeeded by his vice president, Andrew Johnson of Tennessee, but with Lincoln went the nation's best hope for reconciliation between the North and South and between black and white Americans. **RC**

○ John Wilkes Booth photographed in the years preceding his assassination of President Abraham Lincoln.

◐ Official escorts stand alongside Lincoln's body, displayed in an open coffin for public viewing inside New York City Hall.

"And in the end it's not the years in your life that count. It's the life in your years."

Attributed to President Lincoln

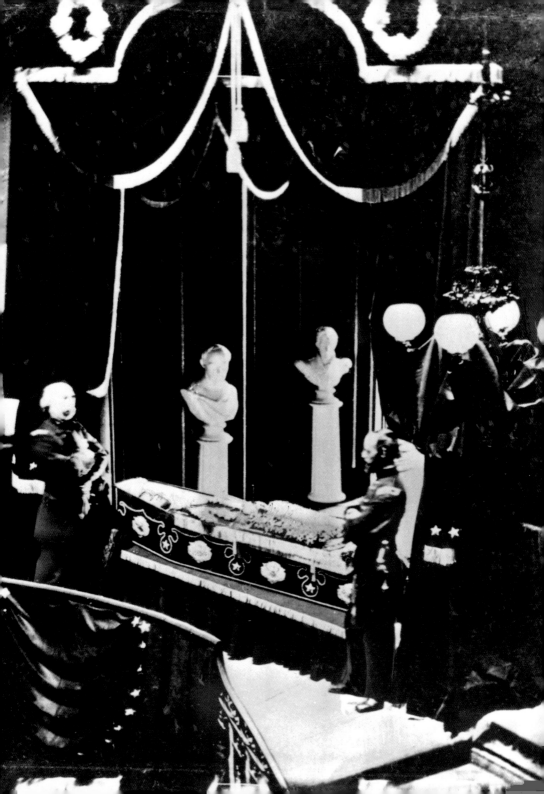

War and Peace Published

The publication of the first part of Leo Tolstoy's Russian epic War and Peace *transforms Russian and European literature.*

Leo Tolstoy devoted five years to completing the first part of *War and Peace*. He drafted the manuscript seven times, until, in 1865, Book I appeared serially. The English translation came in 1866, and all six volumes were published in 1869. An epic on a human scale, it revolutionized Russian and European literature. Nobody had seen a work like this before, in which nearly 500 characters, from serfs to tsars, were woven in multiple storylines, behind a backdrop of bloody battlefields, sophisticated soirées, and peasant homes. To this, Tolstoy added his own penetrating insight into the human condition and voiced his theme of free will versus predestination.

The story portrays two Russian households—the Rostovs, impoverished county squires, and the *noblesse oblige* Bolkonskys—during Napoleon's invasion of Russia in 1812. Tolstoy wrote from experience, having served in the Crimean War in an artillery regiment during the 1850s. The battle scenes vividly portray the chaos and carnage of war, and seem to argue Tolstoy's fatalism that great currents of history sweep mankind along. One man who was inspired by the book, and opened up a correspondence with Tolstoy, was Mahatma Gandhi, who went on to adopt his doctrine of pacifism and nonresistance. Like other Russian aristocrats, Tolstoy owned serfs, but he involved himself in their social conditions and education on his vast estate in the Volga Steppes. Later in life he attempted to give up all his worldly possessions to lead a simpler life. **JJH**

○ The great Russian writer Leo Tolstoy in Yasnaya Polyana, the home where he was born and lived until his death.

○ Alexander Apsit's 1964 illustration for Leo Tolstoy's novel *War and Peace*.

Slavery Abolished

Amending the U.S. Constitution protects the rights of former slaves.

In September 1862, during the long, exhausting, and tragically violent U.S. Civil War, in which slavery had been the defining issue, President Lincoln issued his decisive Emancipation Proclamation. It declared free all those slaves who lived in states that formed part of the Confederacy and effectively banned slavery in the North as well. It was, however, a presidential decree and was only partial in its operation. It did not free slaves in the border states of Kentucky, Missouri, Maryland, Delaware, and West Virginia, nor in Tennessee, which was already under Union control.

Several of the exempt states undertook to abolish slavery while the war continued. Kentucky and Delaware, however, held out. Slavery could not legally be abolished until the Constitution had been amended, and Lincoln made it a large part of his presidential reelection campaign in 1864 that he would amend the constitution to make abolition permanent. It would be the first amendment since 1804. He forced the measure through Congress early in 1865 and, despite his assassination, the states ratified the measure. By the time Georgia accepted it on December 6, twenty-seven of the thirty-six states had ratified it, the requisite three-quarters of the states had signed, and, as Secretary of State William Henry Seward proclaimed on December 18, 1865, slavery was finally abolished in the United States and its territories. Kentucky, though, where there were still 40,000 slaves in 1865, had refused to ratify and did not do so until 1976. Delaware held out until 1901, whereas Mississippi did not ratify it until 1995.

The Thirteenth Amendment and two further amendments dealing with the protection of the civil and voting rights of former slaves are together known as the Reconstruction Amendments. **PF**

Prussia Gains Control

The Austrian army suffers a crushing defeat at the Battle of Königgrätz.

In the summer of 1866, some 400,000 men prepared for battle. At stake was the future of Germany. At that time, thirty-nine states constituted a loose German Confederation, dominated by the Austrian Empire and the kingdom of Prussia. Prussian Chancellor Otto von Bismarck maneuvered Austria into a war he was confident the Prussian army could win.

The highly professional Prussian general staff used railways to deploy a mass of conscript troops at unprecedented speed. The Prussians advanced as three armies, two committed to a frontal assault and

> ## "I would never seek foreign conflicts just to get over domestic difficulties."
>
> **Prussian Chancellor Otto von Bismarck, 1862**

the third maneuvering to attack from the flank. The frontal advance was a desperate business, and had Austrian commander Ludwig Benedek been less hesitant, he might have delivered a decisive counterattack. But the Prussian soldiers were armed with Dreyse rifles, capable of five times the rate of fire of the Austrian arms. The Austrians had already suffered heavy casualties when the Prussian assault on their flank struck home. From then onward the issue was beyond doubt. The Austrians lost 45,000 men, compared with 9,000 Prussian casualties. Austria was in no condition to fight on, and an armistice was arranged. The peace treaty gave Prussia control of northern Germany, and excluded Austria from German affairs. A giant step had been taken toward a Prussian-dominated united Germany. **RG**

Weaknesses of Capitalism Exposed

Karl Marx publishes the first volume of Das Kapital.

Das Kapital.

Kritik der politischen Oekonomie.

Von

Karl Marx.

Erster Band.

Buch I: Der Produktionsprocess des Kapitals.

Das Recht der Uebersetzung wird vorbehalten.

Hamburg
Verlag von Otto Meissner.
1867.
New-York: L. W. Schmidt. 24 Barclay-Street.

◐ The title page for Karl Marx's extensive *Das Kapital*, published in Hamburg in 1867.

"*Capital is dead labor, which, vampire-like, lives only by sucking living labor.*"

Karl Marx, *Das Kapital*

In 1867, the first volume of Marx's *Das Kapital* (*Capital*) was published in German, well behind schedule. The book was an extensive treatise on the political economy, in which Marx declared that the driving force behind capitalism was the exploitation and alienation of labor. Marx argued that employers paid workers the market value for their labor in producing commodities whose final value in the marketplace exceeded the value given to the labor force. This surplus value was taken by the employers because they claimed that, as the owners of capital, they were entitled to the profit. This increased the amount of capital held by the employers, and thus perpetuated the conditions whereby capitalism could continue the exploitation of the labor force.

Das Kapital focused on the structure and contradictions within the capitalist system, rather than class antagonisms. As such, it does not advocate revolution. Instead, Marx argued that if the right conditions prevail, successive crises of growth, followed by collapse, followed by growth can create the conditions for revolution, or at the very least, transition to a new mode of production. Marx claimed that *Das Kapital* was an attempt to analyze the political economy to the point where it could be dialectically represented, and thus provide a scientific justification for the modern labor movement. His aim was to show how capitalism was the natural precursor of a new, socialist form of production in which the workers took control of the means of production.

Although Marx died before subsequent volumes of *Das Kapital* were published in 1883 and 1885, the book can still be seen as the scientific culmination of the arguments he proposed in his most famous work, *The Communist Manifesto*, published in 1848, and written with Friedrich Engels. **TB**

A Lamb to the Slaughter

Emperor Maximilian of Mexico is murdered after a failed coup.

The younger brother of the emperor of Austria, the well-meaning Archduke Maximilian, arrived in Mexico with his young wife, Carlota, in 1864 to be crowned emperor. Quite wrongly, he believed that he had been accepted by what he henceforth regarded as "his people." In reality, he had been infiltrated into the country with the support of a French army, in furtherance of French imperialist ambitions, and in cahoots with rich Mexican landowners and the Roman Catholic Church. They wanted the new emperor to get rid of President Benito Juarez, who was threatening their wealth and power.

To the outrage of his backers, Maximilian showed a dismaying concern for the well-being of the downtrodden peasantry, and refused to undo Juarez's reforms. The French army, however, almost drove Juarez across the U.S. border into Texas before the U.S. government demanded their withdrawal under the Monroe Doctrine. In 1866, Napoleon III of France announced that his troops would be withdrawn. Carlota traveled to Europe to plead for help from him, but in vain. The French left the following year. Maximilian would not abdicate and run, though, because he thought such action dishonorable. His army of 9,000 men was hemmed in by Juarista forces at Queretaro, north of Mexico City, and starved and betrayed into surrender.

Maximilian was held prisoner in a convent. An escape was planned involving one of his courtiers, the American-born Princess Agnes zu Salm-Salm, who was supposed to seduce a certain Colonel Palacios. She failed and so did the plot. Maximilian, who was thirty-four, was sentenced to death and executed early in the morning by firing squad. Juarez returned to Mexico City the following month, and Mexico returned to being a republic. **RC**

○ When Napoleon III withdrew his troops from Mexico in 1867, Maximilian was ousted and eventually executed.

" . . . nobody has any right to lick Mexico except the United States."

Artemus Ward, 1865

Eastern Ethics, Western Technology

The Meiji Restoration begins the modernization of Japan.

🔾 *Reading a Newspaper* (1877) by Yoshitoshi; the text of this satirical cartoon compares the woman to a cat in heat.

"All classes shall be united in vigorously carrying out the administration of affairs."

Meiji Charter Oath, April 1868

The forced opening of Japan to the world by commodore Perry's U.S. naval squadron in 1853 was followed by fifteen years of political conflict between traditionalists and modernizers. In the 1850s, Japan was still a feudal society under the military government of the Tokugawa shoguns of Edo (Tokyo). Honored but purely ceremonial figures, the emperors reigned in powerless serenity from the imperial palace at Kyoto.

The failure to prevent the U.S. violation of Japan's official isolation began to undermine the authority of the shogunate. The financial burden of strengthening coastal defenses and the effect of opening Japan's economy to foreign trade caused increasing hardship, and a spate of rebellions broke out. In 1863, the shogun Iemochi was forced to attend the imperial court to seek the emperor's support for his rule, the first time any shogun had done so for over 200 years. In late 1867, the shogun resigned and samurai rebels, armed with Western rifles, overthrew the military government and returned power to the young Emperor Meiji, who would reign until 1912. The coup was formalized by imperial proclamation on January 3, 1868. Characterized by the slogan of Sakuma Shozan, "Eastern ethics and Western technology," the restoration of imperial rule was followed by an avalanche of change. Feudal jurisdictions and the privileged status of the samurai were abolished. A modern education system, a conscript army and navy, a written constitution, Western clothing, electricity, railways, income tax, postal service, and parliamentary government were all adopted within twenty years. Westernization was enforced from above by a government that remained autocratic and militaristic and that employed the ancient Japanese Shinto religion to create a divine emperor cult. **JH**

Classification of the Chemical World

Mendeleev publishes his periodic table of elements.

Dmitri Ivanovich Mendeleev formally presented his periodic table of elements for the first time to the Russian Chemical Society in 1869. However, some members ridiculed his prediction that there would be discoveries of more radioactive liquids. Mendeleev had the last laugh, though, when gallium was discovered in 1875 and germanium in 1886. These discoveries confirmed Mendeleev's theory of element periodicity.

Mendeleev's table demonstrated recurring, or periodic, properties in chemical elements. The elements were listed in order of increasing atomic number, with elements demonstrating similar chemical properties arranged in vertical columns.

Although Mendeleev is credited with being the creator of the first version of the periodic table, at least two other scientists had also been working on their own tables of elements. Lothar Meyer published a proposal, in 1864, describing twenty-eight elements. Unlike Mendeleev, Meyer did not use his table to predict new elements. Then, in 1865, John Newlands published his Law of Octaves, in which he noticed that elements with similar physical and chemical properties occurred at intervals of eight, leading him to use the analogy of octaves in music. However, Newland's idea failed on two counts: it was not valid for elements with masses higher than calcium, and there was no space to accommodate new elements, such as the noble gases.

The periodic table is an important discovery of modern chemistry, providing a valuable framework with which to classify and compare the behavior of chemical compounds. Continually revised as new elements are discovered and new theories developed, the table has also found important applications in many branches of science and industry. **TB**

○ A photograph of Dmitri Mendeleev (1834–1907), taken in the 1900s at the close of his distinguished career in chemistry.

"Atomic weight belongs not to coal or diamond, but to carbon."

Dmitri Mendeleev on his periodic table

The Golden Spike

Two tracks meet in Utah and create the first transcontinental railroad in the States.

◯ The driving of the golden spike ceremony in Utah signified completion of the first transcontinental route.

It has been suggested that the railroads played as important a role in the development of the United States as the political parties. They were certainly a key factor in making a single united country out of such a vast area. The first railroads were built in the 1820s and 1830s, and by the 1850s were moving west from the east coast. In the 1860s, the Central Pacific Railroad began to build east from California and the Union Pacific Railroad west from Omaha, respectively employing armies of Chinese and Irish laborers.

The single most dramatic moment in U.S. railroad history came when the two lines met at Promontory Summit in Utah. A golden spike had been made to complete the final link. It was to be driven into a special tie of California laurel. On the day, the last rail was laid by eight Chinese laborers, to loud cheers. Two locomotives, Union Pacific No. 119 and Central Pacific No. 60, drew up facing each other, with only the width of a single tie between them. The golden spike was tapped gently into the hole by the head of Central Pacific, Leland Stanford, to create the United States's first transcontinental railroad.

Estimates of how many people witnessed the event range up to about 3,000. The golden spike and the laurel tie were removed immediately and replaced with a normal tie and an iron spike.

At 12:47 P.M., the single word "done" was sent around the country by telegraph. The Golden Spike National Historic Site, which has working replicas of the two locomotives, was established in 1957. **RC**

Inauguration of the Suez Canal

The dream of a new, shorter trade route between Europe and Asia becomes a reality.

○ A fleet of ships enters the Suez Canal at its inauguration, November 17, 1869.

The realization of the Suez project, by which a canal was made linking the Red Sea and the Mediterranean, was the work of one man, the visionary former French diplomat Ferdinand de Lesseps. De Lesseps was inspired by reading accounts of attempts to cut through the desert in the Ancient World, and when a former acquaintance, Said Pasha, succeeded as *Khedive* ("ruler") of Egypt he hastened out to secure permission to realize the dream. Granted a charter within days, de Lesseps set about raising funds, with the aid of a French national loan.

De Lesseps himself turned the first spadeful of sand in 1859, and more than ten years later—thanks to the forced labor of thousands of Egyptian peasants— the canal was completed at Suez. Some 101 miles

(163 km) long, the canal slashed trade times between Europe and the Near and Far East, cutting the need for voyaging around the South African Cape. The canal was opened with a great international celebration in November 1869.

Despite initial British opposition to the French operation, Prime Minister Benjamin Disraeli used Rothschild money to buy the Egyptian government's shares in the canal for Britain, which then became a joint Anglo-French enterprise. The Suez Canal continued to enrich Britain and France until it was nationalized by President Gamal Abdul Nasser in 1956. Immobilized by the Suez War of that year, and by the 1967 and 1973 Arab-Israeli wars, the canal is now once again an international waterway. **NJ**

Spiritual Truth or Temporal Tactic?

The doctrine of papal infallibility reinforces the pope's battle against the forces of democracy and liberalism.

Conform not to the standards of this world, St. Paul had advised. Pope Pius IX had no intention of doing so, especially when this world was increasingly secular, nationalistic, and anti-papal. Already, in 1864, he had condemned such "pernicious" errors as "progress . . . and modern civilization," and now his First Vatican Council added to the pope's antiliberal armory the doctrine of papal infallibility. This is an easily misunderstood dogma. It does not mean that the pope is always right, but that when he is speaking specifically *ex cathedra*—in the discharge of his office as shepherd and teacher of all Christians, and by virtue of his supreme apostolic authority—on matters of faith or morals, his view is binding. The doctrine was promulgated on July 18, 1870, amid events that would rob the pope of much of his authority in Rome, not as a new discovery but as the statement of a timeless truth.

Pius had become pope in 1846. He was a surprise choice. As Austria's leader Metternich joked, "We were prepared for anything, except a liberal pope." But his liberalism was ended by the violent revolutions of 1848 and the loss of the Papal States to the new kingdom of Italy in 1861. The withdrawal of the French garrison from Rome in July 1870 soon made the Eternal City the new Italian capital.

Some German-speaking Catholics preferred schism, but the majority of Catholics accepted the doctrine, which was in fact seldom used. The pope's temporal power had waned, so that in 1871 he occupied only 109 acres (44 ha) in Rome, but his spiritual power over the faithful had increased. **RP**

◑ A full-length portrait of Pope Pius IX, *c.*1860, before the loss of papal land and power that led to the First Vatican Council.

Bismarck Triumphs

The proclamation of the new Germany creates Europe's most powerful nation.

At noon, to a roll of military drums, William I of Prussia entered, followed by other German rulers and generals. There was a short religious ceremony, after which his prime minister, Otto von Bismarck, read out a proclamation and it was all over. William I of Prussia was now William I, the German emperor, and Bismarck was the German chancellor. The proclamation of the new German Empire did not take place in Germany but, paradoxically, on foreign soil, in the Hall of Mirrors at Versailles, France. In fact, the new German state, although talked about for decades, was hastily improvised during Prussia's recent war with France. It was only the French declaration of war in July 1870, which unleashed intense nationalistic feelings, that enabled Bismarck to secure acceptance of the new Reich, for neither the new emperor, nor the German princes, nor the German liberals wanted what they were getting.

William I of Prussia doubted the new imperial title was a step up in the world. Certainly he would not accept the crown from the gutter—meaning from the people—and Bismarck had to bribe the Bavarian king into offering it to him. Even then, he would not speak to Bismarck on the day of the ceremony. As for the princes, inevitably they would be sacrificing power, although at least under the new federal structure they would still be recognized as princes. Perhaps the liberals got the least: there would be universal suffrage and the appearance of democracy, but real power lay with the emperor's ministers, not the parliamentarians.

The unification of Germany was of momentous historical significance. Unified by war, the new state became a politically immature military colossus that continued to seek expansion in Europe. **RP**

Communards Defeated

The two-months-old Commune of Paris is destroyed by the French government.

In the eastern suburbs of Paris on May 28, 1871, a solitary defender fired his final rounds and walked away as French government troops took possession of the last of the communards' barricades in the city.

Out of the confusion of the defeat of Napoleon III the previous year, the siege of Paris by the Prussian army, and the uncertainty about the future government of the country, sections of the population of Paris had created their own city government, the Commune de Paris, on March 28. Harking back to the revolutions of 1792 and 1845, with their Jacobin,

---

"This is all-out war, between parasites and workers, exploiters and producers."

Central committee of the National Guard

---

socialist, and anarchist origins, the commune made a new kind of government, introducing women's suffrage and the separation of church and state.

Such activity, revolutionary in spirit and organized by a self-proclaimed city authority, was not acceptable to the French government. The unity of France and the authority of its ruling class were threatened. Its leader, Alphonse Thiers, ordered the army to take the city. Amid violent fighting between government and communards, parts of the city were set on fire. Hostages were taken on both sides, and many were shot. After the surrender the authorities took revenge. Some 25,000 communards were executed; many were deported. Such bloodshed, unprecedented in modern French history, polarized the left and right in French politics for several generations. **NK**

Chicago on Fire

The Windy City begins to burn and the blaze becomes unstoppable.

One of the most devastating disasters of the nineteenth century, the fire of Chicago began on October 8. Its cause is unknown; one story has it that a cow belonging to immigrant Catherine O'Leary kicked over a lantern, but this was a journalist's fabrication. Various alternatives have been put forward, but none has won universal assent.

The fire department, which had dealt with twenty fires the previous week, responded slowly to the alert, and by the time firefighters arrived, a large number of wooden houses and barns were in flames and strong winds were fanning the fire beyond control. Wooden buildings, a large amount of lumber in the city, and wooden sidewalks helped the blaze. It crossed the Chicago River and destroyed the waterworks, which further hampered the firefighters. By early in the morning of Monday, October 9, it had ravaged the central commercial district and destroyed the new opera house and the courthouse. Thousands fled the flames before the fire burned itself out, having destroyed about a third of the city's property, left 100,000 homeless, and claimed up to 300 lives. The so-called "Burnt District" was some 4 miles (6.4 km) long and three-quarters of a mile (1.2 km) wide, encompassing some thirty-four blocks and more than 2,000 acres (8 sq km), including over 28 miles (45 km) of streets, 120 miles (190 km) of sidewalks, and more than 2,000 lampposts.

Rebuilding began immediately and proved the trigger for Chicago's growth in the late nineteenth century. Fifteen years later there were few signs of fire damage anywhere in the city. **PF**

◗ The burned-out Field, Leiter, and Co. store stands over a sea of rubble and metal detritus after the Great Chicago Fire.

Dr. Livingstone?

Stanley finds Stanley Livingstone and saves the missionary's life.

It was David Livingstone's third expedition to Africa, this time to find the source of the Nile and spread the Word, and the antislavery message. It would also be his last. Reports of his death were exaggerated, but he was in a bad way: he was bleeding from painful hemorrhoids, had tropical ulcers on his feet, and was suffering from intestinal bleeding and diarrhea. His breathing was affected by earlier pneumonia. He had rested for seven months at Bambarre, where he read the Bible four times, and managed to cross Lake Tanganyika to reach Ujiji on November 5, 1871. Yet his

> ## "I walked up . . . took off my hat and said: 'Dr. Livingstone, I presume?'"
>
> **Henry Morton Stanley, explorer**

future looked bleak, until, on November 10, he met Henry Morton Stanley, from the *New York Herald*.

Stanley had run away from a Welsh workhouse at fifteen, crossed to the United States, was looked after by a New Orleans merchant, and became a journalist. Finding the missing missionary would be a scoop. He set out from Zanzibar with two other Europeans, who died, and 192 African porters, most of whom also died. Advancing toward Livingstone, he saw that "he was pale, that he looked weary and wan."

Stanley took charge of making meals for Livngstone, who gradually regained his strength. They got along surprisingly well, but Livingstone refused to return to Britain. They parted on March 14, 1872, Livingstone carrying on his work in Africa until his death in May 1873. **RP**

Unmanned and Adrift

What happened to the Mary Celeste is one of the sea's most enduring mysteries.

The *Mary Celeste,* a small two-masted cargo vessel, sailed from New York bound for Genoa, Italy, on November 7, 1872. She carried a cargo of industrial alcohol, and ten people, including her master, Captain Benjamin Briggs, his wife, Sarah, and their two-year-old daughter, Sophie. None of those aboard were ever seen again.

The ship was next seen near the Straits of Gibraltar on December 4 by the *Dei Gratia,* a British merchant ship that had left New York a week after the *Mary Celeste*'s departure. Her skipper, David Morehouse, who knew Briggs, saw that, although under full sail, she was unmanned. He sent a boarding party, which found the ship sailable but waterlogged, with one lifeboat missing. The ship had evidently been abandoned suddenly but with no signs of panic or violence. A skeleton crew sailed her to Gibraltar, where a court of inquiry suggested that the *Dei Gratia*'s crew had themselves been responsible for disposing of the *Mary Celeste*'s crew—a finding dismissed by most historians. Morehouse was given just a fraction of the prize money that was his due.

Theories about the *Mary Celeste*'s fate range from a mutiny to a sudden storm or earthquake. Many modern writers, however, suggest that Captain Briggs ordered her to be hurriedly abandoned, fearing that her cargo had become unstable and liable to explode. The lifeboat was subsequently lost at sea with all hands.

The mystery of the *Mary Celeste* was taken up by the novelist Arthur Conan Doyle, before he acquired worldwide fame with his Sherlock Holmes stories. Conan Doyle changed the name of the ship to *Marie Celeste* and suggested that warm cups of tea and a sleeping cat were found by the boarding party. These and other details were pure imagination. **NJ**

🌢 A hoax account from an Abel Fosdyk claimed that all the crew fell into the sea and were eaten by sharks, apart from himself.

"The stove was knocked out of its place, and . . . utensils were strewn around."

Oliver Deveau after *Mary Celeste*'s discovery

First Successful English Channel Swim

Captain Matthew Webb's aquatic endeavors turn him into an instant celebrity.

Barrel-chested Matthew Webb, one of a doctor's twelve children from Dawley, Shropshire, England, learned to swim in the River Severn, but he first demonstrated his aquatic ability when, as second mate on the Cunard liner *Russia*, he dived into the mid-Atlantic in a vain bid to rescue a man who had fallen overboard—an act that won him £100 and the Stanhope Gold Medal of the Royal Humane Society.

In 1873 he read of an unsuccessful attempt to swim the English Channel by J. B. Johnson and, resolving to do better, quit the Merchant Navy and started to train at London's Lambeth Baths. On August 12, 1875, he made his first attempt, but was turned back by strong winds.

On August 24 he dived from Dover's Admiralty Pier and set off on the ebb tide, swimming a steady breaststroke through the night. Coated with porpoise fat, sustained by beef tea, and supported by three boats, Webb was badly stung by jellyfish but landed near Calais after twenty-one hours and forty-five minutes in the water, without once resting or touching a support vessel. He had completed the first successful Channel swim, unassisted and without the benefit of artificial swimming aids.

The feat brought Webb instant fame, and his image, heavily moustached and in a striped swimsuit, endorsed a whole range of commercial products from matchboxes to patent medicines. A testimonial fund at the London Stock Exchange raised almost £2,500 for him, and he traveled widely in the United States performing aquatic feats for money. He wrote a book, *The Art of Swimming*, but on July 24, 1883, while attempting to swim the Niagara River under the famous falls for a £10,000 ($48,000) prize, he was sucked under by a whirlpool and drowned. His Channel crossing was not emulated until 1911. **NJ**

◐ After his feat, a newspaper called Captain Webb "probably the best-known and most popular man in the world."

"The sensation in my limbs is similar to that after the first day of the Cricket season."

Captain Webb on swimming the Channel

First Words Transmitted by Telephone

The telephone is patented and the world of modern communications is born.

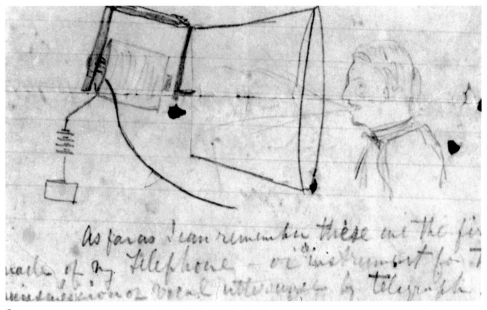

○ This sketch was drawn by Alexander Graham Bell to help explain how his new invention worked.

Alexander Graham Bell's Patent No. 175,465 has been called the most valuable single patent ever issued. Bell had just celebrated his twenty-ninth birthday. A Scotsman from Edinburgh, he, like his father, was fascinated with communications systems. As a boy he tried to teach his Skye terrier to growl in words, and, with his elder brother, made a "speaking machine." It was modeled on a lamb's larynx and, when blown into down a tube, emitted noises that, although meaningless, did sound human.

Bell and his parents emigrated to Canada in 1870, where Bell made himself a career teaching deaf children to speak. For the rest of his life he always listed his occupation simply as "teacher of the deaf." In 1871, he moved to the United States, to Boston, where, teaching as a professor of vocal physiology, he carried out experiments at night. By 1874 the principles of the telephone had taken shape in his mind, and in 1875, spurred on by Chicago inventor Elisha Gray's similar work, he redoubled his efforts and hired an assistant called Thomas A. Watson.

In 1876 Bell was granted a patent for his device and three days later he sent Watson, in the next room, the world's first sentence transmitted by telephone. Years of wrangling with Elisha Gray and other inventors lay ahead, but in 1877 the Bell Telephone Company was organized by Boston businessman Gardiner Greene Hubbard while Bell was honeymooning. By then, telephone messages were traveling more than 100 miles (160 km). **RC**

Victory at Little Big Horn

Native Americans defeat and kill General Custer, but their fate is sealed.

⬤ A drawing of the Battle of Little Big Horn, one of a series by Chief Red Horse, a Minneconjou Sioux.

The battle was a brilliant victory against the whites for the Native Americans of the Great Plains. They were being destroyed by white pressure, white farmers, white townships, the railroads, the extermination of the buffalo, and the influx of gold miners. It was the 1874 discovery of gold in the Black Hills of South Dakota, and the invasion by white miners, that set off a full-scale war. George Armstrong Custer, who had a brilliant reputation as a Civil War cavalry leader, was now in command of the 7th U.S. Cavalry. He was opposed by an alliance of Sioux and Cheyenne, who mustered 3,000 warriors. Their principal leaders were Sitting Bull and Crazy Horse.

Though hugely outnumbered, Custer ordered some of his cavalry, under Major Reno, to attack the Sioux and Cheyenne camp on the Little Bighorn River, while he and five troops got behind them, driving off their ponies. This maneuver was exactly what the Native Americans were waiting for. Custer and his men were attacked head-on by warriors under Crazy Horse, while others, under a chief named Gall, blocked their retreat. Caught in a vise, Custer and his party were killed, and Reno's men retreated with heavy losses to the hills, where they were besieged for thirty-six hours until reinforcements arrived.

Custer's defeat was the birth of a legend, but the Native Americans were doomed. Most would be penned in reservations, and their braves, including Sitting Bull himself, would be forced to make a living appearing in Buffalo Bill's Wild West show. **RC**

Debut of the Ring Cycle

The Festspielhaus *in Bayreuth is the scene for the first complete performance of* The Ring of the Nibelung, *Richard Wagner's epic cycle of four operas.*

In the Bavarian town of Bayreuth, the *Festspielhaus* (Festival Theater), constructed to Richard Wagner's own designs, was crowded and hushed as the curtain rose on the first act of *Das Rheingold*. For the next two evenings the audience would see performances of *Die Walküre* and *Siegfried*, and finally on August 16, *Götterdämmerung*, a five-hour opera. This last offering brought to a triumphant close the first complete performance of *The Ring of the Nibelung*.

Wagner had conceived his idea for a cycle of operas, based loosely on the Norse sagas and the medieval German epic poem of the *Nibelunglied*, twenty-five years earlier in Zurich, having been forced to leave Germany for his part in a revolutionary uprising in 1849. After long years of exile Wagner was on the brink of financial ruin when, in 1864, "mad" King Ludwig II invited him to Munich. Ludwig was infatuated with medieval romance—he later built the fairy-tale castle of Neuschwanstein in the Bavarian Alps—and he supported Wagner financially so that he could complete writing *The Ring*, even when the composer had to leave Munich after starting a scandalous affair with a married woman, Cosima von Bülow. Wagner married Cosima in 1870, set up home in Bayreuth, and dedicated himself to raising the money to building the *Festspielhaus* to house his operas. He died in Venice in 1883, a few months after his final opera, *Parsifal*, was premiered at Bayreuth. A summer festival is held at Bayreuth every year solely for the performance of Wagner's operas. **NK**

○ Austrian soprano Amalie Materna was the first to perform Brünnhilde, one of the Valkyries in Wagner's *Ring* cycle.

○ Bayreuth's *Festspielhaus* was designed by Wagner and opened in 1876 with a performance of his four operas.

Zulu Triumph

Well-armed British forces suffer a terrible beating at Isandhlwana.

The defeat at Isandhlwana was the result of British hubris and the incompetence of their commander, Lord Chelmsford, as much as it was down to Zulu courage and their superior tactics and numbers.

Shaka, the founder of the Zulu nation, had forged his people into a war-winning machine in the 1820s. When his nephew, Cetshwayo, ascended the throne in 1873, Zululand was threatened by the British, who aimed to unite South Africa as a white-ruled colony. When Cetshwayo rejected a British ultimatum to end Zulu sovereignty, Britain invaded. Chelmsford and his

---

"Have mercy . . . when you have come to take our country and eat us up?"

Saul David, *Zulu*, 2004

17,000-strong army pitched his interim camp at the foot of the Isandhlwana mountain. But he neglected to draw his wagons into a defensive *laager* to protect the camp. Reinforcing one of his cavalry scouts who had encountered a force of 1,500 Zulus, Chelmsford divided his column, leaving some 1,700 men at Isandlhwana under Lieutenant Colonel Pulleine.

On January 22 Pulleine was told Zulus were advancing on the camp. The Zulu army of 20,000 fell on the unprepared British, overwhelming them. Only around 350 survived. The dead were ritually disemboweled by the victors in a custom to free their souls. The Zulus lost some 1,500. Isandhlwana dealt a blow to Victorian imperialism at the height of its pomp, and was almost entirely attributable to Chelmsford's underestimation of his enemy. **NJ**

Struggle for Guano

A fight for guano wealth begins between Peru, Bolivia, and Chile.

The liberation of Latin America in the 1820s had proceeded with such speed that many border issues remained unresolved until later in the century. One such problem was Bolivia's access to the sea through the Atacama Desert between Chile and Peru, a region rich in guano, a major source of the valuable nitrates used in saltpeter and fertilizer production.

Bolivia's demand for taxation and seizure of the Chilean Antofagasta Nitrate and Railway Company in February 1879, brought military retaliation by the Chilean army. Peru, which had signed a secret alliance with Bolivia in 1873, was drawn into the dispute, forcing Chile to declare war on both countries.

The Bolivian army was in no condition to put up an effective fight, but control of the sea quickly became a vital factor in the conflict. For six months the Peruvian navy inflicted considerable damage on the much larger forces of its southern opponent. On October 8, however, Chile defeated Peru's Admiral Grau and seized vital control of the sea. They followed up this action with an invasion of Peru, which culminated in the occupation of the capital, Lima, in January 1881 (during this time the Peruvian National Library was looted and 30,000 books were taken to Chile—about 4,000 volumes of which were eventually returned in 2007).

The war continued for several years as Peru resisted—with tacit U.S. assistance—until a peace treaty was signed in 1883. According to the treaty's terms both Bolivia and Peru had to cede mineral-rich territory to Chile, and the provinces of Tacna and Arica were to vote in ten years on their nationality. Peru and Bolivia had suffered hugely, both physically and economically, from the war, and tensions between the combatant countries still exist. **PF**

The First Electric Light Bulb

The incandescent light bulb is perhaps Thomas Alva Edison's greatest invention.

◐ Thomas Edison exhibits a replica of his first successful incandescent lamp, which gave sixteen candlepower of illumination.

Thomas Alva Edison, the supreme U.S. inventor of his day, was born at Milan in Ohio in 1847. He had almost no schooling, but set up a laboratory in the basement at home when he was ten. He obtained his first patent in 1866, when he was nineteen, for an electric vote recorder. It was the first of more than 1,000 patents he took out in his lifetime. He made enough money from a "ticker" he devised for sending stock exchange prices across the country to set up his own research laboratory in New Jersey. Although beaten to the telephone by Alexander Graham Bell in 1876, he made important improvements to the telephone system and, in 1877, invented the phonograph (later the gramophone, and then record player), which set off the whole new era of recorded sound.

Edison then began working on the light bulb, at a time when the principal form of artificial lighting was by gas. A thin carbonized filament of sewing cotton mounted on an electrode gave off a glow that lasted for forty-five hours without overheating. He and his assistants proceeded to try out 6,000 other materials before finding a bamboo fiber that gave a bulb life of 1,000 hours. They went on to lead the way in the development of efficient electric generators and cables for carrying power, as well as devising an electricity meter.

Edison later helped to invent the motion-picture projector. When he died at age eighty-four in 1931, the account of his life and achievements in the *New York Times* ran over four and a half pages. **RC**

The Emancipator Is Assassinated

The assassination of Alexander II in 1881 hastens the day of revolutionary reckoning.

◗ The assassination of Tsar Alexander II was the most ambitious act of terrorism in the nineteenth century.

For some the tsar was the "Great Liberator," who emancipated the serfs in 1861, but for the People's Will he was another Romanov—exploiting the impoverished many for the parasitic few. Alexander II was aware of assassination attempts and was preparing reforms, including an elected Duma, to appease the opposition. But on March 13, as he approached the Winter Palace, an assassin threw a bomb under his ironclad carriage. Members of his entourage were wounded, and the perpetrator, Nikolai Rysakoff, was seized. The tsar alighted and was approaching Rysakoff when another terrorist, Ignacy Nryniewiecki, threw a second bomb, which wounded both himself and the tsar. Cadets returning from parade lifted Alexander from the snow to a sledge and covered his shivering body with their tunics. He was dead within a few hours.

The People's Will was a few dozen young men, grouped into secret cells and obeying their leaders without question. Their aim was to destroy the state and return Russia to its people. The assassination of Alexander II was their most successful attack.

Alexander II may have been a timid reformer, but he was the most liberal of Russia's nineteenth-century rulers. His successor tore up plans for a parliament. Henceforth, no tsar tried voluntarily to introduce reforms, and the revolutionary initiative passed to better organized and supported groups than the People's Will, with precise socialistic aims. Russia was on the high road to revolution. **RP**

Gunned Down

President Garfield is shot by a lone fanatic while waiting for a train.

One of a succession of comparatively undistinguished U.S. presidents, James A. Garfield, had been in office for only four months when, waiting at the Baltimore and Potomac railway station in Washington, D.C., for a train to take him on vacation, he was shot and incapacitated for what little was left of his life.

The killer was thirty-nine-year-old Charles J. Guiteau, a former member of a Perfectionist religious sect in New York State, which promoted the belief that sin and death were illusions, and had a tolerant attitude toward sexual promiscuity. Guiteau was not

"I presume the President was a Christian and he will be happier in Paradise."

Charles J. Guiteau, Garfield's assassin

liked in the sect and left. In the intervals between failing to pay his debts and serving a jail sentence for fraud, he tried to infiltrate himself into Republican politics and wrote a speech for Garfield. He expected a diplomatic appointment as a reward, but was rejected. At this point he received what he thought was a message from God that Garfield had to be "removed" to prevent another civil war in America.

Buying a .44 caliber pistol, Guiteau went on the hunt. Presidents had no protection or bodyguards at that time, and Guiteau was able to fire two bullets into the president's back in the station waiting room. Arrested by a policeman before he could get away in a cab he had waiting, he was hanged in Washington in June 1882. Garfield was dead by then, after lingering on until September 1881. **RC**

Alexandria Burns

The bombardment marks the beginning of Britain's domination of Egypt.

The attack came after rising tension between the nationalist forces of warlord Arabi (Urabi) Pasha, supported by the Muslim Arab population, and its minority of Europeans and Coptic Christians, protected by Britain and France, with Egypt's nominal ruler, the Khedive Tewfik, caught in the middle. The completion of the Suez Canal in 1869 increased Anglo-French interest in Egypt, and Arabi Pasha rose to power as a reaction to foreign influence.

In 1882, Arabi's militia occupied the ancient port of Alexandria and reinforced the city's forts as an

" ... the appearance of a city of the dead. It almost puts one in mind of Pompeii."

William Gill, British traveler in Alexandria

Anglo-French fleet sailed into the harbor, which exacerbated tensions, and in bloody riots in June, Muslim mobs attacked Christian areas of the city, killing more than 50 Europeans and 125 Egyptians. Britain's Admiral Beauchamp Seymour demanded the Egyptians cease fortifying the city or be bombarded. The French took no part in the subsequent fighting.

No response received, the British fired on the forts on July 7. Some 700 Egyptians were killed as well as one British officer. The forts were damaged and surrounding areas reduced to rubble. The Egyptians retaliated by burning down the city's foreign quarters. The British landed and established martial law, the prelude to General Garnet Wolseley's defeat of Arabi Pasha at the Battle of Tel-al-Kebir, and the declaration of a British protectorate over Egypt. **NJ**

Creation of the Ashes

The oldest rivalry in cricket begins when the Australian team beats England on English soil for the first time.

Matches between the two nations had been held for five years before the sole match in the 1882 series, played at the Kennington Oval in south London, saw a fast bowling spell, by Fred Spufford, that left England stranded seven runs short of their target, having lost six wickets for twelve runs. The crowd was shocked, and the press described it as the worst sporting performance in living memory. Two days later the *Sporting Times* newspaper carried a mock obituary: "In Affectionate Remembrance of ENGLISH CRICKET, which died at the Oval on 29th AUGUST, 1882, Deeply lamented by a large circle of sorrowing friends and acquaintances R.I.P. N.B.—The body will be cremated and the ashes taken to Australia."

On the following tour to Australia, the English captain, the Hon. Ivo Bligh, talked of "regaining the Ashes" (which he did), and the tradition was formed.

There were no actual ashes, but at some point during the 1882–1883 tour of Australia, the English captain was given a velvet bag in which to carry the "imaginary ashes," and then Florence Murphy, who became Bligh's wife, gave him a terra-cotta urn about 6 inches (15 cm) high. Its exact contents are in some doubt, although they are probably cricket-related. A short poem from *Melbourne Punch*, celebrating Bligh's success, is glued to the outside of the urn.

Bligh kept the urn until his death, but in 1927 his wife gave it to the MCC (Marylebone Cricket Club), then English cricket's governing body. It is normally kept in the museum at Lord's Cricket Ground, and, as it is not an official trophy, a replica, rather than the original urn, is awarded to the winning side. **PF**

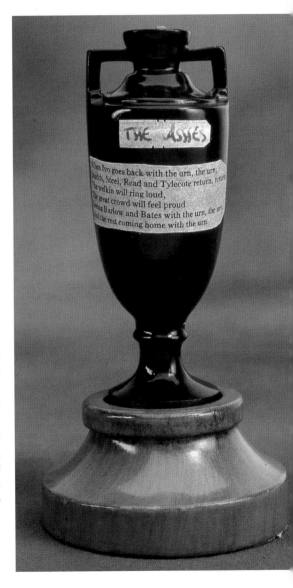

❍ Differing accounts suggest that the contents of the small terra-cotta urn are the ashes of a ball, a stump, or a bail.

Eruption of Krakatoa

The enormity of the volcanic eruption on Krakatoa is felt around the world.

○ A color lithograph of the volcano from the Royal Society's *The Eruption of Krakatoa and Subsequent Phenomena* (1888).

"I stood there ... and felt an endless scream passing through nature."

Edvard Munch after the Krakatoa eruption

The island of Krakatoa between Java and Sumatra had long been known for its violent volcanic eruptions. There were recorded outbreaks in 416, 535, and the 1680s. Nothing, however, could have prepared the world for the vast explosion that blew the island apart in August 1883 and produced the loudest sound in recorded history. The explosion has been estimated as being 13,000 times louder than the atomic bomb at Hiroshima.

After months of rumbling, steam emissions, and small explosions from the island's three volcanic cones, a series of four mighty blasts roared out, unleashing tsunamis more than 100 feet (30 m) high. The blasts were heard 2,200 miles (3,500 km) away in Perth, Australia, and sent columns of smoke and ash spiraling up 50 miles (80 km) into the atmosphere. A rain of hot ash fell on Sumatra, killing a thousand people outright. Most of the island collapsed into the sea in a vast caldera, and all living creatures on the remaining land area were wiped out. The tsunamis killed an additional 35,000 people, as well as utterly destroying 165 villages and settlements and damaging a similar number.

The huge eruption caused significant climate change around the world. In the year after the eruption, average global temperatures fell by 2° F (1.2ºC). Weather patterns continued to be chaotic worldwide until the end of the 1880s. Spectacular sunsets, caused by the ash and gas trapped in the upper atmosphere, were noted far from the location of the explosion—most famously in Oslo by Edvard Munch, as depicted in his masterpiece *The Scream*. The catastrophe has been the subject of many films and books, notably 1969's *Krakatoa: East of Java* (a singularly ill-named work because the island actually lies west of Java). **NJ**

Khartoum Falls

The death of "Chinese" Gordon at Khartoum raises the ire of Queen Victoria.

General Charles Gordon, a capable and energetic, if eccentric, military engineer with mystical Christian views, was popular with the public for his role in suppressing the bloody Taiping rebellion in China and for his evangelical missionary work among poor boys in London. He was sent to Sudan by the Gladstone government in January 1884. Appointed governor-general upon arriving at Cairo, his brief was to evacuate women and children from a Khartoum threatened by advancing Islamic forces under the charismatic religious leader Mahommed Ahmed, the Mahdi (the awaited one).

Gordon succeeded in evacuating more than 2,000 civilians down the Nile before Khartoum was surrounded and besieged by the Mahdists. The government expected him to leave, but Gordon exceeded his orders and put the city into a state of defense. Khartoum was converted into a walled fortification, with a lookout tower in the center from which Gordon himself often kept watch.

Prodded by public opinion, Gordon's predicament finally forced the government to organize a relief expedition under General Wolseley. Despite a dash across the desert, the expedition arrived just too late. Two days before, after a siege of more than 320 days, one of Gordon's Egyptian officers had opened the city to the Mahdists. Gordon was either shot or speared to death and his severed head paraded in triumph. An angry Queen Victoria blamed Gladstone for his tardiness in organizing the relief, and Gordon became a posthumous martyr.

The incident, which occurred while the European powers' colonial "Scramble for Africa" was at its height, has been interpreted as a key moment in the conflict between self-confident Western imperialism and resurgent Islam. **NJ**

◐ *General Gordon's Last Stand* (1885) by George William Joy epitomizes Britain's heroic interpretation of the event.

> ## "I fear . . . treachery in the garrison, and all will be over by Christmas."
>
> **General Gordon, December 1884**

Karl Benz Patents the First Motorcar

Benz invents and markets the forerunner of the modern car.

🔵 Karl Benz's *motorwagen* had a one-cylinder internal combustion engine and traveled at about 9 miles per hour (14.5 kph).

The two fathers of motoring were Germans born 60 miles (100 km) and one decade apart, who, working simultaneously but in complete ignorance of each other, in the early 1880s, invented the car. The internal combustion engines developed by Gottfried Daimler and Karl Benz were not the first powered vehicles—contraptions driven by steam and electric power preceded them by more than a century. However, in demonstrating the practicality of an engine powered by gasoline or diesel, Benz and Daimler pioneered the mass production of the motorcar, the vehicle that arguably revolutionized transport more than any other single invention. It is appropriate, therefore, that the names of these two geniuses who never met should have been coupled together in 1926 when their firms merged to form Daimler-Benz, now Germany's largest company.

Daimler invented the internal combustion engine with his assistant Wilhelm Maybach, working in great secrecy in a greenhouse in Bad Cannstatt, Stuttgart. In 1885, he attached their half-horsepower, two-stroke "Grandfather Clock" engine to a bicycle, thereby creating the first motorcycle.

A few miles away and a few months later in Mannheim, Karl Benz unveiled the first motorcar— the three-wheeled *motorwagen*. Benz invented many of the devices that form the car to this day, including the battery, spark plugs, the accelerator, the gearbox, and the clutch. Daimler and Benz made the fast modern world possible. **NJ**

Violence in Chicago

Tensions within the capitalist system lead to a riot in Haymarket Square.

○ An engraving of the police charging the protesters in Haymarket Square, with portraits of the seven policemen killed.

The growth of the labor movement in the United States was spurred on by industrialization, urbanization, and immigration from Europe. It prompted some fierce clashes as the leaders were suspected to be foreign revolutionaries bent on destroying the U.S. system. On May 1, 1886, there were demonstrations in many U.S. cities to demand an eight-hour day, and if necessary a general strike. In Chicago a strike against the McCormick Harvesting Machine Company turned ugly when strikers attacked blacklegs who tried to cross the picket lines. On May 3 the police intervened, and at least one striker was killed and others were injured. There was a peaceful protest against police brutality in Haymarket Square the next day, but when the police moved to disperse the crowd, someone threw a bomb, killing one of the policemen. The police opened fire and a riot erupted that ended with six more policemen dead and around sixty injured, along with an unknown number of demonstrators.

Eight labor leaders were convicted of conspiring with a murderer, despite the absence of evidence. They were all socialist or anarchist agitators and mostly foreign born, which evidently weighed with the jury. Four of the convicted were hanged in November 1887, and another killed himself. The remaining three were pardoned in 1893. By that time, however, the American Federation of Labor had been founded and labor unions would become an accepted part of the U.S. economy and politics. **RC**

Statue of Liberty Is Dedicated

Symbol of freedom and democracy, the statue was a gift from the French.

◔ The statue began as this clay model by Frédéric Auguste Bartholdi. His mother was possibly the model for the face.

◑ The components of the statue were assembled at the Paris manufacturing site before being shipped to New York.

"Give me your tired, your poor, your huddled masses yearning to breathe free..."

Emma Lazarus, *The New Colossus*

The United States of America's most famous statue, and one of the most readily recognized icons in the entire world, stands on an island at the entrance to New York Harbor. Here it sits as a symbol of freedom and democracy, and a tribute to the vast number of immigrants from Europe who poured into the United States in the nineteenth century in search of a better life. Emma Lazarus in her famous poem on the base called the statue "Mother of Exiles."

The figure holding up her welcoming torch is more than 150 feet (45 m) tall. She was the brainchild of a group of French intellectuals who hugely admired the United States and wanted to commemorate the centennial of the Declaration of Independence of 1776. They were led by Édouard-René Lefebvre de Laboulaye, the author of a large three-volume history of the United States, who wanted to establish a republic on U.S. principles in France. In 1875, Laboulaye and some of his friends gained political power in France and founded the Third Republic. Laboulaye called Liberty's torch "a beacon which enlightens."

The statue was constructed in Paris by the sculptor Frédéric Auguste Bartholdi, who started with a model in terra-cotta, which was enlarged in four stages until it reached its present size. It was supported by an iron framework designed by Gustave Eiffel, of Eiffel Tower fame. In 1884, it was officially accepted by the U.S. government, taken apart, and shipped in crates to New York. The campaign to raise the money to build the statue's base was led by Joseph Pulitzer, the newspaper magnate, and in 1886, the statue was formally dedicated by President Grover Cleveland. There are 354 steps up to the figure's crown, and it is visited by six million people every year. **RC**

Murder Most Foul

A murder in Whitechapel, London, heralds the work of Jack the Ripper.

In the early hours of August 31, 1888, Charles Cross walked to work along Buck's Row, behind Whitechapel station in London. As he avoided the puddles, he stumbled across a body later identified as that of Mary Ann Nichols. She was 5 feet, 2 inches (1.57 m) tall, with brown eyes and five teeth missing. Her face and neck were bruised, and she had two gashes along her throat and knife wounds to the lower abdomen. According to the postmortem doctor, she had probably been murdered in a five-minute attack by a left-handed man with anatomical knowledge.

"A terrible gash . . . as far as the diaphragm, from which the bowels protruded."

East London Observer, September 1, 1888

Often known as "Polly," Mary Ann had been born in 1845. Her marriage had broken down in 1880, and her children lived with their father. She sometimes worked as a domestic servant and a prostitute. She walked along Whitechapel Road on August 30, and was drinking in the Frying Pan pub after midnight. Later she was turned out of a common lodging house because she did not possess the small fee for a night's rest. A few hours later she was dead.

This was probably the first murder by "Jack the Ripper." He killed at least five women between August and November 1888. The hunt was taken up in the press, becoming a worldwide sensation, inspiring books, novels, musicals, and even an opera. The mystery of his true identity has inspired "Ripperologists" all over the world. **RP**

Symbol of Glory

The controversial Eiffel Tower is the star attraction of the World Fair.

Around thirty million people attended the *Exposition Universelle* (World Fair), held in Paris from May 1889 to commemorate the centenary of the French Revolution, but there was only one exhibit everyone was talking about, the Eiffel Tower. It was the world's tallest man-made structure, at 1,051 feet (320 m), and was illuminated by 2,000 gas lights. It comprised 15,000 pieces of welded metal and weighed 7,000 tons (7,112 tonnes). The panoramic views from the summit could extend to 45 miles (72 km).

What better symbol could there be, asked Gustave Eiffel, the engineer who not only designed it but also officially opened it by planting a tricolor flag on its summit, of France's glorious past and also of its still more glorious future. For here was the embodiment of the new age of secular, scientific, and industrial modernity. It was also one in the eye for France's rivals, for what other capital could boast such a structure? Not that everyone was convinced, even in Paris. Skeptics prophesied that visitors would get vertigo and might even be struck by lightning, while an august group of French artists had protested, during the building, "with all our energy . . . against the erection in our capital of the useless and monstrous Eiffel Tower." Yet it was the star attraction at the fair and people flocked to it.

The tower was due to be demolished in 1909, but was spared because it was the ideal situation for the antennae needed by the new science of radio telegraphy. In later decades it went on to become the universal symbol of Paris and today, is one of the world's greatest tourist attractions. **RP**

◗ The tower, seen here on October 17, 1888, was completed on March 31, 1889, with the hoisting of a flag to its top.

Suicide in the Wheat Fields

Van Gogh's early death goes unremarked after a life full of difficulty, drama, and tragedy, ending a painting career of astounding originality.

He ate his lunch quickly that Sunday, as there was work to be done. Many considered him a failed artist, who had sold only a single painting, but undeterred he walked up to the Chateau d'Auvers, where he had left his easel. Then he strolled down a path along the chateau wall and took out a revolver. He needed it, he told people, to scare away the crows. This time, however, he pointed it to his chest and shot himself.

The incident was not unexpected, for the Dutchman's life had always been tempestuous. In the 1870s, he had given away his worldly goods and tried to live a Christlike life. From 1880 his "mission" was painting, and he produced hundreds of canvases with extraordinary rapidity and a gloriously intense use of color. But he was subject to acute depression and hallucinations, and he had voluntarily entered an asylum after hacking off an ear in December 1888.

The wounded Van Gogh staggered back to town. The doctors were reassured that the bullet had missed the heart and vital organs. They did not send him to the hospital. The next day his brother and patron Theo arrived. Infection was setting in, and Vincent was struggling for breath. Theo cradled his brother's head in his arm. "I wish I could pass away like this," Vincent said. He died half an hour later, at 1:30 A.M. on Tuesday July 29, 1890, at age thirty-seven.

The death of a little-known artist was barely noted, but Van Gogh was soon to be recognized as one of the greatest postimpressionists, and as one of the great cultural heroes of modern times. **RP**

◗ Van Gogh painted *Self Portrait with Bandaged Ear* (1889) after he cut off part of his ear during an episode of mental illness.

◖ The painting *Wheat Field with Crows* (1890) balances a sense of foreboding with an intense appreciation of nature.

The Last Stand

The Wounded Knee massacre signals an end of war against Native Americans.

One of the consequences of the destruction of the Native American way of life was the emergence of the Ghost Dance religious cult. It was believed that performing the dance would restore the Native American world, bring back the buffalo, and restore the dead to life. The Sioux of the Black Hills of South Dakota thought that when the great day came, the whites would disappear and the world would be only for Native Americans. Some wore special Ghost Shirts they believed made them bulletproof. The cult made settlers and the Bureau of Indian Affairs nervous.

"Our safety depends upon the total extermination of the Indians."

L. Frank Baum, *Aberdeen Saturday Pioneer,* **1891**

On December 15, the great Sioux chief Sitting Bull was killed on the Standing Rock Reservation in South Dakota by Native police, trying to arrest him. At Wounded Knee Creek on December 29, a battalion of the U.S. 7th Cavalry surrounded a camp of 350 Sioux they were trying to round up and send to Nebraska. One Sioux tribesman's refusal to surrender his rifle, unless he was paid for it, set off a sudden explosion of firing, in which the cavalry fired Hotchkiss machine guns.

In the end, twenty-five cavalry troopers lay dead along with more than 150 Sioux men, women, and children. In the hail of fire, some of the troopers are believed to have been killed by "friendly fire" from their own side. Twenty Medals of Honor were awarded to the cavalry. **RC**

Female Suffrage

New Zealand becomes the first country in the world to give women the vote.

Nineteenth-century New Zealand's political system was the most advanced in the world. It had an elected chamber, the House of Representatives, from 1853, and although the vote was restricted to male Europeans with property, about three-quarters of the male European population met these criteria. An 1860s gold rush brought in thousands of miners who were also given the vote, and native Maori had four seats. All adult men were allowed to vote in 1879. The Electoral Act of 1893 gave the vote to women—making New Zealand the first country to do so.

"The ladies and their smiling faces lighted up the polling booths most wonderfully."

The Christchurch Press, 1893

This followed a long campaign. Women had been voting in local elections since the 1860s, and attempts to give women the parliamentary vote in the 1870s had only narrowly failed.

The women's suffrage movement outside Parliament focused on the Women's Christian Temperance Union led by Kate Sheppard. She organized a series of petitions—one in 1893 had nearly 32,000 signatures, almost a quarter of New Zealand's European adult female population. The first election under the legislation was held on November 28, 1893. Some women, alarmed at the idea of entering the polling booth unescorted, argued that women should vote by mail. In the event the election was described as the "best-conducted and most orderly" ever held in the colony. **PF**

Cause Célèbre

Captain Dreyfus's trial exacerbates differences dividing the Third French Republic.

⬥ Captain Dreyfus (standing by chair, right) faces the Council of War at Rennes that was to banish him to Devil's Island.

On December 22, 1894, Alfred Dreyfus, a Jewish officer in the French army, was sentenced to "deportation for life" for leaking military secrets. Despite his protests ("I am innocent! Long live France! Long live the army!"), he was stripped of his military rank, amid hoots from the crowd of "Dirty Jew," and dispatched to Devil's Island as the only inhabitant apart from his jailers, who were ordered not to speak to him. Eventually, L'Affaire divided France more than anything since the revolution of 1789.

His family was convinced of Dreyfus's innocence, as was the journalist Bernard Lazarre. It was said that he had been a victim of anti-Semitism. Commandant Picquart found evidence of a cover-up; saying it was Major Esterhazy who had passed military secrets. But Picquart was silenced, and a court martial found Esterhazy not guilty in 1898. The following month, however, the novelist Emile Zola published an open letter to the French president titled "J'accuse!" sparking a massive crusade that divided French society into "Dreyfusards" and "Anti-Dreyfusards."

Dreyfus was a symbol of what divided France. Hence it did not seem to matter much that he was pardoned in 1899 and declared innocent in 1906. The scandal still smoldered. At least the French were united during World War I, when Dreyfus came out of retirement and won the Légion d'Honneur. But in 1946, when Marshal Pétain was convicted for his role in the collaborationist Vichy government, he insisted, "It is Dreyfus's revenge!" **RP**

Oscar Wilde Found Guilty

Playwright, novelist, and poet Oscar Wilde is imprisoned for gross indecency.

○ Oscar Wilde's sartorial style and lifestyle were criticized as encouraging effeminate dandyism in young men.

On Saturday May 25, 1895, the courtroom in the Old Bailey was cramped and suffocatingly hot. The celebrated playwright and wit Oscar Wilde had been charged with several counts of gross indecency, and public interest in the trial was at fever pitch. The jury retired at 3:30 P.M. to consider the evidence. Two hours later, the first of seven verdicts of "Guilty" rang out. Mr. Justice Wills pronounced this the worst case he had ever tried, and that Wilde had been at "the center of a circle of extensive corruption of the most hideous kind among young men." Deciding against lecturing him on the evils of his conduct, for "people who do these things must be dead to all sense of shame," Wills peremptorily sentenced Wilde to the maximum penalty of two years' hard labor.

Wilde's fall had been headlong. His greatest triumph had come in February that year, with the first performance of his masterpiece *The Importance of Being Earnest*, but the most witty and sparkling play in the English language had been written during a crisis in Wilde's personal life. The father of his lover was threatening to denounce him publicly as a homosexual, and against his better judgment Oscar was persuaded to sue for defamation. Unsurprisingly, he lost the case and was subsequently arrested for homosexual offenses. Out of Wilde's suffering came more masterworks: his best poem, "The Ballad of Reading Gaol," and the remarkable confessional letter *De Profundis*. By this time, his health was in severe decline, though, and he died in 1900. **RP**

Wilhelm Röntgen Detects X-rays

A physicist's discovery revolutionizes diagnostic medicine.

○ Wilhelm Röntgen chose never to profit from his discovery, saying that its benefits should be freely available to all.

◑ The hand of Bertha Röntgen, X-rayed by Wilhelm, with her ring and other objects blocking the passage of the rays.

> *"Oh, my God . . . it makes me somehow feel that I'm looking at my own death!"*
>
> **Bertha Röntgen on seeing her X-rayed hand**

Wilhelm Conrad Röntgen (1845–1923), professor of physics at the University of Wurzburg, Bavaria, opened up a new vista in the history of medicine by making it possible, for the first time, to explore the internal structures of the body without having to resort to invasive surgery. Like so many earth-shattering discoveries, it was accidental.

Röntgen discovered this new form of radiation while experimenting one evening with cathode rays in his laboratory. Passing an electric current through a glass vacuum tube covered with heavy black paper, he spotted an unexpected green glow on a little screen lying on his bench. He quickly realized that some sort of invisible rays were leaving the tube, going through the paper, and causing the screen to become luminous. He named them "X-rays," because in mathematics "X" denotes an unknown quantity. He soon showed these rays could pass easily through wood, cloth, and paper, but not denser material. One of Röntgen's first experiments in 1895 was to film his wife Bertha's hand, showing that X-rays could even pass through the skin to reveal the bones beneath.

The news of Röntgen discovery spread quickly throughout the world. Scientists everywhere could duplicate his experiment because the cathode tube was well known during this period. Within the year, an X-ray department had been set up at the Glasgow Royal Infirmary, Scotland, which produced the first X-ray of a kidney stone and an X-ray showing a penny in the throat of a child. In the same year an American, Walter Cannon, used a barium meal with X-rays to track the passage of food through the digestive system. Within five years X-rays would be used on wounded soldiers in the Boer War to locate bullets, and X-ray machines even began to appear as curiosities in theatrical shows. **JJH**

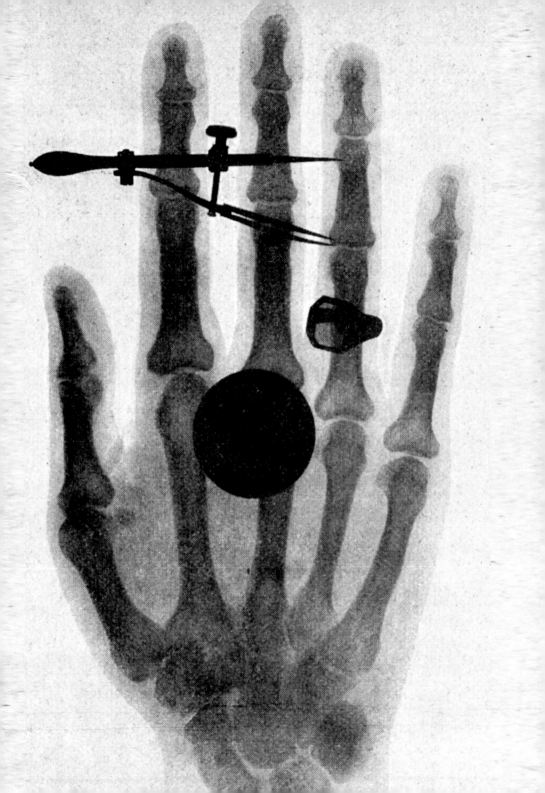

The First Moving Pictures Show

The Lumière Brothers demonstrate moving pictures before returning to stills.

The basement room of the Grand Café on the Boulevard des Capuchins, Paris, was the scene for a crowded gathering of people who had paid to sit in darkness to watch ten short movie sequences, each one around forty seconds long, on such themes as "jumping on the blanket," "baby's meal," and "bathing in the sea," combining direct observation with gentle slapstick. The evening was a triumph, and queues for subsequent viewings stretched around the block. One sequence, filmed a short while after this historic screening, showing a steam train running diagonally across the screen and had the audience screaming and diving for cover.

The entrepreneurs were Alphonse and Louis Lumière, the sons of a photographer and portrait painter in Lyon, who were in their early thirties. Their father, inspired by a demonstration of Edison's peephole kinetoscope in 1894, encouraged them to experiment with moving pictures, and they soon invented the system of sprocket holes to run the film through the camera. Early in 1895 they patented their "cinematograph," a compact all-in-one camera, developer, and projector. Their first film was of workers leaving their father's factory, which they showed privately on March 22, 1895, but the first commercial outing for the technology, and for projecting moving pictures, was at the Grand Café.

The brothers hired assistants to show their device across the world, opening theaters (they called them "cinemas") in which to show their films. In 1900 one was projected onto a huge screen at the Paris Exhibition. Despite the invention's success Louis Lumière soon declared the cinematograph "an invention without a future," leading to the brothers selling the rights to their device and concentrating instead on color photography. **PF**

◑ Auguste (left) and Louis Lumière are credited with both cinema and the Autochrome color photography process.

◑ One of the Lumière brothers' first movies was of a train arriving at La Ciotat station and collecting passengers.

> ## *"The motion picture entertains the whole world. What could we do better . . . ?"*
>
> **Louis Lumière, movie pioneer**

A Humiliating Defeat

At Adowa the Ethiopians deal a telling blow to Italy's African hopes.

Italy invaded Ethiopia—apart from Liberia the only independent African country at the high tide of nineteenth-century European imperialism—to create its own empire in the Horn of Africa along with its colonies of Somalia and Eritrea. The Italian commander, General Oreste Baratieri, was reluctant to attack the numerically superior Ethiopian army (80–150,000 men) under Emperor Menelik II, who barred the path to his 17,700-strong force. But goaded by the taunts of his subordinates, he ordered a three-pronged night march across mountainous

> ## "Italy would prefer the loss of two to three thousand men to a dishonorable retreat."
>
> **Brigadier Vittorio Dabormida, killed at Adowa**

terrain to be followed by a dawn assault. Spies told Menelik that the Italians were on the move, and he moved his men into ideal ambush positions.

The Italians lost their way and at dawn blundered into the enemy. Although the Italians and their native Ethiopian *askari* auxiliaries fought bravely, they were slaughtered, losing 7,000 dead and 1,500 wounded, with 3,000 taken prisoner, compared with Ethiopia's 5,000 dead and 8,000 wounded. Baratieri retreated to Eritrea with the remnants of his army, abandoning all their guns and equipment to the victors. The Italian prisoners were well treated, but captured *askaris*, regarded as traitors to Ethiopia, had one hand and one foot amputated. The victory preserved Ethiopian independence for another forty years, until Mussolini's war of revenge for Adowa in 1936. **NJ**

The Olympics Revisited

The first modern Olympiad opens, re-creating a great sporting tradition.

The French Baron Pierre de Coubertin wished to foster athletic excellence and international harmony, and, inspired by recent archeological finds at Olympia in Greece, looked to the ancient Greek Olympic Games for inspiration. In 1894, he set up an International Olympic Committee to establish the Games, choosing Athens as the initial venue. The "Games of the I Olympiad," as they were officially known, opened in April 1896 and ran for ten days. Some 241 athletes from fourteen nations took part—all the athletes were male, and all were amateurs, attending not as a national team but as private individuals at their own expense.

The ancient Panathenaic Stadium, dating from the fourth century B.C.E., was restored, with this and other facilities mainly paid for with money raised in Alexandria by businessman Georgios Averoff. The opening ceremony on March 25 saw 80,000 people packed into the stadium, the competitors assembled in national groups on the field, and massed bands and choirs playing the Olympic hymn, watched by King George of Greece. There was as yet no Olympic Flame because it was not introduced as part of the ceremony until 1928. The first event, the triple jump, was won by U.S. athlete James Connolly.

The games were a huge success, with Greek athletes gaining one fewer medal than the most successful nation, the United States (winning athletes were awarded a silver medal, rather than the now traditional gold). The most famous race was the marathon, won by the Greek runner Spiridon Louis, a previously unknown shepherd. **PF**

○ The German gymnast Hermann Weingärtner practices on the rings during the first Olympic Games in Athens, Greece.

Gold Is Struck in the Klondike

U.S. gold prospectors turn their attention north to Canada.

○ Prospectors pose near the Chilkoot Summit during the short-lived Klondike Gold Rush of 1896–1898.

> *"There are strange things done in the midnight sun by men who moiled for gold."*
>
> **Robert Service, *The Cremation of Sam McGee***

In August 1896, three people fishing the Klondike River saw an unmistakable gold gleam on the river bottom at Rabbit Creek, subsequently renamed Bonanza Creek. The following day, the trio, Native American "Skookum Jim" Mason Keish, his sister Kate, and her husband, George Carmack, staked a claim in Carmack's name. News of the strike spread, and 1,500 people sailed north from Seattle within ten days of hearing the news. In San Francisco, tickets for steamers heading to the frozen north sold for $1,000. By 1898 the population of Dawson City, the "instant town," which sprang up around the first claims, had reached 40,000, making it the largest Canadian town north of Winnipeg—a size that imposed severe strains on the scanty food resources of the remote area (salt fetched nearly as much as gold) and sometimes threatened famine. Law and order was maintained by the local "Mounties" under their resolute chief, Sam Steele.

Fortunes were made—a Dawson City barber dug up gold worth $40,000 in a single day—and in Harry Ash's saloon an enterprising prospector made $275 simply by sweeping the fallen gold dust off the floor. Of an estimated 100,000 people who set out for the Klondike, only half arrived. Some 5,000 of these successfully staked claims, but only a few hundred made their fortunes. Many became victims of exhaustion, disease, starvation, and human predators. The sheriff of Skagway, on the Canadian border, Jefferson "Soapy" Smith, was said to "cheat and fleece all comers and kill anyone who argued." Mounties at the frontier pass turned back any prospectors with less than a year's supply of food. The rush ended as quickly as it had begun. By 1900, the best of the gold was gone, although commercial digging continued until 1966. **NJ**

Death of Mr. Dynamite

Alfred Nobel's will ensures that his greatest positive influence will be posthumous.

When the Swedish industrialist, chemist, and philanthropist Alfred Nobel died of a stroke at his Italian holiday residence in San Remo, he could look back on a life unusually rich in achievement, but also one that had failed to bring him much in the way of personal happiness.

As an industrialist, Nobel had turned the Bofors steel mill into a successful armaments factory, and as a chemist in 1867 he had developed dynamite as a safer form of the explosive nitroglycerine. After an explosion at his plant killed Nobel's younger brother Emil and four other workers, however, he invented an even safer and more powerful explosive—gelignite. A sensitive soul, Nobel found time to write plays and poetry in between amassing a fortune in arms manufacture, explosives, and oil.

Shaken by a premature obituary in 1888 headlined "The merchant of death is dead," which described him as having become rich by finding ways to kill more people faster than ever before, and influenced by his correspondence with the Austrian writer and pacifist Bertha von Suttner, Nobel resolved to leave his vast fortune to endowing the prizes that bear his name to encourage peace and progress in the arts and sciences. Among recipients of the annual Prizes for Peace, Literature, Physics, Chemistry, Medicine, and Economics have been Winston Churchill, Albert Camus, and Samuel Beckett (Literature); Albert Einstein (Physics); Linus Pauling (Chemistry); and U.S. Presidents Teddy Roosevelt and Woodrow Wilson, along with Mother Teresa, Henry Kissinger, and Martin Luther King (Peace). The founder of the Red Cross, Henri Dunant, and Bertha von Suttner herself (who had become an active figure in the radical peace movement internationally) were among the first winners of the Peace prize. **NJ**

◔ Nitroglycerine was invented by Italian chemist Ascanio Sobrero in 1846, but Nobel patented a way to use it safely.

> ### *"Alfred Nobel—pitiable half-creature, should have been stifled."*
>
> **Nobel, in letter to his brother Ludvig, 1887**

God Save the Queen

Britain's monarchy reaches its zenith with Queen Victoria's Diamond Jubilee.

○ Queen Victoria, photographed on the occasion of her Diamond Jubilee, inspired fierce devotion in her subjects.

○ Victoria's carriage passes the National Gallery and jubilant bystanders in Trafalgar Square, London.

> ## "The cheering was deafening, and every face . . . filled with real joy."
>
> **Queen Victoria in her diary**

Could the celebrations for Victoria's Diamond Jubilee possibly equal those for her Golden Jubilee of 1887? It seemed unlikely, for the seventy-eight-year-old, and increasingly curmudgeonly, queen insisted that she would not alight from her carriage during the planned procession, she would not spend any of her own money on the festivities, and that on no account were any of Europe's crowned heads to be invited. On Sunday June 20, the actual anniversary of her accession, celebrations were, by royal command, muted. At 11:00 A.M., every church, chapel, and synagogue in Britain held a special service, Victoria herself attending St. George's Chapel in Windsor. She confessed in her journal that she felt "rather nervous about the coming days, and that all should go off well." She need not have worried, for what followed was a dazzling imperial spectacle.

Victoria described June 22, the climax of the festivities, as a "never-to-be-forgotten day." From the moment she pressed the button that telegraphed her jubilee message to the empire, all went gloriously well. The sun came out as the guns in Hyde Park announced that she had left the palace, and the actual procession, though routed through some of the poorer parts of the city, elicited a tremendous response. "No one ever, I believe, has met with such an ovation as was given to me, passing through those six miles of streets." It was the greatest ceremonial occasion in British history.

According to the socialist Keir Hardie, it was "bread and circuses without the bread." But it was effective. Another socialist, Beatrice Webb, noted that people were "drunk . . . with hysterical loyalty." Britain was becoming a democracy and the crown had almost no political power left, but monarchy had never been as popular. **RP**

JEUDI 13 JANVIER

Directeur
ERNEST VAUGHAN

ABONNEMENTS

	Un an	Six mois	Trois mois
Paris	20 »	10 »	5 »
Départements et Algérie	24 »	12 »	6 »
Étranger (Union Postale)	35 »	18 »	10 »

POUR LA RÉDACTION :
S'adresser à M. A. BERTHIER
Secrétaire de la Rédaction

Adresse télégraphique : AURORE-PARIS

L'AURORE

Littéraire, Artistique, Sociale

Directeur
ERNEST VAUGH

LES ANNONCES SONT REÇUE
142 — Rue Montmartre —
AUX BUREAUX DU JOURNAL

Les manuscrits non insérés ne sont pas

ADRESSER LETTRES ET MANDAT
à M. A. BOUIT, Administra

Téléphone : 102-88

J'Accuse...!

LETTRE AU PRÉSIDENT DE LA RÉPUBLIQU

Par ÉMILE ZOLA

LETTRE A M. FÉLIX FAURE

Président de la République

Monsieur le Président,

Me permettez-vous, dans ma gratitude pour le bienveillant accueil que vous m'avez fait un jour, d'avoir le souci de votre juste gloire et de vous dire que votre étoile, si heureuse jusqu'ici, est menacée de la plus honteuse, de la plus ineffaçable des taches?

Vous êtes sorti sain et sauf des basses calomnies, vous avez conquis les cœurs. Vous apparaissez rayonnant dans l'apothéose de cette fête patriotique que l'alliance russe a été pour la France, et vous vous préparez à présider au solennel triomphe de notre Exposition universelle, qui couronnera notre grand siècle de travail, de vérité et de liberté. Mais quelle tache de boue sur votre nom — j'allais dire sur votre règne — que cette abominable affaire Dreyfus! Un conseil de guerre vient, par ordre, d'oser acquitter un Esterhazy, soufflet suprême à toute vérité, à toute justice. Et c'est fini, la France a sur la joue cette souillure, l'histoire écrira que c'est sous votre présidence qu'un tel crime social a pu être commis.

Puisqu'ils ont osé, j'oserai aussi, moi. La vérité, je la dirai, car j'ai promis de la dire, si la justice, régulièrement saisie, ne la faisait pas, pleine et entière. Mon devoir est de parler, je ne veux pas être complice. Mes nuits seraient hantées par le spectre de l'innocent qui expie là-bas, dans la plus affreuse des tortures, un crime qu'il n'a pas commis.

Et c'est à vous, monsieur le Président, que je la crierai, cette vérité, de toute la force de ma révolte d'honnête homme. Pour votre honneur, je suis convaincu que vous l'ignorez. Et à qui donc dénoncerai-je la tourbe malfaisante des vrais coupables, si ce n'est à vous, le premier magistrat du pays?

⁂

La vérité d'abord sur le procès et sur la condamnation de Dreyfus.

Un homme néfaste a tout mené, a tout fait, c'est le colonel du Paty de Clam, alors simple commandant. Il est l'affaire Dreyfus tout entière, on ne la connaîtra que lorsqu'une enquête loyale aura établi nettement ses actes et ses responsabilités. Il apparaît comme l'esprit le plus fumeux, le plus compliqué, hanté d'intrigues romanesques, se complaisant aux moyens des romans-feuilletons, les papiers volés, les lettres anonymes, les rendez-vous dans les endroits déserts, les femmes mystérieuses qui colportent, de nuit, des preuves accablantes. C'est lui qui imagina de dicter le bordereau à Dreyfus; c'est lui qui rêva de l'étudier dans une pièce entièrement revêtue de glaces; c'est lui que le commandant Forzinetti nous représente armé d'une lanterne sourde, voulant se faire introduire près de l'accusé endormi, pour projeter sur son visage un brusque flot de lumière et surprendre ainsi son crime, dans l'émoi du réveil. Et je n'ai pas à tout dire, qu'on cherche, on trouvera. Je déclare simplement que le commandant du Paty de Clam, chargé d'instruire l'affaire Dreyfus, comme officier judiciaire, est, dans l'ordre des dates et des responsabilités, le premier coupable de l'effroyable erreur judiciaire qui a été commise.

Le bordereau était depuis quelque temps déjà entre les mains du colonel Sandherr, directeur du bureau des renseignements, mort depuis de paralysie générale. Des « fuites » avaient lieu, des papiers disparaissaient, comme il en disparaît aujourd'hui encore; et l'auteur du bordereau était recherché, lorsqu'un *a priori* se fit peu à peu que cet auteur ne pouvait être qu'un officier de l'état-major, et un officier d'artillerie : double erreur manifeste, qui montre avec quel esprit superficiel on avait étudié ce bordereau, car un examen raisonné démontre qu'il ne pouvait s'agir que d'un officier de troupe. On cherchait donc dans la maison, on examinait les écritures, c'était comme une affaire de famille, un traître à surprendre dans les bureaux mêmes, pour l'en expulser. Et, sans que je veuille refaire ici une histoire connue en partie, le commandant du Paty de Clam entre en scène, dès qu'un premier soupçon tombe sur Dreyfus. A partir de ce moment, c'est lui qui a inventé Dreyfus, l'affaire devient son affaire, il se fait fort de confondre le traître, de l'amener à des aveux complets. Il y a bien le ministre de la guerre, le général Mercier, dont l'intelligence semble médiocre; il y a bien le chef de l'état-major, le général de Boisdeffre, qui paraît avoir cédé à sa passion cléricale, et le sous-chef de l'état-major, le général Gonse, dont la conscience a pu s'accommoder de beaucoup de choses. Mais, au fond, il n'y a d'abord que le commandant du Paty de Clam, qui les mène tous, qui les hypnotise, car il s'occupe aussi de spiritisme, d'occultisme, il converse avec les esprits. On ne croira jamais les expériences auxquelles il a soumis le malheureux Dreyfus, les pièges dans lesquels il a voulu le faire tomber, les enquêtes folles, les imaginations monstrueuses, toute une démence torturante.

Ah! cette première affaire, elle est un cauchemar, pour qui la connaît dans ses détails vrais! Le commandant du Paty de Clam arrête Dreyfus, le met au secret. Il court chez madame Dreyfus, la terrorise, lui dit que, si elle parle, son mari est perdu. Pendant ce temps, le malheureux s'arrachait la chair, hurlait son innocence. Et l'instruction a été faite ainsi, comme dans une chronique du quinzième siècle, au milieu du mystère, avec une complication d'expédients farouches, tout cela basé sur une seule charge enfantine, ce bordereau imbécile, qui n'était pas seulement une trahison vulgaire, qui était aussi la plus impudente des escroqueries, car les fameux secrets livrés se trouvaient presque tous sans valeur. Si j'insiste, c'est que l'œuf est ici, d'où va sortir plus tard le vrai crime, l'épouvantable déni de justice dont la France est malade. Je voudrais faire toucher du doigt comment l'erreur judiciaire a pu être possible, comment elle est née des machinations du commandant du Paty de Clam, comment le général Mercier, les généraux de Boisdeffre et Gonse ont pu s'y laisser prendre, engager peu à peu leur responsabilité dans cette erreur, qu'ils ont cru devoir, plus tard, imposer comme la vérité sainte, une vérité qui ne se discute même pas. Au début, il n'y a donc de leur part que de l'incurie et de l'inintelligence. Tout au plus, les sent-on céder aux passions religieuses du milieu et aux préjugés de l'esprit de corps. Ils ont laissé faire la sottise.

Mais voici Dreyfus devant le conseil de guerre. Le huis clos le plus absolu est exigé. Un traître aurait ouvert la frontière à l'ennemi, pour conduire l'empereur allemand jusqu'à Notre-Dame, qu'on ne prendrait pas des mesures de silence et de mystère plus étroites. La nation est frappée de stupeur, on chuchote des faits terribles, de ces trahisons monstrueuses qui indignent l'Histoire, et naturellement la nation s'incline. Il n'y a pas de châtiment assez sévère, elle applaudira à la dégradation publique, elle voudra que le coupable reste sur son rocher d'infamie, dévoré par le remords. Est-ce donc vrai, les choses indicibles, les choses dangereuses, capables de mettre l'Europe en flammes, qu'on a dû enterrer soigneusement derrière ce huis clos? Non! il n'y a eu, derrière, que les imaginations romanesques et démentes du commandant du Paty de Clam. Tout cela n'a été fait que pour cacher le plus saugrenu des romans-feuilletons. Et il suffit, pour s'en assurer, d'étudier attentivement l'acte d'accusation lu devant le conseil de guerre.

Ah! le néant de cet acte d'accusation! Qu'un homme ait pu être condamné sur cet acte, c'est un prodige d'iniquité. Je défie les honnêtes gens de le lire, sans que leur cœur bondisse d'indignation et crie leur révolte, en pensant à l'expiation démesurée, là-bas, à l'île du Diable. Dreyfus sait plusieurs langues, crime; on n'a trouvé chez lui aucun papier compromettant, crime; il va parfois dans son pays d'origine, crime; il est laborieux, il a le souci de tout savoir, crime; il ne se trouble pas, crime; il se trouble, crime. Et les naïvetés de rédaction, les formelles assertions dans le vide! On nous avait parlé de quatorze chefs d'accusation : nous n'en trouvons qu'une seule en fin de compte, celle du bordereau; et nous apprenons même que les experts n'étaient pas d'accord, qu'un d'eux, M. Gobert, a été bousculé militairement, parce qu'il se permettait de ne pas conclure dans le sens désiré. On parlait aussi de vingt-trois officiers qui étaient venus accabler Dreyfus de leurs témoignages. Nous ignorons encore leurs interrogatoires, mais il est certain que tous ne l'avaient pas chargé; et il est à remarquer, en outre, que tous appartenaient aux bureaux de la guerre. C'est un procès de famille, on est là entre soi, et il faut s'en souvenir : l'état-major a voulu le procès, l'a jugé, et il vient de le juger une seconde fois.

Donc, il ne restait que le bordereau, sur lequel les experts ne s'étaient pas entendus. On raconte que, dans la chambre du conseil, les juges allaient naturellement acquitter. Et, dès lors, comme l'on comprend l'obstination désespérée avec laquelle, pour justifier la condamnation, on affirme aujourd'hui l'existence d'une pièce secrète, accablante, la pièce qu'on ne peut montrer, qui légitime tout, devant laquelle nous devons nous incliner, le bon dieu invisible et inconnaissable. Je la nie, cette pièce, je la nie de toute ma puissance! Une pièce ridicule, oui, peut-être la pièce où il est question de petites femmes, et où il est parlé d'un certain D... qui devient trop exigeant, quelque mari sans doute trouvant qu'on ne lui payait pas sa femme assez cher. Mais une pièce intéressant la défense nationale, qu'on ne saurait produire sans que la guerre fût déclarée demain, non, non! C'est un mensonge; et cela est d'autant plus odieux et cynique qu'ils mentent impunément sans qu'on puisse les en convaincre. Ils ameutent la France, ils se cachent derrière sa légitime émotion, ils ferment les bouches en troublant les cœurs, en pervertissant les esprits. Je ne connais pas de plus grand crime civique.

Voilà donc, monsieur le Président, les faits qui expliquent comment une erreur judiciaire a pu être commise; et les preuves morales, la situation de fortune de Dreyfus, l'absence de motifs, son continuel cri d'innocence, achèvent de le montrer comme une victime des extraordinaires imaginations du commandant du Paty de Clam, du milieu clérical où il se trouvait, de la chasse aux « sales juifs », qui déshonore notre époque.

⁂

Et nous arrivons à l'affaire Esterhazy. Trois ans se sont passés, beaucoup de consciences restent troublées profondément, s'inquiètent, cherchent, finissent par se convaincre de l'innocence de Dreyfus.

Je ne ferai pas l'historique des doutes, puis de la conviction de M. Scheurer-Kestner. Mais, pendant qu'il fouillait de son côté, il se passait des faits graves à l'état-major même. Le colonel Sandherr était mort, et le lieutenant-colonel Picquart lui avait succédé comme chef du bureau des renseignements. Et c'est à ce titre, dans l'exercice de ses fonctions, que ce dernier eut un jour entre les mains une lettre-télégramme, adressée au commandant Esterhazy, par un agent d'une puissance étrangère. Son devoir strict était d'ouvrir une enquête. La certitude est qu'il n'a jamais agi en dehors de la volonté de ses supérieurs. Il soumit donc ses soupçons à ses supérieurs hiérarchiques, le général Gonse, puis le général de Boisdeffre, puis le général Billot, qui avait succédé au général Mercier comme ministre de la guerre. Le fameux dossier Picquart, dont il a été tant parlé, n'a jamais été que le dossier Billot, j'entends le dossier fait par un subordonné pour son ministre, le dossier qui doit exister encore au ministère de la guerre. Les recherches durèrent de mai à septembre 1896, et ce qu'il faut affirmer bien haut, c'est que le général Gonse était convaincu de la culpabilité d'Esterhazy, c'est que le général de Boisdeffre et le général Billot ne mettaient pas en doute que le fameux bordereau fût de l'écriture d'Esterhazy. L'enquête du lieutenant-colonel Picquart avait abouti à cette constatation certaine. Mais l'émoi était grand, car la condamnation d'Esterhazy entraînait inévitablement la revision du procès Dreyfus; et c'était ce que l'état-major ne voulait à aucun prix.

Il dut y avoir là une minute psychologique pleine d'angoisse. Remarquez que le général Billot n'était compromis dans rien, il arrivait tout frais, il pouvait faire la vérité. Il n'osa pas, dans la terreur sans doute de l'opinion publique, certainement aussi dans la crainte de livrer tout l'état-major, le général de Boisdeffre, le général Gonse, sans compter les sous-ordres. Puis, ce ne fut là qu'une minute de combat entre sa conscience et ce qu'il croyait être l'intérêt militaire. Quand cette minute fut passée, il était déjà trop tard. Il s'était engagé, il était compromis. Et, depuis lors, sa responsabilité n'a fait que grandir, il a pris à sa charge le crime des autres, il est aussi coupable que les autres, il est plus coupable qu'eux, car il a été le maître de faire justice, et il n'a rien fait. Comprenez-vous cela! voici un an que le général Billot, que les généraux de Boisdeffre et Gonse savent que Dreyfus est innocent, et ils ont gardé pour eux cette effroyable chose. Et ces gens-là dorment, et ils ont des femmes et des enfants qu'ils aiment!

Le colonel Picquart avait rempli son devoir d'honnête homme. Il insistait auprès de ses supérieurs, au nom de la justice. Il les suppliait même, il leur disait combien leurs délais étaient impolitiques devant le terrible orage qui s'amoncelait, qui devait éclater, lorsque la vérité serait connue. Ce fut, plus tard, le langage que M. Scheurer-Kestner tint également au général Billot, l'adjurant par patriotisme de prendre en main l'affaire, de ne pas la laisser s'aggraver, au point de devenir un désastre public. Non! le crime était commis, l'état-major ne pouvait plus avouer son crime. Et le lieutenant-colonel Picquart fut envoyé en mission, on l'éloigna de plus loin en plus loin, jusqu'en Tunisie, où l'on voulut même un jour honorer sa bravoure, en le chargeant d'une mission qui l'aurait fait sûrement massacrer, dans les parages où le marquis de Morès a trouvé la mort. Il n'était pas en disgrâce, le général Gonse entretenait avec lui une correspondance amicale. Seulement, il est des secrets qu'il ne fait pas bon d'avoir surpris.

A Paris, la vérité marchait, irrésistible, et l'on sait de quelle façon l'orage attendu éclata. M. Mathieu Dreyfus dénonça le commandant Esterhazy comme le véritable auteur du bordereau, au moment où M. Scheurer-Kestner allait déposer, entre les mains du garde des sceaux, une demande en revision du procès. Et c'est ici que le commandant Esterhazy paraît. Des témoignages le montrent d'abord affolé, prêt au suicide ou à la fuite. Puis, tout d'un coup, il paye d'audace, il étonne Paris par la violence de son attitude. C'est que du secours lui était venu, il avait reçu une lettre anonyme l'avertissant des menées de ses ennemis, une dame mystérieuse s'était même dérangée de nuit pour lui remettre une pièce volée à l'état-major, qui devait le sauver. Et je ne puis m'empêcher de retrouver là le lieutenant-colonel du Paty de Clam, en reconnaissant les expédients de son imagination fertile. Son œuvre, la culpabilité de Dreyfus, était en péril, et il a voulu sûrement défendre son œuvre. La revision du procès, mais c'était l'écroulement du roman-feuilleton si extravagant, si tragique, dont le dénouement abominable a lieu à l'île du Diable! C'est ce qu'il ne pouvait permettre. Dès lors, le duel va avoir lieu entre le lieutenant-colonel Picquart et le lieutenant-colonel du Paty de Clam, l'un le visage découvert, l'autre masqué. On les retrouvera prochainement tous deux devant la justice civile. Au fond, c'est toujours l'état-major qui se défend, qui ne veut pas avouer son crime, dont l'abomination grandit d'heure en heure.

On s'est demandé avec stupeur quels étaient les protecteurs du commandant Esterhazy. C'est d'abord, dans l'ombre, le lieutenant-colonel du Paty de Clam qui a tout machiné, qui a tout conduit. Sa main se trahit aux moyens saugrenus. Puis, c'est le général de Boisdeffre, c'est le général Gonse, c'est le général Billot lui-même, qui sont bien obligés de faire acquitter le commandant, puisqu'ils ne peuvent laisser reconnaître l'innocence de Dreyfus, sans que les bureaux de la guerre croulent sous le mépris public. Et le beau résultat de cette situation prodigieuse, c'est que l'honnête homme là-dedans, le lieutenant-colonel Picquart, qui seul a fait son devoir, va être la victime, celui qu'on bafouera et qu'on punira. O justice, quelle affreuse désespérance serre le cœur! On va jusqu'à dire que c'est lui le faussaire, qu'il a fabriqué la carte-télégramme pour perdre Esterhazy. Mais, grand Dieu! pourquoi? dans quel but? Donnez un motif. Est-ce que celui-là aussi est payé par les juifs? Le joli de l'histoire est qu'il était justement antisémite. Oui! nous assistons à ce spectacle infâme, des hommes perdus de dettes et de crimes dont on proclame l'innocence, tandis qu'on frappe l'honneur même, un homme à la vie sans tache! Quand une société en est là, elle tombe en décomposition.

Voilà donc, monsieur le Président, l'affaire Esterhazy : un coupable qu'il s'agissait d'innocenter. Depuis bientôt deux mois, nous pouvons suivre heure par heure la belle besogne. J'abrège, car ce n'est ici, en gros, que le résumé de l'histoire dont les brûlantes pages seront un jour écrites tout au long. Et nous avons donc vu le général de Pellieux, puis le commandant Ravary, conduire une enquête scélérate d'où les coquins sortent transfigurés et les honnêtes gens salis. Puis, on a convoqué le conseil de guerre.

⁂

Comment a-t-on pu espérer qu'un conseil de guerre déferait ce qu'
seil de guerre avait fait?

Je ne parle même pas du ch
jours possible des juges. L'idé
rieure de discipline, qui est
sang de ces soldats, ne suffit-e
firmer leur pouvoir même d
Qui dit discipline dit obé
Lorsque le ministère de la
le grand chef, a établi publiqu
aux acclamations de la représ
nationale, l'autorité absolue de
jugée, vous voulez qu'un con
guerre lui donne un formel d
Hiérarchiquement, cela est imp
Le général Billot a suggestio
juges par sa déclaration, et ils
comme ils doivent aller au fe
raisonner. L'opinion préconçu
ont apportée sur leur siège est
ment celle-ci : « Dreyfus a é
damné pour crime de trahison
conseil de guerre; il est donc co
et nous, conseil de guerre, n
pouvons le déclarer innocent;
savons que reconnaître la culp
d'Esterhazy, ce serait proclam
nocence de Dreyfus. » Rien ne
les faire sortir de là.

Ils ont rendu une sentence ini
à jamais pèsera sur nos cons
guerre, qui entachera désorm
suspicion tous leurs arrêts. Le
conseil de guerre a pu être in
gent, le second est forcément cr
Son excuse, je le répète, est que
suprême avait parlé, déclarant l
jugée inattaquable, sainte et
rieure aux hommes, de sorte q
inférieurs ne pouvaient dire
traire. On nous parle de l'honn
l'armée, on veut que nous l'ai
que nous la respections. Ah!
oui, l'armée qui se lèverait à
mière menace, qui défendrait l
française, elle est tout le peu
nous n'avons pour elle que ten
et respect. Mais il ne s'agit pas
dont nous voulons justement
gnité, dans notre besoin de jus
s'agit du sabre, le maître qu'o
donnera demain peut-être. Et
dévotement la poignée du sa
dieu, non!

Je l'ai démontré d'autre part
faire Dreyfus était l'affaire des b
de la guerre, un officier de l'état-
dénoncé par ses camarades de
major, condamné sous la pressi
chefs de l'état-major. Encore un
il ne peut revenir innocent, san
tout l'état-major soit coupable.
les bureaux, par tous les moyen
ginables, par des campagnes de p
par des communications, par d
fluences, n'ont-ils couvert Est
que pour perdre une second
Dreyfus. Ah! quel coup de ba
gouvernement républicain devra
ner dans cette jésuitière, ainsi q
appelle le général Billot lui-mêm
est-il, le ministère vraiment f
d'un patriotisme sage, qui ose
y refondre et tout y renouveler
de gens je connais qui, devan
guerre possible, tremblent d'ang
en sachant dans quelles mains
défense nationale! et quel n
basses intrigues, de commérages
dilapidations, est devenu cet
sacré, où se décide le sort de la p
On s'épouvante devant le jour te
que vient d'y jeter l'affaire Dr
ce sacrifice humain d'un malheu
d'un « sale juif »! Ah! tout ce qu
agité là de démence et de sottise
imaginations folles, des pratiqu
basse police, des mœurs d'inqui
et de tyrannie, le bon plaisir de
ques galonnés mettant leurs bott
la nation, lui rentrant dans la
son cri de vérité et de justice, so
prétexte menteur et sacrilège
raison d'État!

Et c'est un crime encore que d
tre appuyé sur la presse immonde
de s'être laissé défendre par tou
fripouille de Paris, de sorte que
la fripouille qui triomphe insolemm

"J'accuse!"

Émile Zola's article exposes the true guilty parties of the "Dreyfus Affair."

Émile Zola's famous article, published in the *L'Aurore* newspaper under the explosive headline "J'Accuse!" —contributed by the radical politician Georges Clemenceau—caused a furor. Identified with anti-clerical, liberal opinion, Zola's open letter to President Felix Faure accused leading army officers of engaging in a conspiracy to convict Alfred Dreyfus, a Jewish staff officer, of espionage for Germany; sending the innocent man to the Devil's Island penal colony; and then deliberately covering up their crimes.

The letter was the catalyst that blew the Dreyfus Affair open and triggered the long process of judicial revision that eventually—despite internal divisions and the fall of several governments—resulted in Dreyfus's exoneration and the exposure of Esterhazy, the real spy, whom France's conservative military and clerical establishment had combined to protect.

The letter had appalling personal consequences for Zola. In 1899 he was convicted of defamation and was forced to flee to London to escape jail. He spent a year there in exile with his mistress and children before the growing evidence of Dreyfus's innocence allowed him to return. In Zola's words, "Truth is on the march and nothing can stop it."

However, in 1902 Zola died in his Paris apartment after being overcome by fumes from a faulty stove. It was later alleged that anti-Dreyfusards had deliberately blocked the stove's chimney to kill the novelist. In 1908 after Dreyfus had finally been reinstated in the army, Zola's remains were transferred to the Pantheon in Paris, where France's greatest heroes are honored. **NJ**

◔ Zola's open letter to the president occupied all of the title page of the newspaper *L'Aurore* on January 13, 1898.

Maine Is Sunk

The ship's loss provides a casus belli *for the U.S. to end Spanish rule over Cuba.*

USS *Maine*, an aging battleship, had been sent to Havana by President William McKinley. It was there to show the flag and protect U.S. citizens threatened by rioting in the Cuban capital between Spanish authorities and pro-independence Cuban nationalists who had been fighting an inconclusive guerrilla war in which some 100,000 Cubans had died.

The ship arrived on January 25, and the violence subsided. Then, on the evening of February 15, a massive explosion in the bows of the *Maine* sank her within minutes. Some 260 mainly enlisted sailors

"Please remain. You furnish the pictures. I'll furnish the war."

William Randolph Hearst to his press artist

died instantly, and six died later of their injuries. Captain Charles Sigisbee and most of his officers, quartered in the stern, survived.

U.S. public opinion, fanned by the press, was outraged and blamed Spain for sinking the ship. War fever was encouraged by the rival press barons William Randolph Hearst and Joseph Pulitzer, and after a navy inquiry concluded that a mine had sunk the *Maine*, war was declared on Spain.

The subsequent Spanish-American War ended Spanish rule in Cuba, replacing it with a U.S. presence, which lasted until Castro's takeover in 1959. The cause of the *Maine's* sinking is a mystery, although a 1976 investigation by U.S. Admiral Rickover concluded that spontaneous combustion in a coal bunker had ignited the ship's powder magazine. **NJ**

A Deadly New Weapon

The Battle of Omdurman demonstrates the machine gun's lethal potential.

After the killing of General Gordon by Mahdists at Khartoum in 1885 and the death by natural causes of the Mahdi the same year, the British waited fourteen years before moving to reassert their control over the Sudan. But in 1898 the *Sirdar* (commander) of the Anglo-Egyptian army, Sir Herbert Kitchener, moved with 27,600 Egyptian troops and 8,000 British regulars, supported by a flotilla of twelve Nile gunboats, on the Mahdist capital Omdurman, outside Khartoum, where the Mahdi's successor Khalifa Abd Allah had established his capital. The gunboats bombarded

"Whatever happens, we have got / The Maxim gun and they have not."

Hilaire Belloc, poet, writer, and historian

the city, symbolically reducing the Mahdi's tomb to rubble in a brutal show of force.

Assembling on an arc of hills north of Omdurman, the Mahdist Dervish warriors, armed with spears and rifles, attacked at dawn. They were mown down by newly delivered Maxim machine guns, and the rout was completed by a charge—the last large-scale cavalry charge by a European army—of the Twenty-First Lancers, including the young Winston Churchill. Some 20,000 Mahdists died, with minimal British losses. Three of the British force were awarded the Victoria Cross, and Kitchener received a Barony.

Churchill's self-aggrandizing account of the campaign in his first book, *The River War*, was to promote the Battle of Omdurman as a high-water mark in British imperialism. **NJ**

The Fashoda Incident

The last colonial rivalry between Britain and France is peacefully resolved.

Fashoda, a small town on the White Nile in eastern Sudan, stood directly on two intersecting lines representing conflicting French and British ambitions in Africa. The British were extremely anxious to join up "the Cape to Cairo," thus connecting their southern and central African territories with their northern annexations in Egypt and the Sudan. But the French were equally keen to link their west African empire with their eastern possessions on the Horn of Africa via the Saharan trade routes.

On July 10, 1898, Major Jean-Baptiste Marchand arrived at Fashoda and swiftly claimed the town for France. He had set out from Brazzaville in the French Congo fourteen months earlier accompanied by 150 colonial soldiers. Two months after his arrival, on September 19, a more powerful British force, under the command of Sir Herbert Kitchener, arrived via the Nile. Less than three weeks after his triumph over the Mahdist forces at Omdurman, Kitchener was in no mood to compromise with a colonial rival, and after weeks of tension Marchand reluctantly obeyed orders received from Paris to withdraw from Fashoda. The French force left on November 3.

The new French foreign minister, Theophile Delcassé, had resisted quite significant nationalist pressure for war with Britain, realizing France's inherently weak position, divided as she was by the notorious Dreyfus affair. Delcassé wanted to build an anti-German alliance, and he quietly defused the crisis with an agreement made in March 1899, limiting British and French spheres of influence in Africa to the Nile and Congo rivers, respectively. His diplomacy bore fruit in the creation of the Entente Cordiale, the Anglo-French alliance that was eventually victorious in the Great War. **NJ**

Pathway to the Unconscious

The ideas of Sigmund Freud trigger a revolution in perceptions about human psychology and sexuality that continue to influence our thinking today.

It was finished in September 1899 and published very quickly, on November 4, faster than the publishers expected, for they inscribed the year 1900 on the title page. Not that the error mattered because *Die Traumdeutung* (The Interpretation of Dreams), by an obscure Viennese psychologist, was very definitely a financial flop. Only 600 copies were printed, and it took eight years to sell them. Yet Dr. Sigmund Freud was thrilled with the book. "Insight such as this," he rejoiced, "falls to one's lot but once in a lifetime." He had long been fascinated by his own dreams, believing they held a deep psychological significance. Now, after years of clinical practice and research, he was ready to publish his findings. It was his opinion "that night dreams are just as much a wish fulfillment as day dreams."

Freud believed that human beings are governed by sexual passions, such as the Oedipus complex, of which the conscious mind is but dimly aware. Even in sleep, the mind's libido seeks discharge; and thus the kernel of every dream, even those made somewhat confusing by a form of mental censorship, is the attempted realization of some desire. Here, in embryo, was a whole theory of the human psyche.

Freud's work continued at a tremendous pace. He constructed theories that seemed to shed light not only on neurotic illnesses but on the human mind itself, and thus on every aspect of human culture. Ten years after 1899, his work was far better known. A second edition of *The Interpretation of Dreams* was prepared, and translations were sold all over the world. The public had discovered that Freud was a brilliant prose stylist who could be read, enjoyed, and argued about, not to mention simplified and distorted, by everyone. **RP**

○ Asked whether his cigar-smoking habit had any significance, Freud is said to have replied, "Sometimes a cigar is just a cigar."

> ## *"I am by temperament nothing but a conquistador —an adventurer . . ."*
>
> **Sigmund Freud to Wilhelm Fliess, February 1890**

DECEMBER

A Merry Christmas to you all!
I'm off to join the WAACs,
And serve the country that I love
Until the Axis cracks!

S	M	T	W	T	F	S
		1	2	3	4	
5	6	7	8	9	10	11
12	13	14		16	17	18
19	20	21	22	23	24	25
26	27	28	29	30	31	

The artist Alberto Vargas combines pin-up glamour with a patriotic message in a calendar for the year 1943.

1900–1949

Airship Makes Its First Flight

Count Zeppelin's faith in airships transforms twentieth-century aviation.

◐ A postcard of the first Zeppelin LZ1 taking to the skies over Bodensee, Germany.

Count von Ferdinand Zeppelin, a Prussian army aristocrat, was introduced to lighter-than-air flight in 1863 during the American Civil War. An observer with the Union army, he witnessed observation balloons. In 1891, back in Germany, he retired early to create airships for civil and military use. The zeppelin made its maiden flight on July 2, 1900.

Founding a factory at Friedrichshafen, Zeppelin had used the wealth of his wife Isabella to finance the development of an enormous balloon, 420 feet (128 m) long by 38 feet (11.5 m) across. It was filled with 399,000 cubic feet (11,298 cubic meters) of hydrogen in seventeen separate gas cells covered by rubberized cloth. Cotton cloth held the light metal framework together. The zeppelin was steered by two rudders fore and aft, and driven by two 215-hp Daimler engines, each rotating propellers. Two gondolas under the balloon held the passengers.

On the zeppelin's first flight, the crew of five steered her over nearly 4 miles (6 km) during the eighteen-minute outing, at an altitude of 1,300 feet (396 m). By the beginning of World War I, zeppelins had carried 35,000 people across Germany without an accident. Used to bomb Britain and France in the war, the zeppelin proved vulnerable to attack. zeppelin's death in 1917 and the fatal crashes of the R101 in 1924 and *Hindenburg* in 1937 meant that the future of flying rested with the airplane—although Zeppelins were still made at the original Friedrichshafen factory until 1997. **NJ**

The End of an Era

Queen Victoria's death inspires national mourning in Britain.

○ Large crowds turned out to see Queen Victoria's elaborate funeral procession.

Despite failing eyesight and poor mobility, the aged Queen Victoria, eighty-one in 1900, attended assiduously to her duties. She kept up a voluminous correspondence with her ministers, making them all aware, for instance, that the prospect of Home Rule for Ireland did not amuse her at all. She also took a special interest in her empire: to her the Boers were "horrid people, cruel & over-bearing," and she never doubted Britain's cause in the South African War. But December 1900, at Osborne House on the Isle of Wight, was a cruel month. Her last diary entry was for January 12, recording a "good night." A few days later she had difficulty speaking, and soon her children and grandchildren arrived at her bedside. She died at 6:30 on the evening of Tuesday January 22, 1901.

Ten days later, a funeral of impressive military pomp began. Many thousands of soldiers and sailors conveyed her coffin in stately procession from Osborne, first across the Solent to Portsmouth, then to London, where spectators massed up to half a mile deep in Hyde Park, and finally to Windsor, where the funeral service was held in St. George's Chapel on February 2. Two days later, she was buried at Frogmore next to her husband, Prince Albert, who had died forty years earlier.

In death as in life, Victoria, a woman with her share of human frailties, was transformed by royal propaganda and spectacle almost into a goddess. It was this illusion, and the reverence it inspired, that was key to the monarchy's survival in Britain. **RP**

McKinley Assassinated

An anarchist shoots President McKinley, but the bullet is never found.

William McKinley, twenty-fifth president of the United States, became governor of Ohio in 1891 and secured a massive victory for the Republican Party in the presidential election of 1896. During his first term, the Spanish-American War ended with the destruction of the Spanish fleet in Cuba and the U.S. annexation of the Philippines and Puerto Rico. He was reelected with another substantial majority in 1900. In the following year, the city of Buffalo, on the Niagara Falls, staged a Pan-American Exhibition, which the president amiably attended. It was while greeting his citizens that he was shot.

The line of people waiting to shake the president's hand at a public reception in the Temple of Music included a twenty-eight-year-old anarchist from Cleveland, Ohio, named Leon Czogolz, whom even other anarchists regarded as a dangerous lunatic. His heavily bandaged right hand concealed a gun, and when the smiling president offered his hand, Czogolz fired. The bullet was deflected by a button on McKinley's waistcoat and the anarchist instantly fired again. The second bullet hit the president in the stomach, and Czogolz cried out, "I have done my duty." The president's guards seized Czogolz, took his gun, and hit him. McKinley said faintly, "Be easy with him, boys."

The president died in Buffalo on September 14. He was only fifty-eight, but the surgeons said they could not find the bullet in his abdomen because he was so fat. He was succeeded by the vice president, Theodore Roosevelt. Czogolz was tried and found guilty of murder, and went to the electric chair the following month, perfectly calm and saying, "I killed the president because he was the enemy of the good people—the good working people." **RC**

Radio Transmission

Marconi sends a wireless signal and ushers in a new age of communications.

In 1899 Guglielmo Marconi transmitted a signal across the English Channel. In the same year his wireless technology sent out a genuine SOS message and saved a sinking ship in the North Sea. In December 1901 Marconi announced that he had successfully transmitted the Morse Code letter "S" from Poldhu in Cornwall to a receiver at St. John's in Newfoundland. He had achieved this using a 400-foot (121 m) radio antenna supported by box kites. It was the modest dawn of a revolution in communications that within the century was to transform the world totally.

Born in Bologna, of an Italian father and Scottish mother, Marconi was frustrated in his early efforts to develop wireless telegraphy in his native country. (As a teenager he experimented with sending electric signals across his parents' garden between aerials.) Aged only twenty-one, he came to Britain with his mother in search of potential sponsors. He secured the support of Sir William Preece, the Post Office's chief electrical engineer, who helped publicize Marconi's "wireless telegraphy" system. In addition, he began a series of increasingly powerful radio transmissions of Morse Code signals over both land and water.

His radio made Marconi a wealthy man, but the commercial development of his invention was bedeviled by disputes with rivals, both technical and commercial. An insider-dealing scandal in Marconi shares nearly brought down the British government in 1912. Marconi later returned to Italy, where he became an enthusiastic supporter of fascism—dictator Benito Mussolini was best man at his second wedding in 1927. He died of cancer in Rome in 1937 at age sixty-three. **NJ**

Caruso Records His First Disc

Caruso is one of the first singers to record his voice on a gramophone disc, helping to establish a whole new form of entertainment.

Enrico Caruso made his first recording in 1902 in a studio belonging to the Gramophone and Typewriter Company in New York. His recording of "Vesti la Gubbia" in 1907 became the world's first million-selling record and ensured the supremacy of the gramophone record over other competing technologies for recorded music.

Caruso, born in Naples in 1875, was the outstanding tenor of his time and for seventeen years was the principal tenor of the Metropolitan Opera House in New York. While rehearsing the part of Rodolpho in *La Boheme*, he visited the composer Giacomo Puccini to ask for his comments on his interpretation. Caruso sang a few bars and the composer asked, "Who sent you to me? The Almighty?"

Caruso's fame was guaranteed as one of the first recording stars. Since Edison's original recording of "Mary Had a Little Lamb" on a wax cylinder in 1877, various alternative technologies had been developed. Emile Berliner developed a system of recording onto a gramophone disc, which had many advantages over the cylinder and the phonograph. Although the recording quality was no better, it was easier to make multiple copies through molding and pressing. The gramophone also needed less adjustment and could carry a recording on both sides of the disc. All of Caruso's 450-plus recordings were made for it, and it became the most desirable and popular domestic entertainment system in the first half of the century.

Caruso's recordings, low fidelity by today's standards, give only a partial impression of the power, range, and delicacy of the great man's voice. **NK**

◯ Photograph of Caruso in full costume as the Duke in *Rigoletto*, taken circa 1903.

The First Tour de France Begins

An arduous cycling race rescues a failing newspaper.

○ Maurice Garin, French racing cyclist, won the first Tour de France in 1903.

What has often been described as the world's greatest free sporting event began as a promotional event by a newspaper, *L'Auto*, whose editor Henri Desgranges, a champion cyclist, was engaged in a struggle with a rival journal, *Le Velo*. The concept was the brainchild of Desgranges's assistant Henri Lefevre, who did most of the organization en route.

The first race began on July 1, 1903, outside a café called Le Reveille Matin in Paris. It covered a total of 1,500 miles (2,400 km) and took nineteen days to complete in six formidable stages, some of which involved all-night rides: from Paris to Lyon, no less than 290 miles (467 km), Marseille, Toulouse, Bordeaux, Nantes, and then back to Paris, with rest days between each stage. Of sixty competitors from France, Belgium, Germany, and Switzerland, including professional team riders and freelance amateurs, just twenty-one finished the grueling course. Some 10,000 spectators saw Frenchman Maurice Garin, "the Little Chimney-Sweep," who had led throughout, finish first in the Parc au Princes, Paris. His winning margin was three hours, averaging more than 15.5 miles per hour (25 kph) for the course. Garin won a prize of 6,000 francs. The last finisher came in two days behind.

The celebratory issue of *L'Auto* sold hundreds of thousands—the following year *Le Velo* went out of business. The second race was marred by riots and bribery. Garin won again, but he and the next three finishers were disqualified for cheating—Garin was supposed to have taken a train part of the way. **PF**

The Wright Brothers Take Flight

The bicycle repair brothers make the first powered flight and create history.

○ Orville Wright is in the cockpit while Wilbur watches the first successful flight.

Orville and Wilbur Wright, hometown bicycle repair engineers from Dayton, Ohio, became interested in powered flight in the 1890s. Their great breakthrough was to devise a flexible wing that allowed the pilot to steer by warping it—an idea derived from observing seagulls in flight. After experiments with gliders and a homemade wind tunnel, they added a purpose-built engine in December 1903, before taking their wood, paper, and wire machine, which cost them less than a thousand dollars to construct, to the remote sand dunes at Kitty Hawk, North Carolina. On December 14, Wilbur made the first attempt to pilot it, but the *Flyer* (later known as the *Kitty Hawk*) stalled in takeoff and needed repairs. Three days later, at 10:35 A.M. in a gusting wind, the first flight, now with Orville aboard, covered 120 feet (39 m) in 12 seconds. In the fourth flight of the day, Wilbur flew 852 feet (279 m) in 59 seconds, about 10 feet above the ground. After this, the wind turned the *Flyer* over, smashing it. Just five passersby had seen them, and the next day a single local newspaper briefly reported their achievement.

Continuing experiments the following year met with mixed success, but the brothers learned to control the craft in flight and experimented with catapults to resolve the vexed problem of takeoff. Their own secretive style, based on fear of being copied, and a lack of interest locally meant it was not until 1908—at an air show in Le Mans, France—that their work received the attention it deserved. **PF**

Work on the Stalled Panama Canal Restarts

The United States takes control of the construction of the Panama Canal.

○ USS *Ohio* (left) passes USS *Missouri* in the Panama Canal, July 1915.

The possibility of a canal through the Panama isthmus had been discussed since the sixteenth century, because it would save an 8,000-mile (12,875 km) journey around Cape Horn. The need for one was felt particularly urgently by the United States after the sinking of USS *Maine* off Cuba in 1898. France's attempt to build a canal had stalled, and in 1902 U.S. President Roosevelt began negotiations with Colombia, which controlled Panama, to purchase the concession.

In November 1903, the Panamanians declared independence from Colombia and then sold control over the canal zone to the United States for $10 million. The agreement was ratified in February 1904, and the United States formally took possession of the incomplete French effort in May that year. A workforce of 40,000 men moved more than 70 million cubic feet (2 million cubic meters) of rock per month, while an equally large effort went into providing living accommodation and draining the mosquito-infested swamps. (The French workforce had been devastated by mosquito-borne yellow fever and malaria, which caused the deaths of more than 5,500 men.)

The 51-mile-long (82 km) canal was complete by late 1913, a year ahead of schedule. A grand official opening planned for the following year had to be canceled because of the outbreak of war in Europe, but the first ship to traverse it, the cargo ship *Ancon*, on August 15, 1914, marked the effective opening of the canal to traffic. On the last day of 1999, the United States returned control of the canal to Panama. **PF**

Bloody Sunday in St. Petersburg

The massacre of workers at the Winter Palace helps trigger the Russian revolution.

○ Soldiers in Palace Square open fire on the protesters as they flee on Bloody Sunday.

During the Russo-Japanese war of 1904 to 1905, conditions in St. Petersburg were dire, with employers forcing overtime on the poorly paid workforce. A strike at the Putilov industrial plant spread, and by mid-January, 80,000 workers were idle and the city was without electricity or newspapers. Father Georgi Gapon, an orthodox priest who had founded a workers' organization, announced a demonstration to the tsar's Winter Palace in January 1905 to petition Nicholas II for an end to the war and a restoration of the eight-hour day. Gapon was a highly ambiguous figure who, although in the pay of the tsarist secret police, the Okhrana, seems to have genuinely wanted better conditions for the poor. The protest itself was peaceful, with the workers and wives and children carrying religious icons and singing hymns of loyalty to the tsar. Gapon's men weeded out extremists.

As the march approached the palace, the tsar's Imperial Guard panicked and fired into the crowd. The death toll of the shooting and crowd stampede ranged from 90 (the official figure) to 4,000 (Gapon's estimate). Most historians believe around 1,000 died. The slaughter caused outrage, transforming the strike wave into the 1905 revolution. It also discredited the tsar's rule and increased hatred of the regime. Gapon fled to Switzerland, but when he returned to Russia in October, his role as a police agent was revealed and he was found hanging in a Finnish cottage after a "kangaroo court" organized by his social revolutionary comrades. **NJ**

Battle of Tsushima

The defeat of Russia's Baltic fleet signals the arrival of Japan as a world power.

The Battle of Tsushima demonstrated Russia's military incompetence and damaged Russian prestige. It ensured that Russia lost the war and helped spark the 1905 revolution. Conversely, it put Japan on the map.

After Russia excluded Japan from exploiting the resources of Manchuria, Japan's fleet under Admiral Heihachiro Togo launched the Russo-Japanese war by neutralizing the Russian Pacific fleet with shellfire and torpedo strikes at Port Arthur and Chemulpo in Korea. Incensed, Tsar Nicholas II sent the Russian Baltic fleet, under Admiral Zinovy Rozhdestvensky,

> ## "Japan expects this day the courage and energy of every officer and man in the fleet."
>
> **Admiral Heihachiro Togo, May 27, 1905**

around the world avenging the attacks. After a farcical incident in the North Sea when the Russians fired on British fishing vessels, mistaking them for the Japanese, Rozhdestvensky arrived west of Japan. His fleet of eight battleships, eight cruisers, and nine destroyers faced Togo's four battleships, eight cruisers, twenty-one destroyers, and sixty torpedo boats—all newer than their Russian counterparts.

Togo ambushed the Russians between the islands of Honshu and Tsushima. Within an hour, he had disabled the Russian flagship *Suvorov* and wounded Rozhdestvensky. Three more Russian battleships were sunk before the Japanese torpedo boats began on the survivors. Some 10,000 Russian sailors died. One Russian cruiser and two destroyers survived. Only three Japanese torpedo boats and 1,000 men were lost. **NJ**

It's All Relative

Einstein's Special Theory of Relativity changes thinking on space and time.

Albert Einstein described his Special Theory of Relativity as an attempt to reconcile the laws of mechanics with the laws of electro-magnetism. Published in June 1905, it altered the view of the universe first formulated by Isaac Newton. The theory replaced the linear view of time with a much more complex model. Einstein postulated that, if the speed of light is the same for all observers irrespective of their motion relative to the light source, then all other dimensions of time and space could not be absolute but must vary in relation to the motion of the observer and observed bodies. The measurements corresponded closely to the mechanistic Newtonian model of physics at lower speeds, but diverged sharply at high speeds.

Among the many implications of this theory were that no physical body could travel at or faster than the speed of light and that matter and energy were ultimately interchangeable, which was the basis of the development of nuclear power.

Einstein's theory was formulated in a Swiss journal of physics while he was in a lowly position in the Swiss Patent Office and attracted little attention. The Special Theory of Relativity was one of three groundbreaking papers published by Einstein in 1905. Yet it was only after he attained posts in Prague and Berlin and had developed his General Theory of Relativity in 1916 that his thinking became famous.

Einstein, who was Jewish, left Germany for the United States after the Nazis seized power in 1933 and spent the rest of his life at Princeton University, working for world peace and the state of Israel, and continuing his world-changing scientific labors. **NJ**

◐ One of the world's greatest physicists, Albert Einstein photographed "at work" in 1905.

Mastery of the Seas

The HMS Dreadnought *gives Britain the lead in the race for global naval supremacy.*

○ Postcard of the formidable Royal Navy steamship, 1906.

As Britain's new warship HMS *Dreadnought* slid into the water at Portsmouth dockyard in 1906, the nature of the world's navies changed. All existing battleships were now obsolete. Its design was so radical that it gave its name to a whole new style of ship. Inspired by the thinking of Admiral Fisher, once commander-in-chief of the Mediterranean fleet and now First Sea Lord, the professional head of the Royal Navy, the design brought together all the recent developments in propulsion, armor, and gunnery to create a fast, powerful ship capable of destroying any other ship. All future British warships would follow this model.

Other maritime nations—including the United States, France, Japan, Italy, and Russia—were obliged to follow this design if they were to project maritime power. But the major repercussions were felt in the new German Empire, where Kaiser Wilhelm II, supported by his navy minister, Admiral Tirpitz, had a policy of naval rivalry with Britain in the hope of challenging her predominance in the world's oceans. Both nations invested in more such ships with ever more sophisticated designs. The imperial German ship program was a major worry for the British. In World War I, the two fleets would eventually face each other at the Battle of Jutland, although the outcome proved inconclusive.

The *Dreadnought* concept dominated the world's navies until the new technologies of submarines, aircraft, and carriers. By the end of World War II, the *Dreadnought* was obsolete. **NK**

Earthquake in San Francisco

The city endures the United States's worst twentieth-century natural disaster.

◑ Residents of Golden Gate, near Hyde, continue to go about their business after the 1906 earthquake.

At 5:12 A.M. on April 18, the first tremors were felt on the San Andreas Fault. Just two minutes later, the quake, its epicenter in the bay 2 miles (3 km) from the center of San Francisco, had shaken the city violently. A survivor described the quake as like the waves of the ocean, but swift and choppy, with a grinding noise like an enormous train. Wooden buildings crashed down, cable-car tracks collapsed, and streets caved in. The gas mains burst and fires broke out and raged for four days, destroying 500 city blocks and killing more people than the quake itself, perhaps as many as 20,000 (certainly more than the 567 reported at the time by a government with keen antennae for a potential public relations disaster). Most buildings were insured against fire but not earthquakes, and many of those damaged by the quake suffered arson attacks. The city authorities took firm control, with the fire department dynamiting buildings in an attempt to keep the fire from spreading. Hundreds of looters were shot. In the end, between half and two-thirds of the 400,000 population were left homeless and took to the city parks. But rebuilding took months rather than years.

For the first time after such an event, pictures were seen around the world (although many were retouched to hide the scale of the destruction), and the new science of seismology had a welter of data on which to build, discovering the fault had ruptured for almost 300 miles (483 km), and measuring the quake as around 7.8 on the Richter scale. **PF**

Dreyfus Cleared

The loose ends of the political scandal that divided France are finally tied up.

On this day, three courts sitting together in Paris as the Courts of Cassation cleared Alfred Dreyfus of spying for Germany and high treason, for which he had been sent to Devil's Island in 1894.

Dreyfus's powerful opponents in the army, the Church, and the anti-Semitic press had fought against reopening the case, despite mounting evidence of Dreyfus's innocence. The scandal had already brought down several governments. Dreyfus returned to France after his supporters conclusively demonstrated that the charges were false and were

> *"No, messieurs, no. I beg of you. 'Vive la France!'"*
>
> **Dreyfus rebukes fans shouting "Vive Dreyfus!"**

part of a conspiracy by high-ranking officers, partly because he was a Jewish officer on the anti-Semitic General Staff and partly to protect the identity of the real spy, Charles Esterhazy.

After the court's verdict, the French Parliamentary Chamber and Senate voted to restore Captain Dreyfus and Colonel Georges Picquart—the officer who first proved Dreyfus's innocence and had been dismissed—to the army. Dreyfus was inducted into the Legion of Honour in a courtyard adjacent to the parade ground where he had been degraded before a howling mob eleven years earlier. This time the crowd shouted, "Vive Dreyfus! Vive Picquart!" On October 15, twelve years to the day after his first arrest, Dreyfus reported for duty at the Vincennes Fort near Paris. The Dreyfus affair was over. **NJ**

Immigration Controls

The United States Immigration Act seeks to hold back the tide of humanity.

In the hundred years after 1815, some thirty-five million people entered the United States in what Hugh Brogan has called "the largest peaceful migration in recorded history." Americans began to feel threatened and demanded stricter controls. The 1907 Act of Congress created a new Border District in Arizona, New Mexico, and Texas as a barrier to Mexicans, and authorized refusal to laborers from China and Japan.

The 1890 census showed nine million foreign-born in a total population of sixty-three million. There was anxiety about arrivals from eastern and southern

> *"Will it make our difficulty the less that our human garbage can vote?"*
>
> **Henry George, U.S. economist, 1883**

Europe, the infiltration of Mexicans, and the thousands of Chinese and Japanese coolies sneaking in under loads of potatoes or inside bales of hay. The 1907 Act provided for the exclusion of those with any mental or physical defect that would prevent them from working, and of unaccompanied children. An amendment gave President Theodore Roosevelt the power to deny entry to anyone.

The Act of 1917 required immigrants to be able to read and write in their own languages. In the 1920s a quota system limited the numbers of each nationality allowed in by reference to its numbers already settled in the United States. However, the United States successfully persuaded newcomers to regard themselves as Americans while preserving their own national traditions. **RC**

Drillers Strike Oil

The enormous deposits of oil discovered in Persia will prove a mixed blessing to world politics and economics.

The discovery of the vast oilfields of southern Persia (today's Iran), the second largest after Saudi Arabia's, was made in 1908 by drillers working for a syndicate set up by the British entrepreneur William Knox D'Arcy, one of the founders of the Anglo-Persian Oil Company (APOC), today's British Petroleum (BP).

Knox D'Arcy, a lawyer who made his first fortune in an Australian gold-mining syndicate, agreed to fund a search for oil and minerals in Persia. In May 1901, he secured a concession from the shah and drilling began. It was an expensive and at first fruitless enterprise. In 1903 the costs of drilling consumed £500,000 ($2.5 million) of Knox D'Arcy's wealth, and the following year he was forced to find £100,000 in funding from Burmah Oil, who put up the money in exchange for much of Knox D'Arcy's stock.

In 1908 drilling took place at Masjid-I-Sulaiman in southern Persia, but by May, with no oil found, the venture was close to bankruptcy. Then, on May 26, at 1,180 feet (360 m) down, the drillers finally struck oil. By 1911 a pipeline had been linked to a refinery in Abadan on the Persian Gulf.

Oil would go on to largely dictate the politics of Iran and the wider Middle East for a century and beyond. When APOC was nationalized by the government of Premier Mussadiq in the 1950s, an Anglo-American organized coup overthrew him and installed the pro-Western Shah Reza Pahlavi. The shah in turn was overthrown by the 1979 revolution and replaced by an anti-Western Islamic Republic, which has made the future flow of oil from the wells of Iran ever more problematic. **NJ**

◗ Oil spurts high into the air after a successful drilling at Masjid-I-Sulaiman, Persia, in the early 1900s.

It Came from Outer Space

A giant meteorite explodes in Siberia.

○ Taken in 1910, this photograph shows the damaged landscape of the Tunguska region two years after the explosion.

About 7:15 A.M., hunters near the Tunguska River in central Siberia saw a bright blue streak flash across the sky, followed by a flash and a loud knocking noise. This was followed by a series of explosions, each one accompanied by a shock wave. The forest was destroyed and almost 100 million trees burned over an area 50 miles (80 km) across. From afar, the event registered as equivalent to a major earthquake, and the night sky was lit up for several days, as far away as Europe.

It has been calculated that the explosion was about 1,000 times greater than that of the Hiroshima bomb, making it the largest explosion in modern geological history. It is fortunate that it occurred in such a remote region. It was not until the 1920s that scientists investigated what happened. They concluded it was a large meteorite impact and for decades continued to search in vain for the crater, although they found traces of minerals associated with meteorites. Geologists determined the meteoroid—whether it was an icy comet or a stony asteroid is still debated—probably exploded a few miles above the Earth's surface. Patterns left in the ground resembled those left after a nuclear explosion.

The event led some Siberians to think the end of the world might be near, and there are many alternative explanations for it—some involving UFOs, and others involving exotic astronomical phenomena such as small black holes. It has also inspired many fiction writers to speculate on its causes. **PF**

Launch of the Universal Car

The Model T Ford goes on sale for the first time.

O One of the first Model T automobiles, manufactured in 1908.

The motorcar was one of the key developments of the twentieth century, and the greatest figure in its transformation from a luxury item to one that plenty of people could buy was Henry Ford. A semiliterate Michigan farm boy, he learned engineering through apprenticeships and began building a car in his backyard in Detroit. His first model, in 1896, had a two-cylinder gasoline engine, a wooden chassis, a bicycle seat, and bicycle tires, and could reach a top speed of 20 miles per hour (30 kph). Rival machines rarely exceeded 5 miles per hour (8 kph).

In 1905, he started the Ford Motor Company and launched the Model T in 1908 at $825. With a 20-hp engine and a steel chassis, it cruised at 25 miles per hour (40 kph). He called it "a motor car for the great multitude" and advertised it as the "Universal Car," claiming, "No car under $2,000 offers more, and no car over $2,000 offers more except trimmings."

The Model T was well made and it sold. Ford developed and refined his mass production methods, which reduced the worker to a cog in a machine, cut the time needed for manufacture—reducing chassis assembly from twelve and a half hours to two hours and forty minutes by the end of 1913—and brought prices down. Ford put wages up and cut working hours. A Model T started coming off the production line every twenty-four seconds, and the price was down to $290 by the time production stopped in 1927. More than fifteen million had been sold; the world's love affair with the automobile had begun. **RC**

Peary Reaches North Pole

U.S. explorer Robert Peary claims he is the first person to reach the North Pole, although many doubt his word.

A U.S. naval officer who explored Greenland in the 1890s and 1900s (during which time he lost eight toes to frostbite), Robert Edwin Peary became determined to reach the North Pole. After several failures, he set out from Cape Columbia on Ellesmere Island on March 1, 1909, with an assistant, Matthew Henson, and twenty others—including several Inuit—on wooden sledges drawn by dog teams. Peary and Henson and four Inuit undertook the last five-day stage of the journey, and thirty-seven days after setting out, they reached the pole, or so Peary maintained.

Returning to Labrador in September, Peary announced he had reached his goal but became involved in a bitter wrangle with another American, Frederick Cook, who claimed to have got there the year before. Cook's veracity was very much in question, but Peary's claim was also doubted because it seemed impossible to do the journey in thirty-seven days. In 1926 the pole was reached by a party who flew over it in an airship. They were led by Roald Amundsen, the Norwegian discoverer of the South Pole.

However, in 2005 a British party of five set out in Peary's tracks, starting from a large signpost he had left behind him, pointing to the North Pole. Using dogs and the same type of sledges, they reached the pole in the same thirty-seven days, taking a few hours less than Peary did and arriving in temperatures of seventeen degrees below zero Fahrenheit (-27° C). Peary's reputation now seemed reestablished, sixty-five years after his death. **RC**

◗ Polar explorer Robert Peary photographed around the time of his journey to the North Pole.

◖ Some of the members of the expedition: Oogueah, Ootah, Henson, Equinquah, and Seegloo.

An Empire Crumbles

The Ottoman Turkish Sultan Abdul Hamid is deposed.

Ousted from power in 1909, Abdul Hamid is remembered as a cruel tyrant who hastened the end of the Ottoman Empire. In reality he staved off his empire's inevitable collapse by playing off European powers against each other. He tried to coax his country into modernity without compromising his powers. According to historian F. A. K. Yasamee, he was a combination of "determination and timidity; insight and fantasy held together by immense practicality."

In 1875 Abdul Hamid harshly repelled revolts in the Ottoman Balkan provinces of Bulgaria, Bosnia, and Macedonia, but defeat to Russia in the 1877 to 1878 war led to the crippling Treaty of San Stefano, which

"My God take my hand in these troubled times. My God be my helper . . ."

Poem by Abdul Hamid

granted independence to the Balkans. He was unable to stop Britain from becoming the dominant power in his former domains of Egypt, Sudan, and Cyprus.

Soon afterward, the Young Turk movement, made up of university students and young army officers, agitated for a return to the constitution that Abdul Hamid had granted in 1876, then suspended. In 1909, Young Turk soldiers marched on Istanbul and replaced Abdul Hamid with his brother Mehmed, a puppet of the Young Turks. Turkey then allied with Germany against the Entente powers of Britain and France—a policy that culminated in her taking the losing side in World War I, which ended in the dissolution of the Ottoman Empire. **NJ**

Radical Budget

Lloyd George's "People's Budget" proves controversial with the British parliament.

Members of Britain's House of Commons expected something unexpected from the chancellor David Lloyd George's budget of 1909. Indeed there were so many items to be extracted that his speech took more than four hours to deliver. He began with the need to raise revenue: new battleships had to be constructed; old age pensions, introduced in 1908, were costing more than anticipated; and further provisions were needed to help the sick and unemployed. As a result, taxes would rise. Income tax would increase and a "super-tax" on higher incomes was introduced. There were other revenue-raising measures, including land tax. It was the most radical budget in British history.

"It is for raising money to wage implacable warfare against poverty . . ."

David Lloyd George

The Liberal party had a majority in the Commons, but the Conservatives controlled the House of Lords, which could reject all bills except budgets. Emotions were high, with landowners considering the budget an attack. The Lords rejected the budget—to their regret, as Lloyd George introduced legislation to remove their power over budgets and limit their bill veto to two years' duration.

It took two general elections in 1910 and a threat from the king to create many more peers, but the Lords eventually passed the budget and the new Parliament Act. The "People's Budget" proved a landmark in the growth of the welfare state and in the evolution of the British constitution. **RP**

Dr. Crippen Arrested at Sea

The denouement of an Edwardian domestic murder is a triumph for new technology.

○ Crippen (right, in handcuffs and mask) is taken into custody after his attempt to flee the country fails.

The Crippens were an ill-matched pair. She was an outsize, blowsy, third-rate movie star with Russian, Polish, and German roots who went under the name Belle Elmore; he was a midwestern American, myopic, shy, homeopathic quack. Nonetheless, Dr. Crippen was arrested on July 31, 1910, for the murder of his wife. A jury took less than half an hour to find him guilty, and he was hanged at Pentonville Prison, London, on November 23.

The Crippens had settled at 39 Hilldrop Crescent, Holloway, North London, where Belle taunted her husband with her affairs. That is until Ethel Le Neve, a slim dark beauty, became Crippen's receptionist and his lover. Suddenly, Belle vanished. Crippen said she had returned to the United States, and died. Police and Inspector Walter Dew searched Crippen's house three times without result. Crippen, however, panicked. He disguised Le Neve as a boy and sailed on the SS *Montrose* for New York. Dew searched the house again and found chunks of Belle's dismembered body buried in the cellar. Although at sea, the diminutive doctor was caught thanks to a trans-Atlantic wireless message, a device invented less than a decade before. The *Montrose*'s master, George Kendall, had radioed his suspicion about two of his passengers after seeing Crippen cuddling the boyish Le Neve. Dew overtook the *Montrose* on a faster ship and, dressed as a pilot, confronted Crippen in Canada's St. Lawrence seaway. Meek as ever, Crippen held out his hands for the cuffs. **NJ**

Mexican Revolution Begins

President Diaz is overthrown at the start of Mexico's haphazard revolution.

○ Pancho Villa and Emiliano Zapata surrounded by their supporters.

Under the rule of Porfirio Diaz, who had been president of Mexico since 1876, Mexican industry developed and infrastructural projects multiplied with foreign investment. But the injustices of society had become entrenched, with a gulf between rich and poor, and state-sponsored violence, as Diaz sought what he called "order followed by progress."

Francisco I. Madero tried to stand against Diaz for the presidency, but was jailed. He then escaped and fled to the United States. On November 20, 1910, he called for Diaz's overthrow and agrarian reform. Madero won the 1911 elections but failed to enact his program of social and economic reform. In 1913 he was overthrown by Victoriano Huerta, a military follower of Diaz. Conflict in the country intensified,

with several groups threatening military coups. These included Pancho Villa, conservative Venustiano Carranza, and followers of Emiliano Zapata, a Native American who ran a guerrilla peasant army and sought radical land reform. In 1914 Huerta was forced into exile, and Carranza, promising political and economic reform, became president. Carranza failed to deliver on his promises and his assassination in 1920 is often seen as the end of the revolution, but instability and violence continued until the 1940s.

The revolution saw a rise in Mexican nationalism and opposition to foreign political and economic intervention in the country, and opposition to the Catholic Church. Beyond this, the ideological aims of the protagonists were rarely well defined. **PF**

Amazing Fortress Discovered in the Andes

The "lost city" of Machu Picchu is discovered in Peru.

The discovery of Machu Picchu, the most famous Inca site and one of the best-known archeological sites in South America, high in the Andes Mountains of Peru, caused a sensation. It certainly made the name of its thirty-five-year-old discoverer, Hiram Bingham, an academic at Yale University and specialist in Latin American history. Originally from a Hawaiian missionary family, Bingham had married a Tiffany heiress and consequently had plenty of money to go exploring in South America. After expeditions in Colombia and Venezuela, Bingham turned his attention to Peru and had the good fortune to be led by local guides to the remains of an amazing, mysterious fortress, palace, and temple, which had been forgotten by the outside world for centuries.

Bingham contemplated various theories with regard to his "lost city." He thought it might be the original center of Inca civilization or the mysterious Vilcabamba, the Incas' final refuge from the conquering Spaniards, or perhaps even the home of Inca sacred virgins. It is now considered most likely that it was actually the fifteenth-century country retreat of the Inca Pachacutec and may have been left to fall slowly into ruin after his death. Without doubt, it is a magnificent example of Inca architecture and craftsmanship.

Bingham made many more South American expeditions and, although nothing in his later career remotely matched the discovery of Machu Picchu, he became a respected authority on Latin American history and geography, as well as a U.S. senator for Connecticut in the 1920s and 1930s. His discovery had a powerful influence on the growth of interest in South American history in the United States, and later worldwide. **RC**

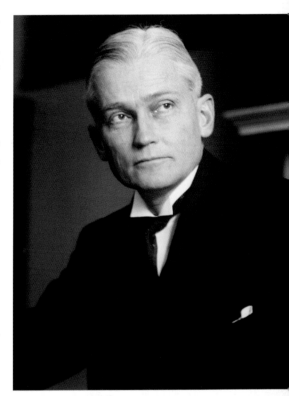

○ Bingham at his desk in 1925, having been sworn into the office of senator of Connecticut.

○ The expedition makes its way along the Urubamba canyon toward Machu Picchu.

> *"This wall and the temple ... were as fine as the finest stonework in the world."*
>
> **Hiram Bingham,** *Lost City of the Incas,* **1948**

Amundsen Reaches the South Pole

Roald Amundsen dresses in Inuit clothes, eats his animals, and reaches the South Pole thiry-five days before the rival British expedition.

Roald Amundsen never intended to be the first man to reach the South Pole when he chartered his ship the *Fram* from fellow Norwegian explorer Fridtjof Nansen. His original goal was the North Pole, but when he heard that the United States's Robert Peary had got there first in 1909, he sailed south.

Only on reaching Madeira did he tell his crew of his intentions, and famously cabled Captain Robert Scott, a British explorer bent on the same objective. Reaching the Bay of Whales on the Ross Ice Shelf on January 14, 1911, Amundsen laid a series of supply depots for his assault on the Pole. On October 19, 1911, he left with four companions and fifty-two Greenland Husky dogs. Using the Axel Heibig glacier route and consuming their dogs as they went, the Norwegians reached the Pole with sixteen dogs on December 14—thirty-five days before Scott. Leaving a tent, a letter, and a Norwegian flag as evidence, they returned to their base on January 25, 1912, after a ninety-nine-day round-trip.

Amundsen beat Scott because he did not stop for scientific observations; he dressed in traditional Inuit furs; he used a faster route to his goal; and he did not encounter the fierce blizzards that doomed the British return from the Pole. Also, Scott did not eat his animals, thus weighing himself down with food. Amunsden continued to explore the polar regions from the air until 1928, when his plane crashed while he was searching for survivors from a downed French balloon over the Bering Sea. **NJ**

◐ Amundsen reaches the South Pole and plants the Norwegian flag as evidence of his triumph.

◑ Taken on January 17, 1912, this photograph shows Scott and his expedition having discovered Amundsen's tent.

Emperor Abdicates

The ex-emperor of China survives prison to die as a palace gardener.

Born in 1906, Pu Yi was the twelfth and last emperor of the Manchu Qing dynasty, which had ruled China since 1634. Chosen by the dowager Empress Cixi, on her deathbed, the baby Pu Yi was accompanied into Beijing's Forbidden City with his wet nurse, Wang, amid a court of eunuchs and mandarins. He did not see his mother again for six years.

In 1912, the regent Empress Longyu was forced to abdicate under pressure from Sun Yat-Sen's republican revolutionary movement in southern China. But Pu Yi retained the title of emperor and

"I have nothing in the world except you, and you are my life."

Pu Yi to his last wife, Li Xin

his apartments in Beijing, where his Scottish tutor, Reginald Johnson, proved to be a stabilizing influence.

Restored to the throne by a warlord in 1917, Pu Yi moved to Manchuria under Japanese control in the 1920s and was proclaimed puppet Emperor Kang De of the Japanese protectorate of Manchukuo in the 1930s. Deported to Japan and then to house arrest in a Soviet dacha after World War II, Pu Yi was returned by Stalin to China and imprisoned by Mao Zedong for fifteen years for collaborating with the Japanese.

Freed in 1959, Pu Yi was kept as a curiosity by Mao's communists, working as a gardener in the Forbidden City where he had reigned. Permitted to marry an "ordinary" Chinese nurse, Li Xin, after a lifetime of unhappy unions with approved royal brides, he died of cancer on October 16, 1967. **NJ**

Polar Explorer Dies

Beaten to the South Pole, Captain Scott dies a hero.

Captain Robert Scott, a British naval officer, was on his second Antarctic journey when disappointment, then tragedy, overtook him. Learning late in the day that Norway's Roald Amunsden was racing him to the South Pole, Scott refused to be hurried and spent a great deal of time on the scientific research that was the ostensible chief goal of the expedition. He also persisted in using a variety of means of transport: ponies and man-hauling, as well as the faster Husky dogs relied on by the Norwegians. British sentimentality about butchering their animals also

". . . I do not think I can write more. For God's sake look after our people."

Scott's last journal entry

slowed Scott down because he and his companions had to carry food supplies for the entire expedition.

The final factor that doomed the trip was the abnormally severe weather that Scott and his team—Edward Wilson, Henry Bowers, Lawrence Oates, and Edgar Evans—encountered on their outward and return journeys to the Pole. After the discovery that they had lost the race, injury, frostbite, and blizzards took their toll. Following the death of Evans and the self-sacrifice of the weakened Oates, who left the party and walked to his death rather than slow them down, the others were marooned in their tent, not knowing that they were only a few miles from a food depot and salvation. Here they died of starvation and exposure, with Scott's journal furnishing the materials for the creation of his heroic and enduring myth. **NJ**

Titanic Sinks on Maiden Voyage

The Titanic *strikes an iceberg and sinks, taking 1,517 people with her.*

The newly built *Titanic*, 52,000-ton flagship of the White Star Line, was the largest ship afloat when she left Southampton on England's south coast on her maiden voyage to New York on April 10, 1912. She never arrived. Four days later, at 11:40 P.M., this enormous Edwardian edifice of opulence and symbol of technological triumph, while steaming at high speed on a calm sea on a clear night, struck an iceberg. The collision tore a long, deep slash along *Titanic*'s side, flooding one by one the separate watertight compartments that supposedly made the enormous ship totally unsinkable.

After two hours and forty minutes of gradually mounting panic, the *Titanic* upended to an angle of 65 degrees and slid, bows first, beneath the icy waters of the Atlantic. Her complement of just twenty lifeboats was enough to carry only half her 2,200 crew and passengers, and some of them were launched half empty. The next morning the liner *Carpathia* rescued 705 survivors, but 1,517 people, including *Titanic*'s captain Edward Smith, went down with the ship. The crew of the *California*, a ship in the vicinity of the disaster, was criticized for mistaking the *Titanic*'s SOS flares for celebratory maroons. Some male survivors, including White Star's managing director Bruce Ismay, were attacked for not letting women and children go in their place, and the dead included a high proportion of "steerage" passengers from the lower decks who had been emigrating to the United States in search of a new life.

In 1985 an American-French consortium led by Robert Ballard located the wreck at a depth of around 2.5 miles (4 km). Since then, thousands of objects have been recovered from the site, which includes a large forward section of the hull, and photographs and movies of the wreck have been produced. **NJ**

○ A newspaper seller broadcasts the news outside the headquarters of White Star in London.

◑ Watercolor postcard of the *Titanic* as she set sail on her one and only voyage.

> " . . . *the event* . . . *woke [the world]* . . . *with less peace, satisfaction and happiness.*"

Jack B. Thayer, *Titanic survivor*

Ballet Evokes Outrage

The premiere of Igor Stravinsky's The Rite of Spring *in Paris causes a riot.*

○ *The Rite of Spring* by Igor Stravinsky was first performed by the Russian Ballet.

At the end of the first decade of the twentieth century, the twenty-eight-year-old exiled Russian composer Igor Stravinsky was the toast of Paris. Although modern in his approach, he seemed firmly anchored in the tonal traditions of his compatriot Tchaikovsky, as his popular ballets *The Firebird* and *Petrouchka* had shown. However, in May 1913, he produced a musical revolution that reverberated throughout the century and has still not died away.

When Sergei Diaghilev, the flamboyant impresario of the Russian Ballet that had wowed the Western world with its outlandish, extravagant productions and the seemingly superhuman leaps and bounds of its principal dancer Nijinski, commissioned Stravinsky to write a new ballet, no one was prepared for the shock he had in store. The score was so complex that it required a hundred rehearsals and the premiere had to be delayed for a year. When it opened on May 29, a veritable riot resulted. The discordant music and the savage story of crude pagan peasants sacrificing a maiden to greet the renewal of spring outraged even the sophisticated Parisian audience, whose yells and catcalls escalated to fully fledged fistfights. The riot drowned out the music, Stravinsky stormed from the theater, and the performance ended in chaos. The following year, when the piece was presented again, the production passed off peacefully and the revolutionary work entered the musical canon as an instant and lasting classic. **NJ**

Suffragette Trampled to Death

Emily Davison's death at the Derby reveals the implacable spirit of the suffragettes.

◐ Emily Davison is fatally injured as she tries to grab the reins of the king's horse; the horse was not hurt.

Spectators were amazed on Derby day in 1913 to see a soberly attired, middle-aged woman dive under the rails at Epsom horse-racing track in England and rush toward the runners. She ran in front of the king's horse, Anmer, and was trampled. The horse was unharmed and the jockey slightly injured. Police used newspapers to stem blood flowing from the woman's skull, but she did not regain consciousness. She had two flags of the Women's Social and Political Union (WSPU) pinned inside her coat. Emily Wilding Davison was the first suffragette martyr.

Born in 1872, Davison had studied at Oxford before becoming a governess and teacher. In 1906 she became one of the first members of Emmeline Pankhurst's WSPU and had found a cause to live for.

Over the next few years she was arrested several times and went on hunger strikes. One time, rather than submit to force-feeding, she barricaded her cell and refused to emerge even after a hose pipe had drenched the room. She was arrested for the last time in 1912 for horsewhipping a man she mistakenly believed to be the chancellor of the exchequer.

To many, Emily Davison was an unbalanced suffragette whose suicide at the Derby was typically neurotic. Yet it is possible that she was securing publicity for her cause simply by pulling up the king's horse. The coroner's verdict was "death by misadventure." Davison was certainly prepared to risk death for her cause. Such determination helped women win the vote in Britain in 1918. **RP**

Archduke Franz Ferdinand Dead

The assassination in Sarajevo becomes the pretext for declarations of war.

○ Archduke Franz Ferdinand and his wife, Sophie, pictured one hour before they were fatally shot.

At 10:50 A.M. on a Sarajevo street, nineteen-year-old Gavrilo Princip stepped up to the car containing Archduke Franz Ferdinand, heir apparent to the Austro-Hungarian Empire, and fired shots into the interior. Princip was a Serbian nationalist and member of a terrorist organization called "Black Hand," whose aim was independence for southern Slav peoples in the Austro-Hungarian Empire. It was led by a Serbian secret intelligence colonel who coordinated the assassination attempt. A bomb was thrown as the archduke and his wife, Sophie, drove to a reception, but the device bounced off their car and exploded under the following vehicle. Despite the shocking lapse in security, precautionary measures for the return trip were ill planned. The driver missed his turn and stopped right beside Princip and a fellow conspirator. Princip seized the moment and shot the duke in the neck and the duchess in the stomach, killing them both. Princip then tried to shoot himself but was tackled by onlookers. He was sentenced to life imprisonment in an Austrian prison, where he died of tuberculosis four years later.

In the meantime Austria-Hungary accused Serbia of complicity and secured Germany's support in delivering an ultimatum that would effectively strip Serbia of its independence. With just two minutes to go before the end of a forty-eight-hour deadline, the Serbs acceded to almost all the demands and offered to accept international mediation. The offer was rejected. World War I had ground into gear. **JJH**

Germany Invades Belgium

This violation of Belgian neutrality is the opening act of World War I.

◐ The German army marches through Brussels at the start of World War I.

The nightmare of World War I began on August 4, when the German armies streamed over the Belgian border. After Britain had demanded in vain that the Germans withdraw, she declared war at 11 P.M.

By 1914 the division of Europe into two rival armed camps was well advanced. Fearing encirclement and Russia's growing military strength, the Central Powers of Germany and Austria-Hungary were convinced that they could win a preemptive war against the allies Russia and France without Britain joining in. Britain was concerned by German belligerence, demonstrated in the Agadir and Panther crises, and by the building of Germany's High Seas fleet to challenge British naval dominance. Britain's loose Entente Cordiale of 1904 with France had recently included conversations about British military support for France in the event of a German invasion.

When Germany used the assassination of the Austrian heir apparent Archduke Franz Ferdinand by a Serb nationalist as a *casus belli* to provoke Serbia's ally Russia into war, her own war plans had long been laid. The plan involved violating Belgian neutrality to invade France and seize the Channel ports. Both Britain and Germany were guarantors of Belgian neutrality—a treaty now contemptuously referred to by German Chancellor Theobald von Bethmann-Hollweg as "a scrap of paper." Germany gambled that Britain would not declare war and that, even if she did, Germany would be able to crush France before British power was brought to bear. **NJ**

Christmas Truce in the Trenches

Soccer and socializing temporarily ease the tension in No Man's Land.

○ British and German troops mingle during the temporary cease-fire of Christmas 1914.

The truce that arose spontaneously in No Man's Land between the trench lines in the first winter of World War I is one of the most poignant episodes of the tragic conflict. The trench lines had solidified after the mobile warfare that had opened the war, and by Christmas 1914 there were calls for a temporary truce—notably from the newly elected Pope Benedict XV. Although rejected by the governments, the call was echoed in the frozen trenches, where an MP turned soldier, Captain Valentine Fleming, told his friend Winston Churchill, "On both sides every single man wants it [the war] stopped at once." On Christmas Eve, it did, briefly, stop.

The future writer Henry Williamson, serving south of Ypres, saw the Germans place a Christmas tree on their parapet. Soon afterward the strains of the carol "Silent Night" drifted across No Man's Land. Shouted Christmas greetings were followed by some bold spirits venturing into No Man's Land to shake hands and share cigarettes with their enemies. The truce continued on Christmas morning along much of the front line, although it was noted that the easier-going Saxon, Swabian, and Bavarian regiments were more inclined to observe a cease-fire than the more militarist Prussians. On Christmas afternoon, an impromptu soccer match was played between the two sides. The truce continued until Boxing Day and in some places until New Year's Day. When the news reached high command, a dim view was taken and similar fraternizations were strictly forbidden. **NJ**

Allies Land at Gallipoli

Allied forces land at Anzac Cove in Turkey.

⭕ Troops disembark at Anzac Cove, squeezing onto the narrow beach from which they would make little headway.

The Gallipoli campaign was a bold strategic plan—typical of Winston Churchill—but disastrously flawed in execution. The aim was to take control of the Gallipoli peninsula, thereby cutting off Turkey from her German and Austrian allies and possibly forcing her out of the war. Once victorious, the Allied Powers would then open a new front in the Balkans from where to strike at the "soft underbelly" of the Central Powers. Britain's cabinet approved the plan in January, but the crucial element of surprise was lost when ships bombarding the Dardanelles forts struck mines, giving the Turks time to reinforce the defenses.

Allied troops—principally the Australian and New Zealand Army Corps (Anzacs) and Britain's Royal Naval Division—landed at Anzac Cove on April 25, 1915. Turkish troops fought hard and a bloody slogging match ensued on the sheer cliffs in baking heat and atrocious conditions. Another Anglo-French landing at Cape Helles likewise failed to make headway, and the campaign degenerated into a savage stalemate. A third landing at Suvla Bay also failed, and in November 1915 the cabinet bowed to the inevitable and ordered an evacuation. In contrast to the shambolic campaign, the evacuation was a textbook operation.

Gallipoli had cost the British Empire casualties of 205,000 killed, wounded, missing, or dead of disease, and the French 47,000. The Turks lost 250,000. The campaign left a sense of lasting bitterness among Australians at British military incompetence and (briefly) also cost Churchill his glittering career. **NJ**

Lusitania Sunk

Torpedoed by a U-boat, the ship gives the United States cause to enter the war.

World War I was into its second year and German submarines operating from Kiel and Bremerhaven were sinking millions of tons of Allied shipping, especially in the Atlantic. Across the ocean, the U.S. government maintained its policy of neutrality. However, on May 7, 1915, the sinking of the *Lusitania* prompted the United States to enter the fray, although not until 1917.

As far as the German Embassy in Washington, D.C., was concerned, the rules of engagement for naval action were perfectly clear. Vessels flying the

"It would have been impossible for me, anyhow, to fire a second torpedo . . . "

Walter Schwieger, alleged entry in war diary

flag of Britain, or any of her allies, were liable to destruction in the zone of war—and that included the waters adjacent to the British Isles. The 31,500-ton British passenger liner *Lusitania* was one such vessel making the crossing from New York harbor to Liverpool with close to 2,000 passengers and crew. Reports of increased German submarine activity prompted the British Admiralty to wire warnings to the ship to adopt zigzagging maneuvers and other evasive actions. The warnings went unheeded and Kapitänleutnant Walter Schwieger ordered a torpedo to be fired from submarine *U-20*. It exploded amidships on the *Lusitania* starboard side, followed by a heavier explosion in the engine room boilers. Only twenty minutes later the ship sank with 1,198 passengers perishing, including 128 U.S. citizens. **JJH**

Death of a Patriot

The execution of Edith Cavell provokes a popular outcry in Britain.

Edith Cavell, a clergyman's daughter from Norfolk, was appointed matron of a nursing school in Brussels in 1907. After the German army occupied most of Belgium in 1914, she volunteered to operate an escape line, which sent hundreds of Belgian men liable to be conscripted—and later escaped Allied prisoners of war and stray soldiers—to the neutral Netherlands under the cover of her hospital work. Neglecting elementary security, she allowed her charges to drink in nearby cafés and was inevitably discovered by the Germans, who arrested her a year after the outbreak of war on August 5, 1915. She was tried under martial law, admitted her actions, and was condemned to death.

Despite strong warnings from U.S. diplomats representing Britain in Brussels about the adverse effect her execution would have on neutral opinion, the sentence was confirmed and carried out at a Brussels shooting range on October 12. Her famous last message, "Patriotism is not enough. I must have no hatred or bitterness for anyone," now inscribed on her statue in London, was given to the Reverend Gahan, an Anglican clergyman, on the night before her execution. The German doctor who certified her death was the Expressionist poet Gottfried Benn.

Allied propagandists made much of the "barbarity" of Nurse Cavell's death, although under military law the Germans were entitled to execute her, as British diplomats privately acknowledged. Nevertheless, she was converted into the war's most celebrated martyr and cause célèbre, illustrating German "frightfulness." Many children born in the war (including French singer Edith Piaf) were named in her honor. After the war, her body was returned to Norfolk and reburied at Norwich cathedral. **NJ**

German Attack on Verdun

The savagely wasteful Battle of Verdun in France begins; lasting ten months, it is the longest battle in history and one of the bloodiest.

Although aimed at France, the real goal of the German attack on Verdun in World War I, according to its architect General Erich von Falkenhayn, "was to knock England's best sword from her hand" by drawing France into a battle of attrition that would "bleed her to death." Falkenhayn chose the fortress town of Verdun, on the River Meuse, as his target. It was surrounded by a ring of forts, though these had been stripped of many of their guns.

The attack opened with a furious bombardment by 1,220 German guns on a narrow 8-mile (13 km) front. Falkenhayn's plan saw this section of the Western Front turned into a "mincing machine" as artillery inflicted slaughter on an industrial scale. German losses soon began to match those of France, however, and although the Germans took two key forts, Verdun itself did not fall. The longer it held out, the greater its symbolism became for both sides. France funneled in fresh troops and supplies and appointed a skilled defensive commander, Pétain. In the autumn, after pressure had been removed from Verdun by the mainly British offensive on the Somme, two more aggressive French commanders, Nivelle and Mangin, prepared counterattacks that retook almost all the ground lost to the Germans.

Falkenhayn's plan failed, but Verdun's debilitating effect corroded the French army's morale, contributing to widespread mutinies the following year. In the long term, it also played a part in sapping the French will to fight another war with Germany in 1940. **NJ**

○ Fallen German soldiers and their equipment fill a trench overcome by a French attack during the protracted battle.

○ Exposed French troops duck for cover during an explosion near their position on the shell-blasted battlefield.

Easter Rising

The rising lights the way toward Irish independence from British rule.

The Easter Rising in Dublin against British rule was the work of the secret Irish Republican Brotherhood (IRB), a clandestine organization dedicated to achieving an Irish republic by physical force. The IRB had infiltrated and gained a commanding position in the Irish Volunteers, the legal paramilitary wing of the majority Irish Parliamentary Party, which worked for Home Rule by constitutional means.

The rising had been planned since the outbreak of the Great War, with promised support from Britain's enemy, Germany. Early in 1916 the socialist James Connolly's tiny Irish Citizen Army was included in the plot, and Connolly was co-opted on to the seven-man military council directing it.

On April 24, some 1,250 rebels rose in Dublin, seizing the general post office as their headquarters and occupying other commanding strong points. IRB leader Padraig Pearse read a proclamation of Irish independence. Six days of fierce fighting followed in which British artillery laid waste to much of central Dublin and hundreds were killed on both sides. After the inevitable surrender, fourteen of the rising's leaders, including Pearse and Connolly, were shot— the latter propped up in a chair because of wounds sustained in the fighting. The executions fueled a wave of public sympathy for the previously widely despised rebels, and by the 1918 postwar election, surviving Easter veterans returning from British internment, including Eamonn De Valera and Michael Collins, were voted into power and formed their own parliament, the Dail Eireann, beginning the final campaign to win independence. Although defeated within a week, the rising was the spark that lit the fuse for the rapid achievement of the long-sought goal of Irish independence from British rule. **NJ**

Sharing Arab Lands

The Sykes-Picot agreement between France and Britain is sealed in secret.

The Sykes-Picot agreement was a diplomatic deal between France and Britain negotiated in the midst of World War I to divide up the territories of the Turkish Ottoman Empire between British, French, and Russian spheres of influence. This cynical "divvying up" of Arab lands between European powers still provokes mistrust in the Middle East to this day.

Negotiated in London between Sir Mark Sykes, a pro-Turkish diplomat, and his French counterpart Francois Georges-Picot, uncle of the future French president Giscard d'Estaing, the deal laid out that a

> ## *"I recognize that we may have to sell our small friends to pay for our big friends . . . "*
>
> **T. E. Lawrence, letter to Sir Mark Sykes**

swathe of territory comprising today's Syria, Lebanon, southeast Turkey, and northern (Kurdish) Iraq should be within France's zone of influence, whereas Britain would be responsible for central and southern Iraq, Jordan, and Palestine. The agreement, later ratified as the treaty of San Remo in 1922, also made provision for Russian access to the Persian Gulf.

At first kept secret for fear of offending the Arabs, who had been induced by the British to rise in revolt against the Turks, the deal became public knowledge when it was publicized by Lenin after the Russian revolution to embarrass the Allies. Criticized for its imperialism and failure to acknowledge Arab aspirations to self-rule, the agreement nonetheless became the blueprint for the postwar settlement in the Middle East. **NJ**

Two Mighty Navies Clash

The German navy fails to break Britain's dominance of the oceans despite inflicting heavy losses on the Imperial and Royal navies at the Battle of Jutland.

Beginning on May 31, 1916, Admiral Sir John Jellicoe, commanding the Royal Navy's Grand Fleet, fought the only fleet action of World War I against the German Imperial Navy, commanded by Admiral Reinhard Scheer. For twenty years before the outbreak of war, the German Empire had challenged the British command of the oceans, and in particular of the North Sea, by an aggressive construction program of the new Dreadnought battleship.

In a running battle across the seas off Denmark, the Royal Navy lost three capital ships, three cruisers, and eight destroyers. More than 6,000 sailors died. The Imperial Navy lost two dreadnoughts, three cruisers, and four destroyers, with the loss of 2,500 sailors. Kaiser Wilhelm II proclaimed a great victory. Indeed the battle had not produced the decisive result that the British, heirs to the traditions of Nelson and Trafalgar, had expected. Weaknesses in ship design, weaponry, and signaling had all been made apparent.

Nonetheless, on June 2, Jellicoe reported from his base in the Orkney Islands that his fleet was ready to leave harbor at four hours' notice. Scheer, however, reported to the kaiser that the German fleet would not be ready for action until the beginning of August. Twice more that year the German Imperial Fleet sortied from its bases, and twice it returned home when the presence of the British fleet was reported. Jutland had ensured that the British would retain their strategic and psychological dominance of the North Sea for the remainder of World War I. **NK**

⊙ A convoy of navy ships in the Battle of Jutland in World War I, May 31, 1916.

⊙ A German warship firing its guns on May 31, 1916, during the Battle of Jutland.

The Bloodiest Morning

The Battle of the Somme begins.

July 1, 1916, was the blackest day in British military history since Hastings in 1066. Despite months of preparation, the British offensive against German positions north of the Somme was almost a total failure. By dusk there were 57,000 casualties—more than 19,000 of them dead. They were the victims mainly of German machine guns, which had been rushed up from deep dugouts where they had "sat out" the preliminary bombardment, to rake the slowly advancing lines of British infantry. Most of the casualties were men of Kitchener's New Armies—the volunteers who had answered his call in 1914.

The main successes on July 1 came in the French sector, where the French, learning from Verdun, mounted more limited "bite and hold" attacks with small groups of men moving under cover of local artillery. Eventually the British would learn these tactics, too. The strategy behind the Somme had been to take the pressure off the French defense of Verdun and reduce the Germans by attrition. To this end, and despite the horrendous losses, the British Commander Haig ordered that the offensive be continued. It went on for four months, taking a few square miles of woods and open ground and a handful of battered villages, at the cost of additional devastating losses.

The latter stages of the battle were notable for the introduction of the first tanks, although their success was limited. The New Armies were reinforced by men from South Africa, Australia, Canada, and New Zealand. By the time Haig called off the offensive in the mid-November rains, his armies were still some way short of Bapaume, the town that had been the original objective. The British Empire had lost 414,000 casualties, their French allies 195,000, and the Germans a similar number. **NJ**

◔ A German soldier prepares to hurl a hand grenade toward advancing British forces on the first day of the battle.

◑ British troops abandoned their trenches and "went over the top," many of them encountering machine-gun fire.

"Enemy forces engaged on the battle front had been severely shaken."

Sir Douglas Haig, December 23, 1916

Rescued!

Shackleton makes it back to Elephant Island and his stranded comrades.

Ernest Shackleton was a showman. A reckless adventurer, but an extraordinary leader of men, he epitomized the Edwardian obsession with polar exploration and personified the idea that playing the game was more important than winning it. Even after Amunsden conquered the South Pole and Scott had died on the same quest, Shackleton managed to raise the money and men for another expedition to cross Antarctica in the middle of World War I.

Shackleton was just as adept at getting his men into tight corners as at leading them out again. His ship *Endurance* was crushed and sank in the pack ice of the Weddell Sea before he had even reached the coast of Antarctica. Marooned on the desolate Elephant Island, Shackleton and a few companions set off in a tiny open boat, the *James Caird*, to summon help. After a 700-mile (1,126 km) voyage, they reached the island of South Georgia and were faced with a march over sheer mountains to reach the nearest whaling station. They made it, and Shackleton traveled to Chile to find another vessel, the *Yelcho*, for the perilous voyage back to Elephant Island. Once again, he battled through and rescued the twenty-two remaining members of his expedition, who had almost exhausted their food but never abandoned hope that "the boss" would come to their rescue. Ironically, having survived the expedition, several of Shackleton's men died in the trenches on their return to war-torn Europe. Shackleton died in 1921 of heart failure during yet another expedition—this time an attempt to circumnavigate Antarctica. He was buried on South Georgia. **NJ**

⬤ The dramatic moment when *Endurance* becomes firmly trapped in the ice and Shackleton decides to abandon ship.

"Mad Monk" Murdered

After numerous failed attempts, the mystic Rasputin is finally killed.

Grigory Efimovich Rasputin, an illiterate Siberian peasant credited with mystical powers of healing and prophecy, established a strong hold on the affections of the Russian Imperial family. He also held firmly on to life, and many murder plots failed before he was killed on December 31, 1916.

Despite his religious leanings, Rasputin had a well-founded reputation for drunkenness, dirt, and debauchery. Arriving in St. Petersburg in 1904, his image as a genuine holy man was boosted by the patronage of some Orthodox priests, and despite (or

"There was something appalling and monstrous in his diabolical refusal to die."
Prince Felix Yusupov

because) of his rough-hewn ways he attracted a following of aristocratic ladies. Rasputin established an unassailable hold on the strong-willed but stupid Tsarina Alexandra—and, through her, Tsar Nicholas II—by stanching the internal bleeding of the tsar's eldest son, Alexei, when he was at death's door.

After Russia entered World War I, Rasputin's interference in politics became more marked, and he was targeted by a conservative, nationalist clique. Led by Prince Felix Yusupov and the politician Vladimir Purishkevich, the plotters lured Rasputin to Yusopov's palace, where they murdered him—with much difficulty thanks to his robust will to live—by feeding him cyanide-laced cakes, repeatedly shooting and battering him, and finally by plunging his still-living body under the ice of the River Neva. **NJ**

The Code Is Broken

Germany's ill-judged attempt to lure Mexico into World War I backfires.

The Zimmerman telegram was at once a diplomatic blunder and a triumph of code-breaking. The sender was German foreign minister Arthur Zimmerman, and the intended recipient Heinrich von Eckardt, Germany's ambassador to Mexico. Britain's ground-breaking naval intelligence department in Room 40 of the London Admiralty had long since broken Germany's diplomatic codes, and so Zimmerman's reckless attempt to lure Mexico into war against the United States was in the hands of the Allies long before Von Eckardt set eyes on it.

The telegram was a gamble born of Germany's desperation to keep the United States out of the war. Berlin knew that Washington's patience would be sorely tried by Germany's sinking of neutral (including U.S.) shipping after its declaration of unrestricted submarine warfare (USW). The telegram tried that patience to the breaking point. In it, the newly appointed Zimmerman declared that should USW draw the United States into war, then Germany would encourage Mexico to declare war on its northern neighbor. Mexico's bait was Germany's promise to restore the "lost territories" conquered or annexed by the United States in the nineteenth century: the states of Texas, New Mexico, and Arizona.

After the telegram had been decoded by cryptanalysts, Admiral Reginald "Blinker" Hall, Britain's preeminent spymaster, delivered it to foreign secretary Arthur Balfour. Overjoyed, Balfour passed it to the U.S. ambassador in London, Walter Page, who duly forwarded it to Washington. An outraged President Woodrow Wilson's declaration of war against Germany followed in April. Historians believe that the duplicitous malice of the telegram was the decisive factor in tipping a reluctant Wilson into war. **NJ**

Leader Returns

Lenin arrives at St. Petersburg to take charge of the Russian Revolution.

The liberal Russian Revolution of February 1917 took many by surprise, not least Vladimir Ilyich Ulyanov (Lenin), leader of the Russian Marxist revolutionary "Bolshevik" faction. He had predicted the event for years, but doubted he would see it in his lifetime.

The "first" Russian revolution found Lenin in Zurich where he had been waiting out World War I in neutral Swiss exile, attending socialist peace conferences, writing withering polemical articles against the war, and fuming in frustration. After the overthrow of the tsarist regime and the formation of a moderate socialist government, Lenin entered into negotiations with the Germans to smuggle him and a group of his Bolshevik comrades into Russia to foment a second revolution that would decisively remove Russia from the war.

They agreed that Lenin's party would travel on a "sealed train" to St. Petersburg. The deal was brokered by wealthy Bolshevik sympathizers and agreed to by the German government, which, although detesting Lenin's revolutionary plans, was desperate to remove Russia from the war before the United States entered it.

After an arduous journey, Lenin arrived at St. Petersburg's Finland Station late on the night of April 16. Spurning a welcoming bouquet and the fawning words of his comrades, Lenin launched into a bitter attack on his own party, fiercely upbraiding the Bolshevik leaders—including Stalin—inside Russia who had cooperated with Kerensky's parliamentary regime. Instead, said Lenin, they should launch an immediate revolution on a program of "land, peace, and bread" under the "guidance" of the Bolsheviks alone. At first derided, the "April theses" became the blueprint for the violent Bolshevik seizure of power six months later. **NJ**

Mata Hari Executed

Secret agent, double agent, or scapegoat—fate finally catches up with the ultimate femme fatale, Mata Hari.

Many historians have suggested that Mata Hari was a scapegoat. Her execution on October 15, 1917, came at a time when France, wracked by military setbacks and the mutinies of its armies, was sorely in need of someone to blame.

Born Margarethe Zelle in August 1876, Mata Hari married Dutch officer Rudolf MacLeod at the age of eighteen and left Amsterdam for Java in the Dutch East Indies. The marriage fell apart, however, and by 1905 she was in Paris working as a circus performer. She took the stage name Mata Hari (Javanese for "sun") and developed an erotic striptease act based on Indonesian dances, which she performed to sensationalist press acclaim.

Her bold personality and the sensuality of her near-naked dances won her fame and a host of high-placed lovers. When World War I came, her military lovers, her neutral Dutch nationality, and her consequent ability to travel freely in all belligerent countries drew her into the murky world of espionage. She may have worked as a genuine French secret agent, but she may also have been a double agent for Germany. Arrested and questioned by the British secret service in London, she claimed to be spying for France and was released. However, in February 1917 she was arrested in Paris after the French supposedly intercepted messages from the German military attaché in Madrid identifying her as a German spy. Mata Hari indignantly denied the charges but was convicted of treason and shot at Vincennes. **NJ**

◑ A mugshot of Mata Hari in profile before her execution on October 15, 1917.

◑ Indian sitar players accompany Mata Hari as she practices her Javanese temple dance.

Balfour Declaration

The British government commits to the idea of a Jewish "home" in Palestine.

O A Jewish colony in Palestine, which was built after the Balfour Declaration.

Few documents capable of achieving momentous consequences have been as brief as the Balfour Declaration of 1917. It came in a one-page letter from British foreign secretary Lord Balfour to Lord Rothschild, a leader of Britain's Jewish community, notifying him that the cabinet would support the establishment of a Jewish "home" (not explicitly a state) in Palestine, "His Majesty's Government view with favour the establishment in Palestine of a national home for the Jewish people . . . it being clearly understood that nothing shall be done which may prejudice the civil and religious rights of existing non-Jewish communities in Palestine." The ambiguity and apparent contradiction of these words have bedeviled progress in the Middle East ever since.

The declaration came at a crucial moment in World War I when Britain was in simultaneous talks with Arab leaders, who were being encouraged to rise against Britain's Ottoman Turkish enemies, and Zionist lobbyists led by Chaim Weizmann. Weizmann had developed a process to synthesize acetone, a vital constituent of the explosive cordite—much needed during the war. In return, he asked for British support in establishing a Jewish home in Palestine.

After the war, Britain controlled Palestine under a League of Nations mandate and permitted Jewish emigration into Palestine. As this increased in the 1930s with the rise of anti-Semitism in Europe, and faced with an Arab revolt in Palestine, Britain endeavored ineffectually to limit Jewish entry. **NJ**

Bolsheviks Take Control

The October Revolution is an old-fashioned seizure of power by an armed minority.

○ Panic sets in amid violent street fighting in St. Petersburg.

Since Lenin's return from exile in April 1917, the Bolsheviks—the extreme wing of Russia's Marxist Social Democrats—were committed to taking power by force from Kerensky's provisional government. They had made one botched attempt in July, known as the "July days," and had been preparing their cadres for a second attempt ever since. On November 7, on the prearranged signal of a blank gunshot from the cruiser *Aurora*, armed Bolshevik sailors, soldiers, and workers seized key points in St. Petersburg.

The provisional government was increasingly unpopular because of its failure to either end the war or improve Russia's desperate economic crisis. Supported by the Left Social Revolutionaries, the Bolshevik central committee voted ten to two in favor of another attempt at seizing power. Active preparations were placed in the hands of Leon Trotsky, a recent charismatic defector to the Bolsheviks from their more moderate Menshevik rivals. He headed up a military revolutionary committee and directed events from the Bolshevik headquarters in the Smolny Institute, a former girls' boarding school.

The October Revolution's greatest coup was the taking of the tsar's Winter Palace, the seat of the provisional government, which was guarded by young military cadets and a battalion of women soldiers. By the end of the day, the city was in Bolshevik hands and the first stage of their takeover of the country had been successfully achieved. **NJ**

French Ship Explodes

The biggest human-made explosion to date takes place in Canada.

○ Dock workers trudge through the snow to assess the damage in the aftermath of the explosion.

Halifax, Nova Scotia, was a major World War I convoy port crowded with merchant ships. Among them was a Norwegian vessel, the SS *Imo*, on her way to New York to pick up relief supplies for Belgium. On December 6, 1917, behind time and possibly traveling faster than normal on her way out of the inner harbor, she collided with a French ship from New York, the SS *Mont Blanc*, which was loaded with a lethal cargo of TNT, guncotton, ammunition, and picric acid (used in making artillery shells). She also had drums of high-octane fuel piled on her deck.

When the two ships collided, sparks flew and some of the *Mont Blanc*'s fuel drums caught fire. Her crew abandoned ship on the orders of their captain and the French ship drifted up against a pier in the harbor, where she suddenly exploded in a blinding white flash of light. The whole ship was blown completely to pieces. The blast totally flattened the immediate area, devastating the surrounding 325 acres (132 ha) and smashing most of the windows in the town.

The blast killed some 1,600 people and wounded thousands more. It caused a huge pressure wave that sank some of the smaller ships in the harbor. Shrapnel raining down caused numerous injuries, whereas rumors spread that Halifax had been bombed by German zeppelins. Rescue parties did a courageous job, but that night came the worst blizzard in years and yet more deaths. The total death toll was reckoned at more than 2,000. **RC**

Treaty of Brest-Litovsk Is Signed

The Bolsheviks buy their way out of World War I.

⊙ Military officials greet each other at Brest-Litovsk, in today's Belarus, having agreed to sign the peace treaty.

When the Treaty of Brest-Litozsk was eventually signed on March 3, 1918, it imposed extremely harsh conditions on Russia. The country lost one-quarter of its territory, half of its industry, and nine-tenths of its coal-mining capacity.

The Bolsheviks had come to power in November 1917 determined to extract Russia from the Great War. The Germans were equally determined to levy a lethally high price for peace from the struggling revolutionary regime. The result when the two sides met at Brest-Litovsk was deadlock. The German military commander, General Max Hoffmann, insisted on terms so harsh—including the loss of Poland, the Ukraine, Finland, and the Baltic states—that the new Soviet commissar for foreign affairs Leon Trotsky broke off the talks, declaring that the Russian armies would neither fight the Germans nor make peace.

The Germans resumed their advance into Russia, and within a fortnight had grabbed all the land they demanded and were menacing the very survival of the regime. A prostrate Russia and her new Bolshevik masters hastily signed the Treaty of Brest-Litovsk.

Within nine months, the treaty was null and void. A defeated Germany was itself wracked by revolution, and the areas abandoned by its armies in the east were filled by competing armies of Whites, Reds, and local nationalists fighting a vicious civil war. The Reds reconquered the Ukraine and Belarus, but Poland, Finland, and the Baltic states managed to establish a shaky independence from Russian rule. **NJ**

Death of the Red Baron

Richthofen's death removes the biggest single threat to Allied airmen.

◐ Richthofen was a minor Prussian aristocrat; a large crowd turned out for his funeral procession.

Freiherr Manfred von Richthofen, feared by his enemies as the "Red Baron" from the blood-red color of his squadron's planes, was a killer. When he was shot down and killed on April 21, 1918, his British foes buried him with full military honors, such was the extent of their respect.

Richthofen was an enthusiastic hunter of game and transferred his lethal shooting prowess to the skies when the Great War began. He was Germany's highest-scoring ace. A colorful and charismatic leader, he often took his Danish hound Moritz aloft with him as a mascot. Before he set out on his final flight, Richthofen had had some near misses—notably in July 1917 when he had been shot down and severely wounded in the head. He resumed the leadership of his famous "Flying Circus" squadron in August 1917 and continued to kill. Nevertheless his death was attributable to his own errors of judgment as much as to the skill of those who shot him down. An inexperienced British pilot, Lieutenant Wilfred May, broke away from a dogfight with Richthofen when the guns of his Sopwith Camel jammed. Richthofen pursued May, chasing him down near ground level. Canadian flyer Captain Roy Brown steered his own Camel in pursuit: "Dived on pure red triplane which was firing on Lt. May. I got a long burst into him and he went down vertical and was observed to crash." Credit for Richthofen's death was also claimed by an Australian machine-gun unit, which fired on the distinctive low-flying plane from the ground. **NJ**

Tsar and His Family Murdered

The horrific execution of the imperial family draws a line of blood in Russian history.

○ Family portrait of Nicholas II and Alexandra with their five children, taken in 1915.

After abdicating in the wake of the first revolution in February 1917, the tsar and his family were held at a series of country retreats. Following the Bolshevik takeover, the conditions of their detention hardened, and they were moved to the Ipatiev House, near Ekaterinburg, where they were executed in July 1918.

As anti-Bolshevik forces approached the area, Bolshevik leaders Lenin and Sverdlov cabled their local allies in Ekaterinburg, ordering the killing of the imperial family. At 12:30 A.M. on July 17, the Romanovs were awakened, led to a cellar, and told they were to have their photograph taken. A firing squad opened fire, but many of the bullets bounced off jewels sewn into the clothes of the tsar's daughters. They were bayoneted and finished off with pistols. The Romanov family's corpses were mutilated to prevent identification and thrown down a mineshaft. Later, they were moved to a nearby shallow grave. After the collapse of communism in 1991, the remains of the tsar, tsarina, and three of their children were recovered, identified with DNA samples taken from living royal relatives, and reburied in 1998 in St. Peter and Paul cathedral, St. Petersburg. In August 2007 it was reported that the remaining Romanovs, the bones of the hemophiliac Tsarevich Alexei and his sister Maria, had also been found in Ekaterinburg.

The Ipatiev House was demolished on the orders of Boris Yeltsin. A cathedral has since been built on the site, and the cellar where the family died is now an Orthodox shrine. **NJ**

Damascus Falls

The capture of the Syrian capital by an Allied army ends Turkey's dominance.

🔾 General Allenby makes his formal entry into Jerusalem in January 1918, seven months before taking Damascus.

> *" . . . we killed as though the deaths and running blood could slake our agony."*

T. E. Lawrence, *Seven Pillars of Wisdom*

The Allied commander in the Middle East, General Allenby, opened a final offensive against Turkish-held northern Palestine and Syria on September 20, 1918. By October 1, the Allied armies had secured a victory, although Allenby himself entered Damascus on October 3 and missed the mayhem.

Pushing ahead of this final advance was a mounted Arab column under Colonel T. E. Lawrence and the Amir Faisal, whom Lawrence hoped to place on the throne of Syria in defiance of the Sykes-Picot agreement. Lawrence's orders were to occupy Dera and cut off the Turkish retreat, but he intended to occupy Damascus itself to demonstrate Arab independence and establish Faisal in power.

However, the Arab column was weak and diffuse. Maddened by evidence of atrocities committed by the fleeing Turks, Lawrence's Arabs slaughtered captured Turkish troops indiscriminately. Meanwhile, Allenby was advancing on Damascus in a pincer movement, aided by aircraft and cavalry, planning to take the city in simultaneous attacks from the south and east. Soldiers of the Australian 3rd Light Horse were the first to arrive in the city on September 30, and they were greeted by cheering Damascenes offering food and cigars. The next day, Lawrence's Arabs entered but were too weak in numbers and too preoccupied with looting and shooting Turks to maintain order. By October 2, the Australians had ended the anarchy, and the Allies staged a victory parade in celebration of their triumph. This effectively meant the end of Turkey's part in World War I and the end of five centuries of Ottoman rule over the Arabs.

Disappointed, Lawrence obtained Allenby's permission for home leave and returned to Britain determined to lobby for the Arab cause, which he had adopted so enthusiastically as his own. **NJ**

Abdication of Kaiser Wilhelm II

The announcement marks the end of imperial Germany.

Although the words were delivered on November 9, 1918, "I herewith renounce for all time claims to the throne of Prussia and to the German imperial throne connected therewith," strictly speaking, Kaiser Wilhelm II did not actually abdicate that day. The decision was officially announced on his behalf but without his consent by his distant cousin Prince Max of Baden. The prince was the last chancellor of imperial Germany and was struggling to stave off a full-blown revolution in Berlin in the dying days of the Great War. Wilhelm himself was in distant Spa, a small wooded town in Belgium that had become the war-time headquarters of his army.

Characteristically, Wilhelm was torn by indecision about what to do as his armies fell back on Germany's frontiers. The crews of his beloved High Seas fleet were holding widespread mutinies, and striking workers and revolutionaries stormed official buildings in Berlin. Initially blustering, he threatened to lead his armies to forcibly put down the revolution. He soon changed his mind when he was gently told that only two out of twenty commanders consulted could answer for the loyalty of their men. When the kaiser reminded the generals of their oath to him, General Wilhelm Groener curtly told him, "In such circumstances, sire, oaths are just words." Even the loyal commander-in-chief von Hindenburg mutely agreed that the kaiser's presence was in fact hindering peace and stability.

In a royal huff, Wilhelm retired to his imperial train and sometime during the night ordered it to journey across the neutral Dutch frontier. On November 28, he formally "suspended the use of his royal prerogative." He remained in exile until his death in the midst of another war in June 1941 and never saw Germany again. **NJ**

◊ Formal photographic portrait of Kaiser Wilhelm II in full military uniform.

> *" . . . the deepest, most disgusting shame ever perpetrated by a people . . . "*
>
> **Kaiser Wilhelm II, on his forced abdication**

Goodbye to All That

The armistice ending World War I is signed in a railway carriage in France.

○ Delighted crowds throng the streets in central Paris to celebrate the end of World War I.

◗ A military truck carries its troops through London, just moments before the armistice officially takes effect.

> ## "Whether you sign an armistice or not, I do not stop until I reach the Rhine."
>
> **Marshal Foch to the German delegation**

The armistice that brought World War I to an end was signed in a railway carriage at a siding in the forest of Compiègne, northwest of Paris, shortly after 5 A.M. on November 11, 1918. It would come into effect at 11 A.M. that day—"the eleventh hour of the eleventh day of the eleventh month."

The armistice was requested on November 7 by the German High Command under Paul von Hindenburg. The German armies had not been defeated nor Germany invaded, but the economy was in ruins and the government was under pressure from the collapse of the armies, mutinies in the navy, and the threat of revolution at home. A German delegation—led by the Catholic Center Party politician Matthias von Erzberger—crossed the front lines near La Capelle in a small motorcade and was taken by train across the northern French battlefields.

An Allied delegation led by France's Marshal Ferdinand Foch and Britain's Admiral Rosslyn Wemyss laid down non-negotiable demands, including Germany's withdrawal from France and Belgium, demilitarization of the Rhineland, and surrender of the German fleet. Erzberger prevaricated but, pressured by the new Social Democratic government in Berlin, which had replaced the departed Kaiser, he signed. Initially the armistice was for just thirty days, but it was renewed regularly until the Treaty of Versailles of June 28, 1919.

While Britons celebrated, many in Germany felt, as Hitler (then a corporal) later wrote, deeply let down, as all German-occupied territories were to be abandoned, and previous treaties signed with Russia (at Brest-Litovsk) and Romania were annulled. Germany also gave up a large amount of materiel, railway wagons, and all its submarine fleet, while most of the surface fleet was interned. **NJ**

Spartacus Week

A Bolshevik-inspired revolt in Berlin is swiftly crushed by the government and the Freikorps soldiers, sworn to put down revolution at all costs.

January 5, 1919, was supposed to begin a German repeat of the 1917 Bolshevik revolution in Russia, but instead it turned into the bloody fiasco of Spartacus Week. The weakness of German communism opened up the way to the total suppression of the German Left by the paramilitary Freikorps.

After Germany's collapse at the end of the Great War, a power vacuum was filled by the competing forces of the revolutionary left—mutinous soldiers, sailors, and striking workers and a small body of communist militants called the Spartacus League. They were opposed by the newly formed social democratic government in tactical alliance with the army and new military formations known as Freikorps.

The Spartacists founded the Communist Party of Germany (KPD), and their leader, Karl Liebknecht, against the advice of his more cautious comrade Rosa Luxemburg, proclaimed a government on January 5 and seized Berlin's strong points. In response, war minister Gustav Noske ringed the city with 5,000 army and Freikorps soldiers and moved them toward the center, systematically crushing Spartacist resistance. Flamethrowers, artillery, and machine guns were used as government forces retook key points and finally the Spartacist headquarters. On January 11, Noske wrote, "The nightmare which hung over the city is dispersed." In the wake of Spartacus Week scores of leftists—including Liebknecht and Luxemburg—were hunted down and murdered in cold blood, a sinister portent for the future of German history. **NJ**

🔾 Karl Liebknecht presides over the mass burial of some of those killed during the riots in Berlin.

🔾 Spartacists encounter government troops in a violent clash on the streets of Berlin.

Amritsar Massacre

A British massacre of demonstrators fans the flames of Indian nationalism.

Jallianwalla Bagh was a public square at the heart of the Punjab holy city of Amritsar. To many Indians, its gardens were a refuge from the crowded bazaars of the city. On April 13, 1919, it was a place of protest, when 10,000 Indians gathered to defy the British ban on public meetings. Soon, when General Dyer and his Gurkha rifleman arrived, it became a scene of indescribable panic and mass murder.

Dyer ordered his men to kneel, take aim, and fire into the crowd. The shooting went on for ten minutes, until the ammunition began to get low. The British

"Yes, I think it quite possible that I could have dispersed them perhaps without firing."

General Dyer to the Hunter inquiry

said that 397 died, although Indians spoke of 800 or more. Forty-year-old General Reginald Dyer believed that authority had to be reimposed in India in general, where nationalism was growing, and in Amritsar in particular, where five Englishmen had recently been killed and an English missionary, Miss Sherwood, had been molested. He was heard saying that "he felt like reducing the rebellious city to a heap of ashes." He was subsequently forced to retire but faced no charges for the atrocity.

In India, news of the massacre killed British efforts at constitutional reform and made many moderate, collaborationist, middle-class Indians into committed nationalists. The moral basis of British rule had been destroyed—it was now, in Gandhi's words, "a satanic regime." The days of the Raj were numbered. **RP**

Einstein Verified

Arthur Eddington demonstrates Einstein's Theory of General Relativity.

Albert Einstein's epochal Theory of General Relativity, first propounded before World War I, remained obscure until the British astrophysicist Arthur Eddington verified it in May 1919. He observed stars near the sun during a solar eclipse and took photographs to illustrate Einstein's theory.

Born in 1887 to Quaker parents of modest means and losing his father at an early age, Eddington's education was funded by scholarships granted for his precocious scientific brilliance. Awarded a degree by Trinity College, Cambridge, he became director of Cambridge University's observatory in 1913. He refused military service in World War I because of his Quaker beliefs.

The year after the war, he traveled to the island of Principe in the Indian Ocean on a research trip to watch the solar eclipse on May 29. His series of photographs confirmed Einstein's hypothesis that stars around the sun appeared to have shifted slightly as their light had been curved by the sun's gravitational field—an effect visible only during an eclipse when the sun's brightness no longer obscures the neighboring stars.

Eddington's findings were widely reported and for the first time Einstein's theory was disseminated in the public consciousness. His gift for explaining the complex theory in simple layman's terms was praised by Einstein himself as "the best presentation of the subject in any language."

Eddington spent much of his later career attempting to devise a "Fundamental Theory" uniting quantum physics, relativity, and gravitation, which he believed obeyed the same fundamental laws. Knighted and made a member of the Order of Merit, Eddington died in November 1944. **NJ**

Through a Difficult Sky

Alcock and Brown fly the Atlantic nonstop.

○ Alcock and Brown pictured taking a turn over Newfoundland, June 15, 1919.

The first nonstop flight across the Atlantic was made in a Vickers Vimy bomber with twin Rolls Royce engines by John Alcock and Arthur Whitten Brown. Alcock, the pilot and leading spirit, had persuaded the Vickers Company to provide the plane. He was a twenty-six-year-old Englishman who had gained most of his flying experience as a bomber pilot in World War I. Like his Scots navigator, Brown, who was six years older, he had spent time as a prisoner of war.

They took off from Lester's Field in St. John's, Newfoundland, on June 14 with some sandwiches, a little whisky, and a bottle of beer to keep them going. After a difficult flight of virtually 1,900 miles (3,040 km) in almost sixteen hours, they crash-landed in a bog in Ireland, near Clifden in Connemara. Their average speed had been 115 miles per hour (185 kph) and their altitude varied from sea level up to 12,000 feet (3,658 m). On the way they had had to contend with engine trouble and with fog, snow, and ice. Brown had climbed out onto the wings to clear ice that was clogging up the engine air intakes, while Alcock had coped with desperately poor visibility in an open cockpit full of snow. The bog looked like a green field from the air, but neither man was hurt when they landed. When the locals asked where they had come from, they said "America." They were welcomed as heroes and both were knighted by King George V. Sadly, Alcock was killed before the end of the year, when his plane crashed in France. Brown lived on until 1948. **RC**

Treaty of Versailles

Germany reluctantly signs a treaty designed to cripple the country financially.

○ Georges Clemenceau signs the treaty in the Hall of Mirrors at the Palace of Versailles, France.

There are two opinions of the treaty that was dictated to Germany at Versailles in the spring of 1919: too severe and not severe enough. The main clauses of the treaty ending World War I were decided on by the leaders of the chief Allies—U.S. President Woodrow Wilson, British Prime Minister David Lloyd George, and French Premier Georges Clemenceau. The treaty stripped Germany of her overseas colonies and chunks of German-speaking territory to the west and east. In addition, she lost her navy and her air force, and her army was limited to 100,000 men. She was forbidden from making or using heavy artillery or tanks and was ordered to pay crippling reparations. Most humiliating of all, Germany was required to accept sole responsibility for starting the war.

The treaty's terms caused outrage and mass protests in Germany. The foreign minister resigned rather than sign. Only the credible threat by the Allies to resume military hostilities and occupy Germany forced a reluctant National Assembly to vote for signing. On June 28—the anniversary of the Sarajevo assassination that had touched off the war—the Germans finally signed. Public opinion in the United States and Britain thought the terms too harsh. Only in France, where bitterness over four years of German occupation still ran high, were they regarded as too mild. Resentment at Versailles helped fuel the rise of Hitler, and when he came to power, he tore up the treaty's clauses one by one, rearmed, and eventually, by launching World War II, took his revenge. **NJ**

Two Minutes' Silence of Remembrance

An Australian journalist advocates an annual silence to pay respect to the war dead.

○ Passengers at Paddington Station, London, stop to observe the first two minutes' silence on November 11, 1919.

The solemn commemoration of the war dead, through war cemeteries, memorials across the land, symbolic tombs of "unknown warriors" for those with no known grave, and annual ceremonies of public remembrance, are among the important legacies of World War I in all combatant nations. The practice began just a year after the armistice.

The tradition of an annual national silence to remember the dead was the idea of an Australian-born journalist and war veteran named Edward George Honey. The journalist had been shocked by what he saw as irreverent wild celebrations that marked the armistice on November 11, 1918. Honey had a letter published in the *London Evening News* on May 8, 1919, advocating an annual five-minute silence

to remember the dead: "Five minutes only. Five silent minutes of national remembrance." Honey called it "a very sacred intercession." His idea was a popular one and was echoed by the South African statesman Sir Percy Fitzpatrick, who wrote to King George V in October suggesting that such a silence "May help to bring home to those who come after us, the meaning, the nobility, and the unselfishness of the great sacrifice by which their freedom was assured." The king's advisers supported the idea, but shortened the length of the silence to two minutes.

In the United States a similar practice began in 1921 with the burial of an unknown soldier in Arlington Cemetery; in 1954 November 11 was renamed Veterans' Day. **NJ**

Your Friendly Neighborhood Speakeasy

The prohibition era begins in the United States.

○ Federal agents make a public display of emptying bottles of whiskey down the drain.

The Eighteenth Amendment to the American Constitution, which came into effect on January 16, 1920, banned the manufacture, sale, barter, transportation, export, or import of any intoxicating liquor. It was the work of a temperance movement that had been growing steadily since the nineteenth century. The temperance cause allied Bible Belt Protestants with businessmen and concerned citizens, who had seen firsthand that working-class drunkenness brought with it poverty, the loss of many working hours, and alarming levels of domestic violence. Calls for temperance led readily into a demand for complete prohibition. By 1861 thirteen states were dry, and the Prohibition Party fought its first presidential election in 1880.

World War I sharpened the prohibitionists' teeth. They argued that national sobriety was essential if the war was to be won. Historians disagree about whether the effect of prohibition was a decrease or an increase in the consumption of alcohol, but no one is in much doubt that it was a serious disaster. Crime levels soared. Liquor was manufactured in people's cellars, brought into the country by bootleggers, and sold in illegal bars called "speakeasies." Millions of dollars were put into the pockets of criminals, and organized crime entered a position of power from which it has never been dislodged. Prohibition lasted until the Twenty-First Amendment came into force in 1933, legalizing the sale and consumption of alcohol. **RC**

The Dublin Dail Approves Anglo-Irish Treaty

The treaty splits Ireland into two states, North and South, and embitters Irish politics.

○ Eamonn De Valera's speech against the Irish Free State Treaty attracts a mass of followers in Dublin.

The debates that culminated in the ratification of the treaty setting up the Irish Free State ended one war—the struggle with Britain for Irish independence—but triggered another, the Irish Civil War of 1922 to 1923. The treaty was negotiated in London by the British, headed by Prime Minister David Lloyd George and war minister Winston Churchill, and Irish plenipotentiaries, led by Arthur Griffith and Michael Collins. Signed in January 1922, it guaranteed Irish independence from Britain, but as a dominion of the Crown rather than as an Irish republic. It also gave the chiefly Protestant northern counties of Ulster the chance to opt out of the new state, which they took.

Militant Irish republicans, led by President Eamonn De Valera, saw the treaty as a betrayal of their struggle, whereas the pro-treaty side argued that it left the door open to achieve full freedom later. After a week of passionate debates in the Dublin Dail (the unofficial "Assembly of Ireland" established by Irish MPs who refused to sit in the British House of Commons), the treaty was narrowly ratified by sixty-four votes to fifty-seven.

Collins and Griffith both died during the civil war, which was nevertheless won by the pro-treaty forces. Over the next twenty years, De Valera led the republicans back from illegality and skillfully used the Free State institutions to achieve a republic—though not yet a united Ireland. The pro- and anti-treaty factions gave birth to the two parties, Fine Gael and Fianna Fail, that still dominate Irish politics. **NJ**

Mussolini's Propaganda Coup

The "March on Rome" is not the heroic coup d'état of fascist legend.

○ Mussolini (center) leads the "March on Rome" surrounded by his Blackshirt supporters.

October 28 was a day of historic significance, so supremely important that 1922 was recalibrated as year one in the fascist era. According to the version of events trumpeted by fascist propaganda, the massed ranks of virile supporters of Benito Mussolini marched on Rome and seized power from the decadent democratic regime. As many as 3,000 gave their lives fighting so that, once again, Italy would be great and Mussolini would found a new Roman Empire. The reality, however, was rather different.

A march on Rome had indeed been planned, although fascist support was weak and Mussolini was preparing to flee if King Victor Emmanuel III declared martial law. Instead, fearing civil war, the king refused and on October 28 invited Mussolini to Rome. It seemed unthinkable that the king would offer Mussolini, whose party had won only thirty-five seats in the previous general election and whose hold on the fascist party was wavering, a ministerial position, and yet on October 29, he declared Mussolini prime minister. The next day, some 30,000 Blackshirts arrived in the capital. The so-called "March on Rome" took place after Mussolini had come to power, not before, and it was bloodless.

By 1926 Mussolini had become Italy's dictator and, according to the brilliant fascist propaganda machine, its savior. His great mistake was to enter World War II. Propaganda invented Italian victories but, in the end, could not disguise utter Italian defeat nor Mussolini's ignominious death. **RP**

Discovery of Tutankhamun's Tomb

Howard Carter opens the inner doorway of Tutankhamun's tomb and finds a wealth of artifacts that had remained undisturbed for centuries.

The tomb had been discovered three weeks earlier, but its opening was delayed until Lord Carnarvon could reach the Valley of the Kings in Luxor. Back in 1899, Howard Carter had discovered the looted tomb of Queen Hatshepsut. Would this, too, be an empty cache? Around 2 P.M. that Sunday afternoon in 1922 Carter made a tiny breach in the top left-hand corner of the inner doorway. He lit candles and the interior of the chamber was dimly visible. He was at first struck dumb with amazement. The hole was then made bigger until the two men could stare in wonder at "the marvellous collection of treasures." There was no doubt about it, this was the grave of Tutankhamun.

Howard Carter had become fascinated with the artifacts of ancient Egypt as a boy, and from 1907 his work had been financed by amateur archeologist Lord Carnarvon. In 1922 Carter was given one more season's finance. After the discovery of the tomb in November, the two men catalogued the contents of the antechamber, and on February 16, 1923, they opened the sarcophagus of Tutankhamun.

In the spring, Carnarvon died of septicemia. Soon the myth of "Tutankhamun's curse" began. Carnarvon had given *The Times* exclusive rights to the story of the tomb, and in retaliation other newspapers spread the myth of the curse—which Carter dismissed as "tommy-rot." The significance of Carter's work was historic, not supernatural, for the world could now enjoy the best preserved of all pharaonic tombs. **RP**

◗ The archeologists catch their first glimpse of the sarcophagus through the doors to the shrine.

◗ Howard Carter is about to lever off the lid of Tutankhamun's coffin and reveal the mummy.

Creation of the U.S.S.R.

The Union of Soviet Socialist Republics is formally proclaimed in Moscow.

The decision in 1922 to create the U.S.S.R., or Soviet Union, ended a debate within the Communist Party over how much autonomy to give the various nationalities ruled by Russia. Essentially, the Union was a re-creation of the old tsarist Russian Empire shorn of Poland and Finland, which had wrested their independence in a civil war following the 1917 Bolshevik revolution.

Always dominated by Russia, the U.S.S.R. was initially composed of just four republics—Russia, Ukraine, Belorussia, and Transcaucasia—but as the Bolsheviks consolidated their control, more republics

"We want . . . a union which precludes any coercion of one nation by another."

V. I. Lenin proposes the U.S.S.R.

joined: Armenia, Azerbaijan, Georgia, Kazakhstan, Moldavia, Uzbekistan, Tajikistan, and Turkmenistan. In World War II, the Baltic republics of Estonia, Latvia, and Lithuania were forcibly annexed, too.

After Stalin became dictator in 1929, the U.S.S.R. rose to be the world's second superpower, despite the dislocations of famine, forced collectivization, industrialization, and the devastation of World War II. It extended communist control over Eastern Europe and communist influence across the entire world.

Eventually the cost of maintaining arms parity with the United States and the inherent inefficiency of the communist command economy undermined the U.S.S.R. After Gorbachev's failure to reform the sclerotic system in the 1980s, his successor, Boris Yeltsin, let the constituent republics go their own way in 1991. **NJ**

Japanese Quake

Earthquakes, fires, and tsunamis destroy Yokohama and most of Tokyo.

In the bustling port of Yokohama, thousands of rickshaws picked their way through streets teeming with dockworkers, foreign diplomats, sailors, traders, and travelers. In residential areas filled with flimsy wooden restaurants and houses, locals were lighting gas stoves in preparation for the midday meal. At two minutes before noon a massive earthquake measuring 7.9 on the Richter scale reverberated from an epicenter in Sagami Bay, just southwest of Tokyo Bay.

From the Hakone Mountain peaks to the shipping lanes of Yokohama Bay, and north to the city of

"The fires seemed to cover the whole city [and] burned all day and all night."

Eyewitness account

Tokyo, the shock waves unleashed a devastating chain of events. Gas lines were severed; lighted charcoal spilled from cookers and lit up hundreds of fires in the old, crowded communities. Broken water mains made firefighting virtually impossible, and public parks and open areas were too small in size and number to form natural breaks. The fires raged for three days, the flames fanned by hot winds that created flash cyclones.

Although not the largest earthquake to ever hit Japan, its proximity to Tokyo and Yokohama had devastating consequences. More than three million people lost their homes, around 104,500 were killed, and 52,000 were injured. Remarkably, rebuilding began at a breathtaking speed, and by 1932 Tokyo and Yokohama were modern, vibrant cities. **JJH**

The German Mark Becomes Worthless

Hyperinflation in Germany in 1923 destroys the currency and rocks political stability.

○ In 1923 the German mark was worth more as waste paper than as a monetary currency.

○ German children get their hands on the worthless bank notes and put them to good use as they play.

> ## "Germany is collapsing in an eerie, step-by-step manner..."
>
> **Journal of Victor Klemperer, October 9, 1923**

Economists are unable to tell us when precisely inflation becomes hyperinflation, but the people of Germany had no difficulty whatsoever in recognizing that their currency—and their savings—were worthless. In November 1923, a loaf of bread that had cost just over half a mark in 1918 now cost around 100 billion marks. At the same time there were a massive 4 trillion marks to the dollar—and rising. The situation had been bad for some time; now it was ludicrous. Those who bought a cup of coffee found that by the time they had drunk it, the price had doubled. The currency was literally not worth the paper it was printed on. No wonder bartering was becoming widespread—a haircut could be bought for eggs, a cinema ticket for coal—and beggars were a common sight on the streets.

What had caused the problem? Many Germans blamed the Treaty of Versailles and the need to pay reparations to the victors of World War I. The Nazis pointed to international Jewish financiers, but the real culprits were successive German governments. They had taxed too little and printed too much money during the war, and they continued to do so after 1918. In January 1923, when the French occupied the Ruhr, the German government called for passive resistance and blithely printed wages for those on strike, thus making the curse of inflation into the catastrophe of hyperinflation.

A remedy arose after Gustav Stresemann formed a coalition in September 1923. Passive resistance was called off, and in 1924, with the Dawes Plan implemented, Germany voluntarily accepted reparations payments and instituted a new currency. The crisis was overcome, although traumatic memories and political uncertainty lingered on and helped destabilize the Weimar Republic. **RP**

King's Speech Broadcast on Radio

King George V's first radio broadcast boosts the popularity of the British monarchy.

🔊 George V makes his Christmas radio broadcast in 1934 from a room at Sandringham.

> " . . . the broadcast went well . . . and was the biggest thing we have done yet."

John Reith, diary entry, April 23, 1924

The British Empire Exhibition, on a specially constructed site at Wembley, was bigger than the Great Exhibition of 1851 and was attended by four times as many people. It was opened on St. George's Day, April 23, 1924, with a speech by King George V. "We believe the Exhibition will bring the peoples of the Empire to a better knowledge of how to meet their reciprocal wants and aspirations," he intoned, "and we hope further that the success of the Exhibition may bring lasting benefits not to the Empire only, but to mankind in general." The sentiments were platitudinous, but the public interest was tremendous because this was the king's first speech to be broadcast. Crowds turned out to hear it on the streets, solemn courts suspended their sittings, and in all ten million people listened in. It was a great success, despite George's dislike of the newfangled broadcasting apparatus.

On royal occasions George V was packaged as regally as his predecessors, but he had never tried to become popular and had resisted calls to exploit the new medium of radio. In October 1923, John Reith, head of the British Broadcasting Company (BBC), which had been set up a year earlier, urged George to deliver a Christmas message to the people. Although the king turned down this request, not even George V could refuse to broadcast a message at the start of the prestigious Imperial Exhibition.

It was the first of several broadcasts on ceremonial occasions. Their immediate popularity prompted George to relent and allow the BBC to transmit a speech on Christmas Day, 1932. This first message began a tradition that has continued until the present day. Royalty, it was decided, could be heard as well as seen. No political figure could afford to ignore the power of radio. **RP**

Holy City Seized

Ibn Saud enters Mecca, laying the foundation for the Kingdom of Saudi Arabia.

The capture of Mecca, Islam's holiest city, in 1924 by the well-prepared forces of Abd al-Aziz Ibn Saud was not held to be of very great importance at the time. However, from the perspective of the twenty-first century, faced with resurgent Islam and the continuing importance of oil worldwide, the seizure now appears to be one of the pivotal events of the last hundred years.

Ibn Saud was born to a powerful ruling family in Riyadh, in the desert province of Nejd, in 1880. However, In 1891, when Ibn Saud was just eleven years old, the family was expelled by the Rashidis, a rival family that contested the Sauds' power, and Ibn Saud disappeared into exile in Kuwait. In 1902, at age twenty-one, he led sixty warriors on a raiding party near his birthplace. With just twenty men, he captured Riyadh and took his revenge by personally slaughtering the head of the Rashidi dynasty.

Ibn Saud consolidated this success and made his clan the dominant power in the Arabian peninsula by allying with the austere and extreme Wahhabi Islamic sect. He also organized his followers as a properly trained army—the Ikhwan. In December 1915, Britain, hoping to draw Ibn Saud into its ongoing struggle against the Ottoman Turks, forged an alliance with him. After the war, Ibn Saud attacked the rival Hashemite clan, driving them from the Hejaz province and crowning his triumph by seizing Mecca in October 1924.

Ibn Saud proclaimed himself the first king of Saudi Arabia in 1932. His power was enhanced by the discovery of huge oil deposits in the kingdom in the late 1930s. He agreed to let the U.S. oil company Aramco exploit the deposits in return for vast sums of money paid to his court. Ibn Saud died in 1953; his sons still rule the kingdom he founded. **NJ**

◔ Abd al-Aziz Ibn Saud, pictured in 1917, forged an alliance with Britain by respecting British protectorates in the region.

> *" . . . he founded a kingdom where previously there had been . . . incipient chaos."*
>
> **Leslie McLoughlin, author**

The Expanding Universe

Edwin Hubble announces the discovery of other galaxies, revealing that the universe is much larger than we thought.

Until the 1920s, it was widely assumed that the galaxy of stars of which our sun is one was the only galaxy in existence. Astronomers, however, had already begun to suspect that there might be other structures farther out in space. One such astronomer was a young American from Missouri, Edwin Powell Hubble. He focused on nebulae—clouds of interstellar dust and gas—and from 1919 studied them at the Mount Wilson Observatory in California. He discovered that some objects thought to be nebulae were actually large-scale aggregates of stars, or galaxies like our own. In 1923, for example, he found thirty-six stars inside the Andromeda nebula, which he subsequently calculated to be 900,000 light years away from us and an enormous distance beyond our own galaxy's edge. The astronomer published his research results on the first day of 1925.

Hubble classified the galaxies into three main types—spiral, elliptical, and irregular. He not only demonstrated that the universe is immensely bigger than previously thought, but went on to show that it is expanding, meaning that the other galaxies are moving away from us. In 1929, he found that the speed at which the galaxies recede increases with their distance from us (Hubble's Law) and established a ratio (Hubble's Constant) between the speed and the distance. Subsequent investigations suggest that the ratio has not always remained the same, but over time has decelerated and accelerated.

Hubble continued working at Mount Wilson virtually until his death in 1953. The Hubble Space Telescope was named in his honor. **RC**

◗ Earlier in his career, Edwin Hubble poses with a telescope at the home of his friend John Roberts in Silver Hills, Indiana.

Apes and Ancestors

The "monkey trial" pits the theory of evolution against the Book of Genesis.

The teaching of evolution was illegal in Tennessee when John Scopes, a biology teacher in Dayton, was backed by the American Civil Liberties Union to test the law's constitutionality. The subsequent trial in July 1925 attracted attention across the United States.

The trial pitted against each other two of the most redoubtable figures of the day. Clarence Darrow, leading for the defense, was the United States's most renowned trial lawyer. William Jennings Bryan, a former Democratic presidential candidate, was recruited for the prosecution as a seasoned

"It is better to trust in the Rock of Ages than to know the age of rocks."

William Jennings Bryan

crusader against the theory of evolution. Bryan's first speech, on July 16, was greeted with an enthusiastic ovation. However, Bryan proved no match for Darrow, who called him to the witness stand as an expert on the Bible and, as it were, made a monkey of him. The lawyer mercilessly showed up Bryan's ignorance of geology, archeology, and the modern trends in biblical criticism. Bryan had to admit that he doubted whether the sun really stood still in the sky for Joshua. A reporter at the trial said, "Darrow never spared him. It was masterful, but it was pitiful."

Nonetheless, the jury still found Scopes guilty on January 26. Although Bryan died in Dayton five days later, the fundamentalist cause was far from lost because the Tennessee Supreme Court upheld the law as constitutional. **RC**

Hitler's Struggle

Mein Kampf reveals the key to Hitler's muddled and malevolent thinking.

"Every great movement on this earth owes its growth to great speakers, and not to great writers." Was this Adolf Hitler's veiled apology in his autobiography, *Mein Kampf* (My Struggle), for his turgid, disjointed, and, in places, unreadable prose? Not at all. Elsewhere in the book, there are huge dollops of self-praise, such as when he wrote—quite inaccurately—that at school he was a "juvenile ringleader who learned well and easily." As an autobiography, the book is neither accurate nor truthful. Nor are its ideas well thought out or substantiated with evidence. The book mainly consists of passionate assertions: Hitler hated the Jews, detested communism, and loathed democracy. Germany's electorate was "mostly stupid and has a very short memory." Yet Hitler contrived to believe in the historic destiny of a racially pure Germany. The future was clear—all Germans should be gathered in a single state and then they would have to acquire *lebensraum* (living space) in the east, unleashing a massive war that would decide the future of the world.

Mein Kampf was dedicated to the "fallen heroes" of the Beer Hall Putsch of November 1923. Hitler's attempt to seize power had ended in bloodshed and his own imprisonment in Landsberg Fortress. There he reconsidered Nazi tactics, "We must hold our noses and enter the Reichstag," and there he dictated his autobiography. The first volume appeared, in an initial print run of only 500 copies, in July 1925, with a second volume published the following year.

As the Nazis gained popularity and power, *Mein Kampf* became a best-seller, making Hitler's views widely known, even to potential enemies. It was never a blueprint for Nazi policy, but it was a chilling revelation of Hitler's most destructive intentions. **RP**

Transmission of Live Moving Images

John Logie Baird gives the first public demonstration of television.

The world-transforming phenomenon television has many fathers, but no one has a stronger claim to its invention than the Scottish engineer John Logie Baird. On January 26, 1926 Baird gave his first public demonstration of the transmission of live moving images in his London laboratory at 22 Frith Street, Soho before an audience of fifty scientists from the Royal Institution and a reporter from *The Times*. Pictures were transmitted at a rate of 12.5 a second.

Baird had perfected a workable television system almost a year earlier in his home in Bexhill-on-Sea, England. He built his first TV set out of a hatbox, scissors, darning needles, bicycle light lenses, a tea chest, and large quantities of sealing wax and glue. Using a semimechanical analogue system, Baird demonstrated the transmission of moving silhouette images at the department store Selfridges in London in March 1925. By October, he was successfully transmitting televised pictures of a ventriloquist's dummy he named "Stooky Bill" within his laboratory. A neighbor, William Taynton, was the first person to have his image transmitted by television.

In 1927, Baird successfully sent a long-distance TV signal between London and Glasgow using telephone wires, and in 1928 he transmitted the first trans-Atlantic signal between London and New York. In July of the same year, he gave the first-ever demonstration of color television. Baird's mechanical method was rapidly overhauled by an electronic cathode tube system developed by the U.S. Marconi company, which was adopted by the BBC in 1935 after comparative trials with Baird's system. Baird founded his own television company, but made little commercial profit from his brainchild. An inveterate inventor, he experimented with radar, a glass razor, pneumatic shoes, and a thermal undersock. **RP**

○ An assistant displays the heads of ventriloquist's dummies used by Baird as subjects for transmission by "televisor."

○ Baird poses in front of the apparatus that he demonstrated in total darkness to members of the Royal Institute.

"The image . . . formed on the screen with unbelievable clarity. I had got it!"

John Logie Baird, *Memoirs*

First Rocket Launched

The first liquid fuel rocket makes the prospect of space travel a possibility.

Rocket experiments go back to the Middle Ages in China, but the chief early pioneer of modern rocketry was a Russian mathematician, Konstantin Tsiolkovski. In 1903, he published a treatise on space travel by rocket that was the first serious scientific treatment of the subject. However, his work was virtually unknown outside his own country, and it was Robert Goddard who launched the world's first liquid-fueled rocket in March 1926.

Goddard was a shy U.S. physicist who had become a professor at Clark University in Massachusetts. There he spent years working on the possibilities of rocketry and space flight, taking out some 200 patents and inventing a sort of early bazooka. In 1919, the Smithsonian Institution published his seminal paper on "A Method of Reaching Extreme Altitudes," which provided mathematical proof that rockets could boost instrument packages into the upper atmosphere. The paper attracted much attention and a mixture of praise and jeers. *The New York Times* accused him of talking nonsense because he had suggested that a rocket could reach the moon. In 1926, Goddard, who was experimenting with liquid oxygen and gasoline as propellants, launched a liquid-fueled rocket from a site near Auburn, Massachusetts. It was 10 feet (3 m) long and took 2.5 seconds to travel 184 feet (56 m) horizontally, reaching a height of 41 feet (12 m).

With encouragement from aviator Charles Lindbergh and funds from Daniel Guggenheim, Goddard created his own rocket-testing site at Roswell in New Mexico in the 1930s. By 1935, his best rocket flew to above 7,250 feet (2,210 m) at a speed of 550 miles per hour (885 kph). He continued his work until his death in 1945 at the age of sixty-two. **RC**

General Strike

The first, and last, general strike in British history begins.

The "national stoppage" was authorized by the Trades Union Congress (TUC) at one minute to midnight on Monday May 3, 1926. One million miners were already out, and now railway workers, dockers, road transport workers, printers, and gas and electricity workers refused to work. When engineers and shipbuilders joined later, a total of 2.5 million people, in addition to the miners, took part in the most complete stoppage in Britain's history. On the first day, the railways ground to a halt, and buses and trams did not run. Thousands of volunteers carried on essential

> ### *"What solidarity! From John O'Groats to Land's End the workers answered the call ... "*
> **A.J. Cook, miners' leader, May 4, 1926**

services, while the government, determined to win the battle for hearts and minds, took steps to control broadcasting and set up its own newspaper.

The General Strike was the culmination of a long history of bitter industrial relations in the mines. When wages were cut and the working day was lengthened, the TUC promised action. Their bluff was called when the government backed out of negotiations, leaving the union with a strike it did not want and for which it had prepared inadequately. The government presented the strike as a challenge to democracy, and the TUC feared it might turn to revolutionary violence. The strike remained solid, but on May 12 the TUC called it off, leaving the miners to fight on alone. The government hammered home its victory in 1927 by declaring future general strikes illegal. **RP**

Death, Fame, and Hysteria

The death of Rudolph Valentino provokes mass mourning—among the female population at least.

The intense reaction to the death of Rudolph Valentino after a brief career says much about the world of Hollywood in the silent movie era. The *New York Daily News* called him "The type-man of the post-war period." Valentino arrived in New York from Italy in 1913, where he worked as a dancing partner. He reached Hollywood in 1917, where he went on to establish himself as a darkly compelling, handsome, Latin-lover type. Women fainted in cinemas at *The Sheikh* in 1921, but a widespread male reaction was summed up by the *Chicago Tribune*, which attacked him under the headline "Pink Powder Puffs."

Falling suddenly and violently ill when visiting New York, Valentino was rushed to the hospital and operated on for acute appendicitis and perforated gastric ulcers. When he came around, he asked a friend, "Did I behave like a pink powder puff or like a man?" Crowds of well wishers gathered outside the hospital, which had to hire extra switchboard operators to cope with the telephone calls. His condition took a fatal turn for the worse.

An estimated 50,000 people filed past the star's casket at a Broadway funeral parlor. On August 30, thousands more watched the hearse on its way to St. Malachy's, with contemporary stars Pola Negri, Mary Pickford, and Constance Talmadge all present. The body was shipped to Los Angeles for a star-studded burial, and an airplane dropped roses over the mausoleum, while rumors spread that Valentino had been murdered by a jealous mistress. A kind of cult developed around the star and the anniversary of his death was commemorated in Hollywood for years. **RC**

◐ Valentino stars as a lieutenant in the Russian army in the silent movie *The Eagle* (1925) directed by Clarence Brown.

Spirit of St. Louis

Charles Lindbergh flies solo across the Atlantic and lands in Paris into a world of unwanted celebrity.

Eight years after Alcock and Brown's first nonstop trans-Atlantic flight came another milestone in aviation history. "The Lone Eagle," as the media dubbed the pilot, made the first solo flight from New York to Paris in May 1927. He won worldwide celebrity and $25,000. In his twenties, Charles Augustus Lindbergh had been a stunt pilot billed as "Daredevil Lindbergh." He was later an airmail pilot operating between St. Louis, Missouri, and Chicago and recruited a group of St. Louis businessmen to back his epic flight.

Many other pilots had made the attempt before, and some had crashed and been killed. Lindbergh took off from Roosevelt Airfield on Long Island on May 20, in a specially built, single-engined monoplane called the *Spirit of St. Louis*. It was so heavily loaded with fuel that it could scarcely take off and led to it being described as "a two-ton flying gas tank." Lindbergh had five sandwiches, but no radio and no parachute. After a flight of 3,600 miles (5,794 km), during which he spent 33½ hours over the Atlantic flying partly through fog and sleet, Lindbergh arrived at Le Bourget Airport, Paris, to a hero's welcome. The president of France bestowed on him the Legion of Honour and New York City gave him a ticker-tape parade down Fifth Avenue.

The flight and the publicity gave the aviation industry a boost and stimulated demand for air travel, but Lindbergh was not comfortable as a media celebrity. He and his wife, the former Ann Morrow, were besieged by journalists and admirers, and in 1932 suffered a hideous tragedy when their eldest son was kidnapped and murdered. **RC**

◐ A photomontage shows Lindbergh flying the *Spirit of St. Louis* past the Eiffel Tower in Paris.

Anarchists on Trial

Sacco and Vanzetti are executed under dubious circumstances.

Whether Nicola Sacco and Bartolomeo Vanzetti were guilty or not is still disputed, but their execution seven years after they had been convicted of murder caused an international outcry. Italians from peasant families, they both emigrated to the United States in 1908. There they became dedicated anarchists and disciples of Luigi Galleani, who advocated assassination and violence in the cause of revolution. The U.S. authorities grew increasingly hostile to revolutionaries, and in 1919 Galleani and some of his associates were deported. His followers retaliated with a terrorist campaign against politicians, judges, and officials. The home of the U.S. attorney general was bombed in 1919, and a bomb set off in Wall Street in 1920 killed more than thirty people.

The extent to which Sacco and Vanzetti were involved is uncertain, but in April 1920, there was a payroll robbery at a factory in South Braintree, Massachusetts, in which two employees were killed. The police rounded up anarchist suspects, and Sacco and Vanzetti were tried before Judge Webster Thayer, who would later describe them as "those anarchist bastards." The lawyer for the defense was thoroughly inadequate, and some of the prosecution evidence was rigged.

At the time, many people believed the two men were convicted not because the evidence against them was convincing, but because of their politics. They were found guilty in July 1921 and sentenced to death. Numerous motions for a new trial were rejected by Judge Thayer, and a committee specially appointed by the governor of Massachusetts found that the trial had been fair. The two went to the electric chair in the state prison at Charlestown. Sacco was aged thirty-six and Vanzetti thirty-nine. **RC**

The First Talkie

Al Jolson gets the honor of delivering the first line in the first talkie.

The first talking, or at least part talking, movie nationally distributed in the United States was *The Jazz Singer*, a Broadway success filmed by Warner Brothers using the new Vitaphone sound process. Most of the picture was silent, but sound was used in the musical sequences and also in some passages of dialogue. The film's success meant that the writing was plainly on the wall for the old silent movies.

The film told the story of a Jewish boy, played by Al Jolson, who rose to stardom singing sentimental, popular songs, much to the horror of his old-

> ## *"Wait a minute, you ain't heard nothin' yet! Wait a minute, I tell ya!"*
>
> **Al Jolson's first audible line in *The Jazz Singer***

fashioned father, who was a synagogue cantor and wanted his son to follow in his footsteps. Jolson was one of the most riveting stage performers of the day and had transformed the comparatively restrained art of vaudeville stage singing by adding lively movement, gestures, and conversations with the audience. He had an electrifying stage presence, and in major Broadway productions he would sometimes stop the action and ask the audience whether they would sooner hear him sing than watch the rest of the performance. When they shouted "yes," which they always did, he would spend the next hour or so putting on a concert for them. In 1928 Jolson starred in *The Singing Fool*, in which he sang "Sonny Boy," the first U.S. record to sell one million copies. **RC**

Steamboat Willie Cartoon Released

The first synchronized sound cartoon short marks the Disney Studio as a global brand.

⬥ An illustration from the animation short *Steamboat Willie*, Mickey Mouse's breakthrough film.

Just under eight minutes of black-and-white animation featuring a rodent called Mickey Mouse transformed the motion picture industry just one year into "talkies." *Steamboat Willie* was not the first Mickey cartoon (*Plane Crazy* came first) nor was it the first animated short to use a synchronized sound track (Betty Boop creator Max Fleisher had used sound, and Paul Terry's *Dinner Time* premiered this technique a few months earlier). What caught the public's imagination was the cute, humanlike mouse and his zany adventures. Cel animation, which eliminated the need to redraw the character, scene, and background for every frame of the film, helped make cartoons a staple of moviegoing by the 1920s, and cartoons often supported the main features.

Walt Disney had set up a studio with Ub Iwerks, but the venture had gone bankrupt, so the two decided to travel to Hollywood to try their luck. Disney started doodling a new character while on a train, and Mickey Mouse emerged. With Iwerks animating the action and a small team inking in the animation cels, Disney quickly oversaw the creation of three Mickey Mouse cartoons. However, he was unable to sell the first two silent efforts, so he added synchronized sound in postproduction to the third. Aside from the great characterization, Disney's animated film demonstrated the effect music could have when it was removed from the background and used instead as a dramatic force for the visual rhythm of the film. **JJH**

Slaughter in Chicago

The St. Valentine's Day massacre is the most notorious gangster killing in U.S. history.

○ Chicago police blamed the massacre on the rivalry between gangs controlling the illegal trafficking of liquor during Prohibition.

Seven men were lined up against an interior wall in a Chicago booze warehouse and slaughtered. Four men, two of them armed with Thompson submachine guns, fired a hail of bullets. The killers had been recruited by a notorious gang figure known as "Machine Gun" Jack McGurn. Two of the men were dressed in police uniforms and arrived at the warehouse in cars that looked like police sedans. This misled the potential victims, who assumed they were being arrested (and particularly angered the Chicago police commissioner). After the killings, the two killers in ordinary clothes came out of the garage with their hands up, led by the two "cops." Six of the dead men were members of an Irish North Side gang led by George "Bugs" Moran, and the seventh

was a mechanic who happened to be on the scene. Just how innocent he was is frequently disputed.

"Bugs" Moran himself escaped, apparently because he arrived at the garage late. He owed his nickname to his violently unstable temper and had long been warring with Al Capone's rival South Side Italian gang. Although Capone was residing innocently at his house in Miami Beach, Florida, at the time, it is generally accepted that he masterminded the killing or that it at least had his approval. "Machine Gun" Jack McGurn was a valued member of Capone's gang and the Moran gang had attempted to kill him not long before. Despite the massacre, Moran managed to keep control of his territory into the early 1930s. **RC**

First Academy Awards Presented

Douglas Fairbanks Sr. presents fifteen golden statuettes, later known as Oscars.

○ Douglas Fairbanks presents the Best Actress Award to Janet Gaynor; the glitz and glamour of Oscar night came later.

"[It had] half his head, that part which held his brains, completely sliced off."

Frances Marion on the Oscar figurine

Initiated by the resoundingly titled Academy of Motion Picture Arts and Sciences, the Academy Awards were introduced as a public relations exercise to boost the image of motion pictures in general. They have since developed into one of the most prestigious recognitions of achievement in the world, and the ceremony at which they are presented is an eagerly anticipated annual event. The first awards were presented by a greatly respected Hollywood figure, the actor Douglas Fairbanks Sr., at a dinner for some 200 people at the Hollywood Roosevelt Hotel in Los Angeles. Fifteen golden statuettes of a man equipped with a knight's sword and standing on a reel of film were awarded for movies made between 1927 and 1928. The trophy was known as The Statuette until 1931, when, so the story goes, the librarian of the Academy, Margaret Herrick, said it looked just like her Uncle Oscar, and Oscar it has been ever since.

The award for the best picture went to a silent film called *Wings*, a story set in World War I about the experiences of two U.S. Air Force pilots in war-torn France. They have brushes with death in spectacular flying sequences and compete for the affections of Clara Bow. The film was directed by William Wellman, and the young Gary Cooper made a brief appearance as a pilot. It had sound effects and background music, but no spoken dialogue, and was the only silent movie ever to win the award. The next two winners were a musical, *Broadway Melody*, and the magnificent *All Quiet on the Western Front*.

In 1929, the award for best actor went to Emil Jannings for his performances in two films (*The Way of All Flesh* and *The Last Command*), and Janet Gaynor won the best actress award for her roles in three (*Seventh Heaven*, *Street Angel*, and *Sunrise*). **RC**

Wall Street Crash

With the crash of the stock market, the roaring twenties become the depressed thirties.

Thursday October 24, 1929, was a cool and rather overcast day; the temperature had reached only about 50 degrees Fahrenheit (10° C) at 10 A.M. when stock market trading began. Nevertheless, the general feeling among traders was one of mild optimism. Share prices had been faltering since the Dow Jones hit a record high of 381 in September that year, but the worst seemed to be over, and traders who had sold were now congratulating themselves on buying back their stocks more cheaply.

The market opened little changed, followed by moderate falls for the first half hour. Then the deluge broke. There was a torrent of selling orders. Anxious crowds soon gathered outside the exchange, at the corner of Broad Street and Wall Street, and leading bankers hastily met and promised to prop up the market. But it was too late; confidence had dried up. Perhaps this was the correction the markets needed? In fact, it was the start of an unprecedented bear run. Falls continued until, in July 1932, 90 percent had been wiped off the value of U.S. stocks.

The root of the problem lay in the 1920s, dubbed by the novelist F. Scott Fitzgerald "the greatest gaudiest spree in history." Speculation had led to a massive inflation in the price of shares that bore little relation to the companies they represented. This did not seem to matter while confidence was high and people were buying, but once confidence sank, there was a massive and infectious panic to sell.

The Wall Street Crash resulted in depression and unemployment in the United States, followed by Roosevelt's New Deal from 1933. In Europe, the consequences were even more severe. As U.S. loans were recalled and the U.S. market for European exports disappeared, fragile democracies collapsed and the era of Nazism, fascism, and war began. **RP**

◐ Crowds gather outside the New York Stock Exchange as news spreads of the economic disaster.

> ## *"The decline carried down speculators, big and little, in every part of the country . . ."*
>
> *New York Times*, October 25, 1929

The Salt March

Gandhi's defiance of the salt laws was a significant step toward independence.

Dandi was a very ordinary fishing village on India's west coast, but there the events of April 5 and 6 were quite extraordinary. On the first day, Mohandas Karamchand Gandhi arrived, head bowed, staff in hand, no doubt footsore from a long march from Ahmedabad, exclaiming that the Gujarati mud felt like velvet. What was truly remarkable, though, was his entourage. He had set off with seventy-eight companions, but now there were thousands of men, women, boys, girls, walkers, cyclists, motorists, minstrels, hawkers, photographers, and newsreel cameramen. They had come to witness an act of historic importance. Early the next day, after the tide had receded from the marshy ground, Gandhi picked up a piece of salt deposited by the sea and thereby publicly defied the mighty British Raj.

The Indian National Congress had voted in 1929 in favor of independence within a year but left to Gandhi the task of achieving it. He chose to defy the law that forced Indians to buy salt from the government and urged his followers to do the same. Here was an issue that everyone could understand. Gandhi reasoned that if Indians refused to cooperate, the Raj would collapse because it depended on Indian collaboration. The Satyagraha, or nonviolent civil disobedience campaign, would end British rule. Gandhi was duly arrested, and soon the jails were full to overflowing.

The Raj did not end because of the salt march. World opinion had been so mobilized, though, that the viceroy, the head of the British administration in India, found it necessary to hold personal talks with Gandhi the following year. The British had recognized a saintly opponent who would be a thorn in their flesh until independence. **RP**

On a Wing and a Prayer

Amy Johnson's solo flight from Britain to Australia makes her a household name.

Known as *Jason,* the plane was a secondhand Moth with a single Gypsy engine. The aircraft was made of wood and fabric, with an open cockpit, and contained only four instruments: an altimeter, an air speed meter, a compass, and an indicator for turning and banking. There was no radio. The pilot was called Amy Johnson, one of the first women in Britain to obtain a ground engineer's license but still a novice pilot. She took with her only bare necessities, including a spare propeller, a revolver, and a knife. She set out on May 5, 1930, and when she reached

> **" . . . I had never ever crossed The Channel. I was rather surprised at my audacity."**
>
> **Amy Johnson**

Darwin on May 24, she had completed an epic flight of 11,000 miles (17,600 km) and become the first woman to fly solo from Britain to Australia. The journey had taken her nineteen days.

World War I had greatly boosted the profile of aviation, and flying feats were in the news. Amy Johnson wanted to beat Bert Hinkler's record sixteen-day flight between Britain and Australia and to show that a woman could succeed in a male-dominated world. The flight aroused worldwide interest. Johnson was decorated by King George V and given £10,000 by the *Daily Mail.* Around a million people lined the streets when she returned home in triumph. **RP**

○ Amy Johnson photographed on May 5, 1930, just before she took off on her historic flight.

Magnificent Skyscraper

The Empire State Building, the world's tallest building, is formally opened.

❶ The skyline of New York is dramatically altered by the construction of the Empire State Building.

"They called it the 'Empty State Building.' . . . No one could afford to rent space."

Irven Brod, president of Empire Diamond Corp.

Rising in art deco majesty 1,250 feet (381 m) above the streets of Manhattan, the Empire State Building was a remarkable statement of confidence in a country sunk in the Depression. On the corner of Fifth Avenue and Thirty-Fourth Street, it was named after New York State and formally opened by a former state governor, Al Smith, whose grandchildren cut the ribbon. Another former state governor, Alfred E. Neumann, was chairman of the construction company, and President Herbert Hoover in Washington was the man who pressed a button that turned on the building's lights.

Begun on St. Patrick's Day in 1930, the construction of the skyscraper required more than 3,000 workmen, 400 tons of stainless steel, and 10 million bricks. The spire at the top was originally intended as a mooring point for airships, although this eventually proved impractical because updrafts from the building made it nearly impossible to make contact with the dock. Designed by Gregory Johnson of the Shreve, Lamb, and Harmon architectural firm, the great edifice was built to survive buffeting by winds of more than 100 mph (160 km/h) at the top. With 6,400 windows and more than seventy elevators, the building provided office space for some 20,000 people and remained the world's tallest construction until 1954.

In a thick fog in 1945, a B-25 Mitchell bomber accidentally crashed into the building seventy-nine floors up, killing fourteen people. One elevator operator fell seventy-five stories inside her elevator and lived to tell the tale. More than thirty people have used the building to commit suicide, and in 1979 a woman who jumped from the eighty-sixth floor was blown back onto the floor below, and survived with only a broken hip. **RC**

"Scarface" Sentenced to Eleven Years

Al Capone is convicted of tax evasion by a federal jury.

The federal government under President Hoover was determined to bring down Al Capone. It succeeded at last when he was convicted of tax fraud in 1931.

The most notorious U.S. gangster, Capone was nicknamed "Scarface" by the media because of a knife wound to the face he had suffered in 1917 while working as a bouncer in a Coney Island bar. His friends called him "Snorky." Capone began to make his reputation after moving to Chicago around 1920 to join another New York Italian, John Torrio, who was running prostitution on Chicago's South Side. With the coming of Prohibition, Torrio was also making a fortune out of bootlegging. He soon retired, and from 1925 Capone took over the leadership of the gang. He expanded into gambling and became increasingly involved in Chicago politics.

Capone talked readily to journalists, many of whom liked him personally, but his growing notoriety focused police attention on his affairs. In 1928, he bought a mansion in Miami Beach, Florida, and his trips to Chicago became increasingly infrequent. In 1929, after attending an organized crime conference in Atlantic City, Capone was arrested and sentenced to a year in prison for carrying a concealed weapon. What finally brought him down, however, was the investigation of the Internal Revenue Service into his finances. In 1931 he was indicted for tax evasion. Found guilty on five of twenty-three counts by a federal jury, he was sentenced to eleven years in prison. The U.S. Supreme Court declined to hear his appeal, and he began his sentence in Atlanta before being transferred to Alcatraz Prison in San Francisco Bay. In 1938, doctors diagnosed syphilis in his brain. He was released the following year and retired to Florida, where he went further downhill before dying in 1947. **RC**

⬥ Capone gives the waiting photographers a sly wink as he leaves the courthouse during his trial for tax evasion.

"A symbol of a shameful era . . . Capone was incredible, the creation of an evil dream."

The New York Times on Capone's death, 1947

Nazi Chancellor

Hitler's appointment as chancellor is the beginning of the end for German democracy.

○ Chancellor Hitler rallies his troops in Erfurt in June 1933.

The meeting was scheduled for 11 A.M. President Hindenburg was familiar with such occasions and, over the previous five years, had appointed five different men to the position. Not that he had any liking for the "Bohemian Corporal," and he became distinctly testy as the minutes ticked away. The delegation arrived shortly after midday. Hindenburg gave a brief address and the new man swore to do his duty, regardless of party interests, for the good of the nation. Hindenburg nodded assent. Adolf Hitler was now the chancellor of Germany. Immediately he launched into a speech, pledging to uphold the constitution. Hindenburg disdained to reply and ended the proceedings with a single sentence, "And now, gentlemen, forwards with God."

It was, in some ways, only to be expected that Hitler would become chancellor. After all, the Nazi party was the largest in the Reichstag, with a third of all votes cast. It was Hitler's turn. Let him wrestle with an unworkable democratic system and an economy teetering on the brink of collapse. Yet this man was the avowed enemy of democracy, and his paramilitary brownshirts had for years been fomenting violence on the streets. No wonder Hindenburg was reluctant to appoint him, but industrialists, fearful of communism, were calling for the appointment.

What harm could Hitler do? His men were in a minority in both parliament and cabinet. Yet within months he was a dictator, and soon the world was made all too aware of exactly what Hitler could do. **RP**

Democracy Goes Up in Flames

The burning of the Reichstag in Berlin helps Hitler on his way to becoming a dictator.

○ The burning of the Reichstag was a pivotal moment for Germany: Hitler was firmly in control and democracy was no more.

At 9:45 that evening, the local fire station received an emergency call—the Reichstag building was on fire. The engines raced to the Köningsplatz and arrived within a few minutes. The firemen certainly did their best, but by the time the fire had been doused, around 12:30 A.M., it was obvious that the debating chamber had been wrecked. Its glass cupola—called by Berliners "the biggest round cheese in Europe"—had cracked with the heat, and the oak-paneled amphitheater had blazed spectacularly. Hermann Göring was the first Nazi on the scene, followed by Adolf Hitler. Göring told the new chancellor that the fire must be the result of a communist conspiracy. It was a theme to which Hitler warmed. At the very moment when a democratic election campaign

was under way, the Reds were attempting to seize power. They must be crushed, and with an iron fist.

The fire was very convenient, and some have argued that the Nazis started the blaze. The probability, however, is that the arsonist was a lone Dutchman, Marinus van der Lubbe. He was a left-winger who wanted to galvanize the working class into a revolt.

The following day, civil liberties were suspended, and leading communists were arrested. In this atmosphere of panic and repression, the Nazis not only won the general election on March 5, but mustered enough votes, when the deputies met, to secure passage of an Enabling Bill giving Hitler dictatorial powers. The Reichstag and German democracy had both gone up in flames. **RP**

Message of Hope

Roosevelt's inauguration as U.S. president begins a period of momentous change.

Despite the United States's depression, the ceremony at the Capitol proceeded as in normal, prosperous times. Or almost. When the bugle sounded at noon on March 4, 1933, the new president could not walk unaided from the Military Affairs Committee Room to the Senate. He had been stricken with polio a dozen years before and so needed his son's support. This time the oath was administered on a Dutch bible that had been in the Roosevelt family for 300 years. "The only thing we have to fear," said Roosevelt, "is fear itself." He promised bold, immediate, and, if

> ## "This nation asks for action, and action now. . . . We must act and act quickly."
>
> **Franklin D. Roosevelt**

necessary, unorthodox action to beat depression and poverty. His firm, resonant, and confident voice gave millions across the United States the message of hope they sorely needed, for more than thirteen million people were out of work, most of the banks were closed, and the farmers were in a desperate plight. Production was less than half that of 1929. If a few feared that Roosevelt might introduce a dictatorship, most hoped that he could prevent mass starvation and get the United States back to work.

Franklin Roosevelt's inauguration began "100 Days" of bold action, which would lead the United States to prosperity after the Great Depression, and through to the verge of victory in World War II. In total, the thirty-second president of the United States served for a record-breaking twelve years. **RP**

Night of the Long Knives

Hitler murders his last possible rivals to take complete control of Germany.

Ernst Röhm and other members of the brownshirted SA (Sturmabteilung) were on vacation at Bad Wiessee in Bavaria. They were asleep at 6:30 A.M. when Hitler and his personal bodyguard burst into the hotel and dragged them from their beds. Hitler confronted Röhm with a pistol. The men were sent to Stadelheim prison in Munich to await their fate, and Propaganda Minister Joseph Goebbels telegraphed a coded signal to Berlin, where Nazi henchmen sent out squads to deal with other SA men. Hitler ticked off the names: his former deputy Gregor Strasser,

> ## "Good chap that Hitler! He showed us how to deal with political opponents."
>
> **Joseph Stalin**

ex-chancellor von Schleicher, Röhm, and perhaps one hundred others. The brownshirts had helped Hitler come to power, but he would not grant them the authority they wanted. Some—the "beefsteaks," red in the middle and brown on the outside—called for a socialist revolution. Others wanted control of the army. Their leader, the scandalous, tough-guy, homosexual Ernst Röhm even criticized Hitler. Something had to be done, especially when Hitler was told the SA were planning an uprising.

Hitler told the Reichstag that the treasonous Röhm and his cronies had been executed. He received applause. When President Hindenburg died, Hitler was made führer of the German Reich, to whom the German army promised "unconditional obedience." No one could stop him now. **RP**

Fascist Aggression in Africa

Mussolini's Italian forces embark upon the conquest of Haile Selassie's Ethiopia, forcing the leader into exile.

In Addis Ababa on October 3, 1935, a war drum brought people running to the palace of Emperor Haile Selassie, ruler of the independent African state of Ethiopia. A court chamberlain announced all Ethiopians must fight. "If you persist in not shedding your blood," they were told, "you will be rebuked for it by your Creator and will be cursed by your offspring." At 5 A.M. a 100,000-strong Italian army crossed into Ethiopia from Italian-ruled Eritrea and Somaliland. Their mission was to extend Italy's African empire for dictator Benito Mussolini's fascist regime.

Although Haile Selassie's forces possessed some modern weaponry, most Ethiopian fighters were armed with outdated rifles or spears. The Italians had total command of the air and attacked Ethiopian soldiers and civilians with high-explosive bombs and poison gas. The fascist regime gloried in its air force—Mussolini's sons Vittorio and Bruno and his son-in law Galeazzo Ciano participated as pilots. The Ethiopians put up a brave fight, but Addis Ababa fell in May 1936, and Haile Selassie fled to exile in Britain.

Ethiopia had been a member of the League of Nations. The fact that the African country did not benefit from joint military action to resist aggression, as promised by the League's charter, left the policy of "collective security" in tatters. Economic sanctions tardily imposed on Italy only pushed Mussolini into an alliance with Hitler. Italy's occupation of Ethiopia lasted five years, Haile Selassie returning in 1941 after Britain's defeat of Italian forces in east Africa. **RG**

◑ Ethiopian tribesman are given weapons as they volunteer to fight against the invasion of the Italian army.

◑ In the north of Ethiopia, Italian troops march toward Adigrat, one of the first cities to surrender to the fascist regime.

End of the Long March

Mao's First Army march for a year across China and establish themselves in Yenan.

○ One of the leaders of the Chinese Communist Party Zhou Enlai, pictured in the Shaanxi province after the Long March.

"The Long March . . . has proclaimed . . . that the Red Army is an army of heroes."

Mao Zedong, 1935

The Long March was an epic episode of endurance in the protracted civil war between the Chinese Communist Party and its Red Army, and the Cuomindang nationalist government led by Chiang Kai-Shek. After traversing 6,000–7,000 miles (10,000–12,000 km), some 8,000 survivors of Mao's First Army arrived in Yenan in October 1935 and successfully established themselves in the remote region.

Almost obliterated by five successive nationalist offensives, the communist leadership in the summer of 1934 had ordered their 84,000 surviving troops under Marshal Zhu Te to break out from their base areas in Jiangxi province in southeastern China and move west before retreating to the remote northern province of Shaanxi, to regroup and form a solid base. Other Chinese communist forces made similar forced marches designed to terminate in Shaanxi.

The Long March was grueling. The communists were continually attacked by their nationalist enemies as they crossed deserts, rivers, and mountain ranges, and had to combat disease, hunger, and the hostility of the peasant populations whose districts they passed through, and whose meager resources they brutally requisitioned. During the year it took his armies to cross China, Mao Zedong established himself as the undisputed leader of the communists, and his devious tactics and ruthless sidelining of rivals on the march, such as Zhou Enlai, Lin Biao, Liu Shao Shi, and Deng Xiaoping, set a pattern he would follow for the rest of his and their lives. Mao himself abandoned his wife and two of his children to their deaths during the course of the march.

Although the march was exaggerated and distorted by communist propagandists and their western apologists, without it the communists could not have survived to master China in 1949. **NJ**

Franco Joins Spanish Revolt

Franco's decision to join the civil war leads to his domination of Spain for forty years.

Would he or wouldn't he? General Francisco Franco came from Galicia and shared the *retranca*, or inscrutability, of many of those born in that region. Perhaps that is why, when he hesitated to support the coup d'état General Emilio Mola was planning, nobody could quite fathom his reasons. He undoubtedly had a grievance against the government, which had just demoted him from chief of the general staff to military governor of the Canary Islands. Did he think the revolt might fail or perhaps that the government might look to him to save Spain? Whatever doubts he may have had, when Mola sent out orders on July 17, 1936, Franco's mind was made up. At 6:10 A.M. on July 18, he telegrammed support to Mola and ordered his troops to besiege the government buildings in Las Palmas. Then, at 3:00 P.M., he flew in a plane chartered from Britain, the *Dragon Rapide*, from the Canaries to Spanish Morocco. Here there was relatively little resistance, yet 189 people were shot.

Franco had joined the Spanish army in 1910 and two years later was posted to Morocco. He quickly made his name with the Army of Africa, whose professionalism owed much to his expertise and discipline. Now their presence was vital on mainland Spain. The Spanish fleet was in Republican hands, but with the help of Mussolini and Hitler, Franco managed to get his entire troop of soldiers across the straits.

The coup in Spain was rapidly becoming a civil war. It was this initial failure of the rebellion that paved the way for Franco's emergence as leader of the nationalists. It was he who presided over victory in the bloody civil war in May 1939. Indeed it was he who ruled as dictator of Spain for so long, until his death in 1975. **RP**

◑ Franco's troops carry out a search for weapons among their captives in Torrejon, Spain.

"Accept the enthusiastic greeting. . . . Blind faith in victory. Long live Spain."

Franco to Mola, July 18, 1936

Jesse Owens Wins Gold

Owens's Olympic victory belies Hitler's belief in Aryan racial supremacy.

The games were undoubtedly a showcase for the Nazi regime. Never before had the Olympics such elaborate and glorious ceremony. Leni Riefenstahl's film *Olympia* later reproduced the spectacle, as well as the fighting spirit of Germany's Aryan youth, and the majesty of the nation's inspirational leader, Adolf Hitler: "the Supreme Being who grants shape to a nation and its people." Not surprisingly Germany headed the medal table. Unfortunately for the Nazis, however, the black U.S. athlete J. C. (Jesse) Owens, a non-Aryan, won four gold medals and was the outstanding success among the 5,000 athletes from fifty-three nations who competed. He won the 100 meters gold in 10.3 seconds, followed by the 200 meters in 20.7 seconds (a new Olympic record), the long jump with 8.06 meters (26 feet 5 inches)—another Olympic record (beating the German athlete Lutz Long into second place)—and led the United States to a world record in the 4 x 100-meter relay.

Newsreels showing Hitler leaving the stadium in a huff after an Owens win have been misleadingly edited. Owens believed that Hitler waved to him and was quite happy with his treatment in Germany. Certainly many German competitors and citizens eagerly congratulated the U.S. athlete.

By his athletic achievements, but also by his charm, modesty, and good manners, Jesse Owens gave the lie to Nazi notions of the master race, and indeed to all delusions of black inferiority. But Hitler did not allow reality to affect his thinking. Belief in the master race led to World War II and the total destruction of the Nazi state. **RP**

◐ Owens in gold medal position having won the long jump; Naoto Tajima took silver and Wilhelm Leichum bronze.

Murder in Moscow

Stalin's show trials inaugurate a regime of terror in the Soviet Union.

The proceedings for this first show trial were held in the October Hall, the lavish ballroom of Moscow's trade union building, in August 1936. In attendance were the sixteen men accused of treason, three uniformed supreme court judges, prosecutor Andrei Vyshinsky, various court officials, and 350 members of the public, sitting on cushioned benches under crystal chandeliers. The world's press was present, as was the regime's leader, Joseph Stalin.

Justice would be done. However, it jarred on Western sensibilities when Vyshinsky called the

> ## "I demand that the mad dogs be shot—every one of them!"
>
> **Andrei Vyshinsky**

accused "liars and buffoons" and "despicable pygmies," and when no evidence was offered. But the defendants confessed, sometimes even denouncing the others. The *New York Times* wrote, "There is free speech in the shadow of the executioner." The high-profile men executed included Grigori Kinoviev and Lev Kamenev, who had played vital roles in the 1917 revolution, and fourteen other old Bolsheviks.

During the trial, the defendants denounced another "nest of Trotskyists." More trials and purges followed, and repression became a way of life for Stalin. Confessions were all that was needed, and there were ways of making people talk. Only in 1956 did the regime admit that Stalin had committed crimes against his own people. **RP**

King Abdicates

Edward VIII relinquishes British crown to marry Mrs. Simpson.

At Windsor castle the director-general of the BBC introduced the speaker as "His Royal Highness, Prince Edward." The empire was being addressed by the now ex-King Edward VIII, who explained that he had abdicated in favor of his younger brother, in order to marry Mrs. Wallis Simpson. "I now quit altogether public affairs, and lay down my burden. . . . God Save the King." The establishment was relieved.

George V may have been a cruel parent who, according to his biographer, did nothing for decades besides kill animals and collect stamps, but he had

> ## "I have found it impossible to carry the heavy burden of responsibility . . . as King."
> **Edward's broadcast of December 10, 1936**

been a model of matrimony. Not like his playboy eldest son, who succeeded him in 1936. Many considered him too sympathetic toward Britain's unemployed and Hitler's Germany, but it was the last straw when he wanted to marry Mrs. Simpson—a "commoner," an American, and according to the prime minister, "impossible." She had been twice divorced and the Church of England, of whom the king was supreme governor, recognized marriage "till death us do part." Edward opted for Mrs. Simpson, and a generous financial settlement, rather than remain monarch without her.

Had Edward remained king and married, there would have been a constitutional crisis. As it was, George VI reigned, while Edward and Wallis married and spent the rest of their lives together. **RP**

Guernica Bombed

The atrocity at Guernica reveals Franco's ruthless attitude toward the Basques.

April 26, 1937, was market day and the Spanish medieval town square was full. At 4:30 P.M. the church bell warned of an air attack, and people hid in the cellars that had been designated shelters. A single plane arrived, a Heinkel 51 bomber of the Condor Legion. It dropped its bombs and left. Guernica had got off lightly, or so it seemed. People emerged from the shelters and helped the injured, but then the full squadron approached and bombs began to rain down. The cellars were not strong enough to withstand the heavier bombs and people ran wildly for the fields, at which point the Heinkel 51 fighter squadron flew in low and strafed them with bullets. Finally, at 5:15 P.M., three squadrons of German Junker 52 bombers arrived. They bombed the town unremittingly for two and a half hours. The Basque government later announced that 1,654 people had been killed and 889 wounded.

The bombing of Guernica served no strategic purpose in the Spanish Civil War. Franco's real aim was to destroy Basque nationalism, for Gernika (in the local language) was the center of the Basque country, Euskal Herria. For Hitler, the exercise was an excellent workout for his planes.

General Franco denied the attack; then he blamed the Basques themselves. But four foreign journalists were in the region, and the truth was soon out. World opinion was shocked. Certainly Picasso was horrified: his gory masterpiece was completed two months later. For many, this massacre, with civilians seen as legitimate targets, signaled a new horrific form of twentieth-century barbarism. **RP**

◗ The desolate streets of Guernica in the aftermath of the bombing, where a lucky dog is the only sign of life.

Zeppelin Bursts into Flames

A spectacular explosion on board the Hindenburg *ends the manufacture of airships.*

◑ It is hard to believe that anyone could have survived such an explosion; miraculously, two-thirds of those on board did.

At one time the sight of a zeppelin would have caused alarm, for these gas-filled rigid airships had been used to carry out air raids during World War I. Now they were accepted as a routine means of passenger transport. Germany's luxurious *Graf Zeppelin* had crossed the Atlantic in 1928, circumnavigated the globe in 1929, and clocked up more than a million miles without incident.

When the *Hindenburg*, the largest flying structure ever built, approached Lakehurst, New Jersey, on May 6, 1937, on a flight from Frankfurt, the crowds massed to see the new marvel, and the landing was being covered on the radio. The disaster that followed was described by a passenger like "a scene from a medieval picture of hell." A thunderstorm delayed the landing, and the *Hindenburg* circled the airfield waiting for the weather to improve. Then, as she dropped her mooring ropes from several hundred feet, there was a muffled boom followed by a huge fireball, visible for many miles. In half a minute the airship was smoldering on the ground. A total of thirty-three people were killed, although sixty-four others were spectacularly rescued from the tangled burning wreckage.

Hitler believed the airship had been sabotaged, but it is more likely that static electricity had ignited the *Hindenburg*'s hydrogen fuel. Whatever the reason, the zeppelin industry could not survive such a debacle. The metal in the airships was melted down and used in fighter aircraft. **RP**

Stalin Attacks the Military

The execution of eight senior officers signals the start of the Red Army purges.

◯ Stalin pictured in 1937 with trusted politicians: Vyacheslav Molotov, Anastas Mikoyan, Marshal Voroshilov, and Mikhail Kalinin.

After a secret trial, Marshal Mikhail Tukhachevsky, first deputy people's commissar for war, and seven other Red Army officers were found guilty of plotting to betray the Soviet Union to Germany and executed. Tukhachevsky, a former officer in the Tsarist Army who had joined the Communist Party in 1918, had been instrumental in transforming the Red Army from a peasant force to a modern, mechanized army and had been made marshal of the Soviet Union in 1935. Joseph Stalin's paranoia had turned him against his military's best and brightest. Using torture, beatings, and sleep deprivation to obtain the confessions of the publicized Moscow show trials of 1936 to 1938, he began a witch hunt to purge the army of "politically unreliable elements," starting at the top.

The losses in the higher echelons were stupendous: three of the army's five marshals, thirteen of its fifteen commanders, eight out of nine admirals, fifty of fifty-four army corps commanders, 156 of 186 division commanders, all sixteen army commissars, and twenty-five of twenty-eight army corps commissars. In all, it is estimated, 30,000 army personnel were executed or sent to labor camps.

The Red Army's weakness resulting from the purges may have influenced Hitler's decision to launch Operation Barbarossa in June 1941. The loss of the experienced officers helped the defeats suffered by the Red Army at the start of the German invasion, until new younger commanders emerged out of the experience of war to replace them. **NK**

Marco Polo Bridge

The Japanese are halted outside Beijing triggering the Sino-Japanese War.

The battle that was responsible for sparking off the eight-year Sino-Japanese war and eventually led to the collapse of Japan's efforts to conquer China in the 1930s and 1940s took place in July 1937 around the medieval marble bridge over the Yongding River south of Beijing. It had been known as the Marco Polo Bridge since its description in the great Venetian traveler's diary as "a bridge of great beauty."

Japan had been steadily expanding its control of northern China from its puppet protectorate Manchukuo (Manchuria) since the Mukden Incident of 1931. From 1932 to 1933 it wrested control of Rehe province around the Great Wall and by mid-1937 controlled the northern, eastern, and western approaches to the ancient Chinese capital. Only the city itself and the southern approach over the Marco Polo Bridge remained in Chinese hands, with the Japanese army, bolstered by its planes and armor, holding the bridge's western end and the numerically superior but ill-trained and underequipped Chinese forces holding out at the eastern end.

At dawn on July 7, the Japanese telegraphed the Chinese requesting permission to cross the bridge and search for a missing Japanese soldier. Permission was refused, and at midnight the Japanese began bombarding the 1,000 Chinese troops defending the bridge. The Japanese overran the bridge, but the Chinese, reinforced, retook it the next day, which was followed by a truce being called.

In negotiations with Japanese commander General Hashimoto, China's General Zhang was given an ultimatum demanding that the Japanese gain the right to enter Beijing, and an apology. General Zhang left the talks and the Japanese launched an assault on the city, which fell on August 18. **NJ**

Rape of Nanking

The Japanese army slaughter Chinese civilians and rape women indiscriminately.

In a century marked by atrocities, the Japanese army's slaughter after the fall of the then Chinese capital of Nanking stands out as perhaps the most bestial single massacre of civilians in wartime.

After the fall of the port city of Shanghai, Japanese troops commanded by General Iwane Matsui moved on Nanking, the capital of Chiang Kai Shek's nationalist government, ordering a scorched earth policy as it retreated. The Japanese responded by slaughtering Chinese on a mass scale in the Yangtze Valley, and when Nanking fell without resistance on December 13, an unparalleled massacre began. First, the Japanese concentrated on Chinese soldiers, but soon they were slaughtering civilians and indulging in the mass rape of females—from infants to the elderly. Between 20,000 and 80,000 women are estimated to have suffered in this way.

Methods of execution included mass shooting, beheadings, burial alive, crucifixion, and hanging by the tongue. Babies were thrown into the air and bayoneted, and Chinese families were forced to commit incest with each other before being murdered. Western witnesses of the slaughter included missionaries, journalists, and the German Siemens businessman John Rabe, who saved many by establishing a safety zone in the city's west, ostensibly for foreigners, but also some Chinese.

The killings and mass rapes continued for more than six weeks into February 1938. It is thought that 300,000 died. Matsui and two lieutenant generals were hanged for the war crime, but few other perpetrators were called to account. China continues to demand in vain, in the face of Tokyo's denial of responsibility, that Japan apologize and make reparation for the bestial behavior of its army in Nanking. **NJ**

Anschluss

Hitler incorporates Austria into the German Reich, demonstrating his contempt for the Treaty of Versailles.

At the end of World War I the Austro-Hungarian Empire of the Habsburg dynasty was dismantled at the Treaty of Versailles. This left Austria as a small country on Germany's border. According to German nationalism, all German-speaking peoples should be united. Hitler, Austrian by birth, made this a reality with the *Anschluss* (union) of 1938.

Although prohibited by the agreements of the Treaty of Versailles, union between Germany and Austria had widespread support in both countries. In 1938 Hitler pressured the Austrian chancellor Kurt

"Thank goodness Austria is out of the way."

Alexander Cadogan, British Foreign Office

Schuschnigg to lift the ban on the Austrian Nazi Party, appoint Nazi ministers, and dismiss the head of the General Staff. Schuschnigg called for a plebiscite on the question of Austrian independence. Hitler demanded that a Nazi government be appointed or he would invade. Schuschnigg resigned and Austrian Nazis took over government offices. On March 12, German army units were welcomed into Austria. A Nazi-controlled referendum gave an endorsement to the union, and Austria became the Ostmark, a province of Greater Germany. **NK**

◗ Kraft durch Freude (KdF: Strength through Joy) supporters from Austria arrive in Berlin, April 4, 1938.

◗ German residents in Britain were ferried a few miles offshore so that they could vote on the *Anschluss*.

The Munich Agreement

The British prime minister agrees to Hitler's demand to annex the Sudetenland.

O Neville Chamberlain (in the long black coat) arrives in Germany ahead of his meeting with Hitler in Munich.

Neville Chamberlain, the British prime minister, returned to England from his meeting with Hitler in Munich to great acclaim outside Downing Street. Waving the document that they had signed pertaining to the Sudetenland, he declared that he had achieved "peace with honor" and "peace for our time."

Having successfully incorporated Austria into the German Reich in March 1938, Hitler had started demanding the incorporation of that part of Czechoslovakia that had a majority of German-speaking citizens, the Sudetenland. The mood of many in Britain and France was against confrontation with Nazi Germany and to avoid armed conflict. They believed that they were not militarily ready to take on the rebuilt and reequipped German army. The agreements made in Munich between the German, Italian, British, and French governments ceded to Germany the majority of the industrial capacity of Czechoslovakia, including the important Skoda arms factory and its western defenses. Without any international support, the Czech government was powerless, and the Germans occupied the Sudetenland without delay. Within six months, the German army moved into Prague, and the country was declared a German protectorate in contravention of Hitler's undertakings to Chamberlain.

This policy of appeasing the fascist dictatorships was bitterly opposed by Winston Churchill, who was convinced that Britain urgently needed to rearm and confront Hitler and Mussolini. **NK**

The Martians Are Coming

Orson Welles's The War of the Worlds *is broadcast, creating panic among listeners.*

○ Orson Welles photographed conducting a rehearsal for the radio broadcast of *The War of the Worlds*.

One of the most famous broadcasts in the history of radio went out in the United States as a Halloween special. Part of a series called "Mercury Theatre on the Air," it was an adaptation of *The War of the Worlds*—H. G. Wells's novel about a Martian invasion of Earth—and was directed with such stunningly believable effect by Orson Welles that some listeners thought it was a factual news report of a real Martian invasion. Lasting for an hour, it was presented as a broadcast of dance band music interrupted by a mounting succession of news flashes and bulletins, starting with reports of strange explosions on Mars. Then came word of a meteorite landing on a farm in New Jersey. The meteorite turns out to be a Martian rocket and the Martians (described as "indescribable")

turn deathly rays on the onlookers. More Martian ships land, spray poison gas, and tear down power lines. The events are commented on by a supposed Princeton professor and a supposed government spokesman. Troops attacking the Martians are swept aside, and people are reported fleeing in panic as the invaders head for New York City. In the end they are defeated, not by force but by earthly germs.

The contemporary newspaper reports of the panic the broadcast caused were exaggerated, but Welles made his name with the program at a time when totalitarian regimes around the world were using radio to spread propaganda. It demonstrated the effectiveness of modern communications in the dissemination of convincing lies. **RC**

Kristallnacht

*The Jewish community in Germany
and Austria is attacked by Nazi gangs.*

The mass of *Kristall* (broken glass) littering the streets on November 9, 1938, gave the outburst its name. At an Old Comrades dinner, Hitler learned of the death of a German diplomat in Paris, Ernst vom Rath, shot by Herschel Grynspan in anger at the failure of his protests against the deportation of 12,000 Polish Jews from Germany to their homeland. Joseph Goebbels, who spoke in Hitler's place, said that Hitler did not authorize demonstrations, but spontaneous outbursts should not be interfered with. This was a signal for a nationwide rampage against the Jewish

"Kristallnacht came ... and everything was changed."

Max Rein, historian

community. In civilian clothes, members of Nazi organizations, the Sturmabteilung (SA) and Schützstaffel (SS), armed with axes and sledge hammers, led the attacks against Jewish premises.

Seven thousand business premises, twenty-nine department stores, and many private homes were wrecked. Synagogues in Germany and Austria were ransacked and Jewish cemeteries desecrated. More than 30,000 German Jews were sent to concentration camps in Dachau, Buchenwald, and Sachsenhausen.

Germany claimed the riots were an expression of spontaneous anti-Semitic anger, but documentation shows that Kristallnacht was a planned campaign. **NK**

⊙ A Jewish synagogue in Berlin still in flames on the morning
after Kristallnacht, November 10, 1938.

Nuclear Fission Found

*Otto Hahn opens the door to nuclear
energy and atomic weapons.*

Otto Hahn, "the founder of the atomic age," was a German scientist who discovered nuclear fission in 1938 as the mounting tensions that would lead to World War II escalated. Fortunately, as an anti-Nazi, his genius was not used by Hitler.

Hahn was born in 1879, graduated from Marburg University in 1904, and worked at University College, London, discovering the isotope radiothorium (thorium 228). Transferring to McGill University, Montreal, in 1905, he worked under Sir Ernest Rutherford before becoming a professor at Berlin University in 1906. There he discovered ionium the "mother substance" of radium, married, and fathered a son. He also began his thirty-year collaboration with Lise Meitner, an Austrian chemist. After being conscripted to develop poison gases in World War I, Hahn wrote the book *Applied Radiochemistry*, which became the "bible" of the U.S. Manhattan Project to develop an atomic bomb.

Hahn's most important discovery was made after he bombarded uranium with neutrons, leading to the splitting of the uranium nucleus into atomic nucleii of medium weight—nuclear fission. In 1934 Hahn resigned from Berlin University in protest at the persecution of Lise Meitner and other Jewish colleagues. He procured Meitner a passport, enabling her to emigrate. Hahn was interned at the end of the war near Cambridge, when the atomic bomb was dropped on Hiroshima. Awarded the Nobel Prize for Chemistry in 1945, Hahn spent the time before his death in 1968 warning against the atomic arms race and the dangers of radioactive pollution. **NJ**

Hitler Invades Prague

The German Nazi regime sets out to incapacitate and destroy a democratic republic as Adolf Hitler extends his power.

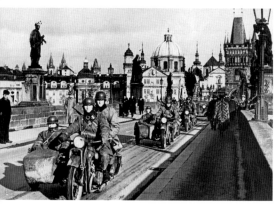

Czechoslovakia, created as an independent, democratic republic from parts of the collapsed Austrian Empire, had been forced in March 1938 to cede the Sudetenland, the part of its territory that had a majority of German-speakers, to Germany. At the same time other smaller regions were ceded to Hungary and Poland. Merely a year later, Hitler and his troops set their eyes on the heart of Czechoslovakia, and on March 15 they occupied Prague.

The Czechoslovak Republic had been fatally weakened in 1938, and the new president, Emil Hácha, was obliged to agree to greater autonomy for the Slovaks. Hitler, keen to extend his control over central Europe and now with his eye on the destruction of Poland and absorption of parts of its territory into the German Empire, needed to destroy what remained of Czechoslovakia. Having lost its frontier defenses in the previous year, together with major parts of its industrial production capacity after Hitler's acquisition of the Sudetenland, the country was in no position to resist. The Eastern Slovak part of the country declared itself independent on March 13, and two days later the German armed forces took Prague. Emil Hácha, under threat of a massive air attack by the Luftwaffe, ordered the Czech military to offer no resistance.

The next day Hitler declared the Czech Republic a German protectorate and recognized Slovakia as an independent nation. The Czech and Slovak parts of the country were reunited in 1945. **NK**

◗ Hitler's Elite Guard marches into Prague; the Czechoslovak army was ordered not to offer resistance.

◖ The German Army enters Prague on motorcycles in March 1939, several months before the commencement of war.

Franco Takes Madrid

The fall of Madrid signals an end to the civil war and legitimizes Franco's reign.

As the Nationalist forces of General Franco entered Madrid, the civil war, which had divided the nation for nearly three years, ended. On April 1, Franco, his administration recognized as the government by Germany, Italy, France, and Great Britain, broadcast a victory speech. Hostilities finally ceased.

Madrid had been besieged since 1936. General Mola, the Nationalist commander, had boasted that his four advancing columns, aided by "the fifth column" of supporters within, would take the city. However, the Republican fighters, most untrained

"Madrid has fallen . . . it is a new formidable victory for fascism."

Count Ciano, Italian foreign minister

but assisted by commanders from Soviet Russia and units from the International Brigades, drove off the regular soldiers of the attacking army.

Although the city was not entirely cut off, conditions and supplies of food, fuel, and ammunition deteriorated. Madrid was regularly bombed by the Nationalist air force. Violence toward Nationalist sympathizers led to more than 10,000 being executed. In 1939, Franco's grip on the city tightened. In March, amid Republican infighting, the Republican prime minister and Soviet advisers left, leaving the local commander, General Casado, to negotiate a surrender. This was rejected by Franco, who insisted the surrender should be unconditional. Over the next four years, many of the Republican defenders of Madrid were imprisoned and executed. **NK**

Nuclear Threat

Albert Einstein sends a stark warning to Roosevelt of the destructive future ahead.

Albert Einstein was the most celebrated scientist of his day. He was also a pacifist, who hoped that the League of Nations would eliminate war, but Nazi Germany in the 1930s changed his attitude. He renounced his German citizenship and settled in the United States. In July 1939, the Hungarian physicist Leo Szilard warned Einstein that the Germans might produce a nuclear bomb. Einstein simply replied, *"Daran habe ich gar nicht gedacht"* ("That, I never thought of"). However, he considered the matter urgent enough to inform the U.S. president.

"Shall we put an end to the human race or shall mankind renounce war?"

Albert Einstein

Szilard had drafted a letter to President Franklin D. Roosevelt, which he discussed with Einstein and another Hungarian physicist, Edward Teller. They decided it should go to the president under Einstein's name. Sent on August 2, 1939, the letter explained that research could lead to the construction of appallingly destructive bombs. The letter suggested that funding for U.S. research on nuclear energy should be increased and implied that the Germans had already begun a nuclear energy program, as indeed they had.

In September, President Roosevelt set up an advisory committee on uranium, which Szilard and Teller, although not Einstein, were asked to join. This action would lead eventually to the development of the first atomic bomb. **RC**

Nazi-Soviet Pact

Europe is stunned by the rapprochement between Germany and the Soviet Union.

Throughout the 1930s it was known that Nazi Germany and Soviet Russia remained antagonistic toward each other. Stalin was suspicious of German ambitions on its eastern frontier and watched with unease the annexation of Austria, the Sudetenland, and the invasion of Czechoslovakia in March 1939. So the signing of the Nazi-Soviet pact in August 1939 came as a deep shock to the rest of Europe.

The agreement openly included a seven-year trade agreement and a ten-year nonaggression pact. There were also secret protocols, by which the two sides

"[Hitler] thinks he has outsmarted me, but it is I who have outsmarted him."

Stalin to Nikita Khrushchev

agreed to the partitioning of the countries between their frontiers. Most of the Baltic states, Estonia, Latvia, and Lithuania would be under Russian domination, whereas Poland would be divided between them.

This agreement gave Germany access to raw materials, as well as security from interference by Russia in its forthcoming invasion of Poland. To Stalin it gave easy access to further territorial expansion in areas that had been part of the Russian Empire before the 1917 revolution. He may also have hoped that the coming war between the liberal democracies and the fascist states would damage them all, allowing for the advance of communist power in Western Europe. For almost two years the pact held firm, until the moment of the German attack on the Soviet Union in June 1941. **NK**

Hitler Invades Poland

Germany's attack on the Poles brings war with Britain and France.

Hitler's foreign policy had always been directed at correcting the perceived injustices of the Treaty of Versailles, incorporating German-speaking areas of Europe within his German Empire and extending control over the Slav populations of central Europe. In 1939, after his successes in Austria and Czechoslovakia, he turned his attention to Poland. In particular he wanted to regain control over the city of Danzig on the Baltic and the Polish Corridor that divided Germany from its province of East Prussia.

His experience of negotiating with the British and French governments had convinced him that they had no appetite for war. In March 1939 Britain and France had given guarantees of support to the Polish government, but as these contained no territorial guarantees, Hitler believed that he could gain his aims without a war on his western frontiers. As the tension mounted, he signed the nonaggression agreement with Soviet Russia, which protected him from Soviet interference.

Faced with rejection of his demands by the Polish government and after fabricated frontier violations, the German army attacked on three fronts aiming at Warsaw. Against German superiority in aircraft, armor, and artillery, the armed forces of Poland retreated toward their southeast border. On September 17, in accordance with a secret agreement in the Nazi-Soviet pact, the Soviet army invaded Poland from the east. A German-Russian border was established within former Polish territory, and Poland ceased to exist as an independent country.

On September 3, Britain and France declared war on Germany in accord with the guarantees they had given to Poland, but failed to take any immediate military action to help the Polish people. **NK**

Gone With the Wind Released

The most expensive movie made to date, at $3.9 million, sets the benchmark for all Hollywood blockbusters to come.

It was the most eagerly awaited film of a bumper movie year for Hollywood (*The Wizard of Oz* and *Mr. Smith Goes to Washington* also premiered). Producer David O. Selznick was behind the movie—an American Civil War epic based on the novel by Margaret Mitchell—having bought the film rights in 1936 for $50,000. Selznick went through fifteen screenwriters, including F. Scott Fitzgerald, and three directors to get the book onto the big screen.

The choice of Clark Gable as roguish male lead Rhett Butler was decided by a public poll, but the

"Where will I go? . . ." "Frankly, my dear, I don't give a damn."

Scarlett O'Hara and Rhett Butler

"search for Scarlett" (O'Hara, the sassy Southern belle) was more problematic. Many of Hollywood's "A" list stars took screen tests, including Bette Davis and Katharine Hepburn, but it was English stage actress Vivien Leigh who scooped the role.

It was a bold move but it paid off. The nearly four-hour epic has grossed more than $390 million worldwide. The feisty romance between Gable and Leigh was pivotal in the movie's success, as were the set scenes, including the burning of Atlanta, and all seven Technicolor cameras available at the time. **JJH**

○ Clark Gable and Vivien Leigh share a passionate embrace during the 1939 film.

○ U.S. audiences stretched around the block in order to catch a glimpse of the most eagerly anticipated film of the year.

Churchill Becomes Prime Minister

Back from the political wilderness, Churchill forms a National Government.

⬥ Winston Churchill in his trademark three-piece suit and hat, pictured a few days after becoming prime minister.

> " ... we shall defend our island, whatever the cost may be ... "

Churchill, House of Commons, June 4, 1940

Winston Churchill took over as Britain's prime minister on the day that the "phoney war" (the period after which war had officially been declared but before heavy fighting began) came to an end with the German assault on Holland and Belgium. Neville Chamberlain had been prime minister since 1937 and had the respect of many of his colleagues, but after six months of war he was beginning to be seen as lacking the drive to be an effective leader. After a disastrous campaign in Norway, dissatisfaction became acute. In a debate in the House of Commons, one of his former colleagues, Leo Amery, quoted Oliver Cromwell: "You have sat too long here for any good you have been doing. Depart, I say, and let us have done with you. In the name of God, go." It was clear that a new prime minister was needed.

On May 10, Churchill was asked by the king to form a government. This he did, inviting members of other parties, particularly Clement Attlee's Labour Party, to join a National Government.

Churchill, a former home secretary, chancellor of the exchequer, and First Lord of the Admiralty, had been politically marginalized for several years before the outbreak of war. Determined in his opposition to the policy of appeasement of the fascist dictatorships of Hitler and Mussolini, he was excluded from any ministerial post. But in September he went back to the Admiralty as First Lord, the post he had held at the outbreak of World War I, where his energy and determination to bring the German and Italian Navies to battle whenever possible was apparent to all. Now taking full charge of the direction of the war, he resisted moves for any accommodation with the enemy, promising little to the British people except short-term pain, but resolute in his belief in ultimate victory. **NK**

Germany Invades Holland and Belgium

Fighting intensifies in World War II as Germany launches a Blitzkrieg.

At nine o'clock on the evening of May 9, 1940, the high command of the German armed forces sent out the codeword "Danzig." This was the agreed signal to begin the offensive in the west at 5:35 the next morning. Breaking the neutrality of both the Netherlands and Belgium, German forces, led by strong Panzer groups, advanced on a broad front. British and French forces moved into Belgium to meet them.

The original plan of attack had been for the German army to push the French and British forces back to the line of the Somme River before redeploying their own troops south to advance toward the heart of France. But somehow these plans had fallen into the hands of the Allies, when a plane carrying staff officers had landed in error in neutral Holland. The German staff had to rethink their intentions. The chief of staff to General von Rundstedt, General von Manstein, proposed "Sichelschnitt" (scythe), a plan to concentrate the armor on the left flank of the attack through the Ardennes Forest. Breaking through the French front on the Belgian-French border, German armor would thrust across northern France for the Channel ports, effectively splitting the Allies in two. Hitler enthusiastically endorsed the plan.

The makeshift plan succeeded beyond all expectation. Crossing the Meuse at Sedan, German armored divisions launched an attack and burst through the French defenses. Ten days after the opening of the campaign, the second Panzer division of General Guderian's XIX Panzer Korps had reached the Channel coast at Noyelles. The French armies in the north, together with the British expeditionary force, were left isolated from the main French armies to the south. **NK**

◑ Soldiers look on as Rotterdam burns in the aftermath of the German attack on the city.

" . . . our soldiers are now accustomed to the German method of attack . . ."

Paris-Soir, **French newspaper report on May 20**

Dunkirk Retreat

Lord Gort evacuates the British expeditionary force from the continent.

When, in May 1940, the German army broke through the French lines on the Franco-Belgian border, it drove directly west toward the Channel, splitting its enemies' forces in two and leaving the British divisions with no way to retreat, but with the possibility of being trapped against the coast. The British commander Field Marshal Lord Gort decided his principal duty was to preserve his army and planned for its evacuation from the beaches of northern France and Belgium.

Requiring sacrificial defenses of the towns and ports on his southern flank, Calais and Boulogne, to hold back the German tanks from overrunning the evacuation beaches, Gort established, with the French army, an ever-shrinking perimeter behind which the navy could evacuate from the port of Dunkirk and neighboring beaches. Incessantly attacked by German planes, with little cover for the withdrawing units or for the ships, Operation Dynamo succeeded between May 28 and June 4 in bringing to England more than 338,000 soldiers, including 120,000 French personnel.

The "Dunkirk spirit" in which the country rallied around in times of trouble was epitomized by the story of the "little ships," private yachts and fishing boats, that contributed to the evacuation effort. Although the army had to be evacuated without its tanks, transport, artillery, or heavy weapons, and was in no state to resist a German invasion, Lord Gort's decision saved the British army from destruction in Europe and provided a base on which the divisions could be rebuilt and reequipped. **NK**

○ The rescue ships could not get close to the beach at Dunkirk, so the soldiers had to wade, neck-high, through the sea.

Germany Takes Paris

The Nazis take the French capital without a fight.

After a meeting between a German staff officer and two French officers to confirm that Paris was an open city and that there would be no resistance, soldiers of General von Studnitz's eighty-seventh infantry division moved in. Units marched down the Champs Elysées, setting up machine gun positions and occupying key sites, including the town hall and the ministry of defense. On June 14, 1940, the city was silent. The government had left for Tours and would later move farther south to Bordeaux. The diplomats had also gone, and many shops and businesses had closed. Large numbers of Parisians had fled.

That evening German radio played triumphal music, and church bells were rung and flags flown throughout the Reich on the direct orders of Adolf Hitler. The French capital, which it had failed to take in four years of fighting in World War I, had capitulated to the German army after a lightning campaign of scarcely more than four weeks.

Paris quickly came back to life—German soldiers were seen behaving as tourists with cameras, the cafés and restaurants reopened, and a semblance of normality returned. The government of Prime Minister Paul Reynaud, realizing that Paris had no military significance, resigned three days later, and the government was entrusted to the veteran Marshal Pétain, who immediately sought an armistice. On June 22, in the same railway carriage in which the French had received the German surrender in 1918, now decorated with swastika flags, General Huntziger signed the armistice document on behalf of the French government. For the French, only General de Gaulle, leader of the Free French Forces, now in London, represented the will to continue the struggle against the invader. **NK**

Trotsky Assassinated

Stalin's last surviving rival is removed as the Russian revolutionary's luck runs out.

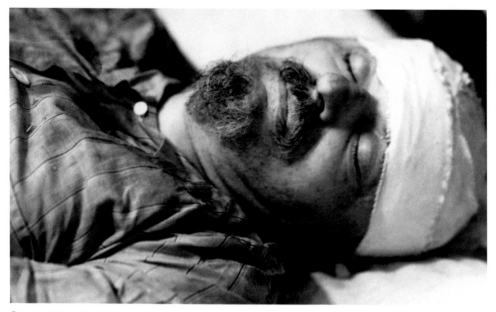

○ Trotsky died in a hospital in Mexico City, having been hacked with an ice ax by one of Stalin's supporters.

Stalin once commented that he never slept better than after arranging the assassination of an enemy. The Soviet dictator must have had particularly sweet dreams on August 20, 1940, after learning that one of his men, Ramon Mercader, had finally tracked down and liquidated Leon Trotsky, Lenin's lieutenant and Stalin's greatest rival and most bitter ideological foe.

Trotsky, the maverick revolutionary who arranged the Bolshevik coup in 1917 and subsequently was largely responsible for winning the Russian Civil War, had lost out to Stalin in the power struggle after Lenin's death. Exiled, he spent years wandering from one hiding place to another as he attempted to evade Stalin's implacable vengeance and organize his own followers as they tried to put into practice his theory of "permanent revolution." Settling in a fortified house outside Mexico City, Trotsky survived one determined assassination attempt when his bedroom was raked by machine-gun fire, and lost his son to Stalin's assassins in 1937.

Finally, a Stalinist agent, Spanish-born Mercader, wormed his way into Trotsky's household via an affair with one of his secretaries, Sylvie Ageloff. On the pretext of asking Trotsky to correct an article, he buried an ice ax in the revolutionary's skull. Trotsky had time to accuse Stalin of the crime before lapsing into a coma. He died the next day. Mercader was released from jail in 1960 and was made a Hero of the Soviet Union. He died in Cuba in 1978 and was buried in Moscow. **NJ**

Discovery of Lascaux Cave Art

An amazing discovery of Stone Age paintings is made in a cave at Lascaux, France.

○ Images of animals feature prominently in the prehistoric cave paintings at Lascaux.

On this day, at Lascaux, in the Dordogne region of southwestern France, four teenage boys were walking on a hillside made treacherous by recent rain. Their dog, Robot, slipped down a hole left by the roots of a fallen tree, and they scrambled after him. Exploring further, they found their way into a large cave. One of the boys shone a lamp across the walls and ceiling to reveal patches of color. They had stumbled upon one of the most magnificent galleries of Paleolithic (Stone Age) cave paintings ever found.

The cavern they had entered (later called "The Hall of Bulls") formed part of a cave system of seven decorated chambers and passages containing 600 paintings and nearly 1,500 engravings. Preserved in astonishing clarity, they are believed to have been made by people living between 15,000 and 17,000 years ago. Continuous friezes of horses, deer, bison, and cattle painted in red, orange, and black mineral pigments run along the walls. Most astounding of all are four huge black bulls, more than 16 feet (5 m) in length—the largest known figures in Paleolithic art.

News of the incredible find soon spread, and the caves were opened to the public in 1948. They were closed in 1963 after it had become clear that the presence of some 100,000 visitors a year was damaging the art, with ominous green patches and white crystals forming on the walls. A visitor center containing an exact facsimile of the caves was opened in 1983, and access to the caves themselves is now severely restricted. **SK**

Worst Night of the Blitz

The City of London endures three hours of heavy bombing just days after Christmas.

Since September 7, 1940, when Germany's Luftwaffe shifted their air attacks from Royal Air Force stations to Britain's cities, London had come under almost nightly aerial bombardment. Londoners got used to air raid sirens and nights in public shelters amid the crump of bombs, the disruption of work and transport, and the loss of many lives and buildings.

After a brief respite over Christmas, the most destructive raid of the Blitz was mounted on Sunday, December 29, targeting the historic heart of the capital, the City of London. In three hours of fire and terror, 120 tons of high explosives and 22,000 incendiaries were dropped. Water mains were fractured, and because the River Thames was abnormally low that night, firefighters were unable to draw water from the river to feed their hoses. The buildings of Sir Christopher Wren, the architect who had rebuilt the city in stone after the great fire of 1666, suffered more than most. Eight of his churches were destroyed, including the beautiful "wedding cake" spire of St. Brides' in Fleet Street. By a miracle, and thanks to fire prevention by the great church's clergy, Wren's masterpiece St. Paul's Cathedral was saved, despite suffering a direct hit.

Other buildings were not so lucky—Guy's Hospital was evacuated, and the whole of Cannon Street, east of Bread Street, was razed. Five hundred people—half of them firemen—were injured and more than 160 died, including eight out of the sixteen firemen killed that night who were crushed when a wall fell on them as they were dousing a fire off Fleet Street. The raid proved to be the climax of the Blitz, and in mid-May 1941, the Germans shifted their offensive once again—this time to Eastern Europe in preparation for the Nazi attack on Russia. London, and Britain, had survived its worst ordeal. **NJ**

◑ Amid the bombed-out shells of buildings, city workers make their way through the rubble and debris of Fore Street.

◐ Remarkably, the iconic landmark of St. Paul's Cathedral stands unscathed after the incendiary bombing.

" . . . like so many people, I felt that while St. Paul's survived, so would we."

Dorothy Barton, in *Wartime Britain 1939–1945*

Enigma Machine Captured

The British Royal Navy retrieves a top-secret German encoding machine and codebooks from a sinking U-boat.

The German forces used a family of machines known as "Enigma" to encrypt and decrypt their radio traffic. Throughout World War II they believed that this system was totally secure. However, Polish intelligence officers had found a way to decrypt some of the German radio traffic before the start of war, and they shared this discovery with their British and French partners. This source of intelligence, known as "Ultra," became key in giving the Allies information on the German order of battle and their operational plans.

One of the most important uses was in directing convoys away from German U-boat "wolf packs" during the Battle of the Atlantic. But the type of Enigma used by the German navy was the most difficult for the British code breakers based at Bletchley Park to break. At the height of battle, changes made by the Germans to their machines meant that the traffic between U-boats at sea and their shore command could not be read at all.

On May 9, 1941, U-110, captained by Lieutenant-Commander Fritz-Julius Lemp, was depth-charged while attacking a convoy in the North Atlantic. Forced to the surface, Lemp ordered the crew to abandon ship, thinking his submarine was about to sink. But before it went down, British sailors from HMS *Bulldog* boarded the U-boat and removed its cipher machines and codebooks. The restoration of the ability to read the German code contributed to the winning of the Battle of the Atlantic, without which Britain would not have been able to continue to fight. **NK**

◑ German signal troops use a teletype encoding machine, the zeros and ones of which lent themselves well to encryption.

◑ The average time taken to decode a message sent on Enigma was one hour, compared to days with other cipher machines.

Hess Flies to Scotland

Hitler's deputy flies to Britain to negotiate peace but is disowned by the Third Reich.

Why Rudolf Hess, Hitler's deputy and the third most senior Nazi leader, flew to Britain on May 10, 1941, is a mystery. Flying in a Bf 110 fighter, he came to land in farmland south of Glasgow in Scotland. Found by local people with a broken ankle, he was taken prisoner by the army and confined for the rest of the war in an English country house.

It is clear that he came with a peace proposal. Hitler was about to embark on his invasion of the Soviet Union, and his geopolitical position would be much improved without a belligerent Great Britain.

"Hess was consigned to the limbo of hush-hush and . . . resolutely suppressed."

Anonymous author in *American Mercury*, 1943

The Hess proposal was that Germany and its Allies would withdraw from all the countries they had occupied. In return Britain would remain neutral in the future German-Russian conflict.

Whether Hess came on the orders of Hitler is not known. Hitler immediately disowned him and declared him insane. It is possible he was tricked by British intelligence services to negotiate with the Duke of Hamilton, a prewar Nazi sympathizer. Was the Duke of Kent, brother of King George V, also a prewar sympathizer, part of the bait to lure Hess to Britain? The official archives on the Hess flight are closed, so no final answers are possible. For Churchill, there would be no negotiated peace. Convicted at the Nuremberg War Trials, Hess died in a prison in Spandau in 1987, the last of the Nazi leaders. **NK**

Barbarossa Launched

Hitler launches a surprise attack to bring about the collapse of the Soviet Union.

Operation Barbarossa was Hitler's plan to subdue Stalin's Russia, and at dawn more than four million German soldiers crossed the frontiers of the Soviet Union. Divided into three army groups, they drove for key objectives. The northern group commanded by Field Marshal Ritter von Leeb advanced through the Baltic provinces toward Leningrad. The center group, led by Field Marshal von Bock, aimed for Moscow, and Field Marshall von Rundstedt led the southern group to the oilfields and the industrial and agricultural economic resources of southern Russia.

"We have only to kick in the door and the whole structure will come down."

Adolf Hitler on invading Russia

The Soviet armies were caught unprepared. Stalin had believed Hitler would not attack before he had subdued his British enemies and refused to accept the intelligence of the impending invasion. The Russians had superiority in tank, artillery, and aircraft numbers, but the training and tactical doctrine of their forces was inferior to the Germans. Hitler's columns advanced through southern Russia, to the gates of Leningrad and Moscow.

Barbarossa was the military incarnation of Hitler's belief that the German people needed more territory and could enslave the inferior Slavs as an economic resource for the production of food. The Russian people held steadfast, and supply problems and the Russian winter prevented Hitler's armies from achieving any of their primary objectives. **NK**

Siege of Leningrad Begins

Leningrad is blockaded by the German army as part of Hitler's Operation Barbarossa.

○ Leningraders leave their bombed homes in 1942. Around 650,000 civilians died that year from starvation, exposure, and shelling.

The lakeside city of Leningrad—previously St. Petersburg, the Tsarist capital of Russia—was one of the three primary objectives of Operation Barbarossa, the German invasion of Russia in June 1941. The German Army Group North cut the final rail link between Leningrad and the outside world on August 31, and the next day began the blockade of the city that would last twenty-nine months. A week later, German and Finnish forces had surrounded the city. Stalin assumed Leningrad was lost.

The city was subjected to endless artillery and aerial bombardment, and the extent of the destruction was estimated to be more severe than the nuclear attacks on Hiroshima and Nagasaki. Public transport ceased; water supplies were destroyed. Food supplies were almost nonexistent. The ration for an unemployed civilian was reduced to 4½ ounces (125 g) of bread per day. Coal and oil stocks became exhausted before the winter began.

The blockade was not complete because large numbers of civilians were able to escape across the frozen Lake Ladoga. Industrial workers were also evacuated to reestablish their factories in unoccupied parts of the country. At the start of the siege, the population was estimated to be 3.5 million. By its close, it was reduced to 750,000, half of whom were serving soldiers, although every civilian who could was required to contribute to the survival of the city. Stalin's pessimism was unfounded. The city held on until it was relieved in January 1944. **NK**

Massacre at Babi Yar

Thousands die during a thirty-six-hour Nazi mass murder on the outskirts of Kiev.

○ The Nazis used Babi Yar ravine as the execution site to prevent news of the killings from filtering back to the Jews in Kiev.

On September 19, 1941, the German army, pushing east into the Soviet Union, entered the Ukrainian city of Kiev after a forty-five-day battle to be met with a series of bomb explosions that rocked the downtown area, killing many German soldiers.

Wrongly blaming Jews for what was probably the work of members of the Soviet NKVD, the SS decided to take retaliatory action against Kiev's entire Jewish population. Orders were issued for all Jews to report on the morning of Monday September 29 at the corner of Melnikovsky and Dokhturov streets, near the Jewish cemetery, with their documents, money and valuables, and warm clothing. Believing that they were to be deported, Jewish men, women, and children spent the day in line waiting to file through the gates of the Jewish cemetery, where they were told to leave their baggage. Then, in groups of ten, they were taken to the edge of a large ravine on the outskirts of the city, known as Babi Yar, and machine-gunned.

The killing lasted thirty-six hours, with nearly 34,000 dead. Bodies piled on bodies, and some of the victims were still alive as the mass grave was hurriedly covered over; only a handful escaped. It was one of the worst single atrocities of the *Einsatzgruppen*, the mobile killing squads of the SS, who are calculated to have murdered up to 1.5 million Jews, Roma (Gypsies), communists, and political activists as the German army advanced through Eastern Europe and Soviet Russia. **NK**

Pearl Harbor

*U.S. neutrality ends when a preemptive
Japanese attack destroys part of its fleet.*

At 7:48 A.M. Hawaiian time, the first wave of Japanese torpedo planes and bombers began the attack on the U.S. fleet, shore installations, and air bases at Pearl Harbor, the base of the U.S. Pacific Fleet. By the time the last flight of the second wave had departed some ninety minutes later, the Japanese had destroyed or severely damaged eight battleships, three cruisers, and three destroyers. In total, 188 aircraft were destroyed and a further 155 damaged. Japanese losses were minimal at twenty-nine aircraft and five midget submarines.

The plan to assault Pearl Harbor had been initiated by Admiral Isoroku Yamamoto, commander of the combined Japanese fleet. He was well acquainted with the United States and he himself feared that provoking the country was to wake a sleeping giant. However, the unprovoked attack on the U.S. naval base was intended to negate a possible U.S. intervention in Japan's forthcoming invasion of British and Dutch colonies, whose reserves of oil and rubber the Japanese considered essential in their plans for domination of East Asia.

Although it was an outstanding tactical success, the attack was a strategic disaster for Japan. It brought the United States into the war alongside Britain and its allies against both the Japanese and the Germans. It failed to destroy the U.S. carrier force, which was at sea at the time of the attack, or to reduce its submarine capability, the two arms of the U.S. navy that would contribute most to the long-term defeat of Japan. The losses suffered in the attack were rapidly made good by U.S. industrial production. **NK**

◖ A small boat rescues sailors from USS *West Virginia* after
she suffered a hit in the Japanese attack on Pearl Harbor.

The Final Solution

*The Wannsee Conference agrees to the
extermination of the Jewish race.*

The Wannsee Conference outside Berlin was a ninety-minute gathering chaired by Reinhard Heydrich, chief of the Third Reich's security services, to confirm the Nazi leadership's decision to evacuate and exterminate Europe's Jews in the conquered regions of Eastern Europe and the Soviet Union.

Fifteen officials from such organizations as the SS, the Foreign Office, and regional authorities were addressed by Heydrich, who reviewed the tightening of anti-Jewish measures and explained that because of the war and the dwindling of resources, the eleven

> ## *"Heydrich . . . is drinking cognac. It is years since I saw him touch alcohol."*
> **Adolf Eichmann, at the conference**

million Jews left in Europe could not remain—nor could they emigrate. Without using the words "extermination" or "elimination," he explained that the Jews would be deported to the east, to be worked to death on construction projects or "treated accordingly," in Heydrich's euphemism, lest they lived to spawn the Jewish race anew. After cognac was served, language became less restrained, according to Adolf Eichmann, who was taking the minutes, and methods were discussed for the mass killing of Jews. Heydrich was assassinated six months later by Czech patriots in Prague. Several other delegates died, killed themselves, or were executed at the end of the war. The last two died in 1982. The conference marks the adoption of mass killing as the Nazis' "final solution to the Jewish problem." **NJ**

Humiliation for the British Empire

The British naval base at Singapore surrenders to a weakened Japanese army.

○ Captured soldiers stand with their hands in the air while Japanese guards fix them with their bayonets.

On February 15, 1942, accompanied by officers carrying a white flag, Lieutenant-General Arthur Percival approached the Ford Motor Factory at Bukit Timah, Singapore, watched by Japanese soldiers. Percival was about to sign what Winston Churchill called "the largest capitulation in British history."

Singapore was well defended from the sea, but defense against landward attack had been neglected. From December 1941, Japanese troops advancing through Malaysia outmaneuvered and outfought British, Australian, and Indian troops. The survivors of this jungle war withdrew into Singapore on January 31, 1942. On the night of February 8, Japanese soldiers crossed to the island on rafts and began infiltrating the defenses. Churchill demanded a fight to the death. His commanders were not so keen. Singapore was under bombardment by Japanese artillery and aircraft, and half of its water supply was under Japanese control. Percival's officers recommended surrender—welcome news to Japanese commander General Yamashita Tomoyuki, whose troops were outnumbered and low on ammunition.

Apart from the Indian soldiers who joined the pro-Japanese Indian National Army, 80,000 troops became prisoners of war. Many would not survive. Around 30,000 local Chinese were massacred by the Japanese in the first fortnight of occupation. Percival survived the war as a POW, but the fall of Singapore destroyed the mystique of the British Empire and the myth of white racial superiority. **RG**

The Battle of Midway

The U.S. Navy wins its first major victory over the Japanese in the Pacific Ocean.

○ The USS *Yorktown* (CV-5) takes a hit in June 1942. After a torpedo attack it later sank, the only U.S. carrier lost in the Battle of Midway.

By the end of June 6, 1942, Admiral Chester Nimitz, commanding the U.S. forces in the Pacific, had won a major victory over the Japanese navy. The Japanese attack on Pearl Harbor had destroyed the U.S. battle fleet, but had left its carrier force intact. The destruction of this force became the major objective of the Japanese admiral, Isoroku Yamamoto.

His plan was to attack the island of Midway, the most westerly island in Hawaii, knowing that the Americans would have to defend it. What he did not know was that U.S. cryptographers had broken their enemy's naval codes and had knowledge of the Japanese intentions and dispositions. The battle spanned three days, with both navies launching long-range attacks by carrier-born aircraft, the ships of the opposing fleets never actually sighting each other. At the end of these exchanges, the Japanese had lost all four aircraft carriers committed to the battle, whereas the Americans had lost just one. More significantly, the Japanese had lost more than 200 aircraft and their combat-experienced crews.

The comparative weakness of Japanese industry meant that they could not replace lost ships and aircraft as quickly as the Americans could, and the highly trained pilots and crewmen lost in battle were irreplaceable. Although a further three years would be needed to force the surrender of the Japanese, after the victory at Midway the impetus in the naval Pacific War lay with the United States, and Japanese hopes for a quick and decisive victory were over. **NK**

Launch of the V-2

Hitler threatens the world with a missile against which there is no defense.

🌀 Images of the V-2—also called Vengeance Weapon 2—in flight in 1946, when its creator was working for the U.S. government.

A brilliant young engineer, Wernher von Braun had been a rocket enthusiast since he was a boy. From 1936 his talents were used by the Nazis to develop the world's first ballistic missile, the V-2. Based at a research center on the Baltic Sea at Peenemünde, his prototype first flew successfully in the autumn of 1942. Engineering problems, connected with propulsion, aerodynamics, and guidance were still unresolved, but by September 1944 the weapon was ready for deployment. Launched from mobile sites, these deadly rockets landed at supersonic speed giving no warning.

Many of the rockets were aimed at the city of Antwerp, a major supply base for the British army in northern Europe. More than 1,400 were fired at London, killing more than 2,700 civilians and wounding another 6,000. Britain's only response was to push the German line back so that they would have no launch sites from which V-2s could reach England. Hitler had hoped that the new rocket, along with his other terror weapon, the unmanned rocket plane V-1, his jet fighters, and new submarines, could turn the war against the Allies. But these weapons were never war winners on their own.

Wernher von Braun surrendered with most of his team to the U.S. Army in 1945, and was taken to the United States, where he began to develop the U.S. rocket program, which would contribute to the nuclear missile deterrent, but also to the building of the rockets that took astronauts to the moon. **NK**

German Army Surrender at Stalingrad

Despite Hitler's protests, a whole German army surrenders to the Russians.

◐ After some of the war's fiercest fighting at Stalingrad, many German soldiers were subjected to long-term imprisonment.

Surrounded by Soviet forces in Stalingrad since November 22 and with no supplies or relief able to get through, the German Sixth Army and commander Friedrich Paulus finally surrendered to the Soviet army. The attack on the city had become a symbol for both Russian and German armies of the struggle between their two countries. Until this surrender, the German army, although never achieving their objective of taking a major Russian city and bringing about the collapse of the regime, had been operationally undefeated by its Russian opponents.

Hitler had determined that the Sixth Army would never surrender and had promoted Paulus to *Generalfeldmarschall* (Field Marshal) knowing that no officer of that rank had ever surrendered in the history of German arms. But numerical inferiority, harsh weather, lack of warm clothing, starvation, and disease made continued resistance impossible. Some 91,000 German soldiers, including twenty-two generals, were marched into captivity in Siberia. The survivors became the last German prisoners of war to be released by the Soviets in 1955, twelve years after their surrender. Only 5,000 were still alive.

Stalingrad was one of the most brutal battles of the century. During the combat, the life expectancy of a private soldier was less than twenty-four hours and a junior officer less than three days. A whole Russian division disappeared in one day during the fight for Mamayev Hill. At least 750,00 casualties were incurred on each side during the battle. **NK**

Battle of Kursk

The Soviet forces demonstrate how to halt the terror of a German Blitzkrieg attack.

◯ Signal flares light a Soviet night attack at Kursk during the biggest tank battle in history; around 6,000 tanks were involved.

The German High Command needed to regain the initiative over the Russians after the Battle of Stalingrad. They decided to launch Operation Citadel, a two-pronged major attack against the Soviets at the city of Kursk. They assembled their largest forces of World War II: 800,000 men, 2,700 armored vehicles, and 1,800 aircraft.

The Russians had good intelligence of German intentions and constructed in-depth defenses in the areas where they expected the attack to fall. They laid large minefields and deployed unprecedented numbers of antitank guns. They outnumbered their opponents with 3,600 tanks and 2,400 aircraft. The Fourth Panzer Army launched attacks on July 4 in the southern sector, and the Ninth Army on July 5 in the northern sector. In the most intensive armored battles of the war on the eastern front, the German armor and infantry made some progress, but could not break through the Soviet defensive lines. The most violent combat took place near the village of Prokhorovka, where the II SS Panzer Corps fought the Fifth Guards Tank Army on July 12.

On July 20, Hitler stopped the battle. U.S. and British divisions had invaded Sicily, and Hitler wanted to move forces to support his Italian allies. The Battle of Kursk may be considered a draw, but the Soviet commanders had demonstrated how to halt a Blitzkrieg attack, and their counterattacks throughout 1943 forced the German army back across central and southern Russia. **NK**

Leningrad Siege Lifted

Russian resistance is victorious as its second city is freed from encirclement.

○ Overcome with emotion the heroes of Leningrad embrace and rejoice at the end of the grueling 879-day siege.

German forces had blockaded Leningrad, the second city of the Soviet Union, since the winter of 1941, but in the first month of 1944, Soviet attacks broke the lock on the city as the enemy retreated.

During the siege, food stocks had been exhausted and the city had been continuously bombed and shelled: schools, hospitals, water and power supplies, and public transport were all destroyed. Disease was rife. More than 1.2 million civilians are thought to have died. However, the city was never completely out of contact with the rest of Russia. During the winters when the ice froze, a road was established across Lake Ladoga over which one million civilians were evacuated and supplies of food, fuel, and equipment brought in. In the summer, waterways were used.

The civilian population of all ages was conscripted into war work; 15,000 children were decorated for their contributions to the defense. The cultural life of the city did not die. The Leningrad Radio Orchestra continued to give concerts and to broadcast. Shostakovich's 7th Symphony, dedicated to the city by the composer in 1941, was performed live and broadcast over loudspeakers in August 1942. The musicians were given extra rations to build up their strength. Leningrad became a symbol of the Russian resistance in the Great Patriotic War against the German invaders, and the raising of the siege was celebrated throughout the Soviet Union. In 1945, the city was awarded the Order of Lenin and in 1965, given the title of "Hero City of the Soviet Union." **NK**

The Longest Day

On D-Day, the largest amphibious force in history storms ashore in France.

◐ The dawn landing of the first U.S. troops at Omaha Beach, Normandy, immortalized by Magnum photographer Robert Capa.

On June 6, over a front of 65 miles (105 km), the leading troops from five seaborne and three airborne divisions of the Allied Expeditionary Force under the command of the American General Dwight D. Eisenhower assaulted the German-held coast of France along the bay of the River Seine in Normandy. By the end of the day, supported by the largest fleet of ships ever assembled, more than 125,000 U.S., British, and Canadian soldiers had disembarked. They were firmly ashore four years after the British had been forced to evacuate at Dunkirk.

For the previous six months, the German commanders along the coast of Europe, under the energetic direction of Field Marshal Erwin Rommel, had worked to strengthen the defenses of the Atlantic Wall, as the Nazi propagandists called it, particularly on the beaches where it was judged the combat would take place. Rommel knew that his armies would be disadvantaged. In order to overcome the shortages of men, tanks, guns, and transport, not to mention the air superiority of the Allied forces, the field marshal decided to try to defeat the invaders as they disembarked.

However, despite inflicting heavy losses, Rommel's soldiers were unable to repel the landings, and by that evening the Allied armies were established on the coast. Over the next ten weeks, the German army in Normandy lost 450,000 men, and then control of France and Belgium, and finally suffered the collapse of its Third Reich. **NK**

Bomb Plot on the Führer Fails

Hitler survives a German assassination attempt at his headquarters.

○ Benito Mussolini joins Hitler at Wolfschanze (the Wolf's Lair) to assess the damage caused by the attempt on Hitler's life.

July 20 was a hot day, and Hitler held his daily conference in a wooden hut on the grounds of his headquarters in Rastenberg, rather than in the usual underground bunker. When the bomb brought into the conference in a briefcase by Colonel Klaus von Stauffenberg, a staff officer from Berlin, exploded, its force was not contained as it would have been in a bunker. The hut collapsed, but Hitler avoided injury.

Whereas the majority of Germany, despite the casualties and deprivations of the war, remained loyal to Hitler and his National Socialist regime, a small number of officers, churchmen, and civil servants had decided that the only solution for Germany was the death of Hitler, a coup d'état, and peace with the British and Americans. Many knew of the activity of the plotters; fewer were prepared to become actively involved, but would have supported the coup had it succeeded.

Stauffenberg saw the explosion and, believing the Führer to be dead, flew to Berlin to initiate the coup d'état. But Hitler rapidly reasserted his control. That night Stauffenberg and his co-conspirators were executed. Hitler, who had never trusted the officer corps or the traditional German establishment, ordered a purge of the plotters, their families, and their sympathizers. Germany's most famous general, Erwin Rommel, who knew of the plot, was forced to commit suicide, and many other officers of all ranks were arrested on the slightest suspicion and killed, often in humiliating and painful ways. **NK**

Ik begin met de foto van Margot en eindig met mijn eigen. Dit is ook Januari 1942. Deze foto is afschuwelijk, en ik lijk er absoluut niet op.

Anne Frank Is Taken

A family's tragedy uncovers a message of hope for the world to embrace.

In the early hours of the morning of August 4, 1944, German security forces, acting on a tip-off from an unnamed source, raided concealed rooms in an Amsterdam office building. They arrested eight Jews, including the Frank and Van Pels families, who had been living in hiding for up to two years. All were taken to concentration camps. One, Anne Frank, who was fifteen years old, was deemed fit to work rather than for immediate dispatch to the gas chambers. However, this was merely a stay of execution, given the way workers were treated in such places. She died in Bergen-Belsen, probably of typhoid, only weeks before the Allies arrived. Her father, Otto, survived, and on his return to Amsterdam found that his daughter's diary, which she had kept from June 1942, had been saved by sympathizers.

Struck by the maturity and insights of his daughter's writing, Otto Frank managed to have it published in 1947, whereupon it caused a sensation. It was the narrative of a young girl living through the stress of a concealed and crowded existence, experiencing her first romantic feelings for young Peter Van Pels and writing of her hopes for the future. Anne's innocence, optimism, and belief in humanity amid overwhelming evil gave the diary its huge impact. The book was widely seen as giving voice to the innocent and oppressed, and providing an inspiration to the weak in the face of ruthlessness. Translated into many languages and the basis of film, stage, and television interpretations, Anne Frank's diary and her name have been cited worldwide to oppose intolerance and discrimination. **JS**

◗ Otto Frank had no idea that his daughter had been writing a diary nor of the depth of the feelings she described.

Paris Liberated

The French Second Armored Division storms back into its capital city.

On August 26, Paris celebrated its liberation. The city had been occupied for four years, and as the German army retreated from Normandy, Paris called for liberation. Hitler had ordered the garrison commander General von Choltitz to destroy the city. The underground resistance was ready to rise up and liberate Paris from within, whereas General Patton wanted to enter the city for the glory of the U.S. army.

Paris was of supreme political importance, and the Allied commander General Eisenhower decided it should be liberated by the one French unit under

> **"Paris must either not fall into enemy hands, or . . . find it a wasteland."**
>
> **Hitler to von Choltitz, August 23, 1944**

his command, the French Second Armored Division, who had fought in North Africa and Normandy. Fighting through German resistance in the western and southern suburbs of the city, three battle groups of infantry and tanks entered Paris on August 25 aiming at key points: the Arc de Triomphe, the Ministry of Defense, and the Hotel de Ville. While the civilian population celebrated, some German units continued to fight. However, von Choltitz did not destroy the city and disobeyed Hitler's instructions to blow the bridges and great public buildings. He surrendered Paris intact to the French divisional commander, General Leclerc.

Charles de Gaulle followed by his soldiers marched from the Arc de Triomphe to the cathedral of Notre-Dame for a service of thanksgiving. **NK**

Disappearance of Glenn Miller

The popular jazz musician is presumed dead; he was on his way to entertain U.S. troops, but his flight failed to reach Paris.

The disappearance of U.S. bandleader Glenn Miller on a routine flight has become an unsolved mystery that overshadows the life it preceded. Miller was at the height of his fame when his plane vanished over the English Channel on a flight to Paris. Miller's brand of big band swing music had made him a household name, giving him a string of hits like "In the Mood," "Little Brown Jug," and "Moonlight Serenade." When war broke out, he enlisted in the U.S. Army, and he and his Army Air Force Band boosted morale with a series of concerts for U.S. troops in Britain.

Offered a spare seat on a Noorduyn Norseman C-64 light plane flying to Paris by Lt. Col. Norman Baessell, Miller spent the night before the flight playing poker at the RAF airfield Twinwood Farm, in Bedfordshire. Miller had qualms when dawn brought thick fog, but Baessell and the pilot, John Morgan, assured him that it was safe to fly, and the trio took off—never to be seen again.

In 1985, British diver Clive Ward found the remains of a Noorduyn Norseman off the French coast, but the absence of serial numbers or human remains made it impossible to definitely establish whether the plane was Miller's. Officially, the disappearance was attributed to the plane's wings icing up, but the lack of a body has led to a number of far-fetched conspiracy theories, including scenarios that the plane did not crash at all and that Miller died in a brothel or of lung cancer. More plausibly, it has been suggested that the plane was hit by "friendly fire" from RAF bombers jettisoning their bomb loads while returning from a raid. **NJ**

◗ Miller's hit "Chattanooga Choo Choo" sold more than one million copies in three months.

Horrors Revealed

The advancing Red Army finds ghastly evidence of atrocities in Polish camps.

A unit of Soviet troops, under the command of Major Anatoly Shapiro, entered a complex of camps around the Polish town of Oswiecim and the village of Brzezinka. They found horrific evidence of one of the largest killing factories of the Holocaust. The Germans had originally opened a camp for Polish, German, and Soviet prisoners, but in October 1941 they opened Auschwitz II at Birkenau, with its gas chambers and crematoria to exterminate Jews. Auschwitz III was opened next as a slave labor camp to exploit Jewish workers until they perished

"I saw the faces of the people we liberated, they went through hell."

Major Anatoly Shapiro, January 2005

from abuse, starvation, and disease. Between one million and four million people were murdered here.

Before fleeing the advancing Russians, the Nazis attempted to conceal their misdeeds. But the crimes could not be hidden. The crematoria and gas chambers were destroyed, although it is possible that this was done by enraged Soviet troops. When most prisoners were forced to march west, a few thousand, too weak to move, were left behind. Their stories included tales of medical experiments on humans, performed by the likes of Josef Mengele. Piles of spectacles, human hair, and shoes, for example, remained. In 1947, the Polish government made parts of the camps a national museum, and in 1979, in recognition of the importance of what the site commemorated, it was made a World Heritage Site by UNESCO. **JS**

Yalta Conference

Allied leaders meet to decide the postwar future of Europe.

At Yalta, the three wartime leaders, President Franklin D. Roosevelt of the United States, Joseph Stalin of the Soviet Union, and Winston Churchill, the British prime minister, met to agree on the shape of Europe after the anticipated surrender of Germany.

Roosevelt and Churchill had particular demands: Roosevelt for a declaration of war by Russia on the Japanese, and Churchill for the territorial and political restoration of Poland. Stalin wanted the expansion of Soviet influence into Eastern Europe. The final agreement divided Germany into three (later four as France was given equal status) occupied zones: the Russians in the East, the British in the north, and the Americans and French in central and south Germany. Berlin, in the Russian zone, would be subject to joint control by the four powers. In Western Europe the frontiers reverted to their prewar boundaries. Austria regained its status as a separate country, but major changes were made in the east, where Germany lost much of its eastern territory, with new boundaries formed by the line of the Oder and Neisse rivers. Poland was reconstituted, but its boundaries moved westward into former Germany. Much of eastern Poland became part of the Soviet Union.

The real outcome of the conference was the opportunity it afforded Stalin to impose communist regimes on the states of Eastern Europe, often against the wishes of their populations. The Polish government in exile, resident in London since 1939 and seen by the British and U.S. governments, as well as the majority of Poles, as the legitimate government, was not allowed by Stalin to reestablish itself in Warsaw. The political shape of Europe laid down at Yalta would last until the collapse of the Soviet hegemony in the east of the continent in the 1980s. **NK**

Bombing of Dresden

A firestorm destroys the center of one of Germany's most historic and beautiful cities.

⌾ A streetcar is still in operation to carry its passengers through the ruins of Dresden.

The night the Royal Air Force bombed Dresden in Eastern Germany, it achieved the objective of all strategic bomber forces, a firestorm. Using a mixture of high explosive and incendiary bombs, the bombers created a self-perpetuating conflagration. The U.S. Air Force followed with further raids the next day, and 13 square miles (33 sq km) of the city were destroyed. Between 25,000 and 40,000 people died. The city, almost untouched by bombing until that night, was one of the jewels of eighteenth-century architecture, the capital of the former Kingdom of Saxony and a baroque masterpiece.

The attack, fourteen weeks before the final German surrender, caused a furor. The Nazi propaganda minister Joseph Goebbels seized on the destruction of the city, which he claimed had no war industries, and the massive civilian casualties (which he exaggerated to 200,000) to accuse the Allies of inhuman behavior.

The reports of the destruction and loss of life caused some people in Britain to question the morality of "terror" bombing. Questions were asked in Parliament. Even Winston Churchill questioned his advisers about the necessity of the attack. The military appreciation was that Dresden had industrial capacity and was a communications and command center for the German army, and that it remained a legitimate target. The debate continued long after the end of the war. Since 1945 the city has been painstakingly reconstructed to its former glory. **NK**

United States Marines Take Iwo Jima

The Stars and Stripes is raised on Japanese soil for the first time in World War II.

○ Rosenthal's photograph appeared on the cover of numerous magazines; it won him the Pulitzer Prize.

Advancing from island to island across the Pacific, the U.S. Marine Corps and Navy were ordered to take Iwo Jima, a small island forming part of the Japanese Home Islands. The need was to secure it as a forward air base from which to heighten the bombing campaign against the cities of Japan.

As the island formed part of their homeland, the Japanese command was determined to inflict as many casualties on the U.S. attackers as they could. They decided to fight for as long as possible, building up the number of troops to more than 21,000.

At 9 A.M. on February 19, 1945, the Third, Fourth, and Fifth Marine divisions went ashore after an intense bombardment from their accompanying ships and aircraft. There was no immediate opposition, but as they moved inshore, they came under intense fire from Japanese infantry and artillery bunkers, beginning some of the most intense combat of the Pacific campaign. In thirty-five days of fighting, the Americans suffered 28,000 casualties. Only 216 enemy troops were captured; more than 20,000 died.

The island was dominated at its southern end by Mount Suribachi. By the fourth day of the battle the marines had isolated it from the rest of the island. On February 23 a small patrol, and later a full platoon, reached the summit and raised the Stars and Stripes, the first foreign flag to be raised over Japanese soil. The moment was captured by Joe Rosenthal from the Associated Press, who took the most celebrated photograph of the Pacific War. **NK**

Franklin Delano Roosevelt Is Dead

The White House announces the death of President Franklin Delano Roosevelt.

○ The president was buried in the Rose Garden of his estate at Hyde Park in Dutchess County, New York.

On March 1, President Roosevelt addressed the U.S. Congress on his return from the Yalta Conference. He remained seated to deliver his speech—"It makes it a lot easier for me not to carry about ten pounds around the bottom of my legs." Many in the audience were shocked by his frail appearance: the stress of the wartime presidency was taking its toll. Even so, few were ready for the news of April 12, 1945, that the president, elected the previous November to an unprecedented fourth term of office, had died from a massive cerebral hemorrhage while staying at his vacation home at Warm Springs, Georgia.

Lucy Mercer Rutherfurd, his former mistress, was with him when he died two hours after collapsing with the words, "I have a terrible headache." In the White House, Eleanor Roosevelt broke the news to Vice President Harry S. Truman, who was sworn in as the thirty-third president of the United States.

Within seconds of the announcement of the president's death, the news had been flashed all over the United States. A newspaper report said, "Not knowing how to express their grief, people wandered out of their homes and began talking with neighbors, in bars, a sudden silence fell, and men and women were unable to adjust their minds quickly to the loss." For millions, the United States without Roosevelt seemed inconceivable. Three weeks later, when Nazi Germany surrendered, Truman dedicated U.S. celebrations to Roosevelt's memory and his commitment to ending the war in Europe. **NK**

Hitler Commits Suicide

The Führer and his wife kill themselves as Russian soldiers close in on their bunker.

◐ Hitler's body is believed to have been buried in the garden behind the Chancellery in Berlin.

As Allied troops drove deep into western and central Germany, Adolf Hitler remained in Berlin surrounded by his entourage of staff officers, guards, secretaries, cooks, doctors, his mistress Eva Braun, and his dog. In his concrete bunker deep beneath the Chancellery in the center of the city, he was awaiting the assault of the Soviet armies on the capital. Ignoring the entreaties of his advisers, he refused to leave Berlin and was determined to fight on or die where formerly he had been all-powerful. He gave orders to broken or nonexistent German forces to destroy the surrounding armies poised to enter the city.

On April 29, with Soviet soldiers advancing nearer to the bunker, he dictated his last testament, appointed Admiral Dönitz, the commander of the German navy, as his successor as Führer, married Eva Braun, and prepared for death. Next day his adjutant gave the Führer's dog a lethal injection. Having had lunch with his dietician and secretaries, Hitler and his new bride then retired to their sitting room, where she administered herself with poison and he shot himself through the mouth.

Hitler had ordered that his body should not fall into enemy hands. His corpse and that of his wife were taken from the bunker by his bodyguards, covered with gasoline, burned, and interred in a shell hole amid falling Soviet artillery rounds and the burning buildings of the doomed city. Their remains were never found. Within nine days, all German forces in Europe had surrendered to the Allied forces. **NK**

First Nuclear Bomb Tested

A nuclear bomb exploded in New Mexico proves its potency as a weapon.

The chief scientist of the U.S. project to build a nuclear bomb, Robert Oppenheimer, judged that, although the theory was sound, he needed to test the first nuclear weapon to ensure that the implosion trigger mechanism would work. In the remote desert of New Mexico at Alamogordo, near the weapons laboratory at Los Alamos, the plutonium fission bomb was successfully exploded on July 16 under the code name "Trinity."

Throughout the 1930s, physicists in Europe and North America had been studying nuclear fission and its potential application as a source of power and a devastating weapon of war. With the rise of fascism, many scientists—some of whom had been doing research in Germany and had moved to the United States—believed it necessary to ensure that the democracies developed the technology before the regimes of Mussolini and Hitler could do so.

The United States, together with Britain and Canada, initiated an urgent and highly secret program to develop the theory, the technology, and the industrial base to manufacture nuclear weapons. This massive undertaking, code-named The Manhattan Project, finally employed 130,000 people.

◐ The giant steel container initially constructed to collect the plutonium in case the nuclear explosion failed to occur.

◖ An image of the famous mushroom cloud from the explosion of the first atomic bomb at the Trinity site in New Mexico.

The team worked to develop the new manufacturing techniques needed to produce plutonium 235 as the fissile material, and new precision engineering methods to ensure that the complex implosion trigger mechanism would work. Anxious that Nazi scientists and engineers were developing their own systems, the authorities placed the work in the charge of General Lesley Groves of the U.S. Army Corps of Engineers, who directed the project and the necessary industrial resources. Robert Oppenheimer was the physicist who headed up the theoretical work and the laboratories. **NK**

"The atomic bomb made the prospect of future war unendurable."

Robert Oppenheimer

Churchill Voted Out

A Labour landslide in the postwar British elections signals the need for change.

Two months after victory in Europe, Churchill was utterly drubbed at the ballot box. But why did the people turn against the leader who had brought them through a world war to victory?

A key factor was the feeling that things had to change. The country was a gas-lit, blitzed-out, cobbled-streeted, coupon-rationed, socially awkward place with outside lavatories and no hot running water. It was still ruled by upper-class Tories out of touch with most of the populace. A feeling for things to be different, to bury the past, was in the air.

"Politics is almost as exciting as war, and quite as dangerous."

Winston Churchill

Trade Union leader Ernest Bevin talked of the gains of socialism for working-class people and struck a chord. Demands for a higher standard of welfare were highlighted by the 1942 Beveridge Report. This blueprint for a free national heath service, full employment, and child allowances was debated in Parliament, where the Tories voted unanimously against immediate implementation.

Labour mustered its forces. At the polls twenty-five million people voted. Labour took 47 percent against the Conservative's 38 percent and the Liberal Party's 10 percent. The Conservative government's 180- to 200-seat majority was turned into a 146-seat Labour landslide. It signaled a British revolution—an endorsement for hopes of job security, social justice, and a decent place to live. **JJH**

Hiroshima Bomb

A U.S. plane drops a nuclear bomb over a Japanese city to devastating effect.

At 8:15 A.M. local time, "Little Boy," the first nuclear weapon, exploded 1,900 feet (580 m) above Hiroshima on the Japanese island of Honshu. Hiroshima had been chosen as the primary target for the raid because it had not previously suffered from any air attack. The bomb was dropped from *Enola Gay*, a B29 bomber captained by Colonel Paul Tibbets. Accompanied by two further planes, one to take photographs, the other equipped with scientific monitoring devices, they had set off from the U.S. base on the island of Tinian. The weapon was armed in flight and the crew removed the safety devices half an hour before the target was reached. The Japanese had tracked the three aircraft approaching their homeland and had put out an air raid warning, but then canceled it. It was not thought that such a small unit posed any threat. No fighters were sent to intercept the raiders.

Dropped at 32,000 feet (9,750 m), the bomb took fifty-seven seconds to fall to the height at which it automatically detonated. The resulting cloud rose 11 miles (18 km) into the sky. The explosion caused total destruction within a 1-mile (1.6 km) radius from the center of the explosion, and 4.4 square miles (11 sq km) suffered damage or fire. Ninety percent of all buildings were either partially or totally destroyed. The Japanese authorities estimated that 255,000 people were living in Hiroshima at the time and that 70,000 were killed by the initial explosion. By the end of 1945, it was estimated that an equal number had died of the effects of radiation. Death and disease resulting from the attack continue to this day. **NK**

◗ The city of Hiroshima was virtually flattened; only buildings constructed to withstand earthquakes survived.

War Is Over

World War II ends as the Japanese army surrenders to the Allied forces.

On board the battleship USS *Missouri*, the Japanese government and military signed the formal act of surrender to the Allied powers.

The Japanese ceased hostilities on August 15. On July 26, President Truman had told Japan that if they did not accept the Potsdam Declaration, which incorporated the terms of the surrender, they would suffer utter destruction. The Japanese rejected this, but after the devastation of Hiroshima on August 6 and Nagasaki on August 9, they broadcast their acceptance and then surrendered to the Americans.

Two weeks later in Tokyo Bay surrounded by the U.S. and British fleets, the Japanese foreign minister Mamoru Shigemitsu and the head of the Imperial General Headquarters Yoshijiro Umezu came to the USS *Missouri* to sign the formal act of surrender. There they met with the Allied commanders headed by General Douglas MacArthur, General Wainright, who led the heroic U.S. resistance in the Philippines, and General Percival, the British commander in Singapore (the latter two recently released from prisoner of war camps). The instrument of surrender was then signed by commanders from all the Allied powers: Britain, France, the Netherlands, Australia, New Zealand, Canada, China, and the Soviet Union as representatives of their respective governments. Japan stood as a ruined country, its economic infrastructure destroyed and two of its major cities flattened. General MacArthur, now the effective ruler of Japan, initiated the drafting and implementation of a new democratic constitution and the beginnings of the economic reconstruction. **NK**

○ New Yorkers in Little Italy celebrate the end of the war with confetti, flags, and banners.

United Nations Created

Out of the ashes of war arises the United Nations, to prevent a third world war.

Its predecessor had proved an abysmal failure. When World War II began in Europe, the League of Nations averted its gaze. The new United Nations would surely do better. The preliminary work had already been done at Dumbarton Oaks, near Washington during 1944, and at San Francisco in 1945. Proposals worked out by the United States, the United Kingdom, the Soviet Union, and China were accepted by the fifty nations that signed the UN Charter.

Now, on October 24, 1945, the new institution was born. There was to be an assembly, mainly consultative,

> ## "If we had had this charter a few years ago . . . millions now dead would be alive."
>
> **U.S. president Harry Truman**

and a council, mainly executive. All peace-loving nations were to be represented with a single vote, whereas the Security Council was to have five permanent members: the United States, the United Kingdom, the Soviet Union, China, and France, and six others, elected for two-year periods. The assembly could pass resolutions by majority votes and the Security Council could insist on action, even military action, although each permanent member could use a veto. International cooperation would be fostered via UN agencies to solve social, economic, and humanitarian problems. The UN had a power imbalance in their favor of the victors of World War II and was constructed as the cold war became frosty. The question still is whether imperfect machinery can be made to work effectively over time. **RP**

First Meeting of the United Nations

The United Nations General Assembly meets for the first time amid high hopes for peaceful cooperation and discussion, but cold war tension is stirring.

London was bomb damaged and food rationed and struggling to accommodate the thousands of visitors descending on it. The venue was the Central Hall in Westminster, one of Britain's largest Methodist churches, now converted into an assembly room. The time was 4 P.M. The action was signaled by two raps with the gavel delivered by Dr. Zuleta Angel of Colombia, the temporary president. Two hundred and twenty-four delegates from fifty-one states were called to attention. The first session of the United Nations General Assembly was under way. Britain's prime minister, Clement Attlee, told the delegates and the press that the United Nations had to become "the overriding factor in foreign policy" to save the world from the scourges of war and poverty.

The United Nations was planned toward the end of World War II and was formed on October 24, 1945. Many had hopes of a new era of justice, freedom, and peace. The first session in London articulated these hopes, but there was also unexpected confrontation. The Americans and West Europeans assumed that Paul-Henri Spaak would be elected as president, but the Soviets nominated a rival candidate. A ballot was held, giving the decision to Spaak by twenty-eight votes to twenty-three votes. When the Security Council met for the first time, on January 19, there were similar East-West divisions.

The United Nations provided no easy solutions to the formidable problems it was set up to combat. Cold war tensions were exacerbated when the UN moved to New York in 1949. Nevertheless it survived, and today there are 192 member states. **RP**

○ Andrev Gromyko, Soviet ambassador to the United States, addresses the delegates at the United Nations assembly.

Peron as President

Juan Peron comes to power in Argentina with popular mistress Eva on his arm.

Argentina was initially neutral in World War II but sympathetic to the United States and Britain, who both had economic interests in the country. However, a coup in 1943 brought a military junta to power that sought the country's economic and political independence and adopted totalitarian measures in pursuit of national unity. One member of the junta was General Juan Peron, who in February 1946 was elected president of Argentina.

As head of the labor department, he built up a power base with the workers by increasing wages,

"Keeping books . . . is capitalistic nonsense. I just use the money for the poor."

Eva Peron

promoting unions, and creating welfare reforms. His popularity was enhanced by a glamorous mistress, the actress Eva, whom he married shortly before winning the presidency at the end of the war.

Peron's policies included nationalizing foreign interests and promoting welfare measures, and his wife, Eva, became head of the welfare program. However, a financial crisis in 1950 led to increased repression and a fixed election in 1951. Eva died of cancer in July 1952, and a bloody uprising against Peron forced him into exile in Paraguay, and then Spain, in 1955.

In 1973, Peron's secretary Hector Campora was elected but resigned when Peron returned to win presidential elections in October. His rule was marked by inner-party conflict, and he died in July 1974. **PF**

Iron Curtain Speech

Churchill's Fulton address calls for Anglo-American strength and unity.

Churchill said it was merely the speech of a private citizen giving counsel in "these anxious and baffling times." He talked about the two threats facing humankind—war and tyranny—the latter happening "in a considerable number of countries." It was important for the United States and Great Britain to maintain a "special relationship," working together for a "grand pacification" of Europe, a continent across which an "iron curtain" had descended. Communist parties were obtaining totalitarian control in Eastern Europe, and communist fifth columns

"This is certainly not the liberated Europe we fought to build up."

Winston Churchill in Fulton, Missouri

were gaining influence in France and Italy. The United States and Britain must remain united and strong and uphold the Charter of the United Nations.

Having unexpectedly lost the 1945 general election, Churchill embarked on a number of major speeches on world affairs. His message was determined by the situation in Europe, but also by his interpretation of the 1930s. There must be no appeasement this time and no military weakness. President Harry Truman fully agreed.

Stalin insisted that Churchill's speech was really a veiled Anglo-American declaration of war. Relations between the West and the Soviet Union were chilly, but Churchill's speech may well have hastened the onset of the cold war. It may also have played a part in preventing a much greater catastrophe. **RP**

The Bikini Modeled in Paris

The first appearance of the bikini signals a liberalization of postwar attitudes.

Although revealing, two-piece garments were worn by women in the ancient world, as can be witnessed in the 1,700-year-old Roman murals in the Villa Casale de Romana in Sicily. The first modern two-piece swimsuits had been seen in the 1930s, but the bikini as we know it today made its debut at a Paris fashion show on July 26, 1946, as the world struggled hard to escape the gray austerity of the postwar period.

It was the brainchild of two Frenchmen: engineer Louis Reard and fashion designer Jacques Heim, who named it after the Bikini atoll in the Pacific Ocean's Marshall Islands, the site of a U.S. nuclear test earlier that month. Heim reckoned that the explosive effect of the new garment would be similar to that of an atomic detonation—and he would be proved right. The two men found that professional models were too modest to parade their sexy invention, but eventually Reard hired a nude dancer, Micheline Bernardini, from the Casino de Paris club to model the garment at the Molitor pool.

Women's fashion took another decisive turn the following year when Christian Dior introduced the "New Look," which consisted of unemphasized shoulders, a natural waistline, and a full skirt with hem lower than previously. Femininity was back.

Over the following decades, the bikini gradually gained acceptance as the swimwear and beachwear of choice for fashionable young (and not-so-young) women across the Western world. Despite conservative outrage, and bans in Catholic countries such as Spain and Malta, the bikini's popularity was boosted by appearances in films such as *And God Created Woman* (1957), starring Brigitte Bardot, and *Dr. No* (1963), in which a statuesque Ursula Andress famously and unforgettably emerges from the sea wearing a white one. **NJ**

◒ The bikini designed by Louis Reard is modeled for an attentive pack of reporters and photographers.

> **"A bikini is not a bikini unless it can be pulled through a wedding ring."**

Louis Reard, its inventor

Terrorist Outrage in Jerusalem

The King David hotel bombing persuades Britain to hand back the Palestine mandate.

It had a reputation for being one of the finest hotels in the world, almost on a par with the Ritz in Paris. In 1946, however, few wanted to stay at the King David hotel unless they really had to, for Jerusalem was the scene of increasingly violent terrorist outrages. A wing of the hotel had been taken over by British administrative and military personnel, and it might have been assumed that the seven milk churns delivered to the kitchens at noon would simply serve their dietary needs. Yet in fact they were packed with explosives, and the deliverymen were in reality members of a Jewish paramilitary organization, the Irgun gang, in Arab dress. At 12:37 P.M. the churns exploded, causing the collapse of six stories and the deaths of ninety-one people: forty-one Arabs, twenty-eight British, seventeen Jews, and five others. Most were hotel workers or clerks, but a few were members of the hated British hierarchy.

Arabs complained that too many Jews were migrating to Palestine, whereas Zionists and their supporters were aghast that Britain was not allowing entry to all Holocaust survivors and other Jews who wished to enter. It was a no-win situation for the British, especially when the violence began to escalate. Aged Zionist leader Chaim Weizmann did his best to deter terrorists from the spectacular attack he suspected was afoot. However, Menachem Begin, the leader of the Irgun (and Israeli prime minister 1977–1983), was adamant: there was little option but to destroy the King David hotel.

The bombing heightened tensions throughout Palestine. It undoubtedly played an important part in Britain's reluctant decision that enough was enough. In February 1947, the future of Palestine was handed over to the United Nations, and the following year the state of Israel was proclaimed. **RP**

⭗ A telephone warning was given but ignored before the bombing of the King David hotel.

> ## "On 22 July, one of the most dastardly and cowardly crimes . . . took place."
>
> **British prime minister Clement Attlee**

Nuremberg War Trials

Senior Nazi war criminals are sentenced to hang during the Nuremberg trials.

The Four-Power International Military Tribunal, popularly known as the Nuremberg war trials, had begun in Nuremberg's Palace of Justice. The United States, the Soviet Union, Britain, and France provided judges and prosecuting staff. The defendants were the twenty-three most important Nazi figures to have survived. The charges included conspiracy to wage war, war crimes, and crimes against humanity. It was, as a British delegate had predicted, "the greatest trial in history." It was also controversial, because the court was scarcely impartial. Nevertheless, three of the accused were found not guilty. Eleven others were to be executed and the rest imprisoned.

" . . . to say . . . not guilty, it would be as true to say that there had been no war."

Robert H. Jackson, U.S. prosecuting attorney

In their defense, the accused said they were simply following orders and did not understand what was going on. Hermann Göring insisted he knew nothing of the Reich's genocidal actions. The blame was placed on those Nazis already dead. The real culprit, said Hans Frank, was Hitler—he was "the devil, and therefore led us all astray."

Göring killed himself with a cyanide pill, but ten others were hanged. Secondary figures were prosecuted until 1949. The trials were not perfect; there was some justice in the defendants' insistence that the victors were also guilty of wanton destruction, but they established benchmarks and precedents for crimes against humanity. **RP**

Dead Sea Scrolls

The find revolutionizes the study of the Old Testament and the old Jewish world.

Mohammed Ahmed el-Hamed, a young Bedouin, was searching the cliffs for a lost goat, on the northwest side of the Dead Sea, and threw a stone into a cave. He heard something shatter and found pottery jars, some of them stuffed with ancient scrolls of leather parchment and papyrus. Scholars investigated the cave and others nearby, and over the next ten years, more than 800 scrolls were found.

Some were manuscripts of the books of the Old Testament, a thousand years older than any others known. Most were in Hebrew, and a few were in Aramaic, the language of Judaea in the first century C.E. It seems likely the scrolls were written in the

"Let your faith and confidence in me never waiver. I am with you, Always."

Fragment found in cave 3

nearby community of Qumran, between about 200 B.C.E. and the first century C.E., and were hidden during the Jewish revolt against the Romans in the 70s, which resulted in the destruction of Jerusalem. Qumran was home to a pious—perhaps celibate—mystical Jewish sect known as Essenes (Saints), who lived as a desert community. Some scholars think it housed a priestly sect known as Sadducees.

The scrolls brought new light on the Old Testament and the Jewish world at the time of Christ, even though none refers directly to Jesus or his followers. To many scholars, they demonstrate the continuity between the teachings of Jesus and those of other Jewish religious leaders of his day. **PF**

Marshall Aid Is Launched

U.S. Secretary of State George C. Marshall offers financial aid to enable Western Europe to rebuild after World War II and resist the spread of communism.

The 296th commencement ceremony at Harvard was a glittering occasion. One eminent figure to receive an honorary degree was T. S. Eliot, the poet who had written that the world would end "not with a bang but a whimper." But U.S. Secretary of State George C. Marshall feared quite the opposite apocalypse. He was introduced as a man "to whom freedom owes an enduring debt of gratitude," and after his speech he was to be owed even more. He emphasized the serious state of world affairs and the impoverished economy of Western Europe following the war. The United States, he said, was prepared to give generous aid, providing the nations of Europe agreed on their requirements and worked together for recovery. Marshall Aid had been launched.

Several motives lay behind Marshall's offer. There was a humanitarian impulse, but also the calculation that, unless the economic health of European customers recovered, U.S. manufacturers would suffer. But the preeminent motive was the fear that, unless the United States shared its wealth, a desperate Western Europe might fall prey to communism. The policy complemented the Truman doctrine of U.S. support of "free peoples . . . resisting attempted subjugation," announced a few months earlier. Marshall Aid was a cold war weapon.

Britain's foreign secretary Ernest Bevin eagerly seized on the U.S. offer and helped found the Organization for European Economic Cooperation. It was, he said, "like a life-line to a sinking man." As a result, sixteen nations shared more than thirteen billion dollars between 1948 and 1951. **RP**

PROSPERITY

THE FRUIT OF CO-OPERATION

EUROPEAN RECOVERY PROGRAMME

○ "Prosperity: The Fruit of Co-operation," a poster promoting the newfound unity between Europe and the United States.

Death of the Raj

Britain quits a divided India in 1947, leading to tension and violence among its people.

○ When India was divided in two, millions of Hindus and Muslims uprooted themselves to rehouse on their own sides of the border.

At a spectacular ceremony at Government House in Delhi, the last viceroy of India, Lord Mountbatten, was sworn in as the country's first governor-general; there were gracious speeches in the legislative assembly, and at 8:30 P.M. the Union Jack was lowered and replaced by the Indian flag. George VI was no longer emperor, the British Raj was no more. Fireworks lit up Delhi, and the party lasted into the next day. A newsreel described the crowds that day, the largest in memory, as "wild with joy."

The British said this was the fulfillment of their rule, which had begun officially when control passed from the East India Company in 1857. It took two world wars and the growth of Indian nationalism to move the British out. Yet when Britain set a deadline for withdrawal, divisions were all too obvious among India's politicians. In the end, deadlock between the Hindu Congress and the Muslim League was broken only by dividing India into two countries. In the new Muslim state of Pakistan, the Union Jack was replaced by the Pakistani flag showing the star of Islam. The dignity of the transfer of power was in many ways cosmetic, masking the furious communal tensions, riots, and slaughter, as millions rushed to get to the right side of the new borders.

The former semi-independent Princely States opted to join one of the two new countries. India became the world's largest democracy, but Pakistan's progress was more problematic, with its eastern wing becoming independent as Bangladesh in 1971. **RP**

Mahatma Gandhi Is Slain

A Hindu fanatic assassinates Gandhi, the father of nonviolent civil disobedience.

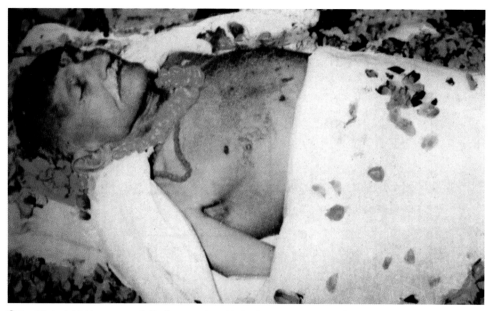

◒ Gandhi's body is laid out, surrounded by flowers and sprinkled with petals.

Mohandas "Mahatma" Gandhi was running late when he left Birla House in Delhi to attend his regular prayer meeting. As an elder statesman, he had been mediating between the prime minister and deputy prime minister of newly independent India. Seventy-eight-year-old Gandhi could not hurry, because he was weak from a fast, the latest undertaken to encourage Hindu-Muslim reconciliation. Two great-nieces were helping him through the crowd when a figure emerged and bent down to touch the Mahatma's feet. In response, Gandhi put his hands together and smiled; but then the man stood up, pulled out a revolver, and fired three shots at point-blank range. Gandhi mouthed the name of the god "Rama," and his frail body slumped to the ground.

Gandhi had known his life was in danger because ten days earlier a bomb had exploded at a prayer meeting. Since his first nonviolent civil disobedience campaign in 1919, he had lived with the possibility of death, seeking "my peace among disorders." After independence, communal tensions were at fever pitch, and it was feared a Muslim might assassinate him, although he was killed by Nathuram Godse, of the right-wing Hindu organization Mahasabha.

The world was shocked, and powerful leaders paid homage to the man who held no political position and had scarcely any possessions. In India, Prime Minister Nehru successfully appealed for calm. Any bloodshed would have been an insult to the saintly figure who embodied nonviolence. **RP**

State of Israel Is Born

The proclamation of Israel leads to an escalation of violence in the Middle East.

There was tight security in the Rothschild Boulevard and the Haganah military police scrutinized everyone at the Museum Hall in Tel Aviv. The Jewish nation had waited 600 generations for this day. Inside, the hall was crowded and hot. At 4 P.M. David Ben-Gurion entered the museum and rapped a gavel on the table for attention. After the singing of the national anthem, the *Hatikvah*, he read out a declaration of independence. The document was then signed by the thirty-seven members of the National Council. Israel was officially in being, with Ben-Gurion as its first prime minister. The goal of establishing a "national home" in Palestine for the Jews had been

---

" . . . we hereby proclaim the establishment of . . . the State of Israel."

David Ben-Gurion

---

proclaimed in 1917 by Britain, which acquired the territory after World War I. Yet the British refused unlimited Jewish immigration—even after the Holocaust—out of concern for the local Arab population and their allies. When violence erupted between the two communities, the matter went to the United Nations, whose recommendation for partition was accepted by the Jews but not the Arabs. Israel's birth was thus highly traumatic.

President Truman of the United States recognized the new state, just ahead of the Soviet Union. But not the Arabs of the Middle East. War would determine the political geography of Israel and scar the region for generations to come. **RP**

White Supremacy

The victory of the Afrikaner National Party opens the door to apartheid.

It was one of the closest general elections in South Africa's history. On one side was the English-speaking United Party led by Jan Christian Smuts, prime minister since 1939 and a pro-British Afrikaner. On the other was the Afrikaans-speaking Herengde Nasionale Party (Reunited National Party) led by Dr. Daniel Malan, a frank pro-Nazi during the war and now a republican. Both parties stood for white supremacy, but Malan championed "native policy" and apartheid (separateness), believing that only whites could be accorded membership of the state.

The Nationalists won the most seats in the virtually all-white election. Smuts lost his seat. The

---

"In the past we felt like strangers . . . but today South Africa belongs to us."

Dr. Malan on becoming prime minister in 1948

National Party had a majority of only five, but this was a turning point of immense significance.

The new government was solely Afrikaner. Great efforts were made to "Afrikanerize" the army, the police, the judiciary, and the civil service. That way Malan could be sure that his new laws would not be sabotaged. Legislation in 1949 and 1950, strongly reminiscent of some of the 1935 Nuremberg Laws against the Jews, was complemented in 1951 by the creation of "homelands" for ten black tribes. Racial segregation had now been extended to the whole of the Union of South Africa. Malan died in 1959, but the era of apartheid was to continue until multiracial elections were held in 1994. **RP**

Immigrants Arrive from Jamaica

The arrival of the Empire Windrush *at Tilbury, England, creates anxiety and signals the start of a multicultural, multiracial Britain.*

She was an ex-Nazi troopship, refitted and renamed *Empire Windrush*. Her voyage had begun in Palestine, with stops in Mexico, Jamaica, Trinidad, Cuba, and Bermuda. Now she was reaching her destination. As she entered the Thames estuary, several stowaways jumped ship, but still she steamed on and eventually reached Tilbury for an unusually public docking. A flotilla of ships surrounded her, including both sightseers and the press—the arrival of a ship carrying 492 Jamaicans was a news story. Aldwyn (Lord Kitchener) Roberts dutifully treated the newsreel cameras to his latest calypso song: "London Is the Place for Me."

West Indian migrants came for a variety of reasons. Some were Royal Air Force pilots, returning from leave. Others, young and optimistic, hoped for well-paid jobs. All had been brought up as British citizens and wanted to see the "mother country." But many British politicians were anxious because this seemed a reversal of the natural order of things. White Britons traditionally emigrated to the colonies, and now blacks from the colonies were emigrating to Britain. It was this attitude that, in 1962, ended the automatic right of entry for all Commonwealth citizens.

Quickly, the West Indians from *Empire Windrush* found jobs, even if it was not the skilled work for which they were qualified, and the fuss made about their arrival died down. The ship's arrival, however, was the beginning of a process that was to transform Britain into a multiracial and multicultural society. **RP**

◗ The former troopship *Empire Windrush* arriving at Tilbury Docks with 492 Jamaicans emigrating to Britain on board.

◗ West Indian migrants contemplate their future after disembarking the *Empire Windrush* in Tilbury dock.

Allies Airlift Supplies to West Berlin

A massive Allied airlift allows Berlin to survive a Soviet blockade and prepares the way for the North Atlantic Treaty Organization.

Bloomers flew from the aerials of military vehicles on Thursday June 24, 1948. "Operation Knicker" was the Anglo-American response to the Soviets' cutting of road and rail links between the western zones of Germany and West Berlin. It involved the "airlifting" of supplies along the three flight paths allocated to the Western Allies in 1945. But was it practicable? A daily minimum of 2,000 tons of food was needed for the 2.5 million people in West Berlin, who had been importing a massive 12,000 tons of supplies every day. Yet the only planes available were one hundred U.S. C-47s and six British Dakotas, each capable of holding no more than 2.5 tons. And what about fuel and coal? Existing supplies would last only months. On the first day of the blockade, Berliners received words of reassurance but only a few tons of supplies.

British foreign secretary Ernest Bevin insisted that the airlift had to work. And it did. By the end of July, the allies were flying in an average of 2,000 tons a day, and by April 1949 that figure had reached 8,000 tons, with around 1,000 planes using the air corridors at any one time. Stalin decided to cut his losses. The blockade was called off in May 1949.

Stalin had instituted the blockade to deter the West from establishing a democratic West Germany. Now, in 1949, he had to accept the inauguration of the Federal Republic of Germany, with an outpost in Berlin. The West had not given way to pressure. Nor would they again, for that same year the North Atlantic Treaty Organization was founded. **RP**

⬤ Citizens of Berlin wait among the ruins as supplies are flown in by a U.S. C-47 plane.

⬤ Dressed as Santa Claus, Lieutenant John Konop of Astoria hands out Christmas presents as part of the relief operation.

Birth of the NHS

The National Health Service (NHS) in Britain provides free health care.

The act had received the royal assent back in November 1946. Everyone in Britain would soon receive free medical care from hospital consultants, general practitioners, and dentists and opticians. Costs would be borne from taxation, and therefore poverty would no longer be a bar to good health. Consultations, treatment, hospital stays, drugs, false teeth, eyeglasses—all would be free at the point of need to anyone who asked.

The inauguration of the National Health Service on July 5 made an enormous difference to people's

"This Service must always be improving; it must always appear to be inadequate."

Aneurin Bevan, June 25, 1948

lives. Previously, medical provision had been patchy and uneven. State insurance had provided most workers, but not their dependents, with free treatment from a doctor, whereas hospital treatment depended on private insurance, local authority provision, or charity. Health secretary Aneurin Bevan had to compromise to win doctors' participation— private medicine would exist alongside state provision, resulting in "pay beds" in NHS hospitals.

Britain became the first Western society to offer free comprehensive medical treatment. There was a tremendous call for this service, which regularly cost more than anticipated. Some charges were imposed from 1951. However, Bevan's confident assumption that private medicine in Britain would "wither away" due to NHS superiority proved sadly mistaken. **RP**

Human Rights Agreed

The United Nations proclaims the Universal Declaration of Human Rights.

An early achievement of the United Nations was to consolidate documents like the French Declaration of the Rights of Man (1789) and the American Bill of Rights (1791) into a single international charter. There was a need for a declaration after World War II, and the UN charter did not define individual rights.

The declaration was the brainchild of the director of the human rights division in the United Nations Secretariat, John Peters Humphrey; and Eleanor Roosevelt, UN human rights commission chair. The thirty articles set out rights such as equality before

"One of the highest expressions of the human conscience of our time."

Pope John Paul II, 1995

the law, liberty, education, and freedom of conscience. It was written as a set of objectives and principles for individual governments to follow and has provided a form of moral pressure that can be brought to bear on a deviant government.

The declaration was adopted with no votes against. Six Soviet bloc countries, Saudi Arabia, and South Africa abstained. It was adopted as international law in 1976. The declaration is sometimes criticized as being insufficiently flexible to allow for cultural variation (not allowing for Sharia law in Islamic countries, for example). Nevertheless, as a milestone on the global acceptance of the rights of individuals against oppressive regimes, it has proved a vital and positive achievement. It has also led to the wider development of human rights law. **PF**

War Criminals on Trial

General Tojo and other Japanese wartime leaders are executed as war criminals.

◎ In the crowded Tokyo courtroom, General Hideki Tojo stands accused of atrocious war crimes.

He was known as "the razor" for his utter ruthlessness. As head of the extreme Tosei faction, Hideki Tojo advocated Japanese expansion into China in the 1930s, joined Germany and Italy in the Tripartite Pact, became prime minister in 1941, and ordered the bombing of Pearl Harbor and a war of savage aggression. Military setbacks forced his resignation in July 1944. Perhaps Tojo's only saving grace was that in the Tokyo courtroom he did not evade blame. On December 23, 1948, he and six other war criminals were hanged at Sugamo prison.

The Allied occupation had begun in September 1945, after the Japanese surrender, and the trials started in May 1946. Twenty-eight Class A war criminals were arraigned before the International Military Tribunal for the Far East. Their crimes included "murdering, maiming, and ill-treating" prisoners of war and civilian internees, "wantonly destroying cities, towns, and villages beyond any justification of military necessity," and "mass murder, rape, pillage, brigandage, torture, and other barbaric cruelties." U.S. prosecutor Joseph Kennan exposed the defendants as "plain, ordinary murderers." Two of them died during the trial, another collapsed mentally, seven were sentenced to death, sixteen to life imprisonment, and two others to jail. By the occupation's end in 1952, Japan had a democratic constitution, the emperor had renounced his divinity, and militarism was a thing of the past. Tojo was largely an inconvenient memory. **RP**

Formation of the People's Republic of China

Mao's victory in China in 1949 creates the world's second communist state.

○ Mao Zedong pauses in reading out the proclamation from the balcony of the Imperial Palace, Beijing.

On October 1, 1949, in Tiananmen Square in Beijing, Mao Zedong proclaimed the formation of the People's Republic of China. Soon the event was commemorated in a gigantic poster: the smiling leader extending his left hand skyward, modern airplanes flying past, and immaculately dressed men, women, and children celebrating. The reality was more prosaic. China was on its knees after two decades of bitter warfare, the population was impoverished, the enemy—Chiang Kai-shek's nationalists—were still not defeated, having withdrawn to the island of Taiwan, and October 1 was just an arbitrary date for the celebrations.

Yet a new state had come into being. Twenty-eight years after helping found the Chinese Communist Party, Mao was leader of communist China. Had Mao been an orthodox Marxist, history may have been different, for experts in Moscow assured him that peasants were a petty bourgeois, almost counterrevolutionary force. Had he been a less skilled leader of guerrilla troops, Chinese communism might not have survived, for the nationalists tried their best to eradicate it. The sides cooperated against the Japanese, but after Japan's defeat, civil war resumed. Even after October 1949, areas of China remained nationalist.

The Soviet Union and then Britain were the first to recognize the new republic. Communist China was a momentous fact of international life. Nationalist China still existed, but only on Taiwan. **RP**

5

6

2

13

9

20

26

27

2

3

An instantly accessible calendar is an entry-level feature of twenty-first-century smartphones.

1950–PRESENT

List of Communists

Senator McCarthy's speech at Wheeling initiates the communist witch hunts.

Joseph McCarthy was a Minnesota farm boy who took up the law and Republican politics. In 1946, he was elected a U.S. senator and at thirty-eight was the youngest member of the Senate. In a speech in 1950 to a Republican women's group at Wheeling, West Virginia, he waved what he said was a list of communist agents known to be working in a government department. A Senate committee investigated the claim and found no grounds for McCarthy's allegations.

Communist successes elsewhere in the world, including China, had been fueling increasingly hysterical suspicions that U.S. government policy had been influenced by communist sympathizers. The Un-American Activities Committee of the House of Representatives, which had existed since 1938, got a new lease on life and held hearings, relying heavily on dubious informers and guilt by association. Their actions turned into a witch hunt as liberal and leftist organizations and individuals were smeared as traitorous "Reds." In January 1950, a former state department official, Alger Hiss, was convicted of perjury for denying under oath to the committee that he had been a Russian agent.

In 1953, McCarthy became chairman of the permanent subcommittee on investigations and used the position to press the "comsymp" witch hunt forward. Some of his suspicions were more securely founded than his critics have cared to admit, but he and his committee's chief counsel, the New York lawyer Roy Cohn, had no regard for evidence and ruthlessly destroyed the reputations of innocent people. To what extent McCarthy believed in his crusade or understood the harm he was doing to his country is still disputed. **RC**

North Korea Strikes

The United Nations has the unique opportunity to act.

In the early hours of the morning, North Korean forces began a full-scale invasion of South Korea with a devastating artillery barrage. The North's leader, Kim Il Sung, claimed he was responding to unprovoked aggression by the South, led by Prime Minister Syngman Rhee. The scale of the offensive, though, was clear evidence of a long-planned campaign to reunify Korea. The original division in 1945 had been intended as a temporary expedient until the United States and the Soviet Union could agree on the future of the country. Two separate governments had emerged, both claiming to be the legitimate authority in Korea. Communists ruled in the North, whereas in the South a corrupt and unpopular, but crucially anticommunist, dictatorship had been nurtured by the United States.

Washington could not allow its own creation to be destroyed and was in a unique position to act. The Soviet Union was boycotting the UN Security Council because the Americans had refused to give the communist regime a permanent seat on the body. Because of this Soviet abstention, and thus their inability to use their power of veto, Washington was able to get Security Council resolutions passed condemning the North Korean invasion and calling on member states to send forces to defeat it. With varying degrees of reluctance and motivated more by their dependence on the United States than by enthusiasm for Korea, fifteen nations contributed forces. Five others sent medical units to a U.S.-led coalition, only nominally under the UN flag, fighting the first open conflict of the cold war. **JS**

◯ Two South Korean soldiers drag a North Korean soldier
out of his hiding place while keeping a lookout for snipers.

China Invades Tibet

Chinese Communist forces storm an isolated and little-known territory.

Claiming to be exercising their sovereign rights and bringing liberation to the people, the People's Liberation Army of China invaded Tibet in the fall of 1950. Chinese emperors had claimed suzerainty over Tibet since the thirteenth century, and for the newly established People's Republic of China that was sufficient pretext to invade. Mao Zedong's regime sought to legitimize its rule by completing what it saw as the reunification of China. Although independent, Tibet, a theocracy under the rule of the Dalai Lama, was too weak to resist.

"We respectfully plead for troops to be sent . . . [to] liberate the Tibetan people."

Purported plea to Mao Zedong, January 1950

There was initially some hope from progressives that the occupation might benefit Tibet. Bringing feudalism to an end could be of advantage to many of the poorest people and bring economic development. However, these hopes soon faded. The Chinese built bridges, roads, and schools, but they also launched a determined campaign to undermine the Buddhist hierarchy's authority. This was accompanied by attacks on traditional culture and the national elite, as well as gross violations of human rights. By 1959 resentment burst into revolt, which was brutally suppressed, forcing the Dalai Lama to flee. The Chinese worked to reshape Tibetan society, not least by attacking the Buddhist religion. Religion, however, remains the symbol of Tibetan national aspirations and its rejection of China. **JS**

Soviet Spy Scandal

"Cambridge Spies" Burgess and Maclean defect to the Soviet Union.

That Friday, as usual, Donald Maclean spent the day at the Foreign Office in Whitehall, London, leaving at 5:30 P.M. for his regular train from Charing Cross to Tatsfield. In fact this was an exceptional day. Not only was it his thirty-eighth birthday, but intelligence had come to light that Maclean was almost certainly "Homer," the spy who had been passing secrets to the Soviets. Maclean was to be interrogated on Monday morning, and MI5 agents followed him to Charing Cross but no further. With his wife heavily pregnant, it was assumed that Maclean would not defect. That evening another spy, Guy Burgess, arrived at the Maclean house and introduced himself to Mrs. Maclean as Roger Styles. Donald then told his wife that he had been called to an important engagement and that he was taking an overnight bag in case he could not get back. The two men raced to the coast, crossed to France, and disappeared. Soon it was revealed they had defected to the Soviet Union.

Burgess and Maclean had been recruited as Soviet agents at Cambridge University in the 1930s, along with a third man, Kim Philby. Maclean had worked in the Washington Embassy from 1944 to 1948, where he leaked intelligence that allowed Stalin to estimate the strength of the West's nuclear arsenal. It was Philby, in Washington, who got wind that Maclean's cover was about to be blown and sent Burgess to warn him.

There had already been several notorious spy scandals in Britain. This fresh one led to the adoption of more vigorous background checks of key personnel. Yet it was not until 1963 that Philby defected, and not until 1979 that another Cambridge spy, Anthony Blunt, was exposed. Both Maclean and Burgess died in Russia. **RP**

Death of Evita

The darling of Argentina, Eva Peron, dies, as does the popular support for her husband, the president of Argentina.

Maria Eva Duarte de Peron, affectionately known as Evita, was still in her early thirties when she died of cancer. Compellingly glamorous and attractive, she was a major influence on Argentine politics as the wife of the dictator Juan Peron. She also made her name as an actress on radio and in movies. In 1943, she met Colonel Peron and became his mistress before marrying him as his second wife in 1945. At his side while he was president from 1946, she created her own charitable organization, the Social Welfare Federation, a bountiful dispenser of patronage that convinced poor Argentines of her warmhearted concern for their well-being, and was a key source of support for her husband. Under her influence, women in Argentina got the vote in 1950. Hugely popular and traveling extensively around the country, she was a crucial channel of communication between Peron and his support in the provinces.

Evita was the first person in Argentina to have chemotherapy. After her death her body was embalmed and her faithful supporters begged the Vatican in vain to canonize her. Without her, Peron rapidly lost support and was forced to flee the country in 1955. Evita's body disappeared and its whereabouts remained a mystery for years. There were stories of it being left in a truck or stored in somebody's attic. In 1971, it was delivered in a van to the house in Spain where Peron was living. It was finally returned to Argentina in 1976 and lies buried in La Recolata Cemetery in Buenos Aires. **RC**

❍ A poster of Evita stuck to the side of a house, after her death, declaring her to be always in the soul of her people.

❍ Mourners pass the glass-topped coffin that houses the embalmed body of Eva Duarte Peron.

Hydrogen Bomb Explodes in Pacific

The hydrogen bomb is tested on an uninhabited island in the Eniwetok Atoll.

⬤ The world's first hydrogen bomb explosion—known as Operation Mike—completely destroyed the islet of Elugelab.

The U.S. project to develop a hydrogen bomb was approved by President Truman in 1950 after the Soviet Union had begun to test its own atomic weapons. A key figure in the program was the physicist Edward Teller, who had earlier worked on the first atomic bomb. What is generally considered the first successful trial of the new weapon was conducted in Operation Ivy at Eniwetok (now Enewatek) Atoll, a group of islets in the Pacific, whose population had been evacuated years before.

The terrifying test, which involved more than 11,000 military and civilian personnel, was carried out at 7:15 A.M. local time on the islet of Elugelab, which was blasted completely out of existence. The explosion produced a yield of 10.4 megatons, with a fireball more than 3 miles (5 km) wide and a mushroom cloud that rose to 23 miles (37 km) and was 100 miles (161 km) wide at the top. Bits of coral fell on ships 30 miles (48 km) away, and the atoll was heavily contaminated by radioactive fallout.

The U.S. Atomic Energy Commission issued a statement on November 16 guardedly reporting a successful test: "In the presence of threats to the peace of the world, and in the absence of effective and enforceable arrangements for the control of armaments, the U.S. government must continue its studies looking toward the development of these vast energies for the defense of the free world."

The atoll was eventually cleaned up, and in 1980 some of the inhabitants were allowed to return. **RC**

Death of a Tyrant

A towering figure on the world stage departs to the dismay of many Soviet citizens.

○ Millions of mourners paid their respects to the dead Stalin; the vast crowds resulted in some mourners being crushed.

On February 28, Joseph Stalin had watched a film with close associates, then he had gone to bed with orders not to be disturbed. When guards investigated his room the following day, he was found collapsed. Medical help was eventually called, but he died on March 5, with political jockeying going on around him and rumors that he had been poisoned. Millions went to see his body lying in state.

For most Soviet citizens, the news that Stalin had died, after twenty-five years or so of unchallenged power over the Soviet Union, left them with a deep uncertainty and fear for the future. Even some inmates of Siberian prison camps were reported to have wept. In the ensuing power struggle, Nikita Khrushchev emerged the victor. To him was left the task of reestablishing the legitimacy of a state bound up for far too long with the whims and desires of one man. The cult of Stalin and the myth of his infallibility had to be dismantled.

There was a period of relative liberalization of Soviet rule, in which many political prisoners were freed and the regulation of culture was relaxed. This culminated in a secret speech Khrushchev gave to the Communist Party congress in 1956, in which he denounced Stalin, a man he had slavishly served for thirty years, as a murderer and a criminal. Khrushchev did not mention the crimes in which he had been involved, but the speech was too big a bombshell to remain secret long. Khrushchev, however, was not destined to succeed to Stalin's full powers. **JS**

Structure of Life Decoded

Crick and Watson present a model of the molecular structure of DNA.

◐ James Watson (left) and Francis Crick with their model of part of a DNA molecule, photographed in 1953.

On April 25, 1953, two scientists, Britain's Francis Crick and the United States's James Watson, announced a huge step forward in our understanding of how life functions are inherited. They presented to the world a model, consisting of two intertwined, helical strands of the molecular structure of deoxyribonucleic acid (DNA), which explained how characteristics could be copied and passed from one generation to another.

Crick was thirty five years old, Watson just twenty-two. Crick had begun his career as a physicist, then moved to biochemistry; Watson began as an ornithologist, then moved on to study viruses. The breakthrough came as Watson studied the X-ray crystallography image of the DNA molecule.

This was very much the dawn of biotechnology, with subsequent researchers able to build on Crick and Watson's work. In the 1970s, Paul Berg and Herbert Boyer devised a means of cutting and pasting together different pieces of an animal's DNA, which paved the way for cutting and pasting DNA from different species. Crick and Watson's work also facilitated the later decoding of entire genomes (the genetic sequence of a species), initially of bacteria, and eventually, once gaps in the available technology were filled, of human beings. From this has come genetic mapping, which is used to identify the genes responsible for inherited diseases and perhaps eventually the genes that influence common diseases and human behavior. **JS**

Mount Everest Is Scaled

Hillary and Tensing scale the world's highest mountain.

🔵 Tensing Norgay and Edmund Hillary relax in their camp on Mount Everest.

They had been cutting steps in the snow of the final ridge for so many hours that their legs would scarcely move. Their original zest had gone; it was now a grim struggle. Hillary then realized that the ridge ahead, instead of rising, fell sharply away. A few more whacks with the ice ax and they made it. It was 11:30 A.M., and Hillary could see on Tensing's face, despite his balaclava, goggles, and oxygen mask, an "infectious grin of pure delight." The two men shook hands and thumped each other on the back until they were almost breathless. They spent fifteen minutes taking photographs before planting the British flag, the Nepalese national flag, and the United Nations flag.

The Tibetans named it Chomolungma, and the Nepalese Sagarmatha, both meaning "Mother Goddess of the World." The British originally called it Peak XV, but renamed it after Sir George Everest, a surveyor-general of India. At 29,028 feet (8,848 m), with variations caused by the fluctuating top level of snow, Everest was the tallest mountain in the world and a provocation to climbers. A dozen well-prepared missions had failed before. Despite using the latest oxygen equipment and specially insulated clothing, an attempt a few days earlier had been beaten back by strong winds. Thankfully, for the New Zealander Hillary and the Sherpa Tensing Norgay (who were climbing as part of a British expedition), the weather for their climb was perfect. The news reached Britain on the eve of the coronation of Elizabeth II, and there was fond talk of "a new Elizabethan Age." **RP**

East German Uprising

Across East Germany, workers strike in protest against the communist regime.

The workers' uprising against communist rule in East Germany in June 1953 was the first of several similar outbreaks—Hungary in 1956, Czechoslovakia in 1968, and Poland in 1970—that demonstrated discontent with Soviet-style puppet states in Eastern Europe.

The rising began after the leadership of the ruling SED (Socialist Unity Party) imposed a 10 percent rise in productivity norms, at the same time freezing wages as a "sixtieth birthday gift" to East Germany's communist leader, Walther Ulbricht. On June 16, 1953, some seventy workers at a Berlin construction site spontaneously struck against the new measures. News of their protest spread quickly, and on the following day 100,000 strikers gathered in the capital, some shouting, "Death to Communism!" The protests spread and affected some 400 cities, towns, and even villages.

The authorities reacted quickly and brutally, ordering sixteen Soviet army divisions (20,000 men) and 10,000 East German "People's Police" (Volkspolezei) to crush the revolt by any means. Tanks rolled down East Berlin's streets, and troops and police opened fire on demonstrators in the central Unter den Linden and Potsdamer Platz areas. At least fifty-five died. After the revolt was crushed, more than 106 death sentences were carried out on condemned protesters, and several thousand people served long terms in jails and labor camps.

Coming only three months after Stalin's death and while the struggle to fill the power vacuum was still in progress in Russia, the Berlin uprising badly shook the leaders of the German Democratic Republic. Repression was their answer—leading to a brain drain to the West and the building of the Berlin Wall in 1961. **NJ**

Mossadeq Out

The CIA engineers a coup in Iran and passes it off as a show of the people's will.

Already Iran's chief of police had been assassinated and a local cleric's home bombed. Now angry crowds demonstrated on the streets of Tehran. It looked very much like a revolution. The shah opted for safety, moving from his summer retreat on the Caspian Sea to Rome—perhaps wisely, for his statues were being pulled down by the mob. Then, on August 19, 1953, came news that he had dismissed the prime minister, Dr. Mohammed Mossadeq, and appointed General Fazollah Zahedi in his place. The wrath of the crowds immediately found a new focus. There were demands for Mossadeq to go, and the fighting became more intense. In its aftermath, 300 people lay dead, Mossadeq fled, Zahedi emerged from the U.S. Embassy as premier, and the shah returned in triumph. It seemed that the will of the people had triumphed. In fact, it was the will of the U.S. and British governments.

The Americans called it Operation Ajax; Winston Churchill preferred Operation Boot. Its origins lay in 1951, when the shah bowed to pressure and named a new prime minister, Mossadeq, who nationalized Britain's massive Anglo-Iranian Oil Company. A plot was then hatched with the U.S. Central Intelligence Agency, whose agents feared communist infiltration of Iran. Large sums of money bought the complicity of various Iranians, including Zahedi. The CIA referred to the shah as "a creature of indecision, beset by formless doubts and fear" who "must be induced to play his role." So induce him it did. The new regime was provided with $5 million, the Anglo-Iranian Oil Company was returned to British hands, and Mossadeq was convicted of treason and imprisoned. The shah reigned until he was deposed in 1979 in favor of the Islamic fundamentalist Ayatollah Khomeini. **RP**

Rock 'n' Roll Hit

"Rock Around the Clock" is recorded by Bill Haley and His Comets and stays at the top of the U.S. charts for eight weeks.

Rock and roll, which got its name in the early 1950s, was rooted in earlier U.S. country music and rhythm and blues. Aimed originally at black audiences, it appealed to whites, too, with their new, rebellious youth culture. In 1951, the singer and guitarist Bill Haley and his band, the Saddlemen, made what he considered the first rock-and-roll record ever, "Rock the Joint." In 1952, the band became the Comets (a play on Halley's Comet), and in 1953 made the first rock-and-roll record to reach the top twenty in the charts ("Crazy, Man, Crazy"), which brought them a contract with Decca.

The band's Decca single "Rock Around the Clock" made no great impression at first, but it took off when it was used in the film *Blackboard Jungle* in 1955, which attracted much attention with its theme of youthful alienation. The best-selling single in the United States for eight weeks, "Rock Around the Clock" became an icon of the new youth scene. In the mid-1950s, Bill Haley and His Comets turned out hit after hit—including "See You Later, Alligator"—and in 1956, they appeared in two rock-and-roll movies, *Rock Around the Clock* and *Don't Knock the Rock*.

From the late 1950s, Haley's path led downhill. Younger stars, such as Elvis Presley and Little Richard, succeeded him in the popular music, youth culture firmament. Hopelessly improvident and loaded with debts, Haley took to drinking and eventually died of a heart attack in 1981. By that time, sales of "Rock Around the Clock" had exceeded twenty-five million. **RC**

◐ The Comets: Joey D'Ambrose, Johnny Grande, Bill Haley (back), Billy Willamson, Marshall Lytle, and Dick Richards.

◑ *Blackboard Jungle* was directed by Richard Brooks and was nominated for four Oscars.

Four-Minute Barrier Is Broken

British athlete Roger Bannister becomes the first person to run a mile in a time of less than four minutes at a meet at the Oxford University track.

The sub-four-minute mile had been the target of middle-distance running for years. In 1923, the great Finnish athlete Paavo Nurmi clocked the distance in just over 4 minutes 10 seconds. Through the 1930s and 1940s, seconds were knocked off the time, and in 1945, a Swede, Gunder Haag, brought the record down to 4:01.3, only a fraction above the target.

On a windy May afternoon in Oxford in 1954, word that a new attempt was to be made in a match between the university and the Amateur Athletic Association (AAA) drew a far larger crowd than usual to the university's athletics stadium. In the mile event, the three principal runners for the AAA were Roger Bannister, Chris Chataway, and Chris Brasher, who had painstakingly planned their tactics. Brasher set the pace for the first two laps and reached the halfway mark in 1 minute 58 seconds. Halfway through the third lap, the diminutive Chataway took the lead, with the tall figure of Bannister looming just behind him. Chataway kept ahead until halfway around the final lap, when Bannister lengthened his stride, passed Chataway with what looked like ease, and thundered thrillingly around the last bend to break the tape. Chataway was not far behind.

The crowd waited in intense expectation while the race announcer deliberately took his time giving the result and then said, "Time . . . " and paused to notch the tension up higher still before announcing, "Three minutes . . ." The rest was drowned in a storm of cheering, but the winning time was in fact 3:59.4. It must have been one of the most exciting events in the entire history of athletics. **RC**

◐ Roger Bannister photographed at the moment he broke the record for the four-minute mile.

French Lose Siege

The communist victory in Vietnam draws the United States into Southeast Asia.

Ho Chi Minh compared the struggle between the French colonial power and his Vietminh guerrillas to that between "an elephant and a grasshopper." France's General Henri Navarre might have agreed when in November 1953 he launched the fortification of the village of Dien Bien Phu, deep in enemy territory. The aim was to lure the guerrillas into an unaccustomed set-piece battle, in which French firepower would win the day. General Giap took up the challenge. As many as 50,000 peasants formed a supply chain, bringing Chinese arms north, and his

"A poor feudal nation had beaten a great colonial power . . . "

General Vo Nguyen Giap

men surrounded the village, shelled the two airstrips, and mercilessly picked off the enemy troops. The siege lasted for fifty-five days until, on May 7, the last French stronghold fell. Only 3,000 French soldiers out of a garrison of 16,000 survived.

The defeat marked the end of France's eight-year battle to recover its former colony. The French had had little enthusiasm for "la sale guerre" in Indochina, and decided instead that Algeria was their prime concern. French negotiators at Geneva agreed to withdraw from Southeast Asia, and Vietnam was divided. The communists, under Ho and Giap, were in control in the north and an anti-communist republic, underwritten by the United States, was established in the south. The seeds were being sown for the bloody Vietnamese War of the 1960s. **RP**

McCarthy Condemned

Senator McCarthy is brought down by the U.S. Senate.

Joseph McCarthy inspired what has been called "the great fear" in the United States. He had a thoroughly damaging impact on the U.S. administration and was a gift to Soviet propaganda. What brought him down in 1954 was his assault on the U.S. Army.

In 1953 his committee investigated an alleged espionage ring in the Army Signal Corps. Not only did the senator fail to produce convincing evidence of an espionage ring, but his contemptuous treatment of a wartime hero, General Ralph Zwicker, offended U.S. patriots, including President Eisenhower.

"McCarthyism is Americanism with its sleeves rolled."

Senator Joseph McCarthy, 1952

March 1954 saw the broadcast of a blistering attack on McCarthy by the respected Edward R. Murrow. Between April and June in televised hearings watched by an estimated 20 million viewers, the army's counsel, Joseph N. Welch, showed McCarthy up to devastating effect as a vicious bully and liar. His celebrated reproach, "Have you no sense of decency, sir, at long last? Have you no sense of decency?" drew applause from the spectators and finally destroyed what was left of the senator's reputation.

In September the unanimous report of a Senate committee denounced McCarthy's behavior as "inexcusable" and "reprehensible," and in December the Senate formally condemned him by sixty-seven votes to twenty-two. He remained a senator, but his day was done and he died in 1957 of acute hepatitis. **RC**

Disneyland Opens Its Doors

Walt Disney opens his first theme park in California.

○ The construction of a dream—building the now-famous castle at Disneyland, in Anaheim California.

Long the reigning monarch of U.S. and international cartoon movies, and also a power in comics, books, and television, Walt Disney had been thinking for a while of building a "Mickey Mouse Park" near his Los Angeles studios. Here, visitors and their children could experience firsthand the Disney universe and the "Disney magic." He acquired land at Anaheim, south of Los Angeles, where construction began in 1954. Costing $17 million, the project's completion was marked by "International Press Preview" on July 17, 1955. Ronald Reagan, later president of the United States, was one of the anchormen on the television coverage of the opening, which suffered from technical faults and a lack of drinking water in very high temperatures (much of the asphalt melted).

Disneyland opened to the public the following day, when an excited crowd gathered in line from 2 A.M. The first paying customer got ticket No. 2— Walt's brother Roy had already snaffled ticket No. 1. The park quickly became hugely popular and famous; it has attracted more than 500 million people. At the center is Sleeping Beauty's Castle. Mickey Mouse, Donald Duck, and other Disney characters appear in costume with great frequency. When it was opened it had five main areas: Main Street USA, a Wild-West town; Adventureland, with a jungle theme; Frontierland; Fantasyland; and Tomorrowland. The Disneyland formula took off, and Disney opened other parks, first in Florida and later near Paris, Tokyo, Hong Kong, and elsewhere. **RC**

Death of James Dean

Screen star and cultural icon James Dean dies in a car crash.

○ The mangled remains of "Little Bastard," the name James Dean gave to his silver Porsche Spyder 550.

James Byron Dean is the only actor ever to win an Academy Award for Best Actor posthumously. He died at the age of twenty-four, having made himself the brooding embodiment of the rebellious youth culture of the 1950s with his performance as a troubled adolescent in *Rebel Without a Cause* in 1955. The film included scenes of teenage gangs, underage drinking, and dangerous car races and was a great hit with young audiences. Dean had starring roles in just two other films, *East of Eden* (1954) and *Giant* (1956).

Dean loved fast cars and car racing. In September 1955, he set off with his mechanic in a powerful, new Porsche 550 Spyder sports car to go racing in Salinas. En route, he was given a ticket for doing 65 miles per hour (105 kph) in a 55-mile-per-hour (90 kph) zone.

Later, he was heading west on U.S. Highway 466 when a 1950 Ford, driven by a twenty-three-year-old man with the improbable name of Donald Turnupseed, tried to cross in front of the Porsche to fork off into a side road. The cars hit each other virtually head-on. Dean was still breathing when the ambulance arrived. The mechanic had been thrown from the car and had a broken jaw. Turnupseed survived with superficial cuts and bruises. He was not prosecuted for the accident. Dean was pronounced dead on arrival at the hospital in Paso Robles, which the ambulance reached just before 6 P.M. He was buried in Fairmount, Indiana, his boyhood home. The death of James Dean created a hysteria that reminded observers of Rudolph Valentino. **RC**

Bus Segregation

Rosa Parks refuses to give up her seat, provoking the Alabama bus boycott.

The black civil rights movement in the United States was making an impact on the South where, in the city of Montgomery, Alabama, "colored" passengers were not allowed to sit at the front of the buses, but had to go to the back instead. The rule was flouted in December 1955 by a respectable, middle-aged, black woman named Rosa Parks, who was active in the civil rights movement. She refused to give up her seat to a white man on the Cleveland Avenue bus because, she said, her feet were tired. The bus stopped, and she was arrested and fined.

Whether this had been planned in advance or not, the effect was electric. Montgomery's black leaders appointed an obscure Baptist minister, the Rev. Martin Luther King Jr., to lead a boycott of the city's buses and secure the maximum publicity. It was an inspired choice, and the outcome vindicated King's principle of nonviolent resistance. More than 90 percent of Montgomery's blacks joined the boycott and organized other ways of getting to work. The bus company and downtown shops complained of losing business. In April 1956, the U.S. Supreme Court ruled against bus segregation, but the local bus company, which wanted to comply, was overruled by the Montgomery police chief. In June, the Montgomery federal district court ruled that the city's segregation ordinances were unconstitutional, and its ruling was upheld by the Supreme Court in November. The city gave way and announced its compliance, and Rosa Parks posed for photographers near the front of a city bus.

The victory in Montgomery was a significant boost for the black civil rights movement across the United States, and saw Martin Luther King on the road to a historic national and international reputation. **RC**

Stalin Denounced

Khrushchev attempts to break with the past by denouncing Stalin.

The 1,355 voting and 81 nonvoting delegates in the Great Kremlin Palace in February 1956 did not know what to expect of the Twentieth Congress of the Communist Party, the first since the death of Stalin in 1953. A broad hint was given on the opening day, when first secretary Nikita Khrushchev asked the delegates to stand in memory of communist leaders (plural) who had recently died. (Stalin in the same breath as Gottwald and Toduka?) Yet no one was prepared for his four-hour, secret session speech on February 25. Khrushchev decried the cult of personality that Stalin had built around himself, revealed Lenin's hostility to him in 1924, and denounced Stalin's role in the destruction of so many innocent people in the purges. Khrushchev claimed that the seemingly infallible leader had in fact been a despot guilty of crimes against the Soviet people. No wonder delegates were stunned and amazed.

Thousands of prisoners were released from the Gulag and statues of Stalin were removed. It seemed like a new dawn, yet there was a backlash. Many saw Khrushchev's speech as a dishonest and cynical attempt to further his own career. The turning point came when Khrushchev sent troops into Hungary, declaring he was a Stalinist in his determination to fight against the class enemy. He had taken two steps forward, but was now taking a long stride back.

Khrushchev's speech was misleading. Western leaders had expected a thaw in the cold war when, in reality, the diplomatic weather was turning rather chilly in Berlin and Cuba. Yet Stalin's reputation never fully recovered from the 1956 onslaught, and, by creating a somewhat more open society in the U.S.S.R., Khrushchev can be seen as a forerunner of *Glasnost* and *Perestroika* in the 1980s. **RP**

Elvis Is Number One

The success of "Heartbreak Hotel" transforms the singer from a local sensation into a national phenomenon and puts rock and roll on the musical map.

"Heartbreak Hotel" was the single that broke Elvis Presley into the mainstream. It was written by Mae Axton and hit the number one spot in the hit parade on April 21, 1956, where it stayed for eight weeks. Axton reputedly told Elvis, "You need a million seller and I'm going to write it for you." The single was released on January 27.

Elvis Aaron Presley was born on January 8, 1935. His early influences were the gospel music of the local church, the rhythm and blues of his black neighbors, and the white country and western on the radio and in school. In 1954, while a truck driver, he cut his first record—a private disc for his mother's birthday. Two days after he had turned twenty-one, in 1956, Elvis had his first recording sessions at RCA's Nashville studios. Colonel Tom Parker, his Svengali-like manager, had paid $40,000 to buy out the singer from his first homegrown record label. Elvis was about to hit the big time.

"Heartbreak Hotel" was inspired by a newspaper story about a young man killing himself. On April 3, Elvis performed it to a massive audience (possibly twenty-five percent of the U.S. population) on *The Milton Berle Show*. Elvis soon became the icon of a new, restless, white, teenage audience and its nascent rock-and-roll tendencies. He may have been clean-cut and eager to please, but he was not staid or safe like the other middle-aged tuxedo- or cowboy-suited performers on television at the time. His hip-swaying, knee-swiveling, lip-pouting performances soon provoked charges of obscenity and vulgarity. "Elvis the pelvis" was shocking the nation. **JJH**

◗ Elvis, photographed in April 1956, holds a framed gold disc of "Heartbreak Hotel."

Nasser Nationalizes the Suez Canal

The nationalization of the Suez Canal provokes conflict with Britain and France.

○ A United Nations soldier from India, photographed in 1956, keeps watch over the canal zone during the Suez crisis.

As many as 50,000 people gathered in the main square of Alexandria to hear President Nasser speak, on the fourth anniversary of King Farouk's exile. Many more were listening on the radio. Some thought he might eat humble pie because his pet project, the Aswan High Dam, might not now be built. In fact, it was an immensely confident speech. Nasser explained how Ferdinand de Lesseps's Suez Canal Company had robbed Egyptians of wealth that was rightfully theirs. But, he insisted, all that was now ending—he was going to nationalize the canal and use its profits to pay for the new dam. If the imperialists did not like it, he told the crowd, "They could choke to death on their fury." By the time he had finished speaking, the deed was done. The words "Ferdinand de Lesseps"

were a coded instruction for Egypt's forces to take control of the canal and of the company's offices.

The Suez Canal had been completed in 1869, allowing ships to pass from the Mediterranean to Asia. Britain became the largest shareholder in 1875 and invaded Egypt in 1882 to protect its investment. Their garrison in the canal zone became a fierce bone of contention after a coup in 1952 by nationalist army officers. It was only in June 1956 that the last British troops left. In the same month, Nasser's friendship with the Soviet Union led the United States to end its financial aid toward the construction of the dam. Nasser's anti-imperialism provoked instant opposition from Britain and France. That he survived their invasion later that year made him a hero in the Middle East. **RP**

Hungary Rises Up Against the Soviets

The uprising in Hungary in October 1956 gives false hopes of an end to Soviet control.

○ Jubilant Hungarian freedom fighters wave their country's flag while standing on a captured Soviet tank.

The Hungarian government had specifically banned demonstrations, but that did not stop the crowds of students, workers, and local soldiers. In October 1956, they came out in open defiance of their Soviet overlords, demanding "Send the Red Army home" and "We want elections." The new dictator, Erno Gero, denounced the demonstrators on the radio, which prompted a siege of the local radio station. Then the city's giant statue of Stalin was pulled down. Surely this was the beginning of a new dawn for Hungary and perhaps for Soviet-controlled Eastern Europe?

Stalin's Red Army had imposed Soviet control on Hungary after World War II. The U.S.S.R.'s grip had seemed to loosen when Khrushchev denounced Stalin and Prime Minister Imre Nagy introduced some progressive reforms in Hungary, but a crackdown followed and Nagy was expelled from the party. The situation was chaotic. Khrushchev withdrew Soviet troops from Budapest, hoping that this concession would end the disturbances. Nagy formed a new government, but when he announced Hungary's imminent withdrawal from the Warsaw Pact, it was the last straw for Moscow. On November 4, some 200,000 Soviet troops and 2,500 tanks were sent to reimpose Soviet domination.

The Hungarian Rising saw at least 3,000 people killed and 13,000 wounded. Nagy was captured by the KGB, tried, and shot. October 23 had been a false dawn, or perhaps a rehearsal for the overthrow of communism in Hungary in 1989 to 1990. **RP**

Conflict at the Suez Canal

Israel's invasion of Egypt is part of an organized plan to remove Nasser from power.

United Nations troops arrive in Port Said in an attempt to restore order to the region.

Israeli troops struck under cover of darkness on October 29, 1956. They entered the Sinai region of Egypt; their mission was to destroy terrorist bases. Soon they were moving westward toward the Suez Canal. Later that day, Britain's prime minister, Anthony Eden, stressed the gravity of the situation to his cabinet. When President Nasser nationalized the canal in June, he had "his thumb on our windpipe," but, with actual warfare in Egypt, the threat to British and international shipping was even greater. Britain had reserved the right to protect the canal if ever its security were in danger. Hence, Eden insisted, they were duty bound to send in military forces to separate the combatants and restore order. France would be Britain's partner in this justified act of international law enforcement.

The Royal Air Force bombed Egyptian airfields, and, on November 5, more than 8,000 British and French troops entered Egypt. Militarily all was going well, and yet the Americans at the United Nations called for a cease-fire, and Nasser blocked the canal by sinking ships filled with concrete. Eden insisted he had "no foreknowledge" of the Israeli attack, but many suspected that Britain, France, and Israel had together concocted an excuse to invade. Eden wanted to remove Nasser and strike a blow in the Middle East against the new Arab nationalist movement.

A massive run on the pound caused Britain to halt the venture and withdraw its forces. Suez was a debacle from which neither Eden nor British imperialism ever recovered. **RP**

Ghana Gains Independence

The creation of an independent Ghana heralds a European scramble out of Africa.

○ Government officials carry Prime Minister Kwame Nkrumah through the crowds after Ghana's independence from Britain.

On the great day in 1957, heavy with anticipation, representatives from all over the world attended the ceremony at Christiansborg Castle in Accra. At midnight, the British flag was lowered and the Black Star was hoisted. The Gold Coast was no more: Ghana, the first African colony to gain independence, had been born. "Jubilation ran riot," reported the press. "With the cheerful din of exploding enthusiasm and the universal exultation of five million triumphant people, died 113 years of imperial dominion."

Power had been transferred peacefully after a series of democratic elections. Britons and Ghanaians were proud of a job well done. The last governor, Sir Charles Arden-Clarke, congratulated the prime minister, Kwame Nkrumah: "This is the end of what

you have struggled for." He was corrected, "It is the end of what we have been struggling for, Sir Charles." Here surely was a model for the rest of Africa to follow, perhaps the rest of the world.

How different the Gold Coast had been before World War II, when it seemed inconceivable to the British that any African colony would be fit for self-government. How different also, in February 1948, when riots in Accra led to the arrest of Nkrumah and other nationalists. Since then, political progress had been breathtaking. Sadly things were very different in 1966. By this time, most colonies in Africa had followed the rapid route to independence, but Ghana was impoverished by corruption, and its dictator, Nkrumah, was overthrown by his own people. **RP**

Free Trade Across Europe

The Treaty of Rome creates the European Economic Community.

○ The signing of the Treaty of Rome—the German delegation signs the papers.

The origins of the movement for European unity can be traced deep into the past, but what really mattered in Rome in 1957 was the experience, not the abstract study, of history. The politicians and the people they represented were painfully aware of the carnage of World War II. Now the past was to be exorcized. Representatives of France, West Germany, Italy, Belgium, the Netherlands, and Luxembourg signed a treaty whose aim was "ever closer union." There would now be a European Economic Community. All tariffs between the six member states were to be abolished, and there would be free movement of goods, capital, and people across their countries.

The Treaty of Rome was the culmination of a series of events, beginning in 1944 when Belgium, the Netherlands, and Luxembourg created the Benelux Union to link their industries and trade. In 1951, the Treaty of Paris set up the European Coal and Steel Community, as well as a council of ministers, a parliamentary assembly, and a court of justice. Then in 1955, at Messina in Sicily, the foundations of the Treaty of Rome were laid. The aims were to abolish war between member states and generate future prosperity. The sacrifice of elements of national sovereignty seemed a small price to pay.

The original six members were soon joined by others. In 2004, the institution now known as the European Union had twenty-seven member states. Its future is one of the most intriguing questions in world politics. **RP**

Soviets Reach Space

The world is amazed at the Soviet Union's scientific prowess.

⬤ The creation of *Sputnik I*, photographed in 1957, was a high point in the career of the Soviet leader Nikita Krushchev.

The world got its first artificial satellite, *Sputnik 1*, courtesy of the Soviet Union. A huge triumph for the Soviet leader, Nikita Khrushchev, the launch caused great consternation in the West. The United States's assumption of technological superiority was badly shaken. The strategic implications appeared to be disastrous. The Soviet Union, it seemed, had a massive lead in the development of intercontinental ballistic missiles. U.S. President Eisenhower was accused of squandering his country's scientific advantages.

Eisenhower, however, was well aware from the intelligence gathered by the U-2 spy plane that the strategic balance stood overwhelmingly in favor of the United States. But he was unable to announce this without revealing the U-2 program. His assurances that the United States was in no danger and that its rocket research was going well were unconvincing. Khrushchev, for his part, was to use this supposed superiority to try to gain advantage in his dealings with the West. He wanted peaceful coexistence and to reduce Soviet military spending, but could not resist wildly exaggerating the strength of his missile forces. It became standard for his trips abroad to be accompanied by a new space launch. It was a bluff, but a believable one. In the end, this was to backfire on Khrushchev. Convinced that U.S. defenses were inadequate and that a missile gap had opened between their nations, Americans demanded that money be found to rectify the situation. This resulted in a very real missile gap, in the United States's favor. **JS**

Mao Announces "Great Leap Forward"

Mao decrees instant industrialization by people power.

○ Mao Zedong's "Great Leap Forward" led to severe poverty, particularly in agricultural communities, and a devastating famine.

The new economic policy announced by China's chairman Mao Zedong in 1958 was nothing if not ambitious. Known as the "Great Leap Forward," it amounted to a new revolution to industrialize China by mobilizing the revolutionary zeal of the masses. In fact, it was a recognition that the industrialization route of the Soviet Union, which squeezed a grain surplus from the peasantry to export and pay for machinery, could not work in China. The Chinese population was so large that what was produced was consumed. Unable to buy technology, the only resource that could be exploited was the peasantry. They were organized into communes and assigned to work brigades. In the belief that China would change instantly, there was initially considerable enthusiasm.

Unfortunately the idea that zeal could substitute for technology proved a fantasy. Backyard furnaces were expected to produce vast quantities of steel. This happened, but the steel was generally of such low quality it was useless. There were very real improvements in the production of goods such as cement, chemicals, and cotton, but the quality was often shoddy. Resources, especially of manpower, were diverted from agriculture. This, coupled with bad weather, caused a famine in which twenty million people had perished by 1960, when Mao was obliged to abandon the Great Leap Forward. This was a major blow to his prestige, forcing him to attempt to reassert his authority through the horrors of the Cultural Revolution in 1966. **JS**

Castro Becomes Prime Minister of Cuba

Castro's army enters Havana, a move that is welcomed by the majority of Cubans.

○ A victorious Fidel Castro and members of his guerilla army drive through the streets of Havana after their successful coup.

Fidel Castro became prime minister in February 1959, but he began his rise to power in Cuba in highly unpromising circumstances. He landed on the southwest coast of Cuba at the end of 1956 with a force of just eighty men. The plan had been betrayed to the Cuban regime, and the invaders were attacked by government troops. Most of them were killed or captured. A few, including Castro, his brother Raul, and Ernesto "Che" Guevara, managed to escape to a hideout in the Sierra Maestra mountains, where Castro told them, "Now we are going to win."

Improbably, he was right. The revolutionaries made effective propaganda use of their radio transmitter to attack the Batista regime and arouse sympathy for their cause abroad. They mounted a guerrilla campaign against the government, and feeling in the country against the regime rose steadily. In July 1958, opposition groups met in Caracas and chose Castro as their leader. A government onslaught on the rebels in the Sierra Maestra failed, and Castro's men launched a counteroffensive. By the time the United States government turned against Batista, the revolutionary army had swelled to some 50,000 men and had gained overwhelming support among the Cuban population.

On New Year's Eve, Batista fled. A military junta replaced him, but quickly collapsed. Army units stopped fighting and Castro's men entered Havana. As prime minister, Castro proceeded to install his Marxist-Leninist regime and ally Cuba with Russia. **RC**

Buddy Holly Dies in Plane Crash

The private plane crashes in an Iowa field minutes after takeoff, killing rock-and-roll star Buddy Holly and his band.

A stainless steel memorial in the shape of a guitar and three records marks the site in an Iowa field where rock and roll's first great legend had his career cut short in a plane crash. Buddy Holly, just twenty-two when he died, created a timeless body of popular music that influenced everyone from the Beatles to Bob Dylan and Bruce Springsteen.

In a bitterly cold February at the end of the 1950s, the Winter Dance Party Tour played to 1,000 people at the Surf Ballroom in Clear Lake, Iowa. This was the early heyday of rock and roll, and top of the bill was Buddy Holly, supported by "The Big Bopper" (J. P. Richardson) and Ritchie Valens. Tired of touring on a bus, Holly had hired a small private plane to fly his band (bassist Waylon Jennings and guitarist Tommy Allsup) to their next gig. But Valens and Richardson hustled for the band's seats and took their places. They took off at 1 A.M. in a snowstorm, with Holly sitting next to the pilot (a rookie with no instrument certification). A few minutes later, visual contact was lost. Everyone on board died in the crash.

Like Elvis, whom Holly met while opening a show for him in Lubbock, Texas, in 1955, Holly was influenced by the blues, rhythm and blues, and country-and-western music. In 1957, with his band The Crickets, Holly headed to New Mexico to record with rising producer Norman Petty. The relationship allowed Holly to blossom and produce a string of pop singles. The string-laden "It Doesn't Matter Any More" became a huge posthumous hit worldwide. **JJH**

◑ The remnants of Holly's plane after the crash; one of the passengers was flung from the wreckage into the snow.

◐ Although his career lasted only eighteen months, Holly's music made a lasting creative impact on early rock and roll.

Dalai Lama Flees

The spiritual and political leader of Tibet is forced into exile in India.

Following growing unrest at the Chinese occupation of Tibet during the early part of 1959, a rumor started to circulate that the Chinese were about to arrest the Dalai Lama. This brought thousands of Tibetans to surround his palace to protect him. Soon the confrontation in Lhasa turned violent, and some 2,000 Chinese troops died. Reinforcements rapidly crushed the insurgency and left the Chinese determined to suppress all opposition.

The Dalai Lama was forced to flee, with some 100,000 countrymen. He was granted asylum in India

"Dalai Lama's reincarnation will appear in a free country and not in Chinese hands."

Statement by the Dalai Lama, July 1999

and set up his government-in-exile at Dharmsala, in the Indian Himalayas. His appeals to the United Nations resulted in a number of resolutions calling upon China to respect human rights in Tibet, but nothing was done to enforce them. The Dalai Lama traveled the world to publicize Tibet's plight and even received the Nobel Peace Prize in 1989 for his nonviolent campaign to end Chinese rule in Tibet. The Chinese government attempted to split Tibetan loyalties by extolling the virtues of the seventeenth Karmapa (a living Buddha of equal status). When he also fled to India in 2000, it was a huge embarrassment to China. As long as the Dalai Lama dwells beyond Chinese control, it could be argued that their grip on Tibet can never be secure. The prospect of them leaving, however, must be deemed remote. **JS**

Wind of Change

Macmillan's speech in Cape Town signals a radical change in British policy.

He had a reputation for being totally unflappable, but even Harold Macmillan, Britain's prime minister, became agitated when he was the guest of the South African premier. Dr. Verwoerd had "horrible ideas," looking upon apartheid as a religion and being convinced that "he alone could be right." Yet on this day Macmillan delivered a speech to the South African Parliament that publicly challenged the Afrikaner regime. He was so nervous that he was physically sick before delivering it. However, the speech had been well prepared. There was a "wind of change" in Africa, he asserted: national consciousness was a political fact of which policy must take account. He praised Afrikaners' nationalism as the first in Africa but insisted that it was not the last, and unless black Africans were treated fairly they would be driven toward communism. He made no direct reference to apartheid but judged that governments should respect individual rights. British policy was changing elsewhere in Africa, he noted pointedly, and might well "make difficulties for you."

The fifty-minute speech was applauded, but South Africans deplored the events that followed. Macmillan's speech foreshadowed the ending of the white settler–dominated Central African Federation. Riots and a damning official report in 1959 had convinced Britain that Nyasaland (Malawi) and Northern Rhodesia (Zambia) should soon have black self-government. South Africa voluntarily left the Commonwealth in 1961 to avoid expulsion.

Macmillan's speech was a somewhat belated recognition that things were changing rapidly in Africa. Nevertheless his words boosted the ambitions of black Africans, at the same time cementing the defensive laager mentality of Afrikaners. **RP**

Ruthless Massacre

Police killings in Sharpeville receive worldwide condemnation.

Racial tension and violence were no strangers in the era of apartheid. Even so, the events in Sharpeville, southwest of Johannesburg, were extraordinary. It started as a demonstration against the 1950 Pass Laws, which required nonwhites to carry identity cards and forbade them from spending the night in a "white" area, even if it was their place of work. Undoubtedly intimidation was used, with some Africans forced to take part. There was also violence and vandalism, but no one expected a massacre.

At the height of the protest, a crowd of several thousand surrounded the local police station. They, at least were unarmed, whereas the seventy-five policemen inside had automatic weapons. Even when the crowd refused to disperse, there was no cause for alarm. Yet the police still decided to open fire, killing 69 and wounding almost 200. Men, women, and children were shot in the back as they ran away. A policeman told reporters that the scene of carnage resembled "a world war battlefield, with bodies sprawled all around."

The government insisted the incident had been caused by the Pan-African Congress (PAC), formed in 1959 and much more radical than the African National Congress (ANC). As many as 20,000 armed Africans had surrounded the police station and they fired first. No one believed them. Instead, on April 1, the United Nations Security Council called for South Africa to end racial segregation. Would the government budge? "We will stand like walls of granite," responded Prime Minister Verwoerd. His government proscribed both the ANC and the PAC, expelled the bishop of Johannesburg, and left the Commonwealth. Isolated, white South Africa survived at the price of radicalizing the struggle. **RP**

Lady Chatterley Trial

Jury decides that D. H. Lawrence's novel is not obscene and can be published.

The defense witnesses went way over the top, describing *Lady Chatterley's Lover* as "wholesome" and "hygienic." The bishop of Woolwich even called the adultery between Lady Chatterley and the gamekeeper, "an act of holy communion." Yet the prosecution barrister, Mervyn Griffith-Jones, contrived to be even more ludicrous. He called no expert witnesses and ham-fistedly attempted to show that the book had no redeeming literary merit. It took the jury three hours to decide that the novel was not obscene and Penguin Books had committed no crime in printing it.

"Is it a book that you would even wish your wife or your servants to read?"

Mervyn Griffith-Jones, to the jury

D. H. Lawrence finished his final version of the book in 1928, describing it as "the most improper novel ever written." It was not pornography, but was simply "a declaration of the phallic reality." It was a distinction too far for the authorities in Britain, where the book was banned. As late as 1955, a bookseller was imprisoned for stocking it. When Penguin printed 200,000 copies in 1959, to mark the thirtieth anniversary of Lawrence's death, the director of public prosecutions instituted what became a show trial.

Not surprisingly, the publicity surrounding the trial made *Lady Chatterley's Lover* a best seller. More than three million Penguin copies were sold within two years. Sexual attitudes and behavior were changing in Britain, and the trial and the book helped usher in "The Swinging Sixties." **RP**

Eichmann Stands Trial for War Crimes

Eichmann's trial shows that war criminals face prosecution long after World War II and the end of the Nazi regime.

All eyes were drawn to the Nazi said to be the embodiment of evil—and yet he did not look the part. In his mid-fifties, small with thinning hair, he looked disappointingly ordinary. This was the man who was charged with having committed crimes against the Jewish people, crimes against humanity, and war crimes. There was a total of fifteen counts, and conviction on any one carried the death penalty. How did he plead? On each count, he insisted that he was "Not guilty in the sense of the indictment."

The trial had been long delayed, for Adolf Eichmann had escaped from captivity in 1946. Only in 1960 was he apprehended by Israeli secret agents, and only now could justice be done, by a three-judge court sitting in the Israeli *Beth Ha'am* (House of the People). It would be done publicly, too, for the audience was packed with journalists, and live coverage was relayed all over the world. The judges were determined that, even in a show trial, due process of law should be scrupulously followed. The attorney general was the prosecutor, but the accused also had a lawyer. Some 1,500 documents were examined and more than one hundred witnesses called, mostly concentration camp survivors who testified to Eichmann's role in sending them to camps.

Eichmann insisted that he had only been "following orders." It was deemed an inadequate defense. He was found guilty on all counts and hanged in May 1962. The message went out loud and clear: Nazi war criminals will be hunted down. **RP**

◒ It was only with Eichmann's trial that much of the world learned the full extent of the Nazi program against the Jews.

◒ Outside the courthouse where Eichmann is being tried, Jews gather to hear news of their notorious persecutor.

First Man in Space

Yuri Gagarin and the Soviet Union leads the United States in the space race.

Vostok 1, the spacecraft whose mission was to carry the first astronaut into space, was launched from Baikonur, Kazakhstan. Aboard was Yuri Gagarin, who would orbit the planet just once, in eighty-nine minutes, reaching a maximum altitude of 187 miles (301 km). The spacecraft was never intended to land. Gagarin parachuted to safety once he had reentered the atmosphere and proved what was suspected, that spaceflight was not fatal to man. With his good looks and ready smile, he instantly became not just a Soviet, but an international superstar.

Gagarin's exploits caused a real headache for U.S. President Kennedy. Ever since the launch of *Sputnik 1* in 1957, there had been a strong feeling that the United States was dangerously lagging behind the Soviet Union in space. Fears had been raised that control of space might mean control of the planet, perhaps through controlling the weather or causing climate change. In his election campaign, Kennedy had castigated his Republican opponents for falling behind in this arena. Now he was under pressure to respond. He did so the following May, announcing a U.S. program to put a man on the moon by 1970. There were doubts about the scientific value of such a mission, and there were suggestions that the money it would cost might be better spent elsewhere. But it was undeniably dramatic. In short, the political value of the mission was far more important than the scientific value. It also had the key advantage that a moon mission was never part of the Soviet space program. This was one race the United States was going to win. **JS**

◗ Yuri Gagarin prepares for blastoff aboard one of the Soviet Union's Vostok 3KA spacecrafts at the Baikonur launchpad.

Cuba Repels Invaders

Castro's troops defeat U.S.-funded Cuban invasion at the Bay of Pigs.

Fidel Castro's triumph in Cuba had given the Soviet Union a reliable ally in the Americas. The prospect of a Soviet military base being established at such close quarters could not be tolerated by any U.S. administration, and the Americans were also worried about Castro's example being followed across the other Latin American countries.

Many Cuban exiles had found refuge in the United States, which broke off diplomatic relations with Cuba in January 1961. In April, the new President Kennedy approved and agreed to fund an invasion of Cuba by anti-Castro exiles. He presented it as an attack on Cuba's modern, Soviet-built military equipment, yet no U.S. troops were directly involved. Planned by the Central Intelligence Agency (CIA) under the previous administration, the plan was an ignominious failure. The Cubans were expecting the attack, and although U.S. planes piloted by Cuban exiles bombed various Cuban airfields on April 15, they had minimal effect. Two days later, a Cuban brigade sailed from Nicaragua to land on beaches in the Bay of Pigs on the southern Cuban coast. The anticipated anti-Castro rising failed to materialize, and Cuban troops, personally and energetically commanded by Fidel Castro, defeated the invaders within forty-eight hours. They took more than 1,000 prisoners, who were eventually ransomed back to the United States in late 1962.

The outright failure of the invasion was a severe embarrassment to Kennedy, not least because it made Castro more popular and drove him even closer to Moscow. Ultimately, the outcome of the attack may have encouraged Soviet leader Khrushchev to raise the stakes by siting nuclear warheads on the island. **RC**

Construction of the Berlin Wall Begins

The Berlin Wall is erected not to keep the West out but to keep East Germans in.

⊙ East German troops begin construction of the wall that eventually would completely surround West Berlin.

Revelers in the early hours of August 13 found the trains were not running; residents on Bernauer Strasse were awakened by the noise of army trucks; workers with pneumatic drills were heard pounding the streets. Soon it was clear that a barbed-wire fence was zigzagging its way through the streets of Berlin. *"Die Grenze ist geschlossen"* (The border is closed), announced the machine-gun-toting soldiers. West Berlin was fenced in with 113 miles (182 km) of barbed wire. The Berlin Wall was being erected, its dividing line running through tenement blocks whose doors opened into one sector and whose windows opened on to another—until they were bricked in.

In 1958, Soviet leader Nikita Khrushchev had remarked that Berlin was "the testicles of the West.

Every time I want to make the West scream, I squeeze on Berlin." In 1949, the West had indeed screamed, when Stalin blockaded the western sectors of the city, but now it was the Soviets' turn to squirm. As many as three million citizens had left East Germany via Berlin between 1949 and 1960, and lately the flow was becoming a flood. Khrushchev insisted the wall was built to prevent spying by the West, but in reality it was designed to stop the exodus of those disaffected with communism.

There was little the West could do besides protest, and in time both sides learned to live with the new dispensation. The wall remained a stark symbol of the cold war, just as its removal in 1989 epitomized its ending. **RP**

Bob Dylan's New York Debut

The boy from Minnesota finds his feet as a solo performer in the big city.

⊙ Appearing here with the Greenbriar Boys, Bob Dylan (center) performed as a sideman before his auspicious solo debut.

At the start of the 1960s, Greenwich Village was already well established as New York's "Left Bank." Here Beat poets, civil rights protesters, and antiwar campaigners headed for the folk clubs—or "basket houses," so-called because the entertainers got paid by passing a basket through the audience. The dark, subterranean Gaslight, opened in 1958, was one of the first and probably most important clubs, and it was here that the young Dylan was drawn to sing, play harmonica and acoustic guitar, hone his stagecraft, and try out new songs. On September 6, Dylan played his first booked set. It included four self-penned songs: "Man on the Street," "He Was a Friend of Mine," "Talking Bear Mountain Picnic Massacre Blues," and "Song to Woody."

According to reports (and a bootleg tape), Dylan sang with great feeling, especially on "Song to Woody," which was his homage to the balladeer of the Depression era. It was his desire to meet Woody Guthrie that had drawn Dylan from remote Minnesota to a bustling live music and recording scene. To begin with Dylan consciously imitated Guthrie, but he soon began to soak up other influences, fine-tuning his stage persona and distinctive nasal delivery.

Low-key folk gigs brought the name Bob Dylan to national prominence thanks to a *New York Times* review by Robert Shelton in September 1961. The glowing piece helped Dylan lever an all-important recording contract with Columbia Records, which proved the critical catalyst to his early career. **JJH**

Mystery Explosion

The death of Dag Hammarskjöld robs the United Nations of its leader.

The DC-6 plane was not far from Ndola airport in modern-day Zambia when the explosion took place. It immediately fell to earth, killing fourteen of the fifteen people on board. Among them was the most distinguished figure ever to hold the position of secretary-general of the United Nations, and the most controversial. "Dag" stood for the rights of small nations, for the UN to be a constructive instrument of peace, and for the secretary-general to be an active executive. The Soviet Union had recently called for his resignation, and inevitably there was speculation that his plane had been sabotaged.

Dag Hjalmar Agne Carl Hammarskjöld held a doctorate from Stockholm University and numerous honorary degrees. Many called the multilingual and multitalented Hammarskjöld a modern Renaissance man. He had worked as an academic, banker, and civil servant before entering the Swedish cabinet in 1951. He also had first attended the UN General Assembly in 1949 and was made secretary-general in April 1953, being reelected unanimously in September 1957. It was a role in which he was highly active and successful. In 1955, he personally negotiated the release of U.S. soldiers captured during the Korean War, and he also pioneered the use of United Nations Emergency Forces and Observation Groups. He was keenly involved with the civil war in the Congo from 1960 onward, and it was on his fourth visit there that he died.

In November 1961, Hammarskjöld was awarded the Nobel Peace Prize "in gratitude for all he did, for what he achieved, for what he fought for: to create peace and goodwill among nations and men." Memorials kept his memory alive, but the UN had henceforth to function without his guidance. **RP**

Algeria Independent

After 132 years Algeria finally gains independence from France.

France first invaded Algeria in 1830 and later incorporated the country into France as part of the French state, although the indigenous populations were not given any political rights. The first stirrings of Arab nationalist feeling in Algeria began between the two World Wars and accelerated greatly after 1945, leading to the first outbreak of insurrectionary activity on November 1, 1954, by the Front de Libération Nationale (FLN). In France the strong Socialist and Communist parties were supportive of Arab aspirations, whereas the right wing parties

> ## "The Algerians will have the free choice of their destiny . . ."
>
> **Charles de Gaulle, January 29, 1960**

argued for the continued unity of Algeria and European France. For eight years the French army fought a campaign of pacification, with increasing brutality on both sides, culminating in outright war against the military wing of the FLN. The army largely gained control, but the political battle could not be won.

In 1958, General Charles de Gaulle came out of retirement with a mandate to resolve the Algerian crisis and bring stability to the French government. De Gaulle recognized that the independence of Algeria was inevitable, and negotiated with the FLN at Evian. After more than a million and a quarter French citizens left Algeria for metropolitan France, the new Algerian government began to revenge itself on those of its citizens who had fought for, or cooperated with, the outgoing rulers. **NK**

First Television by Satellite

The launch of Telstar 1 *enables television transmissions to be sent back to earth by satellite and makes the world seem a little smaller.*

Communication by space satellite, which has today become the basis of a thriving commercial industry and a vital factor in military operations, was first suggested by the writer Arthur C. Clarke in 1945. One of the first to carry the idea forward in the 1950s was a U.S. engineer working for Bell Telephones, John R. Pierce, who played a leading part in the work that led to the launch of the Echo communications satellite in 1960 and *Telstar 1* in 1962.

Echo reflected microwave radio signals back to Earth from its aluminum surface, but *Telstar* was a more sophisticated device, which for the first time allowed television transmissions to be winged back to Earth. It was launched by American Telephone and Telegraph in cahoots with Bell Telephones and the British and French post offices. A gigantic antenna, built in Maine, near Andover, was locked on to the satellite, and subsequent television pictures were relayed across the Atlantic to be received at stations in England and France.

The first pictures from *Telstar* showed the flag at the Andover station, but it was presently transmitting a baseball game between the Chicago Cubs and the Philadelphia Phillies, and President Kennedy used it to give a live transatlantic press conference. *Telstar 1* went out of action in February 1963, possibly affected by radiation from the testing of nuclear weapons. It was replaced by *Telstar 2*. Development continued, and in 1964 the *Syncom 3* satellite relayed pictures of the Tokyo Olympic Games across the Pacific. **RC**

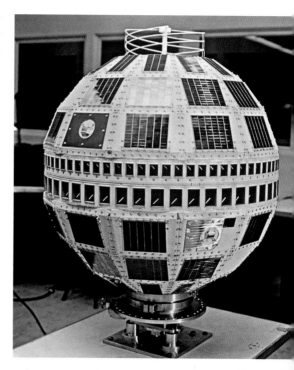

◗ Designed to fit into a Delta rocket, *Telstar 1* was 34.5 inches (880 mm) long, and weighed 170 pounds (77 kg).

◗ Vice President Lyndon Johnson watches the first television transmission to be sent from France via the Telstar satellite.

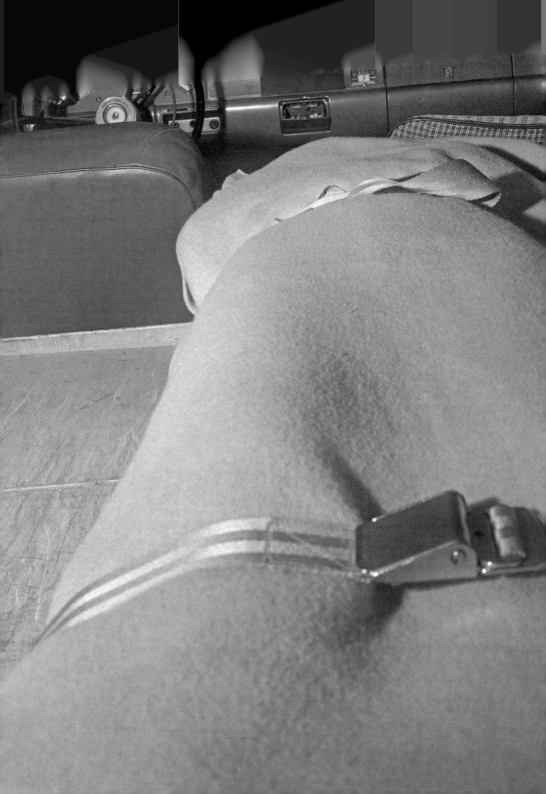

Death of a Goddess

Film star Marilyn Monroe dies of a drug overdose at her home in Los Angeles.

The prosaically named Norma Jean Baker rose from a childhood in foster homes and an orphanage to become one of the world's most famous figures. Discovered by a photographer when she was working in a California factory, she was signed to the film studio Twentieth Century Fox in 1946. After playing a succession of minor dumb-blonde roles, she changed her name to Marilyn Monroe and went on to star in a number of hit movies, including *Bus Stop* (1956), *The Prince and the Showgirl* (1957), and *Some Like It Hot* (1959). Her looks, visible sexuality, and vulnerability made her an international incarnation of feminine desirability, but the strain was great and her private life was largely a disaster.

After a brief first marriage, she married the great baseball player Joe DiMaggio and after him the distinguished playwright Arthur Miller, who wrote her final film *The Misfits* (1961) for her. Her last public appearance of any importance was singing "Happy Birthday, Mr. President" to John F. Kennedy in 1962, in a skin-tight gown with nothing on underneath. At the time, Monroe was signed to star in a film called *Something's Got to Give*. Always notoriously difficult on set, Monroe's behavior had become so impossible by this time—she was now existing on mammoth quantities of prescription drugs—that she was fired. Soon after, she was found dead in bed at her home in Brentwood, Los Angeles. She was thirty-six. Whether her death was suicide or an accidental overdose has been debated ever since. There was also no shortage of theories that she had been murdered by the FBI or the CIA on the orders of the Kennedys. **RC**

◗ Marilyn Monroe's body arrives at the mortuary after she was found dead in her home from an overdose of barbiturates.

Pope Urges Reform

The Second Vatican Council reveals Catholic Church tensions.

The times were changing, even for the Catholic Church. In January 1959, Pope John XXIII insisted that he wanted "to throw open the windows of the Church so that we can see out and the people can see in." On October 11, 1962, he opened the Second Vatican Council to do this. To the 2,400 assembled Roman Catholic bishops, Church dignitaries, and observers from other Christian denominations, and to the representatives of the eighty-six governments or international bodies also present in St. Peter's in Rome, he read an address titled *Gaudet Mater Ecclesia* (Mother Church Rejoices). He rejected the "prophets of doom," always forecasting disaster for the world and the Church. Old thinking would have to change, old doctrine be reformulated, Christian unity promoted. The essential issue, he insisted, was pastoral—how best to teach Christ's timeless message in the ever-changing modern world.

Vatican II was the twenty-first Ecumenical Council, the first since 1870, and the largest in the history of the Church. It lasted until its closure not by John XIII, who died in June 1963, but by Paul VI in December 1965. (Popes John Paul I, John Paul II, and Benedict XVI were also involved with its work.) Yet its reforms were not as momentous as some hoped, as conservatives pitted themselves against progressives.

The Council Fathers enacted four constitutions, nine decrees, and three declarations. There were regrets for past errors, an admission that "many elements of sanctification and of truth" could be found outside Catholicism, and translations of parts of the Mass from Latin into local languages. Certainly Vatican II showed that Catholicism had abandoned the defensive spirit exhibited since the Protestant Reformation of the sixteenth century. **RP**

Kennedy Faces Missile Crisis

The discovery of Soviet missiles on Cuba provokes naval blockade.

⊙ Americans view President Kennedy on department-store televisions as he announces the U.S. blockade of Cuba.

⊙ A U.S. Navy patrol aircraft watches the Soviet missile-carrying ship *Potzunov* as it departs from Cuba after the crisis.

"I call upon Chairman Khrushchev to halt this . . . threat to world peace."

John F. Kennedy, TV address, October 22, 1962

There had been rumors circulating for some time. Now, on Sunday morning, October 14, the proof was obtained. The head of the Central Intelligence Agency, John McCone, had ordered a series of reconnaissance flights to be carried out by U.S. U-2 spy planes. Their photographs of the San Cristóbal area showed that the Soviets were constructing missile sites from which intermediate-range and medium-range ballistic missiles could be launched. This was not the Soviet Union or even its eastern satellites, this was Cuba, the island run by the United States's number one enemy in the Western Hemisphere, the communist Fidel Castro. Missiles, each with a firepower equivalent to one million tons of TNT, were being made operational only 90 miles (145 km) from the United States coastline, and within striking distance of U.S. cities.

President Kennedy was stunned when he heard the news—it was as though the United States had decided to put missiles in Turkey. In fact, as Kennedy was reminded, the United States had done just that. Even so, many people believed that Kennedy should take out the missiles by launching a preemptive air strike, even at the risk of Soviet retaliation. The world held its breath.

On October 24, Kennedy instituted a naval blockade, throwing the onus for starting a war onto the Russians. Three days later, Soviet ships carrying military equipment turned back from Cuba, and on October 28 Nikita Khrushchev agreed to remove the missiles altogether. The following year, as had been secretly agreed behind closed doors, U.S. missiles were withdrawn from Turkey. Advancing to the terrifying brink of nuclear catastrophe taught the superpowers that survival required toughness to be balanced by compromise. **RP**

Slaves Freed

Saudi Arabia becomes the last major country to formally abolish slavery.

The edict of Crown Prince Faisal abolishing slavery in Saudi Arabia came during a modernization period, which introduced education for girls. About 10,000 slaves were freed—estimated as a third of the country's slaves—70 percent belonging to members of the royal family and the rest from other wealthy families. Most were in domestic service.

The first slaves to be freed were thirty-two men and fifty concubines kept by Prince Talal. Faisal had released his own slaves in 1956. He spent tens of millions compensating those who owned slaves.

"Muslim Sharia urges the manumission of slaves, and slavery in modern times . . ."

Prince Faisal, November 1962

Slavery was still present in the Gulf after World War II, but slaves working for international oil companies insisted on keeping what they earned. Qatar abolished slavery with compensation in 1952, but it was abolished without compensation in the Trucial States (United Arab Emirates). In Aden it was abolished by the new communist regime that followed the British withdrawal. Oman abolished slavery in 1970 after a British-supported coup.

Today, many of Saudi Arabia's migrants work under slavelike conditions. In 2005, Saudi Arabia and another fourteen countries around the world were declared by the U.S. government *Trafficking in Persons Report*, "Countries whose governments do not fully comply with the minimum standards and are not making significant efforts to do so." **PF**

Space's First Lady

Valentina Tereshkova becomes the first woman in space.

On June 16, 1963, Valentina Tereshkova entered *Vostok 6*. After completing communications and life support checks, the *Vostok* rocket blasted off, making her the first woman in space. Tereshkova orbited the earth forty-eight times, spending three days in space. With a call sign of *Chayka* (seagull), Tereshkova logged more flying time than all U.S. astronauts during the mission, providing the Soviet Union with a propaganda coup at the height of the cold war.

It was Tereshkova's interest in parachuting that brought her to the Soviet cosmonaut program when

"Once you've been in space, you appreciate how small and fragile the Earth is."

Valentina Tereshkova

it was decided in 1961 to put a woman into space. She was selected alongside four other women from a pool of more than 400 candidates, all linked by this same interest in parachuting. Tereshkova was considered a suitable applicant because of her working class background and because her father had died a war hero in the Finnish Winter War of 1939.

Intensive training lasted several months, during which all five potential cosmonauts undertook weightless flights, prolonged isolation, centrifuge testing, more than 120 parachute jumps, and pilot training in MiG jet fighters. Tereshkova was selected, and the other female cosmonauts never visited space. Nineteen years later Svetlana Savitskaya flew into space in response to U.S. plans to send a female astronaut on board the space shuttle. **TB**

"Ich Bin ein Berliner"

President Kennedy's forthright support for West Berlin ends Soviet attempts to take over the entire city.

The 120,000-strong crowd had been waiting for several hours when President Kennedy appeared on the balcony of Schöneberg *Rathaus* (City Hall) in West Berlin. Their cheers become louder and louder during his speech, for what he said was music to their ears. Their city had been divided and besieged for eighteen years, and now a wall divided citizens and separated families. It was, he insisted, an offense against history and an offense against humanity. Yet the people of Berlin had not been forgotten—their island of freedom was part of the main, and their struggle symbolized that of the whole free world against the tyranny of communism. Freedom was indivisible, and therefore all free men, including Kennedy himself, could take pride in the words *"Ich bin ein Berliner"* (I am a Berliner). There could have been no more defiant affirmation that the West was standing by Berlin until their city and country was reunified. Kennedy's speech was followed by an address by the mayor of West Berlin and the tolling of the Freedom Bell. Finally, the crowds fell silent.

It was one of Kennedy's finest performances. He decided just before the speech to include *"Ich bin ein Berliner,"* the words (written phonetically on a cue card) that summed up his stance.

Kennedy was a morale booster for West Berlin and put an end to Soviet attempts to take over all of the city. It did not directly cause German reunification in 1990, but without such public Western resolution, reunification would have been less likely. **RP**

○ John F. Kennedy delivers his impassioned plea for political freedom to thousands of Berliners hungry for change.

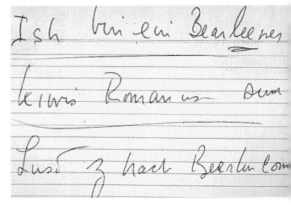

○ One of Kennedy's speech cards has his famous statement written out phonetically to help him avoid mispronunciation.

"I Have a Dream"

Martin Luther King Jr. and civil rights activists march on Washington.

In front of the Lincoln Memorial, Martin Luther King Jr. delivers the speech by which he is now best remembered.

The Reflecting Pool is surrounded by thousands drawn to the city by the March on Washington for Jobs and Freedom.

"If a man hasn't discovered something he will die for, he isn't fit to live."

Martin Luther King Jr., 1963

The progress of the civil rights movement in the United States was demonstrated, literally, when 200,000 marchers assembled in Washington, D.C. The event had been carefully prepared by the civil rights leadership to attract white as well as black support, and care was also taken to keep the Communist Party and other leftist organizations from clawing their way onto the bandwagon. Participation was invited "from only the established civil rights organizations, from major religious and fraternal groups, and from labor unions." The plan was for Martin Luther King Jr. and the other leaders, six black and four white, to walk to the Lincoln Memorial at the head of the marchers. There they were to give their speeches, before going on to the White House for a face-to-face meeting with President Kennedy himself.

Copies of the leaders' speeches had been distributed to the press in advance, but at the last moment King threw away his prepared remarks and spoke to the demonstrators impromptu. His repeated theme was "I have a dream," which was cheered to the echo at each repetition by the huge crowd. "I say to you today, my friends, so even though we face the difficulties of today and tomorrow, I still have a dream. It is a dream deeply rooted in the American dream. I have a dream that one day this nation will rise up and live out the true meaning of its creed—we hold these truths to be self-evident, that all men are created equal." King foresaw an America where whites and blacks would be brothers and where all God's children would be "free at last, free at last, thank God Almighty, we are free at last."

His hearers reacted with mounting fervor to one of the most celebrated orations of the entire century. For better or worse, King had made his mark. **RC**

President John F. Kennedy Assassinated

President Kennedy is shot dead as he rides in a motorcade through Dallas, Texas.

○ Three days after the assassination, President Kennedy is mourned by family members at his funeral in Washington.

◑ A Secret Serviceman shields the Kennedys from further bullets as the dying president's limousine speeds away.

> ## "The sense of something of exceptional hope . . . suddenly cut off in mid-air."
>
> **Isaiah Berlin to Arthur Schlesinger, Nov. 28, 1963**

Ever since that long, dark day in Dallas, conspiracy theories have flourished, attributing the killing variously to the Mafia, the CIA, the Soviet Union, or the Castro regime in Cuba. The official investigation, under Chief Justice Earl Warren, concluded that, like all the other assassinated U.S. presidents, John F. Kennedy was murdered by a lone fanatic. However, the theory that more than one assassin was involved has some distinguished support.

The president and his wife, Jacqueline, were riding in a motorcade through downtown Dallas past welcoming crowds, in a car with Governor John B. Connally of Texas and his wife, when three rifle shots rang out, apparently fired from the Texas Schoolbook Depository overlooking the road. One bullet struck the president in the back and another in the head, and Governor Connally was also wounded. Screaming spectators scattered for cover while the president's car, his distraught wife cradling his head in her lap, raced to the Parkland Memorial Hospital 3 miles (5 km) away. He was pronounced dead there at 1 P.M. At 2:41 P.M., in an impressive demonstration of the American system's strength, Vice President Lyndon B. Johnson, who had also been in the motorcade, was sworn in as president on board the presidential plane, Air Force One, on the way back to Washington, D.C.; Jackie Kennedy stood beside him, her clothes still spattered with her husband's blood.

There was unprecedented national mourning, and it is often said that everyone remembers exactly where they were when they heard the news. The dead president was duly buried on November 25 in the Arlington National Cemetery near Washington. The Dallas police had meanwhile arrested Lee Harvey Oswald for the murder, who was in turn shot dead by another lone fanatic, Jack Ruby. **RC**

Ruby Kills Oswald

Lee Harvey Oswald is shot in front of an audience of millions.

Lee Harvey Oswald's claim to fame was as President Kennedy's murderer, and perhaps it was a desire for fame that motivated him. A persistent truant from school, Oswald dropped out at sixteen, spent time in the U.S. Marines, and developed a love of Marxism. In 1959, he went to the Soviet Union, and tried in vain to gain citizenship. He returned to the United States in 1962, with his Russian wife, living in New Orleans and making no secret of his support for Cuba's communist regime. In March 1963, he ordered a Mannlicher-Carcano rifle from a mail-order company.

In October 1963, Oswald got a job at the Texas Schoolbook Depository in Dallas. It was from the building's sixth-floor window, according to the committee of investigation under Chief Justice Earl Warren, that at 12:30 P.M. Oswald fired the shots that killed President Kennedy and wounded Governor Connally. His rifle was found on the depository floor. He shot dead a Dallas police officer who made an attempt to arrest him, but was caught about 2 P.M. in a movie house.

On November 24, Oswald was being moved from one Dallas prison to another when local nightclub owner Jack Ruby shot him at point-blank range in full view of the police officers escorting Oswald, press reporters, and millions of television viewers. Oswald died at a hospital later that day. Ruby was arrested, but died not long afterward in 1967. Oswald died without confessing to President Kennedy's murder, and there has been speculation that he was shot to prevent him from revealing that he was part of a conspiracy. **RC**

◐ Despite having little chance of escaping from the scene, Jack Ruby lunges forward and shoots Lee Harvey Oswald.

Jerusalem Embrace

The pope attempts to resolve centuries of Catholic-Orthodox rancor.

On the Mount of Olives in Jerusalem, Pope Paul VI embraced the Ecumenical Patriarch, Athenagoras I. This symbolized a reconciliation between the Catholic and Orthodox churches, which had been separated since the Great Schism of 1054 and Latin Christian Crusaders' sacking of Constantinople in 1204. Often conservative, Paul VI reasserted papal primacy over issues such as contraception, priestly celibacy, and the role of women in the Church. But he was a pioneer in ecumenical issues. His pilgrimage to the Holy Land made him the first pope to leave

> ## "They are persuaded . . . to overcome their differences in order to be again one."
>
> **Catholic-Orthodox joint declaration, Dec. 1965**

Italy in 150 years and saw him reach out to Judaism and Orthodoxy. He visited King Hussein of Jordan in Amman and tried to reach doctrinal agreements with Anglicans and Lutherans. He later visited Africa and Southeast Asia and saw improvements in Rome's relations with the communist world.

The meeting meant Orthodoxy and Catholicism became spiritually and symbolically closer than they had been for centuries. It led to the rescinding of the 1054 excommunications of the Ecumenical Patriarch and a number of prominent Roman ecclesiastics. In December 1965, a Catholic-Orthodox joint declaration promised to mend the churches' differences. It did not end the schism, and some Orthodox Christians were not happy with events, but it did show a desire for reconciliation between the churches. **JS**

The Beatles Live on U.S. Television

The band's exposure to the United States spearheads the "British invasion," and their single tops the charts on both sides of the Atlantic.

Already massive in most of Europe because of their genuine grassroots talent and self-deprecating humor, the Beatles had at the end of 1963 yet to "conquer" the United States. In fact, their nominal U.S. label, Capitol, refused to handle their U.K. recordings. Beatles manager Brian Epstein crossed the Atlantic late in 1963 to break the impasse. The Beatles's fourth single, "I Want to Hold Your Hand," was being picked up on U.S. airwaves after a U.S. DJ hustled a U.K. copy from a British air stewardess. Epstein secured $56,000 (£20,000) worth of publicity from Capitol Records and, crucially, top billing on two live telecasts on *The Ed Sullivan Show* for February 9 and 16 the next year. Meanwhile, demand forced Capitol to release the record before the group landed in New York to meet 3,000 fans on February 7, 1964.

Two days later, the Beatles played "All My Loving," "She Loves You," "I Saw Her Standing There," "I Want to Hold Your Hand," and "Till There Was You" to an estimated audience of seventy-three million people. There were 50,000 requests for the studio's 728 seats. It was the biggest transmission of the Beatles in the United States. *The Ed Sullivan Show* was the nation's favorite, and the Beatles brought fun and mayhem into the gloom of Kennedy's assassination and the Vietnam War.

In April, "I Want To Hold Your Hand" became the first single to top the U.S. and U.K. charts simultaneously, and the band's back catalog took up another four positions in the U.S. Top Ten. **JJH**

○ Witty banter with Ed Sullivan helped to consolidate the Beatles's already growing success in the United States.

◑ Ed Sullivan's introduction of the Beatles on his show on February 9 effectively began the "invasion" of British bands.

Mandela Found Guilty

Nelson Mandela is spared the death penalty, but faces life imprisonment.

The death penalty was not imposed, but on that day in Pretoria, South Africa, eight men, including Nelson Mandela, former secretary-general of the banned African National Congress (ANC), were found guilty of sabotage and plotting the violent overthrow of the state. All received life imprisonment. Mandela, an opponent of the apartheid system for years, had originally advocated nonviolent resistance. This changed with the Sharpeville massacre of 1960, when police gunned down more than sixty-nine demonstrators. Mandela founded the ANC's military

"It is not true that the enfranchisement of all will result in racial domination."

Nelson Mandela, to the court

wing, *Umkhonto we Sizwe* (Spear of the Nation), and a sabotage campaign was launched. Mandela was already in prison for leaving the country illegally when a police raid in Rivonia, near Johannesburg, uncovered the arms cache that led to the trial.

Mandela showed dignified defiance throughout the trial, arguing that resistance to oppression was inevitable. Mandela in prison came to symbolize the frustrated aspiration of all black South Africans. His stature grew over the twenty-seven years he was imprisoned. He refused any release that would compromise his beliefs. He became an international leader of the oppressed from his cell. Mandela's name helped mobilize a worldwide campaign against apartheid, which would force the South African government, and its racist policies, to fail. **JS**

"Great Society"

President Lyndon B. Johnson delivers his State of the Union address.

Starting from humble origins in Texas, Lyndon Baines Johnson became Democrat leader in the Senate before running as John F. Kennedy's vice-presidential candidate in the 1960 election. When Kennedy was assassinated, Johnson succeeded him. He wanted to continue Kennedy's "New Frontier" initiatives, particularly to tackle poverty and racism. In a 1964 speech, Johnson announced his desire and intention to "set our course toward the Great Society."

When he ran that year for the presidency in his own right, Johnson secured a massive majority, with

"A President's hardest task is not to do what is right but to know what is right."

President Johnson, State of the Union, 1965

61 percent of the popular vote. In his State of the Union address to Congress, he set out his ideals, "The Great Society rests on an abundance of liberty for all. It demands an end to poverty and racial injustice—to which we are totally committed."

How far Johnson succeeded is disputed. His civil rights acts helped black Americans and Native Americans, billions of dollars were spent on his "War on Poverty," federal support for education increased, and he introduced the Medicare and Medicaid health programs, which some attacked as the introduction of socialism. However, the cost of the war in Vietnam limited government spending on "Great Society" programs and made Johnson unpopular. Thoroughly disillusioned, he declined to run in 1968, and Richard M. Nixon became president. **RC**

Hammer Blows Strike North Vietnam

The United States attempts to stave off the collapse of South Vietnam with a bombing campaign of North Vietnam.

When first introduced, the U.S. Air Force's Operation Rolling Thunder bombing campaign of North Vietnam was designed to prevent supplies and reinforcements from reaching Viet Cong guerrillas. Initially intended to last eight weeks, Rolling Thunder would continue for three years, in the end aiming simply to force the North Vietnamese government to end the war on U.S. terms. In reality, the strength of the Viet Cong came from support among South Vietnamese peasants and did not rely on supplies from the North. The argument that bombing had failed to break the morale of a nation in World War II was ignored, an indication of rapidly growing U.S. frustration at the tenacity of Viet Cong resistance.

In North Vietnam, an elaborate civil defense system and increasingly formidable air defenses (built with Soviet aid) cost the United States dearly; some 700 U.S. aircraft were shot down. Morale in the North remained solid and its military, which had only minimal material needs, remained effective. In the South, the Viet Cong responded by attacking U.S. air bases, and a huge influx of ground troops was needed to protect them. The war not only escalated at an unexpected pace, but became increasingly Americanized. The more the United States took up the burden of fighting, the more the South Vietnamese were willing to stand aside. In the course of Rolling Thunder, one million tons of munitions were dropped, including napalm and anti-personnel bombs. The carnage transformed opinion in the United States and throughout the world, and did much to undermine popular support for the war. **JS**

◑ An aerial view of the bomb damage and impact craters left after a U.S. B-52 bombing strike north of Dai Teng.

Rhodesia Declares Independence

Rhodesia's white minority declares independence and its intention never to accept majority rule, provoking diplomatic and economic sanctions from Britain.

The Unilateral Declaration of Independence of Ian Smith's Rhodesian government was carefully timed to coincide with Britain's Armistice Day celebrations, when the colonial power would be commemorating the dead of two world wars. It was an unsubtle reminder of the past loyalty of the colony, aimed particularly at those in Britain who sympathized with the refusal of white colonists—who were themselves largely of British stock—to accept the rule of the black majority.

However, the position of the British Labour government, and much of the population, was that this was an act of rebellion, and Rhodesian independence would never be recognized until democracy held sway. Diplomatic and economic sanctions were immediately imposed. The United Nations Security Council also condemned the Rhodesian act and imposed sanctions. But British military intervention, for which many African nationalists clamored, was never likely.

Sanctions had little immediate effect. Rhodesia enjoyed the support of Portugal, which was determined to defy African nationalists and hold on to its neighboring colony of Mozambique. The South African government, also, saw Rhodesia as a bulwark protecting its own apartheid regime from African nationalism. But in 1975 Mozambique became independent, and South Africa, suffering sanctions and internal African opposition, was unable to subsidize Rhodesia any longer. By 1979, isolated and exposed, the white minority had no option but to negotiate their submission to majority rule. **PF**

○ Watched by Rhodesian officials, Premier Ian Smith signs the controversial Unilateral Declaration of Independence.

Cultural Revolution Launched

New revolutionary upheavals sweep through China as Mao Zedong pits the zealous youth against anyone with bourgeois ideas or leanings.

By inviting Chinese youths to form Red Guard units and criticize those in authority, Chairman Mao Zedong effectively declared war on his own Chinese Communist Party (CCP). Humiliated and weakened by the dismal failure of his Great Leap Forward in 1958, Mao concluded that the fault lay in the lack of revolutionary spirit within the CCP. The party must have allowed too many bourgeois elements to enter and, like the Soviet Party, was losing contact with the proletariat and peasantry and caring more about its privileges than its responsibilities. Feeling that the young were still true revolutionaries, Mao decided to mobilize them. Red Guards were urged to denounce teachers, writers, anyone involved in the arts, and party members with bourgeois ideas. Denunciations soon turned to humiliation, imprisonment, torture, and murder. China was rapidly reduced to chaos.

The CCP tried to defend itself, but anyone who tried to reimpose discipline over the young was denounced as counterrevolutionary. The CCP therefore mobilized their own Red Guards. An element of civil war developed, with factions of Red Guards engaged in pitched battles. The CCP and even China seemed on the verge of collapse. The army alone was capable of ending the chaos, and although Mao wanted them to support his Red Guards, from 1967 they began to restore order. The Cultural Revolution really ended only after Mao's death in 1976. By then, ironically, any revolutionary enthusiasm left in China had been killed. **JS**

◗ Chairman Mao Zedong shakes the hand of a young Red Guard during his bid to rekindle the revolution in China.

◖ A crowd of Red Guards and students brandish copies of Mao's *Little Red Book* during a demonstration in Beijing.

Verwoerd Assassinated

The strongman of the apartheid regime in South Africa is fatally stabbed.

The South African Prime Minister Hendrick Frensch Verwoerd was fatally stabbed during a session of Parliament in Cape Town, in front of hundreds of witnesses. Verwoerd, a member of the Purified Nationalist Party, often described as the architect of modern apartheid in South Africa, became minister of native affairs in 1950 and premier in 1958. He had overseen much of the legislation that had established apartheid. He had also been responsible for a whites-only referendum establishing the Republic of South Africa, which led to the country's expulsion from the Commonwealth. After he launched a crackdown on internal opposition, at least sixty-nine unarmed demonstrators were gunned down by police in March 1960 in the Sharpeville massacre, the African National Congress was banned, and Nelson Mandela was imprisoned for life in June 1964.

Ironically, given the host of enemies he had made, Verwoerd's assassination may not have been an overtly political act. The motives of his assailant, parliamentary messenger Demetrio Tsafendas, were obscure. Born of a Greek father and a Swazi mother, Tsafendas had somehow been classed as white. This made it illegal for him to marry the woman he had chosen, who was officially classed as colored, unless he could have his own race reclassified. The story suggests that Tsafendas had some grievance against the apartheid system, but he himself claimed that a large worm in his stomach had commanded him to kill. A political assassination would have been embarrassing to the state, so Tsafendas was judged insane and was confined to mental institutions until his death in 1999. Whatever his true motives, his deed was a stark reminder that apartheid rule was opposed and would never be secure. **JS**

Birth of Biafra

Announcement of the breakaway republic triggers clashes in Nigeria.

Colonel Emeka Ojukwu, military head of Nigeria's Eastern Region, unilaterally issued a declaration of independence for what he called Biafra. As this area was the source of Nigeria's only important export, oil, the central government was certain to oppose him.

The origins of the conflict are to be found in Nigeria's colonial past. When carving up the territory, the British had been indifferent to its ethnic character. On independence in 1960, Nigeria was a mix of Muslim and Christian or animist peoples with a history of ethnic tensions. Civilian rule did not survive

> ## "God Bless Biafra. . . . We have emerged triumphant, from all our foes . . ."
>
> **From the patriotic song "All Hail Biafra"**

long, and in 1966 the military took over the government. But economic problems worsened, as did ethnic conflict. The worst friction arose between the Muslim Hausas in the north and Christian Ibo in the southeast. It was the latter, claiming to be the victims of many years of discrimination and atrocities, who sought to establish Biafra as their nation.

This was destined to be one of post-independence Africa's first and bloodiest wars. In the thirty months it lasted, one million refugees fled their homes, and between one and three million are thought to have died in the fighting and the famine it caused. Biafra was defeated, but the problems that gave rise to the conflict remained. Decades later there are still Ibo complaints of discrimination, and renewed conflict remains a distinct possibility. **JS**

Israelis Storm East Jerusalem

The world is staggered by the Israeli victories during the Six-Day War.

⊙ An Israeli convoy heading for the Sinai Desert passes a truck carrying Egyptian soldiers stripped of their uniforms.

On the third day of fighting in their renewed battle with their Arab neighbors, Israeli forces overwhelmed the Jordanians to take the old city of Jerusalem, site of the Dome of the Rock and the only surviving remnant of the ancient Jewish Temple, the Western Wall. A seemingly unstoppable Arab coalition had crumbled in the Israeli onslaught. Realizing that a combined attack was imminent, the Israelis had launched a sudden first strike, destroying much hostile air power on the ground and gaining a vital advantage. In what was to be known as the Six-Day War, Israel stormed across three frontiers, conquering the West Bank from Jordan, the Golan Heights from Syria, and the Gaza Strip and the entire Sinai Peninsula from Egypt. Their victory appeared decisive.

Victory gave rewards. The United States had announced its neutrality, but in reality this marked a strategic partnership, which would provide Israel with unconditional U.S. support. The Egyptians and Syrians would fight again in the 1973 Yom Kippur War, but Egypt's new leader, Anwar Sadat, was willing to abandon dreams of destroying Israel and negotiate for the return of the Sinai. But Israel was now the ruler of great numbers of Palestinians. With the West Bank widely seen as inalienably part of Israel and won by overwhelming force of arms, there was little incentive to seek a compromise. But Israeli occupation would be resisted, and escalating violence would make a permanent settlement of this conflict seemingly impossible to find. **JS**

Revolutionary Hero Shot Dead

Iconic communist hero Che Guevara is hunted down and killed in Bolivia.

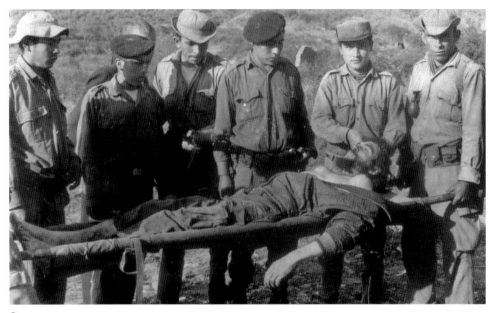

○ Che Guevara's corpse is paraded for the camera after a tip-off led to his execution by a squad of the Bolivian army.

Ernesto "Che" Guevara was thirty-nine years old when he was shot dead by a Bolivian sergeant in a settlement called La Higuera. Argentinean by birth, Guevara trained as a doctor and received his medical degree in Buenos Aires, but he was more interested in revolution. He met Fidel Castro in Mexico, helped establish communism in Cuba in 1959, and held important posts in the Castro government. But he disapproved of the Soviet Union's backing-down in the missile crisis, and the Soviet Union in turn disapproved of his Maoist sympathies. In 1965 Guevara left Cuba in an unsuccessful attempt to export his brand of communism to the Congo. He turned to South America in 1966. With a small band of guerrilla fighters, he established a training camp in the Nancahuazu region of Bolivia, later moving to the Vallegrande area.

Recruits failed to come, however. The local people were suspicious and unfriendly, and Guevara's force never exceeded fifty men. With support, but little direct involvement by the United States, Bolivian army units cornered him and his men in a canyon near La Higuera. Guevara was wounded and held prisoner in the local schoolhouse. There Bolivian soldiers drew lots to decide which of them would execute him. Reputedly, his last words were "Know this, you are killing a man." His body was flown to Vallegrande by helicopter and his death announced to the media. His perhaps most visible legacy to the world is as a popular image on T-shirts. **RC**

First Successful Heart Transplant

South African surgeon Christiaan Barnard performs the first successful human heart transplant and instantly becomes a household name.

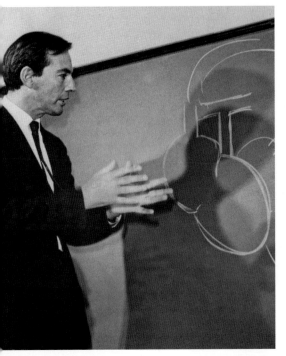

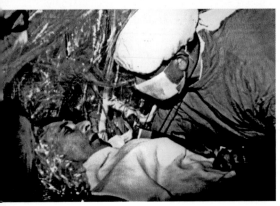

The surgeon Christiaan Barnard studied medicine at the University of Cape Town and cardiac surgery at the University of Minnesota. He had been experimenting with organ transplants in animals for several years, and felt the time had arrived to put these techniques into practice. The recipient was fifty-five-year-old Louis Washkansky; the donor, twenty-five-year-old Denise Darvall, who had been killed in a traffic accident. The operation, which lasted nine hours, involved a thirty-strong surgical team. Barnard, who had not expected the operation to attract much interest, had not even informed the hospital superintendent of his intentions. But at a time when any heart surgery was deemed very risky, his achievement attracted enormous publicity. To his surprise, he was instantly and internationally famous, and went on to be feted by film stars, politicians, and even the pope.

Washkansky survived only eighteen days. The drug used to keep his body from rejecting the new organ also reduced his resistance to infection, and he contracted pneumonia. Only in 1974 did a Norwegian researcher produce the drug cyclosporine, which avoided this complication. Barnard's pioneering work paved the way for the perfection of heart transplant techniques. He continued his research and in 1974 performed the world's first double heart transplant. Indeed, within twenty years of his first operation this surgery had become routine. Barnard retired from surgery in 1983 because of arthritis, and died in 2001, ironically from heart disease. **JS**

◗ Christiaan Barnard explains at a press conference how
   he performed his pioneering heart transplant procedure.
◗ Barnard monitors Louis Washkansky's progress after
   the groundbreaking heart transplant operation.

Tet Offensive Begins

The shock Tet Offensive in South Vietnam leaves the U.S. forces reeling.

The Vietnamese New Year festival, or Tet, was celebrated by Viet Cong guerrillas with an explosion of coordinated attacks in every city of South Vietnam. U.S. forces were stunned at the scale and ferocity of the fighting, which saw a battle fought within the grounds of the U.S. Embassy in Saigon and thousands of civilians perish. The Tet Offensive had been long planned and was intended to disrupt South Vietnam totally. Until then, U.S. leaders thought the war was winnable and felt secure in the cities, if not in the countryside. North Vietnamese General Vo Nguyen

> ## "It is increasingly clear ... that the only rational way out ... will be to negotiate."
> **Walter Cronkite, U.S. broadcaster**

Giap intended to show they were wrong. At best he hoped this offensive would spark a popular rising that would drive the Americans from Vietnam. At least he hoped to force the Americans to negotiate.

In military terms, the U.S. triumphed in the Tet Offensive. The Viet Cong suffered major losses, and henceforth the North Vietnamese army would have to take up the major burden of the fighting. In political terms, the consequences were different. In the United States, the Tet Offensive was perceived as a defeat, and U.S. public opinion turned against what it now saw as a hopeless cause. Although the bloodshed would continue until the 1973 peace agreement, from this point on the Americans were clearly trying to find a way to extricate themselves from the conflict without too great a loss of face. **JS**

Massacre in Vietnam

The My Lai atrocity feeds international revulsion toward the Vietnam War.

The U.S. troops, under the command of Lieutenant William Calley, were sent to root out Viet Cong guerrillas and their sympathizers, believed to be hiding in the village of My Lai. The slaughter that followed was unprovoked and indiscriminate, resulting in the massacre of old men, women, and children. Later military investigations concluded that 347 had been murdered, although the Vietnamese claimed it was 504. The incident was initially covered up and reported as a military engagement in which 128 enemy combatants had been killed. Rumors began to spread, though, and one soldier, Ron Ridenhour, reported the atrocity to several political figures, including President Nixon. It was impossible to conceal, yet Calley was the only man convicted for the crime. Initially sentenced to life imprisonment for premeditated murder, he served only a derisory three and a half years under house arrest.

With the use of defoliants, napalm, and massive bombing campaigns, the Americans, it seemed to many Vietnamese, were destroying South Vietnam in order to save it. The U.S. presence was widely detested, and U.S. troops met hostility at every turn. This encouraged them to assume that any Vietnamese who was killed was automatically Viet Cong. Unable to find their invisible enemies and suspecting all peasants of colluding with them, U.S. troops could easily come to hate all Vietnamese. Such an atrocity as My Lai was hardly surprising, and the horrifying news, when it finally broke, would galvanize and unify the antiwar U.S. movement. It accelerated the shift in U.S. public opinion in general against the war. It also, arguably, convinced many South Vietnamese that perhaps communist rule might be preferable to being the United States's battlefield. **JS**

Martin Luther King Jr. Assassinated

The United States loses a formidable leader, resulting in a surge of anger.

O Five days after King's assassination, more than 50,000 people attended his funeral procession in Atlanta, Georgia.

The U.S. civil rights movement's most famous and effective leader, who had adopted Mahatma Gandhi's principle of nonviolence and won the Nobel Peace Prize in 1964, was shot dead in Memphis, Tennessee. He had visited the city several times to support a strike by black sanitation workers, and, at a meeting on April 3, speaking about rumors of threats against his life, he said, "Like anybody I would like to live a long life. Longevity has its place. But I'm not concerned about that now. I just want to do God's will."

Next evening, King was standing on the second-floor balcony of the Lorraine Motel when there was a loud bang, like a car backfiring. It was actually a rifle shot, fired from the window of a nearby house. Soon after, King was found lying on the balcony with a fatal wound to the head. He was still just alive and his friends put a bedspread from one of the rooms over him, but his life ebbed away before the ambulance could reach him. He was thirty-nine years old.

The news of King's death caused a storm of grief and rage. In riots in Washington, D.C., and other cities, blacks from the ghettoes went on the rampage, looting and burning. It took thousands of troops to restore order. King himself would not have approved of the violence and it did no good whatsoever.

The killer was a white Southerner and petty criminal from Tennessee, James Earl Ray. He fled to England, but was caught in London and returned to Memphis. There, in 1969, he was given a ninety-nine-year sentence. He died in 1998. **RC**

Riots in Paris

Revolutionary outbursts are once again seen in the French capital.

○ Angry students protest on the streets of Paris—their riot spearheaded a general strike that lasted for a fortnight.

A new French revolution seemed imminent. After several days of running battles between students and riot police in Paris, the situation became even more dangerous for the government when striking workers joined in the protests. The trouble originated with a series of confrontations between university and high school authorities and students in March, generally over the intrusive regulations and archaic and bourgeois values that were taught. The French government's response was heavy-handed, and the Sorbonne was surrounded by police. Students were arrested, beaten, and attacked with tear gas. Street battles in Paris's Latin Quarter caused widespread working-class indignation against the police, and an unofficial general strike spread, involving more than ten million workers. It paralyzed France for two weeks. The government appeared close to collapse.

Assessing the loyalty of its troops and reputedly moving tanks to the outskirts of Paris, the government was clearly preparing for the worst. However, the situation evaporated as quickly as it had arisen. The French workers, it turned out, had little sympathy for revolutionary student rhetoric. Major concessions in pay, working conditions, and trade union rights ended the general strike and defused the insurrection. President de Gaulle called a quick general election, which produced a major increase in his support and left the students isolated. Old attitudes toward education and youth had been challenged, though, bringing change not just in Paris but across Europe. **JS**

Robert Kennedy Shot

Senator Robert Kennedy is assassinated in Los Angeles, California.

Three assassinations in the United States in five years took the lives of John F. Kennedy, Martin Luther King Jr., and Robert F. Kennedy. In 1957, Robert Kennedy had been chief counsel to the Senate committee investigating labor racketeering, and in 1960 he ran his brother's successful campaign for the presidency. As attorney general in his brother's administration, he supported the civil rights campaign and led a vigorous fight against organized crime. In 1964, after John F. Kennedy's death, he was elected a Democratic senator for the state of New York and quickly made

---

"My brother need not be idealized . . . in death beyond what he was in life . . ."

Senator Edward Kennedy

---

himself a significant political figure in his own right and a leading opponent of the Vietnam War.

Kennedy announced his candidature for the presidency in 1968, and by June 4 he had won five out of six Democratic primaries, including the one that day in California. As he spoke to his supporters in the Ambassador Hotel, Los Angeles, it looked as if he might well become the second member of his family in the White House. However, leaving through a crowded passageway, he was shot, and he died in a hospital the following day, aged forty-two.

The murderer was a Palestinian-born immigrant, Sirhan Sirhan, who objected to Kennedy's pro-Israel sympathies. He was sentenced to death in 1969, but a plea from Senator Edward Kennedy helped get the sentence commuted to life imprisonment. **RC**

Birth Control Rejected

The pope's condemnation of birth control provokes a crisis of authority.

In a move that dismayed liberal Roman Catholics of the time, Pope Paul VI's encyclical, *Humanae Vitae* (Human Life), emphatically condemned all means of artificial birth control. Arguing that birth control was a violation of natural law and inherently evil, the pope warned that its use would increase marital infidelity, would debase moral standards, and would devalue women into mere instruments of pleasure. Sex within marriage, he argued, that artificially excluded its basic purpose of procreation, was unnatural.

This stance came as a considerable shock to many, who had expected the Church to take a more liberal position in response to the introduction of the contraceptive pill. Indeed, control of fertility was seen as a vital measure in reducing poverty levels throughout the world, especially in the less developed world. The later spread of AIDS would add to the urgency of such arguments. In the Western world, birth control would increasingly be viewed as a matter of personal conscience, rather than an issue for the Vatican's judgment. Procreation, it was claimed, was not the sole purpose of marriage. The pope's ruling would increasingly be ignored.

Although many Catholics agreed with the pope and subsequently have claimed that his warnings have been proved correct, with abortion and illegitimacy rates soaring, in general the response was so hostile that Paul VI was dismayed and he never issued another encyclical. But Pope John Paul II reaffirmed his judgment in 1984. Arguments for birth control were met with demands of obedience to Catholic authority. In reality, the Church lost credibility as a teacher of sexual ethics, and selective dissent against *Humanae Vitae* was to fuel broader dissent against the Vatican's authority. **JS**

Soviet Troops Enter Czechoslovakia

Soviet-led forces make a move to suppress the reforms of Alexander Dubček's Czech government, which is deemed to undermine the stability of communist Europe.

The invasion of Czechoslovakia by a Soviet-led coalition brought to an end the Prague Spring, a period of liberal reforms by the Czech government of Alexander Dubček. Economic stagnation and widespread demands for political reform had led to the ousting of Czechoslovakia's unreformed Stalinist leader, Antonin Novotny, in January. He was replaced by Dubček, who announced a raft of reforms. Although he never intended to allow the party to lose control of Czechoslovakia, threaten Soviet security, or withdraw from the Warsaw Pact, he did insist that socialism needed a human face. He proposed to permit legalized opposition parties. He ended censorship and wanted to normalize diplomatic and trade relations with West Germany. The tragedy was that Dubček did not understand how reforms in Czechoslovakia impacted the communist world.

In Poland there were demonstrations demanding similar reforms. Moscow feared such agitation could spread to the Ukraine. This was unacceptable, but Dubček did not take demands that he rein in reforms seriously. He thought the assurances of loyalty he gave at a summit of Warsaw Pact leaders in July would placate Soviet concerns. The invasion was their reply. The West denounced the invasion, but took no action. Within the communist world a clear message was received. Real change and communist rule were incompatible. If communism was unable to reform itself, therefore, perhaps reform could come only if communism was disposed with. **JS**

○ People in Prague, keen to adopt Dubček's more liberal policies, show their opposition to the military invasion.

◑ Soviet-led forces ride their tanks through the streets of Prague to seize control of Czechoslovakia from Dubček.

Earth Seen from the Moon

The Earthrise photograph is taken eight months before the first landing on the moon.

○ William Anders's breathtaking photograph of Earth as it appears from the vantage point of the moon.

The *Apollo 8* mission carried astronauts Frank Borman, William Anders, and Jim Lovell into lunar orbit. It was the first occasion on which humans had traveled beyond the gravitational field of Earth to that of another body. Their task was to photograph the lunar surface, but as they rolled the spacecraft and came around from the far side of the moon, they saw the distant Earth rising above the vast, inert surface of the moon. Both Borman, the mission commander, and Anders caught the moment on film. Borman captured Earth in monochrome just as it emerged over the lunar horizon; Anders with it risen a few degrees into the black sky, in color, a swirl of blue and white. The picture showed, for the first time, Earth from distant space, a small planet partly shrouded in darkness: a fragile, fluid, integrated world, fascinating and attractive, in contrast to the monolithic, gray, and inert moon , that Lovell described as "like plaster of Paris or grayish beach sand." He added, "The vast loneliness is awe-inspiring and makes you realize just what you have back there on Earth."

In fact, because the moon keeps the same face continually turned to Earth, Earth does not "rise" or "set" from the surface, but remains at the same point in the sky permanently.

The Earthrise photograph was taken up by the developing environmental movement and proved a powerful graphic image for the notion, proposed by James Lovelock, of "Gaia," Earth as a self-correcting, almost intelligent organism. **PF**

Aeronautical Triumph

Concorde, the world's first supersonic airliner, takes to the skies.

○ The first flight of Concorde, flown by pilot Andre Turcat, taking off from the airport in Toulouse.

On a bitterly cold afternoon in Toulouse, France, test pilot Andre Turcat took the Anglo-French airliner Concorde on its first flight. It was a short flight, and the aircraft was not taken to supersonic speeds. As Europe's most ambitious technological project to date, the flight was greeted with immense enthusiasm. Research into a supersonic airliner had begun in the 1950s, but it was soon clear that the cost would be immense and require international cooperation. The British and French governments signed a treaty in November 1962 to share the project. As the costs escalated, there was doubt that Concorde would ever fly. The blaze of publicity for the first flight was intended to reassure British and French taxpayers that they were gaining value for their money.

In the event, the project made a huge loss and overran its development budget several times. Only fourteen aircraft were built for commercial use, and British Airways was able to buy its seven (Air France took the others) only with a government subsidy. Production delays ensured they did not enter service until 1976. Concorde could fly the Atlantic in less than 3.5 hours, though, and became an icon of the aviation industry. Unfortunately, limited fuel capacity rendered the aircraft unable to fly the lucrative Pacific routes, and environmentalists opposed their landing at several U.S. airports because of noise pollution. Concorde remained in service until October 2003, when rising costs and falling revenue in the wake of 9/11 made them commercially unviable. **JS**

Mankind Takes a Giant Leap

Neil Armstrong becomes the first man to set foot on the moon.

Watched by a worldwide audience of 450 million, at 2:56 A.M. GMT, the blurry, black-and-white pictures showed a figure moving indistinctly down a ladder. A mechanical voice was heard over the radio, "That's one small step for man, one giant leap for mankind."

Neil Armstrong, a thirty-eight-year-old NASA test pilot, had put his left foot on the moon, the first man ever to set foot on a natural object other than Earth. He took photographs and collected samples of dust; twenty minutes later he was joined by Buzz Aldrin, who exclaimed on stepping onto the lunar surface, "Beautiful. Beautiful. Magnificent desolation." They practiced jumping in the moon's low gravity before planting a U.S. flag and a plaque with President Nixon's signature and the inscription, "Here men from the planet Earth first set foot upon the moon July 1969 A.D. We came in peace for all mankind." Shortly after, Armstrong took a telephone call from Nixon.

They had blasted off in *Apollo 11* on July 16 from the Kennedy Space Center and had taken three days to reach lunar orbit. Armstrong and Aldrin manned the lunar module *Eagle*, which was to descend to the surface of the Sea of Tranquillity, while the third crew member, Michael Collins, remained in orbit on the larger command module, *Columbia*. As they appeared to be overshooting the planned landing site, Armstrong overrode the computers and landed the craft manually, with just thirty seconds' supply of fuel left.

After twenty-one hours on the moon, the *Eagle* blasted off once more to rejoin *Columbia* in lunar orbit, and begin the return journey. It splashed down in the Pacific on July 24. Armstrong spent much of the rest of his career in the Department of Aerospace Engineering at the University of Cincinnati, declining to use his unique experiences for personal celebrity or political power. **PF**

○ Lunar module pilot Buzz Aldrin's bootprint on the surface of the moon during the *Apollo 11* mission.

◐ Astronaut Buzz Aldrin walks on the surface of the moon in a photograph taken by Neil Armstrong.

"Houston, Tranquillity Base here. The Eagle has landed."

Neil Armstrong on landing the lunar module

Woodstock Rock Festival Begins

Over 450,000 attend the most publicized counterculture "happening" of the decade.

⬤ A couple take it easy on their car as the festival ends and the huge crowd begins to file out of the site.

The Monterey International Pop Festival in 1967 had pushed the hippie ideals of the "Summer of Love" onto a wider stage and Woodstock cemented that vibe into the national consciousness. The "Woodstock Nation" came together in hope and optimism against the prevailing doom of race riots, political assassinations, and the grueling Vietnam War.

The twenty-something organizers were pop promoters Artie Kornfeld and Michael Lang, wealthy businessman's son John Roberts, and lawyer Joel Rosenman. They flew in the "Wavy Gravy Hog Farm" commune from New Mexico to provide low-key security, bad LSD advice, medical tents, portable toilets, and water. They oversaw the world's then-biggest outdoor stage, which was supposed to

revolve, but broke down. So did a lot of the planning, and the organizers had to declare it a free festival (around 186,000 tickets had been sold in advance).

The thirty-one performers were paid anything from $18,000 (Jimi Hendrix) to $2,500 (the Grateful Dead). For some it was a leap to stardom, for others a validation of their rock credentials, but for all it was a triumph over a fuzzy sound system, stormy weather, and poor scheduling to create one of the defining moments in the history of rock music. Despite being on the brink of disaster all weekend—with ankle-deep mud, seventeen miles of bumper-to-bumper traffic, shortages of water and sanitation, and three reported births and deaths—Woodstock succeeded in delivering "three days of peace and music." **JJH**

"Houston, We Have a Problem"

Apollo 13 *is forced to abort its lunar mission after an onboard explosion.*

○ Astronauts Fred Haise, John Swigert, and James Lovell wait to be hauled to safety after their splashdown in the Pacific Ocean.

The first moon landing in 1969 was followed by further space missions that explored the moon's surface and brought back samples of soil and rocks. Most of them went well, but things went badly wrong with the *Apollo 13* mission, which blasted off from Cape Kennedy on April 11, 1970. Two days later, when the spacecraft was about 200,000 miles (322,000 km) from Earth and nearing the moon, there was what the commander called "a pretty loud bang." An oxygen tank had exploded in the command module, drastically reducing the supplies of oxygen, electricity, and water. Mission control at Houston decided to abort the planned lunar landing.

The spacecraft continued around the moon before starting the 250,000-mile (400,000 km) journey back to Earth. The three astronauts aboard used the lunar module as living quarters. Reentry into Earth's atmosphere was achieved on April 17 and, to everyone's profound relief, the spacecraft splashed down neatly in the Pacific, 4 miles (6.5 km) away from the recovery vessel, USS *Iwo Jima*.

The moon missions were undertaken largely for political reasons, because the United States seemed to be being outdone and shown up by the Soviet Union in the exploration of outer space. However, improvements in American-Soviet relations, not to mention the mounting cost of the program, caused the United States to reevaluate its space program. The lunar missions were ended after the successful return of *Apollo 17* in 1972. **RC**

Death of Jimi Hendrix

The guitarist leaves behind a totally original take on electric blues and a look that has come to epitomize the 1960s.

Hendrix was a black, left-handed guitarist who in his lifetime created a whole new vocabulary of sonic effects. He was never comfortable, though, reconciling his white rock image and adulation with a relative lack of connection with his black roots audience.

James Marshall Hendrix was born on November 27, 1942, in Seattle, Washington, and got his first guitar at age twelve. His early recordings and performances were with southern bluesmen and black urban rhythm and blues and soul bands (including B. B. King, The Isley Brothers, and Little Richard). From these roots, he honed a mesmerizing, flamboyant, and hitherto undreamt-of rock style for mainly white audiences.

After seeing him in a New York nightclub, Chas Chandler, ex-bassist with The Animals, chaperoned him back to England. Here he added Mitch Mitchell on drums and Noel Reading on bass to form the three-piece Jimi Hendrix Experience. Hendrix's live act, which included playing the guitar with his teeth and behind his neck, left his English guitar peers totally fazed. His fluid style of playing, with plenty of improvisation, coupled with his unique sound that often sought to harness feedback from the amplifier, completely refigured rock's sonic landscape.

His premature death was a tawdry affair, fueled by a fatal mix of drugs and alcohol. Hendrix died en route to the hospital choking on his own vomit. It was a disappointing end for the most innovative electric guitarist of the rock era, whose influence continues to reverberate to this day. **JJH**

○ Hendrix was unhappy with his legendary performance at the Isle of Wight Festival, England, two weeks before his death.

○ Miles Davis, who also performed at the Isle of Wight Festival, attends Hendrix's funeral with his wife (*left*) and a friend.

Cyclone Strikes

A cyclone accompanied by major floods inflicts huge losses on East Pakistan.

With winds reaching 115 miles per hour (185 kph), the cyclone that struck East Pakistan was equivalent to a Category 3 hurricane. The death toll of more than 300,000 was mainly caused by a storm surge that flooded the densely populated Ganges delta. A warning was broadcast, but it did not mention flooding. In the district of Tazumin, it is estimated that forty-five percent of the population perished.

In all, some 3.6 million people were affected by the cyclone. Much of the fishing fleet, which supplied East Pakistan with its main source of protein, was

"I'm very satisfied that everything is being done and will be done."

President Yahya Khan, November 1970

devastated. In a tragedy of this scale, a rapid relief operation was crucial. Yet it was here that Pakistan's government, based in West Pakistan, was severely criticized. Only one helicopter was available, and the government was slow to provide more. They blamed Indian obstruction for the delay, which the Indian government hotly denied. The Pakistani government refused to allow Indian aid to be flown into the country, and it arrived slowly over land. Crop-dusting aircraft in East Pakistan were offered for relief work, but it took two days for the government to accept them. Such incompetence quickly gave a major electoral boost to separatist political parties such as the Awami League. This, in turn, would take East Pakistan far along the road toward a war of liberation and the creation of an independent Bangladesh. **JS**

Brandt Pays Homage

Germany acknowledges its Nazi past through a symbolic act by its chancellor.

Willi Brandt's kneeling in homage to the victims of Nazism in the Polish capital of Warsaw marked Germany's most decisive break with the Hitler era and—though very controversial in Germany itself—began the rapprochement that culminated in German reunification in 1989.

Brandt, born Herbert Frahm in Lubeck in 1913, had opposed Nazism as a young socialist. When the Nazis gained power in 1933, he fled to Norway, adopting Norwegian citizenship and his new name. Returning to Germany as a German citizen after the war, he rose rapidly within the Social Democratic Party. As mayor of Berlin he received President Kennedy during his visit to the divided city in 1961.

Brandt became chancellor of West Germany in 1969 and embarked on a controversial *Ostpolitik* ("East policy"), opening contacts with East Germany and other communist countries in a process he hoped would lead to the spread of democracy. Ostpolitik almost brought his government down. In one crucial parliamentary division, it is believed that only bribes distributed by the East German Stasi secret service secured the votes Brandt needed.

Ostpolitik culminated in a treaty that relaxed relations between the two German states. Symbolically, Brandt atoned for Nazi crimes when he knelt in Warsaw before the memorial to victims of the 1944 Warsaw uprising—a revolt by Polish patriots that was bloodily crushed by the Nazis. Some Germans saw the act as a national humiliation, with even the left-leaning *Spiegel* magazine demanding, "Should Brandt have knelt?" But the gesture caused *Time* magazine to name Brandt as their Man of the Year for 1970, and the following year he was awarded the Nobel Peace Prize. **NJ**

Bangladesh Declares Independence

East Pakistan secedes, provoking a military response from its western counterpart.

○ Indian troops entering Dacca (Dakha) are hailed as victors by people of the newly named Bangladesh.

When East Pakistan's political leaders issued a declaration of independence from Pakistan, the move came as no great surprise. Since its creation in 1947, Pakistan was an unlikely political entity, with two territories separated by more than 1,000 miles (1,600 km) of Indian land. Apart from the Islamic religion, the two parts had little in common. West Pakistan politically dominated the two-winged state. The more populous East received much less than half of government spending, was underrepresented in the military, faced discrimination in the award of government contracts, and had its political leadership marginalized. The inept government response to the 1970 cyclone was for many the final straw. In the elections, the separatist East Pakistani Awami League won a landslide victory and had an overall majority in the National Assembly. The military simply refused to accept the results. The declaration of independence was an expected reply.

The government in West Pakistan, of course, was not prepared to leave such a challenge unanswered. It had already begun to launch a brutal campaign of repression. A primary victim was the Hindu minority. The hurriedly raised Mukti Bahini (Liberation Force) fought back using guerrilla warfare. The issue would eventually be decided by India, who, incensed by the attacks on Hindus and by the military buildup in the East, intervened in December. They rapidly advanced and took Dacca (Dakha) within days. The new nation of Bangladesh had become a reality. **JS**

Bloodbath in Northern Ireland

The "Bloody Sunday" shootings by a British force provoke an international outcry.

🔴 Youths subject a British army vehicle to a hail of stones during the Bloody Sunday confrontation.

In the Northern Ireland city of Derry (Londonderry to Ulster unionists), British army paratroopers entered the republican Bogside area and opened fire on civil rights demonstrators. Fourteen people were killed. The army declared that they had been under sustained gun and nail-bomb attack from the Irish Republican Army (IRA) and had fired only in self-defense. But no soldiers were injured, and local civil rights activists insisted that the shootings were unprovoked murder and that the demonstrators had been unarmed. A judicial report from Lord Chief Justice Widgery in April exonerating the paratroopers was greeted with considerable skepticism, even in Britain.

British troops had been deployed in Northern Ireland in 1969 to quell sectarian violence and were initially welcomed by the Catholic, republican population as protectors, but relations had soured. By early 1972, Catholic-supported civil rights demonstrations regularly ended in confrontations. In Derry, the confrontation was petering out when paratroopers were sent in to make arrests. They were warned that the IRA used such demonstrations as cover for snipers, but the scale of the violence that resulted has never been explained. The consequences were disastrous. There was worldwide condemnation of British actions, and an enraged mob burned down the British Embassy in Dublin. Sectarian hostilities were hardened, the IRA received a major boost in support, and the scene was set for political deadlock and terrorist atrocities that persisted for decades. **JS**

Nixon Meets Mao

The U.S. president pulls off an astonishing diplomatic coup.

When President Richard Nixon flew to meet Mao Zedong, the United States did not even extend diplomatic recognition to the People's Republic of China. A hard-line anticommunist, Nixon appeared an unlikely envoy of goodwill toward communist China. But he had an advantage over previous cold war presidents. Nixon could recognize that the communist world was not the monolithic bloc under the command of Moscow others had assumed. The tensions between Moscow and Beijing had been exposed by fighting along their frontier on the Ussiri River in March 1969. This was a conflict the United States might exploit. Also, Mao could see the advantages of a friendly superpower to counterbalance Soviet hostility. In April 1971 the first hints of changing attitudes were dropped, when Beijing issued a surprise invitation to the U.S. table tennis team to visit China. U.S. spokesmen were soon hinting that the president would be delighted by an invitation himself.

Of course, diplomacy was not spontaneous. U.S. national security adviser Henry Kissinger conducted intense discussions with the Chinese in advance. The major problem was Taiwan, recognized by the United States as having the legitimate government of China and seen by Mao as a rebellious province. As neither side could concede on this matter, a formula to evade the issue had to be agreed. In reality, this prepared the way for the official recognition of the People's Republic, which saw China gaining a permanent seat on the United Nations Security Council. Moscow was the big loser in this diplomatic game, suddenly seeing itself isolated, and was forced to make concessions to the United States over such issues as strategic arms limitation. Nixon's coup led to a significant relaxation of cold war tensions. **JS**

Spies in Watergate

The Watergate break-in is the seed that will lead to President Nixon's downfall.

Richard Nixon's narrow victory in the 1968 U.S. presidential election was greeted with dismay by many liberals and opponents of the Vietnam War. Nixon and his close associates were paranoid about the opposition, and in 1971 a special unit, known as "the plumbers," was set up to spy on and frustrate the machinations of the regime's enemies. Among the spies were Gordon Liddy and Howard Hunt, who had both formerly worked for the CIA. In June 1972 the United States was propelled into an internal crisis when several of the plumbers were arrested in the

> *"Play it rough. That's the way they play it and that's the way we are going to play it."*
>
> **President Nixon to H. R. Haldeman**

Democratic National Committee's headquarters in the Watergate complex, Washington, D.C., where they had installed bugging equipment. Liddy and Hunt were both involved.

People assumed that the president would not have known about it, and in November Nixon was reelected by a huge majority. Investigations by the *Washington Post*, however, were beginning to reveal disquieting information about administration skulduggery. The Watergate plumbers pleaded guilty to burglary and were convicted in January 1973, but one of them wrote to the trial judge to say that the White House had been covering up its role in the affair. It was growing ever clearer that the White House had been involved, and the scandal would ultimately bring President Nixon down. **RC**

Massacre in Munich

Horror visits the Olympic Games's celebration of peace when athletes are taken hostage and their rescue is catastrophically bungled.

Carnage descended on the Munich Olympic Games when a shootout between Munich police and Palestinian terrorists killed all nine of the Israeli athletes who had earlier been taken hostage. Eight members of the Black September organization had entered the Olympic Village, where security measures had been light, and struck at the Israeli residences, killing two athletes before taking their hostages. The terrorists demanded the release of more than 200 Palestinians held in Israeli prisons. West German authorities, aghast at the prospect of more Jewish blood being spilled on German soil, were initially willing to offer the kidnappers an escape route, but in the end made a rescue attempt. This was a fateful decision because, like most police forces in Europe, the Munich police had little experience of terrorism and less of hostage rescue. The attempt was mishandled, with poorly placed snipers, a police team on the aircraft who abandoned its mission, and poor communication. The hostages, one policeman, and five terrorists were killed. Three terrorists were captured, but they did not remain in custody long. A few weeks later, they were released after a German airliner was hijacked by their colleagues.

Controversially, the games went ahead, but the tragedy was a clarion call to the West of the dangers of modern terrorism, and countermeasures were instigated. It also put the Palestinian issue at the center of relations between the West and the Arab world, where it subsequently remained. **JS**

◗ A member of the Palestine Liberation Organization on the balcony of the Israeli athletes' dormitory.

◖ Grieving relatives of the eleven murdered athletes arrive in Munich to receive their coffins.

Abortion Legalized

The Supreme Court's judgment in Roe v. Wade *legalizes abortion in the U.S.*

The feminist movement had steadily gained ground in the United States in the 1960s, alongside the civil rights movement. One factor was the greater independence of women, far more of whom now had jobs outside the home. Another was the new permissive climate that now allowed sexual matters, including abortion, rape, and homosexuality, to be discussed more openly.

In 1971 and 1972, the Supreme Court moved to uphold the equality of women before the law under the Civil Rights Act of 1964. The following year, the court reached a highly controversial judgment in the case of *Roe v. Wade*. The law in Texas, as in most other states, banned abortion except on medical grounds to save the mother's life. Jane Roe was the pseudonym of a young Dallas woman, unmarried and pregnant, who challenged the Texas law's constitutionality. She and other plaintiffs appealed to the Supreme Court against the decision of the Dallas district attorney, Henry Wade, to continue to bring prosecutions in cases of abortion. The court acknowledged the sensitivity of the issue and the strong emotions on both sides, but ruled in effect that, under the Fourteenth Amendment, a woman could not legally be prevented from having an abortion during the first six months of her pregnancy solely on the grounds that her life was not considered to be in danger.

President Carter later stated that, although he was personally opposed to abortion, he also opposed interfering with the Supreme Court's decision. He came under fierce attack from those in the United States who denounced abortion as tantamount to murder, and the issue was a factor in the triumph of the Republicans and Ronald Reagan in 1980. **RC**

Cease-fire in Vietnam

An agreement is reached between the United States and North Vietnam.

The peace talks between U.S. and North Vietnamese officials, aimed at ending the Vietnam War, finally bore fruit after five long years. Massive U.S. bombing campaigns had been launched, and heavy casualties had been inflicted by both sides. All the while antiwar protest within the United States put further pressure on President Nixon to reach a settlement. The aim of the United States had always been to withdraw, but to leave a stable and independent South Vietnam behind. The North Vietnamese wanted the Americans to go, leaving them free to decide the destiny of all of

> ### *"We have concluded an agreement to end the war and bring peace with honor."*
> **President Richard Nixon, January 1973**

Vietnam. The final agreement seemed initially to be in the United States's favor. An immediate cease-fire came into effect. Both sides agreed that the South Vietnamese people had an absolute right of self-determination in their system of government. Reunification of North and South would be addressed only through negotiation.

However, in the agreement, the North Vietnamese forces stationed in the South were not mentioned. This meant they could stay in place and pose a permanent threat to the stability and security of the South. Once it seemed certain that nothing would persuade the Americans to return to Southeast Asia, the North Vietnamese would feel free to brush aside their agreement and reunify the nation by force. In April 1975, this is precisely what happened. **JS**

A Brutal Coup in Chile

Socialist President Allende is ousted from government and the severe regime of General Pinochet descends on Chile.

Salvador Allende was a Marxist from his youth and a founder of the Chilean Socialist Party in 1933. He ran for president several times in the 1950s and 1960s before at last succeeding in 1970 as the candidate of a group calling itself Popular Unity, supported mainly by socialists and communists. Allende put Chile on friendly terms with the communist regimes in Cuba and China, and Fidel Castro paid a long visit to Chile in 1971. But Allende's attempt to make Chile a socialist country seriously weakened the economy and roused such fierce opposition and violence that the president declared in August 1973 that the country was on the brink of civil war. Just how far the United States contributed to Allende's ousting is disputed, but the CIA was certainly authorized to spend millions of dollars trying to bring him down.

Early September saw huge rival demonstrations in Santiago until leaders of the Chilean army, navy, air force, and national police carried out a brutally effective coup. Announcing "the liberation of the fatherland from the Marxist yoke," they arrested many left-wing leaders, took military control of factories and working-class areas in cities, and declared martial law. Trapped in the presidential palace, Allende ordered a white flag to be flown in surrender. Two shots were heard and his dead body was found with a machine gun, allegedly a present from Fidel Castro. All resistance in the palace ceased and General Augusto Pinochet, the head of the army, was proclaimed the country's new president. **RC**

⊘ President Allende photographed in February 1973, seven months before he was murdered.

◗ Salvador Allende on his last day as president—photographed a few hours before the coup overthrew him.

Arabs Strike During Yom Kippur

A surprise attack during the religious holiday leaves Israel reeling.

○ Egyptian soldiers languish under guard after being taken prisoner by Israeli troops during the short-lived Yom Kippur War.

Egyptian and Syrian forces used the Jewish religious festival of Yom Kippur (Day of Atonement) to launch a surprise attack on Israel. Syrian forces pushed into the Golan Heights, while the Egyptians stormed across the Suez Canal into Sinai. In the first few days, the Israelis seemed in desperate trouble, suffering heavy losses and frantically trying to mobilize their reserves. They were to be saved in part by poor coordination between their enemies, a massive airlift of U.S. equipment, and the prompt supply of U.S. intelligence on enemy dispositions. The Syrians were beaten back, and a counterattack across the Suez Canal trapped the Egyptian Third Corps. A cease-fire favorable to Israel was agreed upon less than three weeks after the first shot.

The Yom Kippur War, although short, was important. For Israel it was a warning that the days of easy victories were over. The Arabs had hoped to regain territory lost in 1967, and their failure stung. Importantly, though, they had broken the strategic and diplomatic deadlock that had gripped the region since 1967. The war had threatened to cause a major confrontation between Moscow and Washington, and both wanted to avoid risking renewed hostilities in the region. The Organization of Petroleum Exporting Countries (OPEC) imposed crippling sanctions on the West, convincing Europeans of the need for peace. Even hard-line Israelis recognized that a settlement, at least with their most formidable enemy, Egypt, would have to be negotiated. **JS**

Crude Oil Supplies Halted

OPEC makes the West pay a high price for supporting Israel.

○ A crowd of cars at a Brooklyn, New York, gas station during OPEC's embargo on selling oil to the United States and its allies.

When Israel won victory over its Arab neighbors in the Yom Kippur War, the Arab world struck back. The Organization of Petroleum Exporting Countries (OPEC), the international cartel dominated by Middle East countries, used its oil supplies as a weapon for the first time, announcing a total embargo on the supply of crude oil to the United States. The embargo was soon extended. Western allies faced an immediate 70 percent rise in the price of gasoline, throwing them into economic recession. In reality, OPEC's actions were not simply a show of solidarity with Egypt and Syria, but were based on a deeper resentment against Western exploitation. Western economic growth had been based on cheap energy prices. Crude oil suppliers had long been paid a mere pittance for what was generally their only export. OPEC was formed to enable its members collectively to resist Western pressure to keep their price down. A major price rise, it was argued, was long overdue.

The short-term consequences of OPEC's decision were harsh. The West experienced inflation and economic stagnation. Unemployment rose and gasoline prices quadrupled. The exporters gained vast wealth, much of which remained in the hands of the political elite or was spent on arms. But U.S. support for Israel did not falter, and alternative sources of oil were developed. Within a month, Congress approved the construction of the Trans-Alaskan oil pipeline, capable of delivering two million barrels per day. OPEC's power faded within a decade. **JS**

Carnation Revolution

A left-wing military coup ends the era of authoritarian government in Portugal.

⊙ MFA troops in Lisbon, three days after the coup, wear red carnations as a symbol of Portugal's peaceful revolution.

Shortly after midnight on April 25, 1974, Portugal's state-controlled radio broadcast "Grandola, Vila Morena," a song by folk-protest singer Zeca Afonso. Casual listeners were surprised because the right-wing government of Prime Minister Marcelo Caetano had banned Afonso as an alleged communist. To junior officers in the Portuguese armed forces, however, this was a long-awaited moment: The song was the signal for a revolutionary coup to begin.

In the course of the night, the Movimento das Forças Armadas (MFA) moved to occupy key points throughout the country. The Portuguese people awoke to hear the announcement of a coup and an appeal for calm. Despite instructions from the MFA to stay at home, crowds gathered in the center of Lisbon. Many carried red carnations picked up at the flower market, and hundreds of these were slipped into the barrels of rifles carried by soldiers on the street. The flowers came to symbolize the revolution, carried out with an almost total lack of violence. Caetano fled to Brazil and a respected officer, General António Spínola, was installed in power.

For more than forty years Portugal had stagnated under the "New State" instituted and presided over by António Salazar. It was clinging to an African empire, fighting costly wars against guerrillas in Angola, Mozambique, and Guinea-Bissau. Transition to a new regime would not be easy. Spínola soon fell out with the left-wing MFA, but after a turbulent period the country emerged in 1976 as a liberal democracy. **RG**

Nixon Forced to Resign Over Watergate

Facing impending impeachment, President Nixon resigns.

⭘ President Richard Nixon photographed in the process of delivering his resignation speech on television.

The Senate had set up a committee to investigate the Watergate affair. It discovered that President Nixon possessed tape recordings that revealed his personal involvement. He refused to hand over the tapes and tried to prevent officials from being questioned, but John Dean, one of the president's counsel, told what he knew and implicated two of Nixon's closest aides, John D. Ehrlichmann and H. R. Haldeman. They attempted to deny their own and the president's involvement, but it became apparent that President Nixon had been lying. In July 1974, the Judiciary Committee of the House of Representatives voted to recommend three articles of impeachment.

The game was up and the president resigned. He was succeeded by the vice president, Gerald Ford, who issued Nixon a full pardon. Meanwhile, investigations by Congress, the FBI, and the media had implicated government officials and agencies in a catalog of illegal activities—from campaign "dirty tricks" and fraud to wiretapping—which had involved the employment of the FBI, the CIA, and the tax authorities against the regime's "enemies." Past illegal activities were also brought to light. The CIA was discovered to have plotted the assassination of foreign politicians, including Fidel Castro, and to have been hand in glove with the Mafia. It became clear that lawless underground operations had been going on at top level in the United States for years. Mounting public hostility contributed to the defeat of Ford by Jimmy Carter in the 1976 election. **RC**

Microsoft Founded

So begins a fortune and arguably the greatest accumulation of "soft" power ever.

○ Paul Allen and Bill Gates photographed in 1981 after signing their contract with IBM.

It started in 1975 when a nineteen-year-old Harvard student and his school friend produced a BASIC interpreter for a newly released computer known as the Altair 8800. To concentrate on making it, the two moved to Albuquerque, New Mexico, and formed their company, Micro-soft. The trademark (without the hyphen) was registered in November 1976.

The breakthrough came in 1980 when computer giant IBM approached Microsoft to write an interpreter for their new personal computer (PC). Eventually Microsoft were contracted to supply its operating system, known as MS-DOS. The popularity of the IBM PC and its clones made Microsoft a dominant force in software, a position confirmed by its release of the first version of Windows in 1985.

Many of their products were sold "bundled" with PCs. Soon Microsoft controlled a huge proportion of the world market for computer operating systems, as well as for the software used on personal and business computers. Despite complaints about their stranglehold on the software market, and about flaws in their products, Microsoft went on to achieve an unparalleled global ubiquity.

The two men who founded the company were Bill Gates and Paul Allen. Allen's poor health meant he withdrew from close involvement in Microsoft in the mid-1980s, but he remained a major shareholder. Gates would go on to become the world's wealthiest man, whereas Allen would merely be one of the richest in the United States. **PF**

Pol Pot Takes Control in Cambodia

The Khmer Rouge takes Phnom Penh and begins to exact revenge on its opponents.

○ Khmer Rouge guerrillas drive a jeep through the streets of Phnom Penh on the day they took control of Cambodia.

Carpet-bombing of Cambodian territory by U.S. forces in an attempt to cut supply routes used by the Viet Cong guerrillas against South Vietnam seriously destabilized the country in the early 1970s. This, combined with the end of U.S. aid to the Cambodian government after the cease-fire in Vietnam in 1973, helped the communist guerillas of the Khmer Rouge to finally take the nation's capital, Phnom Penh. When the Khmer Rouge began their offensive in January, resistance soon crumbled. By February, they had taken control of the banks of the Mekong River and cut supplies to the capital. As food and ammunition ran out, government resistance collapsed.

Initially it was hoped that the Khmer Rouge would rule moderately. Such hopes were soon dashed. The Khmer Rouge leader, Pol Pot, announced the arrival of Year Zero, marking a complete break with the past. The Cambodian people were to establish the perfect revolutionary society, which to Pol Pot meant a peasant society. Cities were cleared of their inhabitants. They found themselves enslaved and starving in gigantic collective farms. Money, education, private property, and religion were forbidden. In its short life, Pol Pot's regime murdered between one and three million of its own people. But it was not its murderous criminality that brought down the regime, but its hostility toward the Vietnamese. An invasion in December 1978 forced the Khmer Rouge back into the mountains, where they mounted a renewed guerrilla war. **JS**

U.S. Withdrawal

The United States evacuates Saigon, leaving South Vietnam to its fate.

The largest helicopter-born evacuation in history took place when the United States withdrew its embassy from Saigon as North Vietnamese forces closed in on the city. Thousands of South Vietnamese citizens who had supported the United States's presence in South Vietnam were also evacuated, but many thousands more were left behind. South Vietnam had in reality been living on borrowed time. Since the cease-fire of January 1973, which had left North Vietnamese troops in position in the South, only the threat of a U.S. return had prevented their

"The options before us are few. . . . We cannot . . . abandon our friends."

President Gerald Ford, April 1975

final push to reunify the country. When, in 1974, U.S. aid to the South was substantially reduced, it was clear there was no such commitment. The northern offensive was launched in December 1974, and southern forces were soon in a desperate position.

Despite the appeals of President Gerald Ford, it was clear that Congress would never sanction the redeployment of U.S. forces. This open abandonment was in itself enough to destroy South Vietnamese morale. Although North Vietnamese forces made no attempt to prevent the U.S. evacuation, pictures of frantic South Vietnamese crowds desperately trying to enter the U.S. Embassy and get a seat on a flight out came to symbolize a humbled superpower. The most powerful military force in the world had been defeated by a lightly armed peasant army. **JS**

Thrilla in Manila

Muhammad Ali rewrites the rules of professional boxing.

One of the most famous boxing matches of all time was the rematch between the two former world champions, Smokin' Joe Frazier and the thirty-three-year-old Muhammad Ali. On the two previous occasions, in 1971 and 1974, each boxer had won one fight, so all was square.

Ali had been recognized as an exceptional boxer since 1960, when he won an Olympic gold medal, as Cassius Clay. However, his cock-sure personality and outspoken style led to him being denounced by some whites. This view was reinforced for many when he converted to Islam and abandoned his "slave name." He then refused to serve in the U.S. Army, for which he was stripped of his title in 1967.

The rivalry between the two fighters had begun well before the first match, when Ali represented those who opposed the Vietnam War and Frazier the pro-war establishment. Ali arrived at the match somewhat underprepared. Frazier, on the other hand, was resentful of the verbal abuse he had received from Ali (who had called him a "white man's champion" and suggested he was no more than a gorilla) and had trained determinedly.

The grudge contest began with an onslaught from Ali, but Frazier withstood it and continued to come forward as Ali began to tire. After the tenth round, however, with both boxers virtually exhausted, Ali was able to reassert his authority. In the fourteenth, Frazier boxed practically blind, resolutely refusing to throw in the towel, but the fight was stopped at the end of the round. After his historic victory, Ali himself collapsed from exhaustion. **PF**

○ Frazier takes a blow to the head as Ali begins the determined onslaught that eventually brings the fight to a close.

Spain Embraces Democracy

Juan Carlos I is crowned king of Spain as years of dictatorship come to an end.

🅞 Crowds in Madrid read of Franco's death; on his deathbed the dictator asked the Spanish people to support the new king.

> *"[To restore democracy and become] King of all Spaniards without exception."*

Juan Carlos, first speech to Parliament, 1975

When Juan Carlos came to the throne in 1975, Spain had been living in a postwar time warp thanks to the longevity of its dictator, Franco, and the country was facing serious problems. The centralized economy was badly exposed by the worldwide economic recession and further hit when Britain, Spain's major trading partner, joined the EU in 1973. Soaring domestic inflation hit the normally quiescent middle class hard, and unrest among university students and manual workers became vociferous. Workers attempted to establish trade unions to protect their rights against the state-controlled syndicates. Opposition to U.S. air bases in Spain was also vocal (it was in U.S. interests to support the fascist status quo against communism). A large body of priests openly supported worker demonstrations, encouraged by the social teachings of Pope John XXIII. Meanwhile ETA, the militant Basque separatist movement, stepped up its campaign of violence and allegedly assassinated Franco's vice president, Carrero Blanco, in 1973. This, coupled with the overthrow of the friendly fascist regime in Portugal in 1974, put further pressure on Franco's ailing health. Prime Minister Carlos Arias Navarro, an archconservative, only exacerbated the situation by dithering over reform.

In a sense, Franco's death on November 20, 1975, was merely the prelude. He had already named his successor six years earlier, Juan Carlos de Borbón, the son of the legitimate heir to the throne, Juan de Borbón. Juan Carlos was considered a supporter of Franco's policies and had sworn an oath of allegiance to the fascist party (El Movimiento National). But he also held aspirations toward reform. The shift would not happen overnight, however, despite the opening up of political debate and party activity for the first time since the 1930s. **JJH**

Apple Computer Company Founded

Apple Inc. challenges Microsoft's dominance of the world of computing.

Apple was founded in 1976 by Steve Wozniak, an electronics hobbyist working for Hewlett-Packard in Silicon Valley, near San Francisco, and Steve Jobs, then a video games designer. Wozniak designed a computer for his personal use on an integrated circuit board, and Jobs persuaded him they should produce a commercial model. In April 1976, they set up a company, the Apple Computer Co., to do just that.

The name was chosen to be at the head of the alphabetical list of computer companies, ahead of the much larger Atari. Their first product, produced in Jobs's bedroom and garage, was the Apple I, one of the first personal computers to reach the market. It incorporated novel features, including a TV display and a keyboard, and sold for $666.66. An updated version, the Apple II, came out the following year, with higher-resolution graphics allowing the display of pictures.

In January 1984, they released the first version of the Apple Macintosh, a computer with a monitor in a single box. It incorporated a "graphical user interface" and a mouse at a time when PCs used the more unfriendly DOS operating system. The Apple Macintosh was sold as a direct and more stylish competitor to the cheaper PC, and from this time onward, Apple generated and sustained a solid reputation for well-designed—though niche— products, employing the vertical integration of hardware and software that made them particularly attractive within the creative industries.

In April 1981, Wozniak was involved in a plane crash that left him with temporary amnesia. Sadly, he was obliged to give up his position as Apple's product development supremo. He left full-time employment at Apple in 1987. Jobs left Apple in 1986, but returned to become its chief executive officer in 1997. **PF**

○ Steve Jobs demonstrates a chess game on the monitor of an Apple II computer in 1979.

> *" . . . everything an apple represents, healthy, personal, in the home."*
>
> **Steve Wozniak**

Student Protests in Soweto

South African police overreact to student demonstrations concerning the use of the Afrikaans language in schools.

What was intended as a peaceful student rally in the scattered townships of Soweto ended in violence and saw twenty-three people killed. The object of the students' protests was the 1974 Afrikaans Medium decree. The South African government, alarmed at the declining use of Afrikaans—the language of white settlers of Dutch origin—had ordered that the language must be used to teach half of the subjects in all schools. Not only was Afrikaans a language of limited practical use, but it was widely seen as the language of the oppressor. In April, the students at Orlando West Junior School had gone on strike over the issue, and protests had spread. The rally was secretly planned and took the police by surprise. Tear gas was deployed, which was answered by stone-throwing. The police fired random shots.

Some form of challenge to apartheid should have been expected. The victories of nationalist movements, such as Frelimo in Mozambique in 1975, showed that it was possible for Africans to defeat white colonial rulers. Within South Africa, there was a new spirit of defiance and self-confidence among the young. The language issue, representing as it did the frustrations and resentments felt by African youths, politically mobilized an entire generation. South African security forces were never again able to impose the peace and stability previously known. The struggle for liberation had begun in earnest. By the end of the year, up to 700 people had been killed in civil upheavals. South Africa was facing worldwide condemnation, tightening boycotts, and growing economic instability. **JS**

○ Rocks in hand, schoolchildren in Soweto take to the streets to join the rioting.

Victory at Entebbe

Israeli commandos show the world how they deal with hostage takers.

In a spectacular display of military skill, Israeli commandos ended the hostage drama at Uganda's Entebbe airport. The drama began a week earlier when four militants, two from the Popular Front for the Liberation of Palestine (PFLP) and two from Germany's Red Army Faction, hijacked an Air France airliner en route from Israel to Paris. When it arrived at Entebbe, it was met by Ugandan dictator Idi Amin, who gave a speech in support of the PFLP. The militants released most passengers, but kept the Israeli citizens and those with Jewish names. They

"This operation will certainly be inscribed in the annals of military history . . ."

Israeli Prime Minister Yitzhak Rabin, July 1976

demanded the release of fifty-three other militants held in five different countries and threatened to kill the hostages, now held in the airport building. The Israeli military swiftly planned their response.

Three Hercules transport aircraft, carrying about 200 soldiers, swept down on the airport. They immediately stormed the airport building. All the militants and some twenty Ugandan soldiers were killed. The Israelis suffered a single fatality, their commander, Lieutenant Colonel Yonatan Netanyahu. They destroyed eleven MiG 17 fighters on the ground to prevent pursuit and flew back to Israel via Nairobi, where some of the wounded were hospitalized. The dazzling success of the raid was to be a source of enormous pride to Israelis. For Amin it was widely seen as the beginning of the end of his dictatorship. **JS**

Salute to Modernity

The Centre Pompidou arts center opens its doors in Paris.

The long-awaited and much-criticized Centre Pompidou, which opened in the Beaubourg area of Paris in 1977, was the brainchild of Georges Pompidou (French president from 1969 to 1974), who wanted to create a modern space into which visual arts, music, theater, cinema, and literature could be brought together and enjoyed by all. The main architects, Renzo Piano and Richard and Susan Rogers, were relatively unknown, but their design was definitely innovatory.

To maximize space in the building, which reached seven floors, electricity cables, water pipes, and the like were confined to brightly colored pipes on the outside of the building. Escalators also ran on the outside, in clear plastic tubes, offering magnificent views of Paris. Critics described the building as having been turned inside out, whereas admirers lavished praise on the vision and radicalism of the design.

The center housed a huge public library, which eventually covered three floors. There was also a museum of modern art that grew to hold 50,000 works, a center for music, a conference center, and restaurants and children's areas. The plaza outside became a popular meeting area for Parisians and a venue famous for street performers. It had been intended as a place where people of all ages and backgrounds could equally enjoy modern culture. In many ways, it must be judged successful. It became the most popular tourist attraction in Paris, averaging 25,000 visitors every day. In fact, it was so popular that during the 1990s, it had to close for more than two years for renovations, which included moving offices outside to enlarge the display areas. If many continue to hate it, it has nonetheless become an international icon to the modern world. **JS**

Star Wars Opens

The first installment in George Lucas's epic saga is released in U.S. theaters.

George Lucas, one of a group of Hollywood brats (the rising generation of ambitious directors that included Steven Spielberg and Francis Ford Coppola), wrote and directed the space fantasy adventure which has become one of the most successful and influential film concepts of all time. It was also the first of six films in the series to be made (though the fourth in the narrative sequence). The films were released in the form of two trilogies, the first of which comprised *Star Wars* (later renamed *Star Wars: A New Hope*), *Star Wars: The Empire Strikes Back* (1980), and *Star Wars: Return of the Jedi* (1983). The second trilogy was released between 1999 and 2005.

Lucas, inspired by a wide range of mythological and action stories in print and on film, conceived the idea of Star Wars in 1974 but found it hard to find a Hollywood studio willing to invest in the project until Twentieth Century Fox took it on. Though primarily adventure films, the stories are dressed up with pop psychology and pseudo-mythology. Much of this centers on the concept of a mysterious omnipresent Force, an epic conflict between good (embodied by the main character Luke Skywalker) and evil (embodied by Darth Vader, who turns out to be Skywalker's father), and the cult of the Jedi Knights, a cosmic force for good.

The concept of Star Wars moved from popular culture to international politics in March 1983 when U.S. president Ronald Reagan announced a futuristic plan for a space-based defence system, the Strategic Defence Initiative, against the threat of Soviet missile attack. Requiring much untried technology, this was dubbed Star Wars by those who believed it would exist only in the realm of science fiction. **PF**

Death of Elvis Presley

The "King of Rock 'n' Roll" dies of a heart attack at home in Graceland.

The "King of Rock 'n' Roll"—or just "The King"—died ignominiously at the age of forty-two, bloated with junk food, painkillers, sleeping pills, and sedatives, on his bathroom floor at Graceland, his estate in Memphis, Tennessee. The cause of death was given as cardiac arrhythmia. For years he had suffered a range of bowel and liver disorders.

The next day, 50,000 people flocked to the house, where mourners were permitted into the hall to view the body in its copper coffin. The same day, twenty million copies of his records were sold.

> ## "Elvis Presley's death deprives our country of a part of itself."
> **President Jimmy Carter, 1977**

Although he was initially buried next to his mother, the grave was tampered with the following month and thereafter the coffin was moved to the grounds of Graceland. Meanwhile, some fans claimed he had not died but gone into hiding, and Elvis sightings were reported for years across the United States.

Elvis had continued recording and performing until shortly before his death. The boy from Mississippi had been the ultimate symbol of teenage rebellion and unfettered sexuality in the 1950s. He had brought black music to the attention of millions of white youngsters and had become a rhinestone icon of conservative America, campaigning against what he saw as the dangerous influence of the Beatles. A television broadcast in 1973 was said to have had a larger global audience than the moon landing. **PF**

Steve Biko Dies in Police Custody

South African police deny murdering the anti-apartheid activist Steve Biko while he was in police custody in Pretoria.

When the internationally respected anti-apartheid activist Steve Biko died in police custody in Pretoria, his was the twentieth such death in eighteen months. Biko had become politically active as a medical student at the University of Natal and was expelled because of it. An articulate speaker and writer, Biko preached nonviolent resistance to apartheid, but still fell foul of the security services. In March 1973, he was issued with a banning order. This meant his movements were restricted, he was forbidden to publish or even to speak to more than one person at a time, and nobody was permitted to quote his words. His influence was such, though, that he was still seen as an inspiration to the protests that led to the 1976 Soweto riots.

In August 1977, he was arrested at a police roadblock and charged with terrorist offenses. He was kept naked and chained in a cell in Port Elizabeth, until he was rushed to Pretoria for medical treatment, where he died. The police claimed his death was the result of a hunger strike, but he was found to have massive head injuries consistent with a savage beating. Any wounds he suffered, the police insisted, must have been self-inflicted. The South African Attorney General judged that, as there were no witnesses, there were no grounds to charge any police officer with his death. This did not save South Africa from international condemnation. More to the point, however, South African attempts to cow opposition failed. Biko's main message, that Africans must be proud, still served to inspire resistance long after his death. **JS**

◐ A protester at the gates to the Palace of Justice, Pretoria, where a judicial inquiry was held into the death of Biko.

Smallpox Conquered

The last case of naturally occurring smallpox is confined and cured.

One of the great scourges of humankind, smallpox, became the first disease officially to have been wiped out across the world—at least as a naturally occurring disease. This has been described as the greatest single medical achievement in a century that saw extraordinary advances.

Twenty years earlier smallpox was endemic in about twenty-five countries and there were ten million cases a year across the world, half of them in India. In 1958 the World Health Organization called for a campaign against the disease. The project began in earnest in 1967 and included surveillance to spot new outbreaks quickly, containment or isolation of those with the disease, and widespread vaccination. Progress was quickly made in Latin America and West and Central Africa, but South Asia and especially India proved initially reluctant, partly because of the cost. The obstacles were cleared by the early 1970s, and in 1975 officials were surprised to find India had already achieved "smallpox zero" status. In October 1977 the last case occurred in Africa, in Somalia, when Ali Maow Maalin, a twenty-three-year-old hospital cook, contracted the disease. Almost 55,000 people were vaccinated in the two weeks after his diagnosis; the outbreak was confined, and Maalin recovered.

The final WHO declaration that the world was smallpox-free was made in May 1980. The entire program cost a little more than $300 million, and the savings in medical costs were enormous. Ironically, however, small stocks of smallpox virus were kept by several countries, partly to make vaccines in case the disease were to recur and partly to make biological weapons. Fear that these might become available to terrorist organizations or "rogue states" abounded in the early 2000s. **PF**

Camp David Talks

An agreement at Camp David appears to offer a solution to the Middle East conflict.

When Jimmy Carter assumed the U.S. presidency in January 1977, he gave peace in the Middle East his highest priority. The real breakthrough came with the Egyptian president Anwar Al Sadat's startling visit to Israel in November 1977, which at least implied diplomatic recognition of that country. This opened the way for bilateral negotiations. Subsequent talks were held at Camp David in September 1978, and Carter played a crucial role in refusing to allow negotiations to fail. The biggest stumbling block was the Palestinian territory of the West Bank and the

> *" . . . this area can become a model for coexistence and cooperation among nations."*
>
> **Camp David Accords, September 1978**

Gaza Strip. The Israeli prime minister, Manachem Begin, was willing to restore the Sinai Peninsula to Egypt in return for a peace treaty, but was obdurate in his refusal to leave these occupied lands. Eventually, Sadat decided to pursue Egyptian national interests rather than wider Arab interests. Two main documents were produced, which provided a framework for peace between Egypt and Israel, in which the Sinai was returned in exchange for a peace treaty in 1979.

A wider framework for the Middle East talked of some form of autonomy for Palestinians at some point. The Israelis gained much—without Egypt, no hostile coalition could threaten their survival—but this did not provide peace on other borders. Sadat was accused of betraying the Arab cause and was assassinated by Islamists in October 1981. **JS**

Mass Suicide at Jonestown

The mass suicide in Guyana of the Jonestown cult known as the People's Temple Christian Church shocks and bewilders the United States.

In Jonestown, Guyana, 913 U.S. citizens, led by Jim Jones, committed mass suicide. The dead made up virtually the entire cult known as the People's Temple Christian Church and included 276 children. The People's Temple had been in decline until Jones moved it to San Francisco in 1972, where the cult became racially mixed and undertook considerable charity work. However, its newfound preeminence was accompanied by scandals and eventually an investigation for tax evasion. In response, Jones leased a stretch of jungle in Guyana and built Jonestown.

Grueling labor and an inadequate diet caused discontent within the cult. It was alleged that Jones used a regime combining drugs, intimidation, and brutal punishments to keep the disaffected in line. There were rumors that some members had been murdered for trying to desert. Hearing this, Leo Ryan, a U.S. congressman, began an investigation and led a group of representatives from the media, the government, and families to Jonestown.

Reports of what followed are confused, but it seems that several cult members insisted on leaving with Ryan. However, when the party reached the local airstrip, they were attacked and Ryan and four others were killed. Thereupon most of the cult docilely lined up and committed suicide by taking a cocktail of Valium and cyanide. Only a handful fled; some were shot in the attempt. That a cult leader could exercise such domination appalled the United States and did much to discredit cults everywhere. **JS**

◒ People's Temple follower Larry Layton standing with police following his arrest for the shootings on the local airstrip.

◓ The deaths occurred in bizarre circumstances; Jonestown is the largest mass suicide in modern history.

Ayatollah Khomeini Returns

Exiled cleric Ayatollah Khomeini returns to lead the Iranian revolution.

○ After fifteen years in exile, Ayatollah Ruhollah Khomeini arrives back in Teheran.

The Ayatollah, Ruhollah Khomeini, returned to a delirious welcome in Teheran. He had long been at the forefront of Islamic opposition to Shah Muhammed Reza Pahlavi. He had denounced the shah's so-called "white revolution" in 1963, which involved land reform, enfranchising women, and allowing non-Muslims to hold government office. He was exiled in November 1964, eventually residing in Paris. From there he launched a ceaseless bombardment of tracts and sermons against the shah, which were banned in Iran but still widely circulated and increasingly influential. By the late 1970s political opposition was widespread, and increasingly the shah relied on oppression to survive. But by January 1979, amid mass protests and growing

chaos, even this would no longer suffice. The shah announced that he and his family were leaving Iran for a holiday. It was really his abdication.

It was unclear how the Iranian revolution would proceed. Islamists had certainly been at the forefront of the opposition. But so had liberals, socialists, and even communists, and many wanted democracy and a secular state. The flight of the shah had left a provisional government under a secularist, Shapoor Bakhtiar. But Khomeini was determined to be the sole arbiter of Iran's fate. He named his own follower, Mehdi Bazargan, as a rival prime minister and announced that any who defied him were defying Allah. He swept aside Bakhtiar and set Iran firmly on the road toward becoming an Islamic theocracy. **JS**

Breakdown at Three Mile Island

The most alarming nuclear power accident in U.S. history occurs in Pennsylvania.

⊙ There was a great deal of confusion around the issue of evacuation, and some women and children moved to a local sports center.

No one seems to have discovered exactly why, but at 4 A.M., the main feedwater pumps in the Unit 2 reactor at the Three Mile Island plant near Middletown, Pennsylvania, failed. The emergency pumps also failed and the supply of water transferring heat from the water circulating in the reactor core was cut off. The core closed down automatically, but a succession of instrument malfunctions and human errors caused a substantial loss of the water cooling the core. The core itself began to melt and give off radioactive gases.

Surprisingly little radioactivity escaped into the atmosphere and the accident caused no immediate ill effects. None of the plant workers nor the 25,000 people living within 5 miles (8 km) suffered any harm, and evacuation plans were deemed unnecessary.

The accident was frightening all the same, and seven other similar nuclear reactors were immediately closed, temporarily. President Carter ordered an investigation, as did the Pennsylvania House of Representatives. The authorization of new nuclear reactors was halted for the time being and the incident cast a pall over the U.S. nuclear industry for years. The Unit 1 reactor at Three Mile Island, which had not been affected, was not restarted until 1985, and the attempt to repair Unit 2 was given up in 1990 because it was still too unsafe to walk into.

The accident inevitably heightened fears about nuclear power in the United States and elsewhere. It stimulated public opposition and strengthened the arm of the antinuclear protesters. **RC**

Thatcher Elected Prime Minister

Margaret Thatcher becomes the first woman to enter Downing Street as prime minister of the United Kingdom.

When Margaret Thatcher outmaneuvered her political colleagues to win the leadership of the Conservative Party in 1975, she became the first woman party leader in British politics. Four years later, aged fifty-three, she made even greater waves by leading the Conservatives into government to become the first woman elected prime minister in European history.

With the support of her wealthy businessman husband, Dennis Thatcher, she assiduously pursued politics, eventually being elected to Parliament in 1959. Although rising in the 1970s to become minister for education and science in Ted Heath's government, she had hardly looked like a leader in waiting.

Now she had to take on Prime Minister Callaghan and the Labour Party. Thatcher cleverly articulated the middle classes' despair of the power of the unions, high inflation, growing unemployment, and the perceived failure of Britain as a superpower. A giant billboard campaign featuring a picture of a long line of unemployed people shuffling under a slogan "Labour Isn't Working" proved particularly effective. Mrs. Thatcher also promised to cut income tax, reduce public expenditure, make it easier for people to buy their own homes, and curb the power of the unions.

Despite her slick campaign, her popularity ratings were to fall. This has led to speculation that Mrs. Thatcher did not win the election because of her popularity, but rather inherited it because of Labour's overwhelming unpopularity. **JJH**

◗ Margaret Thatcher is all smiles as she arrives at her new home; she was yet to build her reputation as the "Iron Lady."

◗ In Chelsea, London, Thatcher celebrates the first of her three general election victories.

Proud Pilgrimage

The Polish pope makes a triumphant return to his homeland.

Pope John Paul II, the first Polish pope and the first non-Italian to hold that office since 1522, knelt and kissed the ground when he landed at Okecie military air base in his native land. Two million cheering Poles lined his route to Warsaw, where he celebrated an open Mass before 250,000 more.

Born Karol Jósef Wojtyła, in Wadowice near Krakow in 1920, he had been a talented sportsman with aspirations to be an actor and playwright in his youth. German occupation in 1939 transformed his life. He found his vocation and began his theological

---

"It was like a carnival, a . . . campaign, a crusade, and an enormous Polish wedding."

Time magazine, June 1979

---

studies secretly in 1942. He was ordained in 1946 and, after rapid promotion, by 1967 he was cardinal.

The election of a Polish pope at this particular time was to be a fateful decision. The peoples of Eastern Europe were growing impatient with the economic and political stagnation of communist rule. There was a yearning for change. The Polish government's welcome to the pope was ambivalent. They hardly desired to give such a harsh critic a hero's welcome, but could hardly refuse him one. He insisted his visit was purely spiritual, but he obviously realized its political importance. The Catholic Church received a huge boost in popularity and confidence. The pope's visit has also been credited with inspiring the formation of the independent trade union Solidarność (Solidarity) in August 1980. **JS**

U.S. Embassy Stormed

In an illegal act, the Ayatollah Khomeini's followers seize the U.S. embassy in Iran.

A shouting mob of Iranian students, all fanatical followers of the Ayatollah Khomeini, stormed the U.S. embassy in Teheran, where they took hostage sixty-six diplomats and embassy staff. The crisis arose after the administration of Jimmy Carter allowed the deposed shah, Muhammad Reza Pahlavi, to enter the United States to seek medical treatment for cancer. The shah had been a loyal ally to Washington, but this step incensed public opinion in Iran, where his return for trial and execution was demanded.

The students, publicly supported by the ayatollah once it was clear that no immediate military retaliation would follow, demanded the return of the shah and his wealth and an admission of past U.S. misdeeds against Iran, along with an apology and an undertaking not to repeat them. Most of the women and African-American hostages were released, but fifty-two were held hostage for 444 days.

This was a terrible humiliation for Carter, who could do little beyond freezing Iranian assets in the United States. In April 1980, U.S. Special Forces launched Operation Eagle Claw, an ill-conceived rescue attempt that ended in confusion and tragedy, with aircraft colliding and eight U.S. servicemen killed. To the Iranians, this was divine intervention.

The ayatollah used the crisis to brush aside opponents and establish an Islamic theocracy in Iran. To Carter, it was the final blow to his credibility, and he lost the presidential elections a few months later by a landslide. Eventually, to secure the release of the hostages, the Americans were obliged to pledge noninterference in Iranian affairs and unfreeze the Iranian assets on U.S. soil. The hostages were released on January 20, 1981, which was also the last day of Carter's office as U.S. president. **JS**

Soviet Intervention in Afghanistan

The Soviet invasion of Afghanistan begins a dangerous adventure.

○ Soldiers from the Mujaheddin stand on an abandoned Soviet helicopter.

The Soviet invasion of Afghanistan opened a new battleground in the cold war. The U.S.S.R.'s involvement began in 1978, when the pro-Soviet People's Democratic Party of Afghanistan (PDPA) seized power in a coup d'etat. Determined to erase feudalism, the PDPA rode roughshod over the religious sensitivities and traditions of rural Afghans. An Islamic backlash soon reduced the country to chaos, and it looked like the PDPA was unlikely to survive. This was a problem for Moscow. The Iranian revolution of 1979 was a stark warning of the dangers of Islamic fundamentalism, which unchecked might spread to the Islamic peoples of Soviet republics, such as Uzbekistan and Turkmenistan. Intervention could be risky, but a pro-Soviet regime in Afghanistan could act as a buffer state against Islam. The decision was made to invade, install a leader in Babrak Karmal, and withdraw.

Military operations were successful, but Moscow had made political miscalculations. The first Mujaheddin (resistance) groups appeared, and the United States was eager to arm them. Volunteers from across the Islamic world (including Osama bin Laden) flocked to fight in this jihad (holy war). Soviet forces were bogged down in a guerrilla war. The increasingly obvious failure of the Soviet military discredited the regime in Moscow and played a crucial role in the eventual downfall of the Soviet Union. The war also spread, and helped to unify an Islamic fundamentalism that was as hostile to the Americans as it was to the Soviets. **JS**

Strike in Gdańsk Shipyard

The solidarity of Polish workers issues a dramatic challenge to communist rule.

○ Strike leader Lech Wałęsa speaks to supporters at the gate of the Lenin shipyard in Gdańsk, Poland.

In the Lenin Shipyard, Gdańsk, simmering resentments finally came to a head with an unofficial and illegal strike. Workers demanded pay rises and improved family allowances. An electrician, Lech Wałęsa, soon emerged as leader of the strikers. He persuaded the strikers to keep occupying the shipyard and, with the help of the Catholic Church, turned the strike into a national campaign with the foundation of a new, independent trade union, Solidarność (Solidarity). Through Solidarity, a general strike was organized and demands for political freedom were articulated alongside economic grievances. Poland was in turmoil, and the government began to negotiate.

The mere existence of Solidarity was, however, a challenge to communist rule. The Communist Party claimed to stand for the working class, but was now being repudiated by it. This was unacceptable in Moscow, and Soviet leaders made it clear that if the Polish authorities did not restore order, they would. Fearing an invasion, army leader General Wojciech Jaruzelski became premier in December and imposed martial law. Solidarity was banned, thousands were arrested, and several were killed in clashes with the security services. But an underground movement survived, and Solidarity continued to hold the loyalty of ordinary Poles. Jaruzelski's government enjoyed little popular support, and by 1989, unable to implement needed reforms, he began negotiations with Solidarity, unwittingly beginning the process of dismantling communist rule in Poland. **JS**

John Lennon Killed in New York

The former Beatle and prominent campaigner for world peace is shot dead.

○ Thousands of fans and peace campaigners gather in New York to hold a vigil for John Lennon.

John Lennon was struggling to free himself from some of the frustrations of his relationship with Paul McCartney, engaging in peace campaigning, primal scream therapy, and life as a househusband, when he was assassinated by a fan. Having been half of the most successful song-writing partnership in history and, with the Beatles, having turned pop music into a global phenomenon, Lennon set about destroying his achievements by forming a partnership with Japanese-American performance artist Yoko Ono. The boys' club of the band could not withstand this demanding female interloper, and by the time the Beatles formally split in 1970, Lennon and Ono had married and formed a new creative and domestic partnership based in New York.

At 10:50 P.M. on December 8, 1980, Lennon was returning to the Dakota apartments in New York when he was approached by a fan, Mark David Chapman, for whom he had signed an autograph just a few hours previously. Chapman called out to Lennon and shot him four times in the back—the singer was dead on arrival at the hospital.

Chapman, who claimed he had heard voices telling him to kill Lennon, read a copy of J. D. Salinger's *Catcher in the Rye* while he waited for the police to arrive, and said later that he identified strongly with the book's main character, Holden Caulfield. He pleaded guilty and was sentenced to life imprisonment. Three weeks after Lennon's death, "(Just Like) Starting Over" hit the top of the charts. **PF**

"Gang of Four" Face Trial

The trial of four Mao supporters in China marks the end of the Cultural Revolution.

○ Wang Hongwen admits his crimes in court while Jiang Qing maintains her innocence.

The "Gang of Four," put on trial in 1981 for "anti-Party activities," comprised Mao Zedong's widow, Jiang Qing, and her associates Wang Hongwen, Zhang Chunqiao, and Yao Wenyuan. They rose to prominence as Mao's faithful supporters during China's Cultural Revolution, which began in 1966, and became closely associated with the violence and chaos that ensued. Among the party hierarchs they persecuted was Deng Xiaoping, who was purged, whereas his son Deng Pufang was tortured. Deng proved to be a vengeful man and returned to the hierarchy in 1973 as Mao's health began to decline. In the confused political in-fighting that followed, Deng emerged as the victor. The four were arrested in October 1976, after Mao's death, accused of attempting to seize power. In their trial, Jiang was notably defiant and, along with Zhang, denied all charges. Wang and Yao confessed and repented. It made little difference. All were given long prison sentences but were released a few years later, their power destroyed.

In reality, the trial marked the rejection of permanent revolution in China. Deng recognized that the nation needed stability and prosperity. From 1978, he introduced a "socialist market economy," which in fact meant abandoning Mao's ideology, but without admitting it, and retaining political power in the hands of the Chinese Communist Party. Criticisms of Mao were permitted, and China developed the fastest-growing economy in the world. Yet political freedom was never permitted. **JS**

First Personal PC

IBM starts manufacturing its personal computer and it is an instant success.

One of the most important innovations of the twentieth century was the computer. It gradually progressed from an enormous, unwieldy machine to a small personal computer that could be used in offices and at home. A key event in this development was the introduction by the International Business Machine (IBM) company of a new personal computer in 1981. The computer, named the 5150 was not the first of its breed by any means, but IBM's solid reputation for quality and reliability made it a strong seller and gave the use of personal computers a powerful boost. They were no longer a trendy fad, but something people increasingly thought they ought to have.

IBM had a history in this general field. It created the world's first floppy disk in 1967 and in 1975 unveiled its 5100 portable computer, which was probably the first self-contained portable computer system. Around 1980, the company marketed its Datamaster all-in-one desktop word processor. Like the 5100, it was expensive (around $15,000) and sales were low. The 5150 was a different story altogether. It was reasonably affordable at around $3,000 and it offered more memory than its rivals, whose makers promptly began copying it, producing what were initially known as "IBM clones" and later simply as PCs. In August 1982, after a year of manufacturing, the two hundred thousandth model was shipped out.

The first 5150 contained the Intel 8088 CPU (central processing unit), a single floppy disk drive, and 64 KB of RAM and was the brainchild of engineer Don Estridge. The decision to supply the computer with Microsoft's DOS operating system was the foundation for that company's domination of the software market. **RC**

Falklands Invaded

The Argentine invasion of a British dependency proves a desperate gamble.

For Argentina's military junta under Leopoldo Galtieri, the invasion of the Falkland Islands in 1982 seemed the ideal opportunity to divert attention from severe economic problems and mounting internal unrest. Sovereignty over the Falkland Islands, a British dependency in the South Atlantic known to the Argentineans as the Malvinas, had been disputed since the nineteenth century. Negotiations between the two countries had opened in 1965, but the British did not show any real interest in reaching a solution. In 1981, however, Britain's last naval presence was withdrawn, and a new bill in Parliament suggested full British citizenship for the 1,800 islanders would be withdrawn.

Galtieri surmised that regaining the Malvinas for Argentina would give the junta immense popularity. The British, it seemed, had no interest in the islands and would accept a military fait accompli. This was a serious miscalculation. Britain's prime minister, Margaret Thatcher, was at the time deeply unpopular for her divisive economic reforms. She, too, could gain popularity at home through a successful military operation. Urged on by a Royal Navy eager to prove its current value, she sent a naval task force to re-conquer the islands.

The seventy-four-day conflict ended in a decisive defeat for Argentina. It left more than 900 British and Argentinean servicemen killed and 2,000 wounded. Some 11,000 Argentinean soldiers surrendered. The Argentinean junta could not survive the humiliation, and democracy returned in 1983. Thatcher also won a landslide election victory that year. **JS**

○ An explosion on board the HMS *Antelope* on May 24 during an attempt to defuse an undetonated bomb.

Massacre in Beirut

Israel denies complicity in the butchery of Palestinians at refugee camps.

🌑 Innocent victims were ruthlessly gunned down, stabbed, or hacked to death and their bodies left to rot in the searing heat.

The civil war in Lebanon, which first began in 1975, plumbed new depths of horror when Israeli troops, who had intervened in June 1982 to expel the Palestinian Liberation Organization (PLO), surrounded the Chatila refugee camp and its adjoining Sabra neighborhood, while Christian Phalangist militiamen entered and began a three-day orgy of atrocity and mass murder. Perhaps 3,500 defenseless civilians perished. The Phalangists believed that Palestinians had assassinated their leader, Bashir Gemayel, although his murder had in fact been organized in Syria. The Israeli defense minister, Ariel Sharon, claimed that the PLO, which had withdrawn from Beirut, had left concealed guerrillas behind. The Israeli military denied being aware that a massacre was actually taking place, but survivors alleged their active complicity. There was subsequent speculation that Sharon wanted to drive not only the PLO but the entire Palestinian refugee population out of Lebanon.

Whatever the truth, there was an international outcry against the massacres, especially in Europe. In Tel Aviv, 300,000 Israelis demonstrated to show their horror. In December, the United Nations General Assembly condemned the massacre as an act of genocide. In February 1983, the Kahan Commission in Israel exonerated all Israeli troops but found Sharon personally responsible through negligence. Sharon was forced to resign, but returned to the center of Israeli politics as prime minister in 2001. In 2002, an attempt to prosecute Sharon failed. **JS**

Reagan Announces "Star Wars" Initiative

The United States embarks on a sophisticated defense policy.

⬤ Reagan's proposal to launch missiles from outer space forces Gorbachev to open negotiations to end the cold war.

In March 1983, Ronald Reagan announced the Strategic Defense Initiative, popularly nicknamed "Star Wars," which proposed using missiles based in outer space. A former Hollywood film actor who had been an effective governor of California, Reagan had won the U.S. presidential election of 1980 for the Republican Party at a time when the United States seemed to many U.S. voters dismayingly weak. A sophisticated defense policy was vital.

The new administration believed that something close to an undeclared war was in progress against what Reagan called "the evil empire" of the Soviet Union and its allies. He was determined to offer assistance to anticommunist forces all around the globe and oversaw a massive buildup of U.S. military might. The Defense Department budget, for example, which was set at $136 billion in 1980, had grown to $244 billion five years later. A new generation of immensely powerful nuclear missiles and weapons was created, some of which were installed in Europe. The technical feasibility of the new Star Wars initiative was doubtful, but it alarmed the Soviet Union's leadership. The world seemed to be nearing a nuclear war, but Reagan's threat worked and the Soviets backed down as the new Soviet premier, Mikhail Gorbachev, realized that the U.S.S.R. could no longer afford the huge expense of an arms race. Gorbachev opened successful negotiations with Reagan, bringing the cold war to an end as the Soviet system tottered toward collapse. **RC**

European Protests

Europe-wide demonstrations condemn the deployment of cruise missiles.

On this day, millions took to the streets across Europe to protest against the decision to deploy U.S. "Pershing 2" cruise missiles in Europe. In Germany, about 1.2 million people formed a 64-mile (102 km) human chain from Stuttgart to New Ulm. In London, protesters claimed one million marched. Protests were also seen in Rome, Vienna, Stockholm, Paris, Brussels, Madrid, and Dublin. Opposition to cruise missiles had begun in early 1982, when the decision to deploy ninety-six of them at Greenham Common, England, had led to the establishment of a permanent peace camp, limited to women and children only, outside the base, much to the annoyance of the British government. The problems with Pershing 2 were that they were small (35 feet [10 m] long), carried on mobile launch vehicles, and cheap (about $2 million without the nuclear warhead). They therefore represented a nightmare for arms control agreements because of the difficulty in verifying their numbers and locations. A total of 572 were expected to be stationed in Europe. In addition, U.S. President Ronald Reagan and his loyal partner British Prime Minister Margaret Thatcher were widely regarded by peace activists as hard-line Cold Warriors and too hawkish to be trusted with such weapons.

The European demonstrations showed the depth of feeling against intensifying the cold war. Governments, however, remained unmoved. The deployment of Pershing 2 carried on. They were finally removed in March 1991 only as a result of the 1987 Intermediate Nuclear Forces Treaty between the United States and the Soviet Union, negotiated, ironically, by Reagan. The Greenham Common peace camp, however, remained until 2000, acting as an inspiration to peace activists across the world. **JS**

Suicide Bombings

Lebanese suicide bombers in Beirut shatter Western efforts.

Two Lebanese Shi'a suicide bombers wrought carnage on U.S. and French troops. The troops were part of a multinational force sent to provide stability in Lebanon and help end a ruinous civil war. A number of militant Shi'a groups, who would later form Hezbollah, believed that the foreign troops were imperialists and defenders of the mortal enemy, Israel. At the U.S. Marine base at Beirut International Airport, a bomber crashed his truck into the lobby of the main building, where most of the marines were sleeping, before detonating a massive bomb. The

> ### *"You have a force . . . unable to protect itself. It was a disaster waiting to happen."*
> **Caspar Weinberger, September 2001**

building collapsed and 242 marines perished. It was the worst loss the U.S. Marines had suffered in a single day since World War II. Simultaneously, a similar bomb was detonated in the basement garage of the French base, killing fifty-eight paratroopers.

The U.S. defense secretary, Caspar Weinberger, insisted the United States would not be intimidated by terrorists and its Middle East policy would not change. This sentiment was echoed by French President Francois Mitterrand, but U.S. Marines were withdrawn in February 1984, and the rest of the multinational force followed in April. A heavy-handed response would have brought the Americans more hostility from the Arab world. In 2003, a U.S. court ruled that the Iranian government was responsible, but nobody has ever been held accountable for these killings. **JS**

The Golden Temple Is Stormed

A violent attack on a sacred Indian shrine in the state of Punjab risks a dangerous backlash from Sikhs in India and elsewhere.

When the Indian army stormed the Golden Temple of Amritsar, the most sacred shrine of the Sikh religion in the Indian state of Punjab, it was pursuing militant Sikh separatists of the Damdami Taksal and its leader, Jarnail Singh Bhindranwale, who had taken shelter there. Bhindranwale had been calling for the creation of an independent Sikh state. His popularity and influence were growing among Sikhs, and the Indian government was unwilling to allow such a threat to Indian unity to persist. Operation Blue Star, as the attack was named, was authorized by Prime Minister Indira Gandhi, after several days' siege in which supplies were cut to the militants and thousands of Sikh pilgrims were trapped inside. When the army moved in, there was heavy fighting, resulting in many casualties and considerable destruction.

As journalists had been expelled from the area, details of what followed are hotly disputed. The army claimed 83 soldiers and 492 in the complex, including Bhindranwale, were killed. Sikh sources insist that most of the inhabitants were massacred and that parts of the complex, including the irreplaceable Sikh reference library and the Akal Takhat (the traditional seat of Sikh secular power adjacent to the Golden Temple itself) were deliberately destroyed. Sikhs everywhere were enraged. Many moderates in India were appalled at an act that could only feed extremism. Thousands of Sikhs were arrested after the Golden Temple was stormed. This was followed by a cycle of terrorism and repression that lasted for years, which Gandhi herself did not live to see. She was assassinated by her own Sikh bodyguards. **JS**

◯ Protests among furious Sikhs reach fever pitch after the sacred Golden Temple is attacked.

Indira Gandhi Assassinated

The Indian prime minister pays the price for sacrilege against a Sikh sacred shrine.

○ Although mob violence broke out after the assassination of Indira Gandhi, her funeral was solemn and dignified.

Beant Singh and Satwant Singh, the two men who gunned down India's prime minister, Indira Gandhi, were members of her own bodyguard. As Sikhs, they had been outraged when Gandhi had authorized the storming of their most sacred shrine, the Golden Temple of Amritsar, the previous June. The attack was always a risky move, but Gandhi was convinced it was necessary. Sikh separatists of the Damdami Taksal and their leader, Jarnail Singh Bhindranwale, had been campaigning for a Sikh theocratic republic and now sought refuge in the Golden Temple. Such a challenge to Indian national unity had to be suppressed. Inevitably, the operation resulted in many deaths and much damage to the temple complex. Many Sikhs believed stories that the Indian army had massacred thousands and had deliberately destroyed parts of the complex. The crackdown on Sikh separatism that followed only fed a cycle of terrorism and reprisal. Gandhi was calmly fatalistic about any threat to herself. When asked about the wisdom of keeping Sikh bodyguards, she pointed to Beant Singh, who had guarded her for ten years, saying this was a man she trusted utterly.

While Gandhi was walking in her garden, the two shot her thirty-one times. Beant Singh was shot dead on the spot. Satwant Singh was wounded and later executed. When news of the assassination was released, there were sectarian riots across India. Enraged Hindus hunted down Sikhs. It added a new level of bitterness to the Sikh separatist struggle. **JS**

Poisonous Gas at Bhopal

Thousands of Indians die horribly in a poison gas leak from a Union Carbide plant.

O Workers collecting bodies for mass burial or cremation soon lost count of the number of victims.

In the Indian city of Bhopal, a leak of poisonous gas from a pesticide factory owned by U.S.-based multinational Union Carbide killed thousands in one night. Some 39 tons of the highly toxic gas, methyl isocyanate, perhaps mixed with cyanide gas and the most lethal gas of World War I, phosgene, were accidentally released while the city slept. The final death toll is much disputed, but perhaps 30,000 perished as a result of the worst industrial accident in history. Some 150,000 were disabled and as many as 500,000 may have suffered some form of poisoning. Contamination of drinking water supplies led to excessive rates of cancers, breathing disorders, and birth defects. Union Carbide, it is claimed, had refused to build the plant away from the city because of the additional cost. In the 1980s, as demand for pesticides fell, the plant was allegedly subject to stringent cost-cutting measures that undermined maintenance and safety standards.

Union Carbide fought a long legal battle to avoid paying damages and only agreed on a settlement in 1989. Most bereaved families received just $2,200 compensation. Many of the disabled received little or nothing. In 1992, the Bhopal Court of Justice issued an arrest warrant for culpable homicide against Warren Anderson, at the time of the accident Union Carbide's chief executive officer. U.S. authorities failed to extradite him. The incident, however, raised serious questions about the conduct of Western multinationals in the less-developed world. **JS**

Miners Admit Defeat

The National Union of Miners votes to end industrial action in Britain.

🔵 Miners' leader Arthur Scargill faces the camera after announcing the failure of the strike to secure a deal over pit closures.

After fifty-one weeks, the National Union of Miners (NUM) finally called off its national strike. A special delegate conference voted ninety-eight to ninety-one to end the industrial action. At many collieries, returning miners tried to put a brave face on things, marching back to work behind brass bands. But this could not disguise the scale of the defeat of the most powerful trade union in Britain, one that in 1974 had brought down the Conservative government.

In reality Margaret Thatcher's Conservative government had prepared for and even welcomed this new confrontation. Victory would crush all effective trade union resistance to Thatcher's radical industrial reforms. Stockpiles of coal were built up and unlimited resources were available to the police to defeat the NUM's tactic of flying pickets, involving sudden, mass blockades of specific targets. The government's cause was further helped by the NUM leader, Arthur Scargill, who, fearing to lose a ballot on the strike, illegally refused to hold one.

The consequences of defeat were severe. Within twenty years an industry employing 187,000 miners was reduced to just six collieries, employing less than 4,000. Even in the East Midlands, where the collieries were modern and profitable and there had been little enthusiasm for industrial action, the miners were not spared. Countrywide, whole communities, utterly dependent economically on the collieries, were devastated. But Thatcher could celebrate a defeat for all trade unions. **PF**

Rainbow Warrior Sunk

An act of sabotage by France forces the end of its own nuclear testing program.

○ New Zealand's prime minister David Lange decried the sinking as "a sordid act of international state-backed terrorism."

At 11:45 P.M., an electric-blue flash was seen in Auckland Harbor, New Zealand, followed by two explosions. Four minutes later, a 131-foot-long (40 m) former trawler sank. Ten of the crew managed to get to safety, but one, Portuguese photographer Fernando Pereira, was drowned in his cabin as he went to retrieve his equipment. The ship, the *Rainbow Warrior*, belonged to the environmental campaign group Greenpeace, which was engaged in a protest against French plans to test a nuclear warhead on the Polynesian atoll of Mururoa. The plan was to sail from New Zealand, an ally of France but a country with a nuclear-free policy, to Mururoa and disrupt the test.

A few days earlier, two French secret agents had visited the *Rainbow Warrior* and planned to sink her by means of two limpet mines attached to her hull— they were not intended to cause loss of life. Pleading guilty to manslaughter, they tried to argue that the *Rainbow Warrior* was carrying espionage equipment and that Pereira was a spy for the KGB. They were sentenced to ten years in prison but returned to France a few years later.

In the outcry that followed the sinking, a flotilla of private boats sailed from New Zealand to Mururoa Atoll, and France's nuclear testing program was abandoned for ten years. New Zealand's nuclear-free policy became strongly confirmed, and Greenpeace's popularity and profile internationally soared. It was later revealed that the French president, Francois Mitterrand, had authorized the bombing. **PF**

Live Aid Helps Ethiopia

Urged by promoter Bob Geldof, musicians perform for free in a global charity event.

⬤ A vast crowd faces the stage at the historic and globally televised Live Aid concert at Wembley Stadium, London.

At 12:02 P.M. on a sunny day at Wembley Stadium, London, Francis Rossi of Status Quo began the proceedings in front of 72,000 fans. Across the Atlantic, 90,000 fans at JFK Stadium, Philadelphia, saw their stateside concert kick off at 1:51 P.M. An estimated 1.5 billion people watched the shows live on television in 160 countries. This was Live Aid, raising money and awareness for an appalling famine in Ethiopia by "switching on" a global jukebox.

The atmosphere was euphoric, with Bono of U2 escaping into the crowds and picking up a dancing partner, and Freddie Mercury and Queen rampaging though their greatest hits. But nonmusical moments remain equally embedded in the collective consciousness—the videos of starving Ethiopian children (the reason the event was happening at all), and the emotionally charged expletive outbursts of thirty-two-year-old Irish co-organizer Bob Geldof as he exhorted people to get on the phone and pay.

Without Geldof, Live Aid would not have happened. After watching harrowing televised reports of dying Ethiopian children in October 1984, the lead singer of The Boomtown Rats had sparked off a social concern missing from both international politics and the music scene. Indifferent governments bowed to Geldof's indomitable pleas and filibustering to "do something." Live Aid was a huge success: people around the world donated money or their talents and services for free and the event raised £48 million ($62 million) for the Ethiopians. **PF**

Rock Hudson Dies

The death of the popular movie star focuses attention on the growing threat of AIDS.

○ Rock Hudson's name appears In a patchwork quilt created in Washington in 1996 to commemorate victims of AIDS.

Rock Hudson was an exceptionally good-looking, and to all appearances thoroughly heterosexual, actor whose successful Hollywood career was very much a creation of his agent and the studios. Even his name had been chosen for him—Rock from the Rock of Gibraltar and Hudson from the Hudson River. Hollywood legend had it that Hudson needed thirty-eight takes for his only line in his first film, *Fighter Squadron*, in 1948, but in the 1950s and 1960s he appeared to advantage in a series of enjoyable comedies, many of them with Doris Day.

Quiet and shy in private, Hudson used to say that he did not like himself on the screen. Very few people, and certainly not the general public, had the faintest idea that he was homosexual and that his marriage to his agent's secretary in 1955 had been a sham organized by the studio to keep any prying eyes turned in a different direction. It had lasted three years. Hudson's sexual inclinations were revealed only when he was close to death from AIDS, of which he died with dignity at his home in Beverly Hills shortly before his sixtieth birthday.

He was the first important show business figure to die of the disease. Much of the media coverage was cruel, but at the same time the news helped the growing acceptance of homosexuality. It encouraged the gay rights movement, which had been gaining strength since the 1970s, and heightened sympathetic public realization of the terrible toll that the devastating new disease was taking. **RC**

Space Shuttle Explodes on Takeoff

The Challenger *space shuttle mission ends in tragedy.*

The *Challenger* space shuttle took off around 11:30 A.M. and disintegrated some seventy seconds later. It had reached a height of 9 miles (14.5 km) and a speed of close to 2,000 miles per hour (3,220 kph). All seven of the crew were killed. They were the first Americans to die after takeoff, although three astronauts had perished in a launch-pad fire in 1967.

Perhaps most famously, the crew included a schoolteacher named Christa McAuliffe, the first person ever to be selected in a program to send ordinary civilians into space. The tragedy was made even more harrowing because her husband and children, and the families of the astronauts, were watching as the shuttle lifted off. The disaster made a huge impression on the media and the public, with one study reporting that 85 percent of Americans questioned knew what had happened to the shuttle within an hour of it occurring.

The launch had been postponed several times from Kennedy Space Center on the central Florida coast due to poor weather and mechanical problems. That day, the weather was fiercely cold and ice had to be scraped off the shuttle, delaying the launch a further two hours. Almost immediately after liftoff, flames and smoke were seen on one of the external booster rockets, and soon the booster was surrounded by flames. The shuttle then turned into a red, orange, and white fireball. The crew, meanwhile, had noticed nothing wrong. An inquiry reported that the shuttle's booster rockets had no sensors to warn of problems and that the trouble began when an O-ring in the right booster failed at liftoff.

The disaster was a savage blow to the space program, which was already in difficulty because of excessive costs. The shuttle launches were suspended for close to three years. **RC**

○ The space shuttle *Challenger* (STS-51L) takes off from Kennedy Space Center in Florida.

◑ Seventy-three seconds after blastoff, *Challenger's* rocket boosters and external fuel tank break off and disintegrate.

" . . . they waved goodbye and 'slipped the bonds of Earth to touch the face of God.'"

Ronald Reagan quoting the poem "High Flight"

Swedish Prime Minister Assassinated

Olof Palme is shot dead on the way home from the cinema.

○ The spot in central Stockholm where Olof Palme was murdered is now marked by a brass plaque set into the pavement.

On a cold winter night, Olof Palme, the Swedish prime minister, and his wife, Lisbet, were walking home after a night out at the Grand Cinema in Stockholm. Suddenly, a man approached the couple from behind, drew a handgun, and fired a number of shots. Palme was fatally wounded in the back. Lisbet was also hit, but she survived the attack.

A nearby taxi driver called an ambulance while two young girls rushed over to see if they could help. Palme was rushed to the hospital but was pronounced dead on arrival just after midnight on March 1, 1986. Crucially, there were no bodyguards at the scene, although this was not unusual. Palme's assassin melted into the night, and although Christer Pettersson was convicted of the killing two years later, he was released after an appeal. A number of alternative theories have been put forward. As a result, the assassination that shocked a nation still remains one of the great unsolved mysteries.

More than twenty years later, Palme's legacy is a matter of debate. Although the majority of Swedes feel that he championed the social and economic aspirations of the Swedish people, many individuals openly declared their hatred for him. Palme was a radical, outspoken, and charismatic leader who opposed the Vietnam War and fought vigorously for the rights of many oppressed peoples throughout the world. As prime minister, he defended the welfare state and introduced a number of laws that together were labeled "economic democracy." **TB**

Reagan's Retaliation

The United States bombs Libyan targets in reprisal for a terrorist attack.

⬤ Damaged goods are piled up in a wrecked Tripoli home after a U.S. air strike that was purportedly directed at military targets.

Operation El Dorado Canyon, ordered by the U.S. president, Ronald Reagan, involved the bombing of several positions in the Libyan cities of Tripoli and Benghazi. U.S. authorities insisted that the attacks were directed at military targets, such as the naval academy, the military airport, and army barracks in Tripoli. In the event, there were some civilian casualties, most notably the infant adopted daughter of the Libyan dictator, Colonel Muammar Gaddafi. Tensions between the United States and Libya had been mounting, and a few weeks earlier a naval confrontation between Libyan and U.S. naval forces in the Gulf of Sidra had left thirty-five Libyan seamen dead. Two weeks later, a bomb exploded in a West Berlin discotheque frequented by U.S. servicemen.

Three Americans and a Turkish woman died, and there were 50 Americans among the 230 injured. The Americans claimed to have intercepted signals proving Libyan involvement. The U.S. air strikes were presented as a proportionate response and fully legal under Article 51 of the United Nations charter, permitting national self-defense.

Many Europeans were skeptical about this justification. The attacks provoked outrage in Libya and sympathy from the Arab world. In response, a militant group, the Arab Revolutionary Cells, killed three British and U.S. hostages in Lebanon. In 2001, four people, including one Libyan diplomat, were convicted for the bombing, but little was achieved in stemming the rise of Middle Eastern terrorism. **JS**

Chernobyl Nuclear Plant Explosion

In Ukraine, the Chernobyl nuclear reactor explodes, releasing a radioactive cloud with far-reaching and long-term consequences.

In the early hours of the morning, an explosion ripped through the number four reactor of Ukraine's Chernobyl nuclear power station. The accident happened when the inexperienced night shift carried out tests on the reactor's safety systems. When these failed, the resulting explosion blew holes in the side and roof of the reactor and threw the massive reactor lid into the air. A lethal cloud of radioactive contamination was released into the atmosphere. Initially the reactor crew failed to grasp the magnitude of the disaster and stayed at their posts trying to bring the reactor under control. Local firefighters attempted to douse the flames. None wore protective suits; many were to perish from radiation sickness. The authorities were slow to act. A collective sense of disbelief and denial appears to have gripped those responsible.

The radioactive cloud spread contamination across much of Europe. The Soviet authorities were painfully slow in reacting to the tragedy. Only thirty-six hours later was a decision made to evacuate the 50,000 population of the neighboring city of Pripyat, and then the inhabitants were told it would be only a temporary measure. The May Day parades in Ukraine's capital, Kiev, went ahead as planned. No warnings were given. Eventually a large zone around Chernobyl was quarantined and a sarcophagus erected over the reactor, which would temporarily contain the contamination. Not surprisingly, the tardy response, the inadequate decontamination, and the long-term health problems did much to discredit the Soviet leadership, especially in Ukraine and Belarus. **JS**

◖ Radiation experts in a helicopter measure radioactivity in various parts of Chernobyl's roofless number four reactor.

Primo Levi Dies

Scholars dispute the claim that the Holocaust survivor committed suicide.

The Italian-Jewish writer Primo Levi was found dead in the stairwell of his Turin apartment; the coroner's verdict was suicide, perhaps associated with depression, although some scholars have pointed out that there was no clear evidence for this. The lack of a suicide note has led some to conclude that his fall from the third floor may have been accidental.

The manner of his death is significant, as Levi was famous for his open and positive assertion of the values of life in the face of violence and oppression, and in his writing most famously explored his

"In order for the wheel to turn, for life to be lived, impurities are needed. . . ."

The Periodic Table, 1975

experiences as a survivor of Auschwitz. Trained as a chemist at Turin University, he graduated in 1941 and in 1943 joined the Italian partisan movement fighting Mussolini's puppet "Salo" government. On capture, he was sent to Auschwitz in February 1944, and he remained there until liberation eleven months later, one of only twenty Italian Jews to survive the camp.

After the war, his books, particularly *If This Is a Man* (1947) and *The Truce* (1963), won international acclaim as explorations of the worth of human life in inhuman surroundings, bearing witness to the horrors of the Nazi attempt to destroy the Jewish people. Although he did not show specifically anti-German feeling, he became a leading voice of Italian antifascism and led the opposition to those who attempted to deny the Holocaust. **PF**

Battle for the Party

Gorbachev introduces perestroika, *the radical but risky Soviet reform program.*

In introducing *perestroika* (restructuring) and its associated approach of *glasnost* (openness to scrutiny and discussion), the Soviet leader Mikhail Gorbachev set out how he intended to address the Soviet Union's problems and ensure its long-term survival. By the 1980s, the Soviet-American arms race was placing an increasingly unsustainable strain on the Soviet economy and society. Many sectors of the economy were in recession, alcoholism was becoming endemic, and although the population did not reject the Soviet system, they were becoming

"Perestroika—the process of change in our country— started from above . . ."

Mikhail Gorbachev, Memoirs, 1995

increasingly impatient with its shortcomings. To Gorbachev, the only solution was a complete transformation of the state and party system. It must become more responsive to the wishes of its citizens and be willing to accept their open criticisms. The economy must be modernized and state controls eased. Party conservatives opposed reforms, fearing they could result only in the downfall of the party. They put up a determined bureaucratic resistance to *perestroika* and greatly hindered Gorbachev's efforts. It really was a battle for the life and soul of the party.

The result was a series of half measures that infuriated conservatives and failed to satisfy reformers. Worse, *perestroika* removed the repression that kept the old economic system moving, but failed to provide the incentives to replace it. **JS**

Defiance on the Streets

The start of the Palestinian Intifada is a major challenge to the Israeli occupation.

○ A stone-throwing youth, his face hidden in a scarf to escape prosecution, expresses his opposition to Israeli control.

A traffic accident, in which four Palestinians from the Jabalia refugee camp were killed by an Israeli army vehicle, led to an explosion of protest in the occupied territories. The causes of the Intifada ("shaking off"), though, go deeper than a traffic accident. Since the 1978 Camp David agreement between Israel and Egypt, the prospect of a new Middle East war to end the occupation had evaporated. The Palestinians felt that their cause was forgotten. Rapid population growth, heavy unemployment, and humiliating security measures imposed by the Israelis all fueled Palestinian frustration. In 1987 rioting began in Jabalia and developed into a national uprising. This took many forms, from simple civil disobedience, such as refusing to pay Israeli taxes, to attacks on Israeli soldiers and the killing of suspected collaborators. In July 1989, Israel experienced its first suicide bombing.

In the six years it lasted, the first Intifada saw Palestinians kill 160 Israelis and about 1,000 suspected collaborators. Israeli security forces are believed to have killed 1,162 Palestinians. The Israelis had little experience of crowd control and were internationally condemned for using lethal force against stone-throwing youths. The Intifada convinced many Israelis that direct negotiations with the Palestinians were now necessary. The Palestinians had asserted their national identity and were reaching for nationhood. In 1993, such negotiations ended this Intifada, but many issues regarding nationhood were left unanswered. **JS**

Horror in Halabja

Iraq's use of chemical weapons on its own civilians signals a new level of barbarity.

○ Kurdish corpses lie sprawled on the ground after Saddam Hussein's deployment of chemical weapons on Halabja.

On a day that will be remembered forever by Kurds as "Bloody Friday," the Iraqi army poured a lethal cloud of poison gas on Halabja—one of their own cities. About 5,000 were said to have been killed and 7,000 suffered long-term illnesses from what is thought to have been a cocktail of the nerve agents sarin, tabun, and VX. Halabja, a Kurdish city of around 70,000 people, stands close to the frontier with Iran. Kurdish nationalists had long resisted Iraqi rule. During the Iran-Iraq war (1980–1988), their resistance was met with the genocidal Anfal ("Spoils of War") campaign, under the command of dictator Saddam Hussein's cousin, "chemical" Ali Hassan al-Majid. More than 180,000 Kurds were killed altogether. By 1988, with the United States supporting Iraq as a counterweight to the Islamic fundamentalism of Iran, the war was going badly for Iran. Desperate to open a new front, Iranian troops had supported the Kurdistan Nationalist Front's Peshmerga guerrillas when they seized the city. When conventional artillery failed, Iraq used chemical weapons.

When news of the atrocity began to reach the West, the United States Defense Intelligence Agency initially claimed the attack had been launched by Iran. However, the evidence against Saddam Hussein's regime grew, and he was condemned by the United Nations Security Council. Few, however, showed any interest in bringing the perpetrators to justice at the time. In 2003, the atrocity was one of the issues used to justify a U.S.-led invasion. **JS**

Drug Cheat Disqualified

Ben Johnson is stripped of his Olympic gold after testing positive for a banned drug.

⬥ Ben Johnson races to his astonishing—but unfortunately also drug-enhanced—victory in the Olympic Games at Seoul.

For three days, it was the sensation of the Seoul Games—the photo of a Canadian sprinter slowing as he crosses the finish line in the 100-meter sprint. He set a new world record of 9.79 seconds and finished more than a meter ahead of his rivals in an event where centimeters usually separate gold from bronze.

The 100-meter sprint is the highest-profile event of any Olympic Games, and in this case the rivalry between Johnson and U.S. sprint legend Carl Lewis had reached unusual intensity. Johnson had claimed the world record in Rome in 9.87 seconds the previous September. However, the urine sample given by the Jamaican-born sprinter immediately after the Seoul race tested positive for the anabolic steroid Stanazolol, and three days later he was sent

home in disgrace and banned from athletics for two years. The title was awarded to Lewis, and Britain's Linford Christie won silver. Ironically, both these men later tested positive for illegal drugs in the course of their athletic careers. (Lewis failed three drug tests during the 1988 U.S. Olympic trials for stimulants found in cold medication, but he was allowed to compete at Seoul claiming inadvertent use.) In 1993, Johnson was again found to have taken banned substances and was barred from athletics for life.

Johnson's case was the most high-profile success in the "fight against cheats" and raised awareness of the prevalence of drug-taking among athletes at the highest level. It also gave rise to accusations of victimization that continue to dog the sport. **PF**

U.S. Airliner Blown Up

A bomb planted by unidentified terrorists destroys Pan Am flight 103 over Lockerbie.

⭘ Pan Am flight 103 was destroyed by a bomb in a radio given to a passenger, alerting the authorities to a new kind of threat.

A U.S. airliner, Pan Am flight 103, flying from London Heathrow to New York Kennedy airport, was blown out of the sky by a terrorist bomb. All 259 aboard were killed when 1 pound (450 g) of plastic explosive was detonated in the forward cargo hold just thirty-eight minutes into the flight. The aircraft broke up, and debris and victims were scattered along an 81-mile (103 km) corridor. The horror was compounded when a section of a wing of the airliner plunged into the Scottish town of Lockerbie, blasting a crater 155 feet (47 m) long into the town, killing eleven more.

Investigators concluded that Libyan dictator Colonel Gaddafi was responsible for the outrage, in reprisal for the U.S. bombing of Tripoli in April 1986. Two Libyan intelligence agents, Abdelbaset Ali Mohmed al-Megrahi and Al Amin Khalifa Fhimah, were accused of the crime. After several years of sanctions and threats of more severe reprisals, Gaddafi, still insisting on Libya's innocence, agreed to surrender the two men. They were tried under Scottish law in the Netherlands. In January 2001, after an eighty-four-day trial, Fhimah was acquitted, but al-Megrahi was convicted and sentenced to life imprisonment. In a controversial move, the Scottish government released al-Megrahi on August 20, 2009, on compassionate grounds because he was suffering from cancer and a doctor's report claimed he had only three months to live. Al-Megrahi was given a hero's welcome when he returned to Libya and lived until May 20, 2012. **JS**

Under Sentence of Death

Ayatollah Khomeini orders the killing of Salman Rushdie for his Satanic Verses.

○ Muslims in Bradford, England, set fire to a copy of *The Satanic Verses* after Ayatollah Khomeini's fatwah is announced.

British-Indian author Salman Rushdie was sentenced to death by Iran's religious leader, Ayatollah Khomeini. The fatwah, or religious edict, called upon Muslims to kill Rushdie for blasphemies against Islam. His offense was his fourth novel, *The Satanic Verses*, in which he examined relations between East and West and made comments about the Prophet Muhammad that many Muslims deemed to be deeply offensive. The Iranian government offered a bounty to his killer, and across the world Muslims demonstrated in outrage. Their fury was compounded when it became clear that British law did not allow for the book to be banned. Rushdie went into hiding, and Britain severed diplomatic relations with Iran for inciting the murder of a British citizen.

In the end, Rushdie spent ten years under police protection. Diplomatic relations with Iran were restored in September 1998, after the Iranian government disassociated itself from the death sentence. But the fatwah could be rescinded only by the man who issued it, and Khomeini died in June 1989. His successor, Ayatollah Ali Khamenei, in fact reaffirmed it, and radical Muslims insisted they would carry it out if the chance arose. The controversy re-emerged in June 2007, when Rushdie was awarded a knighthood, and highlighted the growing tensions between the Islamic and Western worlds. The fact that traditional Western rights to freedom of speech were used to defend attacks on Islam helped politicize and radicalize a generation of Muslims. **JS**

Exxon Valdez Oil Disaster

A major oil spill off Alaska alerts the world to the fragility of the environment.

⊙ An oil-skimming operation works to remove oil released by the tanker *Exxon Valdez* in Prince William Sound.

When almost 11 million gallons (42 million liters) of crude oil leaked out of a grounded tanker into the pure water of Prince William Sound in March 1989, the impact on the environment was significant.

The whole question of drilling for oil in the Alaskan wilderness was already controversial when the *Exxon Valdez* left Valdez oil terminal on the evening of March 23 on its way to Washington with 53 million gallons of oil. Three hours later, it hit a reef. A vast slick of oil spread across the sound, and initial attempts by Exxon to break it up failed as the water was too calm. Some limited success was had in burning the oil, and in restricting its spread through the use of booms. A storm blew up a few days later, though, and drove the slick onto the rocky, indented, and remote coast, necessitating a massive cleanup operation. Perhaps half a million seabirds and hundreds of seals died, and many salmon breeding grounds were destroyed. The loss of clams, herring, and seals was a disaster for the local fishing industry.

The environmental impact of the oil, and of the cleanup operation, has been studied intensely, and new techniques developed as a consequence. Although visible signs of the oil had gone after a year, much remains hidden in the soil twenty years later. Exxon was criticized for its initial slow response to the crisis, but took responsibility for the massive cleanup operation. Litigation has continued ever since on the level of damages it should pay. **PF**

Tiananmen Square

Massacre of demonstrators kills hopes for democracy in China.

On this day, soldiers of China's People's Liberation Army attacked peaceful demonstrators in Beijing's Tiananmen Square. Hundreds, perhaps thousands, were slaughtered by soldiers firing indiscriminately and driving armored vehicles over demonstrators. The confrontation arose seven weeks earlier, with a student march in memory of a recently deceased Chinese Communist Party (CCP) leader and known reformer, Hu Yaobang. This occasion brought many discontented Chinese together and allowed them to articulate their grievances. Since 1978, the reforms of leader Deng Xiaoping had brought a market economy to China, but this had not been accompanied by serious political reforms. Further excited by the impending visit of reforming Soviet leader Mikhail Gorbachev, demonstrators occupied Tiananmen Square and refused to leave until democratic reforms were promised.

The CCP's response was confused and indecisive. Initially they pleaded with the demonstrators to leave and promised there would be no violence. Some 1,000 demonstrators joined a hunger strike, which earned them considerable support across China. This was a challenge that the CCP could not ignore. Once Gorbachev had left, troops were brought in from outlying provinces. They attacked without warning. Arrests of activists followed, paralyzing the democracy movement. China and the world were shocked at the ferocity of the crackdown. International sanctions were imposed, but China was too lucrative a trading partner for them to last long. The CCP was left firmly in control of the country. **JS**

◑ A lone citizen blocks the progress of tanks on the Avenue of Eternal Peace in Beijing during the crushing of the uprising.

Chain for Freedom

Baltic Republics join hands to demand an end to Soviet rule.

Perhaps two million people of the Baltic Republics of Latvia, Lithuania, and Estonia—a quarter of their total populations—joined hands on August 23 to form the longest human chain in history. The 375-mile (600-km) chain stretched across all three republics. It was an entirely peaceful protest to mark the fiftieth anniversary of the 1939 Nazi-Soviet pact, which contained secret protocols permitting the Soviet Union to annex these republics, which hitherto had been independent. The demonstration was intended to remind the world of the lingering injustices of that day. The first small Baltic demonstrations against inclusion within the U.S.S.R. were seen after the introduction of *perestroika* (restructuring) and its associated approach of *glasnost* (openness to scrutiny and discussion) by Soviet leader Mikhail Gorbachev. They were broken up by the police, but protesters were becoming emboldened as the Soviet system began to fragment.

Gorbachev was shocked by the demonstration. Although he was prepared to admit that the secret protocols existed, he insisted that the Baltic Republics had joined the U.S.S.R. voluntarily, and he further insisted that they had no grounds to seek secession. However, local people could recall the mass arrests and mass deportations of 1939, greeting German invaders as liberators in 1941, and the brutal reassertion of Soviet power after the German defeat and the mass settlement of Russian colonists that followed. They were as determined on independence as Moscow was on keeping them within the Soviet Union. Gorbachev attempted to keep control through economic sanctions and military force, but the Moscow coup of August 1991 allowed the Baltic Republics to regain their independence. **JS**

Berlin Wall Tumbles

The German people force the nation toward reunification.

The Berlin Wall—the very symbol of the Cold War—was swept away by citizens from both sides of the divide, just over twenty-eight years after its construction. Its creators, East Germany's communist government, had insisted that it was an "antifascist wall," protecting the East German people. Nobody was fooled. It was clearly intended to halt the mass migration of East Germans to more prosperous West Germany, which had reached such a scale that it threatened the survival of East Germany. Although there were ingenious escapes across the Wall over the years, and many were killed making attempts, the Wall did provide East Germany with stability.

By the late 1980s, this stability was under threat. The reforms of Mikhail Gorbachev in the Soviet Union had aroused tremendous excitement in East Germany, where there was a desperate longing for change. But the communist leader Erich Honecker knew that reforms would end with the dissolution of communist rule and refused to follow Gorbachev's example. Growing discontent led to mass demonstrations and a new stampede to escape the regime, this time through Hungary, where the frontier with Austria was opened, allowing thousands to reach West Germany. In October 1989, the Communist Party, in a desperate effort to save East Germany, removed Honecker in favor of Egon Krenz.

Krenz's regime handled the growing crisis with astonishing incompetence. It was announced that regulations to travel to the West would be relaxed, but no details were given. Rumors spread that the Wall would be opened, and thousands gathered at the checkpoints, clamoring to cross. The guards, lacking orders, let them through. The authority of the East German regime collapsed, and in October 1990 the state itself ceased to exist. **JS**

◐ Watched by fellow demonstrators, a man pounds the hated Berlin Wall with a sledgehammer.

◑ People of East and West Berlin celebrate the New Year in 1990 together in front of the city's iconic Brandenburg Gate.

> ## "A combination of the fall of the Bastille and a New Year's Eve blowout . . ."
>
> *Time* magazine, November 1989

Havel Elected

Famed dissident Václav Havel is chosen as the first leader of the new post-communist Czechoslovakia.

Playwright and political dissident Václav Havel was unanimously elected by Czechoslovakia's federal Parliament as his nation's first post-communist president. This came despite the fact that no democratic elections had been held and Parliament was still dominated by communists.

Havel was a surprising choice. Born to a wealthy capitalist family in 1936, he was always under suspicion during communist rule. He had a notable reputation as a playwright by 1968, but was critical of communist rule. He supported Alexander Dubček's reforms of the 1968 "Prague Spring" and was an outspoken critic of the Soviet-led invasion. He was banned from the theater as a result. This simply made him more politically active. He spent several terms in prison and earned national and international renown. During the "Velvet Revolution" in 1989, he was a leading spokesman for democratic reform.

As President of Czechoslovakia (1989–1992) and then of the Czech Republic (1993–2003), Havel was held in high international regard. Domestically, the assessment was more mixed. He failed to persuade the Slovaks to retain a federal union with the Czechs. He oversaw the privatization of the economy, despite preferring a mixed—partly private and partly state-owned—economic model. His amnesty of prisoners, abolition of capital punishment, and apology to Sudeten Germans for their expulsion after 1945 were very unpopular in some quarters. However, he also presided over the transition to democracy and gained entry into the NATO alliance. Overall, his presidency was regarded positively when he stepped down. **JS**

◯ Czecholslovakian students cheer in support of Havel during the "Velvet Revolution."

End of the Long Road to Freedom

Nelson Mandela's release by the South African authorities signals the beginning of the end of apartheid.

At 4:14 in the afternoon, hand in hand with his then-wife, Winnie Madikizela, the slight figure of a seventy-one-year-old man whose name was known the world over, yet whose face and voice had been hidden for almost three decades, walked down the long, straight drive of Victor-Verster Prison at Paarl, near Cape Town. As he reached the gate, he punched the air with his fist and drove away without speaking. Later that day, he made an hour-long speech on the balcony of the city hall of Cape Town. It may not have been the ringing oratory that the world was hoping for, but it assured his listeners of his continuing commitment to the African National Congress, on which a thirty-four-year ban was lifted the same day. He also insisted on the importance of continuing the struggle against the apartheid regime that had sent him to prison in 1964, on charges of treason and sabotage, and convicted of blowing up power lines.

Nelson Mandela, imprisoned in the notorious Robben Island jail for eighteen of those twenty-seven years, had become the symbol of the struggle against apartheid. His principled and dignified refusal to compromise, either personally or politically, with the regime that had offered to release him if he renounced violence, made him the movement's hero. In the coming months, he negotiated the end of the apartheid regime with Prime Minister F. W. de Klerk, led the country into its first multiethnic elections, and as president from 1994 to 1999 steered South Africa through an unexpectedly peaceful transition to majority rule, becoming in the process the world's most respected statesman. **JS**

○ Nelson Mandela and his then-wife, Winnie, give clenched-fist victory salutes in Cape Town after his release from prison.

Hubble Launched

Europe and the United States join forces to launch the pioneering Hubble space telescope together.

○ The Hubble space telescope was reported to be fifty times more sensitive than ground-based telescopes.

"We are going to have the ability to . . . probe the secrets of creation."

Leonard Fisk, NASA

The investigation and exploration of outer space was a major theme in the history of the second half of the twentieth century. The U.S.S.R. sent the first orbiting satellite into space in 1957, and the following year President Eisenhower established the National Aeronautics and Space Administration (NASA) in the U.S., which ran many major space exploration projects. In 1975, the European Space Research Organization and the European Launcher Development Organization were amalgamated as the European Space Agency by thirteen European countries (Austria, Belgium, Denmark, France, Germany, Ireland, Italy, the Netherlands, Norway, Spain, Sweden, Switzerland, and the United Kingdom, with Finland as an associate) to promote research into space and technology.

After many delays and financial obstacles, NASA and the European Space Agency joined forces to put an astronomical observatory into orbit in space. Named after the U.S. astronomer Edwin Hubble, the first person to discover galaxies beyond our own, it has a 95-inch (241-cm) aperture telescope, which was intended to see images unaffected by Earth's atmosphere. It is the only telescope made to be serviced by astronauts.

Soon after it was launched into position approximately 360 miles (580 km) above Earth, a fault was found in the main mirror, which seriously hampered the telescope. This was put right by the first servicing mission in 1993. Since then, the Hubble telescope has been responsible for numerous key discoveries. It provides unprecedentedly deep and clear views of the universe—from our own solar system to faraway galaxies that were formed billions of years ago. **RC**

Iraq Invades Kuwait

Iraq's invasion of oil-rich Kuwait is a challenge to the international order.

In the early hours of the morning, 100,000 Iraqi troops, supported by 700 tanks, swept across the frontier of neighboring Kuwait. Taken completely by surprise, Kuwait collapsed within the day, leaving hundreds dead and thousands of foreigners trapped. The Iraqi dictator, Saddam Hussein, threatened to turn Kuwait City into a graveyard if his conquest and annexation of Kuwait was challenged. The Iraqi government had long claimed sovereignty over Kuwait, which it held was historically part of Iraq's national territory.

The causes of the invasion were more mundane. Iraq had emerged from the Iran-Iraq War (1980–1988) with little but a shattered economy and massive debts. A high price for its only important export, oil, was vital. The Iraqis claimed that Kuwait was flooding the world market, keeping prices low. They also accused Kuwait of stealing oil from Iraq's Ramailah oil field and of stationing troops on Iraqi territory. In reality, Saddam Hussein realized that seizing Kuwait's oil reserves would give him immense power over the market. Unfortunately for him, the international community also recognized this.

There was a considerable degree of unanimity among the great powers and rulers in the region that this invasion was unacceptable. The United Nations Security Council condemned Iraqi aggression and demanded an immediate withdrawal. International outrage was further fueled by reports of Iraqi atrocities within Kuwait. An international coalition, led by the United States, began to assemble a huge army in Saudi Arabia—much to the fury of an Islamic fundamentalist, Osama bin Laden—to defend it from a similar fate and to expel the Iraqis from Kuwait if negotiations failed. In January 1991, that expulsion (Operation Desert Storm) began. **JS**

End of the Cold War

The Conventional Forces Treaty effectively thaws the Cold War.

In Paris, twenty-two nations signed the Conventional Forces in Europe (CFE) Treaty, marking the end of the Cold War. Arms limitation negotiations between East and West first began in 1969 and produced a string of agreements restricting strategic weapons. A conventional forces agreement had always proved elusive, though, not least because the Soviet Union insisted on equal reductions, which would maintain their huge numerical superiority. The United States insisted on reductions to equal levels, which would eliminate that advantage. The question of whether withdrawing Soviet weapons across the Urals, technically outside Europe but easily returned, would be an acceptable fulfillment of treaty obligations remained unanswered.

By the late 1980s, with Mikhail Gorbachev's reforms causing an economic crisis, the Soviet leader accepted that major cuts in military spending were vital. He announced a huge, unilateral reduction of forces in Europe. This paved the way for an agreement to be finalized. The CFE Treaty specified limits on troop numbers and weapons to be held by both NATO and the Warsaw Pact in Europe. Both sides, for example, were permitted 20,000 tanks, 20,000 artillery pieces, 6,800 combat aircraft, and 2,000 attack helicopters. All excess weapons were to be destroyed under strict verification procedures. The collapse of the Soviet Union in December 1991 required the successor states to ratify the treaty. When signed, it was the cause of great optimism that a new era in East-West relations had opened.

In July 2007, then Russian President Vladimir Putin suspended the treaty in protest at the United States's newest missile defense system, which involved radar facilities in Central Europe. **JS**

Iraqis Ousted

Coalition forces drive the Iraqi invaders from Kuwait.

After several weeks of air bombardment and a four-day ground campaign, the liberation of Kuwait was a total success. The Iraqi leader, Saddam Hussein, had hoped that the international community would accept a fait accompli after his invasion and annexation of Kuwait in 1990. Instead, alarmed at the prospect of a single nation controlling so much of the world's oil, the United Nations sanctioned a multinational coalition, which assembled in Saudi Arabia, initially to contain and eventually to expel the Iraqi leader. Saddam's only hope was to break up the

"He panicked, ordering his army's withdrawal. It was not enough for the allies."

Obituary of Saddam Hussein, the *Guardian*

coalition. He planned to separate the Arab nations by transforming the war into an Arab struggle against the common enemy, Israel. When the air attacks began, he launched a number of Soviet-made Scud missiles on Israeli cities. If Israel retaliated, other Arab nations would, he hoped, withdraw from the coalition. Considerable U.S. pressure prevented retaliation.

The Iraqi defeat did not come cheap. The Iraqis inflicted an environmental nightmare on the region. Millions of gallons of crude oil were pumped into the Persian Gulf and 600 oil wells were set on fire. Believing that the coalition would invade Iraq and topple the dictator, there were uprisings among the Shi'a Iraqis in the south and the Kurds in the north. The coalition decided that an invasion would be detrimental and did little to help the rebels. **JS**

Coalition Aids Kurds

The coalition is forced to intervene and relieve the plight of Kurdish refugees.

The plight of up to 1.7 million Kurds in northern Iraq had been ignored. Operation Provide Comfort belatedly recognized the desperate situation and began delivering supplies and protection to the victims of Saddam Hussein's regime.

The Kurds have a long and bloody history of oppression. They never gained their own state of Kurdistan after World War I, and the Kurdish people found themselves partitioned between Iran, Iraq, Turkey, and Syria, all of whom treated them with suspicion. In Iraq, where they were seen as traitors during the Iran-Iraq War (1980–1988), their suffering was appalling. The notorious Anfal ("Spoils of War") campaign, intended to crush Kurdish Peshmerga guerrillas, killed perhaps 180,000 Kurds. Most infamously, the Iraqis used nerve gases on the town of Halabja in March 1988.

Unsurprisingly, therefore, the Kurds anticipated that the liberation of Kuwait by a multinational coalition would be followed by the overthrow of the Iraqi dictator. But the coalition halted its advance, leaving the Kurds in a desperate position. The refugees fled to the northern frontier of Iraq, to the border with Turkey. The Turks, who had been fighting Kurdish separatists since 1984, refused them entry.

The Kurds were left without shelter, clean water, food, and medical supplies in the mountains in the middle of winter. Only when news reports brought the terrible position of the refugees to the attention of the world did the coalition finally move. The Iraqis were ordered not to fly aircraft in northern Iraq. Thirty countries provided aid. For the Kurds, however, coalition protection provided, for the first time perhaps, the prospect of some form of autonomy or even statehood. **JS**

Collapse of a Nation

Croatia and Slovenia declare their independence from Yugoslavia, inciting fears of a civil war with the region's dominant power, Serbia.

Prospects for the survival of communist-ruled Yugoslavia had been uncertain since the death in 1980 of Tito, who led the communist partisans to victory in 1945. By the late 1980s, the economy was stagnating and the Communist Party was discredited. This allowed a middle-ranking party functionary, Slobodan Milosevic, to come forward as a Serb ultra-nationalist. By exploiting old ethnic hostilities and fears, Milosevic rose to the leadership in Serbia. He was able to Serbianize the federal army and overturn the autonomy of the provinces of Kosovo and Vojvodina. He was clearly reaching for a Serbian-ruled Yugoslavia. If he could not attain this, he would settle for a Greater Serbia and seize as much territory as he could. Croatia and Slovenia prepared to resist. Milosevic accused the Croats of plotting genocide against the Serb minority in Croatia.

Croatian and Slovenian independence was followed by immediate war. The federal army met an unexpected defeat in Slovenia, but in Croatia the fighting was bitter. A new term, "ethnic cleansing," entered the English language to describe the brutal expulsion of ethnic groups. A cease-fire was finally reached in January 1992. Then the Serbs turned their attention to Bosnia-Herzegovina, and while the world looked on impotently, repeated atrocities were committed. The savagery continued until 1995, when a Croatian offensive regained all the territory the Croats had previously lost, and the Dayton Accords ended the fighting in Bosnia. **JS**

◑ Soldiers with the new uniform and flag of Slovenia practice for the separatist republic's independence ceremony.

◐ The May 1980 funeral of Josip Tito in Belgrade was, for many, a signal that the Yugoslavian state would not survive.

End of the Soviet Union

The Soviet Union ceases to exist with a simple announcement.

At the end of 1991, the president of Russia, Boris Yeltsin; the president of Ukraine, Leonid Kravchuk; and the president of Belarus, Stanislau Shushkevich, jointly agreed that the Union of Soviet Socialist Republics no longer existed. Since the attempted coup in Moscow the previous August, the Communist Party of the Soviet Union had been compromised and its prestige and power had collapsed.

The Soviet Union and its leader, Mikhail Gorbachev, remained an inconvenient fact for Yeltsin. To get rid of the former would dispose of the latter and secure Yeltsin's power within the Russian Federation. He envisaged that a Commonwealth of Independent States (CIS) would replace the Soviet Union and maintain its world status. However, most of the former Soviet Republics, especially Ukraine, saw the CIS as simply a means to end subservience to Russia. The Baltic Republics of Estonia, Latvia, and Lithuania refused even to join the CIS.

Many Russians were to regret the loss of the power of the Soviet Union, and many could not accept that the split with Ukraine was permanent. Russia's relations with the former Soviet Republics was always to be uneasy, and many strongly resented what they perceived to be Russian interference in their internal affairs. Some twenty-five million Russians found themselves living in foreign nations, where they often faced severe discrimination. Some peoples left within the Russian Federation clamored for their own independence. In 1994, the Chechens declared independence and a savage war broke out. Ultra-nationalist groups appeared within Russia, and there were instances of racially motivated violence. Former Soviet Republics are acutely aware of the yearning of many Russians to regain a lost empire. **JS**

Prospects of Peace

The Oslo Agreement attempts to end the conflict between the PLO and Israel.

The agreement was ultimately signed in Washington by the Israeli Prime Minister, Yitzhak Rabin, and the leader of the Palestinian Liberation Organization (PLO), Yasser Arafat, but its contents had been decided in Oslo. Rabin had been defense minister for much of the first Intifada (1987–1993) and had concluded that Israel had no choice but to negotiate with the Palestinians. The agreement, however, was only a start to the peace process. The PLO agreed to renounce violence and recognize Israel's right to exist. Israel recognized the PLO as the representative

"[This is] a historic event, inaugurating a new epoch of peaceful coexistence."

Yasser Arafat

of the Palestinian people and acknowledged Palestinian rights to self-government. The Israeli military would withdraw from parts of the Gaza Strip and the West Bank, where a Palestinian Authority (PA) would be established. Over the next five years, a permanent settlement would be negotiated.

Arafat was duly elected President of the PA, but little other advancement was made. Far too much had been left unsettled in the Oslo Agreement, and slow progress led to disillusionment. Israeli settlements in the occupied territories expanded rapidly. Palestinian guerrilla attacks resurged and the PA could not, or would not, stop them. In 1996, a new Prime Minister, Benjamin Netanyahu, made further steps in the Oslo Agreement conditional upon the halt of violence, effectively ending all progress. **JS**

Rwandan Genocide

The assassination of the country's President ignites ethnic hostilities in Rwanda, leading to genocide.

President Juvenal Habyarimana of Rwanda was killed when his aircraft was shot down over the capital, Kigali. Habyarimana, a Hutu, had negotiated an uneasy peace with the revolutionary group the Rwandan Patriotic Front (RPF), which mainly represented the minority Tutsi people. Blaming the Tutsis for the assassination, the presidential guard began a massacre of Tutsis that spread out across the country from the capital.

Spurred on by political and military figures, Hutus slaughtered Tutsis and Hutu moderates wherever they could be found. Perhaps as many as 800,000 perished. Hutu death squads, such as *Interahamwe* ("those who fight together"), earned a grim reputation for clubbing or hacking their victims to death with machetes.

Tutsi-Hutu hostility was long-standing and had its roots in economic differences. Belgian colonial rulers from 1916 insisted on treating the Tutsi and the Hutu as different peoples and assumed the Tutsis were superior. Given preferential treatment, the Tutsis soon attracted deep resentment.

When the slaughter began, the international community did little. Many Western countries refused to contribute troops to a United Nations peacekeeping force. In fact, the peacekeepers were withdrawn after a small number were killed. The United Nations thenceforth limited its role to attempts to negotiate a cease-fire. The killings ended, however, only when the RPF took Kigali and installed a new Hutu President, Pasteur Bizimungu. The Tutsi RPF leader, Paul Kagame, became Vice President. Two million Hutus immediately fled, causing serious instability in neighboring states. Strong ethnic hostilities remained. **JS**

○ Skulls and bones lie outside a church that was the site of one of the genocidal massacres.

"We watched as the devil took control of paradise on Earth . . ."

Lieutenant General Roméo Dellaire, UN

Democracy Triumphant in South Africa

South Africa holds its first multiracial elections.

🡒 Two women celebrate the announcement of Nelson Mandela's historic victory.

White rule in South Africa finally came to an end, not in bloody revolution, but in orderly lines at polling booths. Negotiations between Nationalist Party (NP) leader and President Frederik Willem de Klerk and African National Congress (ANC) leader Nelson Mandela had finally ushered democracy into South Africa. A peaceful transition of power was far from guaranteed. White society experienced either relief or rage at the prospect of majority rule. The threats of white extremists taking up arms, or open conflict between the ANC and the Zulu-dominated Inkatha Freedom Party, were very real. The polls remained open for three days to allow all votes to be cast.

The ANC were the clear winners, with more than twelve million votes. The NP received nearly four million and Inkatha some two million votes. A collection of minor parties garnered a few thousand votes each. As had been previously agreed, the three main parties formed a coalition government of national unity. It was a government facing huge expectations. South Africa was experiencing massive unemployment and serious problems of poverty and inequality. Newly enfranchised Africans expected the election to produce rapid and dramatic improvements to their living standards, especially in housing, jobs, and education. In the event, the new government could not deliver all that was expected of it, but its great success was in establishing and maintaining democracy in the country. **JS**

Subway Gas Attack

Members of Aum Shinrikyu launch a lethal sarin attack on the Tokyo subway.

○ Members of Tokyo's emergency services prepare to enter the subway in the aftermath of the sarin nerve gas attack.

The Tokyo subway, notorious for uncomfortable overcrowding, was the target of an attack with a deadly nerve gas during the morning rush hour. Five separate trains were attacked. In each, a plastic bag filled with the gas sarin was punctured just as the doors closed before the train pulled away from the station. Twelve people died and more than 1,000 were injured, 50 of them seriously. Many of the others suffered temporary blindness. The city's hospitals were flooded with victims, and it took several hours for the gas to be identified.

The perpetrators were members of a cult known as Aum Shinrikyu, or "Religion of Truth," which had been set up in 1984 by Shoko Asahara as a meditation group. In the next decade, it gained a considerable following in Japan but was dogged with controversy about its methods of recruitment and funding. In the early 1990s, Aum built up strong connections to Russia. It also declared war on the Japanese constitution and began to collect an armory of conventional weapons and build its own chemical and biological weapons. In 1994 it launched a sarin attack in the city of Matsumoto. It is now believed that the Tokyo attack was launched in anticipation of a police raid on the cult's headquarters.

Asahara fled after the attack, and several other attacks were attempted. Asahara was eventually captured and condemned to death for mass murder. Aum Shinrikyu still exists, but it is now known as Aleph. **PF**

Bombing in Oklahoma

Right-wing extremists Timothy McVeigh and Terry Nichols bomb government offices in Oklahoma City in one of the United States's worst modern-day atrocities.

Revenge for the U.S. government's botched handling of a siege in Waco, Texas, was taken exactly two years later, when a truck bomb blew up just outside federal government offices in Oklahoma City. A gaping hole was blown in the building, and dozens of people were buried in the rubble. The death toll was reported as 168, although, gruesomely, there was one severed leg unaccounted for that suggested there was yet another victim. More than 800 people were injured.

There were thousands of Americans, mostly white men, who belonged to fanatical groups fiercely opposed to the federal government. Suspicion rapidly focused on two of them: Timothy McVeigh and Terry Nichols. McVeigh rented a truck in Junction City, Kansas, on April 15, and the next day the two men left a getaway car in Oklahoma City. They then returned to Kansas, where they used plastic buckets and a bathroom scale to make a bomb (using ammonium nitrate fertilizer and liquid nitromethane, among other ingredients) weighing about 5,000 pounds (2,268 kg), which they put in the truck. McVeigh then drove to Oklahoma City early on April 19, wearing a T-shirt bearing the words *Sic semper tyrannis* (Thus ever to tyrants), words that John Wilkes Booth proclaimed when he assassinated Abraham Lincoln. He lit a two-minute fuse before parking the truck by the building and walking away.

McVeigh was executed in 2001, and Nichols was imprisoned for life. The immediate effect of the atrocity was to dampen right-wing extremism. **RC**

◐ A police photograph of Timothy McVeigh, arrested and eventually executed for the bombing in Oklahoma City.

◑ McVeigh's truck bomb was powerful enough to destroy a side of the glass-fronted Alfred P. Murrah Federal Building.

Muslims Massacred in Bosnia

The United Nations looks on helplessly as Serbian troops massacre thousands of Muslims at Srebrenica.

In April 1993, the city of Srebrenica was declared a "safe area" by the United Nations, but in July 1995 it was taken by the army of Republika Srpska, representing Bosnian Serbs. In the days that followed, more than 8,000 Muslims were massacred.

The area around Srebrenica formed a Muslim enclave within territory conquered by the Serbs, and it had been under siege since March 1993. A United Nations representative, General Philippe Morillon, assured the besieged population, however, that they were under the protection of the United Nations. A safe area was proclaimed and a force of Dutch peacekeepers was stationed to protect it. By early 1995, Bosnian Serb leader Radovan Karadzic was under pressure to end the war and was determined to eradicate this enclave before he submitted. His forces, commanded by Ratko Mladic, closed in.

Within the enclave there were severe shortages, and the Muslim military presence was ill-armed and poorly organized. They had little prospect of defeating a serious attack. The peacekeepers themselves were only lightly armed and had no clear instructions what to do if an attack was made. When the first attacks met little resistance, the Serbs moved in on the city. Threats by NATO forces to launch air strikes were countered with threats against the Dutch soldiers—they had become nothing more than hostages and could only stand by when the killings began. It was a shameful event, but attempts to bring Karadzic and Mladic to justice proved fruitless. **JS**

◗ Body bags containing victims from mass graves in the Srebrenica area line the walls of an underground shelter.

◗ A wall in Tuzla recalls the mostly men and boys killed in the largest mass murder in Europe since World War II.

Princess Diana Killed in Car Crash

The car carrying Princess Diana and Dodi Al Fayed crashes into a pillar in a Paris tunnel.

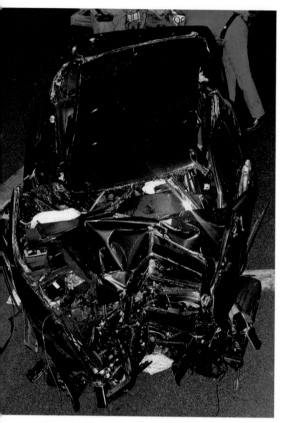

⬭ The wreckage of the limousine in which Princess Diana and Dodi Al Fayed were pursued by paparazzi to their deaths.

"There was no conspiracy to murder any of the occupants of that car."

Lord Stevens, December 2006

Diana, Princess of Wales, was well known worldwide for her tireless work with charities helping children, homeless people, and AIDS sufferers. She also touched the hearts of millions with her charm and charisma, yet was constantly hounded by the media. From her engagement to Prince Charles in 1981 onward, it seemed that the press was prepared to go to extremes to learn details of her private life.

Diana died in a traffic accident in Paris together with her companion, Dodi Al Fayed, the son of Egyptian-born tycoon Mohammed Al Fayed, and her chauffeur, Henri Paul. Her bodyguard, Trevor Rees, survived the crash. They were being driven late at night from Paris's Ritz Hotel to Al Fayed's apartment. The car was traveling at high speed to escape the pursuit of the paparazzi when their Mercedes Benz S280 sedan struck a pillar in the Pont de l'Alma tunnel. Investigators later reported that Paul had been drinking. The news of Diana's death provoked astonishingly sentimental scenes in Britain, with acres of flowers laid at impromptu memorials across the country. An estimated 2.5 billion people worldwide watched her televised funeral at Westminster Abbey.

Conspiracy theories about her death followed quickly, fed in part by a grief-stricken Mohammed Al Fayed, who could not accept that his son's death had such mundane causes. Some held that British agents had assassinated Diana because she threatened the monarchy—perhaps she was carrying Al Fayed's illegitimate child, was going to marry him, or was about to convert to Islam, or any combination of these themes. In April 2008, however, the inquest into her death returned a verdict that Diana had been "unlawfully killed due to the gross negligence of driver Henri Paul and the paparazzi." **JS**

Death of Mother Teresa

Mother Teresa's death is mourned around the world.

Mother Teresa, who spent forty years ministering to some of India's most destitute people, died at the age of eighty-nine. She suffered a heart attack in Calcutta (Kolkata).

She was born Agnes Gonxha Bojaxhiu in 1910 in Skopje, now the capital of Macedonia. At the age of eighteen, she joined the Sisters of Loreto to become a Catholic nun and a missionary in India. She never saw her family again. After a short spell in a convent in Ireland, where she learned to speak English, she arrived in India in 1929. In 1946, after several years' teaching in a convent, she chose to go among the people of the most desperate slums of Calcutta. She began by converting an abandoned Hindu temple into a free hospice, in which the impoverished could die with dignity. She then also took on the task of ministering to lepers and later orphans.

In 1950, she received the permission of the Vatican to establish a new order of nuns, the Missionaries of Charity. Initially this had just thirteen members. By the time of her death, the order numbered 4,000 and was supported by 100,000 lay volunteers. They were involved in running numerous hospices, orphanages, and charity centers across the world. Her tireless work rapidly gained her global renown, and she was the recipient of a host of international awards, including the Nobel Peace Prize in 1979. She was granted Honorary Citizenship of the United States in 1996.

Although Mother Teresa had some critics—who, for instance, alleged that her clinics reused hypodermic needles—they were few in number. She was called by many a "living saint." After her death, Pope John Paul II beatified her (a major step toward canonization or becoming a saint), and she became Blessed Teresa of Calcutta. **JS**

⟁ Members of the Missionaries of Charity pay their respects to Mother Teresa, who founded their order of nuns.

> *"I see God in every human being. . . . Is it not a beautiful experience?"*
>
> **Mother Teresa, 1974**

Human Genome Draft Completed

The map of humanity is drawn.

○ Study of the human genome has revealed the role of genes in most diseases, including individual resistance to infections.

Beginning in the mid-1980s, plans were put forward by James Watson, one of the two men who had made the seminal discovery of the structure of DNA in the early 1950s, to map the entire genome, or genetic blueprint, of the human species. The project officially began in 1990 and had teams working across the world. It was funded mainly by the U.S. Department of Energy and the National Institute of Health.

A rival, privately funded project began in 1998, led by Craig Venter of Celera Genomics. It used a less time-consuming method and allowed the company to retain some control over the uses of the information discovered. Rivalry between the projects perhaps accelerated the work, and the completion by the publicly funded National Human Genome Research Institute of the "rough draft" was announced two years ahead of schedule by Bill Clinton and Tony Blair on June 26, 2000. The draft covered perhaps 97 percent of around three billion chemical base pairs that are assembled into some 20,000 genes bundled into the twenty-four chromosomes in every human cell to form the essential instructions for the building of a living body. Clinton and Blair stressed the medical benefits from the fast-developing understanding of the relationship between genes and diseases.

The complete genome was published three years later, and the project was completed in 2006. It has provided a wealth of data to aid scientists to study in far more detail the interactions of genes and the ways in which they manifest in the body. **PF**

9/11

Terrorists attack the United States and some 3,000 innocent victims lose their lives.

○ With the North Tower burning, the South Tower is engulfed by a fireball as the second hijacked airliner makes its strike.

Often referred to simply as 9/11, the atrocities of that day were the worst of their kind in the history of the United States. Carried out by a group of Muslims inspired by the Islamic terrorist group Al-Qaeda, about 3,000 innocent victims were killed. On the morning of September 11, four teams of terrorists, each with its own pilot, hijacked four planes bound for California from different airports. Two of them were flown to New York City and crashed into the World Trade Center's twin towers. The American Airlines Boeing hit the North Tower at 8:46 A.M., and the United Airlines Boeing hit the South Tower at 9:03 A.M. Many people inside were killed instantly, and television pictures showed the towers wreathed in flames, with people leaping from high floors.

A third airliner was flown to Washington, D.C., and crashed into the Pentagon. In the fourth plane, said to be heading for the Capitol in Washington, D.C., brave passengers resisted the hijackers and tried to regain control of the aircraft. In the struggle, the plane crashed in a field in Pennsylvania, killing everyone on board.

Most of the terrorists came from Saudi Arabia. Al-Qaeda had its origins in the U.S.S.R.'s invasion of Afghanistan in 1979. It was created by Osama bin Laden, a rich Saudi, who fought the Russians with U.S.-funded anti-Soviet forces. In 1998, bin Laden issued an order for his followers "to kill Americans everywhere." The consequence of 9/11 would be a virtual U.S. war against Islamic terrorism. **RC**

Bankruptcy of the Enron Corporation

The dark side of capitalism is revealed as the formerly respected energy company Enron files for bankruptcy amid revelations of fraud and fabrication.

A few months after 9/11 came one of the most spectacular bankruptcies in U.S. history. The Enron Corporation was an energy company that dealt in communications, natural gas, electricity, paper, plastics, petrochemicals, steel, and even "weather risk management." Founded in 1931 in Omaha, Nebraska, as the Northern Natural Gas Company, it expanded and in the 1980s changed its name.

Hailed by *Fortune* magazine for years as "America's Most Innovative Company" and in 2000 as one of the hundred best companies to work for in the U.S., Enron had a 20,000-strong workforce and an opulent head office in Houston, Texas. In August 2001, however, a highly regarded financial analyst, Daniel Scotto, issued a report on Enron called "All Stressed Up and No Place to Go," advising shareholders to sell up and get out. It became clear that Scotto was right when the company filed for bankruptcy. Its profits and assets figures were false—in some cases grossly exaggerated and in others fabricated. Debts and losses had been hidden away offshore. Enron's most valuable asset and the largest source of income was the original Northern Natural Gas Company.

The discovery that this much-admired company had been relying on organized accounting fraud made Enron a byword for corporate greed, ruthless corruption, and the dark face of capitalism. Some of the directors were sued and had to pay damages, and the prominent firm of Arthur Andersen, Enron's accountants, was forced to close down. **RC**

○ Enron's corporate logo outside the company's headquarters in Houston, Texas.

○ In May 2002 members of Enron's Board of Directors were questioned about their role in the collapse of the company.

Bomb Attacks in Bali

A terrorist atrocity in the tropical paradise of Bali shocks the world with its scale and knocks the tourist industry.

It was the worst terrorist crime in Indonesian history. The bomb attacks on the resort-island of Bali killed 202 and injured 209. Although thirty-eight Indonesians were killed, the majority of the dead were tourists, and included eighty-eight Australians, twenty-six British, and seven Americans. The attacks occurred in the crowded Kuta Beach district. A suicide bomber detonated his backpack bomb in Paddy's Pub nightclub while a car bomb outside the Sari Club opposite exploded simultaneously. The results were devastating and horrific. A vast amount of material damage occurred, and many of the wounded suffered such terrible burns that they were flown to Australia for treatment by specialists.

The perpetrators belonged to an Islamic fundamentalist group, Jemaah Islamiah (JI). The U.S. and Australian governments immediately claimed JI had links to Al-Qaeda. Others have questioned this because there are clear domestic roots for Indonesian Islamic fundamentalism. JI's leader, Abu Bakar Bashir, was tried but denied all connections to the attacks. He was acquitted of treason, and his thirty-month sentence for a much lesser offense caused outrage in the United States and Australia. Three others received death sentences for the bombing. One, the purported mastermind behind the attacks, Amrozi bin Haji Nurhasyim, gave a cheerful "thumbs-up" sign when he received his sentence in April 2003. Clearly JI, like similar movements elsewhere, remains unbowed by the prospect of death. **JS**

○ A month after bombs destroyed two nightclubs in Kuta, visitors stand and offer prayers for victims of the attack.

○ Cars and buildings blaze after a car-bomb explosion outside the Sari Club, close to the scene of the first bomb.

Columbia Is Lost

The space shuttle disintegrates and all seven crew members are killed.

The U.S. space program was one of the most remarkable developments of the twentieth century, but, inevitably, there were disasters. One was the loss of the *Challenger* space shuttle in 1986 and another came with the disintegration of the space shuttle *Columbia*. The disaster was caused by a little piece of foam insulation, just 3 feet (1 m) long, which fell off the external fuel tank when the shuttle was launched and set off a succession of problems. *Columbia* had experienced difficulties with foam shedding before, and NASA engineers had become accustomed to it and thought little of it, a phenomenon later solemnly labeled the "normalization of deviance."

"The cause in which they died will continue. Our journey into space will go on."

President George W. Bush, February 1, 2003

When the team in charge of reentry went on duty in the Mission Control Center at 2:30 A.M. on February 1, neither they nor the astronauts in the spacecraft saw any reason for concern about the shuttle and its landing. At 8:15 A.M., the "de-orbit burn" was carried out 175 miles (282 km) up above the Indian Ocean, slowing the *Columbia* down from 17,500 miles per hour (28,164 kph) to begin reentry. The shuttle reentered the atmosphere 76 miles (122 km) above the Pacific at 8:44 A.M., crossed the California coast, and at about 9 A.M. began to break up over Texas. People on the ground reported hearing a loud boom and seeing smoke trails and debris in the sky. All seven of the crew were killed. **RC**

Fall of Baghdad

Saddam Hussein's power collapses as coalition forces take Baghdad.

The invasion of Iraq by a U.S.-led international coalition was proclaimed a great success when Baghdad fell in April 2003. The coalition, facing intense domestic opposition, had initially met surprisingly stiff resistance. The invaders had expected to be greeted as liberators, but the southern Shi'a population, who had been abandoned after their rising following the liberation of Kuwait in February 1991, launched no revolt to help them. It had taken two weeks for British forces to secure Basra, and a hard battle was expected at Baghdad. However, the capital's rapid fall encouraged hopes that all resistance would now collapse. Iraqi leader Saddam Hussein had fled, along with his senior supporters. There was jubilation on the streets of Baghdad, though perhaps not as much as Western reporters suggested. A crowd cheered when a U.S. armored vehicle pulled down Saddam's statue in Firdus Square. They were much less enthusiastic when a U.S. flag was temporarily draped over it.

After disastrous wars and years of economic sanctions, few Iraqis mourned the fall of Saddam. But foreign conquest and occupation were never going to be accepted easily. A rapid recovery and improved living standards, as well as a quick return to civilian government, would be vital. Almost immediately, problems arose and looting broke out. As a result, the National Museum was plundered of thousands of irreplaceable artifacts, and the National Library and Archives were burned. The Americans were quick only to secure the Oil Ministry. Chaos and armed resistance to the occupation developed rapidly. **JS**

◯ A triumphal statue of Saddam Hussein is symbolically dragged to the ground by U.S. occupation forces.

Madrid Bombed

A terrorist outrage threatens the survival of the Spanish government.

A series of explosions brought horror to the Spanish capital. The bombs—it was later established that there were ten explosions—were detonated within and around three railway stations: the mainline Atocha station and two smaller stations at Santa Eugenia and El Pozo. The bombers struck during rush hour to maximize the death toll. In all, 191 people were killed and more than 1,800 injured. So terrible were the injuries that hospitals had to appeal for extra blood donors. Police warned that it might not be possible to match all the body parts to the correct victims. The telephone network nearly collapsed from the number of distraught relatives seeking assurances of the safety of their loved ones.

The Spanish government seemed to have no doubts about the perpetrators, and Interior Minister Angel Acebes announced that the Basque separatist group Eta was definitely responsible. This caused immediate skepticism. The scale of the atrocity and lack of the standard telephone warning made Eta an unlikely candidate. The Spanish government was a strong ally of the United States in its invasion of Iraq, making Islamic fundamentalism a more plausible explanation. When a suspect van near Madrid was searched and evidence suggesting Islamic involvement was found the next day, there was considerable outrage. The government, it seemed, had blamed Eta to conceal the fact that they had not taken the Islamic threat seriously.

In the general elections held three days after the explosions, the ruling People's Party was unexpectedly beaten, and the new Socialist Prime Minister, José Luis Rodriguez Zapatero, immediately confirmed his election promise to withdraw Spanish troops from Iraq. **JS**

Wave of Terror

A tsunami in the Indian Ocean brings widespread catastrophe.

Horror swept across the rim of the Indian Ocean when a tsunami, or massive tidal wave, brought death and destruction to the coastal settlements in its path. It was created by an underwater earthquake, measuring 8.9 on the Richter scale, which caused the seabed off the coast of the Indonesian territory of Aceh to jump some 33 feet (10 m). The devastating tsunami, traveling at nearly 500 miles per hour (800 kph), was the biggest seen in forty years.

The coast of Aceh and its capital Banda Aceh were all but destroyed. In some villages, 70 percent of the population perished and some 500,000 people were left homeless and destitute. In total, more than 130,000 lives were lost in Indonesia. The tsunami rushed on to Burma (Myanmar), Thailand, Sri Lanka, India, and even East Africa, where 200 Somalis died. The total death toll was estimated at around 200,000. Given the popularity of many of these areas as tourist resorts, the victims came from all across the globe. Bodies were still being found months later, and there were fears that polluted water and decomposing bodies would cause epidemics.

The catastrophe shocked the world, and within six months $12 billion in aid had been pledged to the victims. The governments of the region also agreed to develop an early warning system in case of future tsunamis. Attempts to identify the dead brought together an international effort by forensic scientists. Despite such efforts, for the impoverished and homeless, the task of rebuilding proved slow and frustrating, especially for the poorest, who generally had the least access to aid. **JS**

◯ People stare in disbelief as a wave crashes ashore at Koh Raya, part of Thailand's territory in the Andaman islands.

Suicide Bombing in London

London is left reeling by new atrocities caused by terrorist suicide bombers.

CAMERA-14
07:21:54   07/07/05

○ Captured by CCTV cameras at Luton train station, the suicide bombers head to London for their mission of destruction.

◐ The explosion on the bus in Tavistock Square ripped off the roof of the top deck and destroyed the back of the vehicle.

"They are trying to use the slaughter of innocent people to cow us . . ."

British Prime Minister Tony Blair, July 2005

London experienced the horrors of suicide bombers for the first time on July 7. There were four attacks: three on underground trains—one near Liverpool Street station, one in Edgware Road station, and one between King's Cross and Russell Square stations—and one on a bus in Tavistock Square. A total of 56 people died and more than 700 were injured. London's transport system was paralyzed, and cell phone networks jammed as people frantically sought news of their loved ones, further hampering the rescue services.

A previously unknown Islamic group was quick to claim responsibility. Two weeks later another four men attempted to emulate them. Fortunately, their bombs failed to detonate. In a grim response, the police shot dead a suspected bomber at Stockwell underground station the next day, but he was an innocent Brazilian, Jean Charles de Menezes.

What stunned the British public was that the four bombers—Mohammed Sidique Khan, Shehzad Tanweer, Germaine Lindsey, and Hasib Hussain—were all British-born and had never attracted the attention of the police for radical Islamic views. Acquaintances generally remembered them more for their interests in sports than in the Qu'ran. Two of the bombers, Khan and Lindsey, had left behind pregnant wives.

The British were left to ponder how it was possible for ordinary British Muslims to become so alienated from their country that they would commit mass murder. The messages that the suicide bombers left behind made it clear that British foreign policy in the Islamic world played a very large part in their action, citing their committment to Islam and "atrocities" perpetrated against fellow Muslims as their motivation. **JS**

Hurricane Strikes

Hurricane Katrina hits New Orleans, and authorities respond all too slowly.

○ A satellite image of the hurricane as it strengthened to a Category Five (160 miles per hour) before reaching land.

"At least 80 percent of New Orleans was under flood water on August 31st . . ."

National Climate Data Center summary

The birthplace of jazz, the city of New Orleans, took the full force of Hurricane Katrina, one of the fiercest storms in U.S. history. On 28 August, the storm went from a Category Three to a Category Five over the Gulf of Mexico, with a maximum sustained wind of 175 miles per hour (280 kph). Hundreds of thousands of the city's inhabitants fled as the hurricane approached. Some, often the poor and the old, stayed behind. The Superdome football arena was chosen as their refuge of last resort.

The center of the storm passed to the east of the city, but the hurricane wrecked the levee system, which had been built to protect New Orleans from floods. Water poured into the city, and many of those who had remained behind had to swim to safety or were trapped in attics and on roofs. By evening, there were bodies floating in the streets or lying around in debris. Some were left for days, decomposing and making identification very difficult.

The city had no clean water and no electricity. Buildings mostly stood up to the storm well, but it blew many windows out, and beds were reported flying out of the windows of the Hyatt Regency Hotel, the glass exterior of which was completely destroyed. After the hurricane had passed, looting and violence by individuals and groups armed with guns became a serious problem. The police were completely occupied with the task of rescuing residents, meaning that shopkeepers had to try to defend their property by themselves. There were even reports of snipers shooting at rescue workers and police, although whether these stories were true is uncertain. The local, state, and federal governments came under fierce criticism over what was considered a slow and inadequate response to the catastrophe. **RC**

Death of a Dictator

The former Iraqi dictator, Saddam Hussein, is executed for his crimes.

Saddam Hussein, who ruled Iraq from 1979 to 2003, was hanged before dawn in the Baghdad district of Khadimiya in a building his own security services had previously used to carry out many executions in his name. He had been sentenced to death the previous November for the 1982 murder of 148 men and boys in the Shi'a town of Dujail.

The fact that this single crime was the basis of the death sentence, given his ghastly record of atrocities, reflects the chaotic and at times farcical nature of his yearlong trial. Three defense lawyers were assassinated; one fled the country. Saddam at times boycotted the hearings, and on one occasion he was dragged from the court after calling it a "daughter of a whore." Human rights groups were highly critical of the proceedings. Iraqis were generally unimpressed.

Saddam was mocked by his executioners who illicitly filmed his death. Subdued and holding a copy of the Qu'ran, he expressed no remorse. When the execution was announced, there were some celebrations in Sadr City, a Shi'a district of Baghdad, and some protests in his hometown of Tikrit. The Iraqi Prime Minister, Nuri al-Maliki, said that the execution marked the closure of a dark chapter in Iraq's history. Saddam's body was flown by a U.S. military helicopter to his birthplace in Al-Awja, near Tikrit, and buried in a family plot.

U.S. President George W. Bush proclaimed that it was an important step on the road to democracy for Iraq. Most Iraqis, however, seemed indifferent, disbelieving that this would end the violence that plagued occupied Iraq. They were right: The same day, three car bombs exploded in Baghdad, killing thirty-seven people, and across Iraq four U.S. servicemen died. **JS**

◐ A clip from Iraqi television footage filmed minutes before Saddam was hanged.

"You have destroyed us. You have killed us. You have made us live in destitution."

Shouted by a guard at the execution

The Credit Crisis

The collapse of Lehman Brothers signals a worldwide economic recession.

Warnings had been in the air for some months: rising defaults on "sub-prime" mortgages—for people whose credit-worthiness was below the once-accepted standards—were threatening major financial institutions, and they found it harder and harder to raise funds. For the prior ten years, the magic of Wall Street had spread the risk around, raised credit on the thinnest of collateral, and made the economic clouds vanish. Few banks were ready for the storm that was to hit them.

Lehman Brothers, a highly respected 150-year-old Wall Street institution, was one of the most badly exposed. In the second quarter of 2008 its losses were $2.8 billion, causing its share-value to plummet. The bank tried and failed to find a buyer, and on September 15 it filed for bankruptcy protection. After hurried meetings at which the staff heard the news, many of them, once recipients of huge salaries and six-figure bonuses, immediately abandoned their offices, clutching boxes of belongings.

The collapse triggered a further run on the global financial system, leading to the virtual cessation of interbank lending and massive tax-payer investment to prevent the collapse of other major financial institutions in the United States, Britain, and other countries. This was not, however, enough to prevent the collapse of the Icelandic Bank and others, while the result of the crisis was to freeze a high proportion of bank lending to businesses and individuals throughout the world. The outcome was the start of a major world recession—the result of the way in which the bankers had pursued profits out of reselling what now became known as "toxic assets"—and the rest of the world paid the price for bankers' arrogance and greed. **PF**

U.S. President Obama

The inauguration of Barack Obama marks a change of leadership in the U.S.

Two million people, the largest crowd in the country's history, gathered together on a freezing morning on Washington, D.C.'s Mall. The previous day had been Martin Luther King Day, commemorating the birth of the 1960s civil rights leader exactly eighty years earlier. The timing was auspicious, as Barack Obama was to be the first black president of a country where, just a few decades ago, such a thing had seemed impossible. The inauguration also spelled the end of the presidency of George W. Bush who, despite sky-high ratings in the aftermath of the 9/11 attacks, was widely felt to have left the country seriously weakened both at home, economically, and abroad, fighting two wars.

On many scores, Obama offered a break with the past. Campaigning with the slogan "Change we can believe in," Obama set out to redefine and revitalize the American political system. A Chicago lawyer and senator from Illinois, his epic battle with Hillary Clinton for the Democratic Party nomination had honed a reputation for oratory and unflappability, while his complicated family background—with connections in Texas, Kansas, and Hawaii, as well as Kenya and Indonesia—helped win him national support in the election on November 4, 2008 against Republican John McCain.

At the inauguration, the bands played, Aretha Franklin sang, and Yo Yo Ma played the cello. The oath was administered at noon by Chief Justice John Roberts, followed by the long-awaited inaugural address, citing the challenges that would be faced to mark a new start for America. **PF**

⬡ U.S. President Barack Obama waves to his supporters at an Inaugural Ball on the evening of January 20, 2009.

Michael Jackson Found Dead

The "King of Pop" dies weeks before he was to begin a long tour.

○ A fan in the Indian city of Bangalore pays his respects to the dead performer; Jackson's death touched fans around the world.

American singer and dancer Michael Jackson was found dead at his home in Los Angeles at the age of fifty, having apparently been given an overdose of the anesthetic propofol by his personal physician, Conrad Murray, who was treating him for insomnia. At the time of his death, Jackson was preparing for a return to live performance for the first time in many years, having been booked for a season at London's O2 arena, which was due to start in three weeks' time.

Jackson had been in the public eye ever since the age of six, when he was the lead singer in the chart-topping Jackson Five. His solo career in the 1980s, particularly the album *Thriller* (1982), made him a global star, one of the most recognized faces in the world. His behavior, however, became increasingly bizarre, with a series of face-lifts and skin-lightening procedures, while he retreated to his Californian ranch, where he indulged in a fantasy return to childhood. This led to accusations of child abuse, for which he was tried and acquitted in 2005. Thereafter his popularity and fortune declined sharply.

News of the death was first revealed just eighteen minutes after it had been pronounced, on celebrity gossip website TMZ.com. It led to an outpouring of grief around the world comparable to those occasioned by the deaths of John F. Kennedy in 1963 and Princess Diana in 1997. A family ceremony was held, followed by a public commemoration on July 7, where a galaxy of stars offered eulogies; it was watched by a global audience of a billion people. **PF**

Devastation Strikes Haiti

The island nation is hit by a catastrophic earthquake.

⬤ This cathedral in Port-au-Prince was one of thousands of buildings razed to the ground by the earthquake.

One of the most destructive earthquakes ever recorded, measuring 7.0 on the Richter scale, struck the homes of some of the world's poorest people in the Caribbean state of Haiti during the afternoon of January 12.

Huge areas of the capital, Port-au-Prince, were totally devastated. Initial reports suggested a death toll approaching a quarter of a million people, with an equivalent number of injured and a million homeless. Much of the country's infrastructure was itself hit, with damage to many government buildings, public utilities, and hospitals.

A worldwide emergency aid effort was immediately begun, though it was hampered by the plethora of different organizations offering assistance with little coordination between them. Receiving and distributing relief materials was also hampered by the small size of the airport, which itself had been damaged. U.S. forces quickly entered Port-au-Prince to try to maintain order, but many survivors found that it was a week or more before the basic essentials—food, tents, and water—reached them.

The numbers of homeless, and the scale of the need, overwhelmed attempts to provide quick aid, and several months later many were still living in tents in and around the ravaged city. Some countries, including the United States, accepted refugees. International banks offered hundreds of millions of dollars worth of aid, while the World Bank waived debt repayments for five years. **PF**

Deepwater Horizon Oil Platform Explodes

The U.S. suffers its worst environmental disaster since the Dust Bowl of the 1930s.

The world's worst-ever accidental marine oil spill began after an explosion and fire on the Deepwater Horizon oil rig, which was 40 miles (64 km) off the Louisiana coast in the Gulf of Mexico. The explosion, which was later found to have been caused by faulty cement, killed eleven people on the platform and caused it to sink, resulting in a massive oil leak on the sea floor, at a depth of 5,000 feet (1,524 m). Some 50,000–60,000 barrels per day gushed out into the ocean. Repeated attempts by the oil company BP to plug the leak failed, thwarted by the depth of the water. Almost five million barrels of crude oil were released into the Gulf before the well was finally capped on 15 July, 2010, around three months after the initial explosion.

The spillage resulted in a huge oil slick, which was washed up along hundreds of miles of the Louisiana coast, devastating the fishing and tourism industries and threatening environmental disaster despite a huge containment, dispersal, and cleanup operation. Around the Gulf of Mexico, seabirds, turtles, dolphins, crustacea, and many species of fish were affected, and experts have estimated that it may be years before the full extent of the damage is known. Nevertheless, some of the worst permanent ecological harm may have been averted by the relatively speedy dispersal of the oil slick by the wind.

BP's apparent inability to cap the leak, and some clumsy PR by the company's British chief executive, Tony Hayward, brought huge criticism—not least from U.S. President Barack Obama, who pledged to ensure that BP would pay for the damage caused. The company's liability was initially estimated at up to $100 billion, which then led to widespread concerns about the impact of this bill on the British economy. **PF**

> ## "The amount of oil . . . we are putting into [the ocean] is tiny in relation to the total water volume."

Tony Hayward, May 2010

🅞 The Deepwater Horizon oil rig burns as it collapses into the Gulf of Mexico.

🅞 Dispersant clotted oil and fresh crude oil float on the surface of the sea, 9 miles (14 km) from the source of the spill.

Tunisian Government Falls

The Tunisian revolution heralds the start of the "Arab Spring."

> ## "We have only one demand: for the government to fall. They all have to go."

Bassem El Barouni, protester in Tunis

○ A picture of President Ben Ali is burned at a demonstration in Paris to show support for the Tunisians.

◑ Demonstrators run as police throw tear gas to break up a protest in Tunis.

The suicide of street trader Mohamed Bouazizi in protest at his treatment by the police in the city of Sidi Bouzid on December 10, 2010 was the unexpected trigger for a rising tide of protest in Tunisia against the longstanding and autocratic government of President Zine El Abidine Ben Ali. Attempts by the government to suppress the demonstrations were thwarted by the use of social networking, notably via Twitter and Facebook, which allowed the protesters to organize and publicize their activities, and to inform the outside world.

Initially about unemployment, corruption, and freedom of speech, the protests gradually turned into a direct attack on Ben Ali himself. President since a coup d'etat in 1987, he had won 90 percent of the vote at his re-election in 2009.

On January 14, Ben Ali resigned and fled with his family to Saudi Arabia. He was convicted of money laundering in absentia, and sentenced to a long prison term. Protests continued for some weeks until the Tunisian people were convinced that all representatives of the old regime had been driven from power. Elections were called for October.

The Tunisian revolution was the start of the "Arab Spring," which saw mass protests across the Middle East, including in Bahrain, Yemen, and Syria. In Egypt, a fortnight of mass protests (January 25 to February 11) in Tahrir Square, Cairo, toppled Hosni Mubarak after thirty-five years in government. Not all achieved their aims so effectively, though, and in countries such as Syria, retaliation by the government brought widespread and prolonged violence. These events took place with little apparent involvement of outside powers. However, in Libya, a rising against Muammar Gaddafi was assisted by a no-fly zone enforced by NATO until his overthrow in August. **PF**

Tsunami Hits Japan

A combined earthquake and tsunami cause devastation in Japan.

One of the most powerful earthquakes ever recorded occurred at 2:46 P.M. on March 11, about 43 miles (70 km) off the eastern coast of Japan. The quake caused a tsunami up to 26 feet (8 m) high, which hit the coast less than an hour later. An area of more than 220 square miles (550 square kilometers) was destroyed, with houses uprooted and ships, trucks, and huge amounts of debris washed far inland. Many communities were totally devastated, and 15,000 people were confirmed dead, with thousands of others missing and injured. Over four million homes were left without electricity, and damage to dams disrupted water supplies for millions more. Huge damage to roads, rail, and ports hampered the rescue and cleanup efforts. The economic cost of the earthquake and tsunami was estimated at $235 billion, the world's most costly disaster to date.

The site where damage caused the most concern, however, was the coastal nuclear plant of Fukushima, where three aging reactors were hit by both the quake and the tsunami. Damage to the cooling systems caused the cores to melt, resulting in hydrogen explosions and leaks of radioactive material into the atmosphere and water. The area within 12 miles (20 km) of the plants was evacuated, while engineers battled to avert a catastrophe.

The power company and the government were both criticized for their poor handling of the situation and lack of clear information to the public. Although a disaster on the scale of Chernobyl was averted, events at Fukushima caused the government to rethink Japan's dependency on nuclear power. **PF**

◖ Burning houses and wrecked ships are among the piles of debris in Kisenuma city.

Osama bin Laden Killed

The Al-Qaeda leader is killed in a secret U.S. operation in Pakistan.

The most wanted man in the world, Al-Qaeda leader Osama bin Laden had lived a shadowy existence on the run since escaping from Afghanistan in 2001. Occasional audio or video tapes implied that he remained on the move, perhaps living in remote parts of the northwest region of Pakistan, yet investigations by both U.S. and Pakistani security forces turned up nothing. Early in 2011, however, the CIA received reports that he was living in a compound in the Pakistani city of Abbottabad.

Just after midnight local time on May 2, on the orders of U.S. President Obama and without the knowledge of the Pakistani government, a team of

> ## "To those . . . who have lost loved ones to Al-Qaeda . . . justice has been done."
> **President Barack Obama**

U.S. special forces flew in to attack the compound. It proved lightly guarded, and a brief firefight resulted before the U.S. forces entered bin Laden's room and shot him in the chest and head. The body was removed by helicopter, and the raid was over in just thirty-eight minutes. President Obama watched it live on a video link in the White House.

The body was positively identified as bin Laden's, photographed, and then buried at sea. News of the raid was received jubilantly in the U.S. and elsewhere, but the Pakistani government—which viewed the secrecy of the raid as an indication of mistrust—complained vociferously about the U.S. violation of their sovereignty. **PF**

The God Particle Is Revealed

The Large Hadron Collider reveals the elusive Higgs boson at CERN in Switzerland.

Scientists have long understood that mass is a fundamental quality of matter, but have struggled to say exactly what gives matter its mass. Traditionally, it is thought to have been the neutrons and protons in atomic nuclei—but what gives mass to the neutron or proton? Particle physicists had no answer.

In the 1960s the British physicist Peter Higgs suggested that a fundamental mass-carrying particle existed. This was named the Higgs boson but its supposed characteristics made it virtually undetectable, and for many years it was impossible to prove or disprove his hypothesis. Ironically, the search for such tiny particles required huge machines and enormous supplies of energy, which was provided by the Large Hadron Collider, a vast particle accelerator built at CERN in Switzerland that started up in 2008. The first major challenge for the machine was to search for the Higgs boson, which was also a key element in modern descriptions of how the Big Bang produced the universe as we know it.

The elusive Higgs boson was popularly known as "the God particle," after a book published by Leon Lederman in 1993. His original title was *The Goddamn Particle: If the Universe Is the Answer, What Is the Question?* and the first part of the title was changed by the publishers to *The God Particle*. There is nothing else to suggest that the Higgs boson is connected to concepts of divinity, and many scientists object to the appellation, which they see as misleading.

On July 4, 2012, scientists at CERN announced that they had observed results compatible with their predictions of the Higgs boson. They had effectively found an entirely new form of matter. Over the following year the discovery was confirmed and refined, and in 2013 Peter Higgs was awarded the Nobel prize for his work of fifty years earlier. **PF**

"I am quite surprised that [the detection] happened during my lifetime."

Peter Higgs

○ The Large Hadron Collider at CERN, which revealed the Higgs boson and changed our understanding of the universe.

Hurricane Sandy Hits New York

A tropical storm takes an unexpected path and causes mass devastation.

Hurricane Sandy was the largest Atlantic storm on record and the second most costly in U.S. history, after Hurricane Katrina, which struck in 2005. The storm was responsible for more than 200 fatalities and it left many millions of people without power, costing more than $68 billion across twenty-four U.S. states.

It began in late October as a tropical storm in the Caribbean and crossed Jamaica and Haiti before moving north, through the Bahamas, and up the eastern seaboard of the United States. A state of emergency was declared in several areas; flights were canceled, schools were closed, and many communities were evacuated. Similar storms had turned northeast and blown out in the ocean, but on October 29, 2012, Hurricane Sandy turned westward. It made landfall in Atlantic City, New Jersey, and in New York City. The surge at Battery Park, Manhatten, was almost 14 feet (4.3 m) high. The East River burst its banks, flooding much of Lower Manhattan and inundating seven subway lines. Buildings were left without power and the Stock Exchange closed for several days. Seventy-one people died in New York, and the total cost to the city was estimated at $42 billion. In Atlantic City the hospitals and fire stations were evacuated and three towns were under 5 feet (1.5 m) of water. At least 22,000 homes were uninhabitable and there were complaints about the lack of support for the newly homeless.

The hurricane hit a few days before the presidential elections and it became a political issue. The governors of affected states—notably the Republican Chris Christie in New Jersey and Democrat Mario Cuomo in New York—worked with President Obama to limit the damage. The potential link between the unusual path and severity of the hurricane and climate change was debated widely. **PF**

> **"This storm is a killer storm that will likely take more lives as she makes landfall."**
>
> **Martin O'Malley, Governor of Maryland**

◑ A NASA satellite image showing Hurricane Sandy over the Bahamas shortly before hitting New York and New Jersey.

Flight MH17 Shot Down

A tragedy that brought the conflict between Ukraine and Russia into focus.

Ukraine was a part of the Soviet heartlands until it became a nation in 1991. This caused instability, as some Ukrainians looked to the Kremlin for their lead, while others wanted closer ties with the West. In 2014 these tensions exploded as pro-Russian President Viktor Yanukovych was forced out of office. Eastern Ukraine, dominated by Russians, dissolved into civil war. The separatists were supported by Russian equipment and in February 2014, the separatists and Russian forces seized Crimea (a republic within the Ukraine). Two weeks later Russia claimed Crimea and the region was annexed by President Putin.

On July 17, 2014, a Malaysian Airline Boeing 777 passenger jet traveling from Amsterdam to Kuala Lumpur crashed near Hrabove in the rebel-held Donetsk region of Ukraine. All 298 people on board were killed, including 193 Dutch nationals, 43 Malaysians, and 38 Australians. Access to the crash site was difficult and separatists looted the wreckage.

Investigation showed that a Buk surface-to-air missile downed the aircraft. Ukrainian separatists and the Russian government argued that the Ukrainian government shot down the plane using a fighter jet. But separatists were recorded claiming responsibility in phone conversations, and may have had Russian-supplied missiles. The Ukrainian government said that the missile had been launched from Russian territory. Russia then vetoed a Malaysian-backed UN proposal to prosecute those responsible. Four months earlier, the disappearance of Malaysian Airlines flight MH370 had caused the loss of 239 lives. The two incidents resulted in the renationalization of the airline. **PF**

◯ Parts of the aircraft flight MH17 at the crash site near the village of Hrabove in November, 2014.

ISIS Beheading Video

The terrorist group ISIS uses gruesome shock tactics to gain the world's attention.

Several extreme jihadist and Islamist groups emerged from the chaos created by the civil war that broke out in Syria following the government's suppression of democratic protests in 2011, and the weakness of the Iraqi government following the withdrawal of Coalition forces in 2013. The most successful of these was known as Islamic State of Iraq and Levant (ISIL, also known as ISIS, or IS). Having seized large tracts of eastern Syria and western Iraq, acquired considerable resources, including oil wells, and captured much equipment from the Iraqi army, its leader Al-Baghdadi declared a new Islamic caliphate in June 2014.

ISIS was denounced as un-Islamic by many mainstream Muslims. It was a millenarian cult that proclaimed the end of the world was imminent, and it brutally forced civilians to submit to its extreme interpretation of Islam. It was eager to draw the West into a fight and was adept at manipulating broadcast media by using graphic imagery, and using social media to attract new recruits worldwide.

Having taken several Western aid workers and journalists hostage, on August 19, 2014, ISIS released a video of forty-year-old U.S. photojournalist James Foley kneeling on the ground in an orange jumpsuit before being murdered and decapitated with a knife by a masked attacker. The murderer was later identified as a British-born graduate from London who had traveled to Syria two years previously.

Several more beheading videos followed over the coming months, as well as other films showing gruesome and increasingly sadistic executions of both individuals and groups. ISIS sought to create the impression that the organization was relentlessly progressing toward its goals despite months of U.S. airstrikes and drone attacks on its positions. **PF**

Charlie Hebdo Cartoonists Killed

Religious cartoons provoke extremists to attack magazine offices in Paris.

⊙ Parisians gathered on the Republic square in downtown Paris on 7 January in memory of those killed earier that day.

Satirical, left-wing magazine *Charlie Hebdo* was famous in France for irreverent cartoons of authority figures, particularly concerning religion, and in 2013 and 2014, the magazine published several cartoons lampooning Muhammad and Sharia law. Depictions of Muhammad are forbidden in many Islam traditions.

On the morning of January 7, 2015, Said and Cherif Kouachi, brothers of Algerian descent, entered the *Charlie Hebdo* offices in Paris and killed eleven people, including the editor Stephane Charbonnier and other leading cartoonists. They injured several others before killing a policeman outside the building as they escaped. Claiming to be members of al-Qaeda wishing to die as martyrs, the brothers were killed north of Paris the next day after a manhunt.

The attack on *Charlie Hebdo* provoked a huge response from the French public, who saw it as an attack on the values of the country: "liberty, equality, fraternity." Many claimed "Je suis Charlie" ("I am Charlie") to show their solidarity with the victims and assert the right to free speech and to cause offence. Vigils were held in Paris and cities worldwide, and on January 11, two million people attended a march in Paris to show solidarity with the magazine, including French President François Hollande, German Chancellor Angela Merkel, and the prime ministers of many other countries. The subsequent issue of *Charlie Hebdo* sold almost five million copies worldwide, which compared to 35,000 copies for the previous issue. **PF**

Hundreds of Refugees Die in the Mediterranean

The EU cease rescue patrols as a record number of migrants cross the seas to Europe.

○ An image from the Italian coast guard showing an overcrowded boat of hopeful immigrants traveling across the Mediterranean.

The Syrian civil war, ISIS advances, and disturbances in Eritrea combined to create an unusually large refugee crisis in 2014 and 2015. Thousands fled their homelands, setting their sights on Europe, and smugglers were happy to help. A major route was from Libya to the tiny Italian island of Lampedusa. Old and unseaworthy boats were desperately overloaded with passengers who undertook the journey with the expectation that if they arrived, they would be granted asylum, and if not, they would be rescued by EU patrols.

In early 2015 the EU policy relating to patrolling this seaway changed, as it seemed insupportable to continue providing a comprehensive rescue service. But the flow of migrants increased and in mid-April a 70-foot (21-m) boat overturned 60 miles (96 km) from Libya, drowning up to 800 people. Only a few dozen could be rescued.

Throughout the summer tens of thousands of people arrived in Europe via this route and hundreds more died at sea. Others arrived via the Greek islands close to the Turkish coast, or through eastern Europe, overwhelming local communities, border controls, and processing procedures. The EU and its member states had little coordinated policy to deal with this humanitarian crisis, and long-established positions on borders and free movement were challenged. Governments promised to pursue the traffickers but the task seemed hopeless. It was the largest movement of people within Europe since 1945. **PF**

Paris Shootings

Parisians are attacked by jihadi gunmen in seven locations around the city.

Less than a year after the *Charlie Hebdo* incident, Paris was the target of a second major Islamist attack. Seven strikes took place across the city from around 8:20 P.M. on a Friday evening. The targets had been chosen to represent the ways in which young Parisians typically enjoy themselves: drinking with friends; attending a rock concert; watching a football match. Some 129 people died and hundreds were injured.

The attacks were performed by a group, mostly of French origin, based in Belgium. Three suicide bombers tried to attack the football stadium where France was playing Germany—with president François Hollande in attendance—but were unable to gain entry to the ground. Simultaneously, men with Kalashnikov machine guns fired on several bars and restaurants in eastern-central Paris, and others burst into the Bataclan theater, where an American rock band was playing. The following day ISIS claimed responsibility, asserting, "let France and those who walk in its path know that the smell of death will never leave their noses as long as they lead the convoy of the Crusader campaign and . . . are proud of fighting Islam in France, and striking the Muslims in the land of the Caliphate with their planes, which did not help them at all in the streets of Paris and its rotten alleys. This attack is the first of the storm and a warning to those who wish to learn."

A manhunt ensued and France was now at war. President Hollande announced the response would be merciless, ordering heavy bombing attacks on the ISIS capital of Raqqa in eastern Syria. Meanwhile, Parisians asserted their values of life and liberty. **PF**

◐ Mourners hold a vigil on the road opposite the Bataclan in Paris, where some 89 people were killed.

Britain Votes to Brexit

A referendum on British membership of the EU results in a majority vote to leave.

The question of Britain's membership had been a thorn in every government's side since the Treaty of Maastricht (1992) turned the European Economic Community into the European Union (EU). A small band of rebel politicians (dubbed "the bastards" by prime minister John Major in 1993) swelled as Nigel Farage built up the populist UK Independence Party (UKIP). In 2013, prime minister David Cameron, beset by an anti-Europe faction in the Conservative party, promised a referendum after the next election.

After unexpectedly returning to power in 2015, Cameron called the referendum for June 23, 2016. His close allies and friends Michael Gove and Boris Johnson deserted him to lead the Leave campaign, promising to "take back control" of Britain's laws, borders, and legislation, and to stop the flow of money from Britain to Brussels. Cameron, leading the Remain campaign, focused relentlessly on the economic perils of "Brexit." The two campaigns revealed deep and bitter divisions, notably between the liberal metropolitan elite who mainly supported Remain, and the working-class of the towns and cities who felt forgotten by Westminster, threatened by a wave of immigration and badly hit by Cameron's austerity policies.

When the polls closed, Leave campaigners declared that they had lost, but a few hours later it became evident they were wrong. The final count was 51.9:48.1 in favor of leaving the EU. Cameron, who had said he would stay in post whatever the result, resigned the next morning. After a period of political confusion, Theresa May was elected prime minister by the Conservative Party and, declaring "Brexit means Brexit," prepared the country for a dramatic and historic change of direction. **PF**

Trump Towers over America

Donald Trump is inaugurated as the 45th President of the United States

O Donald Trump conducted the most divisive campaign of modern times, but the numbers were still on his side.

"The forgotten men and women of our country will be forgotten no longer."

Donald Trump, November 8, 2016

After eight years of Barack Obama's Democrat presidency, and with the Republicans in chaos through the primary season, many assumed that Democrat candidate Hillary Clinton, former Secretary of State and wife of former president Bill Clinton, would succeed him. The unexpected Republican choice to challenge her was property tycoon and TV celebrity Donald Trump, who had a high profile among the electorate but no political experience. Relying on crude rhetoric and simple language, but making highly effective use of Twitter to get his message across, Trump insulted so many key groups—including women, disabled people, blacks, Muslims, and Mexicans—contradicted himself so often, and behaved so bizarrely at times that he was repeatedly written off as a candidate.

Despite this, his consistent message was to reduce illegal immigration, to bring back Rust-Belt jobs that had been moved abroad under Obama, and to "make America great again." .

On election day, Clinton won the popular vote by three million but Trump, by capturing the depressed industrial states of Pennsylvania and Ohio, won the electoral college. His victory was greeted by shock and fear across the United States and in much of the rest of the world, not least because of a strange combination of bellicose rhetoric toward China and apparent leniency toward Russia. After his election, he attacked what he called the "mainstream media," whom he accused of creating "fake news." At his inauguration, which was beset by arguments about the size of the crowd and violent protests, Trump identified the "American carnage"—the product of unemployment, drugs, gangs, poor education—which he intended to address as president. A new, unpredictable era had begun. **PF**

Buddhist Genocide in Burma

Thousands of Burma's Muslim minority flee as cries of genocide go unanswered.

Burma, or Myanmar, is primarily a Buddhist country comprising ethnic Burmese, but contained a long-established Muslim minority about 1 million people, known as Rohingya, mainly inhabiting the northern coastal state of Rakhine.

Following a crackdown by the army against the Rohingya in 2016, a larger attack began in August 2017 in a response to a series of attacks by the Arakan Rohingya Salvation Army (ARSA) on police posts and bridges in the region. ARSA justified these attacks as an attempt to break a government siege on urban centers.

ARSA was declared an Islamist terrorist organization, and the army attack was supported by a Rakhine Buddhist militia. Hundreds of villages were burned, while widespread rape and massacres resulted in the deaths of an estimated 10,000 people. By early 2018, almost 700,000 Rohingya had fled to neighboring Bangladesh where they were housed in refugee camps.

The attacks were widely reported and criticized internationally as ethnic cleansing and genocide. While the Burmese military had long been immune to international condemnation, the attitude of the Burmese State Counsellor (head of government) Aung San Suu Kyi—who won the Nobel prize in 1991 for her campaign for human rights and democracy in the face of longstanding persecution and house imprisonment at the hands of the Burmese military —now surprised many; she appeared to be doing nothing to restrain the attacks. Aung San Suu Kyi described "a huge iceberg of misinformation," suggesting that the Rohingya were illegal immigrants rather than true Burmese citizens, and querying whether the brutal ethnic cleansing was actually taking place. **PF**

⊙ Thousands of Rohingya refugees fleeing persecution in Burma line the border of Bangladesh at Cox's Bazar.

"Myanmar [Burma] does not fear international scrutiny."

Aung San Suu Kyi, September 19, 2017

Glossary

abba: Aramaic; "father."

Abbasid, Almohad: See Islamic.

aegis: Greek; "shield, breastplate."

ahimsa: Sanskrit; "nonviolence."

A.N.C.: African National Congress. A political movement of black South Africans, which was banned in the 1960s to prevent its protests against the Apartheid regime.

ancien regime: French; "old regime." Aristocratic political system in fourteenth- to eighteenth-century France made up of the monarchy, the clergy, and the nobility.

Angevin: The House of Anjou, which ruled Normandy, England, Aquitaine, and Ireland during the twelfth and thirteenth centuries. See Plantagenet.

Anti-Semitism: Prejudice and hostility toward the Jewish race and religion.

Apartheid: A system of racial segregation enforced by the white minority government in South Africa between 1948 and 1990.

Assyria: An empire located on the banks of the Tigris River in modern-day Iraq. It stretched from the Fertile Crescent to Egypt.

Aztec: An ethnic, Nahuatl-speaking people whose empire dominated Central America in the fourteenth to sixteenth centuries.

Babylon: Ancient city of Mesopotamia located in modern-day Iraq, which was the center of the Babylonian Empire from the rule of Hammurabi (c.1728–1686 B.C.E.).

ballista/ballistae: Latin; "crossbows."

B.C. / A.D., B.C.E. / C.E.: The Gregorian calendar is divided into two eras before and after the traditional date of the birth of Jesus Christ—B.C. "before Christ" and A.D. "Anno Domini" ("year of our Lord"). Today's terms are B.C.E. ("before the common era") and C.E. ("common era").

boule/boulai: Greek; "to will." In ancient Greece, a legislative council.

burh(s): Anglo-Saxon; borough(s) or fortified town(s).

Buwayhids: Persian people who became an Islamic ruling dynasty in the tenth century.

Byzantine: Ornate and often heavily gilded architecture developed in the fifth and sixth centuries. Later a term to describe churches using a traditional Greek rite and subject to Eastern canon law.

Byzantium: Ancient Greek city founded c.667 B.C.E., which in the later Roman period became the center of the Byzantine Empire under the name Constantinople.

caesar: Latin; junior emperor.

Caliph: The head of an Islamic community (caliphate) ruled by Sharia law. The Umayyad, Abbasid, and Ottoman dynasties, among others, were caliphates.

Canaan: An ancient territory, called the "land of Canaan" in the Hebrew Bible, roughly corresponding with present-day Israel, and the Palestinian Territories, parts of Lebanon, Jordan, Egypt, and Syria.

Crusades: Military campaigns, beginning in 1096, waged by Christian armies from Western Europe with the aim of conquering Jerusalem and the Holy Land and freeing them from Islamic rule.

Christendom: Government by Christian rules and institutions. Historically used to mean the Byzantine Empire from 392 until 800 when Charlemagne was crowned Holy Roman Emperor.

deme(s): Greek; village(s) or subdivisions of land in ancient Attica.

democracy: Greek; "rule by the people." See isonomia.

Deus vult: Latin; "God wills it."

diodochi: Greek; "successors," especially of Alexander the Great.

Dutch East India Company: Set up in the Netherlands in 1602, it funded expeditions to seek territories and establish monopolies in overseas trade.

eis ten polin: Greek; "in the city," from which the name Istanbul derives.

Etruscan: Ancient civilization of the Italian peninsula that flourished from prehistory before being absorbed into the Roman empire.

Fatimid: An Arab Islamic dynasty that ruled from the tenth to eleventh centuries and was located in present-day Egypt and the Levant with the city of Cairo as its capital.

Feudalism: A political and social system in medieval Europe under which peasants owed legal and military service to their lords who, in turn, owed service to the crown.

Georgian: The art and culture of Britain under the Hanoverian kings, beginning with George I (r.1714–1727).

Ghazi: Arabic; "valiant for the faith."

Ghaznavid: See Islamic.

Ghurid: See Islamic.

Gupta: The empire occupying northern India around 550 C.E.

Habeas corpus: Latin; "we command you have the body." Legal action enshrined under Magna Carta in 1215 by which anyone can seek relief from unlawful detention. It protects the liberty of individuals from imprisonment without legal sanction.

Hanoverian: The ruling dynasty of Britain from 1714 to 1837, beginning with King George I. Although only 52nd in line for the throne, he was the nearest Protestant according to the Act of Settlement.

Hanseatic League: An alliance of trading guilds centered around northern Europe that linked trading posts in the Baltic area from the thirteenth century onward. The League is said to have begun with the rebuilding of the German town of Lübeck in 1159.

Hellenistic: The architecture and culture of the Greek-speaking world following the death of Alexander the Great in 323 B.C.E.

Heresy: Nonconformist beliefs; heresy in the medieval period usually means deviation from the beliefs of the Christian church. Examples of heresy are Catharism and Gnosticism.

hijra: Arabic; "migration," specifically Muhammad's migration to Mecca.

hoplites: Greek; "infantrymen," usually with spears.

Holy Roman Empire: An alliance of territories in Central Europe in the medieval period under the rule of the Holy Roman Emperor, beginning with Charlemagne in 800.

HUAC (House UnAmerican Activities Commission): An investigative committee of the U.S. House of Representatives set up in the 1930s to investigate Nazi activities. It became a permanent committee in 1945 and focused on investigating suspected communists. In 1947 the committee blacklisted 300 Hollywood writers, actors, directors, and others connected with the entertainment industry for suspected communism.

Huguenot: Sixteenth- to eighteenth-century French Protestants, also known as Calvinists, who criticized the Roman Catholic church for its ritual, hierarchy, and monasticism. Huguenots focused on a more direct, personal interpretation of the Bible. Huguenots were persecuted in France from the late sixteenth century, and many left and settled in England, South Africa, and North America.

Inca: A civilization in the central Andes region in South America, which rose to prominence in the eleventh century and ruled the largest state in pre-Spanish America.

Inquisition: A method of combating heresy used by the Christian church throughout the medieval period to target non-Christians and Protestants. The Spanish Inquisition—established by Pope Sixtus IV in 1483—was probably the most ruthlessly applied, using torture to extract confessions of heresy.

insulae: Latin; term describing apartment blocks in ancient Rome.

Intifada: An Arabic word, which loosely translated into English means "rebellion." Since the late 1980s, the word has come to be associated with Palestinian uprisings against Israeli rule.

Islamic: Abbasid, Almohad, Ghaznavid, Ghurid, Safavid, Sassanid, Timurid, and Umayyad were some of many ruling dynasties that emerged in the Islamic world in the years following the death of the Prophet Muhammad in 632. The influence of Islamic culture was felt throughout the Middle East and as far afield as Moorish Spain.

isonomia: Greek; equal rights for all.

Jacobite: A supporter of the movement calling for the return of the Stuart kings to the thrones of England and Scotland.

Judah / Judaea: The Kingdom of Judah, also known as the Southern Kingdom, was an ancient territory in the south of present-day Israel, with Jerusalem as its capital that lasted from the tenth century B.C.E. until the sixth century C.E.

Khalsa: Punjabi; "pure" referring to a Sikh army.

Khan: Originally the heads of Central Asian nomadic tribes and later adopted by Turkic peoples and Mongols. The most famous ruler to use the title was Genghis Khan (1162–1227) who was known as "Khagan," meaning Khan of Khans.

koan: Japanese; paradoxical questions.

kshatriya: Sanskrit; Hindu ruling warrior caste.

K/T Boundary: The end of the Cretaceous (K) and beginning of the Tertiary (T) periods some 65 million years ago, when some much debated event, such as a meteorite, caused the extinction of many species.

ludi saeculares: Latin; Roman "secular games," involving sacrifices.

McCarthyism: The term refers to the anti-communist sentiments prevalent during the 1940s and 1950s, and was named after Senator Joseph McCarthy, who vigorously pursued anyone he believed to have communist sympathies.

Macedonia: A geographical and historic region of Greece corresponding to the modern-day province of Macedonia. Later the Kingdom of Macedon expanded to include the southern states of ancient Greece, and under Alexander the Great (356–323 B.C.E.) it expanded further to encompass Persia, Egypt, and parts of modern-day India.

Magna Carta: An English charter issued by the nobles in 1215 to curb the powers of the king. It required the king to acknowledge legal process and be bound by the law himself. See habeas corpus.

Mayan: A Mesoamerican civilization that occupied the Yucatán Peninsula of present-day Mexico and beyond in what is now Guatemala, Belize, El Salvador, and Honduras from c.400 B.C.E. to the Spanish Conquest in the mid-sixteenth century. It had the only developed written language of the pre-Columbian Americas.

Medieval: A period from the fifth to the fifteenth century in European history, which is also known as the Middle Ages.

Mesopotamia The area located between the Tigris and Euphrates Rivers, which corresponds to modern-day Iraq. The region has been settled since the fifth millennium B.C.E. and is the location of the most ancient cities in human history, such as Ur and Uruk and the Akkadian and Babylonian empires.

milites Christi: Latin; "soldiers of Christ,"used to describe both monks and Crusaders.

monakhas: Greek; "solitary."

Monroe Doctrine: First stated by President James Monroe on December 2, 1823, the doctrine asserted the neutrality of the United States of America vis-à-vis European powers, and stated that such powers no longer had rights to colonize the United States or interfere in its affairs.

Moors: During the medieval period, Muslims of the Islamic Iberian Peninsula and North Africa.

Mughal: The ruling dynasty of the Indian subcontinent from the sixteenth to the nineteenth century, the Mughals were of Turkic origin and set up a vast Islamic empire. The most famous Mughal ruler was Akbar the Great, who ruled from 1556 to 1605.

noblesse oblige: French; a noble's action must befit his title.

OPEC: The Organization of the Petroleum Exporting Countries, founded in 1960, which is made up of twelve oil exporting nations.

Ottoman: Turkish empire ruling from 1299 to 1922 from the capital Constantinople. At its peak, it spanned three continents—Europe, the Middle East, and North Africa.

panem et circenses: Latin; "bread and circuses." Placating citizens with food and entertainment as a means of distraction.

Papal Schism: Also known as the Great Schism, this term refers to the state of affairs after 1409, when there were three claimants to the papacy: John XXIII, Pope Benedict XIII, and the Roman Pope Gregory XII.

Persia: A region that roughly corresponds to modern-day Iran. The Persian Empire had an ancient history dating back to before 500 B.C.E. Persian culture refers to the history of Iran and its people.

Peloponnesian War: Fifth-century B.C.E. military conflict between the Ancient Greeks of Athens and the Peloponnesian League led by Sparta.

Phoenicia: Ancient maritime culture located in a coastal settlement in what is now modern-day Lebanon, Syria, and Israel.

Plantagenet: A name given to a branch of Angevin rulers of France and England. Geoffrey of Anjou, father of Henry II of England, was known as Plantagenet. See Angevin.

Pliny the Elder: Gaius Plinius Secundus (23–79) was an author, naturalist, and naval and military commander in ancient Rome. His only surviving work is the *Natural History*, which was a reference work of knowledge about medicine, plants, agriculture, architecture, sculpture, geology, and mineralogy. He died witnessing the eruption of Vesuvius, which destroyed Pompeii and Herculaneum in 79.

presbyter: Greek; a minister of the early Christian church.

quriltai: Turkish; "assembly."

rangatira: Maori; "Maori chiefs."

reconquista: Spanish; "reconquest." Christian kingdoms conquering Muslim Spain from the eighth to the fifteenth century.

Reformation: In European history, the word refers either to the Protestant Reformation of the Roman Catholic church begun by Martin Luther in the early sixteenth century, or to the English Reformation begun by King Henry VIII, which resulted in the church in England breaking from the church in Rome.

Renaissance: A cultural movement of the late Middle Ages that started in Italy and spread throughout Europe. It began with a revival of classical learning and influenced art, literature, philosophy, politics, science, and religion.

Restoration: Return of King Charles II to the English throne in 1660 after the end of Oliver Cromwell's Commonwealth.

Roi fainéant: French; "do nothing king," used specifically for Sigebert III and Clovis II.

saeculum novum: Latin; "new age."

Safavid, Sassanid: See Islamic.

sans culottes: French; "without knee-breeches." Poorer members of French Revolutionary society.

satori: Japanese; "sudden enlightenment."

Sejm: Polish; "parliament."

Seljuk: A Turkic people who carved out a huge empire from the mid-eleventh century onward in the Middle East, from present-day Turkey, the Levant, and Persia to Afghanistan, Turkmenistan, and beyond.

Scorched earth: A military tactic that has been used throughout human history that involves the complete destruction of property and infrastructure to prevent the enemy regaining territory.

Shi Huangdi: The king Qin Shi Huang was named Shiu Huangdi, meaning First Emperor. He ruled a unified China in the third century B.C.E.

Shogun: A military commander ruling a "shogunate" or administrative area. Throughout Japan's history since the Middle Ages, powerful Shoguns have determined who ruled Japan as emperor.

Shi'atu 'Ali: Arabic; "the party of Ali" (now known as Shi'a).

sic semper tyrannis: Latin; "thus ever to tyrants."

Silk Road: Series of ancient trade routes between China, India, and Western Europe. In addition to all types of goods, Chinese silk was transported along these routes before the Western world learned the secrets of silk manufacture.

sirdar: Hindi/Urdu; "commander."

Sol Invictus: Latin, "Unconquered Sun." The late Roman sun god.

Sons of Liberty: A group of shopkeepers and artisans in the colonies of British America who successfully campaigned for the abolition of the Stamp Act.

Stuart: Mary Queen of Scots changed the spelling of her family name from Stewart to Stuart. Her son, James VI of Scotland, became James I of England. The last Stuart to rule was Queen Anne (d.1714), who ruled Great Britain.

Sumerian: The ancient culture of the region situated in the fertile land between the Tigris and Euphrates Rivers in present-day Iraq.

Sunnah: Arabic; "example of the Prophet" (now Sunni).

Tacitus: Publius Cornelius Tacitus (c.56–117) was a senator and historian of first-century Rome whose surviving works, the *Annals* and *Histories,* record the reigns of the Roman emperors from the death of Augustus (14) through Tiberius, Claudius, and Nero to the death of Domitian (96).

Taika: Japanese; "great change."

tetrarchy: Greek; "rule by four."

Timurid: See Islamic.

tirthankar(s): "saint(s)." In Jainism, one who has reached spiritual enlightenment.

The Troubles: A lengthy period of conflict (c.1968–1998) between republican (principally Catholic) and loyalist (principally Protestant) paramilitary organizations in Northern Ireland. The roots of the conflict go back to the seventeenth century. The Good Friday Agreement in 1998 was signed by both sides as part of the ongoing Northern Ireland Peace Process.

Tudor: The English ruling dynasty from 1485 to 1603 started by Henry VII after the Battle of Bosworth. He was succeeded by his son Henry VIII, whose daughter Elizabeth I of England was the last Tudor monarch.

Umayyad: See Islamic.

umma: Arabic; "community."

War of the Roses: A struggle for the English throne that lasted from 1455 to 1485 between the House of York, which used a white rose as its emblem, and the House of Lancaster, which used a red rose. The war ended at the Battle of Bosworth when Henry Tudor, later Henry VII, was triumphant.

Warring States Period: The conflict between rival Chinese states lasting from the fifth century B.C.E. until the unification of China under the Qin Dynasty in 221 B.C.E.

General Index

C

Cabot, John 250
Cabral, Pedro Alvares 256
Caesar, Julius 71, 72, 74, 75, 79
Caetano, Marcelo 846
Callaghan, Jim 862
Calley, William 825
Calvin, John 303
Camp David agreement (1978) 858
Campora, Hector 755
Cannon, Walter 598
Cao, Diego 245
Capetians 160
Capistrano, Giovanni da 242
Capone, Al 689, 695
Caravaggio, Michelangelo Merisis da 340
Cardigan, General 538
Cardoso, Benta Banha 271
Carlyle, Thomas 451
Carmack, George 604
Carnarvon, Lord 674
Carolingians 124, 134, 136, 138
Carranza, Venustiano 633
Carter, Howard 674
Carter, Jimmy 842, 847, 858, 861, 863
Cartier, Jacques 334
Caruso, Enrico 616
Casati, Count Gabrio 530
Cassius Longinus, Gaius 75
Castelnau, Peter of 198
Castro, Fidel 793, 799, 806, 823, 843, 847
Catesby, Robert 332
Cathars 198, 199
Catherine II (the Great), Empress of Russia 413, 442, 464
Catherine of Aragon 286, 300
Catholic League 324, 352
Cato the Elder 69
Cavour, Count Camillo 546, 548
Central Intelligence Agency (CIA) 778, 799, 806, 843, 847
CERN 932
Cervantes, Miguel de 331
Cetshwayo, King of the Zulus 581
Challenger space shuttle 880, 914
Chamberlain, Neville 710, 718
Champlain, Samuel de 334
Champollion, Jean-François 458
Chandler, Chas 836
Chapman, Mark David 866
Charbonnier, Stephane 936
Charlemagne, King of the Franks and Emperor 138, 140, 143, 146
Charles I, King of England 359, 363, 365, 366
Charles I, King of France 213

Charles I, King of Spain 268
Charles II, King of England 366, 373, 377
Charles III, King of Naples 405
Charles III (the Simple), King of France 155
Charles IV, Holy Roman Emperor 223
Charles IV, King of Spain 476
Charles V, Holy Roman Emperor 268, 270, 271, 275, 277, 280, 281, 284, 285, 298, 299
Charles VI, King of France 233
Charles VIII, King of France 247
Charles X, King of France 503
Charles XII, King of Sweden 388, 391
Charles the Bald, Holy Roman Emperor 148, 150
Charles Martel (the Hammer) 134
Charlie Hebdo 936
Charney, Geoffrey de 216
Chartism 515
Chartres Cathedral 194
Chataway, Chris 780
Chaucer, Geoffrey 185
Chaumarys, Hugues de 486
Chelmsford, Lord 581
Chernobyl 884, 931
Chiang Kai-Shek 700, 767
Choltitz, General Dietrich von 741
Chongzhen, Emperor of China 361
Chou En Lai 700
Christian VII, King of Denmark 418
Christie, Chris 933
Christie, Linford 888
Christina, Queen of Sweden 370
Christmas Day 105
Christodoulos, Archbishop 169
Church of England 286, 288
Church of Jesus Christ of Latter-day Saints 503, 525
Churchill, Winston 610, 644, 645, 672, 710, 718, 727, 732, 743, 744, 750, 755, 778
Cicero, Marcus Tullius 76
Cistercian Order 178
Clapperton, Hugh 454
Clark, William 472
Clarke, Arthur C. 803
Clarkson, Thomas 507
Claudius, Emperor of Rome 87, 89
Clay, Henry 488
Cleisthenes 42
Clemenceau, Georges 609, 669
Clement V, Pope 216
Clement VII, Pope 227, 284, 286, 288, 295
Clement VIII, Pope 324
Cleopatra VII, Queen of Egypt 77, 79

Cleveland, Grover 590
Clinton, Bill 910
Clinton, Hillary 922
Clinton, Sir Henry 433
Clive, Robert 411, 452
Clovis I, King of the Franks 110
Cluny Abbey 153
Codrington, Admiral Edward 499
Cohn, Roy 770
Colbert, Jean-Baptiste 356
Coleridge, Samuel Taylor 457
Coligny, Admiral de 311
Collins, Michael (American astronaut) 832
Collins, Michael (Irish politician) 648, 672
Cologne Cathedral 206
Columbia space shuttle 914
Columbus, Christopher 214, 248, 249, 256
Compostela 145
computers 848, 853, 868
Concorde 831
Condorcanqui, Jose Gabriel 432
Confucius 42
Connally, John B. 812, 815
Connolly, James 602, 648
Conrad I, King of Franconia 155
Conrad III, King of Germany 182
Constantine, Emperor 89, 100, 101, 102, 103, 104
Constantine XI, Byzantine Emperor 240
Constantinople 103, 115, 116, 194, 240
Conventional Forces in Europe Treaty (1990) 899
Cook, Frederick 630
Cook, James 415, 416, 428
Cooper, Antony Ashley 507
Cooper, Gary 690
Coote, Sir Eyre 411
Copernicus, Nicolaus 296
Cornwallis, Lord Charles 433, 442
Cortés, Hernán 264, 274, 276
Cossacks 318
Coubertin, Pierre de 602
Cranmer, Thomas 286, 300
Crassus, Marcus Licinius 69, 72
Crazy Horse 579
creation, and date of 24
Crick, Francis 776
Crimean War 442, 538, 539
Crippen, Dr. Hawley Harvey 632
Crockett, Davy 509
Crompton, Samuel 400
Cromwell, Oliver 362, 363, 365,

Picture Credits

Every effort has been made to credit the copyright holders of the images used in this book. We apologize for any unintentional omissions or errors and will insert the appropriate acknowledgment to any companies or individuals in any subsequent editions of the work.

22 Science Photo Library/Matthew Bate **23** Science Photo Library/Prof. Walter Alvarez **25** Corbis/Bettmann **27** AKG-Images/Erich Lessing **28** Art Archive/Gianni Dagli Orti **29** Corbis/Gianni Dagli Orti **30** Corbis/Alinari **31** Alamy/Visual Arts Library **32** Art Archive/National Palace Museum Taiwan **33** Corbis/Ali Meyer **34** AKG **36** Art Archive/Bibliothèque des Arts Décoratifs Paris/Gianni Dagli Orti **39** Alamy/Mary Evans **40** Alamy/Christine Osborne **43** Bridgeman/Bibliotheque Nationale, Paris, France **44** AKG **45** Alamy/Visual Arts Library **47** Bridgeman/Bibliotheque des Arts Decoratifs, Paris, France, Archives Charmet **48** Corbis/Bettmann **49** Alinari/Bridgeman **50** AKG **51** Alinari/Bridgeman **53** Art Archive/Hellenic Institute Venice/Gianni Dagli Orti **54** Alinari/Bridgeman **56** Art Archive/Mechitarista Congregation Venice/Alfredo Dagli Orti **57** AKG **59** Alamy/Mary Evans **60** AKG **62** Alamy/The Print Collector **63** AKG/Laurent Lecat **64** Bridgeman/Private Collection, The Stapleton Collection **66** Art Archive/British Library **68** Corbis/Bettmann **70** Bridgeman/Gahoe Museum, Jongno-gu, South Korea **73** Alamy/Visual Arts Library **75** Alamy/Mary Evans **76** Scala **77** Bridgeman/Villa Barbarigo, Noventa Vicentina, Italy, Giraudon **78** Scala/Photo Austrian Archive **80** Art Archive/Rheinische Landesmuseum Trier/Gianni Dagli Orti **81** Bridgeman/Galleria degli Uffizi, Florence, Italy **85** Alamy/Marion Kaplan **86** Scala/courtesy of the Ministero Beni e Att. Culturali **88** Bridgeman/Musee des Beaux-Arts Andre Malraux, Le Havre, France, Giraudon **89** Alinari **90** Alamy/The Print Collector **92** Bridgeman/Musee des Beaux-Arts, Lille, France, Lauros / Giraudon **93** Corbis/Sean Saxton Collection **94** Corbis/Historical Picture Archive **96t** AKG/Reproduced with the cooperation of Irvin Ungar, HISTORICANA, Burlingame, CA www.szyk.com **96b** Alamy/Israel Images **98** AKG **100** AKG **101** Scala/courtesy of the Ministero Beni e Att. Culturali **102** Art Archive/Palazzo Leoni-Montanari Vicenza/Gianni Dagli Orti **103** Corbis/Historical Picture Archive **104t** AKG **104b** Bridgeman/Private Collection **107** Alamy/Mary Evans **109** Alamy/Visual Arts Library **111** Alamy/Visual Arts Library **112** Scala/courtesy of the Ministero Beni e Att. Culturali **113** Scala/courtesy of the Ministero Beni e Att. Culturali **114** Alamy/Mary Evans **117** Alamy/Visual Arts Library **118** Corbis/Summerfield Press **119** Bridgeman **120** AKG/Ullstein Bild **122** Corbis/Stapleton Collection **125** AKG/British Library **126** Illustration from the *Tounomine engi emaki* supplied by Tanzan Jiniya **128** Corbis/Michael Nicholson **130** Bridgeman/Brooklyn Museum of Art, New York, USA, Gift of K. Thomas amd Sharon Elghanayan **133** Alamy/Nick Fraser **134t** Alamy/Mary Evans **134b** Alamy/Visual Arts Library **136** Bridgeman/Bibliotheque Mazarine, Paris, France, Archives Charmet **137** Bridgeman/Private Collection, Giraudon **139** Alinari/Bridgeman **140** Art Archive/British Library **141** Bridgeman/Private Collection, Roger Perrin **143** AKG/British Library **144** Art Archive/Galerie Théorème Louvre des Antiquaires/Gianni Dagli Orti **147** AKG **149** Bridgeman/Private Collection, ©Walker Galleries, Harrogate, North Yorkshire, UK **150** Alamy/Mary Evans **151** AKG **153t** Alamy/Visual Arts Library **153b** Art Archive/Bibliothèque Nationale Paris **154** Corbis/Stapleton Collection **157** Corbis/Gianni Dagli Orti **159** Corbis/Bettmann **160** Corbis/Leonard de Selva **164** AKG/Erich Lessing **166t** AKG/Paul Almasy **166b** Alamy/Dinodia **168** Alamy/ArkReligion **170** AKG/British Library **171** AKG/Erich Lessing **172** AKG **173** AKG **174** Corbis/Michael Freeman **175** Art Archive/Museo Civico Bologna/Gianni Dagli Orti **176** AKG/Erich Lessing **177** Scala/Ann Ronan/HIP **178** Bridgeman/Museo Civico, Prato, Italy **179** Alamy/Visual Arts Library **180** Bridgeman/Phillips, The International Fine Art Auctioneers, UK, Photo © Bonhams, London, UK **182** AKG **183** AKG/British Library **184** Alamy/David Lyons **185** AKG/British Library **186** AKG/British Library **187** Bridgeman/Galleria Civica d'Arte Moderna di Torino, Turin, Italy, Alinari **188t** Alamy/Print Collector **188b** Alamy/JTB Photo Communications, Inc. **190** Alamy/Print Collector **191** AKG/British Library **192** Art Archive/Private Collection Paris/Gianni Dagli Orti **193** Art Archive/British Library **195** Alamy/Visual Arts Library **196** Alamy/Visual Arts Library **197** Bridgeman/Bibliotheque Nationale, Paris, France **199t** Bridgeman/©British Library Board. All Rights Reserved **199b** Scala/HIP **200** Bridgeman/Palacio del Senado, Madrid, Spain, Index **203** Corbis/Summerfield Press **204** Corbis/Bettmann **207** Corbis/Historical Picture Archive **209** Alamy/Mary Evans **211** Bridgeman/Biblioteca Marciana, Venice, Italy, Giraudon **212** Alamy/Mary Evans **213** Art Archive/Galleria d'Arte Moderna Palermo/Gianni Dagli Orti **214** Bridgeman/©British Library Board. All Rights Reserved **215** Bridgeman/Smith Art Gallery and Museum, Stirling, Scotland **217** Bridgeman/©British Library Board. All Rights Reserved **219** Bridgeman/Museo Nacional de Antropologia, Mexico City, Mexico, Ian Mursell/Mexicolore **220** Bridgeman/Louvre, Paris, France **221** AKG/Stefan Diller **222t** Art Archive/Bibliothèque Nationale Paris **222b** AKG/Jérôme da Cunha **224** Getty/Hulton Archive **225** Art Archive/Hamburg Staatsarchiv/Harper Collins Publishers **226** Alamy/Dennis Cox **228** AKG/British Library **229** AKG/British Library **230t** Alamy/Mary Evans **230b** AKG **232** AKG **233** Bridgeman/Private Collection, The Stapleton Collection **235** Art Archive/Santa Maria Novella Church Florence/Gianni Dagli Orti **236** Alamy/Mary Evans **237** AKG/Jérôme da Cunha **238** Scala/courtesy of the Ministero Beni e Att. Culturali **241** Alamy/North Wind Picture Archive **242** Bridgeman/Topkapi Palace Museum, Istanbul, Turkey **244t** Bridgeman/©The Trustees of the Weston Park Foundation, UK **244b** Alamy/Mary Evans **247** Alinari/SEAT **248** Corbis/Stapleton Collection **249** Bridgeman/©Royal Geographical Society, London, UK **250** Corbis/Bettmann **251** Bridgeman/Banco Nacional Ultramarino, Portugal, Giraudon **252** Bridgeman/Museo Nazionale del Bargello, Florence, Italy **253** Alamy/Visual Arts Library **257** Bridgeman/Louvre, Paris, France, Lauros/Giraudon **258** Corbis/Gallery Collection **259** Alinari **260** Scala **261** Scala **263** Alinari **265t** Bridgeman/©City of Edinburgh Museums and Art Galleries, Scotland **265b** Bridgeman/Bibliotheque des Arts Decoratifs, Paris, France, Archives Charmet **266** AKG **267** Bridgeman/Musee Conde, Chantilly, France **268** Alinari/Bridgeman **269** Bridgeman/Topkapi Palace Museum, Istanbul, Turkey, Bildarchiv Steffens **270** Bridgeman/Galleria degli Uffizi, Florence, Italy, Giraudon **271** Alamy/Visual Arts Library **272** Alamy/Leo Macario **273** Corbis/Alinari **275t** AKG **275b** AKG/Joseph Martin **276** Corbis/Stapleton Collection **277** AKG **279** Art Archive/Kalmar Castle Sweden/Alfredo Dagli Orti **280** AKG/Erich Lessing **281** AKG **282** Scala/HIP **283** Alamy/Visual Arts Library **284** Bridgeman/Private Collection **285** Alinari/SEAT **287** Scala **288** Bridgeman/Private Collection **289** AKG **290** Bridgeman/Private Collection, ©Philip Mould Ltd, London **291** Art Archive/Musée du Louvre Paris/Gianni Dagli Orti **292** Scala/HIP **294** Bridgeman/Bibliotheque Nationale, Paris, France, Lauros/Giraudon **297t** Corbis/Hulton **297b** Bridgeman/Private Collection **299** Alinari/Finsiel **300t** Alamy/Classic Image **300b** Alamy/Pictorial Press Ltd. **302** Bridgeman/Chateau de Versailles, France **303** Alamy/Mary Evans **304** Bridgeman/Private Collection, Photo ©Rafael Valls Gallery, London, UK **305** AKG/André Held **306** Art Archive/Eileen Tweedy **307** Bridgeman/©Guildhall Art Gallery, City of London **308** Bridgeman/©Cheltenham Art Gallery & Museums, Gloucestershire, UK **309** Art Archive/Kobe Municipal Museum/Laurie Platt Winfrey **310** Alinari/Bridgeman **311** AKG/Jérôme da Cunha **313** AKG **314** Corbis/Bettmann **316** AKG/Erich Lessing **317** Bridgeman/The Crown Estate **319t** Bridgeman/Private Collection, ©Look and Learn **319b** Bridgeman/State Art Gallery of Kirgiz Republic, Bishkek, Kyrgyzstan **320** AKG **321** Scala/HIP **323** Bridgeman/©Ashmolean Museum, University of Oxford, UK **325** Bridgeman/Private Collection **326** Art Archive/British Museum/Eileen Tweedy **327** Mary Evans **328** Art Archive **329** Art Archive/Pinacoteca Nazionale di Siena/Gianni Dagli Orti **330** Bridgeman/Private Collection **331** Mary Evans/Asia Media **332** Alamy/Mary Evans **333** AKG **334** Art Archive/Culver Pictures **335** Bridgeman/Private Collection, Ken Welsh **336** Alamy/North Wind Picture Archive **337** Bridgeman/National Portrait Gallery, London, UK **338** Scala/Ann Ronan/HIP **339** Alamy/Mary Evans **340** The Art Archive/Galleria Borghese Rome/Alfredo Dagli Orti **341** The Art Archive/San Luigi dei Francesi Rome/Alfredo Dagli Orti **343** Corbis/Christophe Boisvieux **344t** Corbis/Louie Psihoyos **344b** Bridgeman/Private Collection **346** AKG **347** Corbis **348** Alinari/

Bridgeman **349** Bridgeman/Private Collection, The Stapleton Collection **350** Alamy/Print Collector **352** Scala/BPK, Bildagentur fuer Kunst, Kultur und Geschichte, Berlin **354** Bridgeman/Louvre, Paris, France, Peter Willi **355** Art Archive/Tokyo University/Laurie Platt Winfrey **356** Bridgeman/ Musee des Beaux-Arts, Rouen, France, Lauros/Giraudon **358** AKG **360** Bridgeman/Private Collection **362t** Getty/Hulton **362b** Getty/Popperfoto **364** Bridgeman/National Gallery, London, UK **365** Art Archive **367t** Bridgeman/Louvre, Paris, France, Lauros/Giraudon **367b** Bridgeman/Chateau de Versailles, France, Lauros/Giraudon **369** Bridgeman/Santa Maria della Vittoria, Rome, Italy **371** AKG/Electa **372** AKG/Jean-Louis Nou **375** Bridgeman/©Museum of London, UK **376** Alamy/Lebrecht Music & Arts Photo Library **378** Alamy/Mary Evans **379** Art Archive/Musée du Château de Versailles/Gianni Dagli Orti **380** Corbis/Art Archive **382** Alinari/Imagno **384** Corbis/Bettmann **385** AKG **388** Corbis/Bettmann **389** Alamy/Print Collector **390** Bridgeman/Houses of Parliament, Westminster, London, UK **391** Corbis/Bettmann **392** Alinari/Topfoto **393** Bridgeman/St. Paul's Cathedral Library, London, UK **394** Bridgeman/Archives du Ministere des Affaires Etrangeres, Paris, France, Archives Charmet **395** Scala/Art Media/HIP **396** Bridgeman/©Victoria Art Gallery, Bath and North East Somerset Council **397** Getty/Hulton **398** Alinari/ Bridgeman **401t** Bridgeman/National Portrait Gallery, London, UK **401b** Alamy/Mary Evans **402** Bridgeman/Schloss Augustusburg, Bruhl, Germany **403** Bridgeman/©Norwich Castle Museum and Art Gallery **404t** Bridgeman/Courtesy of the Council, National Army Museum, London, UK **404b** Bridgeman/Private Collection **406** Alamy/Classicstock **407** AKG **408** Bridgeman/Pennsylvania Academy of the Fine Arts, Philadelphia, USA **409** Bridgeman/Private Collection **410** Corbis/Bettmann **412** Bridgeman/Private Collection, Phillips, Fine Art Auctioneers, New York, USA **413** Scala **414** Bridgeman/Private Collection **416** Getty/Hulton **417** AKG/British Library **418** AKG **419** Bridgeman/Bibliotheque Polonaise, Paris, France, Bonora **421** Bridgeman/American Antiquarian Society, Worcester, Massachusetts, USA **422** Getty/Hulton **423** Art Archive/Private Collection Paris/Alfredo Dagli Orti **424** Alamy/Stockmontage Inc **424b** Art Archive/Marc Charmet **426** Corbis/PoodlesRock **427** Alamy/Select Images **428** Bridgeman/©Dixson Galleries, State Library of New South Wales **429** Getty/Hulton **430** Alamy/Print Collector **431** Bridgeman/Ecole Nationale des Ponts et Chaussees, France, Archives Charmet **432** Art Archive/Coll Diaz Peru/Mireille Vautier **434** AKG **437** Bridgeman/Pennsylvania Academy of the Fine Arts, Philadelphia, USA **438** Bridgeman/Musee de la Ville de Paris, Musee Carnavalet, Paris, France, Giraudon **439** Alamy/Visual Arts Library **440** Bridgeman/©British Library Board. All Rights Reserved **441** Alinari **443t** Corbis **443b** Getty/Popperfoto **444t** Bridgeman/Musee de la Ville de Paris, Musee Carnavalet, Paris, France, Giraudon **444b** Scala/Ann Ronan/HIP **446** Bridgeman/Private Collection, Ken Welsh **447** Art Archive/Musée Lambinet Versailles/Gianni Dagli Orti **448** Getty/Hulton **449** Corbis/Art Archive **450** Corbis/Burstein Collection **451** Getty/Time & Life Pictures **453** Bridgeman/Academie Nationale de Medecine, Paris, France, Archives Charmet **454t** Getty/Time & Life Pictures **454b** Bridgeman/ Private Collection **456t** Getty/Hulton **456b** Art Archive/Eileen Tweedy **459** Getty/Hulton **460** AKG/Erich Lessing **463t** Getty/Hulton **463b** AKG **464** AKG **465** AKG **466** Corbis **469** Bridgeman/Louvre, Paris, France **470** AKG **471** Alamy/Mary Evans **472** Bridgeman/Private Collection **473** AKG/Erich Lessing **474** Art Archive/Eileen Tweedy **475** Bridgeman/Bibliotheque Nationale, Paris, France, Lauros/Giraudon **476t** AKG **476b** Bridgeman/Prado, Madrid, Spain **478** Bridgeman/State Central Artillery Museum, St. Petersburg, Russia **479** Bridgeman/Private Collection, Photo©Bonhams, London, UK **480** Alamy/Visual Arts Library **481** Corbis/Bettmann **482** AKG **483** Alamy/Visual Arts Library **484** Bridgeman/ Private Collection, The Stapleton Collection **485** Bridgeman/Private Collection **487** Bridgeman/Bolivar Museum, Caracas, Venezuela, Giraudon **488t** Bridgeman/.©Collection of the New York Historical Society, USA **488b** Alamy/North Wind Picture Archives **490** Art Archive/Bibliothèque Marmottan Boulogne/Gianni Dagli Orti **491** Art Archive/Museo Nacional de Historia Lima/Gianni Dagli Orti **492** Art Archive/Biblioteca National do Rio de Janiero Brazil/Gianni Dagli Orti **493** Corbis/Bettmann **494t** Bridgeman/National Portrait Gallery, London, UK **494b** AKG **496** Alamy/Visual Arts Library **497** Corbis/Bettmann **498** Bridgeman/Gernsheim Collection, University of Texas, Austin, USA, Archives Charmet **499** Art Archive/ Museum der Stadt Wien/Alfredo Dagli Orti **500** Scala/HIP **501** Getty/Hulton **502t** Getty/Hulton **502b** Alamy/Mary Evans **504** Bridgeman/©The Royal Institution, London, UK **505** Getty/Hulton **506t** Corbis/Bettmann **506b** Science Photo Library **508** Bridgeman/Guildhall Library, City of London **509** Getty/Hulton **510** Alamy/Mary Evans **511** Bridgeman/State Russian Museum, St. Petersburg, Russia, Giraudon **512** Getty/Hulton **513** Corbis/Bettmann **514t** Alamy/INTERFOTO Pressebildagentur **514b** Alamy/Mary Evans **516** Science & Society Picture Library/NMeM **517** Bridgeman/Courtesy of the Council, National Army Museum, London, UK **519** © Antiques & Collectables / Alamy **521t** Corbis/Bettmann **521b** Scala/HIP **522** Alamy **524** Bridgeman/Private Collection **525** Getty/Hulton **527** Corbis **528t** AKG **528b** AKG **530** Scala **531** Bridgeman/ Private Collection, The Stapleton Collection **532** Corbis/Bettmann **533** Scala/HIP **534** Corbis/Bettmann **535** Bridgeman/Private Collection, Giraudon **536** Scala/National Portrait Gallery Smithsonian/Art Resource **538** Corbis/Bettmann **539** Alamy/ClassicStock **540** Getty/Felice Beato/ Hulton **541** Getty/Hulton **542** Science Photo Library **543** Corbis/Hulton **544** Corbis/Hulton **545** Bridgeman Art Library **547** Scala **549** Corbis/ Hulton **550** Corbis/Bettmann **551** Art Archive/Musée National de la voiture et du tourisme Compiègne/Gianni Dagli Orti **553t** Corbis **553b** Corbis **554** AKG **555** Corbis/Hulton **556** Alamy/Ultimate Group LLC **557** Corbis/Bettmann **558t** Corbis/Bettmann **558b** Getty/Time & Life Pictures **560** AKG/RIA Novosti **561** Corbis/Bettmann **562** Corbis **563** Corbis/Bettmann **564t** AKG/RIA Nowosti **564b** AKG/RIA Nowosti **566** AKG **567** Corbis **568** Corbis/Asian Art & Archaeology, Inc. **569** Alamy/Print Collector **570** Corbis/Bettmann **571** Getty/Hulton **572** Alinari **574** Corbis/Bettmann **576** Alamy/Mary Evans **577** Alamy/Mary Evans **578** Alamy/Print Collector **579** Corbis/Stapleton Collection **580t** Alamy/Lebrecht Music & Arts Photo Library **580b** Corbis/Hulton **582** Corbis/Bettmann **583** Getty/Hulton **585** Getty Images **586** Alamy/Mary Evans **587** Bridgeman/©Leeds Museums and Galleries (City Art Gallery) UK **588** Corbis/Bettmann **589** Corbis **590** AKG **591** Art Archive/Culver Pictures **593** AKG **594t** Bridgeman/©Samuel Courtauld Trust, Courtauld Institute of Art Gallery **594b** Corbis/Francis G. Mayer **596** Corbis/Bettmann **597** Alamy/ Pictorial Press Ltd. **598** Corbis/Bettmann **599** Alamy/Print Collector **600** Corbis/Sygma **601** Kobal Collection/Lumiere **603** AKG **604** Corbis **605** Corbis/Bettmann **606** Corbis/Hulton **607** Alamy/Mary Evans **608** AKG **611** Corbis **614** Alamy/Mary Evans **615** Getty/Hulton **617** Corbis/ Bettmann **618** Rex Features/Roger-Viollet **619** Corbis/Bettmann **620** Corbis **621** AKG **623** Alamy/Print Collector **624** Alamy/Mary Evans **625** Rex Features/Tony Davis **627** Getty/Hulton **628** Science Photo Library/RIA Novosti **629** Getty/Time & Life Pictures **630t** Getty/Popperfoto **630b** Getty/Hulton **632** Getty/Hulton **633** Art Achive/National History Museum Mexico City/Gianni Dagli Orti **634** Mary Evans/Rue Des Archives **635** Corbis/Bettmann **636t** AKG/Ullstein Bild **636b** Corbis/Hulton **638** Rex Features **639** Art Archive/Ocean Memorabilia Collection **640** Rex Features/Roger-Viollet **641** Corbis/Hulton **642** Corbis/Bettmann **643** Corbis/Bettmann **644** Art Archive **645** Corbis/Hulton **647t** AKG/Ullstein Bild **647b** Getty/Hulton **649t** Rex Features **649b** Alamy/INTERFOTO Pressebildagentur **650** Art Archive/Imperial War Museum **651** Getty/ Popperfoto **652** Corbis **655t** AKG **655b** Getty/Popperfoto **656** Rex Features/Roger-Viollet **657** Alamy/Print Collector **658** Corbis/Bettmann **659** Corbis/Hulton **660** Corbis/Bettmann **661** AKG **662** Corbis/Hulton **663** Corbis/Bettmann **664** Corbis/Hulton **665** Alamy/Print Collector **666t** Corbis/ Bettmann **666b** Getty/Hulton **668** Getty/Hulton **669** Corbis/Bettmann **670** Science & Society Picture Library **671** Corbis/Bettmann **672** Corbis **673** Getty/BIPS/Hulton **674t** Corbis/Hulton **674b** Getty/Time & Life Pictures **676** Corbis/Bettmann **677** AKG **678** Getty/Hulton **679** Getty/Time & Life Pictures **680** Science Photo Library/Emilio Segre Visual Archives/American Insitute Of Physics **682** Alamy/Mary Evans **683** Corbis/Bettmann **685** Alamy/Pictorial Press Ltd. **686** Corbis/Bettmann **688** Rex Features/SNAP **689** Corbis/Hulton **690** Corbis/Bettmann **691** Corbis/Bettmann **693** Getty/Hulton **694** Corbis/Bettmann **695** Corbis/Bettmann **696** AKG **697** UPPA/Photoshot **699t** Corbis/Bettmann **699b** Corbis/Bettmann **700** Getty/AFP **701** Corbis/Bettmann **702** Getty/Popperfoto **705** Getty/Hulton **706** Corbis/Bettmann **707** Corbis/Bettmann **709t** AKG **709b** Corbis/Hulton **710** Getty/Time & Life Pictures **711** Corbis/Bettmann **712** Paul Popper/Popperfoto/Getty Images **714t** Corbis/Bettmann **714b** ©Corbis **717t** Kobal Collection/Selnick/MGM **717b** Kobal Collection **718** Getty/Hulton **719** Corbis **720** Getty/Bert Hardy **722** Rex Features/

Roger-Viollet **723** © François Pugnet/Kipa/Corbis **724** Getty/Hulton **725** Corbis **726t** Corbis **726b** Getty/Ian Waldie **728** AKG **729** Getty/Hulton **730** Getty/Hulton **732** Getty/Popperfoto **733** Corbis **734** Getty/Hulton **735** Alamy/Mary Evans **736** Alamy/Mary Evans **737** Getty/Hulton **738** Magnum/©2001 Cornell Capa **739** Getty/Time & Life Pictures **740** AKG **742** Corbis/Hulton **744** Corbis/ Bettmann **745** Corbis **746** Getty/Time & Life Pictures **747** Getty/Hulton **748** Corbis **749** Corbis **751** Corbis/ Bettmann **752** AKG **754** Corbis/Bettmann **756** Rex Features/Sipa **757** Corbis/Hulton **759** Corbis **760** Getty/Popperfoto **761** Alamy/Print Collector **763t** Getty/Hulton **763b** Getty/Popperfoto **764t** Getty/Time & Life Pictures **764b** Corbis/Bettmann **766** Getty/AFP **767** Getty/AFP **771** Corbis/Bettmann **773t** AKG/Paul Almasy **773b** Corbis/Bettmann **774** Science Photo Library/Los Alamos National Laboratory **775** Getty/ Popperfoto **776** Science Photo Library/A. Barrington Brown **777** Alamy/ Royal Geographical Society **779t** Getty/Michael Ochs Archive **779b** Corbis/ CinemaPhoto **780** Alamy/Mary Evans **782** Rex Features/Everett Collection **783** Alamy/Pictorial Press Ltd. **785** Getty/Time & Life Pictures **786** Corbis/Hulton **787** AKG **788** Getty/Popperfoto **789** Corbis/ Bettmann **790** Getty/Hulton **791** Getty/AFP **792** Alamy/INTERFOTO Pressebildagentur **793** Getty/Popperfoto **794t** Corbis/Bettmann **794b** Getty/Michael Ochs Archive **797t** Getty/Popperfoto **797b** Corbis/ David Rubinger **798** Getty/AFP **800** Getty/Popperfoto **801** Getty/Hulton **803t** Corbis/Bettmann **803b** Corbis/Bettmann **804** Corbis/Bettmann **806** Getty/Time & Life Pictures **807** Getty/Time & Life Pictures **809t** AKG **809b** Corbis/Reuters **810** Corbis/Bettmann **811** Getty/Time & Life Pictures **812** Getty/Hulton **813** PA Photos/James W. Ike Altgens/AP **814** Rex Features/Everett Collection **816t** Corbis/Bettmann **816b** Getty/ Hulton **818** Corbis/Tim Page **819** Corbis/Bettmann **820t** Corbis/ Bettmann **820b** Getty/AFP **822** Corbis/Bettmann **823** Corbis/JB Russel/ Sygma **824t** Corbis/Bettmann **824b** Getty Images **826** Corbis/Bettmann **827** Rex Features/Sipa **829t** Corbis/Libor Hajsky/EPA **829b** Rex Features/ Edwin Walter **830** NASA **831** Getty/AFP **832** NASA **833** NASA **834** Corbis/Bettmann **835** Getty/Time & Life Pictures **836t** David Redfern/ Redferns **836b** Getty/Time & Life Pictures **838** Corbis/Christian Simonpietri/Sygma **839** Magnum/Gilles Peress **841t** Getty Images **841b** Getty Images **843t** Getty/AFP **843b** Corbis/Dmitri Baltermants **844** Rex Features/Sipa **845** Allan Tannenbaum/Time & Life Pictures/Getty **846** Corbis/Henri Bureau/Sygma **847** Getty/Hulton **848** Rex Features/Sipa **849** Getty/AFP **851** Corbis/Bettmann **852** Getty/Hulton **853** Getty/Time & Life Pictures **854** Alamy/Peter Jordan **856** Getty/Hulton **857** Corbis/ Selwyn Tait/Sygma **859t** Getty/David Hume Kennerly **859b** Getty/David Hume Kennerly **860** Corbis/Bettmann **861** Getty/Time & Life Pictures **862t** Corbis/Hulton **862b** Getty/Hulton **864** Corbis/Alain DeJean/Sygma **865** Corbis/Bettmann **866** Getty/Hulton **867** Rex Features/Sipa **869** Getty/Hulton **870** Corbis/Michel Philippot/Sygma **871** Corbis **873** Corbis/Kapoor Baldev/Sygma **874** Corbis/David Turnley **875** Corbis/ Kapoor Baldev/Sygma **876** Getty/ David Levenson **877** Getty/AFP/Patrick Riviere **878** Getty/Georges De Keerle **879** Corbis/Larry Downing/Sygma **880** Getty/Hulton/MPI **881** Rex Features/Sipa **882** Getty/AFP **883** Rex Features/Mr. F. Zabci **884** Corbis/ Igor Kostin/Sygma **886** Corbis/Peter Turnley **887** Rex Features/Sipa **888** Getty/Steve Powell **889** Corbis/Bryn Colton/Assignments Photographers **890** Corbis/Sygma **891** Getty/AFP **892** Corbis/Reuters **894** Corbis/Reuters **895** Corbis/Wolfgang Kumm/ DPA **896** Corbis/Peter Turnley **897** Rex Features/Sipa **898** Corbis **901t** Getty/AFP **901b** Corbis/Bettmann **903** Getty Images **904** Corbis/David Turnley **905** Tokyo Shimbun/Corbis Sygma **906t** Rex/Sipa Press **906b** Rex/Sipa Press **907t** Corbis **907b** Corbis **908** Rex Features/Sipa Press **909** Pablo Bartholomew/Gamma Liaison **910** Florence Durnad/Sipa Press/Rex Features **911** Sean Adair/Reuters/Corbis **912t** James Nielsen/Getty Images **912b** Stephen Jaffe/AFP/Getty Images **913t** Corbis **913b** Darma/ AFP/Getty **915** Partick Baz/AFP/Getty **917** John Russell/AFP/Getty **918** 2005 Metropolitan Police **919** Balkanpix.com/Rex Features **920** Rex Features **921** Ali Haider/EPA/Corbis **923** Corbis/Chris Gardner **924** Jagadeesh NV/epa/Corbis **925** Getty **926** Christopher Berkey/epa/Corbis **927** MCT via Getty Images **928** AFP/Getty **929** Christophe Ena/AP/Press Association Images **930** STR/epa/Corbis **932** Richard Juilliart/AFP/Getty Images **933** NG Images/Alamy Stock Photo **934** Ettore Ferrari/epa/Corbis **936** Dimitar Dilkoff/AFP/Getty Images **938** Haytham PicturesAlamy Stock Photo **939** REX Shutterstock **941** SK Hasan Ali/Alamy Live News

Contributors

Tony Bunting (TB) is a postgraduate research student at the University of Central Lancashire specializing in twentieth-century international relations.

Richard Cavendish (RC) is a historian who regularly covers anniversaries of past events in *History Today*.

Peter Furtado (PF) (General Editor) has edited many reference works on world history, including the *Atlas of World History*. He is a fellow of the Royal Historical Society.

Reg Grant (RG) is the author of more than twenty books on historical and military subjects, including *Flight: 100 Years of Aviation* and *Soldier: A Visual History of the Fighting Man*.

James J. Harrison (JJH) writes on history and culture. He was a contributor to *History The Definitive Visual Guide* and Editorial Consultant on *1000 Makers of the Millennium*.

John Haywood (JH) is an honorary research fellow at Lancaster University and writes on ancient and medieval history. His books include *The Dark Ages: Building Europe*.

Nigel Jones (NJ) is a writer and historian. He has written studies of the Great War and is currently working on a book about prominent prisoners of the Nazis.

Nick Kennedy (NK) studied history at Oxford. After a career in publishing, he now concentrates on the military history of the twentieth century.

Susan Kennedy (SK) studied history at Oxford. She worked in publishing and at the BBC and now edits and writes works of historical reference for adults and children.

Robert Pearce (RP), formerly Professor of Modern History at the University of Cumbria, is the author of more than twenty books and the editor of *History Review* magazine.

John Swift (JS) is a Senior Lecturer in History at the University of Cumbria. His publications include *The Palgrave Concise Historical Atlas of the Cold War* (2003) and *Labour in Crisis: Clement Attlee and the Labour Party in Opposition, 1931-40* (2001).

Acknowledgments

Quint**essence** would like to thank the following:
Sales Helena Baser **Editing** Jemima Dunne, Ben Hubbard **Copy Editing** Joe Fulman **Indexing** Ann Marangos